The Waite Group's

MICROSOFT®
QUICKC®
PROGRAMMING

The Waite Group's

MICROSOFT®
QUICKC®
PROGRAMMING

SECOND EDITION

Mitchell Waite, Stephen Prata, Bryan Costales, Harry Henderson

PUBLISHED BY
Microsoft Press
A Division of Microsoft Corporation
One Microsoft Way, Redmond, Washington 98052-6399

Library of Congress Cataloging-in-Publication Data

Microsoft QuickC programming.

　　　1. C (Computer program language)　2. Microsoft
QuickC (Computer program)　　I. Waite, Mitchell.
QA76.73.C15M53　　1989　　　　005.13'3　　　　89-14556
ISBN 1-55615-258-2

Printed and bound in the United States of America.

1 2 3 4 5 6 7 8 9　FGFG　3 2 1 0 9

Distributed to the book trade in Canada by General Publishing Company, Ltd.

Distributed to the book trade outside the United States and Canada by Penguin Books Ltd.

Penguin Books Ltd., Harmondsworth, Middlesex, England
Penguin Books Australia Ltd., Ringwood, Victoria, Australia
Penguin Books N.Z. Ltd., 182-190 Wairau Road, Auckland 10, New Zealand

British Cataloging in Publication Data available

IBM®, PC/AT®, and PS2® are registered trademarks
of International Business Machines Corporation.
Microsoft®, MS-DOS®, and QuickC® are registered trademarks
of Microsoft Corporation.

Project Editor: Eric Stroo
Technical Editors: Dail Magee, Jr.
　　　　　　　　　Doug Henderson
Manuscript Editor: Rebecca Pepper

To Bobbie Lee,
who touched me in a way no one ever has
Mitchell

Contents

PART III: Intermediate C Topics

Preface

Change comes quickly in the computer industry—just a year and a half ago the first edition of *Microsoft QuickC Programming* hit the bookstore shelves. It quickly became a bestseller for The Waite Group and for Microsoft Press.

The Waite Group chose to write the first edition because we were inspired by a beta version of a low-cost C compiler from Microsoft that offered lightning-fast point-and-click compiling, a friendly interface, and full compatibility with the libraries of the Microsoft C Professional Development System. As an authoring group fiercely interested in education, we saw a book on QuickC as a great opportunity to teach the powerful but cryptic C language to beginners and professionals alike. So our four experienced authors brought The Waite Group's time-tested interactive, top-down, stepwise tutorial approach to QuickC.

Since we wrote the first edition, QuickC has gone through a number of revisions and has acquired powerful new features. QuickC version 2.5 boasts an improved interface that features new windows, a notepad, and the ability to cut and paste text. It features an improved debugger, customizable editor, expanded graphics libraries that include business graphics and a variety of fonts, and an enhanced hypertext-based on-line help system. QuickC now supports virtually all memory models, it compiles incrementally to disk for increased speed, and it lets you write programs that will run under Windows and OS/2. This friendly C compiler even includes an in-line assembler so that you can embed assembly language code into your C programs, and the new MASM-compatible QuickAssembler, which lets you write separately compiled assembly language modules directly from the QuickC environment! All this at a cost that makes this compiler accessible to hackers and students as well as professionals.

In this second edition, *The Waite Group's Microsoft QuickC Programming* gives full coverage to these powerful new enhancements. You'll also notice that all programs have been updated for compatibility with ANSI C. This book will appeal to new readers and to those who purchased and enjoyed the first edition.

We think you will find that this book goes beyond most other C books on the market (including our own). If you have any comments, questions, or suggestions for new books, we'd love to hear from you. Address your correspondence to

> The Waite Group
> 100 Shoreline Highway, Building A, Suite 285
> Mill Valley, California 94941

You can reach Mitchell Waite on the following networks: Compuserve (75146,3515), BIX (mwaite), usenet (hplabs!well!mitch), MCI Mail (Mitch), and AppleLink (D2097).

Mitchell Waite
Stephen Prata
Bryan Costales
Harry Henderson

Acknowledgments

The authors would like to take this opportunity to thank the people at or associated with Microsoft Press for helping to make this book a success: Jim Brown and Dean Holmes for making possible this second edition and for responding patiently to our numerous requests, Rebecca Pepper for her meticulous editing, Doug Henderson for his technical review, and the excellent editorial and production staff for their technical assistance and careful attention to detail. Also, thanks to the many readers whose letters and kind words have helped make this second edition even better than the first. And finally, thanks to Scott Calamar for coordinating this project for The Waite Group.

PART I

Introduction to C

Introduction

Why Learn C?

If you have experience with C, you are probably familiar with its advantages over alternatives such as BASIC or Pascal, and you may want to skip to the next section, which discusses the specific advantages of QuickC for C programmers. Here we compare C with two other popular languages, BASIC and Pascal.

Although Pascal has its enthusiasts, and our old friend BASIC certainly has been improved in many ways (Microsoft's QuickBASIC for example), C has quickly become the premier language for professional programming both on micros, such as the IBM PC family, and on larger machines, such as those running the UNIX/XENIX operating system. Why is C so popular?

3

Portability and Standards

One reason is portability. The core of standard C is so designed that the same program runs on an IBM PC, a VAX mini, and an IBM mainframe.

Portability results from adhering to standards that guarantee common language features and functions, regardless of the vendor, implementation, or hardware environment. The first, informal C standard was proclaimed by the famous "white book," Brian W. Kernighan and Dennis M. Ritchie's *The C Programming Language* (New Jersey: Prentice-Hall, 1978). The specifications in that book have been widely adopted in the design of C compilers, but the definitions are not comprehensive and specific enough to provide a true standard. Therefore, the American National Standards Institute (ANSI) proposed a draft standard for the C language. The final version of this standard was finally adopted in January 1990. Most current and future C compilers will be written to conform with the ANSI standard. QuickC is compatible with the ANSI standard. It also permits you to verify that your code uses only ANSI-compatible functions and definitions or to identify nonstandard features, such as those needed to support functions specific to MS-DOS and to IBM hardware.

Another reason for the popularity of C is its close ties to the UNIX operating system. UNIX was written in C, and a variety of standards support the use of C in the UNIX environment. QuickC is functionally compatible with the UNIX System V standard library specifications. But what does all this standardization mean to you, the QuickC programmer?

A C program written under QuickC on an IBM PC can, if it uses only ANSI-standard features, be moved, or "ported," to an Apple Macintosh, and you can compile it with an ANSI-standard Macintosh C compiler and run it in the new environment.

This level of standardization is not common in programming languages. Pascal is only partially standardized: A Turbo Pascal program for the IBM PC, for example, cannot run under standard IBM Pascal without modification. In the IBM PC world, the ubiquitous BASICA program has offered a kind of standard, but other models of computers are provided with quite different dialects of BASIC, and you must do an extensive conversion to get a BASIC program written on one machine to run on another manufacturer's hardware.

Notice that this discussion applies specifically to the "core" of C: the control structures, data structures, and basic input/output functions. Outside of this standard core, a number of areas of a C implementation are machine-dependent, such as the storage size of various kinds of numbers, the keyboard codes, the video screen, graphics, and features of the operating system that handle files.

To be worth its salt, a C compiler that runs on the IBM PC must include functions that give programs access to MS-DOS features, the underlying BIOS, and the hardware. Similarly, a C compiler for the Macintosh must include functions that give a program access to such elements as the machine's system toolbox. These functions are hardware-dependent and implementation-specific—by definition, they are not portable, but they are essential to getting the most out of your machine. C, as you will discover, provides a way to gather the machine-dependent parts in an organized manner, something most other languages can't do.

BASIC and, to a lesser extent, Pascal approach hardware dependence by customizing the language itself to include commands or functions that take care of the machine-dependent features. For example, a BASIC statement to control the speaker might be called PLAY. Another version of BASIC might call it MUSIC. The problem with this approach is apparent when you try to convert a program to run on a different machine; you cannot easily find the parts of the program that you must change to manipulate the features of a given machine. Also, such hardware-dependent statements may work differently on computers with different hardware configurations.

A Modular Approach

The programmer's task is more manageable with C. Each C compiler includes files of definitions, called include files, and collections of precompiled functions, called function libraries, which you can use to supplement the core of C to take full advantage of the features of a given machine. Your QuickC function library includes a rich collection of definitions and functions for every significant PC graphics standard, including MDA, CGA, EGA, MCGA, VGA, and Hercules; presentation (business) graphics; the whole set of low-level MS-DOS function calls; and much more.

The result is that a C programmer has several choices. If you don't need graphics or machine-specific features, you can write an ANSI-standard text-only C program and easily move it to other machines and operating systems. If you do need machine-dependent features in your program, you can first develop the "no-frills" version of the program and then add graphics and other hardware-dependent features in easily identified include files and libraries. For a particular hardware environment, you can then merge the appropriate include files and libraries into your program. Figure 1-1 on the following page illustrates the concept of portability.

Portability requires many trade-offs. In general, the less portable (in other words, the more hardware-dependent) a program is, the faster it runs, and the more it takes advantage of graphics and other special hardware features. On the other hand, the more portable a program is, the easier it is to maintain it, to modify it, or to convert it to work with new hardware.

Throughout this book, we point out portability issues and suggest ways to deal with them. For example, we note those features of QuickC that are compatible with ANSI and UNIX System V. We also look at portability versus performance in the MS-DOS world. For example, we discuss alternative ways for dealing with devices such as the keyboard and video display on MS-DOS machines (standard I/O, console I/O, and BIOS) and point out the portability trade-offs involved with each.

(A) BASIC—A SNUG FIT BUT NOT PORTABLE

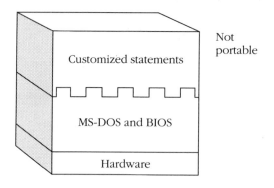

(B) C—A PORTABLE CORE

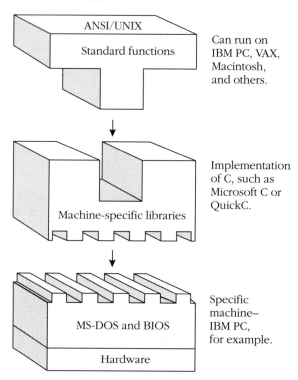

Figure 1-1. *Portability in C.*

C Is Powerful

Portability is desirable, but you also want to write code that takes full advantage of the hardware. In this age of drop-down menus, windows, mice, and help screens, users expect a lot more out of software than they did only a few years ago. As a programmer, you are often pushing the limits of the hardware, whether in processing speed, I/O, or graphics.

When it comes to harnessing the hardware, C really shines. For example, other languages try to hide the fact that you are manipulating the contents of memory when you write code; with C pointers, you can easily manipulate memory directly. With Pascal, you can also directly manipulate memory with pointers, but the syntax is not as simple or as powerful as that of C. And in BASIC, you can use PEEK and POKE to access memory, but they lack the flexibility of pointers.

Another important indicator of the power of a language is its ability to use machine resources efficiently. All high-level compiled languages translate program statements into machine instructions. With most languages you have little control over the efficiency of the resulting machine instructions. You are at the mercy of the assumptions the compiler or interpreter makes about your program and how it will be used. Suppose, for example, that your program uses one or two variables frequently in a loop that will be executed many times. In C, you can declare register variables that are stored, whenever possible, in internal CPU registers; thus, C can help you avoid delays in loading or retrieving their values in memory. The result is greater execution speed.

Another important feature of C is its ability to compile programs using a variety of memory models. A memory model describes the way RAM is used during compilation and the way program code and data are shared in RAM. With most older BASICs you can use only 64 KB of memory to hold program code and data. Today, most MS-DOS machines have at least 256 KB of memory (and often 640 KB or more). Thus, newer compilers for BASIC, Pascal, and other languages often allow access to a larger amount of RAM. But C compilers go a step further: You—the programmer—decide how the computer will allocate memory.

Depending on the needs of your program, you can choose to use most of the machine's memory for storing compiled instructions, you can use most of the memory to store data (such as arrays, structures, or lists), or you can allocate varying numbers of 64-KB memory segments to both. Figure 1-2 on the following page shows the concepts of pointers, register variables, and memory models.

Pointers, register variables, and memory models are only some of the options C gives you for controlling the machine. In addition, most C compilers let you improve, or "optimize," the machine code generated from your program. You can optimize for program size (a smaller .EXE file) or for faster execution or for a combination of these. For example, QuickC performs some optimization for you and lets you choose other features as appropriate. In addition, you can use QuickC in combination with Microsoft C (the professional, industrial-strength C compiler) to provide optimization that is truly the state of the art.

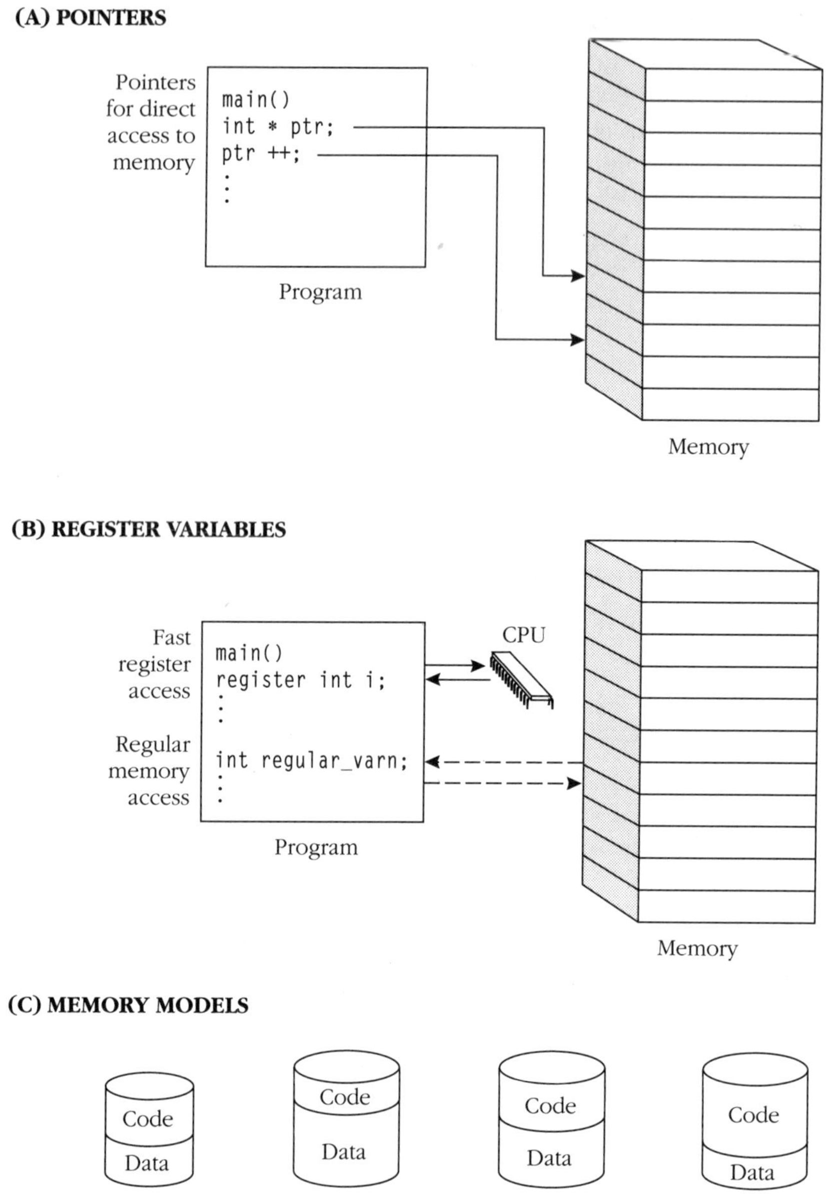

(A) POINTERS

Pointers
for direct
access to
memory

```
main()
int * ptr;
ptr ++;
:
:
```

Program

Memory

(B) REGISTER VARIABLES

Fast
register
access

```
main()
register int i;
:
:
```

Regular
memory
access

```
int regular_varn;
:
:
```

CPU

Program

Memory

(C) MEMORY MODELS

Code

Data

Code

Data

Code

Data

Code

Data

Figure 1-2. *C gives you control of the machine.*

C Is Extensible

C also lets you customize the contents of include files and libraries so that they contain only the definitions and functions your program needs. These custom files can contain functions for anything from manipulating a database to formatting text. After you write and test these definitions and functions, your main program can use them as easily as it can use the standard include files and libraries provided with your compiler. On large real-world programming projects, teams of programmers can receive specifications for each set of routines needed, and each team can create resources that can be used anywhere in the project. Although most languages offer a version of this building-block methodology, the C approach is the simplest, the most flexible, and the easiest to use.

The very popularity of C enhances the value of such language extensions. Hundreds of vendors have created C function libraries for almost every imaginable task. Figure 1-3 shows conceptually how you can use function libraries from both QuickC and

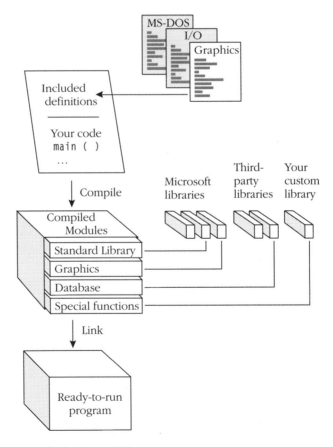

Figure 1-3. *Using include files and libraries.*

other vendors in your programs. You can easily integrate vendor libraries into your own code, and because they are the products of professional C programmers, they are likely to be fast and efficient. You can almost always avoid the age-old problem of reinventing the wheel.

C Is Structured

The syntax of the C language itself supports structured programming. C provides the control structures of a modern structured language, such as *if/else*, *for*, *while*, *while...do*, and *switch*. (The last is like Pascal's *case* statement.) If you are experienced in Pascal or in one of the newer BASICs (such as Microsoft QuickBASIC), you will find these control structures conceptually familiar. However, you will have to learn syntax differences for C, and boxes in this book help to highlight them. If you are used to one of the older BASICs, you will be pleasantly surprised at how these structures enable you to avoid those *goto* statements that can so easily lead to disorganized "spaghetti code."

C Is Concise

Although C is a well-structured language, it encourages concise rather than verbose statements. For example, it uses braces to begin and end blocks of code, rather than Pascal's *begin* and *end*. C provides shorthand operators for assigning values to variables and for incrementing variables. To show the flavor of C, the following table presents a few comparisons of C, Pascal, and BASIC assignment statements:

Some Comparisons of BASIC, Pascal, and C

Task	BASIC	Pascal	C
1. Set a, b, and c to 0	a = 0	a := 0;	a = b = c = 0;
	b = 0	b := 0;	
	c = 0	c := 0;	
2. Set i to i + 1	i = i + 1	i := i + 1;	i++;
3. Set a to a + 5	a = a + 5	a := a + 5;	a += 5;

The conciseness of C speeds the typing of programs and makes C source files more compact and easier to edit. C functions are more accessible than their Pascal counterparts and much more efficient than the awkward subroutine mechanism of BASIC.

The C preprocessor also helps you write concise programs. You can, for instance, create macro definitions, which let you use short, descriptive, easy-to-remember names in your source file; the preprocessor replaces them with expressions or whole blocks of code prior to compilation.

This brief overview of the general features of C should suggest why the language is so popular. Let's now look more closely at the product with which this book is concerned, Microsoft QuickC, and see how its particular features and advantages make programming in C even more attractive.

Why QuickC?

Traditionally, C has had one big drawback compared with interpreted languages such as BASIC—a complex compilation and debugging process. You probably know that C is a compiled language, and MS-DOS–based compiled languages traditionally have required that you go through a lengthy series of steps to produce an executable file. The steps to compiling a traditional C program are the following:

1. Start a text editor or word processor and write a program.

2. Save the program to disk and exit the editor.

3. Run the compiler program by issuing a command line from the DOS prompt, usually with several filenames and cryptic options that tell the compiler what memory model to use, whether to generate a listing file, and so forth.

4. Look at the listing produced by the compiler, and study every error message.

5. Print this error list for reference.

6. Start the editor again, open your C program file, and for each error try to find the exact line in which the error occurred and correct the program.

7. Go back to step 3 and try again until the program compiles without errors into an object code file.

8. Now run the linker and tell it what libraries to combine with your object code file to produce an executable program (an MS-DOS .EXE file). If you used an incorrect function name or failed to specify the correct libraries, you will now get a new batch of error messages, this time from the linker. (They might, for example, report an "unresolved external," which probably means that the name you used for a function in your code did not match the name of the function defined in the library.) To fix these errors, you might need to look at listings of include files. Or you might have to go back to the editor and correct your program. In any case, you must recompile and then try to link again.

9. When the code links without errors, you can finally run the program. Did it execute as you expected? No? Do you want to make some changes? Well, go back to the editor and try again.

Just reading through these steps suggests how tedious a traditional compiled language can be. With interpreted languages, such as BASIC, LOGO, or HyperTalk, you can type a line or two of code, execute it immediately, and see the results. If your line of code contains errors or if you want to add or change something, the interpreter usually provides a simple text editor or line editor you can use immediately.

But interpreted languages have one critical drawback—they're slow. Each line in an interpreted language program has to be translated into machine-executable instructions each time it is encountered. Therefore, only the simplest interpreted-language applications run fast enough for use in the real world.

The philosophy behind QuickC is to provide a programming environment that is as easy to use as an interpreter, but that offers the execution speed obtainable only with a compiler. With QuickC, writing and testing programs is so easy that C can be a beginning programmer's first language.

The QuickC Programming Environment

With QuickC, you do all of your program development in and from the same place—the QuickC integrated programming environment. (Figure 1-4 shows the QuickC screen with the Run menu pulled down.) This environment offers many advantages:

- You can open a file for editing by using the Open command on the File menu, or you can simply start typing a new program. The QuickC full-screen editor is immediately available, with insert/delete, cut/paste, indention—all the features you need to type a program as easily as you type a letter with a word processor. And you never really "leave" this editor. You merely select whatever service you need from the menus.

- Are you used to another editor? The default editor uses WordStar-compatible commands, but you can select alternative "key files" that set up the editor to use the command keys for the Microsoft Editor, BRIEF, EMACS, or Epsilon. You can even use the MKKEY utility to define your own command keys. As an alternative, you can have the integrated environment use an external editor.

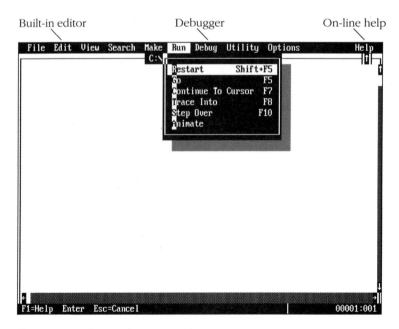

Figure 1-4. *The QuickC integrated programming environment.*

These features allow you to customize the QuickC environment so that it looks like the one with which you're already comfortable.

■ To run the program you can click the mouse or use the keyboard. When you work with a program that has not yet been compiled, the compiler and linker are called as needed. There are no complex command-line options to type. If your program is error free, the program runs in seconds on the output screen.

QuickC compiles your program code very quickly, as fast as 22,000 lines per minute. How does it do this? While older compilers have to recompile the entire source code file each time you change your program, QuickC by default compiles "incrementally," recompiling only those functions you have changed. This can speed up the cycle of program development (testing, debugging, and recompiling) considerably. It also makes it easier for you to experiment with programs by making small changes and observing the results—a good way to learn any language.

■ As you review a series of error messages, the cursor follows along through your program text; you can instantly correct each error with the built-in editor. No printed listings to pore over; no error numbers to look up!

■ Suppose your program compiles correctly but doesn't work as you expected. Without leaving QuickC, you can turn on the debugging and trace features, rerun your program, and then watch the changing values of selected variables, follow the flow of execution, and check the values being passed to and from functions called by your program.

What about multiple-module programs—C programs that have several separately compiled libraries and code files? Traditionally, you had to run a special "make" program and create a file with a unique syntax that tells the compiler how to rebuild your program whenever you change a file. With QuickC's program list feature, you simply tell QuickC what libraries and source code files you want to use. QuickC keeps track of all the other details, such as the relationship between modules and the date each module was last compiled.

■ Do you need access to MS-DOS? Need to make a new directory or back up some programs? Maybe you want to run some previously compiled C programs from MS-DOS. With a traditional, command-line-driven C compiler, you exit the program code editor, work in MS-DOS, and then run the editor again and figure out where you left off. With QuickC, you never leave the integrated programming environment. Using the DOS Shell feature, you exit to MS-DOS, take care of your business, and return to QuickC where you left off.

You can select many other features from the QuickC programming environment in the same easy way. With a command-line compiler, most features require that you type obscure flags or option switches on the command line or create batch files to simplify complicated compiler commands. With QuickC, you select with a mouse or with a few keystrokes such features as the error warning level, language extensions, and optimization. But don't let the convenience deceive you—underneath the covers, QuickC is constructing the proper list of options so that you can use the same linker that the Microsoft C Professional Development System uses. (QuickC also includes a command-line-driven compiler for those times when you have a special need, such as examining preprocessor output.)

QuickC Performs

QuickC is faster in almost all cases than its nearest competitors, and it beats them hands down in floating-point operation. QuickC also is fully compatible with its "big brother," the Microsoft C Professional Development System. Any program that compiles under QuickC compiles under Microsoft C. Therefore, you can develop programs with QuickC and then effortlessly recompile under Microsoft C to fine-tune them, using a variety of optimization techniques.

QuickC: Standard and Comprehensive

Earlier we discussed ANSI and other official standards for C. There are also unofficial industry standards that are almost as important. When you use QuickC, you have the advantage of full compatibility with the compiler that has become the industry standard for PCs: Microsoft C. Thus, dozens of third-party C code libraries work with your programs because the programs you write are compatible with the ANSI or UNIX System V standards or with the MS-DOS–specific features of Microsoft C.

The extras that come with the QuickC product are also impressive. Each standard-model library (tiny, small, medium, compact, large, and huge) supports the 8087 and 80287 coprocessors. There are libraries for every kind of PC graphics from monochrome and CGA to the latest VGA graphics for the IBM PS/2. The QuickC Graphics Library features easy-to-use routines for drawing points and lines and manipulating complete images, all with impressive speed. QuickC also has libraries that allow your programs complete access to MS-DOS and BIOS calls. And, because of QuickC's UNIX compatibility, you can also use UNIX System V functions for writing programs that can be ported to work in the UNIX environment.

Hardware Requirements

To run QuickC you need an IBM PC/XT, PC/AT, PS/2, or compatible computer with at least 512 KB of RAM and a hard disk. Although you can run versions of QuickC prior to version 2.01 with two floppy-disk drives, we recommend that you have a hard drive. Compiling or linking to disk with floppy disks is time-consuming compared to using hard disks. Also, fitting onto two standard floppy disks all the files you need for developing programs can be tricky. But because some of you will be using floppy-disk-based systems, we will give you some tips later that should help you make the best of the situation.

We also recommend (but don't presuppose) that you use QuickC with a compatible mouse. You can handle all QuickC functions from the keyboard, but why get bogged down learning the keystroke combinations? With a mouse in hand, you simply point at what you want and select it.

On the other hand, many people don't have (or choose not to use) a mouse. With QuickC, you can use short keystroke combinations. For example, Alt-R-G selects the Run menu's Go option to compile and run a program. (Even if you have a mouse, typing is sometimes faster.)

Graphics capability is optional for most of this book. Chapter 15, which deals with graphics, requires at least a CGA, of course; for advanced graphics, you need an EGA; and the VGA section requires a PS/2, or a VGA board for older PCs. (If you have the new VGA, you also have CGA and EGA capability.) Even if you have only the basic monochrome adapter, you can enhance your QuickC programs in interesting ways with the built-in IBM graphics character set.

Finally, we recommend that you have a printer (although a printer is not required for executing the programs in this book).

Knowledge Requirements

Some programming experience—with BASIC or Pascal, for example—will help. But thanks to the ease of use of QuickC, C *can* be your first programming language, although you may have to work a bit harder than an experienced programmer.

Because many of you have programmed in BASIC (such as BASICA or Microsoft QuickBASIC) or Pascal (Microsoft QuickPascal or Borland's Turbo Pascal, for example), we scatter "asides" throughout the text for BASIC and Pascal programmers. These point out the ways in which C is similar to and different from those languages. Familiarity with another language is a two-edged sword when it comes to learning C. On the one hand, you already know many programming concepts used in C. On the other hand, differences in syntax and usage can trip you up if you aren't careful.

If you are a UNIX programmer, you will feel right at home—as soon as you get used to QuickC's much more comfortable living room! The QuickC environment is far easier to use than the UNIX *cc* compiler and *ln* linker, and you won't have to write any *make* scripts. You probably already know the fundamentals of C, but watch out for features that are different in the IBM PC/MS-DOS environment, especially graphics and MS-DOS system calls. But as we noted, with a few minor exceptions Microsoft C supports the standard I/O and other library functions used on UNIX systems. Occasional boxes point out matters of interest to UNIX programmers.

Conventions and Style

We have chosen the following typographical conventions for discussing C programs in the text:

■ Names of ordinary (local) variables are lowercase italic. Examples: *count, sum*

■ Names of external or global variables are also italic, but the first letter is capitalized. Example: *Model*

- Underscores join the words of multiple-word variable names. Examples: *Grand_total* (an external variable), *line_count* (an ordinary variable)

- Constants created with *#define* are uppercase italic. Example: *PI*

- Macro definitions are uppercase italic. Example: *PRINT_ERROR(MSG)*

- Names of functions supplied with QuickC (such as *printf()*) are lowercase italic. Names of functions created by the programmer are italic with an initial cap. Example: *Count_lines()*

  You'll also notice keywords and function names that are preceded by an underscore character. Microsoft provides these keywords and functions (the graphics functions, for example), but they do not have the portability guarantees of ANSI-standard features. Example: *_getvideoconfig()* (a Graphics Library function)

- Built-in "keywords," or reserved words, of the C language are italic when they occur in text. Examples: *int*, *do*, *while*

- Filenames (except header filenames) and pathnames are uppercase roman. Examples: \LIB\GRAPHICS.LIB, SCREEN.DAT

- Names of special keys are spelled as they appear on the standard IBM PC extended keyboard. Examples: Enter (not Return), Ctrl-C, the Esc key

Program Listings

Program listings are set off from the text in a monospace font. Constants, variables, and function names are capitalized as indicated in the preceding list, but no italics are used in listings, of course.

In many cases, we provide a sample session that demonstrates how a program interacts with the user. In these sample sessions, user input is italic, as illustrated below.

```
C>guess ─────────────────────── Run the GUESS program
What number am I thinking of? ─── Program response
7 ────────────────────────────── User input
Wrong! Try Again?
3
Right! You win!
```

NOTE: The comments at the right in the sample session above are not part of actual program dialogue. Rather, they help describe what is going on.

Program Style Conventions

A clear, consistent typographical style makes programs easier to read. No single style is universally accepted for C program listings. Ultimately, you fashion your own, based on your judgment and the prevailing usage. In some cases, more than one kind of syntax can be used. Although C itself doesn't care about spacing between the elements of a statement or an expression, we use a space between elements unless removing the space is clearer. Also, we use a 4-space indention for nested statements and the braces that enclose them.

We always align braces ({ and }) vertically—a major stylistic departure from the style adopted by Kernighan and Ritchie. That is, we use

```
while (condition)
    {
    /* body of loop */
    }
```

rather than

```
while (condition) {
    /* body of loop */
    }
```

We believe this style enables you to read the listings and identify blocks of code more easily. Be warned, however, that you will find many C listings that exhibit the second (K&R) style.

Finally, because experienced C programmers often make a virtue of saying a lot with a little, we point out concise, idiomatic coding styles that you are likely to see in program listings from various sources, and we sometimes show two or more ways to code a statement.

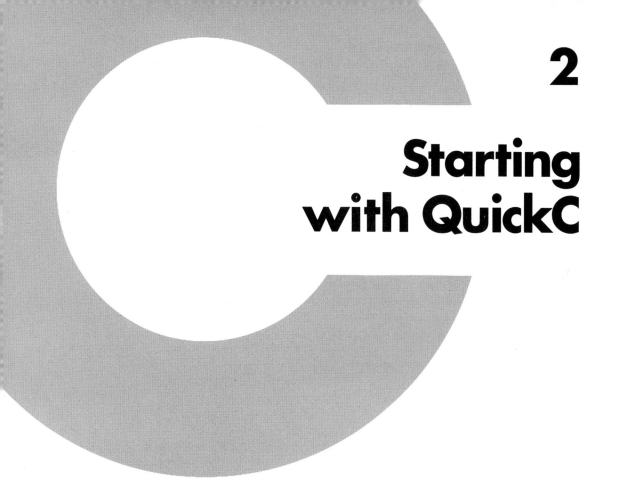

2

Starting with QuickC

You are now ready to explore the QuickC environment. In this chapter we describe the environment, show how to set up QuickC on your computer system, present an overview of the QuickC menus and dialog boxes, and help you create and run your first QuickC program. We also show how to get help from QuickC and how to fix program errors. When you've finished this chapter, you will be comfortable with QuickC and ready to learn the C language itself.

Our Book and Their Book

QuickC comes with an excellent user manual that details the mechanics of using QuickC. It explains how to configure the system, how to use the menus and understand the options they contain, and how to use the programs that comprise the QuickC programming tools. The package for the QuickC program also includes a tutorial book, *C for Yourself,* that discusses a number of aspects of C programming and summarizes the run-time library. Although the topics in the tutorial overlap those covered in this book, *Microsoft QuickC Programming* goes into much greater depth and detail and includes more sample programs.

Because Microsoft clearly documents the details of using QuickC, we are able to devote most of this book to the art and science of programming in C with QuickC. We will summarize the details of using QuickC as needed, however, so that you won't have to spend time flipping between books. Use the documentation provided by Microsoft when you want to find detailed information about using the editor, compiler, linker, and other utilities.

Directories and Files Used by QuickC

Programming in C usually involves combining several files to eventually form an executable program. These files include definitions of data structures and functions (header files), libraries of precompiled functions, and your own program code. The QuickC environment uses several directories to organize the files into distinct groups according to purpose, such as function libraries, include files, and so on. QuickC also uses distinctive filename extensions to identify files that are used or created in the compiling and linking process.

Why So Many Files?

If you use languages such as BASIC or some versions of Pascal, you might wonder why QuickC needs such an elaborate system of files and directories. With most versions of BASIC, for example, you need only two files: the BASIC interpreter program that creates and runs your programs, and the file that contains your BASIC program. Although the QuickC environment can look quite complicated by comparison, QuickC sets up most of the directories and files for you and makes it easy for you to move among all the files of a programming project. Nevertheless, it is important to understand how QuickC organizes files, especially if you need to modify the default organization to avoid conflicts with existing directories or for some similar reason.

To explain the "environment" you work in, we must examine QuickC's directories and the files they contain. We use the QuickC default names in our discussion because the actual names and locations of the directories depend on how you invoke the SETUP program.

The Base Directory and Subdirectories

QuickC installs directories as subdirectories of a single base directory. If you use QuickC by itself, the base directory is usually C:\QC25; thus, the actual pathname for the \BIN directory is probably C:\QC25\BIN. The other critical QuickC directories (also located in \QC25 by default) are \INCLUDE and \LIB. Let's look at these and at some optional directories that you might find useful.

The \BIN Directory, Compiler, and Linker Programs

The \BIN directory contains the program QC.EXE, which runs QuickC, provides the integrated programming environment, and lets you write, compile, link, and execute QuickC programs. (The name "BIN," by the way, is short for "binary." The \BIN directory is usually reserved for "binary files," or files containing executable programs.)

The QuickC package actually contains two compiler programs: QC.EXE, which comprises the integrated programming environment with its editor, menus, and so on; and QCL.EXE, the "command-line" version of the QuickC compiler. (To help distinguish between the programs, think of QCL as "QuickC Line-oriented.") QCL is much like the traditional C compiler we described in Chapter 1. Rather than using menus and dialog boxes, you compile a program by going to the MS-DOS prompt and typing a command line with options. Another program in the \BIN directory, called QLINK.EXE (or LINK.EXE in earlier versions), combines your compiled programs and stand-alone libraries into a single executable program. QuickC usually performs this linking as an invisible process, although you can specify linker options when necessary. When you use QCL, you can control the linker directly with a series of command-line options.

QC.EXE, with its integrated programming environment, is more convenient to use than QCL.EXE, and we assume in most parts of this book that you will use it to compile and run your programs. However, the command-line compiler is very useful for doing what are called batch compilations and is often more convenient than the integrated environment for setting specific combinations of compile options, compiling with alternate memory models, or using an alternative program editor. QCL also lets you use "make" files created with the Microsoft C Professional Development System, version 4.0 or later. (Make files are files that keep track of the compilation of multiple program modules. QuickC offers an easy-to-use alternative called "program lists," which we discuss in Chapter 12.)

The \INCLUDE Directory and Header Files

The "core" of C is greatly extended by compiler vendors who develop new sets of predefined constants, macros, data structures, and functions for such areas as graphics, device I/O, and MS-DOS. Some of these elements are standard (ANSI standard or UNIX System V standard) and are found in virtually all compilers; others are specific to the IBM PC or to Microsoft. The QuickC \INCLUDE directory contains many text files of both types. These are known as "include files" because your program can include definitions from one or more of these files. (They are also known as "header files" because their names must be specified at the beginning, or head, of a program.) This is also where you'll put include files that come with any third-party libraries you obtain.

Include files are not executable files or complete C source programs; they are ordinary text files that contain useful definitions. Their purpose is to provide an interface between your program and the compiled code in stand-alone libraries. When a program references an include file, the code in the include file is inserted into and compiled with the code you actually typed in.

For example, the include file stdio.h contains many of the most commonly used input and output functions, and graphics.h contains definitions for data structures and functions in the Graphics Library. The following table lists the standard QuickC include files. Note that include files have filenames with the .h extension. (Don't worry about understanding this comprehensive list yet; we will discuss many of the include files in detail as we use them in programs throughout the book.)

In QuickC, the \INCLUDE directory also contains a subdirectory called \SYS. This subdirectory contains system-specific include files for IBM personal computers and compatibles.

QuickC Include Files

File	Main Purpose
assert.h	Debugging expressions
bios.h	Interface to the IBM BIOS (basic input/output system) hardware functions
conio.h	PC-specific console (keyboard) and port (device) I/O
ctype.h	Character testing and conversion
direct.h	Creating, removing, and changing MS-DOS directories
dos.h	Setting and reading 8086 registers for MS-DOS calls
errno.h	System-wide error numbers
fcntl.h	Opening MS-DOS files with various modes
float.h	Implementation-dependent values for advanced floating-point operations
graph.h	Microsoft-specific data structures and functions for monochrome (MDA), CGA, EGA, MCGA, and VGA graphics
io.h	Low-level file-handling and I/O routines
limits.h	Implementation-dependent values for sizes and ranges for data types, etc.
locale.h	Localization routines
malloc.h	Memory allocation functions
math.h	Definitions used by math library
memory.h	Memory manipulation routines (buffer setup, etc.)
pgchart.h	Functions for charting (presentation graphics)
process.h	Used with routines that allow a program to "spawn" (run) another program as a "child process"
search.h	Sorting and searching routines
setjmp.h	Used for saving and restoring the program state during a "long jump" (jump to a different memory segment)
share.h	Flags that control sharing of a file among several users (i.e., on a network)
signal.h	Values for "signals" that can be sent to interrupt handlers, etc.
stdarg.h	Routines that let a function use a variable number of arguments (ANSI style)

(continued)

File	Main Purpose
stddef.h	Miscellaneous constants, types, and variables
stdio.h	UNIX-compatible standard I/O, such as functions to get and put characters to the console or a file
stdlib.h	Definitions for miscellaneous library functions
string.h	Definitions for string manipulation functions
time.h	Data structures used for accessing system time
varargs.h	Routines that let a function use a variable number of arguments (XENIX-style)

The \SYS subdirectory of \INCLUDE contains:

locking.h	Flags for locking files (for networks)
stat.h	Structure definition used to return status of an MS-DOS file or directory
timeb.h	Types used by *ftime()* (used to get current time)
types.h	Types used in values returned by functions for time and file status information
utime.h	Used by *utime()* to update access and modification times for MS-DOS files

The \LIB Directory and Libraries

Much of C programming involves writing code that uses standard C functions to perform such tasks as getting a character from the keyboard or sending a text string to the screen. Microsoft has already compiled these functions for you and has placed them in files called "libraries." The \LIB directory contains these library files, which have the filename extension .LIB. As noted earlier, when QuickC starts, it includes in memory the code for a considerable number of commonly used functions.

If you examine the PACKING.LST file on the QuickC Product disk, you will see many libraries with similar names, such as SLIBCR.LIB, SLIBFP.LIB, or MLIBCR.LIB. Why are there so many libraries? The architecture of the Intel 8086 and 80286 processors used by the IBM PC family requires that memory be divided into 64-KB segments. As a result, special instructions are needed to access program instructions or data that go beyond a single segment. The designers of C compilers address this problem by providing programmers with multiple memory models, each containing a different allocation of segments for code and data. (QuickC uses tiny, small, compact, medium, large, and huge memory models.) Additional libraries handle floating-point (decimal) calculations: Some use the 8087 floating-point coprocessor chip, others use software that emulates its functions. Also included are two optional graphics libraries: GRAPHICS.LIB, the general graphics library; and PGCHART.LIB, the presentation graphics (charting) library.

Combined Libraries

You can use libraries in two ways. When you compile, you can tell the linker to include specified libraries (a memory-model library, a floating-point library, a graphics library, and so on). Although you can use a program list to identify the necessary libraries, the process can involve a bit of bookkeeping. The easier way to use libraries is to employ the SETUP program (discussed later in this chapter) to build one or more combined libraries. A combined library is a package that contains one library for the floating-point option, one standard library for the specified memory model, and some general-purpose "helper" libraries. It can also contain the optional libraries GRAPHICS.LIB and PGCHART.LIB. The advantage of creating a combined library is that QuickC uses it by default, so you don't have to specify library names when you compile and link. The \LIB directory contains any combined libraries you create with the setup process. (QuickC 1.0 also used a subdirectory called \TMP to store temporary files created during compilation. With QuickC versions 2.0 and later, you no longer need this subdirectory.)

The \SAMPLES and \TUTORIAL Directories

The QuickC SETUP program creates a \SAMPLES directory on your hard disk and stores in it several sample programs. You can use these to practice loading, editing, compiling, and running QuickC programs. The SETUP program also creates the \TUTORIAL directory, which contains the files used by the QuickC on-line tutorial (described later).

The \PROG or \SOURCE Directory

By default, QuickC stores your programs in the current directory when you invoke the compiler. All other files created by the compiling and linking process are also stored there. You can create your own directories to store the source code (the actual program text) for the C programs you write and the various files QuickC builds from your source files. Although this is entirely optional, it makes for a more orderly directory and helps you organize and find your programs more easily.

Whatever your current directory, the process of writing, compiling, and linking programs creates the following kinds of files, depending on the compiler and linker options you select:

NAME.C—Source code for the C program NAME

NAME.OBJ—Object code produced by the compiler for the C program NAME

NAME.EXE—The compiled and linked object code for the program NAME, which can be executed by typing *name* at the MS-DOS prompt

NAME.MAK—A "make" file containing instructions that QuickC uses to recompile or "rebuild" your program if you change it

NAME.ILK—A file used to keep track of what has been changed in the source program (used by the incremental linker)

NAME.SYM—A symbol table used to resolve internal references

NAME.MDT—Information about the incremental compilation of each source file

Figure 2-1 summarizes our tour of QuickC directories and files. Without listing all the QuickC files, the chart shows a typical directory structure for QuickC on a hard disk.

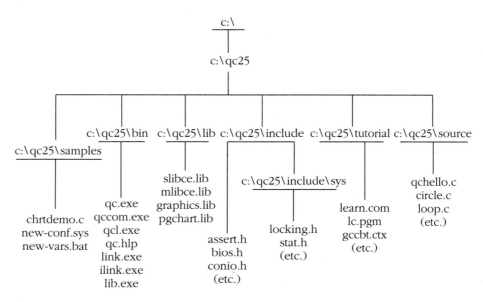

Figure 2-1. *Typical directory structure for QuickC versions 2.0 and later.*

From Source to Object: An Overview

Now that we've surveyed the compiler, the linker, include files, and libraries, let's see how they work together when you run a program with QuickC. Let's assume your program uses two include files, stdio.h and graph.h. When you "run" or "start" the QuickC compile/link phase, the compiler starts by "reading" your source code in the editor buffer. First it sees the instructions to add the include files. The compiler then loads the stdio.h file and compiles the code found there. (The code in an include file is not already compiled.) Next it loads and compiles graph.h. These include files contain, among other things, declarations of functions that are implemented in libraries. (The standard library for each memory model implements the functions declared in standard header files such as stdio.h; GRAPHICS.LIB implements the functions in graph.h.) As it compiles the include file, the compiler notes these references to library code and passes them to the linker.

After the compiler generates the object code for the part of the program you wrote yourself, the linker "resolves" all library references: It extracts from the appropriate libraries the "modules" that contain the necessary code and combines them with the rest of the code. QuickC then creates the files mentioned in the discussion of the \PROG directory in the previous section. Finally, it creates the executable file. If you had asked QuickC to run the program rather than simply compile it, the executable file would then run, and you would be able to view any resulting screen output. Figure 2-2 on the following page summarizes this process graphically.

QuickC creates executable files with the extension .EXE, unless you specify the tiny memory model, which produces executable files with the extension .COM. You can run an executable file created by QuickC by typing its name at the DOS prompt.

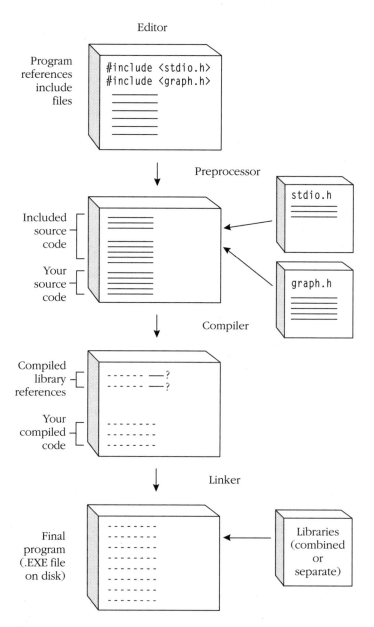

Figure 2-2. *Compiling and linking with include files and libraries.*

Running the QuickC SETUP Program

Microsoft distributes QuickC on either 5.25-inch or 3.5-inch floppy-disk sets. These disks contain the two compilers (integrated-environment and command-line), a full set of libraries for each memory model with a choice of 80x87 hardware support or emulation, a rich assortment of more than 30 include files, several utility programs, and many other support files. The QuickC SETUP program lets you set up a working environment that contains only the files and directories you need and that affords automatic access to critical directories. SETUP performs the following operations:

- Sets up variables and commands in the MS-DOS environment that tell the operating system where to find all QuickC programs and files

- Sets up a home directory for QuickC on your hard disk, creates the \BIN, \INCLUDE, \LIB, \SAMPLES, and \TUTORIAL subdirectories, and moves files from the floppy disks to these directories

- Creates one or more combined libraries, depending on the memory model(s) and form of floating-point support you specify

MS-DOS Variables and QuickC

As we mentioned above, QuickC uses some MS-DOS environment variables, which specify the locations of system resources. When you boot an MS-DOS disk, the operating system calls on two files to configure the system: AUTOEXEC.BAT and CONFIG.SYS. Commands in these files control the environment that QuickC uses.

When you run the SETUP program for a hard-disk system, SETUP creates two files: NEW-VARS.BAT and NEW-CONF.SYS. You can rename these files and use them as is or insert their contents into your existing AUTOEXEC.BAT and CONFIG.SYS files respectively. We recommend the latter procedure unless there are serious conflicts with your existing settings. If you have no AUTOEXEC.BAT, use the MS-DOS command RENAME to rename NEW-VARS.BAT as AUTOEXEC.BAT.

You can use any editor (such as Sidekick or Edlin) to insert NEW-VARS.BAT in your AUTOEXEC.BAT file. The resulting file might look like this:

```
setclock ───────────────────── Set system clock
fastopen c: ──────────────────── Install file access cache
sk ───────────────────────────── Run Sidekick
PATH=c:\;c:\wp;c:\qc25\bin;a:\ ─── Combined with your old path
set INCLUDE=c:\qc25\include
set LIB=c:\qc25\lib
```

After you insert the PATH and SET commands found in NEW-VARS.BAT, you will probably have two *PATH*= commands in your AUTOEXEC.BAT file. Combine the directories in the path provided by SETUP with your existing path, as shown in Figure 2-3. You can normally use the SET commands without modification. (By default, MS-DOS permits only 128 bytes of space for storing MS-DOS variable values. If this amount proves insufficient, modify it as described in the box on page 29.)

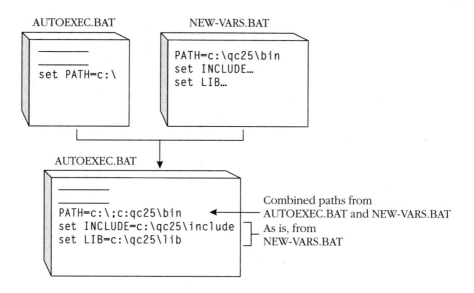

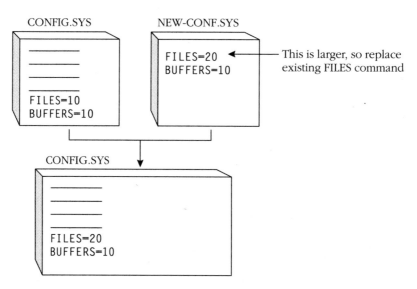

Figure 2-3. *Editing AUTOEXEC.BAT and CONFIG.SYS.*

Here's what the NEW-VARS.BAT commands do. PATH is an MS-DOS command that specifies the directories that MS-DOS searches to execute a program. Whenever you tell MS-DOS to execute a program on your hard disk (such as the QuickC linker or library manager), it first looks in the current directory and then checks the specified directories in the order they are listed. The next command tells QuickC that include files are in the \INCLUDE subdirectory of the base QuickC directory. Similarly, the last command (*set LIB=c:\qc25\lib*) specifies that the libraries needed to link your programs are found in \QC25\LIB.

Setting Up QuickC

Now let's set up the QuickC working environment. The QuickC manual should be your source for detailed information about setup procedures and the various options involved, but here are "quick start" instructions that can simplify the process and probably save you time.

The basic steps you should follow are:

1. Check the PACKING.LST file on the first QuickC distribution disk. Be sure you have a complete set of disks and manuals.

2. Back up the QuickC disks to floppy disks. (Use the MS-DOS DISKCOPY command to ensure you have an exact copy.) Then use the backups during the setup process.

3. Use the command *MORE < README.DOC* to read about last-minute changes to the QuickC documentation. The README.DOC file is on the Setup disk. At this point you're mainly looking for matters pertaining to the installation of QuickC, so you can read the first section only and skip the rest for now. Later, you might want to print a copy of this file for reference. You can also display the README file from the on-line Help system.

4. Run the SETUP program.

Before you run SETUP and before you use QuickC to develop programs, be sure that you have at least 512 KB of free memory (448 KB for version 2.0). QuickC may appear to run fine with somewhat less than 512 KB until you try to compile certain programs.

Out of Environment Space?

If your current AUTOEXEC.BAT has many SET commands or a long *PATH=* statement, you might get an MS-DOS "out of environment space" error when you add the QuickC variables. If this happens, expand the available environment space by putting this command in your CONFIG.SYS file:

```
shell=c:\command.com /e:size/p
```

For MS-DOS versions 3.0 and 3.1, *size* is the number of 16-byte "paragraphs" you want to reserve for the MS-DOS environment variables; for MS-DOS versions 3.2 and later, it is the actual number of bytes. The default *size* is 10 paragraphs, or 160 bytes. To set the environment to 256 bytes, use

```
shell=command.com /e:16/p ———————————— MS-DOS version 3.0 or 3.1
shell=command.com /e:256/p ——————————— MS-DOS version 3.2 or later
```

To verify the amount of free memory, enter the CHKDSK command at the MS-DOS prompt. To increase the amount of free memory, you might be able to change your AUTOEXEC.BAT file so that some memory-resident programs are not loaded. Then reboot to free the memory those programs were reserving.

CHKDSK will also tell you how much space is available on your fixed disk. To install QuickC, you need about 2.75 MB of available space, depending on whether you include the tutorial (which is recommended), and on how many libraries you choose to install. If you install all of the libraries and documentation files, you need about 6 MB.

Setting Up QuickC for Hard-Disk Systems

The QuickC installation program, SETUP, is very easy to use. It is menu driven and gives an on-screen explanation of each question it asks. You simply press the Enter key to accept the default shown in brackets, or type a different response if needed. The following discussion therefore touches on only a few of the more important SETUP options.

When you are asked for the following:

```
Math options:  Emulator [Y]:     8087 [N]:
```

accept the defaults unless you will want to compile programs that require the presence of a numeric coprocessor chip (8087, 80287, or 80387). These chips allow much faster processing of program instructions that involve floating-point calculations. If you specify y for the 8087 option and you want to generate code that can also run on a system with no numeric coprocessor (if you are writing commercial software, for example), you should also accept the default y for the Emulator option.

Are You Using Both QuickC and the Microsoft C Professional Development System?

If you use both QuickC and the Microsoft C Professional Development System, you can install both compilers on your fixed disk without causing any conflict. Because both compilers use the same library and include files, and because both compilers use the same environment variable names to locate these files, you won't have to create separate directories for each compiler's library and include files. Simply install the QuickC libraries and include files in the directories that you set up for a prior installation of the professional system. The only planning and organizational work you'll need to do is to organize the compiler files and the source code files.

QuickC's fast compiler can save time in program development, and then the sophisticated optimizations of the larger compiler can speed the execution of your program. Further, if a program is syntactically correct but uses features of the larger compiler (such as certain compiler directives), QuickC simply checks your syntax and then ignores those features when you run the program.

The kinds of programs you will be able to compile can be affected by the memory models you choose in the following option:

```
Memory Models:  Small [Y]:    Medium [N]:    Compact [N]:    Large [N]:
```

As was mentioned in Chapter 1, memory models allow you to determine what memory segments will be used to store your program's instructions and data. Since each memory model has its own set of libraries, specifying models that you will not be using wastes considerable space on your fixed disk. For learning purposes, the default small model is fine. (In QuickC 1.0 the default [and only] memory model supported in the integrated environment was the medium model.)

You can install additional models later by running SETUP again with the *setup /l* command. This causes SETUP to prompt you for new models without repeating the rest of the setup process. (You can also use the */h* option with SETUP, which causes SETUP to omit the on-screen help information that accompanies prompts.)

Watch for the following prompt:

```
Include in combined libraries: GRAPHICS.LIB [N]:    PGCHART.LIB [N]:
```

Because this book presents programs using QuickC's general graphics functions and its new presentation graphics (charting) functions, we suggest you change both of these responses to *y*. That way you won't have to worry about linking these libraries separately each time you compile a graphics program. If it turns out that you won't be using graphics, you can run SETUP with the */l* option and re-create your libraries without the graphics components to save fixed-disk space.

QuickC provides full mouse support but does not require a mouse. When you see the following item:

```
Install Microsoft Mouse [Y]:
```

change the answer to *n* if you don't have a Microsoft (or Microsoft-compatible) mouse. If you do have a compatible mouse, accept the installation and try it out—the choice of mouse or keyboard is mainly a matter of individual preference. The MOUSE.COM driver supplied with QuickC is the latest version, so you should install it even if you have an earlier version of MOUSE.COM or MOUSE.SYS. Be sure that your AUTOEXEC.BAT file runs \QC25\BIN\MOUSE.COM. If you have an older driver that is installed via a DEVICE statement in your CONFIG.SYS file, be sure to remove or comment out that statement.

If you are using MS-DOS 3.2, watch out for this item:

```
Copy the DOS patch files [N]:
```

This version of MS-DOS has bugs that can affect your program's handling of floating-point operations. If you have MS-DOS 3.2 or PC-DOS 3.20, we recommend responding *y* to this installation option. After installing QuickC, read the .DOC files in the \QC25\BIN\PATCH directory that this option creates. They will tell you whether you need to install one or both patches, and how to do so.

When you are asked whether you want to copy the sample programs and the tutorial files, we recommend that you respond *y* unless your disk space is very limited. The tutorial is a very useful introduction to QuickC, and the sample programs are good educational tools, especially for learning how to use the graphics functions. You can, however, run these files from copies of your distribution disks.

Finally, if you will be using the full Microsoft C Professional Development System in addition to QuickC, check your documentation and README file for instructions about specifying directories for the include files and libraries to ensure that you install the latest versions of these files.

After you respond to all the prompts, SETUP creates the QuickC directories, places header files in the \INCLUDE subdirectory, creates a "combined library" for each specified memory model using the floating-point option you selected, and places the

Setting Up QuickC for Floppy-Disk Systems

Versions of QuickC prior to version 2.01 can be installed and run on a system that has two floppy-disk drives and no hard disk drive. With any version of QuickC, however, the size and complexity of the program create difficulties for the floppy-disk user.

If you are installing QuickC on floppy disks, see the appropriate section in the Microsoft documentation. The README file for version 2.0 gives a sample setup for floppy-disk users. When you run SETUP, the combined libraries of your choice will be created on separate floppy disks (if space allows); have the disks ready before you begin. The documentation also explains how to create the \INCLUDE and \LIB directories "by hand" and how to set the required MS-DOS variables. (SETUP does not create the NEW-VARS.BAT or NEW-CONF.SYS files for floppy-disk installation.) Be sure that your CONFIG.SYS file sets minimum values of *FILES=20* and *BUFFERS=10*.

When you run QuickC, you will occasionally have to swap disks when the compiler or linker can't find a needed file. The suggested setup provided by Microsoft is designed to minimize swapping and works well with small programs, such as the examples in this book. The examples in the book do, however, assume you have a hard disk with QuickC residing in a directory in drive C. To use the same sample programs on a floppy-disk system, substitute references as follows:

Fixed Disk	*Floppy Disk*
C:\QC25\BIN	A:
C:\QC25\INCLUDE	A:\INCLUDE
C:\QC25\LIB	B:

combined libraries in the \LIB subdirectory. These libraries are called your "standard libraries" because they contain compiled versions of all the standard C routines (with specified options, such as graphics).

If you have already edited your MS-DOS AUTOEXEC.BAT and CONFIG.SYS files, your QuickC environment is now set up and ready to use.

Starting QuickC

Now we're ready to start using QuickC. If you have QuickC on a fixed disk and have correctly included \QC25\BIN in the PATH variable in the AUTOEXEC.BAT file, run QuickC by entering

qc

at the C> prompt. (If you haven't changed your PATH variable to include \QC25\BIN, you must change to this directory before you can run QuickC.)

Improving the QuickC Display

When you enter *qc* on the MS-DOS command line, QuickC assumes you have a color monitor. If you have a monochrome monitor, this default setting can reduce the contrast of the characters on your screen and make them hard to read. To fix this, exit QuickC by selecting Exit from the File menu and start QuickC in its "black-and-white" mode by entering *qc /b*. To produce the same effect, choose Color from the Options menu and select LCD. QuickC saves color settings from session to session.

If you use a computer that refreshes the screen at a faster rate than that of standard ATs, as some higher-performance models of COMPAQ computers do, you can speed screen displays by using the command *qc /g* to start QuickC.

If your computer has an EGA or VGA card, you can set the screen to display 43 or 50 lines, instead of the normal 25, by starting QuickC with the *qc /h* command. The \h option sets the maximum number of lines your video hardware can support. Unless you have a high-resolution monitor, however, text can be hard to read in this mode.

If your display does not support high-intensity colors (as is the case with LCD monitors on many laptops and with some Amdek color monitors), start QuickC with the command *qc /nohi*, or choose Color from the Options menu and select Color 3.

You can combine mode options by separating them with a space. For example, the command *qc /b /g* starts QuickC in monochrome mode and accelerates the screen refresh rate. You can also put the *qc* command and options in a batch file so that you don't have to type them each time you start.

If you have a specific program that you want to load into the editor when QuickC starts, simply include the filename of that program in the *qc* command. You don't need to specify the .C extension, but you do need to supply the pathname if the file is not in your current directory. For example, the command *qc /b newprog* specifies the monochrome video display and loads the program NEWPROG.C from the current directory. Notice that options such as */b* must precede the filename.

Overview of the QuickC Screen

If you've used menu-based integrated programming environments, such as Turbo Pascal and Microsoft QuickBASIC, the QuickC screen, shown in Figure 2-4, should look familiar.

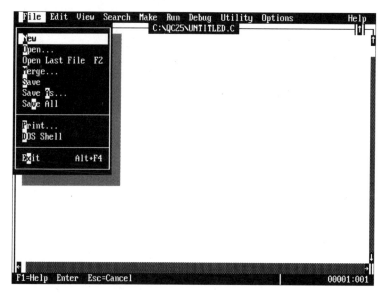

Figure 2-4. *QuickC startup screen with the File menu open.*

Notice the following screen elements:

- The menu bar across the top of the screen lists the following options: File, Edit, View, Search, Make, Run, Debug, Utility, Options, and Help.

- The title bar displays the name of the program currently loaded into the editor. (Because we haven't created and saved a program yet, the title now reads *UNTITLED.C.*)

- The main area of the screen, now blank, is the workspace for your program editing.

- A menu (the File menu) is currently pulled down. If the File menu on your screen shows fewer options, choose Full Menus from the Options menu.

- Two scroll bars, a vertical one on the right side of the screen and a horizontal one near the bottom of the screen, give you the option of using a mouse to scroll text up and down or side to side.

- The small arrow below the word *Help* on the menu bar controls the size of the current window. If you click on it with the mouse, the window will expand to full-screen size; click on it again, and the window will shrink. When only one window is open (as is the case in the figure), this function does not work.

■ The line at the bottom of the screen has two parts. On the left is a list of shortcut keystrokes appropriate to the current situation. Wherever an equal sign appears (as in *F1=Help*), you can also select that function by clicking on it with the mouse. The right side of the bottom line shows the current position of the cursor, in the format *line:column*.

Trying Out QuickC: The On-Line Tutorial

QuickC versions 2.0 and later come with an on-line tutorial that introduces you to the basic elements of using QuickC. The tutorial has four main lessons. The first one shows you how to use the tutorial itself. The lesson called "Getting Around in QuickC" shows you how to move among the menus and windows in the environment and how to get on-line help. The other two lessons cover creating programs (loading, compiling, and running them, and using program lists) and debugging.

You can install the tutorial when you run SETUP or you can choose Customize Menu from the Utility menu, type the pathname to the tutorial, and choose Save. After you install the tutorial, you can run it at any time by choosing Learn QuickC from the Utility menu. Alternatively, you can run the tutorial by putting the disk labeled "Learning the Microsoft QuickC Integrated Environment" in drive A and entering *a:learn* at the MS-DOS prompt. (On 3.5-inch disks, this tutorial program is located on the Setup disk.) We strongly recommend that you go through the tutorial to get a quick, hands-on introduction to each aspect of using QuickC.

Making Selections

The best way to get accustomed to the use of the menus, dialog boxes, and "hot key" shortcuts is to go through the tutorial and skim the Microsoft documentation and on-line help. For the sake of convenience, however, the following table lists some of the shortcut keys commonly used in editing and running programs.

Key	Function
F2	Open the last file used
Alt-Backspace	Undo the last edit
Shift-Del	Cut the marked text
Ctrl-Ins	Copy the marked text
Shift-Ins	Paste the cut or copied text
Del	Clear the marked text
F4	View the output screen
Ctrl-\	Search for selected text
F3	Repeat the last search
Shift-F3	Find the next error
Shift-F4	Find the previous error
Shift-F5	Start the current program
F5	Compile, link, and run the current program

The Mouse

Although you can select all QuickC functions from the keyboard, you might want to try using a mouse if you have one. With a mouse, you need only to point and click to select anything on the screen. Because you don't have to learn all the keystroke combinations for making selections or using the editor, you can concentrate on learning C right away. Further, the mouse makes it easier to select items from a dialog box. You might want to learn both the mouse and keyboard methods and see which one best suits you. Or you can mix them, using the keyboard for making menu selections and the mouse for making selections in dialog boxes, for example.

If QuickC doesn't seem to respond to your mouse, check your AUTOEXEC.BAT file to ensure that the driver MOUSE.COM is being run when you start your system. (Some mice use drivers in the CONFIG.SYS file instead.) Your mouse must be a Microsoft mouse or a compatible one, such as the IBM PS/2 mouse or the Logitech serial mouse.

Writing a Program

Now we're ready to write a simple C program, which we will call QCHELLO.C. First, select the File menu. Note the Exit option on the File menu. Choose this option when you're ready to end your QuickC session. If you select Exit after changing your current program, QuickC first asks if you want to save the changed program. When you exit QuickC, you return to the MS-DOS prompt. If you have a mouse, move the mouse until the pointer on the screen is on the File menu, and click the left button. This reveals the File menu, which is shown in Figure 2-4 on page 34. To reveal the File menu using the keyboard, press the Alt key and then press the *F* key. Notice that each menu item has a highlighted letter (often, but not always, the first letter in the word or phrase). Type this letter to select the menu item.

On the same line as the Exit option is the key combination Alt-F4. This means that Alt-F4 is the hot key for this option. You can press Alt-F4 to exit QuickC without having to use the menu. Any menu option that also has a hot key shows the key combination in this way. Simply noticing these key combinations is a painless way to learn them. Gradually, you may find yourself using more hot keys and fewer menu or mouse selections.

By default, QuickC presents simplified menus showing only the most commonly needed options. If you choose Full Menus from the Options menu, QuickC displays all the menu options. We recommend that you do this.

Selecting a File

Choose the Open option from the File menu—press O or move the mouse pointer to Open and click the left mouse button. When you select the Open option, a *dialog box* appears, such as the one shown in Figure 2-5. QuickC uses dialog boxes to obtain the information it needs to carry out your requests.

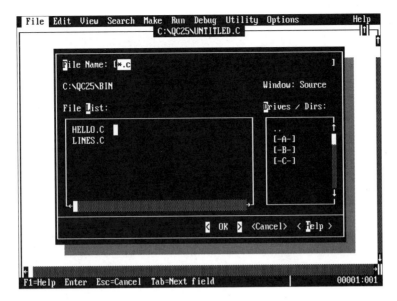

Figure 2-5. *The Open dialog box.*

The box you see is a standard dialog box that appears when QuickC needs you to select a file. (It is also used for other purposes as well, such as saving or merging a file.) You can select a file in two ways. You can type the filename (or a complete pathname) between the brackets that follow the label File Name. The cursor is already waiting at that location.

The other way to select a file is to choose a filename from the file list. Below the File List label is a large rectangle with some names in it. This is a list of the contents of the current directory, which is probably C:\QC25\BIN. Only C program source files, filenames with the .C extension, are listed. To the right, under the label Drives/Dirs, is a smaller rectangle. This lists any subdirectories of the current directory, as well as the drives on the system, such as A and C.

To change the current drive or directory, simply double-click (click the left mouse button twice quickly) on the name of the drive or directory to which you want to switch. With the keyboard, use the Tab key to move into the Drives/Dirs area, and use the Up Arrow and Down Arrow keys to highlight the drive or directory you want. Press Enter to select the highlighted item.

Notice that the symbol .. is included in the Drives/Dirs list. Selecting .. moves you up one level in the directory hierarchy. For example, if you are in \QC25\BIN, selecting .. will change the current directory to \QC25. When you change the current drive, directory, or file, the filename and pathname shown near the top of the dialog box are updated automatically. Practice moving among the files and directories. Try inserting the floppy disk with the QuickC SAMPLES directory in drive A and switching to it.

General techniques for selecting from dialog boxes are as follows:

- With a mouse, move the pointer to the item you want. Click the left button to select the item.

- With the keyboard, use the Tab or back-Tab (shifted Tab) key to move from one section of the dialog box to another. Use the Up Arrow and Down Arrow keys to move the cursor from item to item. Press Enter to select the item.

With the back-Tab or your mouse, move the cursor to the File Name text box. Type *qchello.c* and then press the Enter key. Another small dialog box appears to inform you that this file does not exist. Accept the default of *Yes* to create it.

Typing the Program

You are now ready to type a program. QuickC's default mode is in fact "edit mode," and the large area of the screen with the cursor in it is the Edit window. As you type the text in Listing 2-1, you can use the arrow keys to move the cursor and the Backspace key to make corrections. Press Enter at the end of each line.

```
/* qchello.c -- a simple C program */

main()
{
    printf("Hello, and welcome to QuickC!\n");
}
```

Listing 2-1. *The QCHELLO.C program.*

Saving the Program

To save this program to disk for future reference, open the File menu again. Notice the Save and Save As options. Select Save to write the file to disk using the name you specified when you opened the file. When the dialog box appears, type *QCHELLO.C* and press Enter. Figure 2-6 shows the screen after you save the file.

What Does It Do?

Although we won't look at the structure and anatomy of C until the next chapter, this program gives you a hint of C style. The first line (enclosed by the characters /* and */) is a comment that briefly describes the program. Comments are optional but highly recommended. The word *main()* indicates the beginning of the main function. A function is a group of related statements in a program. (Most C programs have many functions in addition to the main one.) As the name suggests, *printf()* prints the string in the parentheses that follow. The braces, *{* and *}*, set off the group of statements (only one statement in this case) that constitutes the *main* function. So it's easy to see what this program does: It prints *Hello, and welcome to QuickC!* on the screen. (The \n at the end of the string simply moves the cursor to the beginning of a new line.)

```
 File  Edit  View  Search  Make  Run  Debug  Utility  Options          Help
                        C:\QC25\BIN\QCHELLO.C
/* qchello.c -- a simple C program */

main()
{
    printf("Hello, and welcome to QuickC!\n");
}




















 <F1=Help> <Alt=Menu> <Shift+F5=Restart>                        00007:001
```

Figure 2-6. *QCHELLO.C as typed into the Edit window.*

Running QCHELLO.C

Running the program is simple. Select the Run menu. As you probably know, before we can run our program we must first compile and link it. The Go option on the Run menu executes all these steps for you: compiling, linking, and running the program.

QuickC pops up a small box that keeps you informed of the number of lines compiled. If you get any error messages, simply proofread your program to be sure it matches Listing 2-1. (If you still have errors, you have probably installed QuickC incompletely or incorrectly. Review the setup instructions.) Compilation and linking are finished in a couple of seconds, assuming you installed QuickC on a hard disk. With the Go option, QuickC runs your program as soon as it is compiled and linked.

After the program runs, the screen displays the following:

```
C:\QC25\BIN\QCHELLO.EXE
Hello, and welcome to QuickC!

Elapsed time = 00:00:00.05.  Program returned (30).  Press any key.
```

You are now looking at the "output screen." QuickC keeps track of the output screen, which always holds the results of your programs, so you can switch back and forth between it and the QuickC environment screen.

The first line of the output, QCHELLO.EXE, gives the name of the executable (.EXE) file created for your program on disk. We will not bother to show this line in subsequent listings of program output. (In fact, several files—.EXE, .SYM, .ILK, and so on—are created for each program you compile. You will probably want to get rid of all the compiler-created files but the .EXE file eventually, to save disk space.) The program itself generates the next line of output; it is the message specified in the program line beginning *printf*. The last line gives the time it took the program to run (about five hundredths of a second). This value varies with the processing hardware.

Press any key to return to QuickC. For now, don't worry about the return value mentioned in the third output line.

Escaping to MS-DOS

At the File menu, select the item DOS Shell. This option switches the display to the output screen where the MS-DOS sign-on message and prompt appear. You can now run any MS-DOS command, as well as most programs and batch files.

To run QCHELLO.EXE, enter

```
C>qchello
```

Only the program's output (the "hello" message) appears, rather than the additional information shown when the program is run from QuickC. This is because QuickC itself isn't running now. The program is being run directly from MS-DOS.

Now enter the following to return to QuickC exactly where you left it:

```
C>exit
```

Getting Help

We will not cover every feature of QuickC in this book so that we can devote more space to C itself. Although we occasionally refer you to the QuickC documentation, there's another source of help as near as your keyboard—the QuickC Help facility.

QuickC offers help at almost any point when you are using the integrated environment. You can get help directly on any of the following:

- The C language keyword, operator, or library function currently under the cursor in the Edit window

- Any topic listed in the Help contents outline or in an alphabetical index

- The currently selected menu option

- The current dialog box

- Any compiler or linker error message

- The Help facility itself

Because of its many context-sensitive features, Microsoft calls this Help system the Quick Advisor. Once you access the Help system, you can browse its contents using "hyperlinks" to move to related topics. The on-line tutorial shows you how to summon the various kinds of help screens. The sections that follow simply summarize the help features.

Getting Help at the Cursor Position

As you write a program, or examine someone else's, you might find it useful to get an explanation of such things as the *for* statement, the ++ operator, or a library function such as *printf()*. Figure 2-7 shows the Help window for the *printf()* function in QCHELLO.C. To display this information, move the cursor to *printf* in the program code and press F1.

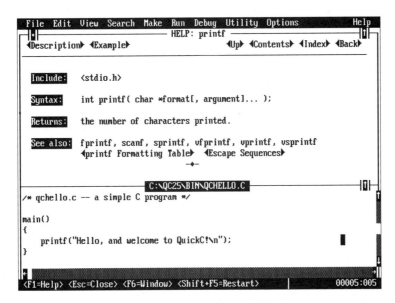

```
 File   Edit   View   Search   Make   Run   Debug   Utility   Options          Help
┌──────────────────────────── HELP: printf ──────────────────────────────┐
 ◄Description► ◄Example►                    ◄Up► ◄Contents► ◄Index► ◄Back►


   Include:    <stdio.h>

   Syntax:     int printf( char *format[, argument]... );

   Returns:    the number of characters printed.

   See also:   fprintf, scanf, sprintf, vfprintf, vprintf, vsprintf
               ◄printf Formatting Table►   ◄Escape Sequences►
                              ─◆─
┌══════════════════ C:\QC25\BIN\QCHELLO.C ═══════════════════════════════┐
/* qchello.c -- a simple C program */

main()
{
    printf("Hello, and welcome to QuickC!\n");             ▌
}

 <F1=Help> <Esc=Close> <F6=Window> <Shift+F5=Restart>         │      00005:005
```

Figure 2-7. *Context-sensitive help for a function in QCHELLO.C.*

Notice the words between wedge-shaped symbols (◄ and ►) at the top of the window. These words are called hyperlinks; they allow you to jump quickly to related topics. You will see hyperlinks on most help screens.

The text in the Help window is the beginning of the help summary for the library function *printf()*. Note that this screen gives a concise description of the kinds of data the function accepts and what it returns. Notice that you are given the opportunity to get a longer description of the *printf()* function, a sample program that uses this function, and tables of codes used with *printf()*.

Have you ever read an explanation that contained a concept or term that in turn required a further explanation? This certainly isn't uncommon in technical fields. One especially nice feature of the keyword Help system is that it even works within a Help window itself. For example, you can get information about a function shown in a sample program that you retrieved while seeking information on another function.

Setting "Bookmarks"

You can go through layers and corridors of the Help system indefinitely. Sometimes, however, you'll want to return to certain screens that explain key ideas. QuickC allows you to set a "bookmark" at the current help screen by pressing Ctrl-K followed by 0, 1, 2, or 3. You can have as many as four bookmarks. To return to a help screen that you have marked, press Ctrl-Q followed by the number of the bookmark.

Pasting from the Help Window

Each library function's on-line documentation includes a sample program. It's often useful to compile and run the program so that you're sure you understand how the function works. (As you will learn later in this book, you can even use the QuickC debugging options to examine the details of how a function works.)

To copy a sample program, get help for a function and select the Example hyperlink. Highlight the program that appears in the window, and choose Copy from the Edit menu. Now press F6 to move to the Edit window, and then press Shift-Ins or choose Paste from the Edit menu. You can now compile, link, and run the program.

Printing Help Text

If you would like a printed copy of any text displayed in the Help window, be sure the Help window is active. (Press F6 if necessary.) Choose Print from the File menu. Be sure your printer is connected, and then choose OK from the dialog box to print the text. This is a handy way to get printed listings of the sample programs from the QuickC Advisor.

Getting Help by Topic (Contents Help)

You are not limited to getting help on the item under the cursor. Figure 2-8 shows a list of topics (a "table of contents") that you can select from the Help menu. Some topics give you a list of relevant library functions, from which you can then choose to see a description of a function that looks interesting.

Notice that the Quick Advisor offers you a number of paths to the same place. For example, if you're interested in knowing which function draws an arc, you can browse down to _arc by using the Contents Help facility. On the other hand, if you're already looking at the _arc function in some program code, you can get specific help on it by using the Keyword Help facility described earlier. In other words, QuickC provides a number of different views of the same information, and you get to the information in a way appropriate to your purposes. This is the essence of the new technology of hypertext, which you will be seeing in an increasing number of programming tools and application programs.

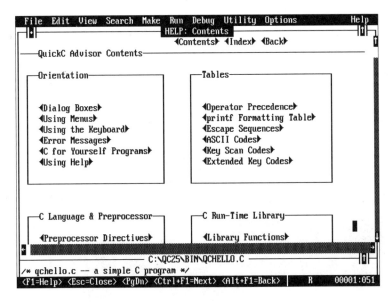

Figure 2-8. *Help by topic.*

Getting Help by Using the Topic Index

Yet another way to look up a topic is to use the alphabetical index. (Choose Index from the Help menu.) Figure 2-9 shows the first screen of the topic index. Notice the row of boxed letters in alphabetical order. Choose a letter to get a list of topics (mainly library functions) beginning with that letter, and scroll to the topic you want.

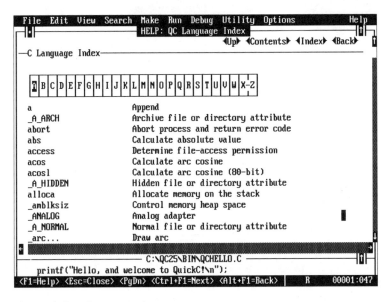

Figure 2-9. *The topic index.*

You can move freely among the various kinds of help without going back to the Help menu and starting over. You can select any kind of help that appears in the list of hyperlinks on the current help screen. Thus, you can usually select Contents help or Index help directly from the current screen. After practicing with the Quick Advisor for a session or two, you will soon be zeroing right in on the help you need.

Getting Help on Menu Items

If you forget what a particular menu option does, you can use the Help facility to refresh your memory. Simply press F1 to get a description of whatever menu option is currently highlighted. Figure 2-10 shows the help screen for the Merge option on the File menu.

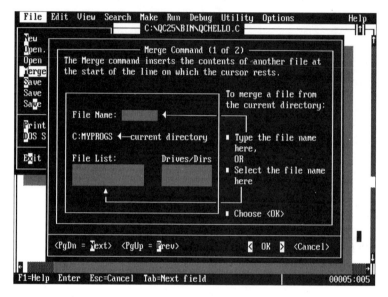

Figure 2-10. *Help screen for a menu option.*

Getting Help in Dialog Boxes

As you have seen, QuickC uses dialog boxes to request information that it needs to complete your commands. Whenever a dialog box is on the screen, you can press F1 to get an explanation of the required information. (You can also click on the Help button in the dialog box.) The help display for a dialog box has the same format as that in Figure 2-10.

Getting Help for Error Messages

Inevitably, you are going to run into errors when compiling or linking your programs. Each error message includes a very brief description of the error, but sometimes that isn't enough to tell you what is wrong. Figure 2-11 shows how you can get help on an error (in this case, a missing semicolon in QCHELLO.C).

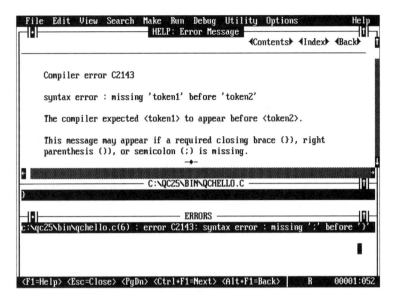

Figure 2-11. *Help screen for an error message.*

Getting Help on Help

Finally, you can get a general description of the Help facility itself, either by choosing Help on Help from the Help menu, or simply by pressing Shift-F1. In addition to reminding you how to use the Help system, this help screen lets you move into the rest of the Help system.

Customizing the QuickC Editor

You might be quite happy with the QuickC editor, especially if you are familiar with WordStar. In any case, most keys—PgUp, PgDn, Del, Ins, Tab, and so on—will work as you would expect. On the other hand, you might already be comfortable with another editor, perhaps BRIEF, Epsilon, or the Microsoft Editor used with Microsoft C. This section tells you how to customize the QuickC editor so that it resembles the editor with which you are most comfortable.

Custom Key Layouts (.KEY Files)

The QuickC editor assigns its command keys by reading a file with the extension .KEY. When you run QuickC, you can use the */k* command-line option to specify any of the .KEY files supplied with QuickC. For example, if you type *qc /k:epsilon.key*, QuickC will run with the editor configured to act like Epsilon. QuickC also saves this configuration: Specify the */k* option again only if you want to change editors.

QuickC also comes with a utility called MKKEY, which is described in the *Up and Running* manual. (See also the first part of the README file for later additions, including additional .KEY files.) Any file that you create with this utility can be loaded with the */k* option described in the previous paragraph.

Adding Editors or Other Programs

As an alternative, you can actually run a different editor within the QuickC environment, rather than simply making the built-in editor "look like" another. To do this, choose Customize Menu from the Utility menu. Select Custom &Editor, choose the Edit command, and then provide the following information:

■ The text that will appear for this item on the Utility menu

■ The pathname for the editor or other program to be run

■ The arguments (option switches, filenames, and so on) that you would type on the MS-DOS command line when running the program directly

■ The directory to be made current when the program is run

In addition, you can decide whether there will be a prompt requiring you to press a key before the program returns to the QuickC environment and whether a hot key should be associated with the program.

The README file has additional information on customizing certain editors, such as BRIEF, Epsilon, and the Microsoft M editor. Note that the degree to which your editor will cooperate with the QuickC environment varies. With many editors, you won't be able to get context-sensitive help from the source code, for example.

You can also install programs other than editors on this menu—for example, a project management program to keep track of your programming time.

Preparing for the Next Chapter

In the next chapter we begin our study of the elements of the C language. Although we discuss additional QuickC features as needed, we do not concentrate on using the QuickC environment. So take some time now to get comfortable with it. We recommend that you try the following:

■ Save QCHELLO.C under another name, and then use the Open option on the File menu to reload QCHELLO.C into the editor.

■ Practice compiling and running programs, using the sample programs provided with QuickC.

■ Use the DOS Shell option on the File menu to exit to MS-DOS, run an .EXE program, and then use *exit* to return to QuickC.

■ Make some errors in QCHELLO.C and try running the program. Observe the error messages, fix the errors, and run the program again. What happens if the last *)* is missing? What happens if you change the word *Hello* to *Hi?*

■ Practice using the editor and the Quick Advisor. Use the Help facilities to assist you in learning the editor. Note that the Microsoft documentation includes an appendix to the *Up and Running* manual that lists the key assignments for four different editors.

Core of C

C Fundamentals

Now that you feel comfortable in the QuickC environment, we can turn our attention to the fundamentals of C. First, let's look at the basic elements of C programs.

Basic Elements of C Programs

The simplest possible C program, which we call TINY.C, is shown in Listing 3-1 on the following page. Type this program into the QuickC editor; then run it with the Go option from the Run menu. (We recommend that you enter and run all the sample programs in this book—this will help you understand and remember the concepts we discuss.)

As you probably suspected, this program doesn't actually do anything when you run it. QuickC generates the message *Program returned (0). Press any key*, but the program produces no output at all. The *main()* function returns the value 0, in this sample, to the operating system. (The return value might be different on your machine.)

This value is significant only if you control it deliberately, as you might want to do when you call a C program from another program.

```
/* tiny.c -- the smallest possible C */
/*          program with comments    */

main() /* Function name and argument list */
{
        /* Function definition in braces */
}
```

Listing 3-1. *The TINY.C program.*

A Program Consists of Function Definitions

As simple as it is, however, this program illustrates a basic element of C—*A C program is essentially a set of function definitions*. A function contains statements (instructions) that the program "calls" to perform specific tasks. A function definition must contain at least the following elements:

■ The function name

■ An "argument list" enclosed in parentheses

■ A group of statements that define the function

In practice, and especially with programs written in the new ANSI C standard, function definitions can be more complicated than this. But this simplest definition is all we need until we look at functions in more detail in Chapter 6.

TINY.C has only one function, *main()*. The argument list, which follows the function and is enclosed in parentheses, contains any parameters, or formal descriptions of information, that the function uses when it is called (executed). Although an argument list can also be empty, as it is in *main()*, the parentheses are still required. Because *main()* contains no function definition statements, the program does nothing when you run it.

The QCHELLO.C program we developed in the last chapter is an even better example of the elements of a C program. Figure 3-1 identifies the parts of QCHELLO.C.

A Function Definition Consists of a Group of Statements

In C, a pair of braces (*(* and *)*) encloses a group of statements. Notice the part of the program between the braces in Figure 3-1. The statement here defines the function *main()*. All stand-alone C programs begin with *main()*. The statements within braces are sometimes called the "function body," to distinguish them from the function name and argument list, which together form the "function header."

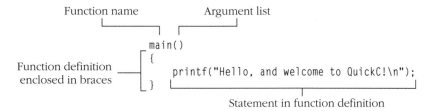

Figure 3-1. *Parts of the QCHELLO.C program.*

The function body can consist of any number of program statements. Note, however, that the braces are still required even if the definition contains no statements. Think of braces as symbols that delimit "paragraphs" of C code.

A Statement Is Like a Sentence

A statement in C consists of keywords, variable and function names, and operators. Like an English sentence, a C statement describes a complete action. A statement always ends with a semicolon. Below are some sample statements and their meanings:

```
printf("This is a statement"); ——— Print This is a statement
count = 1; ————————————————— Set the variable count to 1
getche(ch); ——————————————— Wait for user to type a character, assign it to the
                               variable ch, and echo (display) it on the screen
```

QCHELLO.C has only one statement, *printf("Hello, and welcome to QuickC!\n")*; this statement translates as "Print the string 'Hello, and welcome to QuickC!' and then go to the next line." (The \n specifies a newline character, which moves the cursor to the next line.) This statement completely defines the function *main()* and describes what happens when the program executes the function.

A Statement Can Contain Expressions

Can an expression, such as *count + 2*, be a statement? Well, it doesn't end with a semicolon. But more important, it is not a complete statement. The word and number merely express a quantity ("two more than the value of the variable *count*"); they don't do anything with the quantity.

Although an expression by itself is not a statement, it can be an important element of a C statement. For example, *count = count + 2;* is a complete C statement that assigns the quantity of the expression to the variable *count*.

A Statement Can Call Functions

Let's look at QCHELLO.C in more detail. (See Figure 3-2 on the following page.) What exactly is the *printf()* function at the start of the statement that defines the *main()* function? If you know BASIC, you might say, "It's the command you use to print in C." This isn't really correct, however. In BASIC, *PRINT* is a built-in BASIC command (or keyword) that prints a string or number. In C, *printf* doesn't execute a built-in command; it calls a function named *printf()* and gives (or "passes") the function an argument that tells it what to print.

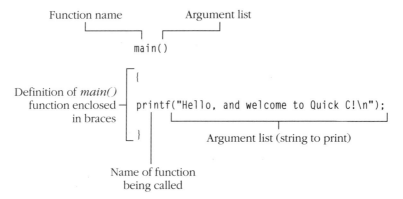

Figure 3-2. *Parts of QCHELLO.C revisited.*

Compare the *printf()* statement with the line containing *main()*. Both consist of a name followed by parentheses: that is, a function name and an argument list—the list for *main()* is empty. (Note that when we show function names in text, we use a trailing set of parentheses to distinguish them from other C elements.)

The *main()* function name and its empty argument list are followed by a pair of braces that enclose the function definition. (Notice in QCHELLO.C that no semicolon follows *main()* because the line isn't a complete statement: It's the header for the function definition that follows.) The line with *printf()*, however, needs no defining group of statements because we are not defining *printf()* there; we're merely using, or calling, the function in a statement. To call a function, simply use its name and argument list in a statement. We refer to statements such as the *printf()* line as "function calls."

Remember that every function must be defined before you can call it; otherwise, QuickC would not know what statements to use when it tries to compile the function name. So where is the definition of the *printf()* function we called in Figure 3-2? The *printf()* function is a library function. Its definition is included in the combined library that was built for you during installation. When you link your program, QuickC inserts the appropriate machine code for printing.

Quick Tip

If you know Pascal, you recognize the similar use of the semicolon to end statements in C. However, there is one important difference between its use in C and its use in Pascal. In Pascal, the semicolon can be omitted if the statement is the last statement in a group (the statement immediately before the word END). In C, *every* statement ends with a semicolon.

Also notice that the braces in C serve the same function as the Pascal keywords BEGIN and END: They delimit a group of statements.

We stress the difference between C's library functions and the built-in commands of languages such as BASIC to emphasize the all-important role that functions play in C. C uses the same syntax in all QuickC library functions, such as *printf()*; functions that you define yourself, such as *main()*; and C libraries developed by Microsoft or other vendors.

The Flow of Execution Starts with *main()*

When you run a C program, execution always begins with the function named *main()*, which must be present. What QuickC executes next depends on the functions that *main()* calls in its definition. In QCHELLO.C, execution starts with *main()*. In the definition of *main()*, QuickC encounters the name *printf()* and executes that function.

Punctuation and Spacing in C Programs

Generally speaking, QuickC lets you break lines of code almost anywhere or insert many spaces (or none) between program elements. For example, you could rewrite the QCHELLO.C program as:

```
main(){printf("Hello, and welcome to QuickC!\n");}
```

or, at the other extreme, you could add line breaks to produce the NARROW.C program shown in Listing 3-2. There are, however, some exceptions to C's tolerance of white space and "free-form" syntax. You can't split a function name across two lines because the compiler reads the newline character at the end of the line as part of the function name. Also, you can't break a quoted string, such as the "Hello, and welcome to QuickC!" in our *printf()* statement, because the compiler won't let you use the newline character in a "string constant" (although you can specify a newline character within a string by using the escape sequence \n, as we have seen).

```
/* narrow.c -- a choppy C program */

main
(
)
{
printf
("Hello, and welcome to QuickC!\n");
}
```

Listing 3-2. *The NARROW.C program.*

Because C is a somewhat cryptic language, you should use spacing and alignment of code to make it easier for other programmers to read and revise your programs. (Remember, after a few weeks you, too, are "another programmer" when you look at your code.) You'll also find that aligning braces vertically helps you avoid errors: The vertical alignment lets you easily match beginning and ending braces.

Using Comments in C

Listing 3-1 on p. 50 contains several lines and parts of lines that begin with /* and end with */; for example:

```
/* tiny.c -- the smallest possible C */
```

These lines are comments, or nonexecuting remarks, that explain how a program works. We strongly encourage you to use comments in your programs; they make programs much easier for a reader to understand. Because QuickC ignores comments, they can follow a program statement on the same line or cover many separate lines. The program examples in this book have introductory comments, and we insert other comments where appropriate.

Below are several different styles you can use for comments:

```
/* Comment line one */
/* Comment line two */
```

or

```
/* Comment line one
comment line two */
```

or

```
/* Comment line one
/* Comment line two
/* Comment line three */
```

However, you can't insert a comment within a comment as follows:

```
/* Comment line one
/* Nested comment line two */
Comment line three */
```

The reason you can't "nest" comments is that once the compiler detects the beginning of a comment (the /*), it considers everything that follows (including another /*) to be part of the comment until it detects */. In the nested comment above, the compiler considers the comment ended at the */ after the word "two." It then treats the word "Comment" on the next line as an undefined function or variable name. Some compilers now allow nested comments, but this is not a standard feature.

Quick Tip

Many versions of Pascal use both /*...*/ and {...} to enclose comments. In C, you can never use braces for comments: They serve only to begin and end groups of statements.

Data Types and Declarations of Variables

Variables are names for memory storage areas used by a program. Variables come in many shapes and sizes. Many BASIC programmers get along reasonably well using only two types of variables: numeric (representing a number) and string (representing a series of characters). A BASIC programmer might write

```
ITEM$="WIDGET"
SERIAL=32767
```

to define two variables. The *$* at the end of *ITEM* signifies a string variable; its absence in *SERIAL* signifies a numeric variable. A BASIC interpreter sets up these variables "on the fly" as it analyzes the lines of code, without allocating space for them in a particularly efficient way.

With C, the situation is more complicated. To use computer memory more efficiently, the C compiler reserves a specific location in memory for each variable. As a programmer, you need to tell the compiler exactly how many bytes of storage to use and how to store the data in those bytes. C offers a wide range of data types, each of which is characterized by such things as the range of numbers that a variable can hold, whether negative values should be accommodated, whether values can be integers only or can include decimal fractions, and so on. If you are a BASIC programmer, this constant attention to data types takes a little getting used to. However, by the end of this chapter, you will know all the fundamental data types and when to use each.

Let's begin our survey of data types by considering some different types of data we might store in variables:

- 30 (the number of students in a class)

- 599,617,814 (the number of seconds since a date in 1970)

- 22.95 (the price of a computer book)

- 1,000,000,000,000.00 (the future U.S. budget)

- a (the letter "a")

As you probably know, data is stored in a computer as patterns of bits: 1s and 0s, "ons" and "offs." In the IBM PC family of computers, bits are organized in groups of 8 (called bytes), in groups of 2 bytes (called words), or in groups of 4 bytes (called double words), depending on the operation involved and the processor used. Figure 3-3 on the following page shows how many bytes are needed to store the different sizes and kinds of numbers in the preceding list. The figure also shows the names (keywords) for the data types that describe the storage involved. The addresses shown were arbitrarily chosen, but they demonstrate how successive items are stored with lower addresses.

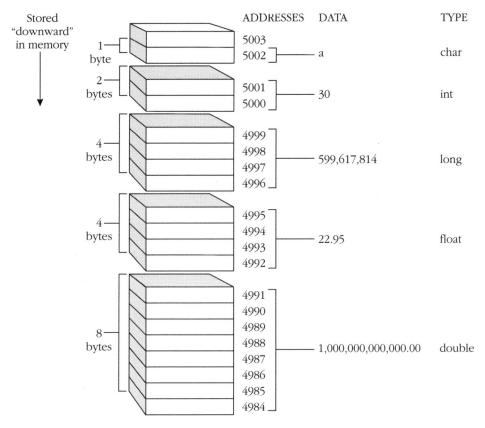

Stored "downward" in memory

	ADDRESSES	DATA	TYPE
1 byte	5003 / 5002	a	char
2 bytes	5001 / 5000	30	int
4 bytes	4999 / 4998 / 4997 / 4996	599,617,814	long
4 bytes	4995 / 4994 / 4993 / 4992	22.95	float
8 bytes	4991 / 4990 / 4989 / 4988 / 4987 / 4986 / 4985 / 4984	1,000,000,000,000.00	double

Figure 3-3. *Storing information in memory.*

The QuickC *sizeof* operator returns the number of bytes that a given data type uses. The program VARSIZE.C (see Listing 3-3) uses this operator and a series of *printf()* statements to print the size (in bytes) of each of the following data types: *char, int, long, float,* and *double.*

```
/* varsize.c -- shows amount of memory occupied */
/*              by various types                 */

main()
{
    printf("Size of a char in bytes is %d\n", sizeof(char));
    printf("Size of an int in bytes is %d\n", sizeof(int));
    printf("Size of a long in bytes is %d\n", sizeof(long));
    printf("Size of a float in bytes is %d\n", sizeof(float));
    printf("Size of a double in bytes is %d\n", sizeof(double));
}
```

Listing 3-3. *The VARSIZE.C program.*

Here's the output of VARSIZE.C:

```
Size of a char in bytes is 1
Size of an int in bytes is 2
Size of a long in bytes is 4
Size of a float in bytes is 4
Size of a double in bytes is 8
```

Declaring Variables

To declare a variable, specify the data type and then the variable name.

Here are some examples:

```
int account_no;
float balance;
double budget;
char acct_type;
```

The first statement declares *account_no* as an integer (*int*) variable. The remaining statements declare variables as floating-point decimal (using the keyword *float*), "jumbo" 8-byte floating-point (*double*), and 1-byte character (*char*) data types.

When you declare a variable, QuickC sets aside the appropriate number of bytes and notes the variable's starting address. The next program, VARADDRS.C (Listing 3-4), declares several types of variables and then prints their starting addresses.

```
/* varaddrs.c -- uses & operator to get */
/*                addresses of variables */

main()
{
    char c1, c2;
    int i;
    long l;
    float f;
    double d;

    printf("Address of c1 %d\n", &c1);
    printf("Address of c2 %d\n", &c2);
    printf("Address of i  %d\n", &i);
    printf("Address of l  %d\n", &l);
    printf("Address of f  %d\n", &f);
    printf("Address of d  %d\n", &d);
}
```

Listing 3-4. *The VARADDRS.C program.*

Although the output of this program varies with different system configurations, it will look something like this:

```
Address of c1 3620
Address of c2 3618
Address of i  3616
Address of l  3612
Address of f  3608
Address of d  3600
```

VARADDRS.C obtains the addresses of the variables by using an ampersand (&) prefix with each variable name. The ampersand is the "address operator"; it returns the starting address for each variable specified. Compare the output of VARADDRS.C with Figure 3-3 to see how variables declared with different data types require different amounts of memory. When QuickC allocates the required number of bytes for a declared data type, the last byte allocated (moving downward in memory) is the variable's starting address. For example, the integer variable *i* has an address of 3616, indicating that it uses 2 bytes (3618 − 3616 = 2); the *double* type variable *d* uses 8 bytes (3608 − 3600 = 8). Note that the compiler allocates 2 bytes for *char* values *c1* and *c2*, although each value requires only 1 byte. The extra byte is convenient for manipulating (2-byte) words in memory.

Rules for Naming Variables

In C, the names of variables and functions are called "identifiers." An identifier can contain any uppercase or lowercase alphabetic characters (A–Z or a–z), digits (0–9), and the underscore character (_). However, the identifier must begin with a letter or underscore. Below are some examples of legal and illegal identifiers:

```
bignum ————————— Legal
BigNum ————————— Legal, and distinct from bignum
_video ————————— Legal, can begin with an underscore
bal_due ———————— Legal, underscore used to separate words
player2 ———————— Legal, number in variable name
8ball —————————— Illegal, can't begin with a number
tally-ho! —————— Illegal, contains hyphen and exclamation point
int ——————————— Illegal, keyword reserved for name of integer type
```

As you can see, you have considerable flexibility in choosing names for your variables. Because QuickC can distinguish the first 31 characters of a variable name, you can use long, descriptive names that help make the program easier to understand and modify. (You might want to use shorter names if you use a compiler that does not support long names.) C distinguishes between uppercase and lowercase characters, so *BigNum* and *bignum* are different variables. Note that you can't begin a variable name with a number, use punctuation marks such as ! or $, or use C-language keywords as variable names. (You can embed a keyword in a variable name, however: *interest* is a legal name even though it contains the keyword *int*.) Fortunately, C has few keywords compared to languages such as BASIC: Most specify data types (such as *int*) or control and decision-branching operations (such as *while* and *if*).

We use specific conventions for naming variables and functions. (See "Conventions and Style" in Chapter 1.) These are not required by QuickC but are used here to differentiate among types of variables and functions. We also begin our variable names with a character other than an underscore—Microsoft uses the initial underscore for some variable and function names declared in the library header files.

Assignment Statements

How do you assign values to variables? In C, the simplest assignment statement consists of a variable name followed by an equal sign (=) and the value to be assigned. Below are some examples:

```
a = 5;
b = a + 5;
c = a + b;
```

In these assignment statements, the value to the right of the equal sign is assigned to the variable on the left. The value can be a number or an expression involving variables and numbers, such as *a + 5* or *a + b*. If the value is an expression, QuickC determines the result and then assigns it to the variable.

You can also assign the same value to several variables at once. Usually, you do this to initialize variables by setting them all to 0 or 1:

```
line_count = word_count = 0;
line_no = page_no = 1;
```

Initializing Variables

Many languages (including most versions of BASIC) automatically initialize numeric variables to 0 and character variables to blank or, perhaps, "null." C does not. For example, if your program has the following two lines:

```
int length;
printf("The length is %d\n", length);
```

and you do not initialize *length*, it might produce the following output:

```
The length is -25480
```

The default value of a C variable is determined by whatever pattern of bits happens to be in the memory locations the compiler allocates to the variable. Therefore, if you want to use a variable named *total*, for example, in a program that keeps track of some quantity, you should assign that variable an initial value of 0. You might modify the declaration above as follows:

```
int length = 0;
```

Because C is a concise language, it lets you combine the declaration and assignment of a variable. That is, you can declare the data type, the variables, and their values in the same statement:

```
int a = 10, b = 50, c = 100;
```

Type *int*

Now that you know how to declare numeric variables and assign values to them, let's look at the *int*, or integer, data type more closely. An integer is a whole number, such as 30, −5, or 93,000,000. In QuickC, an *int* variable can hold numbers in the range −32,768 through 32,767. This rather odd-looking range is established because the *int* type uses 2 bytes (16 bits) of memory. Two bytes can actually hold a range of 0 through 65,535. But, in the regular *int* type, the high (leftmost) bit of the 2-byte combination stores the sign (positive or negative), leaving only 15 bits for the number.

If your variable will never store negative integers, you can use the *unsigned int* type. Because the sign bit is not used, the compiler can use the full 16 bits to store values from 0 through 65,535.

Now let's look at the INTVARS.C program (Listing 3-5), which declares three integer variables, assigns values to them, and then prints values that describe the World War II German battleship *Bismarck*. We declare *length* and *beam* as *int* variables because the length and beam (width) of the ship are each less than 32,767 feet. For the *displacement* variable (the "weight" of the ship), we use the *unsigned int* type because we need a larger number (41,676) than 32,767 (the *int* limit) but a smaller number than 65,535 (the *unsigned int* limit).

```
/* intvars.c -- declares, defines, and prints */
/*              some integer variables         */

main()
{
    /* Declare variables */
    int length, beam;
    unsigned int displacement;

    /* Assign values to variables */
    length = 824;
    beam = 118;
    displacement = 41676;

    /* Print out values */
    printf("The battleship Bismarck was %d feet long", length);
    printf(" with a beam of %d feet\n", beam);
    printf("and displaced %u tons.\n", displacement);
}
```

Listing 3-5. *The INTVARS.C program.*

The next three statements assign the values to the variables, and the three *printf()* statements print the values. Notice that the *printf()* statements use two arguments within the parentheses: a string enclosed by double quotation marks, such as *"The battleship Bismarck was %d feet long"*, followed by a comma and the variable name whose value is to be printed. The *%d* in the string is a *printf()* format specifier: The value of the variable is printed in its place. (The *%d* specifier denotes a decimal [base 10] integer. C uses a variety of specifiers for different types and formats of numbers and characters. We'll discuss them when we look at *printf()*.) When you run INTVARS.C, it generates the output that appears below:

```
The battleship Bismarck was 824 feet long with a beam of 118 feet
and displaced 41676 tons.
```

Long Integer Type

We've seen that *unsigned int* variables can hold values as great as 65,535. But what if you must use larger numbers? Type *long* uses 4 bytes (32 bits) of memory (1 bit is reserved for the sign) and can store numbers from -2^{31} through $+2^{31}$ or −2,147,483,648 through 2,147,483,647 in base 10. Once again, if your variable will contain only positive numbers, you can double the high end of this range by specifying *unsigned long*. This lets you assign your variable a whole number value in the range 0 through 4,294,967,295.

The SCORE.C program (Listing 3-6 on the following page) combines the declaration and assignment of the four *int* variables *home*, *visitors*, *inning*, and *attendance*. Because *total_attendance* has a different data type, *long*, you must declare it in a separate statement. Again, the *printf()* statements display the values assigned to the variables and produce the following output:

```
The score after 7 innings is
Home Team 5, Visitors 2.

The attendance today is 31300.
Attendance this year to date is 1135477.
```

Quick Tip

ANSI C lets you specify any basic variable type as *unsigned*. It also lets you specify *signed* types. Therefore, although QuickC considers the *int* type to be signed by default, the C language doesn't guarantee that all C compilers do so. To write portable programs, you need to specify all variables as either *signed* or *unsigned* types.

```
/* score.c -- defines and prints    */
/*             int and long variables */

main()
{
    /* Declare some int variables and assign */
    /* values to them in the same statement  */

    int home = 5, visitors = 2, inning = 7, attendance = 31300;
    long total_attendance = 1135477;  /* long int */

    /* Print out the values */

    printf("The score after %d innings is\n", inning);
    printf("Home Team %d, Visitors %d.\n\n", home, visitors);
    printf("The attendance today is %d.\n", attendance);
    printf("Attendance this year to date is %ld.",
           total_attendance);
}
```

Listing 3-6. *The SCORE.C program.*

Floating-Point Types

You should store whole numbers as integers whenever possible—integers use the least amount of memory and integer arithmetic is fast. However, many numbers (such as dollars-and-cents amounts) require decimal fractions. In computers, these types of numbers are stored in "floating-point" format.

Consider the number 22.95. This number can be stored by dividing it into two parts: the digits themselves and an exponent showing the magnitude of the number as a power of ten. Thus, 22.95 could be represented as $22.95 * 10^0$. For uniformity in performing operations, however, C always expresses the digits with only one digit to the left of the decimal point. The above number is therefore stored as $2.295 * 10^1$ (which has the same value as $22.95 * 10^0$). C represents this notation with the expression 2.295e+001. The first element, 2.295, is the number's digits (the "mantissa"), and the e+001 represents "exponent 1," or 10^1.

Type *float*

The most commonly used floating-point type in C is *float*. In QuickC, type *float* uses 3 bytes to store digits (the mantissa) and 1 byte to store the exponent. Because exponents can be negative (for example, 1.4e−002 = .014), 1 bit of the exponent byte stores the sign. Converted into decimal terms, this means you can store a mantissa with seven significant digits and an exponent ranging from −38 through +38. In fact, with QuickC's *float* type, you can store numbers as large as 3.4e+038, that is, 34 with 37 zeros after it.

The FLOATS.C program (Listing 3-7) displays three *float* values, each printed in both traditional decimal and exponential formats. The following is the output of the FLOATS.C program:

```
2500.125000      2.500125e+003

0.003300         3.300000e-003

-50.990002       -5.099000e+001
```

Notice that because 0.0033 is less than 1, it has a negative exponent (represented by the minus sign after the *e*). On the other hand, −50.99 is a negative number, but because its magnitude (unsigned value) is greater than 1, it has a positive exponent. FLOATS.C prints each variable first in decimal notation and then in exponential notation by varying the format specifier in the *printf()* statement: The *%f* produces traditional decimal format, and the *%e* produces exponential format.

```c
/* floats.c -- shows floating-point values in   */
/*             regular and exponential formats   */

main()
{
    float f1 = 2500.125, f2 = 0.0033, f3 = -50.99;

    printf("%f\t %e\n\n", f1, f1);
    printf("%f\t %e\n\n", f2, f2);
    printf("%f\t %e\n", f3, f3);
}
```

Listing 3-7. *The FLOATS.C program.*

Type *double*

QuickC provides a "jumbo" floating-point type called *double* for decimal numbers larger than 340,000,000,000,000,000,000,000,000,000,000,000,000. It uses 8 bytes of storage and has a range of (positive or negative) 1.7e−308 through 1.7e+308. That's 308 decimal places before or after the decimal point.

For maximum precision, version 2.5 of QuickC stores *long double* variables in a 10-byte (80-bit) storage space. Previous versions support *long double* as a distinct data type but afford it the same storage space as type *double*.

Precision for Floating-Point Numbers

You must consider more than size, however, when storing numbers in a computer. We referred to a trillion-dollar budget ($1,000,000,000,000.00) earlier in the chapter. If size were the only consideration, we could use *float* to store this number. (A *float* can handle about 10^{38}, and a trillion is merely 10^{12}.)

However, you also must consider the precision available to each data type in order to choose the right type for a given variable. Precision refers to the number of digits guaranteed to be exactly correct after a calculation. The *float* type has a precision of seven digits. Consider the following statements and the resulting output:

```
float trillion = 1000000000000.00;
printf("%f\n", trillion);

999999995904.000000
```

We lost 4096.00 in this operation. Although we might be happy if the government lost only that much of a trillion-dollar budget, we expect full precision in financial calculations and in most scientific calculations. With its seven-digit precision, *float* can't accurately represent a trillion dollars. We attain the required precision by declaring

```
double trillion = 1000000000000.00;
```

Values of type *double* have 15-digit precision, so the result is completely accurate.

Type *char*

Let's look at one last data type, *char* (character). Character values include the upper-case and lowercase letters, the numerals, the punctuation marks, and the nonprinting control characters. On most computers, including the IBM PC, characters are represented by numbers from 0 through 127, according to the ASCII code.

The CHARS.C program (Listing 3-8) shows some examples of ASCII codes. Running the program produces the following output:

```
The character A has ASCII code 65.
If you add 10, you get K.
The character a has ASCII code 97.
```

Type Variations on Different Machines

The C language doesn't define the number of bytes used by the *unsigned int* and *int* types. Instead, the number of bytes is based on the size of number a particular processor can handle in a single operation. In this way, C compilers take advantage of a machine's architecture. Because the IBM PC/XT and PC/AT use the Intel 8086, 8088, or 80286 processor, an *int* uses 2 bytes, or 16 bits. QuickC complies with this implementation. However, on more powerful personal computers, such as those using the Intel 80386 processor, and on many minicomputers and mainframes, an *int* uses 4 bytes, or 32 bits. Even if you program in "standard" C, you must be aware of these differences in implementation and machine architecture if you "port" the program to another machine.

```
/* chars.c -- shows some variables of type char */
/*            as both characters and integers    */

main()
{
    char ch1 = 'A', ch2 = 'a';

    printf("The character %c has ASCII code %d.\n", ch1, ch1);
    printf("If you add 10, you get %c.\n", ch1 + 10);
    printf("The character %c has ASCII code %d.\n", ch2, ch2);
}
```

Listing 3-8. *The CHARS.C program.*

The first line of the *main()* function declares two *char* type variables, *ch1* and *ch2*, and assigns them the values 'A' and 'a', respectively. The 'A' and 'a' are called "character constants," or "character literals," and you assign them to *char* variables the same way you assign numeric constants. (Note that you must use single quotation marks around a character constant.)

Consider the first *printf()* statement in the program:

```
printf("The character %c has ASCII code %d.\n", ch1, ch1);
```

The variable *ch1* is specified twice at the end of the argument list. The first format specifier, *%c*, prints the value of *ch1* as a character. Then the *%d* specifier prints the value of *ch1* as an integer. A character is actually stored as a 1-byte version of an *int* value, and unless you specify that QuickC treat it as a character, it is treated as an integer. This enables us to use the expression *ch1 + 10* in the second *printf()* statement. The variable *ch1* contains an integer value (the ASCII code for 'A', or 65), so adding 10 to it produces 75. When the *%c* specifier is then used to print this value, *printf()* displays the character with the ASCII value 75, or 'K'.

Type *unsigned char*

A *char* value is a signed, 1-byte value that stores values in the range −128 through +127. However, the IBM PC's version of ASCII uses the values 0 through 255 as character codes. The first half of extended ASCII contains the regular ASCII character set. Codes from 128 through 255 consist of special characters and graphics that together are called the "extended character set." You can use the extended character set by declaring variables as *unsigned char* values. For example,

```
unsigned char box = 219;
printf("%c\n", box);
```

displays a rectangular box, or extended ASCII character number 178. (Note that the QuickC Help facility shows the complete extended ASCII character set.)

Summary of Data Types

You don't need to memorize the precise numbers associated with each data type; QuickC's Help facility lets you check which data type you should use in a given situation. Display this summary of QuickC data types by pressing Shift-F1 and then proceeding to the appropriate screen. As you work with various data types in this chapter, consult this summary, shown in Figure 3-4, to refresh your memory.

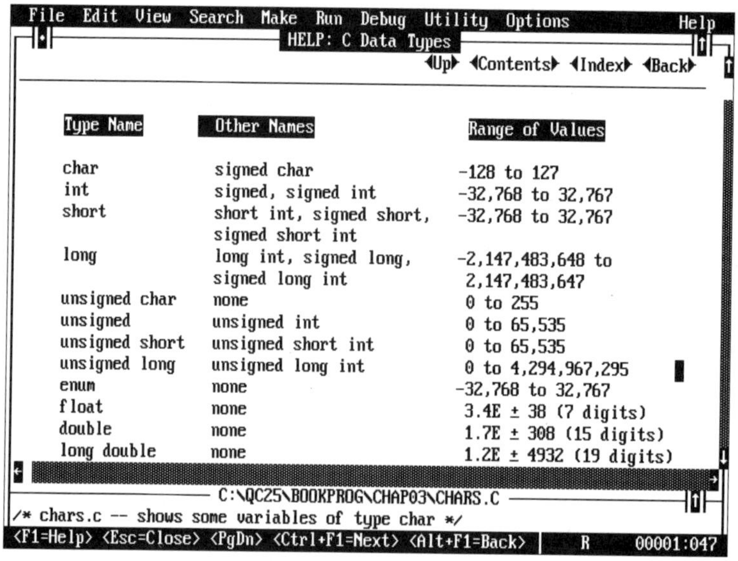

```
 File   Edit   View   Search   Make   Run   Debug   Utility   Options          Help
┌─■┤──────────────────── HELP: C Data Types ─────────────────────────────┤↑├┐
│                                         ◄Up► ◄Contents► ◄Index► ◄Back►      ↑│
│                                                                             │
│   ┌Type Name┐        ┌Other Names┐              ┌Range of Values┐           │
│                                                                             │
│    char              signed char               -128 to 127                  │
│    int               signed, signed int        -32,768 to 32,767           │
│    short             short int, signed short,  -32,768 to 32,767           │
│                      signed short int                                       │
│    long              long int, signed long,    -2,147,483,648 to          │
│                      signed long int            2,147,483,647              │
│    unsigned char     none                       0 to 255                    │
│    unsigned          unsigned int               0 to 65,535                 │
│    unsigned short    unsigned short int         0 to 65,535                 │
│    unsigned long     unsigned long int          0 to 4,294,967,295       ■  │
│    enum              none                       -32,768 to 32,767           │
│    float             none                       3.4E ± 38 (7 digits)        │
│    double            none                       1.7E ± 308 (15 digits)      │
│    long double       none                       1.2E ± 4932 (19 digits)     │
│▒                                                                           ▒│
└────────────────── C:\QC25\BOOKPROG\CHAP03\CHARS.C ──────────────────┤↑├──┘
 /* chars.c -- shows some variables of type char */
 ⟨F1=Help⟩ ⟨Esc=Close⟩ ⟨PgDn⟩ ⟨Ctrl+F1=Next⟩ ⟨Alt+F1=Back⟩   │   R    00001:047
```

Figure 3-4. *Data types help screen.*

Using *typedef*

C lets you rename any data type with the *typedef* statement. For example, if you use variables of type *unsigned char* to hold characters from the full 256-character extended set, you could define an easily remembered mnemonic:

```
typedef unsigned char xchar;
xchar highlight_char, border_char;
```

The *typedef* statement tells QuickC that the word *xchar* (for "extended character") now represents *unsigned char*. Next, we declare two variables, *highlight_char* and *border_char*, as type *xchar*. Note that you can still declare variables as *unsigned char* at any time. Also note that *typedef* does not create new data types; it merely provides synonyms for existing ones.

The HARDWARE.C program (Listing 3-9) ends our survey of QuickC data types. Be sure you understand why we declared the different types. The *printf()* statements display the values of the variables and some descriptive text.

```
/* hardware.c -- shows a mixture of int, */
/*              float, and char types    */

main()
{
    int threads   = 8;          /* threads per inch */
    float length  = 1.25,       /* length in inches */
          diameter = 0.425,     /* diameter in inches */
          price    = 0.89;      /* price per hundred */
    char bin = 'A';             /* kept in bin A */
    long quantity = 42300;      /* number in bin */

    printf("Screws: %d threads/inch\n%f inches long\n",
            threads, length);
    printf("%f diameter\n\n", diameter);
    printf("Price per 100: %f\n", price);
    printf("Stored in bin: %c\nQuantity on hand: %ld",
            bin, quantity);
}
```

Listing 3-9. *The HARDWARE.C program.*

```
Screws: 8 threads/inch
1.250000 inches long
0.425000 diameter

Price per 100: 0.890000
Stored in bin: A
Quantity on hand: 42300
```

Although the program works correctly, it would look better if the output were formatted more neatly. Also, QuickC printed several extra decimal places and filled them with zeros. To gain more control over the appearance of program output, we need to study *printf()* in more detail.

The Power of *printf()*

Thus far, we've used *printf()* statements merely to display values. But *printf()* is actually quite versatile for formatting numbers and character strings.

Using Escape Sequences

Let's look at the parts of the *printf()* statement from QCHELLO.C:

```
printf ("Hello, and welcome to QuickC!\n");
```

This is the simplest *printf()* statement: It merely prints a string; no variables are involved. Earlier, we briefly discussed the one unusual feature of this *printf()* statement, the \n at the end of the string. This combination of backslash and following character is called an "escape sequence." Escape sequences tell *printf()* to print special characters as part of the given string. The \n sequence, for example, adds

PART II: CORE OF C

the newline character, which moves the cursor or printer head to the beginning of the next line. Many languages use two kinds of statements for printing: one to print some information, and a second to print some information and then start a new line. With typical conciseness and versatility, C lets you use one function to print any ASCII character, including newline, tab, and carriage-return characters, giving you complete control of the position of the cursor or printer head.

One QuickC help screen, shown in Figure 3-5, lists all the escape sequences. The newline \n and tab \t sequences are the most frequently used. The \a escape sequence causes the terminal to sound an "alert," or beep.

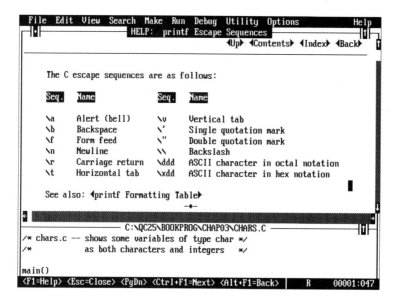

Figure 3-5. *Character escape sequences.*

The ONELINE.C program (Listing 3-10) shows what happens if you don't use the newline escape sequence. When you run the program, the output is all on one line:

```
All displayed onthe same line, with no space unless specified.
```

```
/* oneline.c -- shows how printf() continues */
/*              on the same line              */

main()
{
    printf("All displayed on");
    printf("the same line, with no space");
    printf(" unless specified.");
            /* note the added space in the string above */
}
```

Listing 3-10. *The ONELINE.C program.*

Not only do the strings from all three *printf()* statements end up on the same line, but the word "on" at the end of the first string also runs into the word "the" at the start of the second string. To print two strings on the same line with a space between them, you must include the space in one of the strings. In the third string of ONELINE.C, we added a space before the word *unless*.

The program STRINGS.C (Listing 3-11) demonstrates the two basic ways to print strings with *printf()*.

```
/* strings.c -- shows two ways to print */
/*               a string with printf()  */

main()
{
    printf("This uses a string literal by itself.\n");
    printf("%s", "This plugs the literal into %s.\n");
}
```

Listing 3-11. *The STRINGS.C program.*

The first *printf()* statement has only one argument—the string to be printed including the newline escape sequence. The second statement has two arguments, the format specifier *%s* (for "string") and the string to be printed. It replaces the specifier with the string and prints it. This is the same procedure we used to print numeric variables and literals with specifiers such as *%d* and *%c*.

The STRINGS.C program produces the following output:

```
This uses a string literal by itself.
This plugs the literal into %s.
```

TABS.C (Listing 3-12 on the following page) illustrates the use of the tab escape sequence \t. The TABS.C program prints four sets of data in a neat table. The program prints the table headers first, using \t to tab to the next field. Using \t to position each item at the next tab stop causes the output to be left-justified in each field.

To make the table easier to read, we added a blank line between the header and the data by including an extra \n in the second *printf()* statement. The program then prints the values of the variables in the same tab fields as the headers. The result of all this formatting effort is as follows:

number in bin	size (inches)	threads per inch
338	0.250000	6
57	0.500000	8
1048	0.750000	12
778	1.000000	16

```
/* tabs.c -- shows formatting with the \t */
/*            tab escape sequence          */

main()
{
    int    q1 = 338, q2 = 57, q3 = 1048, q4 = 778,  /* quantity in bin */
           t1 = 6, t2 = 8, t3 = 12, t4 = 16;   /* threads per inch */

    float  s1 = 0.250, s2 = 0.500, s3 = 0.750, s4 = 1.0;
           /* size in inches */

    /* Print table header */
    printf("number\t\t size\t\t threads\n");
    printf("in bin\t\t (inches)\t per inch\n\n");

    /* Print lines of table */
    printf("%d\t\t %f\t %d\n", q1, s1, t1);
    printf("%d\t\t %f\t %d\n", q2, s2, t2);
    printf("%d\t\t %f\t %d\n", q3, s3, t3);
    printf("%d\t\t %f\t %d\n", q4, s4, t4);
}
```

Listing 3-12. *The TABS.C program.*

Formatting Numbers with *printf()*

The *printf()* function can also print numbers in a variety of formats. Let's look at a *printf()* statement from SCORE.C, which is analyzed in Figure 3-6.

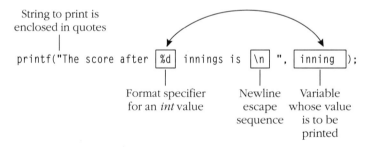

Figure 3-6. *The* printf() *statement from SCORE.C.*

Notice the *%d* in our example, SCORE.C. This, as we have already mentioned, is the format specifier for a decimal integer. The string *"The score after %d innings is"* is followed by a comma and the variable *inning*. Thus, when the *printf()* statement is executed, the string is printed with the value of *inning*. You can also print more than one value in the same string. For example, if you define *int apples = 12, oranges = 9, pears = 3;* and then execute the following *printf()* statement:

```
printf("I have %d apples, %d oranges, and %d pears.\n",
        apples, oranges, pears);
```

you see the following output:

```
I have 12 apples, 9 oranges, and 3 pears.
```

Specifying Formats with *printf()*

Variables are printed according to their data type and the format specifiers used. The QuickC Help facility includes a useful table (Figure 3-7) that shows format specifiers and additional symbols that can specify formats.

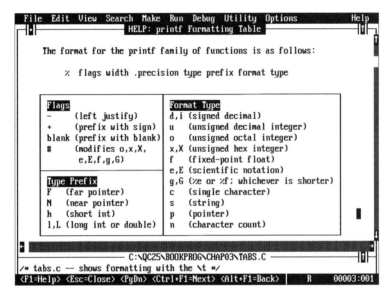

Figure 3-7. *Format specifiers.*

Return and Newline Are Different

If you program in other languages on MS-DOS machines, you might expect \r (carriage return) to move the cursor to the start of a new line. Change the \n in TABS.C to \r and run the program again. What happens? Each line prints over the preceding one. Although many languages on MS-DOS machines incorporate a linefeed in a carriage return, C treats newline and return as distinct operations. The return operation moves the cursor to the beginning of the current line but does not advance it to a new line. A newline operation causes output to start on the next line. Subsequent output starts at the beginning of the next line (rather than directly below the old position) because MS-DOS interprets the newline as though it contains a carriage return as well.

The program SPECS.C (Listing 3-13) prints different types of variables with their appropriate specifiers.

```
/* specs.c -- shows printf() format  */
/*             specifiers for numbers */

main()
{
    int    i = 122;        /* ASCII code for 'z' */
    long   l = 93000000;   /* distance to sun (miles) */
    float  f = 192450.88;  /* someone's bottom line */
    double d = 2.0e+030;   /* mass of sun (kg.) */

    printf("%d\n", i);  /* integer as decimal */
    printf("%x\n", i);  /* integer as hex */
    printf("%ld\n", l); /* long */
    printf("%f\n", f);  /* float as decimal */
    printf("%e\n", f);  /* float as exponential */
    printf("%f\n", d);  /* double as decimal */
    printf("%e\n", d);  /* double as exponential */
}
```

Listing 3-13. *The SPECS.C program.*

Compare the following output with the *printf()* statements in the SPECS.C program:

```
122
7a
93000000
192450.875000
1.924509e+005
20000000000000000000000000000000.000000
2.000000e+030
```

The first *printf()* statement prints the value of the *int* variable *i*, 122, as an ordinary decimal integer, using the now-familiar *%d* specifier. The next statement prints the same value with the *%x* specifier, which prints values in hexadecimal format. Next, we print the long integer value 93000000. Notice that this specifier, *%ld*, combines the *%l* (long) and *%d* (integer) specifiers.

The SPECS.C program then prints the value of the variable *f*, 192450.88, using the *%f* floating-point specifier. In the next statement, we use *%e* to print the same number in exponential notation. Which is better? If the value represents money, the regular decimal format is more appropriate, but remember that both representations are slightly inaccurate because the original value, 192450.88, has eight places and *float* has a maximum precision of seven places. (If you want absolute accuracy in this case, use the *double* specifier.)

We print the final value, 2,000,000,000,000,000,000,000,000,000,000, two ways: as a *double* (note that you can use *%f* for *double* as well as for *float*) and as exponential notation with *%e*. Clearly, the latter is easier to read and understand.

Format Specifiers and Data Types

Remember, the format specifier merely controls how a value is displayed. The data type of the value represents the way in which it is actually stored in the computer. The program FORMATS.C (Listing 3-14) displays the comedy of errors that can occur if you carelessly use the wrong format specifier with a data type. The following is the output of the program; compare it with the *printf()* statements in the program.

```
As integer:      5
As long integer: 41811973

run-time error R6002
- floating-point support not loaded
```

```
/* formats.c -- shows what happens when format */
/*               doesn't match data type        */

main()
{
    int i = 5;
    printf("As integer:      %d\n", i);
    printf("As long integer: %ld\n", i);
    printf("As exponential:  %e\n", i);
    printf("As float:        %f\n", i);
}
```

Listing 3-14. *The FORMATS.C program.*

The program uses four different specifiers to print the value of the *int* variable *i*, which we set to 5. Only the first representation, using *%d*, is correct. Consider the second *printf()* statement, in which we told QuickC to print the value of *i* as a long integer *%ld*. The results vary widely (even from one run to another). Why is this? A long integer uses 4 bytes of memory, but this variable, as an *int* type, uses only 2. When you specify a long integer, QuickC takes 4 bytes starting at the address of *i* and converts them into a long integer. Two of these bytes, however, have nothing to do with the variable *i*. You can see how similar problems arise when we try to interpret an integer variable as a *float*. All this confusion demonstrates that the format specifier must be compatible with the data type being handled. Table 3-1 on the following page correlates the most commonly encountered specifiers and data types.

With improved efficiency, version 2 of QuickC actually alerts you to the problem:

```
run-time error R6002
- floating-point support not loaded
```

Table 3-1. **Compatibility of Specifiers and Data Types**

Specifier	Types
%d	*int* (signed or unsigned) or *char* (ASCII value)
%ld	*long*
%f	*float* or *double* (decimal format)
%e	*float* or *double* (exponential format)
%c	*char* (as character)

After QuickC compiled the program, it "knew" that no floating-point variables were declared. (The only variable declared in the program, *i*, is an *int*.) Therefore, no floating-point routines were loaded. When the code compiled in response to the *%e* and *%f* specifiers was run, an error occurred because these format specifiers perform floating-point arithmetic routines to display the result.

Field Specifiers

We can also improve the appearance of *printf()* output by controlling how many decimal places are printed and how the number is aligned in the output field. To do this, C lets us precede the format specifier with a "field specifier." The field specifier takes the following form:

```
field width.decimal places
```

The *field width* is the total number of character positions that will be printed, and *decimal places* is the number of places printed after the decimal point. (Use the decimal place specifier only for *float* and *double* values.) The following are two examples of field specifiers:

```
"%5.2f"
```
——— *float*; 5 places, 2 of which are decimal places
```
"%8d"
```
——— integer; 8 places (no decimal places)

The program FIELDS.C (Listing 3-15) shows how field specifiers work. The program prints a single variable with varying field specifiers:

```
  123.456001
```
——— %12.6f (field specifier)
```
123.4560
```
——— %8.4f
```
  123.456
```
——— %8.3f
```
  123.46
```
——— %8.2f

In the first *printf()* statement, the field specifier *%12.6f* sets up a 12-character-wide field, 6 characters of which are decimal places. Because the variable has only 10 characters to be printed (9 digits and a decimal point), *printf()* indents the number two spaces. By default, numbers are right-justified (printed starting in the rightmost position of the specified field width). To print numbers that start at the left side of the field (left-justified), put a minus sign in front of the field specifier, *%−4.2f*.

```
/* fields.c -- shows the same number with different */
/*              field widths and number of decimals  */

main()
{
    float f = 123.4560;

    printf("%12.6f\n", f);
    printf("%8.4f\n", f);
    printf("%8.3f\n", f);
    printf("%8.2f\n", f);
}
```

Listing 3-15. *The FIELDS.C program.*

Note also that in the first *printf()* statement we asked for six decimal places, even though the variable *number* contained only the first four places. Although *printf()* prints these extra places, they add nothing to the precision of the number, and, in fact, give a misleading impression of precision. You should specify decimal places only to the expected precision of the value. For example, if you know that a value will range between 0 and 9999 with decimal places, you might specify *%8.3f* because the value can have as many as four places to the left of the decimal point, and a float has only seven places of precision. Thus, a total of seven places (four before and three after the decimal point) displays an accurate value. Specifying *%11.6f* for the same example would give a false impression of precision.

In the second statement, the specifier establishes a field width of 8 (with 4 decimal places). The third statement specifies the same field width of 8, but with only 3 decimal places. Notice that the value's fourth decimal place, the zero, is dropped, and that the number is indented one space because the value has only 7 characters. The last statement again specifies 8 as the field width, this time with only 2 decimal places. The *printf()* function not only drops the third decimal place, but it also rounds up the second decimal place from 5 to 6. Also, because the number has one fewer digit to fit in the 8-character field, *printf()* indents the number another space.

Arithmetic Operators

Like most languages, C offers a complete set of arithmetic operators: + (addition), – (subtraction), * (multiplication), and / (division). C also provides a fifth operator that is less common in other languages—%, the remainder operator, sometimes called the "modulus" operator. This operator returns only the remainder of a division operation. For example, the expression *5 % 2* is 1 (5 divided by 2 has a remainder of 1), and *9 % 3* is 0 (9 divided by 3 has no remainder).

The modulus operator has many uses: You can use it for creating counters that cycle within a specified range or for resetting variables such as line counts by checking for a remainder of zero (if *line_cnt % page_length* is equal to 0, you know that you must start a new page).

Operators are used with values to form expressions that yield new values. Below are some examples:

```
10 * 5 ─────────── Multiply two literals
a / 5 ─────────── Divide value of a by 5
count + 1────────── Add 1 to value of count
(a * 80) + b ────── Multiply value of a by 80, and then add value of b
```

In a program, you combine expressions with other elements to form statements. The MATH.C program (Listing 3-16) contains statements that use expressions involving arithmetic operators.

Each *printf()* statement prints the expression and then its value, as follows:

```
99 + 2 = 101
5 - 12 = -7
7.25 + 3.5 = 10.750000
20 * 20 + 40 = 440
20 * (20 + 40) = 1200
a * a - c + b = 102
a * (a - (c + b)) = 40
Integers: 5 / 2 = 2
Floats: 5.0 / 2.0 = 2.500000
```

The first three statements simply add and subtract literal numbers and print the results. Notice in the third statement that when QuickC sees a number with a decimal point, it assumes a *float* type and prints the answer accordingly (10.750000).

```c
/* math.c -- shows arithmetic and       */
/*           precedence via expressions */

main()
{
    int a = 10, b = 4, c = 2;

    /* Simple arithmetic expressions */
    printf("99 + 2 = %d\n", 99 + 2);   /* ints */
    printf("5 - 12 = %d\n", 5 - 12);
    printf("7.25 + 3.5 = %f\n", 7.25 + 3.5);  /* floats */

    /* Compare precedence */
    printf("20 * 20 + 40 = %d\n", 20 * 20 + 40);
    printf("20 * (20 + 40) = %d\n", 20 * (20 + 40));
    printf("a * a - c + b = %d\n", a * a - c + b);
    printf("a * (a - (c + b)) = %d\n", a * (a - (c + b)));

    /* Compare integer and float division */
    printf("Integers: 5 / 2 = %d\n", 5 / 2);
    printf("Floats: 5.0 / 2.0 = %f\n", 5.0 / 2.0);
}
```

Listing 3-16. *The MATH.C program.*

Operator Precedence

The second group of statements in MATH.C illustrates "precedence," or the rules that determine the order in which operators are applied. Generally, QuickC performs multiplication and division first, then addition and subtraction. If operators have equal precedence (such as division and multiplication), QuickC performs the operations from left to right. The QuickC Help facility lists all the operators in the language (including many covered in later chapters) and arranges them in groups from highest to lowest precedence. Figure 3-8 shows the beginning of this table.

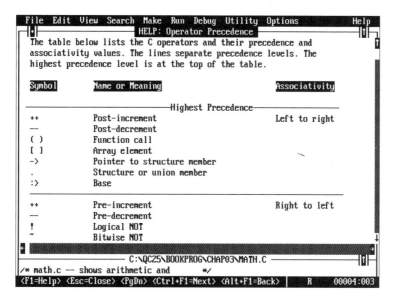

Figure 3-8. *Operator precedence help screen.*

In Listing 3-16 the first *printf()* statement in the second group of statements multiplies 20 by 20, then adds 40, producing a value of 440. However, you can use parentheses to impose a different order of precedence, as shown in the next statement. To evaluate the expression 20 * (20 + 40), QuickC performs the addition first (with a result of 60) and then multiplies 20 by 60 to produce a value of 1200.

The next two statements use combinations of variables. As an exercise, perform the calculations on paper to see whether you get the same results as those produced by MATH.C. Remember to observe the rules of precedence.

The final two statements in MATH.C illustrate a common problem for the unwary beginning C programmer. QuickC divides integer and floating-point types differently. If you specify numbers as integers, as in the first statement, the compiler performs integer division. Accordingly, 5 divided by 2 is 2 because this type of division discards any remainder. (A remainder in division is a fraction, and *int* types cannot represent fractions.) However, when you specify numbers with decimal points,

QuickC treats them as *float* types, producing the answer, 2.5. Variables of *int* and *float* types are handled the same way as the literals above.

The RECEIPTS.C program (Listing 3-17) performs practical calculations with QuickC's math operators. Notice that we declare the *units* variable as an *int* type (you can't sell half a unit!) and the price and tax rates as *float* types.

```
/* receipts.c -- calculates gross and net */
/*                receipts on sales        */

main()
{
    int units = 38;        /* number sold */
    float price = 149.99,  /* price per item */
          rate = 0.06;     /* sales tax rate */

    /* Variables to hold calculated totals */
    float gross, tax, net;

    /* Perform calculations */
    net = units * price;
    tax = net * rate;
    gross = net + tax;

    /* Print results */
    printf("\tSales Report\$n");
    printf("Net sales: \t%6.2f\n", net);
    printf("Tax:\t\t %5.2f\n", tax);
    printf("Gross sales:\t%6.2f\n", gross);
}
```

Listing 3-17. *The RECEIPTS.C program.*

The "calculations" section uses expressions to generate values for the variables *net*, *tax*, and *gross*. The *printf()* statements combine tab escape sequences (\t) and field specifiers to align the output. Specify only two decimal places for money amounts. (Makes cents, doesn't it?) The program produces the following report:

```
        Sales Report
Net sales:      5699.62
Tax:             341.98
Gross sales:    6041.60
```

Arithmetic with Mixed Types

The accuracy of a number generated by QuickC depends on its data type and the format in which it is printed. An additional problem arises when you perform arithmetic operations on literals (constants) or variables of different data types: dividing an *int* by a *float*, for example.

For calculations with mixed data types, C ranks data types roughly according to the number of bytes of storage they require. From highest to lowest, they are:

```
long double  10 bytes
double        8 bytes
float         4 bytes
long          4 bytes
int           2 bytes
char          1 byte
```

Generally, QuickC converts the lower-ranking type to the higher-ranking one before it performs the calculation. Thus, when QuickC divides 49 by 12.5, it first converts 49 to 49.0 (a *float*), then performs the division. (If QuickC chose a lower-ranking type, the calculation would lose precision. The above calculation, for example, would be 49 / 12 = 4 in integer division.) Although the *long* and *float* types both use 4 bytes, a *float* can contain a fractional part that would be lost when converted "down" to a *long*. Therefore, *float* is ranked as the "higher" type. Finally, QuickC converts *float* types to *double* types before it calculates the result.

Although it's convenient that QuickC performs conversions for you, some real problems can occur if you assign the results of a calculation to a variable of an incorrect data type. The following example illustrates such a mistake:

```
int sales, units = 50;
float price = 1.99;
sales = units * price;
printf("Total sales are %d.\n", sales);
```

QuickC calculates *units * price* correctly by converting units from 50 to 50.0 (to make it a *float*) and then multiplying it by the *float* value *price* (1.99). The value of the expression is now the *float* value of 99.50. So far, so good. However, we assigned this value to the variable *sales*, which we declared as an *int* type. As a result, the fractional part of the value (.50) is dropped, making the value of *sales* an incorrect 99.00. The solution to this problem is simple—consider all the potential values for a variable before you declare it. In this case, declare the variable *sales* as a *float*.

QuickC can help remind you of potential problems with data type conversions. If you select the Options menu, then Make, and finally Compiler Flags, the dialog box lets you select one of five levels of compiler warning messages (levels 0 through 4). If you select level 2 before you compile programs, QuickC sends a warning message for each program statement that causes a data type conversion. A typical message follows:

```
warning C4051: type conversion = possible loss of data
```

If you see this type of message, note the statement at which the cursor is displayed, examine the data types involved, and look up the meaning of warning C4051 in the QuickC documentation. There you will note that this is an advisory message. QuickC issues the message for perfectly legitimate conversions, such as the *int* to *float* conversion in our earlier division example.

The MIXED.C program (Listing 3-18) performs operations with mixed data types.

```
/* mixed.c -- shows the effects of mixing */
/*           data types in an expression */

main()
{
    int     i = 50, iresult;
    long    l = 1000000, lresult;
    float   f = 10.5, fresult;
    double  d = 1000.005, dresult;

    fresult = i + f;           /* int + float to float */
    printf("%f\n", fresult);

    fresult = i * f;           /* int * float to float */
    printf("%f\n", fresult);

    lresult = l + i;           /* long + int to long */
    printf("%ld\n", lresult);

    printf("%f\n", d * f);     /* double * float to double */

    fresult = d * f;           /* assigned to a float */
    printf("%f\n", fresult);   /* loses some precision */

    /* Debugging a division problem */

    iresult = i / l;           /* int / long to int */
    printf("%d\n", iresult);   /* whoops! loses result */
    printf("%ld\n", iresult);  /* this won't fix it */
    fresult = i / l;           /* store in float result */
    printf("%f\n", fresult);   /* doesn't work */
    dresult = i / l;           /* try a double */
    printf("%f\n", dresult);   /* doesn't work */
    fresult = (float) i / l;   /* try type cast */
    printf("%f\n", fresult);   /* correct result */
}
```

Listing 3-18. *The MIXED.C program.*

Compare this output with the program statements:

```
60.500000
525.000000
1000050
10500.052500
10500.052734
0
73138176
0.000000
0.000000
0.000050
```

The first pair of statements adds *int* and *float* values and prints the result, which is 60.5, a *float* value. This shows QuickC's default type conversion at work. The second pair of statements shows the same conversion with a multiplication operation. The third pair of statements adds a *long* to an *int*. Note that the result is correct (100,000 + 50 = 100,050), and, from its size, you can guess that it must be a *long*. QuickC converts the value 50 to a *long* before it does the calculation.

Next, the program works with *double* and *float* types. When we specify *d* * *f* in the *printf()* statement, QuickC converts the *float* value *f* to a *double* and calculates a *double* result, which we print. (Remember, you can use the *%f* format specifier with either the *float* or the *double* type.) Because the answer requires nine places of precision, converting from *float* to *double* preserves the accuracy of the value.

Next, we perform the same calculation, but we assign the result to a *float* value, *f*. Notice that the result, 10500.052734, becomes inaccurate starting at the fourth decimal place. Converting from *double* to *float* can produce both large and subtle errors, depending on the numbers involved. To be safe, use a *double* variable to hold the result of this type of calculation.

The last, lengthy, set of statements illustrates various approaches for dividing an *int* value *i* by a *long* value *l*. Only the last method produces the correct result.

Assigning the result of the division to an *int* variable produces a value of 0 because the result is a very small decimal fraction (50/1,000,000) and integer division does not recognize remainders.

In the next statement we assume that the result of the division is a decimal fraction and that we can store it in a *float*. But this doesn't work either. When we add more decimal places by using a *double* variable for the result, we still get a result of 0. The problem here is that when the two integer variables *i* and *l* are divided, the integer portion of the result, 0.000050, is 0. At this point, we can't retrieve the decimal fraction. Assigning the quotient to a *float* or a *double* merely gives us a floating-point representation of 0!

Type Casting

C provides a solution to our division dilemma with a construction called a "type cast." A type cast explicitly converts a value to a specified type before any operations are done on that value. Consider the following example:

```
int i1 = 10, i2 = 3;
printf("%d\n", i1 / i2);
printf("%f\n", (float) i1 / i2);
```

In the first *printf()* statement, we divide the two integers and produce the integer result of 3. In the second *printf()* statement, we add *(float)* before *i1*. This is the type cast: It converts the value of *i1* to a *float*. Because a type cast has a higher precedence than the arithmetic operators, it converts *i1* to a *float* before the division operation. Now the division operation contains a *float* and an *int*! QuickC's default type conversion then converts *i2* to a *float* as well, and the result is the *float* value 3.33333. If you look at the last two statements of the MIXED.C program, you can see we used a type cast in the same way and obtained the correct result of 0.000050.

Type casts are useful for handling variables of lower-ranking data types (*int*, for example) that must occasionally be used in calculations to produce a result of a higher-ranking type (such as *float*). A program can make more efficient use of both storage and processing time by declaring such variables as the lower type and using type casts when necessary. Later, you will find type casts valuable when you must convert values to a specific type, such as a pointer.

Getting Input with *scanf()*

In order to write programs that have real-world utility, we must first understand how a C program gets input from the user. The all-purpose C function for getting input and storing it in a variable is called *scanf()*. Figure 3-9 shows how it works.

Let's assume we have a program with a declared integer variable named *acct_no*. When the *scanf()* statement executes, the program waits for input from the user. After the user types the number and a carriage return, the input is stored in the variable *acct_no*, as if it had been placed there by an assignment statement. Notice that the *acct_no* variable in the *scanf()* argument list is preceded by an ampersand (&). Do you remember when we placed ampersands in front of variable names in the VARADDRS.C program (Listing 3-4 on p. 57) to retrieve the storage addresses of the variables? The *scanf()* function requires as its second argument an address at which it can store the input. The & returns the address of the following variable. If you omit the address operator from the front of the variable name, the *value* of the variable is interpreted as though it were an address, and the user input is stored at that address. This can produce frightful results if it overwrites information that your program needs!

The first argument in the *scanf()* statement in Figure 3-9 is *"%d"*. This looks and works like the format specifiers we used with *printf()*—it specifies the type of the value that the program expects. As with *printf()*, the *"%d"* specifies an integer.

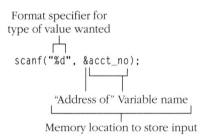

Figure 3-9. *Parts of a* scanf() *statement.*

You can also use most of the other specifiers you used with *printf()*. The following statement, for example, gets a value for the *float* variable *deposit*:

```
scanf("%f", &deposit);
```

Notice that *scanf()*, by itself, does not print a prompt for the user; it merely presents the user with a blinking cursor. Therefore, you should precede a *scanf()* statement with a *printf()* statement that tells the user what information to supply. In the example above, we might precede the *scanf()* statement with:

```
printf("How much is your deposit? ");
```

The cursor now appears following the prompt. You don't need to include a newline character: The cursor will move to the next line when the user presses Enter after typing the input.

You can also use *scanf()* to get values for more than one variable at a time:

```
printf("What are your age and weight? ");
scanf("%d %d", &age, &weight);
```

In this example, the user types an age, a space (to separate the values), and then a weight. Note that the user can also press Enter or Tab for the space.

The CONVERT.C program (Listing 3-19) uses *scanf()* to prompt a user for a temperature in Fahrenheit and then converts the temperature to centigrade.

```
/* convert.c -- converts Fahrenheit temperature    */
/*               to centigrade; gets value from user */

main()
{
    float ftemp, ctemp;

    printf("What is the temperature in Fahrenheit? ");
    scanf("%f", &ftemp);
    ctemp = (ftemp - 32.0) * 5 / 9.0;

    printf("The temperature in centigrade is %5.2f", ctemp);
}
```

Listing 3-19. *The CONVERT.C program.*

We print the prompt with a *printf()* statement and then use a *scanf()* statement with a floating-point specifier *%f* to get the input value for the *float* variable *ftemp*. A sample user dialogue with CONVERT.C follows:

```
What is the temperature in Fahrenheit? 87
The temperature in centigrade is 30.56
```

The AVGTEMP.C program (Listing 3-20 on the following page) averages the daily high temperatures for a week. When you run the program, it prompts you for the high temperature for each day of the week, beginning with Monday.

```
/* avgtemp.c -- finds average temperature */
/*               for the week             */

main()
{
    int t1, t2, t3, t4, t5, t6, t7;
    float avg;

    printf("Enter the high temperature for:\n");
    printf("Monday: ");
    scanf("%d", &t1);
    printf("Tuesday: ");
    scanf("%d", &t2);
    printf("Wednesday: ");
    scanf("%d", &t3);
    printf("Thursday: ");
    scanf("%d", &t4);
    printf("Friday: ");
    scanf("%d", &t5);
    printf("Saturday: ");
    scanf("%d", &t6);
    printf("Sunday: ");
    scanf("%d", &t7);

    /* Calculate and display average */
    avg = (t1 + t2 + t3 + t4 + t5 + t6 + t7) / 7.0;
        /* divide by 7.0 to ensure float result */
    printf("The average high temperature for");
    printf(" this week was %5.2f degrees.\n", avg);
}
```

Listing 3-20. *The AVGTEMP.C program.*

The *int* variables *t1* through *t7* store the daily high temperatures, which are obtained by a series of *scanf()* statements. The program then calculates an average temperature and prints it. A sample dialog with this program appears below.

```
Enter the high temperature for:
Monday: 82
Tuesday: 91
Wednesday: 97
Thursday: 104
Friday: 95
Saturday: 88
Sunday: 78
The average high temperature for this week was 90.71 degrees.
```

It is important to note that *scanf()* does not check to make certain that the input is compatible with the data type of the variable in which it is stored.

Shortcut Assignments, Increments, and Decrements

Now that you know how to assign a value to a variable with the assignment operator (=) and how to use arithmetic operators to calculate new values, we can show you a few tricks and shortcuts. In the course of a program, it is often useful to add a value to a variable repeatedly or to subtract a value from a variable repeatedly. For example, a program that counts lines needs to add 1 to a variable (such as *total_lines*) each time it counts a new line. We could do this as follows:

```
total_lines = total_lines + 1;
```

That's the way most languages do it. However, because changing the value of a variable is such a common occurrence in programming, C provides special, concise "arithmetic assignment operators" for the purpose.

Arithmetic Assignment Operators

The arithmetic operators are +, −, *, /, and %, and the assignment operator is =. The arithmetic assignment operator, as the name suggests, is a combination of an arithmetic operator and the assignment operator: for example, +=. QuickC performs the specified arithmetic on the variable and then assigns the result of the calculation to the variable. Using an arithmetic assignment operator, we can write a shorter version of the statement that increases the value of *total_lines* by 1:

```
total_lines += 1;
```

Listed below are more examples that use arithmetic assignment operators:

```
count -= 1;        Subtract 1 from the value of count
fare += 0.75;      Add 0.75 to value of fare
value *= 10;       Multiply value by 10
```

You can use any arithmetic operator in an arithmetic assignment operation. Table 3-2 lists the five possible arithmetic assignment operators. The addition and subtraction assignment operators are the most commonly used.

Table 3-2.   Arithmetic Assignment Operators

Operator	Meaning
+=	Add to value and assign
-=	Subtract from value and assign
*=	Multiply by value and assign
/=	Divide by value and assign
%=	Get remainder from division and assign

The OPEQUAL.C program (Listing 3-21 on the following page) demonstrates the use of arithmetic assignment statements. The *printf()* statements print several arithmetic assignment expressions and their results.

Be sure that when you read the *printf()* statements in the program you can correctly predict the following output:

```
Starting values: m = 10 n = 5
m += 2 makes m 12
m -= n makes m 7
m *= 2 makes m 14
m = m + 1 makes m 15
m += 1 makes m 16
```

```
/* opequal.c -- shows combination math/assignment */
/*                operators and increment operators */

main()
{
    int m = 10, n = 5;
    printf("Starting values: m = %d n = %d\n", m, n);

    /* Combination of arithmetic and assignment */
    printf("m += 2 makes m %d\n", m += 2);
    printf("m -= n makes m %d\n", m -= n);
    printf("m *= 2 makes m %d\n", m *= 2);

    /* Two ways to increment m */
    printf("m = m + 1 makes m %d\n", m = m + 1);
    printf("m += 1 makes m %d\n", m += 1);
}
```

Listing 3-21. *The OPEQUAL.C program.*

Increment and Decrement Operators

As the last program demonstrated, both *m = m + 1* and *m += 1* added 1 to the value of *m*. If you've done any programming, you know how frequently the value of a variable must be increased or decreased by 1. This is especially true when you create a "counter" variable that keeps track of the number of times a statement in a loop executes. C provides an ultra-concise operator, the *increment* operator ++, to add 1 to the value of a variable. Similarly, the *decrement* operator -- subtracts 1 from the value of a variable.

INCDEC.C (Listing 3-22) shows how the increment and decrement operators change the value of a variable. Compare the program statements with the output that immediately follows the listing:

```
a is 10
++a is 11
--a sets a back to 10
```

```
/* incdec.c -- shows effect of           */
/*              increments and decrements */

main()
{
    int a = 10;

    printf("a is %d\n", a);
    printf("++a is %d\n", ++a);
    printf("--a sets a back to %d\n", --a);
}
```

Listing 3-22. *The INCDEC.C program.*

Note that the increment and decrement operators are really arithmetic assignment statements. They add (or subtract) 1 and assign the resulting value to the variable.

count++; ——— is equivalent to ———count += 1;
index--; ——— is equivalent to ———index -= 1;

(Most programmers do not use a space between the increment [or decrement] operator and the variable name. However, in C it is perfectly legal to use intervening spaces, as in *count + +*.)

Pre-Increment *vs* Post-Increment

In the INCDEC.C program we put the increment or decrement operator in front of the variable name. However, you also can position the operator after the variable name. In either case the variable is incremented or decremented; but there is one important difference. If you put the operator in front of a variable name, the incrementing or decrementing is done immediately. If you put the operator after the variable name, the incrementing or decrementing is not done until *after* the use of the variable. The PREPOST.C program (Listing 3-23 on the following page) shows how this works. The output of the program illustrates how incrementing is delayed:

```
b is 100
b++ is still 100
but after it's used, b is incremented to 101

++b, on the other hand, is immediately 102
```

Notice what happens to *b* if we use the increment operator *after* it rather than before it. The first *printf()* statement with the value *b++* prints the original value of 100, showing that it has not yet been incremented. The next *printf()* statement, however, prints 101.

```
/* prepost.c -- shows effect of pre-increments and */
/*               post-increments (or decrements)  */

main()
{
    int b = 100;

    printf("b is %d\n", b);
    printf("b++ is still %d\n", b++);
    printf("but after it's used, ");
    printf("b is incremented to %d\n\n", b);

    printf("++b, on the other hand, ");
    printf("is immediately %d\n", ++b);
}
```

Listing 3-23. *The PREPOST.C program.*

As a practical matter, the distinction between pre-increments and post-increments (or decrements) is usually important only when the variable is incremented or decremented while it is being used with other operators in a single expression. For example, suppose you want to both increment *counter* and assign it to *total* in the same statement. Assuming *counter* is currently 10,

```
total = counter++;
```

assigns 10 to *total* because *counter* is assigned to *total* but not incremented until the next time it is used. On the other hand:

```
total = ++counter;
```

assigns 11 to *total* because *counter* is incremented immediately and then assigned.

Relational Operators

If you have some programming experience, you know that most programs must make decisions based on the values of certain variables. Variables are tested, or compared, and the result of the test determines which program statement will execute next. The next two chapters cover the variety of "control structures" that C provides for this purpose. Let's build the foundation for those discussions by looking at the operators that C uses for testing or comparing values.

A relational operator compares two values, which can be variables, literal numbers, or whole expressions. A combination of relational operators and values is called a relational expression. An example is *count > 10*, which translates as "Is the value of count greater than 10?" The > in this expression is the "greater than" relational operator. The expression has a value of true or false depending on the current value of the variable *count*. If *count* is 8, for example, the expression is false.

Table 3-3 illustrates the ways we can compare two values, *a* and *b*. The values can be constants, variables, or expressions—anything that expresses a numeric value. (Remember that ASCII characters, too, are essentially numeric values.)

Table 3-3. Relational Operators

Expression	Meaning
a < b	Is *a* less than *b*?
a > b	Is *a* greater than *b*?
a == b	Is *a* equal to *b*?
a != b	Is *a* not equal to *b*?
a <= b	Is *a* less than or equal to *b*?
a >= b	Is *a* greater than or equal to *b*?

We described the value of a relational expression as being "true" or "false." These terms are useful as we follow the logic of a program, but the actual value of a relational expression, like everything else in the computer, is numeric. When an expression is true, its value is 1; when an expression is false, its value is 0. The RELATION.C program (Listing 3-24) uses *printf()* statements to show the values of some expressions that use relational operators. The program generates the following output:

```
a = 5    b = 3    c = 4
Expression a > b has a value of 1
Expression a == c has a value of 0
Expression a > (b + c) has a value of 0
Expression a = b has a value of 3
```

```
/* relation.c  -- shows effect of relational operators */

main()
{
    int a = 5, b = 3, c = 4;

    printf("a = %d\t b = %d\t c = %d\n", a, b, c);

    printf("Expression a > b has a value of %d\n", a > b);
    printf("Expression a == c has a value of %d\n", a == c);
    printf("Expression a > (b + c) has a value of %d\n", a > (b + c));
    printf("Expression a = b has a value of %d\n", a = b);
            /* what happened here? */
}
```

Listing 3-24. *The RELATION.C program.*

Because *a* is 5 and *b* is 3, the expression *a* > *b* has a value of 1, or true. Because *c* is 4, *a* == *c* has a value of 0, or false. The third expression combines relational and arithmetic operators: It calculates the quantity *(b + c)* and then compares the value to *a*. The last expression illustrates a common source of confusion, which is discussed in the next section.

Relational == vs Assignment =

Did you notice that in the preceding listing the last expression, *a* = *b*, is an assignment statement, not a test for equality? In C, a single equal sign, =, is the assignment operator, but a double equal sign, ==, is the relational "equals" operator. In some languages (such as BASIC), a single operator, =, serves both purposes. So if you are familiar with the BASIC usage, you might make errors with these operators until you get used to the difference.

A common symptom of this error is a test in which the result always appears to be either true or false. For example, if you type the assignment *count = 10* instead of the relational *count == 10* and then use the result to control program flow, QuickC always sees the result of the test as "true." Although relational expressions return a value of 1 for "true," QuickC considers any nonzero value to be "true" in this type of test. Because the sample statement with = is actually an assignment, its value is 10 (the number assigned), which QuickC interprets as "true" during a relational test.

Precedence of Relational Operators

In RELATION.C, we used parentheses in the expression *a* > *(b + c)*. If you check QuickC's operator precedence help screen (Figure 3-8 on p. 77), you will see that relational operators have a lower precedence than arithmetic operators. Therefore, even if you don't use parentheses, *b + c* is calculated first, and only then is the result compared to *a*. Nevertheless, it is a good programming practice to use parentheses to clarify an expression.

Assignment and "Equals" Relation

The following table lets you compare the assignment and relational "equals" operators in C to those in other common languages:

Language	Assignment	Relation
C	=	==
BASIC	=	=
Pascal	:=	=
FORTRAN	=	.EQ.
Logo	make	=
COBOL	MOVE	EQUAL TO

Logical Operators

Sometimes it is necessary or useful to test for more than one circumstance in the same expression or statement. For example, you might want to test to see if either the temperature or pressure in a boiler has exceeded a safety limit. Let's assume the test for temperature is *(temp < 900)* and the test for pressure is *(pressure < 5000)*. We can combine the two tests as follows:

```
(temp < 900) && (pressure < 5000)
```

The *&&* is called the AND logical operator. It compares the results of two relational operations and returns a value of true (that is, 1) only if *both* values are true. QuickC first makes the *temp* test, and then it makes the *pressure* test (testing from left to right). Then the && operator checks to see whether *both* tests were true.

The OR logical operator, ¦¦, works as the AND operator does except that it returns a value of true (that is, 1) if *either or both* tests are true. Thus, the statement

```
(ch == 'q') ¦¦ (turn > last_turn)
```

returns a value of true if either the current value of *ch* is 'q' or the current value of *turn* is greater than that of *last_turn*, or both. You could use this statement to check whether a game is over.

Using two logical operators, && and ¦¦, and two possible results of a test (true and false), the TRUTH.C program (Listing 3-25) demonstrates the possible results for a relational statement involving two tests. It makes comparisons using 1s and 0s that represent the results (true or false) of already completed relational tests. Thus, *1 AND 1 is 1* means "true and true is true."

```
/* truth.c -- shows logical operators */
main()
{
    printf("1 AND 1 is %d\n", 1 && 1);
    printf("1 AND 0 is %d\n", 1 && 0);
    printf("0 AND 0 is %d\n", 0 && 0);
    printf("1 OR 1 is %d\n", 1 ¦¦ 1);
    printf("1 OR 0 is %d\n", 1 ¦¦ 0);
    printf("0 OR 0 is %d\n", 0 ¦¦ 0);
}
```

Listing 3-25. *The TRUTH.C program.*

The TRUTH.C program generates the following output:

```
1 AND 1 is 1
1 AND 0 is 0
0 AND 0 is 0
1 OR 1 is 1
1 OR 0 is 1
0 OR 0 is 0
```

Once again, if you check the QuickC operator precedence help screen, you will notice that logical operators, such as && and ¦¦, have a lower precedence than the relational operators, such as < and ==. Therefore, we didn't need parentheses around the relational expressions in our examples because QuickC evaluated them before it checked the logical operators. Again, we used parentheses because they make these complex expressions easier to read.

The last logical operator we need to discuss is !, the NOT operator. Its function is simple enough—it reverses the truth value of a relational expression. For example, if *a* is 10, *a > 5* is true, but *!(a > 5)* is false.

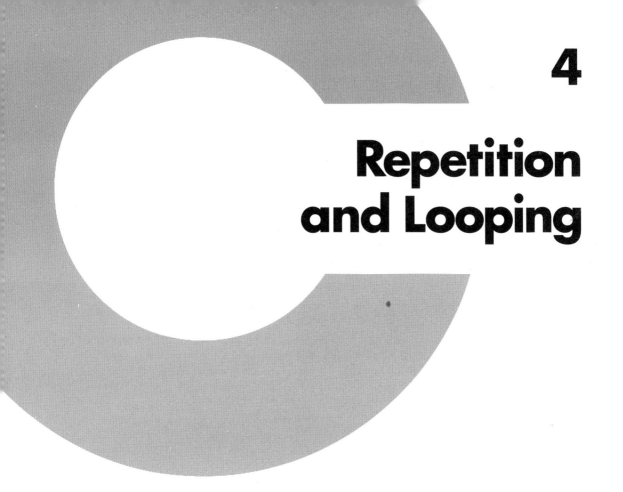

4

Repetition and Looping

In all our programs so far, QuickC has executed the statements sequentially, from the first statement to the end of the program. However, most of the important work in a program involves controlled repetition, in which a group of statements repeatedly does a particular job until the work is done. For example, consider the data-entry routine of a database program. This group of statements (used to receive, validate, and store data) must be repeated as long as the user wants to enter new data records. This set of repeating statements is called a *loop* because it is executed as though the statements were arranged in a circle. However, when the user wants to stop entering data, the program must be able to recognize a "quit" command and stop repeating the data-entry statements.

As you study C, you will find many other examples of the need for controlled repetition. For example, a program that retrieves data from a file must repeatedly read and process data items until it reaches the end of the file. If you program in another language, you probably use loops regularly to initialize and access elements of an array or a set of variables.

C uses three types of loops: the *for* loop, the *while* loop, and the *do* loop. Although these loops are fundamentally similar, they let you control the looping action in different ways to suit different needs. This chapter focuses on how to use these three types of loops and some of their common variations.

The *for* Loop

The *for* loop repeats a group of program statements as long as a specified condition is true. Generally, you use it to specify a fixed number of repetitions: for example, processing the accounts for each month of a year.

The anatomy of a *for* loop is as follows:

```
for (start; condition; update)
    {
    /* statements */
    }
```

In this generalized *for* loop, *start* is one or more statements that initialize the variables used by the loop; *condition* is a relational expression that is tested to see whether the loop should continue to run; and *update* is one or more statements that change the values of variables in the loop. The group of statements between the braces that follow the *for* line is the body of the loop. These statements execute as long as the *condition* in the parentheses is true. (The body can also consist of only one statement, in which case the braces are optional. We tend to use braces for even a single statement, however, because they make the body of the loop easier to distinguish.)

The FORLOOP.C program (Listing 4-1) uses a *for* loop to count from 1 through 10. After we declare the variable *i*, we begin the loop structure with the keyword *for*. The parentheses that follow the *for* contain the control statements for the loop. Notice that semicolons separate the control statements.

The *start* statement establishes the variable *i* as the loop's "control variable." This is the variable whose value is tested to determine when the loop will stop running.

```
/* forloop.c -- a simple for loop that counts to ten */

main()
{
    int i;

    for (i = 1; i <= 10; i++)
        {
        printf("%d\n", i);    /* body of loop */
        }
    printf("All done!\n");  /* executed when i > 10 */
}
```

Listing 4-1. *The FORLOOP.C program.*

(Many people use *i*, j, and *k* for loop control variables. This practice has its roots in FORTRAN programming. However, any valid variable name will do.)

The next statement, *i <= 10*, is the loop's test, or condition. It specifies that the body of the loop execute repeatedly as long as the value of *i* is less than or equal to 10. The test condition is a relational statement that compares the loop control variable to an assigned value and returns a value of 1 (true) or 0 (false).

The last statement in the *for* loop parentheses is *i++*. This "update" statement changes the value of the loop control variable each time the loop body executes. Here we use the ++ increment operator to increase *i* by 1 each time it executes, and, in fact, most *for* loops use update statements that either increment or decrement the control value by 1. Using values other than 1, however, is almost as easy: The statement *value += 10*, for example, adds 10 to *value* each time it executes. You can also use multiplication or division rather than addition or subtraction.

Let's step through FORLOOP.C one statement at a time to see how it works:

■ Set *i* to 1.

■ Check *i* to see if it is less than or equal to 10.

■ Because the result of this test is true, execute the body of the loop. (The body consists of a *printf()* statement that prints the value of *i*.)

■ Execute the update statement, *i++*. (Set *i* to *i* + 1, or 2.)

■ Check the test statement again to see if *i* is still less than or equal to 10. If it is, execute the body of the loop again. Continue the cycle until the test condition is false (when the value of *i* increases to 11).

Figure 4-1 on the following page shows this program as a flowchart. You can follow the arrows to trace the flow of execution.

Why does the loop stop running? Let's look at the situation when *i = 10*: The *printf()* statement in the body of the loop prints the number 10. The update statement then increments the loop by 1 and the test statement executes. Because the value of *i* is now 11, the test fails (returns a "false" value). This causes the program to skip the loop body and execute the next statement, which prints the message *All done!*

Choosing a Control Variable

If you are used to writing loops in BASIC, remember that with C you must declare the loop control variable before you use it in the loop. Select a data type for the control variable that can accommodate the full range of values the variable will hold when the loop is run.

For example, a loop that will run 50,000 times requires a control variable of type *unsigned int* because a signed *int* value cannot exceed 32,767.

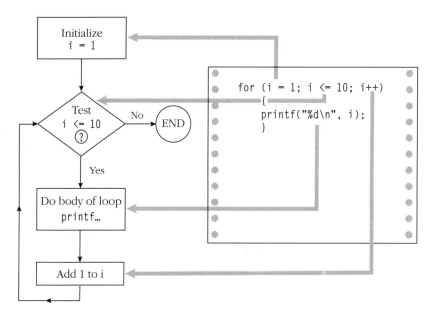

Figure 4-1. *The* for *loop.*

for Loop Style

As with other C statements, the statements within the parentheses of a *for* loop can extend to more than one line if necessary. As noted in our discussion of conventions, we align the braces vertically for the loop body, as shown in FORLOOP.C. An older style aligns the braces as follows:

```
for (i = 1; i <= 10; i++) {
    printf("%d\n", i);
}
```

With this style, the braces can get lost in a long listing, making it difficult to find where the body of the loop begins and ends. Aligning the braces vertically makes them easier to spot and highlights the body of the loop.

Also note that we indent the body of a C loop to the right of the line that specifies it. To indent text in the QuickC editor, simply press the Tab key. The default indention in QuickC is eight characters, but you can change this value in the Options box of the View menu. We use a tab of four characters in our listings.

Pitfalls to Avoid in *for* Loops

An easy mistake to make when writing *for* loops is to put a semicolon *after* the closing parenthesis:

```
for (i = 1; i <= 10; i++);——— Semicolon added
```

This *does not* cause a compiler error: In C, a semicolon by itself is a "null statement." Such a statement does nothing, but it counts as a legal statement. Putting a semicolon after the parenthesis makes the null statement the body of the loop. Adding the semicolon to FORLOOP.C causes the loop to do "nothing" 10 times; the program then prints the value of *i* (which is 11 after the loop exits) and *All Done!*

Always remember to put braces before and after a loop body that consists of more than one statement. If you do not use braces, only the first statement following the parentheses executes as the body of the loop. The remaining statements will execute only once, after the loop terminates. (This is another reason for adopting the practice of putting braces around the statements in a loop body, even when the body has only one statement.)

Multistatement *for* Loops

FORLOOP.C has only one statement in the body of the loop, but most programs are much more complex. Let's develop a program that will print a table of square roots, squares, and cubes for the integers from 1 through 9. Because this program must calculate and print three values for each number, it needs several statements in the body of the *for* loop.

Using QuickC Library Functions

To write such a program, we need a means of determining the square root of a number. Although C does not have operators for calculating squares or cubes directly, we can get these values simply by multiplying a variable by itself two and then three times. To get the square root, however, we must call on QuickC's *sqrt()* function. This function returns the square root of any value you pass to it. For example, if *i* = 4, then *sqrt(i)* = 2.

The *sqrt()* function is an example of a QuickC library function (sometimes called a "library routine"). We've already used two of these library functions, *printf()* and *scanf()*. QuickC can find both these functions automatically, but for most library functions, you must supply the name of the include file containing the function declaration.

The *sqrt()* function is one of many library routines that are defined in the include files (often called "header files") of the \INCLUDE directory. One of the early tasks in learning QuickC is becoming familiar with its external library functions. Fortunately, QuickC makes it easy to explore the function library.

> ## Quick Tip
> Sometimes it is convenient to break out of a loop during its execution. Perhaps you recognize a problem with its output, or perhaps you find yourself in a runaway loop—one whose test will not or cannot fail. To break out of a loop, press Ctrl-Break.

QuickC's extensive on-line Help facility lets you call up a summary of any function to find out how it works and which include files contain its definition. To find out about *sqrt()*, select Index from the Help menu. Next, choose S and then select *sqrt.* When you select this function, a Help window appears at the top of the QuickC screen. The first entry in this window informs you that *sqrt()* is declared in the math.h include file.

QuickC also lets you browse through include files while you are working on a program. Simply select Include from the View menu, select the \INCLUDE directory from the window (if necessary), and then select the include file you want to view. When you finish, select Open Last File from the File menu, and QuickC returns you to the program you were working on.

Of course, the preferred reference for all QuickC library functions is the on-line documentation provided with QuickC.

Using an Include File in a Program

To use functions or other definitions from an include file in your program, you must specify the name of the file you want to call before the start of *main()*. For example:

```
#include <graph.h>
```

includes the file that declares graphics functions and definitions in your program. (The angle brackets that enclose the filename tell QuickC to look for the file in the default \INCLUDE directory, which is identified by the environment variable *INCLUDE*.) This statement is actually a "directive" to the QuickC preprocessor, a program that makes changes in your source file before compilation begins. In this case, the *#include* preprocessor directive reads the contents of the specified include file into your program. Only after it reads and compiles all the include files does QuickC compile your program statements. Note that preprocessor directives such as *#include* are not actually C language statements and do not end with a semicolon.

TABLE.C (Listing 4-2) uses the library function *sqrt()*, which calculates square roots. We use the *#include <math.h>* directive before the definition of the *main()* function to tell QuickC to use the math.h include file in the program. A *printf()* statement then prints the table header. Because we want to print the header only once, we don't place this statement inside the loop!

Quick Tip

If you want QuickC to search for a file in the current directory instead of the default include directory, enclose the filename in quotes: *#include "graph.h"*. If you want QuickC to search another directory, specify the full pathname: *#include "c:\qc25\mydefs\defs.h"*.

```
/* table.c -- prints square root, square, and cube */
/*             for the numbers 1 through 9          */

#include <math.h>   /* include math functions so we */
                    /* can do square root           */

main()
{
    int i;

    printf("i\t sqrt(i)\tsquare(i)\tcube(i)\n\n");
    for (i = 1; i < 10; i++)
        /* beginning of body of loop */
        {
        printf("%d\t", i);
        printf("%f\t", sqrt(i));
        printf("%d\t\t", i * i);
        printf("%d\n", i * i * i);
        }
        /* end of body of loop */
}
```

Listing 4-2. *The TABLE.C program.*

Next comes the *for* loop. The loop specifications establish the test condition as $i < 10$ and the update as increments of 1.

The body of the loop consists of four *printf()* statements: The first statement prints the value of i; the next three print, in order, the square root, the square, and the cube for each value. The program results in the following neatly formatted table:

i	sqrt(i)	square(i)	cube(i)
1	1.000000	1	1
2	1.414214	4	8
3	1.732051	9	27
4	2.000000	16	64
5	2.236068	25	125
6	2.449490	36	216
7	2.645751	49	343
8	2.828427	64	512
9	3.000000	81	729

Multiple Initializations and Calculations in *for* Loops

An almost universal rule in C states that anywhere you can put a single C statement, you can put multiple statements. For example, in a *for* loop, you can initialize two variables in the first part of the loop specification, as follows:

```
for (count = 1, total = 0; count < values; count++)
    {
    total += count;
    }
```

Here we initialize the *for* loop by setting the loop control variable *count* to 1. At the same time, we set the variable *total* to zero. This loop adds all the integers between 1 and the number specified in *values*. Notice that a comma separates the two statements in the initialization: Semicolons separate the three parts of the loop specification (start; condition; update), and commas separate multiple statements within each part.

You can also use multiple calculations in the update portion of the loop specification. For example, we can rewrite the *for* loop as follows:

```
for (count = 1, total = 0; count < values; total += count, count++)
    {;}
```

Here we moved the statement that added each new value of *count* to *total* out of the loop body and put it in the update part of the loop specification. To be valid, however, a loop must have a body, so we added a single semicolon (a null statement) as the loop body. (Using the null statement is a somewhat dangerous practice because you might accidentally delete the stray semicolon. To highlight its importance, we indent the semicolon to the loop body position and enclose it in braces.)

The use of multiple statements and null bodies in loops is a matter of programming style. Many C programmers try to be as concise as possible, so you will often encounter these usages in C code. We present these variants to acquaint you with common C programming practices; you gain no performance advantage by doing all initializations and calculations within the loop specification.

The INFLATE.C program (Listing 4-3) is another example that uses multiple initializations and calculations. At first glance, you might think that the braces in the *for* loop have been forgotten or misplaced.

```
/* inflate.c -- shows multiple initializations */
/*                and calculations in a for loop */

main()
{
    int year;
    float value, rate;

    printf("What do you think the inflation rate will be? ");
    scanf("%f", &rate);
    printf("\nIf the dollar is worth 100 cents in 1990 ");
    printf("and the inflation rate is %2.2f, then\n\n", rate);

    for (year = 1991, value = 1.0; year <= 1999;
        value *= (1.0 - rate),
        printf("in %d the dollar will be worth", year),
        printf(" %2.0f cents\n", value * 100), ++year)
        {;}
}
```

Listing 4-3. *The INFLATE.C program.*

100

The program asks you to estimate the average inflation rate for the next decade or so. (We're sure your guess is as good as ours!) If you enter *.06*, the program generates the following:

```
What do you think the inflation rate will be? .06

If the dollar is worth 100 cents in 1990 and the inflation rate is 0.06, then

in 1991 the dollar will be worth 94 cents
in 1992 the dollar will be worth 88 cents
in 1993 the dollar will be worth 83 cents
in 1994 the dollar will be worth 78 cents
in 1995 the dollar will be worth 73 cents
in 1996 the dollar will be worth 69 cents
in 1997 the dollar will be worth 65 cents
in 1998 the dollar will be worth 61 cents
in 1999 the dollar will be worth 57 cents
```

The program uses *scanf()* to obtain the estimated inflation rate. Then it prints the introduction to the table and enters a *for* loop. Because the table prints yearly values, we call the loop control variable *year*. (Note, by the way, that control variables need not start at 0 or 1.) The initialization part of the loop also sets *value* to 1.0. (In other words, the dollar starts at its full value.) The test part of the loop causes the printing of values for the years 1991 through 1999.

The update part of the loop specification does the work of this loop—the loop has a null body. Each year the current value is multiplied by *1.0 - rate* to show the effects of inflation. The arithmetic assignment operator, *=, causes this new amount to become the new *value*. The *printf()* statements print the amount in cents by first multiplying *value* by 100; the format specifier *%2.0f* rounds it off to whole cents. Finally, *++year* increments *year*, and the loop is ready for another pass.

Nesting *for* Loops

Sometimes it is useful to have one of the statements in the body of a loop be another loop. This is called "nesting" one loop within another. For example, you might design a program to read a data file that is arranged so that each line contains four data fields. An "outer" loop could process each line, and an "inner" loop could process each field. The outline for this program might be

```
Open_file(name);
for (line = 1; line <= last_line; line++)
    {
    for (field = 1; field <= 4; field++)
        {
        Process_field();
        }
    }
Save_file(name);
```

The first, or outer, loop uses the control variable *line* and the test *line <= last_line* to read each line of the file in turn. (In this example, we assume that the number of lines in the file has been previously determined.) The inner *for* loop uses the control variable *field* to step through the four fields of each line.

The body of the nested *for* loop calls the function *Process_field()* to do the actual reading of data. When the last field in the line is processed, the inner loop exits. Because we are still in the body of the outer loop, the outer loop continues by moving to the next *line*; then the inner loop runs again. Only when the inner loop runs for the last *line* does the *Save_file()* statement execute.

Our next sample program, GRAPHBOX.C (Listing 4-4), uses several *for* loops, including a pair of nested loops, to draw a box on the screen using PC graphics characters.

As we mentioned earlier, the IBM PC uses the ASCII values from 128 through 255 to represent the extended character set, which includes many shapes that you can use to create effective graphics. To find the appropriate characters for drawing a box, choose Contents from the Help menu and select the ASCII chart. Scroll down or press PgDn to examine the extended characters. For example, with character number 201 you can draw the upper-left corner of the box.

To display these characters, you must use the QuickC function called *putch()*. Call the function by specifying the ASCII code of the desired character in parentheses. For example, to draw the corner character mentioned above, specify

```
putch(201);
```

A *for* Loop Using Characters

Because the IBM extended character set is merely a set of integer values from 0 through 255, a *for* loop can process characters as easily as it does ordinary integers. For example, the *int* control variable can be initialized by setting it to the character value 'a'. There is no problem with this, because the PC stores 'a' as the integer value 97. Then, by specifying the loop test condition $i <= 'm'$, you determine that the body of the loop will be repeated 13 times, once for each letter in the first half of the alphabet.

```
/* graphbox.c -- defined to use PC-specific graphics characters */

#define NL 10
#define CR 13
#define BLANK 32
#define UPLEFT 201
#define UPRIGHT 187
#define LOWLEFT 200
#define LOWRIGHT 188
#define LINE 205
#define SIDE 186

main()
{
    int i, j, height, width;

    /* Get height and width from user */
    printf("How high a box do you want? ");
    scanf("%d", &height);
    printf("How wide do you want it to be? ");
    scanf("%d", &width);

    /* Draw top of box */
    putch(UPLEFT);
    for (i = 0; i < (width - 2); i++)
        putch(LINE);
    putch(UPRIGHT);
    putch(NL);
    putch(CR); /* go to next line */

    /* Draw sides of box */
    for (i = 0; i < (height - 2); i++)  /* outer loop */
        {
        putch(SIDE); /* left side */
        for (j = 0; j < (width - 2); j++) /* inner loop */
            {
            putch(BLANK);
            }
        putch(SIDE); /* right side */
        putch(NL);
        putch(CR); /* move to next line */
        }

    /* Draw bottom of box */
    putch(LOWLEFT);
    for (i = 0; i < (width - 2); i++)
        putch(LINE);
    putch(LOWRIGHT);
    putch(NL);
    putch(CR); /* box is done; move cursor to new line */
}
```

Listing 4-4. *The GRAPHBOX.C program.*

Using #define

Our box-drawing program uses many different characters to represent the corners and sides of the box, plus the newline, return, and blank characters. Remembering the ASCII codes for all these characters is a difficult task, and relying on memory could lead to coding mistakes. The C language, however, has a feature that helps eliminate this problem.

C provides a mechanism for assigning symbolic names to frequently used values in a program. The preprocessor directive *#define* lets you specify a name and assign a value to it, as in the following example:

```
#define UPLEFT 201
```

Before QuickC compiles your program, the preprocessor finds each occurrence of the name UPLEFT and replaces it with the number 201. You remember the name; QuickC remembers the number. You can also use *#define* with characters. If you use the definition *#define color "green"* and you use the statement *printf(color);* in your program, the preprocessor translates the statement into *printf("green");* before QuickC compiles it.

#define vs Variables

You might ask why you should use *#define* when you could do the same thing more easily with ordinary variables. After all, you could declare *int nl = 10;* and then use *putch(nl);* (to simplify punctuation) and thereby avoid the preprocessor step. But there are two reasons why this isn't a good idea.

First, you create more efficient code with *#define* than you do with a variable. When your program uses variables, QuickC must compile extra machine instructions to store, change, or fetch the needed values. With *#define*, on the other hand, the preprocessor compiles the values directly into the compiled code: The program doesn't need any extra instructions. As a result, your compiled code is faster and more compact.

Second, a variable should represent a quantity that is subject to change by the program. The ASCII value 10 for a newline character, however, is a constant. Using *#define* guarantees that the value you define cannot accidentally be changed while the program is running.

Incidentally, the new ANSI C standard creates the keyword *const* to let you avoid *#define* directives. Using the new keyword, you might declare the constant *nl* as follows:

```
const int nl = 10;
```

Always place *#define* directives before the definition of *main()*, and do not end them with a semicolon. (If you use a semicolon, the preprocessor will treat it as part of the value to be substituted. This often leads to a bug that causes a compiler error.)

In general, you can use *#define* directives to make your code more readable. For example, you could use *NL* for the newline character instead of 10, the newline ASCII value. Also, *#define* makes it easy to change many values in a program without having to change many individual statements.

To continue with the previous example, if you convert your program to run on a mainframe that uses a non-ASCII character set, you need only to change the value of *NL* in the *#define* statement to reflect the new character value throughout the program.

When you run the GRAPHBOX.C program, it asks

```
How high a box do you want? 8 ────── Enter height in lines
How wide do you want it to be? 20 ────── Enter width in characters
```

Figure 4-2 shows the graphics box that this program generates on your screen.

Figure 4-2. *Character graphics box produced by GRAPHBOX.C.*

The program begins with nine *#define* statements that name the needed characters and their values. The first section of *main()* prompts the user for a height and width. Then a call to *putch()* displays the character for the upper-left corner of the box. Next, a *for* loop prints a graphics double-line character *width − 2* times. (We print 2 less than *width* characters to leave room for the upper-left and upper-right corner characters.)

The third section of *main()* draws the sides of the box. After subtracting the top and bottom lines, we want to print *height − 2* lines. This is provided for by the test statement in the next *for* loop. For each line, the program prints the *SIDE* character (the double bar) and then uses a nested *for* loop to print *width − 2* blank characters to position the cursor at the right side of the box. Another *SIDE* character completes the line; then an *NL* and a *CR* move the cursor to the next line.

The statements that print the bottom line are the same as those that printed the top line, except that they use the special characters for the lower-left and lower-right corners of the box.

The *while* Loop

C contains another loop structure, called the *while* loop, which takes the following general form:

```
while (test)
    {
    /* statements */
    }
```

Structurally, the *while* loop is a *for* loop with only the test part of the specification, its condition, in parentheses. You initialize loop variables in a statement before the *while*, and you update or increment the loop with a statement in the loop body. Thus, although the *for* loop features compactness and holds the entire loop specification in the parentheses, the *while* loop is easier to read because the parentheses contain only the test expression. The WHILE.C program (Listing 4-5) shows a simple example.

```
/* while.c -- a simple while loop */

main()
{
    int count = 1;

    while (count < 11)   /* loop condition */
        /* Body of loop */
        {
        printf("%d\n", count);
        count++;
        }
    printf("Done!\n");
}
```

Listing 4-5. *The WHILE.C program.*

The program produces the following output:

```
1
2
3
4
5
6
7
8
9
10
Done!
```

The statement *int count = 1;* declares and initializes the loop control variable. At the *while* statement, the condition *count < 11* is tested. Because the result is true, the body of the loop executes. The body consists of a *printf()* statement that prints the current value of *count*, and the statement *count++;* which increments *count*. The test condition is then checked again, and the loop continues printing numbers until *count* reaches 11. At this point the test fails, the loop terminates, and the statement *printf("Done!\n");* executes. Figure 4-3 shows a flowchart of this *while* loop.

At this point you might ask why you need *while* statements if they are merely variant forms of *for* loops. The answer is simple. A *for* loop is designed to work with a specific series of values (such as numbers from 1 through 10 or 1 through *total_lines*), and it usually counts up or down. A *while* loop, however, is designed to run indefinitely as long as some condition remains true. It also can test many kinds of conditions.

For example, suppose you want to write a program that draws endlessly changing graphics patterns until the user presses a key to stop it. A *while* loop is ideal for this purpose when used with the QuickC library function *kbhit()*, which returns a 1 (true) if a key is pressed and a 0 (false) if no key is pressed. (A loop that waits for some external event to take place is called a "polling loop.") The main loop of your graphics program might appear as follows:

```
while (!kbhit())
    {
    /* draw statements */
    }
```

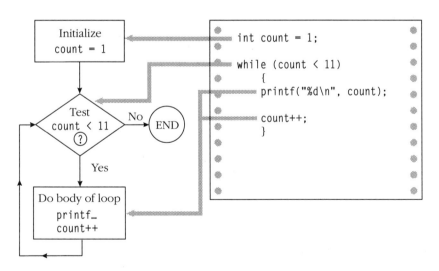

Figure 4-3. *The* while *loop.*

The *draw* statements create the graphics while the test part of the *while* loop specification polls the keyboard. As long as the user does not press a key, the *kbhit()* function returns a 0, or false. Notice that we use an !, which is the logical not operator, in front of *kbhit()*. "Not false" is the same as "true," so the test for the *while* loop is satisfied and the body of the loop executes as long as the user doesn't press a key. If you find this reverse logic difficult to understand, try translating the loop specification into words:

```
while————— "As long as"
!————— "no"
kbhit()——— "key is pressed"
```

When the user presses a key, *kbhit()* returns "true," but the logical NOT operator reverses the result into "not true," or 0, and the loop ends.

Notice that a polling *while* loop needs no counter variable or incrementing. The *while* loop needs only to test a condition that will eventually change. (If the condition never changes, the program never stops.)

Using *while* to Animate a Character

We can nest *while* loops in the same way that we nested *for* loops. The ANIMATE.C program (Listing 4-6) uses a set of nested *while* loops to produce simple animation—making a character appear to move back and forth across the screen.

When you run ANIMATE.C, a double arrow graphics character (» or «) and the flashing cursor move back and forth across the screen until you press a key.

ANIMATE.C starts with *#define* statements that specify the right arrow and left arrow PC graphics characters as well as the blank and backspace characters, which we use for moving the cursor back and for erasing the previously drawn arrow.

The outer loop uses *while (!kbhit())*, which keeps the program running until you press a key. The expression *!kbhit* is true as long as no key has been pressed. Checking the result of a call to a function such as *kbhit()* is an important technique in C. The inner *while* loop moves the arrow to the right by repeatedly

1. Displaying the right arrow character

2. Backing up the cursor

3. Erasing the previously displayed arrow by printing a blank character in its place

4. Incrementing *pos* to keep track of the cursor position (Remember, the blank moves the cursor to the position at which the arrow is to be displayed next.)

A *while* loop then tests *pos* to stop the arrow when it reaches the right side of the screen (position 79).

```
/* animate.c -- animates a graphics character */
/*              until a key is pressed        */

/* Special characters */
#define RTARROW 175
#define LFTARROW 174
#define BLANK 32
#define BACKSPACE 8

main()
{
    int pos, i, j = 1;

    while (!kbhit())
        {
        pos = 1;
        while (pos < 79)
            {
            putch(RTARROW);
            i = 1;
            while (i < 1000)
                {
                j = i + 10;
                i++;
                }
            putch(BACKSPACE);
            putch(BLANK);
            pos++;
            }
        while (pos > 1)
            {
            putch(LFTARROW);
            i = 1;
            while (i < 1000)
                {
                j = i + 10;
                i++;
                }
            putch(BACKSPACE);
            putch(BLANK);
            putch(BACKSPACE);
            putch(BACKSPACE);
            pos--;
            }
        }
}
```

Listing 4-6. *The ANIMATE.C program.*

Notice the two nested *while* loops that we use to slow the display so that the eye can follow it. These loops simply count to 1000. We often use delay loops such as these to slow a program to accommodate human perception or peripheral devices that cannot keep up with the CPU. (Sophisticated delay loops read and use the system clock.) If you have a fast machine (such as an 80386), try changing *i < 1000* to *i < 10000* and recompile the program; the animation will then be slow enough to follow with your eyes.

Another set of *while* loops moves the arrow from the right side of the screen to the left side. You should have little trouble figuring out how it works. Note that the arrow must move backward on the return trip, so we decrement (rather than increment) *pos* and test for *pos > 1* to see when the arrow reaches the left side of the screen.

What happens when the arrow reaches the left side of the screen? The body of the outer loop finishes, and control returns to the test statement in the outer loop. Assuming no key has been pressed, the body of the loop then executes again.

Combining *while* and *for* Loops

The following program, MIXLOOPS.C (Listing 4-7), accepts a character from the user and counts through the alphabet until it reaches the character, beeping once for each increment. The loop continues to accept characters until the user enters a blank. (Note: As written, the program works only with lowercase alphabetic characters; you can extend it to accept others by changing the starting value of the variable *i*.)

```
/* mixloops.c -- reads characters, beeps for */
/*               ASCII count, uses a while    */
/*               loop and a for loop          */

#include <conio.h>

main()
{
    char ch;
    int  i;

    while ((ch = getche()) != ' ') /* get a character */
        {
        printf("\n");
        for (i = 'a'; i <= ch; ++i) /* count up to alpha position */
            {
            printf("In FOR loop!\n");
            printf("\a");  /* sound beep each time */
            }
        }
}
```

Listing 4-7. *The MIXLOOPS.C program.*

A session with MIXLOOPS.C might run as follows:

```
c—————————— User enters character
In FOR loop!—————— Beeps each time line is printed
In FOR loop!
In FOR loop!
————————————— User enters blank to end program
```

The outer loop, a *while* loop, contains the test:

```
while ((ch = getche()) != ' ')
```

This introduces another QuickC library function called *getche()*, which stands for "get character with echo." This function accepts a character from the user and echoes (displays) it on the screen. Because this function is declared in conio.h, you must add the appropriate *#include* line before the definition of *main()*.

An important feature of this loop is its use of a function call whose value is both assigned to a variable and tested in the loop condition. We'll learn more about function calls in the next chapter.

When the user enters a character, the assignment *ch = getche()* assigns the ASCII value of the character to the variable *ch*. The not-equals operator, !=, then compares the character value to the ASCII value for the blank character, specified as ' '. This results in a true or false value that the *while* loop tests.

If the user does not enter a space, the *for* loop, which makes up the body of the *while* loop, executes. The *for* loop tests for *i <= ch*. Thus, if the user enters the character *f*, the loop counts from the ASCII value of 'a' to that of 'f': The body of the *for* loop executes one time each for the values 'a' through 'f', and you hear six beeps.

MIXLOOPS.C is a good example of the appropriate use of *while* and *for* loops. The outer loop, a *while* loop, waits indefinitely for a condition to change (the user enters a space); the inner loop, the *for* loop, counts to a definite value (the ASCII value of the character entered in the *while* loop).

The *do* Loop

The third (and final) C looping structure is the *do* loop, which takes the following general form:

```
do
    {
    /* statements */
    }
while (test);
```

The *do* loop is very similar to the *while* loop, with one major difference—the *while* loop performs the test and then executes the body of the loop; the *do* loop executes the body of the loop and then performs the test. Thus, the body of a *do* loop always executes at least once, even if the result of the first test is false.

The DOLOOP.C program (Listing 4-8) demonstrates a simple *do* loop that performs the now-familiar task of counting from 1 through 10.

```
/* doloop.c -- a simple do-while loop */

main()
{
    int i = 1;

    do
        {
        printf("%d\n", i);
        i++;
        }
    while (i < 11);
    printf("Done!\n");
}
```

Listing 4-8. *The DOLOOP.C program.*

Of the three C looping structures, the *do* loop is by far the least used. Usually when you test for a change in condition, a *while* loop is more appropriate because you want the program to react immediately to user input, especially a "quit" command.

Use the *do* loop to repeat an action until some condition changes only when the test need not be made immediately. A good example is the TIMER.C program (Listing 4-9). This program lets you specify a time in seconds, after which the program beeps three times and prints *Time's Up!*

The TIMER.C program uses the library function *time()*, which, when given the address of a *long* type variable, stores in that variable the number of seconds that have elapsed since Jan. 1, 1970, as measured by your PC's clock. As you would expect, the function also returns this value for use in the calling statement.

After the initial messages are printed and the user enters a number, the program calls the *time()* function. Because this function, like *scanf()*, requires an address as its parameter, you must call the function as *time(&ltime)*, using the address operator & to specify the address of the *long* variable *ltime*. The returned value, the elapsed seconds from Jan. 1, 1970, to the second the user enters a number, is assigned to the variable *start*. We add the number of seconds specified by the user to this variable

---

Quick Tip

Pascal programmers should note the similarity of C's *do* loop and Pascal's *repeat until* loop. The difference is that the *do* in C construct repeats the body of the loop until the specified condition is *false*, whereas the Pascal loop repeats the body until the condition is *true*.

```
/* timer.c -- uses do loop to    */
/*              check elapsed time */

#include <time.h>

main()
{
    long start, end, /* starting and ending times measured */
                     /* in seconds since Jan. 1, 1970       */
         ltime;      /* used to get a value from time() */
    int seconds;     /* elapsed time to be set */

    printf("QuickC Egg Timer\n");
    printf("Enter time to set in seconds: ");
    scanf("%d", &seconds);
    start = time(&ltime);   /* get system elapsed seconds */
                            /* since Jan. 1, 1970 */
    end = start + seconds;  /* calculate alarm time */

    do
        {;}                           /* null statement for loop body */
    while (time(&ltime) < end);   /* wait for alarm time */

    printf("Time's Up!\a\a\a\n");
}
```

Listing 4-9. *The TIMER.C program.*

and store the result in the variable *end*. This variable thus contains the number of seconds which must elapse before the program terminates.

The *do* loop then begins. Because this is a timer program and the user wants to wait some period of time, the test does not need to be performed before the body of the loop executes, so the *do* loop is appropriate. The body of the loop is a null statement—all we want to do is wait. The test *while (time(&ltime) < end)* repeatedly calls *time()* and checks the returned value until the time exceeds the value in *end*.

Debugging and Loops

It's rare for a program to work correctly the first time you run it. Debugging is the art of knowing what to look for in a program that has errors and of correctly interpreting what you see. Some common errors in C programs that involve elements we have already discussed include

■ Syntax errors

■ Uninitialized variables

■ Wrong or incompatible data types

■ Incorrectly specified loops

Throughout this book we point out common programming errors. Syntax errors are the easiest to fix: The compiler enforces the rules of C syntax and informs you when and where you have erred. (Sometimes, though, you must sort out the real problems from the syntax errors that occur as a result of an earlier error!)

True bugs are much harder to detect and fix because they cannot be detected by QuickC. We'll define a "logic bug" as an error that does not violate the rules of C but generates program results that are either completely or partially incorrect. For example, C contains no rule that a variable must be initialized. Nor is there a rule that prevents you from assigning the result of a *double* calculation to an *int* variable (but QuickC will often warn you when you mix data types in a statement). And loops, with their sometimes complex conditions and specifications, offer plenty of opportunity for bugs, such as the problem that arises when you use a semicolon immediately after a *for* loop specification.

Until recently, debugging a C program was a tedious process that involved putting *printf()* statements at strategic locations in a program to reveal the values of key variables or the order in which program statements executed (or both). Then came programs called "debuggers" that could run and report on a C program. QuickC represents the next step in the evolution of debugging: The debugging features are built into the QuickC environment itself.

The BUGS.C program (Listing 4-10) is a bug-ridden program that we will fix using the QuickC Debug menu and facilities. The program features a *while* loop and is supposed to let the user enter as many as five numbers and get their total and average.

```c
/* bugs.c -- for practice with debugger */

main()
{
    char response;
    int number, max_numbers = 5, count = 0, total = 0;
    float average;

    printf("Continue (y/n)? ");
    response = getche();
    while ((response != 'n') && (count < max_numbers))
        printf("\nEnter a number: ");
        scanf("%d", &number);
        total += number;
        printf("Continue (y/n)? ");
        response = getche();
    average = total / count;
    printf("\nTotal is %d\n", total);
    printf("Average is %f\n", average);
}
```

Listing 4-10. *The BUGS.C program.*

Type this program exactly as shown. (If you spot some bugs along the way, give yourself a star. But please type the program as shown so you can step through the debugging exercise properly.) When you run the program, this is what happens:

```
Continue (y/n)? y
Enter a number:
Enter a number:
Enter a number:
```

The program is running out of control. To break out of it and return to the QuickC environment, press Ctrl-Break. Because the program uses a *while* loop, it seems likely that something is causing one statement of the loop to be repeated endlessly.

The Debug menu is shown in Figure 4-4. The debugger allows you to step through your program as well as view and change the values of variables. By default, QuickC has debugging on. (If, for some reason, it is not on, choose Make from the Options menu, and then activate Debug in the Select Build Flags option box.) Restart the program by pressing Shift-F5 (the same as Restart on the Run menu). This tells QuickC to start the program from the top but to wait for you to specify how much of the program to run. To "step through" the program, press F8 (the same as Trace Into on the Run menu). One statement of the program will be executed each time you do so.

As the program runs, notice that the statement currently being executed is highlighted. (If you have a color monitor, you can change colors by selecting Color from the Options menu.) The first *printf()* statement executes and is followed by the *scanf()* statement that solicits a response. Type *y* to continue.

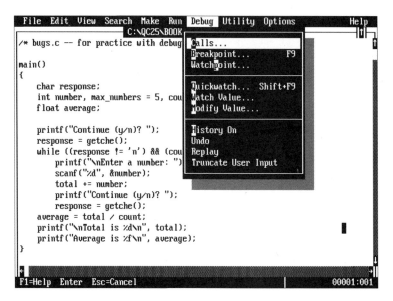

Figure 4-4. *The Debug menu.*

Notice that the loop specification line and the next *printf()* line execute continually. Do you see why? We didn't use braces to mark the beginning and end of the loop body. Therefore, the *printf()* line is executed as the body of the loop. Because this statement doesn't get or change values for either of the loop's two control variables, *response* and *count*, the loop test never becomes false, and the loop never terminates. Now you can insert the braces before and after the indented lines.

This example illustrates how easy it is to use the QuickC debugger. You simply turn on the debugging features, observe the problem, and go back to the program to fix it. Because everything is done in the QuickC environment, you don't have to save or reload any files.

Now run the program again one step at a time. As the highlight moves on the screen, notice that the whole body of the loop executes. That's an improvement. You now can run BUGS.C and enter a series of numbers to be totaled and averaged. Let's say you enter three numbers: 8, 12, and 10. This is what happens:

```
Continue (y/n)? y
Enter a number: 8
Continue (y/n)? y
Enter a number: 12
Continue (y/n)? y
Enter a number: 10
Continue (y/n)? n
run-time error R6003
- integer divide by 0
```

Clearly the program still doesn't work right. A look at the listing shows that the program is supposed to add each new number to *total* and, after the last number is entered, divide *total* by *count* to get *average*. Apparently *count* is still zero when the loop exits, thus triggering the divide-by-zero error. Why? To find out, let's use another feature of the QuickC debugger, "watch variables."

Move the cursor in the text area to the variable name *count*. Select Watch Value from the Debug menu. The window shown in Figure 4-5 appears. The Watch window is a device that lets you designate program variables for QuickC to monitor. When the value of one of these variables changes, QuickC displays its new value in a window at the top of the screen. This eliminates the need to put extra *printf()* statements in your program to monitor variables.

Because you already selected it with the cursor, the word *count* appears in the window. Select Add from the bottom of the dialog box to set a watch on the variable *count*. (Note that you can select Delete to remove the currently selected watch value, or Clear All to remove all watch values.)

You can also specify another display format for the value of the watch variable by adding a comma and a format specifier to the variable—for example, *count,d*—which specifies an integer format display for *count*. The format specifiers are similar to those you used with *printf()* and *scanf()*.

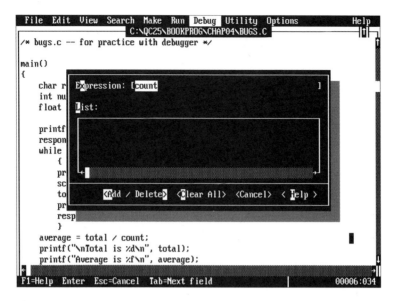

Figure 4-5. *Adding a watch variable.*

Now, let's set a breakpoint, a location in the program at which you want execution to stop. This lets you examine the status of the watch variable. Move the cursor to the last line in the body of the *while* loop—*response = getche();*—and press F9 or choose Breakpoint from the Debug menu and select Add.

Controlling the Debugger from the Keyboard

It is often easier to use keyboard commands rather than menu selections to debug a running program. You can use the following QuickC keyboard commands while debugging a program:

Function Key	Result
F8	Execute next statement, trace through function
F10	Execute next statement, trace around function
F7	Execute until current cursor position is reached
F4	Display the output screen

(When a statement calls a function you have defined elsewhere, F8 traces through the definition of the function. F10, on the other hand, does not detour to trace a called function.)

Now you're ready to run the program again, this time at full speed. Again, the program prompts you for numbers. The program stops at the breakpoint at the end of the body of the loop. At the top of the screen, a small window lists the current value of the watch variable.

To examine the values of other variables, you can add variable names to the Watch window, or you can use the Quickwatch feature, introduced in QuickC version 2.5, to display the current value of any variable or expression. For example, at the breakpoint press Shift-F9 to display the Quickwatch window. Type *number* in the Expression text field and select Evaluate to display the current value of the variable *number*. Figure 4-6 shows the screen with the value of *number* displayed by Quickwatch.

Now add *number* to the Watch window by selecting Add Watch. Do the same for *total*, and select Continue from the Run menu (or press F5) to resume execution.

As the loop cycles, notice that *number* accepts the value of the number you entered. Check the value of *total*; notice that it grows as you add new numbers. But *count* always remains zero. Have you figured out why? We forgot to put a statement in the body of the loop that increments *count*. Adding *count++;* after *total += number;* completes our debugging of the program.

You can do more complex things with the debugger, so be sure to read Chapter 17 of this book for more information. For example, when you learn about arrays and structures, you can use watch variables to display them, too. Meanwhile, you also can use the debugger as a learning tool for tracing the flow of programs in this book, the sample programs provided by Microsoft, or other C programs.

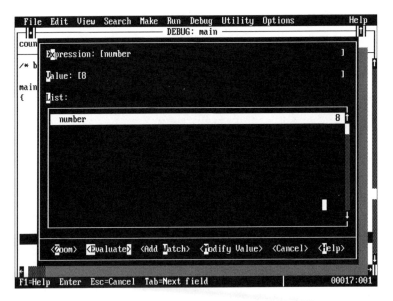

Figure 4-6. *Debugging in progress.*

Decisions and Branching

All programming languages must be able to perform controlled "branching." Branching uses the result of a test or condition to determine which statement (or group of statements) will execute next. In this chapter we discuss the variations of branching in C and learn how to use them with looping statements.

The *if* Statement

In C, as in most languages, the *if* keyword introduces a branching statement. The following structure is the simplest form of branching:

```
if (condition)
    /* statement(s) */
```

An *if* statement, like a *while* loop, evaluates a condition first. The condition can be any combination of values and relational or logical operators that yields a true (nonzero) or false (zero) value—*answer* == 'y', for example. If the condition is true, the subsequent statement (or group of statements in braces) is executed. (As with loops, the statement or statements controlled by the condition are called the body of the statement.) If the condition is false, the subsequent statement or group of statements is not executed, and execution continues with the next statement or group of statements. A simple example follows:

```
if (balance < 0)
    printf("Your account is overdrawn!\n");
printf("Your current balance is %8.2f\n", balance);
```

If the customer's balance is less than zero, the first *printf()* statement executes, telling the customer the account is overdrawn; then the second *printf()* statement, which prints the current (negative!) balance, executes. If the customer's balance is zero or more, the condition is false, and the first *printf()* statement does *not* execute—the program skips it. Only the second *printf()* statement executes.

In the above example, we indent the first *printf()* statement to show that the *if* controls it—it is the body of the *if* statement. (In C, we indent statements for our benefit only: The compiler doesn't require indention.) Always enclose the condition in parentheses, and do not use a semicolon directly after the parentheses—the complete *if* construct includes the *if* keyword, the condition, and the statement body.

The IF.C program (Listing 5-1) features the *if* statement. The program asks the user if he or she wants to continue. The test expression

```
ch = getche() == 'y'
```

gets the response character, assigns it to *ch*, and tests it.

The *if* statement represents a fork in the road: One of two possible courses is followed, depending on the result of the test. The flowchart in Figure 5-1 depicts such a branch, with the test shown in a diamond-shaped box.

```
/* if.c -- simple if statement */

main()
{
    char ch;

    printf("Do you want to continue (y/n)? "); /* prompt */
    if (ch = getche() == 'y')
        printf("\nLet's continue...");          /* if true */
    printf("\nAll done.\n");                     /* always executed */
}
```

Listing 5-1. *The IF.C program.*

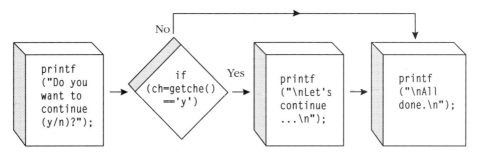

Figure 5-1. *Flowchart for the* if *statement.*

The program generates one of two responses:

```
Do you want to continue (y/n)? y ———— User types y
Let's continue...
All done.
```

or

```
Do you want to continue (y/n)? n ———— User types any character other than y
All done.
```

Note that the program prints *Let's continue...* only if the user types *y*; however, it always prints *All done.*

Comparing *if* and *while*

Notice the structural similarity of the following two statements:

```
if (score > 90)
    printf("Excellent!");
```

and

```
while (question <= total_questions)
    Ask_question();
```

Quick Tip

If you know BASIC or Pascal, you might notice that C does not use the *then* keyword before the body of the *if* statement. Most other languages use the following form for the *if* statement:

```
if (condition)
    then statement(s)
```

If you mistakenly use *then* with *if*, the QuickC compiler will catch the error, of course, and you will soon stop making it.

Both statements test a condition and, if the condition is true, execute the statement body. The important difference between the two constructions is that the *if* statement executes the body of the statement only once; but the *while* statement executes the body repeatedly (as long as the test continues to yield a "true" result).

If you think about the two statements, you can see why each is appropriate for its assigned task. A statement that prints the final score of a quiz needs to be executed only once. On the other hand, a statement that calls a function that asks the next question in the quiz must be executed repeatedly.

Using a Group of Statements with an *if* Statement

The body of an *if* statement can contain any number of statements. Consider the following example:

```
if (choice == 'd')
    {
    printf("How much do you want to deposit? ");
    scanf("%f", &deposit);
    balance += deposit;
    printf("Thank you. Your new balance is ");
    printf("%8.2f", balance);
    }
```

When *choice* is *'d'*, the program executes all five statements between the braces. Notice that we use the same indention for the braces and the statements.

Nested *if* Statements

Just as the body of a loop can contain another loop, the body of an *if* statement can contain another *if* statement. For example, a simple text formatter might use the following code fragment:

```
if (pos == line_length)
    if (++line_count > lines_page)
        {
        Print_footer;
        putch(FF); /* advance to next page */
        ++page_number;
        Print_header;
        }
```

If the first *if* statement is true (the character position equals the line length), the program executes the body of the statement, which is itself an *if* statement. This statement increments *line_count* by 1, and if the result is greater than *lines_page*, the body of the inner *if* statement is executed. These statements print a footer on the current page, send the printer a "formfeed" character, add 1 to the page number, and print a header for the next page. (Because we must repeatedly test for the end of line and the end of page, we would actually place these *if* statements inside a *while* loop. As you might expect, you will often use *if* statements inside loops, and we will show you examples of these later in this chapter.)

Providing Alternatives with *else*

The *if* statement has an adjunct—*else*—that is useful for executing a statement or group of statements only if the given condition is false. The general form of the *if-else* statement is simply an extension of the simple *if* statement:

```
if (condition)
    */ statement(s) */
else
    */ statement(s) */
```

Consider the following example:

```
if (age >= 18)
    {
    printf("To vote, enter number of candidate: ");
    scanf("%d", &candidate);
    }
else
    printf("Sorry, you must be at least 18 to vote.\n");
```

The first group of statements is executed only if *age* is greater than or equal to 18. The statement following *else* is executed only if that condition is false. An *if-else* statement lets you provide an appropriate response for both true and false results.

Note that we align the *else* with its corresponding *if* because together they form one *if* statement of two parts. Correspondingly, we also indent the statement body controlled by the *else* to match the statements under the *if*.

The IFELSE.C program (Listing 5-2 on the following page) uses an *if* statement with an *else* to simulate the logon sequence for a bulletin board system.

If the user replies *y* to the question *Are you a new user?*, the statements following the *if* are executed. If the user types *n* (or any other character), the statements following the *else* are executed instead.

Here is a sample dialogue:

```
Are you a new user (y/n)? y

You must register to use this
bulletin board. Please read
Bulletin #1 first. Thank you.

Are you a new user (y/n)? n

Enter your secret number: 31415
```

```
/* ifelse.c -- an if construct with else */

main()
{
    char ch;
    int num;

    printf("Are you a new user (y/n)? ");
    if (ch = getche() == 'y')
        {
        /* Executed if test condition is true */
        printf("\n\nYou must register to use this\n");
        printf("bulletin board. Please read\n");
        printf("Bulletin #1 first. Thank you.\n");
        }
    else
        /* Executed if test condition is false */
        {
        printf("\n\nEnter your secret number: ");
        scanf("%d", &num);
        }
}
```

Listing 5-2. *The IFELSE.C program.*

Matching an *else* to an *if*

As you write more advanced programs, you will need to use more complex *if* statements, such as:

```
if (temp < 900)
    if (temp > 750)
        printf("Warning! Boiler overheating!\n");
else
    printf("Start emergency shutdown!\n");
```

This program is meant to check the temperature and print a warning if the temperature is between 750 degrees and 900 degrees, or print an emergency alert if the temperature is greater than 900 degrees. It might look correct, but it's not.

When this *if* statement is actually executed, it prints nothing if the temperature exceeds 900 degrees, and it prints the emergency warning if the temperature is less than 750 degrees! We actually want the *else* to go with the outer *if* to print the emergency warning only if the temperature exceeds 900 degrees. Although we physically aligned the *else* so that it appears to go with the outer *if*, the compiler reads the statement differently. It considers the *else* to belong to the inner (nested) *if* statement.

Always remember that QuickC matches a given *else* with the preceding unenclosed *if* that is not already paired with an *else*. Now that we understand this rule, we can fix the program by enclosing the inner *if* in braces so that the *else* is not attached to it.

```
if (temp < 900)
    {
    if (temp > 750)
        printf("Warning! Boiler overheating!\n");
    }
else
    printf("Start emergency shutdown!\n");
```

The Conditional Assignment Statement

Compared to BASIC or even Pascal, C might seem to be a sparse language that provides the essential tools for programming but few frills. However, we've already seen several elements of C (such as the special increment and decrement operators) that simplify commonly encountered programming chores. Another such common programming task is assigning one of two values to a variable, depending on the result of a test. For example, suppose we want to set the variable *max* to the larger of the values of the variables *n1* and *n2*. Of course, we can use an *if* and *else*, as follows:

```
if (n1 > n2)
    max = n1;
else
    max = n2;
```

But we can also use C's "conditional assignment" statement to do the job in a single line of code. The general form for the conditional assignment statement is

```
variable = (expression) ? value1 : value2;
```

QuickC evaluates the expression in parentheses first. In this form of assignment statement, if the expression is true (nonzero), *value1* is assigned to *variable*; if the expression is false (zero), *value2* is assigned to *variable*. Notice that a question mark (?) follows *(expression)* and a colon (:) separates the two values.

We can now rewrite our earlier statement for assigning a value to *max* as follows:

```
max = (n1 > n2) ? n1 : n2;
```
— Assign if false
— Assign if true
— Expression to test
— Variable to receive value

This translates to "If *n1 > n2*, then assign the value of *n1* to *max*; otherwise, assign the value of *n2* to *max*." Although this statement looks odd, it's really quite handy.

Assigning Truth Values

If the two possible values for a variable are actually "true" and "false," you don't need to use the conditional assignment statement. Simply assign the result of the expression to the variable. For example,

```
frozen = (temp <= 32)
```

sets the value of *frozen* to true (nonzero) if the temperature is less than or equal to 32 and sets *frozen* to false (zero) otherwise.

The SHORTIF.C program (Listing 5-3) illustrates some shorthand and conditional assignments.

First, the program gets a number from the user. Then it tests the number to see whether it is positive. Notice that we do this by assigning the result of the expression *(num >= 0)* to the variable *pos*. This value now contains "true" if the number is positive, or "false" if it is not. (Remember that the result is actually a numeric value, 1 or 0, that has the logical effect of "true" or "false" when used in tests.)

Next, the program uses a conditional assignment statement to calculate the absolute value of the number. (The absolute value of a number is its value disregarding its sign. Thus, both 5 and −5 have an absolute value of 5.) Recall that a conditional assignment statement assigns one of two values to a variable, based on the truth result of an expression. However, you can also use a single variable that has a truth value instead of an expression. Because the variable *pos* was assigned a truth value earlier, we can use it here as the test for the conditional assignment.

Now let's look at the assignment statement and the *if-else* branches. If the entered number (*num*) is positive, *pos* contains "true," and the statement assigns *num* to the absolute value *abs*. In other words, the absolute value of a positive number is simply the number itself.

If *num* is negative, however, then *pos* contains "false," and the statement assigns the second value, −*num*, to *abs*. The negative of a negative number is a positive number, which the program can report as the absolute value. The following examples

```
/* shortif.c -- shows 'shorthand' if-else;    */
/*              gets absolute value of number */

main()
{
    int num, pos, abs;

    printf("Enter a whole number: ");
    scanf("%d", &num);

    pos = (num >= 0); /* is number positive? */

    abs = (pos) ? num : -num;  /* assigns negative of */
                               /* number if number is negative */
    if (pos)
        printf("The number is positive.\n");
    else
        printf("The number is negative.\n");
    printf("Absolute value of number: %d\n", abs);
}
```

Listing 5-3. *The SHORTIF.C program.*

demonstrate the output when the program is run twice—first with a positive number and then with a negative number:

```
Enter a whole number: 23
The number is positive.
Absolute value of number: 23

Enter a whole number: -58
The number is negative.
Absolute value of number: 58
```

Multipath Branching

Thus far, we've discussed simple branches (the single *if*) and two-way branches (the *if* and *else*). Simple branches are most useful for testing a condition that can have only one of two values—typically "true" and "false." But what about those situations in which you must test for one of several values? This commonly occurs in a menu from which a user must choose one of several items.

Consider, for example, a program that lets the user get data from a home weather station. Let's say the user can choose among readings for temperature, humidity, barometric pressure, and wind velocity. Here's one way to set up the menu:

```
printf("Enter reading wanted (t = temp;  h = humidity;\n");
printf("p = pressure;  w = wind velocity): ");
ch = getche();
if (ch == 't')
    printf("Current temperature is %5.2f degrees C\n", temp)
else
    if (ch == 'h')
        printf("Humidity is %5.2f percent\n", humidity);
    else
        if (ch == 'p')
            printf("Barometric pressure is %7.2f millibars\n", pressure);
        else
            if (ch == 'w')
                printf("Wind velocity is %d knots\n", wind);
            else
                {/* default */
                printf("Invalid choice. Choose ");
                printf(" t, h, p, or w.\n");
                }
```

Such a chain of *if* statements, each hooked to the preceding statement's *else*, will work, but this approach has many disadvantages. Its many levels of nesting are difficult to read. Also, the many indentions eventually run the code off the edge of the screen, requiring awkward line breaks.

This type of code also creates a conceptual problem. The structure of these statements suggests that each *if* statement is dependent on all of the preceding *if* statements. The implication is that we are checking for some kind of special case that is true only if all the *if* statements in the series are true. But nothing is further from the truth—we merely want to compare *ch* to four possible values and provide a branch for each value. (We also need a default branch to handle invalid user-entry values.)

We can improve the visual organization of our branches in the following manner:

```
if (ch == 't')
    printf("Current temperature is %5.2f degrees C\n", temp)
else if (ch == 'h')
    printf("Humidity is %5.2f percent\n", humidity);
else if (ch == 'p')
    printf("Barometric pressure is %7.2f millibars\n", pressure);
else if (ch == 'w')
    printf("Wind velocity is %d knots\n", wind);
else { /* default */
    printf("Invalid choice. Choose ");
    printf("t, h, p, or w.\n");
    }
```

This arrangement is clearer and more compact. All of the branches now have the same level of indention, showing that they are coequal and not dependent on each other. Note, however, that *else if* is not a distinct statement: Changing indention doesn't change the way the compiler handles this code.

The *switch* Statement

C offers a special *switch* statement that simplifies the writing of multiple branches. The general form of *switch* follows:

```
switch (variable)
    {
    case 'constant1':
        /* statement(s) */
        break;
    case 'constant2':
        /* statement(s) */
        break;
    case 'constant_n':
        /* statement(s) */
        break;
    default:
        /* statement(s) */
    }
```

Specify the name of the variable to be tested in parentheses after the word *switch*. As with the other loops and branches, don't use a semicolon at the end of the first line: The entire structure constitutes one statement.

The body of the *switch* statement (enclosed in braces) is a list of possible branches. Each branch consists of the word *case* followed by a constant value (a number or character) in parentheses. During execution, this constant is compared with the *switch* variable: If they are equal, the statements for that *case* execute. Notice that single quotation marks enclose each constant and that the line ends in a colon.

One or more statements follow each *case* line. (Do not enclose a group of statements in braces—the compiler handles all statements under a given *case* as a single unit.) The last statement in each branch is the keyword *break*. The *break* statement immediately ends execution of the *switch* statement; program execution resumes at the statement that follows the body of the *switch* statement. Usually you will conclude each *case* in a *switch* statement with the keyword *break*. If a *switch* statement behaves erratically, look for missing *break* statements in the individual cases. Also, include a *default:* to handle invalid choices.

Sometimes, however, you will want to execute a set of statements if the *switch* variable has any one of several values. You can do this by placing the set of statements after a series of *switch* values, as in the following:

```
switch (ch)
    {
    case 'q':
    case 'Q':
        Show_score();
        End_game();
        break;
    case ...
    }
```

No statement is associated with *q*, so execution falls through to the code for *Q*, the *Show_score()* and *End_game()* functions execute, and *break* is encountered.

A *switch* statement can contain any number of branches, which is why the last branch in our format description uses the notation *constant_n*. A special case, *default:*, is an optional branch that is usually placed after the last explicit *case* in the *switch* statement. It specifies the branch that executes if none of the conditions for the other cases match the value of *variable*.

Let's use the *switch* statement to rewrite our weather station menu:

```
switch (ch)
    {
    case 't':
        printf("Current temperature is %5.2f degrees C\n", temp)
        break;
    case 'h':
        printf("Humidity is %5.2f percent\n", humidity);
        break;
    case 'p':
        printf("Barometric pressure is %7.2f millibars\n", pressure);
        break;
    case 'w':
        printf("Wind velocity is %d knots\n", wind);
        break;
    default:
        printf("Invalid choice. Choose ");
        printf("t, h, p, or w.\n");
    }
```

Figure 5-2 illustrates this *switch* statement. The multiple branches suggest tracks in a railroad switching yard, the probable origin of the name.

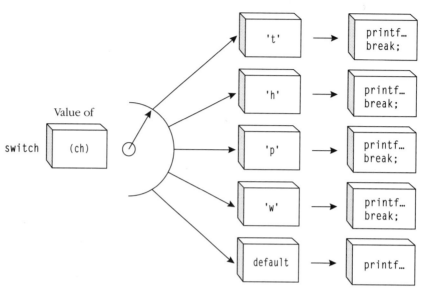

Figure 5-2. *The* switch *statement.*

The *break* Statement

The *break* statement has uses other than serving as the last statement in each *case* of a *switch* statement. A *break* statement can also be used with the three looping statements: (*for*, *while*, and *do*). In all cases, however, *break* has the same effect—it immediately breaks out of the enclosing structure and causes execution to resume after the end of the *switch* or loop structure. The BREAK.C program (Listing 5-4) uses *break* to exit from a *while* loop.

```
/* break.c -- shows how to get out of loop with break */

#include <stdio.h>
#define TRUE 1

main()
{
    int number;

    while (TRUE) /* endless loop */
        {
        /* Get a random number between 0 and 32,767 */
        number = rand();
        printf("%d\n", number);
```

Listing 5-4. *The BREAK.C program.*   *(continued)*

Listing 5-4. *continued*

```
        /* Break out of loop if random number is greater than 32,000 */
        if (number > 32000)
            break; /* exit while loop */
        }
    printf("Broke out of the while loop.\n");
}
```

This program uses the *rand()* library function to generate a series of random numbers. On each pass through the *while* loop, the program generates and displays one random number in the range 0 through 32,767. The statement

```
if (number > 32000)
    break;
```

terminates the *while* loop if the program generates a random number greater than 32,000. The output might look something like the following:

```
41
18467
28145
16827
491
2995
11942
5436
32391
Broke out of the while loop.
```

The last value, *32391*, triggered the *break* statement. The *while* loop terminates, and the *printf()* statement following the body of the *while* loop executes.

The SWITCH.C program (Listing 5-5, which begins on the following page) shows you how to create a simple menu using a *while* loop that contains a *switch* statement. The program asks the user to select one of four math routines (octal representation, hex representation, square, or square root), prompts for a number to be converted, and prints the result. The user types *q* to exit the program.

The following is a sample dialogue with SWITCH.C:

```
Select a math routine:
o = octal   h = hex   s = square
r = square root  q = quit: o
Enter a whole number: 30
Result: 36

Select a math routine:
o = octal   h = hex   s = square
r = square root  q = quit: r
Enter a whole number: 10
Result: 3.162278
```

(continued)

continued

```
Select a math routine:
o = octal   h = hex   s = square
r = square root   q = quit: q
```

```
/* switch.c -- demonstrates switch statement; prints */
/*             values according to user's choice      */

#include <math.h> /* for sqrt() */
#define TRUE 1

main()
{
    char choice;    /* routine wanted by user */
    int number;     /* number entered by user */

    while (TRUE)    /* endless loop */
    {
        printf("\nSelect a math routine:\n");
        printf("o = octal   h = hex   s = square\n");
        printf("r = square root   q = quit: ");
        choice = getche(); printf("\n");

        if (choice == 'q')
            break; /* exits the while loop; ends program */

        /* Rest of program executed if choice <> 'q' */
        printf("Enter a whole number: ");
        scanf("%d", &number);

        switch (choice) /* print according to choice requested */
            {
            case 'o':   /* print octal */
                printf("Result: %o\n", number);
                break;  /* break here in each case     */
                        /* exits the switch statement */

            case 'h':   /* print hex */
                printf("Result: %x\n", number);
                break;

            case 's':   /* square */
                printf("Result: %d\n", number * number);
                break;
```

Listing 5-5. *The SWITCH.C program.*   *(continued)*

Listing 5-5. *continued*

```
        case 'r':   /* square root */
            printf("Result: %f\n", sqrt(number));
            break;

        default:
            printf("Choice must be o, h, s, r, or q\n");
        }
    }
}
```

We enclose the menu in an endless *while* loop because the user will be making choices indefinitely. Notice that we use *while (TRUE)* instead of *while (1)*. Both have the same effect, but the code is clearer when we use a *#define* statement to make TRUE equal to 1 and use the descriptive name in the program.

After the program displays the menu and *getche()* gets the user's choice, an *if* with a *break* statement tests for the possibility that the user wants to quit. If the user quits, the *while* loop terminates and the program ends.

If the user did not enter *q*, the program obtains the number to be processed. A *switch* statement then processes the number. The constants in the various cases correspond to the menu options so the *switch* statement can match the user's choice with the appropriate *case*. If the choice is *o* or *h*, a format specifier returns the appropriate value; if the choice is *s* or *r*, the value is calculated.

The *default:* case handles any value not specified in the menu by printing a list of valid values. Note that the *default:* case needs no *break* because there are no further statements in the *switch* statement that can be executed.

switch vs if-else

Using *switch* gives you code that is at least as clear as the series of *else if* statements shown earlier, because each *case* is clearly distinct. The *switch* has the additional advantage that the variable to be compared is stated clearly once, at the beginning of the structure, rather than being buried inside the individual tests.

Whether you decide to use *switch* or the *else if* form is a matter of style. A good rule of thumb is to use *switch* whenever the program is testing for four or more possible values (including a default). In fact, a *switch* might even be clearer than *else if* branches for three possible values.

There are, however, situations in which you cannot use *switch*—even when you want to represent many possible branches. A *switch* statement can be used only to test simple constant values. You cannot, for example, use a *switch* for the decisions that follow.

```
switch (expenditure)
    {
    case < 10.00:———————————————— Relational expression
        printf("petty cash");            is illegal in a switch
        break;
    case < 100.00:
        printf("see office manager");
        break;
    case < 500.00:
        printf("see district manager");
        break;
    default:
        printf("see head office");
    }
```

Unlike many versions of the Pascal *case* statement and similar structures in other languages, the C *switch* statement cannot compare a value against *ranges* of values. It also cannot be used with relational expressions. For these programming tasks, you must use multiple *if-else* structures.

The *continue* Statement

Under some conditions we might need to skip some of the statements in the body of a loop and return to the loop's test condition. For example, if a program offers a menu operation that has potentially irrevocable consequences (such as overwriting the contents of a file), you might want to ask *Do you really want to overwrite this file?* If the user answers *no*, the program must skip the remaining statements and return to the menu. The *continue* statement lets you extricate yourself from a loop in this way.

A *continue* statement takes the following general form. We illustrate it here with a *while* loop, although you can use it in any kind of loop (but not a *switch*).

```
while (condition)
    {
    */ some statements */
    if (condition)
        continue;
    */ rest of statements */
    }
```

The *if* statement tests a condition as usual: If its condition is true, the *continue* statement executes. This restarts the loop before the rest of the statements in the body of the loop execute, and the *while* loop condition is tested again.

The CONTINUE.C program (Listing 5-6) uses a simple example of a *continue* statement. The program also illustrates a "toggle switch" variable, *sw*. A toggle switch alternates between two values each time you use it. If it's "on," it switches "off" the next time you use it.

```
/* continue.c -- shows continue statement in a loop */

main()
{
    int sw = 0;
    char ch;
    while (1) /* endless loop */
        {
        /* print current status */
        if (sw)
            printf("\nSwitch is ON\n");
        else
            printf("\nSwitch is OFF\n");

        printf("Do you want to quit? ");
        if (ch = getche() == 'y')
            break;     /* exit loop on yes */
        printf("\nDo you want to toggle the switch? ");
        if (ch = getche() != 'y')
            continue; /* restart loop on no */

        sw = !sw;      /* toggle switch */
        }
}
```

Listing 5-6. *The CONTINUE.C program.*

The body of the endless *while* loop first prints the current status of the *sw* switch. Next, the program uses a *break* statement to give the user an opportunity to quit. The program then asks the user whether the switch should be toggled. If the answer is not *y*, a *continue* statement skips the last statement in the loop body and the switch is not toggled. If the answer is *y*, the *continue* statement isn't executed, and the last statement, *sw = !sw*, toggles the switch. (Recall that the negation operator [!] reverses the truth value of the associated variable.)

The next program, BIGM.C (Listing 5-7 on the following page), demonstrates various combinations of *for* loops and *if* statements and includes a *continue* statement. The program draws a letter M within the dimensions specified in the *#define* statements at the beginning of the program.

The Appropriate Use of *continue*

The *continue* statement is rarely used in C programs. Often your intent in using a *continue* statement is better expressed by an *else* branch for the relevant *if* statement or by a new *if* statement. However, if you have a complicated, multiply nested set of *if-else* statements, using a *continue* statement might simplify the program flow.

```
/* bigm.c -- draws a letter M using     */
/*            if and continue statements */

/* Define characters */
#define CH 'M'      /* character to "draw" with */
#define BLANK ' '
#define NL 10
#define CR 13
#define LEFT 20     /* left side of M    */
#define RIGHT 46    /* right side of M   */
#define BOTTOM 21   /* last line to use */

main()
{
    int pos, line;

    /* Space to left side */
    for (line = 1; line <= BOTTOM; line++)
        {
        for (pos = 1; pos < LEFT; pos++)
            {
            putch(BLANK);
            }
        putch(CH); /* draw left side */

        /* Are we past midpoint? */
        if (line > ((RIGHT - LEFT) / 2))
            {
            /* Yes, so draw only right side */
            for (pos = LEFT + 1; pos < RIGHT; pos++)
                {
                putch(BLANK);
                }
            putch(CH);
            putch(NL);
            putch(CR);
            continue; /* start loop over, do next line */
            }
        /* Not past midpoint, check for interior */
        for (pos = LEFT + 1; pos < RIGHT; pos++)
            {
            if ((pos == (LEFT + line)) || (pos == (RIGHT - line )))
                putch(CH);
            else
                putch(BLANK);
            }
        putch(CH);
        putch(NL);
        putch(CR); /* could also use printf("\n"); */
        }
}
```

Listing 5-7. *The BIGM.C program.*

The BIGM.C program generates the following output:

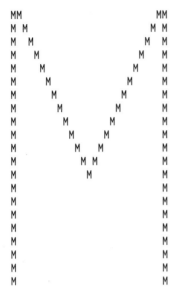

```
MM                      MM
M M                    M M
M  M                  M  M
M   M                M   M
M    M              M    M
M     M            M     M
M      M          M      M
M       M        M       M
M        M      M        M
M         M    M         M
M          M  M          M
M           MM           M
M            M           M
M                        M
M                        M
M                        M
M                        M
M                        M
M                        M
M                        M
M                        M
```

Drawing the letter *M* involves drawing two distinct sections—the V-shaped inner part and the straight-sided outer part. The overall control for drawing all the individual lines resides in the outermost *for* loop. Each line is started by a small *for* loop that moves to the left side of the M and prints the character *M* there.

What happens next depends on whether the current line number is in the top or bottom part of the M. We determine this by testing to see if the distance down the screen in lines is greater than half the distance across the M in characters. (This test is arbitrary. Feel free to try other formulas and to vary the size of the M by changing the *#define* directives.)

If we are below the bottom of the V part of the M, the *for* statement in the body of the *if* moves to the right side, which is then drawn. The *continue* statement (which doesn't require an *if* here) then skips the rest of the statements, which aren't needed.

If the *if* statement is false, we are still in the upper portion of the M: The body of the *if* is skipped, and the rest of the statements in the body of the outer loop execute. The *if* statement works on the principle that the inner lines of the M are drawn one space further to the right and to the left from the sides of the M for each line further down the screen. Thus, the appropriate positioning for the inner lines is found by adding or subtracting the current line number.

The *goto* Statement

C's *goto* statement transfers control to the line containing the specified *label*. For example, you might use *goto* with an *if* statement, as follows:

```
printf("Do you want to continue?\n");
if (ch = getche() == 'y')
    goto yes;
printf("Goodbye\n");
    goto end;
yes: printf("Let's continue...\n");
end:
```

Here, if the user enters *y*, the *goto* statement immediately causes execution to skip to the *printf()* statement that follows the label *yes:* (which must end with a colon). If the user does not enter *y*, the second *goto* skips the "yes" branch.

If this looks confusing, that's because it is. You can do the operation much more clearly with an *if* and an *else*:

```
printf("Do you want to continue?\n");
if (ch = getche() == 'y')
    printf("Let's continue...\n");
else
    printf("Goodbye\n");
```

Nearly all contemporary computer scientists discourage the use of *goto* because it obscures program logic and makes code difficult to decipher, as anyone who has ever tried to debug an old-style BASIC program knows. If your programming background is in the older versions of BASIC or FORTRAN, resist the impulse to use *goto* statements. Examine the logic of your program: You will probably see, as in the above example, that an *if-else* with appropriate conditions (or a *switch*, *break*, or *continue*) lets you implement the operation more clearly. That's why you can go for months without encountering a *goto* in C programs. (An occasional exception is the *goto* that breaks out of a multiply nested loop. You can't use *break* in this situation because it only breaks out of the current loop. But even in this case, you can avoid a *goto* by redesigning the program to use flag variables, which we will discuss later.)

More Complex Conditions for Branching

Because we have been concentrating on the mechanics of branching, we have used only simple test conditions in our branching statements. In the last chapter, we showed you how to use logical operators (&& and ¦¦) to create multiple conditions for controlling loops. You can also use these compound conditions to control the execution of *if* statements.

The next program, PIXELS.C (Listing 5-8), introduces the QuickC Graphics Library. It generates random positions for pixels (points of light on the screen) and uses a compound condition to display only selected pixels.

```
/* pixels.c -- creates shapes from random pixels */

#include <graph.h> /* for graphics  */

main()
{
    int pixels, xpos, ypos;

    /* Window coordinates */
    int xmin = 100, xmax = 540;
    int ymin = 50,  ymax = 150;

    srand(0);                   /* init random nums */
    _setvideomode(_HRESBW); /* CGA 640 x 200     */
    _setcolor(1);               /* white foreground */

    /* Generate random pixel locations */
    for (pixels = 1; pixels < 10000; pixels++)
        {
        xpos = rand() % 639;
        ypos = rand() % 199;

        /* Set pixel if within window */
        if ((xpos > xmin && xpos < xmax) && (ypos > ymin && ypos < ymax))
            _setpixel(xpos, ypos);
        }
    getch(); /* freeze screen until key pressed */

    /* Restore original video mode */
    _setvideomode(_DEFAULTMODE);
}
```

Listing 5-8. *The PIXELS.C program.*

Running the Program

We've already included header files in several programs. The machine code associated with these header files was in the standard library (such as SLIBCE.LIB, the small memory model with floating-point emulation), so you need only specify *#include* and the appropriate header file. QuickC knew where to find the default library.

To use graphics, however, you must specify the graph.h header file. The functions it declares reside in a separate library, GRAPHICS.LIB. If, when you ran the SETUP program, you did not build a combined library that includes GRAPHICS.LIB, then you need to tell QuickC where to find the Graphics library. As with the TABLE.C program in the last chapter, you need a program list. To create a program list, refer to "QuickC Program Lists" in Chapter 12, pp. 378–89.

PIXELS.C starts by including the graph.h header file, which contains definitions for graphics modes at every resolution and color supported by the IBM graphics adapters (CGA, EGA, VGA, and so on, each with several modes). We discuss graphics modes and graphics routines in Chapter 15. Here, simply note that the statement _setvideomode() in PIXELS.C sets the video mode to the constant _HRESBW, which represents the two-color high-resolution CGA mode with a resolution of 640 pixels by 200 pixels. The _setcolor() statement sets the foreground color (the color of the displayed pixels) to white.

The values *xmin*, *xmax*, *ymin*, and *ymax* contain the coordinate positions of the screen "window" in which the program plots pixels. Figure 5-3 shows some sample output for the PIXELS program.

The heart of the program is the *for* loop that plots 10,000 random pixel positions. Notice that we use the % (modulus) operator to select values in the range 0 through 639 for *x*-coordinates, and 0 through 199 for *y*-coordinates. (This corresponds to the 640-by-200 resolution for the specified CGA high-resolution mode.)

The *if* statement checks for an *x* and a *y* position within the window specified by *xmin*, *xmax*, *ymin*, and *ymax*. Notice that the && logical AND operator ensures that each value is greater than or equal to the minimum and less than or equal to the maximum. The && between the two expressions in parentheses tests the random value to see if it fits in *both* the *x* and *y* ranges.

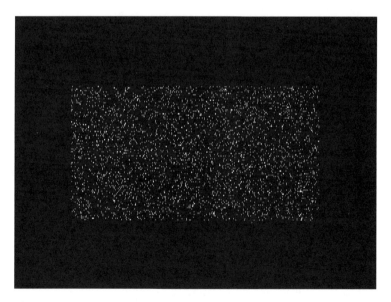

Figure 5-3. *Screen output for PIXELS.C.*

Variations of PIXELS.C

You can create many interesting shapes by substituting different conditions in the *if* statement. The GALAX.C program (Listing 5-9) establishes a center point (*center_x*, *center_y*) and a *radius*. The *if* statement in the *for* loop uses a formula that determines whether a point is within the circle—if it is, the program plots the pixel.

The result of running GALAX.C (Figure 5-4 on the following page) looks more like an ellipse than a circle because in the 640-by-200 mode pixels are more densely spaced horizontally than they are vertically. Because the program must calculate many square roots, it runs slowly. We use an *if (kbhit())* statement to let you stop the program by pressing a key.

```c
/* galax.c -- creates an ellipse by selecting */
/*            from random pixels               */

#include <graph.h> /* for graphics */
#include <math.h>  /* for sqrt() */
#include <conio.h> /* for kbhit() */

main()
{
    int pixels, radius = 50;
    double center_x = 320, center_y = 100, xpos, ypos;

    srand(0);
    _setvideomode(_HRESBW);
    _setcolor(1);

    /* Draw filled ellipse, a circle distorted by */
    /* pixel ratio of high-resolution screen      */
    for (pixels = 1; pixels < 25000; pixels++)
        {
        /* Generate random location */
        xpos = rand() % 639;
        ypos = rand() % 199;

        /* Is distance within radius? */
        if (sqrt((xpos - center_x) * (xpos - center_x)
            + (ypos - center_y) * (ypos - center_y)) < radius)
            _setpixel((short) xpos, (short) ypos);
        if (kbhit())
            break; /* exit if key pressed */
        }
    getch(); /* freeze screen until key pressed */
    _setvideomode(_DEFAULTMODE);
}
```

Listing 5-9. *The GALAX.C program.*

Figure 5-4. *Output of GALAX.C.*

Functions and Function Calls

One of the great advantages that C offers a programmer is its huge variety of library functions, which cover everything from manipulating text to controlling memory allocation. The seasoned C programmer soon learns that the C library contains most of the tools needed to perform a given task. However, the real power of C derives from the ease with which you can design customized C functions that perform the specific and unique operations your program requires. In this chapter, we will show you how to create and use these functions.

Functions and Program Design

Every C program must have at least one user-defined function, the *main()* function. Most C programs, however, consist of many user-written functions, because the procedure for processing data usually involves many different steps. A program that calculates statistics, for example, might have to ask the user for data, check the data for validity, store the data in memory or on disk, process the data (often according to several criteria), and report the results, possibly in a variety of formats. If all this

143

program code were in the *main()* function, the resulting jumble would hamper a programmer trying to visualize where one step ends and the next one begins. Debugging the program would be nearly impossible because you would have difficulty figuring out which of the intertwined parts worked correctly and which ones did not. And if you decided to revise the program to add new capabilities, you could not easily find the appropriate place to add new code.

Most experienced programmers design programs using a "top-down" approach. This method resembles the way you would write an outline for a report. First, list the principal ideas or steps. Then divide those ideas or steps into subtopics, and continue subdividing until you feel ready to write the actual sentences. If this approach is used, the *main()* function for our statistics program might read:

```
main()
{
    Data_menu();
    while (More_data)
        {
        Get_data();
        Check_data();
        Store_data();
        }
    Process_data();
    Report_menu();
    Do_report();
}
```

Each of the names followed by parentheses in the definition of *main()* is a call to a user-defined function. (We will capitalize the first letter of the names of user-defined functions such as *Data_menu()* to distinguish them from library functions provided by QuickC, such as *printf()*. This capitalization isn't required by the C language, however.) Notice how this "outline" clearly shows the overall flow of the program. First, the program offers the user choices in a data-entry menu; then it enters a loop that receives, validates, and stores data as long as more data is entered. The data is then processed. Another menu lets the user generate a specific type of report, and finally the program prints that report.

Note that using functions does more than merely keep the parts of a program conceptually separate; it also provides an orderly way of communicating information between different sections of the program. Each function receives information, such as the values of certain variables, and after it finishes executing, it returns the transformed information to the part of the program that called it.

In a C program, any function can call any other function. This means that your user-defined functions can call other user-defined functions as well as C library functions. For example, the definition of *Do_report()*, shown on the opposite page, might call other user-defined functions, each of which prints a different kind of report, corresponding to the choices offered in the *Report_menu()* part of the program.

```
Do_report()
{
    switch (choice)
        {
        case 'b':
            Bar();
            break;
        case 'p':
            Pie();
            break;
        case 'l':
            Line();
            break;
        case 't':
            Table();
            break;
        }
}
```

Normally, you declare the user-defined functions in *main()* before the program calls them. The function definitions usually follow the definition of *main()*. (You also can define groups of functions in separate files: We will discuss this approach in Chapter 12.) Figure 6-1 proposes a general outline for a program that declares and uses three user-defined functions.

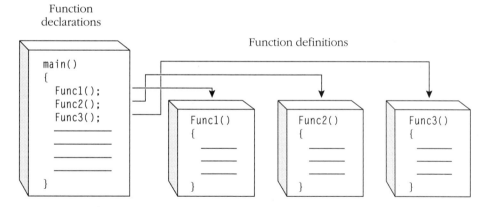

Figure 6-1. *Outline for a C program with functions.*

Dividing a program into logically organized user-defined functions also lets you develop the program one piece at a time. You can start by putting "stub" definitions in the functions, such as:

```
Pie()
{
    printf("executing Pie()\n");
}
```

By using stub functions, you can test the overall control structures of the program (the loops, branches, and switches) before you write the actual routines that perform the various tasks. Then you can replace functions one at a time with their real definitions. After you are certain that a function works properly, you can move to the next function. The basic philosophy of this type of programming is "divide and conquer."

Declaring and Defining a Function

Now that we've discussed the advantages of user-written functions in program development, let's look at the mechanics of declaring, defining, and using your own functions. Always remember that you must declare your functions before you use them. In earlier chapters, you used the *#include* directive to supply declarations of C library functions in your program. For functions you create yourself, however, you must provide the declaration and a definition.

Declaring a Function

Let's declare and define a function that prints an error message. The general format of a simple function declaration is as follows:

```
return_type name();
```

In the declaration, *return_type* refers to the data type (*int*, *float*, and so on) of the value that the function returns. Our first example is a function that displays error messages; it does not return a value, so we use the special word *void* as the return type. (The word *void*, in this instance, doesn't mean "invalid," but rather "empty.")

```
void Error();
```

The function name—*Error*, in our example—must be followed by parentheses, which hold the parameters the function is designed to use. For an error message function, parameters might include a string to print and values that would indicate that the message be printed in high-intensity text, accompanied by a beep, and so on. You must always include parentheses—even if, as in the case of our *Error()* example, you use no parameters. (The compiler uses the parentheses to distinguish a function from a variable.) Notice also that you must use a semicolon at the end of the line.

> ## Ways of Defining Functions
>
> We will first discuss the "classic" method of declaring and defining functions in C. You will see this method used in many older C programs. It has the virtue of simplicity, but it also has disadvantages that will soon become apparent. Therefore, we will soon switch to the use of the more complete "prototyping" method that is recommended for use with QuickC.

As with variable declarations, you can declare several functions of the same type on one line:

```
void Error(), Greeting(), Warning();
```

Usually, programmers place the declarations for user-defined functions in the definition of *main()*, before any other statements (except possibly comments).

```
main()
{
    void Error(); /* function declaration */
    */ other function declarations */

    */ statements */
}
```

However, if a program has many user-defined functions, you might want to put the declarations before *main()*. This practice enables you to see the declarations more easily and separates them from the code of *main()* proper.

Defining a Function

After you declare a function, you must define it with statements that will execute when the program calls the function. The first line of the function definition essentially repeats the original function declaration:

```
void Error()
```

However, remember that with a definition you use no semicolon at the end of the line. The next line contains an opening brace (*{*), and then come the statements that define the function. The definition ends with a closing brace (*}*). Thus, we write our *Error()* function definition as follows:

```
void Error()
{
    printf("Error!\a\n");
}
```

When a statement calls this function, it prints the word *Error!* and sounds a beep. (Notice the \a [alert] escape sequence, which is listed in Figure 3-5 on p. 68.)

Calling the User-defined Function

We call our user-defined *Error()* function the same way we call a library function like *printf()*—by naming it in a statement in *main()* or in the body of another function. Consider the following example:

```
main()
{
    :
    if ((number < 1) || (number > 9))
        Error(); /* function call */
}
```

The *if* statement calls the *Error()* function only if *number* is either less than 1 or greater than 9. Note that the function call ends with a semicolon and includes the parentheses with the function name.

The DBLBAR.C program (Listing 6-1) calls the user-defined function *Line()* to print a double bar before and after a program title. Notice that we declare *Line()* before the statements in *main()*, that we call *Line()* twice from within *main()*, and that we define *Line()* following the end of *main()*. Figure 6-2 shows the flow of control in this program.

You can also follow the flow of this program by using QuickC's debugging facilities. Press F8 to select Trace Into from the Run menu. When you run the program, you see the highlighted statement move through *main()* until it reaches the first call to *Line()*. QuickC then highlights the statements in *Line()*. Highlighting returns to *main()* with the statement following the call to *Line()*. Control shifts in the same manner when the program encounters the second call to *Line()*.

```
/* dblbar.c -- prints header using */
/*             Line() function      */

#define DOUBLE_BAR 205

main()
{
    void Line();        /* declare Line() function */

    Line();             /* call Line() function */
    printf("dblbar.c -- prints header using\n");
    printf("           Line() function\n");
    Line();             /* call Line() again */
}

void Line()             /* function definition */
{
    int pos;

    for (pos = 1; pos <= 40; pos++)
        putch(DOUBLE_BAR);
    printf("\n");
}
```

Listing 6-1. *The DBLBAR.C program.*

148

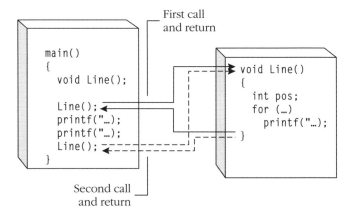

Figure 6-2. *Flow of control in DBLBAR.C.*

A Disadvantage of Using Functions

The double-bar program demonstrates the advantage of using functions—they reduce the size of the program. Any time we need to draw a line, we simply call *Line()* rather than repeat the whole *for* loop. However, using functions has a potential disadvantage. At the machine-code level, each time the program calls a function the current status of the calling program (including the contents of CPU registers) has to be saved, information must be passed to the function (normally via a memory area called the "stack"), and various other housekeeping operations must be performed to return control to the calling statement. Therefore, calling a function involves a lot more "overhead" than does merely using a copy of the desired code wherever you need it in your program. (The performance difference is not noticeable with only a few function calls, but you might notice it when you execute a function call thousands of times within a loop.) The loss of efficiency is not critical in most cases and usually is far outweighed by the benefits of using functions. But keep in mind that the more function calls you use, the more important the overhead factor becomes.

Passing Information to a Function

Our user-defined function *Line()* did not require that any information be passed to it. Most functions, however, require one or more items of information called arguments, or "parameters." This is often true of the QuickC library functions: *printf()* needs to know what to print and how to print it, *scanf()* needs to know what information to get from the user and where to store it, and so on. Indeed, because it uses no parameters, the *Line()* function in Listing 6-1 is extremely limited. As it stands, it always prints a line of 40 characters. However, suppose we want 20 or 60 characters. Let's define this function so that when you call it, a parameter tells it how long the line should be.

149

```
void Line(length)     /* length is parameter    */
    int length;       /* declaration of parameter */
{
    int pos;
    for (pos = 1; pos <= length; pos++)
        putch(DOUBLE_BAR);
}
```

When you call this function, the *length* parameter (placed in parentheses in the function definition) receives the current value of the variable *length*. The items named in the definition of a function are called "formal parameters." The definition of the *Line()* function includes one formal parameter, *length*. When you call a function, you must include an actual value, such as a constant or a variable, for each formal parameter the function requires. Thus, if we use the statement *Line(10);* to call the *Line()* function, the value *10* is the "actual parameter" corresponding to the formal parameter, *length*. Inside the *Line()* function, *length* becomes a variable of type *int* with the value 10.

Notice that we declare the parameter *length* as an *int* in the function definition for *Line()*. This declaration serves the same purpose as the declaration of an ordinary variable: It tells the compiler what type of data the parameter represents. Notice also, however, that unlike the declaration of an ordinary variable, which follows the opening brace of the function definition body, the declaration of a function parameter *precedes* the opening brace. The new ANSI C standard places the parameter type before the name within the parentheses, as in the following:

```
void Line(int length)
```

This kind of declaration is called a "function prototype" and is discussed in more detail later in this chapter. Note that when a function uses parameters, the parameter should also be put in the declaration of the function in or before *main()*. Thus, in a program that uses *Line()*, the declaration would be

```
main()
{
    void Line(int length);
    ⋮
}
```

or

```
void Line(int length);
```

It's easiest to use the same form for the function declaration as for the first line of the function definition—but remember that the declaration ends with a semicolon, whereas the definition does not.

After you declare the parameter *length*, the *Line()* function refers to it as though it had been declared and initialized as an ordinary variable. In our example, *length* sets the limit for the loop condition, thereby controlling the length of the line.

Parameters make functions versatile. The program now can call *Line()* and set the length of the line with any appropriate value: a number, a variable name, a *#define* constant, or an expression.

By the way, you can call the *Line()* function using a variable with the same name as the parameter (*length*). The variable in the function that calls *Line()* belongs to the calling function, and the parameter "belongs" to the called function. They are, in effect, separate local variables—the only connection between them is the value.

Let's look at the ALERT.C program (Listing 6-2), which uses a function with a parameter. The *Beep()* function uses a parameter named *times* to control the number of times a beep is sounded. When the function is executed, the *if* statement checks to see whether *times* has a value in the range 1 through 4. If the value is out of the range, the program prints an error message. Notice that the error message prints the name of the function and the value that *length* passed to it. Including this type of information helps you debug your programs.

```
/* alert.c -- sounds alarm by calling a      */
/*             Beep() function with a parameter */

main()
{
    void Beep(int times);  /* function declaration */

    printf("*** Alert! Alert! ***\n");
    Beep(3);       /* call Beep() with parameter */
}

void Beep(times)
    int times;   /* declare function parameter */
{
    int count;

    /* Check that parameter is in the range 1 through 4 */
    if ((times < 1) !! (times > 4))
        {
        printf("Error in Beep(): %d beeps specified.\n", times);
        printf("Specify one to four beeps");
        }
    else /* sound the beeps */
        for (count = 1; count <= times; count++)
            printf("\a");   /* "alert" escape sequence */
}
```

Listing 6-2. *The ALERT.C program.*

If the value of *times* is in the correct range, a *for* loop with the limit of *times* generates the correct number of beeps. Try changing the calling statement in *main()* to *Beep(0)* or *Beep(100)*.

How Parameters Work

Now that you know how to use parameters, let's take a detailed look at how they work. Figure 6-3 shows what happens when a program calls a function that has a parameter. When it executes the function call *Line(small)*, QuickC places the value of the variable *small* on the stack and passes control to the *Line()* function. The *Line()* function "knows" from its definition that it should expect one parameter, called *length*. It also knows that it is an *int* value. Thus, the function reads 2 bytes (an *int*) from the stack and creates a temporary storage location for them. This value can now be accessed by *length* within the *Line()* function. It is basically a variable that behaves as if it had been declared and initialized within the function definition.

Note that the parameter in a function call is not normally affected by the operation of the function. The function operates with a local variable it creates, not with the variable in the calling statement.

Passing Parameters in Registers

Version 2.5 of QuickC introduced an optional method of passing parameters. Rather than placing the parameter values on the stack, the compiler uses storage locations on the processor called registers. Because access to the register contents is immediate, functions that use this method of parameter passing—fastcall functions—execute more quickly if the code is compiled with the Microsoft C Optimizing Compiler version 6. A fastcall function can receive as many as three 16-bit parameters in registers.

To identify a fastcall function, declare it with the keyword *_fastcall*, as in the following example:

```
int _fastcall Quick_draw(x, y);
```

You can also compile your program with the option /Gr to cause all appropriate functions in the program to be compiled as fastcall funtions. Functions that are not appropriate for fastcall compilation are *main*, all the run-time library functions, and any function prototyped with an attribute that conflicts with *_fastcall* (such as *_cdecl* or *_pascal*).

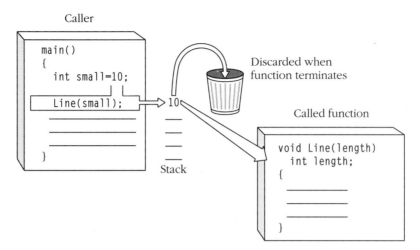

Figure 6-3. *Function parameters and the stack.*

Functions That Return Information

Sending values to a function is only one way that information flows between a calling program and a function in C. A function can also send information to the program. For example, in the expression

```
ch = getche()
```

getche() returns a value (the character) to the calling statement, which in turn assigns the value to the variable *ch.* To have a function return a value to its caller, add a statement to the function definition that consists of the keyword *return* with the value to be returned enclosed in parentheses, as follows:

```
return (value);
```

Replace *value* with any information you want the function to return—the value of a variable, the result of a calculation, a character the function has read, or anything else that can be expressed using a C data type. When the flow of execution reaches a *return* statement, the function immediately terminates, returning the specified value to the calling statement. (A function can have several *return* statements to return different values under different conditions; the branches of an *if* or *switch* statement, for example, might contain separate *return* statements. The function always terminates at the first *return* statement it encounters, however.) In the calling statement, the returned value replaces the function call, and execution of the statement continues.

Let's look at a very simple example, a function that accepts a quantity in yards, converts it to feet, and returns the result:

```
int Ytof(yards)
    int yards;
{
    return(yards * 3);
}
```

This function takes the number of yards passed to it through its formal parameter *yards*. The *return* statement calculates the number of feet (*yards * 3*) and returns the value to the caller. Suppose the calling program uses the following statement:

```
distance = Ytof(course_length);
```

and assume that the user supplies a *course_length* of 750 yards. When the statement calls *Ytof()*, it passes the value of *course_length* to the *Ytof()* function. The function returns 2250 (750 * 3), which replaces the function call in the statement. The statement is now equivalent to

```
distance = 2250;
```

and the assignment operator assigns this value to *distance*.

Also notice that the definition of the *Ytof()* function begins not with the type *void* but rather with the type *int*. The return type *void* signifies that the function does not return a value. (We also must declare the parameter *yards* to be an *int* in the definition of *Ytof()*.)

Now let's look at a more useful example. Some languages have a built-in exponentiation operator; C does not. However, the math.h include file contains a function, called *pow()*, that you can call as *pow(x, y)*. The *pow()* function raises the first parameter (*x*) to the power specified in the second parameter (*y*). Because this function uses *double* values, it can handle both integer and floating-point values with great precision. The EXPO.C program (Listing 6-3) creates an integer version of this function that can respond to various types of input.

The *Expo()* function takes two parameters (the number to be raised to a power and the power to raise it to) and returns a value to the calling statement. However, part of designing functions that return values is deciding how to handle special cases. This program must be able to handle three special cases: an exponent less than 0 (negative), an exponent equal to 0, and an exponent equal to 1. Thus, we designed EXPO.C to respond to valid inputs, special inputs, and error conditions with appropriate messages and return values.

Raising an integer to a negative exponent results in a fraction that is less than 1. For example, 2 to the −3 power is the same as:

$\frac{1}{2^3}$ which is equal to $\frac{1}{8}$ or 0.125.

```
/* expo.c -- uses exp() function to */
/*          calculate powers       */

main()
{
    int Expo(int number, int power);
    int number, power;

    printf("Enter a number: ");
    scanf("%d", &number);
    printf("Raise to what power? ");
    scanf("%d", &power);

    printf("Result: %d", Expo(number, power));
}

int Expo(int number, int power)
{
    int count, value;
    int total = 1;      /* store value of calculation */

    if (power < 0)      /* reject negative exponents */
        {
        printf("Error in Expo(): negative exponent\n");
        return(0);
        }

    if (power == 0) /* any number to 0 power is 1 */
        return(1);

    if (power == 1) /* any number to 1 power is itself */
        return(number);

    /* Calculate for power > 1 */
    for (count = 1; count <= power; count++)
        total *= number;
    return(total);
}
```

Listing 6-3. *The EXPO.C program.*

This function handles only positive powers because it uses *int* type variables that can't handle fractions. The first *if* statement tests the *power* parameter and prints an error message if it is less than zero. The *return* statement returns a value of 0 to the calling program, and the function terminates.

Now let's look at the remaining two cases in *Expo()*. If the power specified in the call to *Expo()* is 0, a *return* statement returns 1. (Any number to the zero power is 1.) If the power specified is 1, *Expo()* returns the number itself.

Finally, a *for* loop calculates all other cases (positive powers greater than 1). Because we initialized *total* to 1 at the beginning of the function, the assignment statement *total *= number* in the *for* loop multiplies *number* by itself *power* times.

The *main()* function simply lets you test the *Expo()* function by passing it a number and a power.

Function Prototypes

We've seen that you can declare a prototype for a function at the beginning of your program, as in this example:

```
int Expo(number, power);
```

This declaration tells QuickC that your function returns an *int* value. That takes care of the value coming out of the function. The definition also specifies data types for the parameters.

We might, of course, design a function to work with integer values and then accidentally give it some *double* values as real parameters. If you don't specify any parameters in the function prototype, QuickC isn't even aware of the potential problem.

The MIXTYPES.C program (Listing 6-4) shows what can happen when the type of data passed to the function does not match the expected type. The *Examine()* function expects a parameter of type *int*. In *main()*, however, we declare the variable *n* as *float* and then call *Examine()* with the parameter *n*.

We wrote this program in the older C style. In that style, you can actually skip the declaration of a function entirely, and the compiler will assume that it returns an *int* value. We've done better than that, however, declaring the *Examine()* function with its *int* return type but with no mention of its parameter (*num*). We left out a key item,

Special Return Values and Error Numbers

Why return a value if an error occurs? Because the value returned can warn the caller that an error has occurred. The warning value selected is a value that the function will not return by normal operation. If normal operation of the function returns a positive number, a number such as 0 or −1 sometimes indicates an error. For functions that don't normally return a number, the return value usually indicates something relevant about the function's operation: For example, the return value of *scanf()* is the number of data fields read, and a 0 indicates an error. Other functions return 0 if their operations were successful; a nonzero return value not only indicates an error but also represents an error number that specifies the precise problem. As you continue to work with QuickC, you will become familiar with many library functions and learn the meanings of their return values.

```
/* mixtypes.c -- shows problem with calling function */
/*               with wrong type parameter           */

main()
{
    int Examine();
    float n = 5.0;
    float i;

    printf("n in main() is %f\n", n);
    i = Examine(n);    /* pass float to function */
                       /* but it's expecting an int */
    printf("Examine() returned n as %f\n", i);
}

int Examine(num)  /* function didn't declare parameter type */
{
    printf("Examine() says n is %d\n", num);
    return(num);
}
```

Listing 6-4. *The MIXTYPES.C program.*

however: the data type for the parameter. The *Examine()* function merely prints its parameter. (It expects its parameter to be of the default *int* type, hence the *%d* format specifier in the *printf()* control string.)

What happens when you run MIXTYPES.C?

```
n in main() is 5.000000
Examine() says n is 0
Examine() returned n as 0.000000
```

The *printf()* statement in *main()* verified a *float* type. But when we try to print the value of this parameter inside *Examine()*, we see that its value is now 0. Because we didn't specify a type for the *num* parameter in *Examine()*, the *float* was passed to the function without comment. However, because the function expects *num* to be an *int* (the default), the *float* is fetched from the stack as if it were an *int*. (Treating the 4-byte value 5.0 as a 2-byte int returns two zero bytes, or 0.) Finally, *Examine()* returns this incorrect value to *main()*.

How can we avoid this problem? In Chapter 3, we discussed strategies for ensuring sensible type conversions, such as using type casts. Here we need to tell QuickC the data type of the function's parameters. You do this by providing a complete function prototype. Function prototypes are a key feature of the new ANSI standard for C because they help to prevent type mismatches such as the one in MIXTYPES.C.

A function prototype declares the name of the function, its return type, the data type of each parameter, and, optionally, the parameter's name. Below are some sample declarations:

```
int Factorial(int number);
int Expo(int number, int power);
void Line(int x1, int y1, int x2, int y2, int color);
char Getyn(void);
```

Some of these are functions we used earlier in this chapter; you will see the others later. Although you have already used return type declarations, the full ANSI proto-types add an additional specification—the data type for each formal parameter. The prototype for *Factorial()* indicates that it returns a value of type *int* and accepts one parameter of type *int*. The prototype for *Expo()* specifies that it returns an *int* and accepts two *int* parameters.

The *Line()* function uses a return type of *void* because it does not return a value; it does, however, take five *int* parameters. Notice that the keyword *int* appears with each parameter—unnecessary repetition if we were simply declaring variables but required in a parameter list. Finally, *Getyn()* returns a *char* but has the parameter *void*, which signifies that the function takes no parameters. In addition, the proto-types specify the names of the parameters. (Although the names are optional—you could say, for example, *int Factorial(int)*—we recommend using the parameter names in the declaration so that all the information is in one place.)

The beginning of the function definition should also contain the function return type, the function name, and the types and names of formal parameters, as in the following:

```
int Factorial(int number)
int Expo(int number, int power)
void Line(int x1, int y1, int x2, int y2, int color)
char Getyn(void)
```

You also could declare the parameter types separately on the following lines. (Notice that the function definitions do not end with semicolons.)

Type Checking in Pascal and C

In the type-mixing situation just described, a Pascal compiler would show an error. Pascal checks actual parameter types against the expected parameter types and is very strict about making you define types for everything. Tradi-tional C philosophy, on the other hand, expects the programmer to anticipate problems carefully, so the compiler permits the mixing of function parameter types. Thus, because C does not force you to declare types for function pa-rameters, it often cannot tell you that anything is wrong when the types of the actual and expected parameters don't match. If you follow modern C program-ming practice and define function return and parameter types, the compiler will alert you to many potential problems.

Advantages of Using Prototypes

Using prototypes might involve a little more thought and a little more typing, but it offers many advantages, which is why the ANSI C standard and QuickC support it. First, the complete prototype contains all the information you need to use the function: what you can put in and what you can expect to get out. Indeed, if you look up a library function using the on-line help, you will find the complete prototype prominently displayed.

If you use prototypes, QuickC checks both the type and number of the parameters in your function calls against the type and number of the parameters you specify in the prototype. In cases where types are mixed, QuickC tries to promote smaller to larger types. (See the examples in Chapter 3.) If you use the wrong number of parameters, QuickC displays an error message.

The PROTO.C program (Listing 6-5) is a revision of the program MIXTYPES.C, rewritten to use full function prototypes. This program produces more reasonable output than that produced by MIXTYPES.C:

```
n in main() is 5.000000
Examine() says n is 5
Examine() returned n as 5.000000
```

With the prototype, QuickC knew that *Examine()* needed an *int* parameter. When the program tried to pass it a *float* value, QuickC converted the value to an *int* before passing it to the function. (Some conversions can cause variables to lose precision, but the resulting value is much more likely to be acceptable.)

```
/* proto.c -- demonstrates function prototyping */
/*             and parameter checking           */

main()
{
    int Examine(int num);  /* parameter type specified */
    float n = 5.0;
    float i;

    printf("n in main() is %f\n", n);
    i = Examine(n);     /* pass float to function */
                        /* but it's expecting an int */
    printf("Examine() returned n as %f\n", i);
}

int Examine(int num)  /* definition includes parameter type */
{
    printf("Examine() says n is %d\n", num);
    return(num);
}
```

Listing 6-5. *The PROTO.C program.*

Multiple User-written Functions

The TIMER2.C program (Listing 6-6) illustrates the use of several functions in one program. It uses a function named *Delay()* to improve the timer program we used in Chapter 4. The *main()* function asks the user for the number of seconds to be timed and the interval by which the program should count off the time, beeping once at each interval. The *while* loop repeatedly calls *Delay(interval)* to wait for *interval* seconds; then it sounds the beep (by calling the *Beep()* function) and prints the elapsed seconds. Be sure you understand the positions and components of the function declarations, the function definitions, and the prototypes for the *Delay()* and *Beep()* functions.

```
/* timer2.c -- interval timer; calls   */
/*             Delay() and uses Beep() */

main()
{
    /* Function declarations */
    void Beep(int times);
    void Delay(int seconds);

    /* Variable declarations */
    int seconds, interval, tick;

    printf("Set for how many seconds? ");
    scanf("%d", &seconds);
    printf("Interval to show in seconds? ");
    scanf("%d", &interval);
    printf("Press a key to start timing\n");
    getch();

    tick = 0;                /* run "clock" for */
    while (tick < seconds)   /* specified time  */
        {
        Delay(interval); /* wait interval seconds */
        tick += interval;
        printf("%d\n", tick);
        Beep(1);
        }
    Beep(3);
}
```

Listing 6-6. *The TIMER2.C program.*   *(continued)*

160

Listing 6-6. *continued*

```
void Delay(int seconds)
    /* Wait for number of seconds specified. */
    /* See TIMER.C in Chapter 4 for details  */
    /* on the library function time().        */
{

    long start, end, /* starting and ending times */
                     /* measured in seconds since */
                     /* Jan. 1, 1970 */
         ltime;      /* used to get val from time function */

    start = time(&ltime);  /* get system elapsed seconds */
                           /* since Jan. 1, 1970 */
    end = start + seconds; /* calculate alarm time */

    do
        {;}                          /* null statement for loop body */
    while (time(&ltime) < end);   /* wait for end of time  */
}

void Beep(int times)
{
    int count;

    /* Check that parameter is in range 1 through 4 */
    if ((times < 1) !! (times > 4))
        {
        printf("Error in Beep(): %d beeps specified.\n", times);
        printf("Specify one to four beeps");
        }
    else /* sound the beeps */
        for (count = 1; count <= times; count++)
            printf("\a");  /* "alert" escape sequence */
}
```

Passing Parameters in Pascal and C

In Pascal, you can pass either the value of a variable or its address in a parameter. (The first is a "call by value"; the second is a "call by reference.") In C, function parameters are always passed by value; the variable itself is never passed. The value can, however, represent the address of a variable. In this case the variable itself, and not merely the value, can be accessed and changed by the called function. (A value that represents the address of a variable is called a "pointer," which we discuss in Chapter 8.)

The *Delay()* function has the same code as the TIMER.C program in Chapter 4, except that it adds the parameter *seconds* to the current time to determine what time should be compared with the system time in the *do* loop. A sample run follows:

```
Set for how many seconds? 30
Interval to show in seconds? 5
Press a key to start timing
5 ─────────────────────────────── Beeps after each number
10
15
20
25
30
```

Putting User Functions in an Include File

Notice in TIMER2.C that the definition of the *Beep()* function follows that of *Delay()*. We've used the *Beep()* function before, and we will use it again in several other programs. You would save program space if you put the definitions of *Beep()* and related functions (perhaps *Line()*, another function that prints characters in reverse video, a function that draws a box around a string, and so on) in an include file. Then you could include these functions in any program without typing or pasting them in by hand. Simply save the definitions in a file that uses the traditional .H extension (hilite.h, for example). Then insert the line *#include "hilite.h"* at the beginning of your program. (You can use the existing INCLUDE subdirectory, but your file system would be better organized if you created a subdirectory called INCLUDE\USER to hold these user-written include files.)

As an alternative, you will learn in Chapter 12 how to turn a group of functions into a library like the ones distributed with QuickC. In that case, your custom include file will contain only declarations for variables and functions (and perhaps constants and macros). The actual function definitions will be in the compiled library. This will allow you simply to link in the functions you need, rather than recompiling them each time you build a program. It would also allow you to distribute your functions commercially without the source code.

Functions with Many Parameters

Functions can use any number of parameters. The actual parameters specified in the function call parentheses are assigned, in order, to the corresponding formal parameters in the function definition.

As a general rule, however, functions that use more than five parameters become cumbersome. If you must use more than this number, reconsider the operations your function performs and try to do the operations in two or more simpler functions. After all, one of the chief benefits of using functions is that they keep each piece of a program at a manageable size. The LINES.C program (Listing 6-7) uses five parameters in its *Line()* function, which draws a colored line on the screen. (To run this program, you need an EGA or VGA display.)

```
/* lines.c -- calls Line() with */
/*              five parameters    */

#include <graph.h>

main()
{
    void Line(int x1, int y1, int x2, int y2, int color);

    int x1, x2, y1, y2, i, color;

    _setvideomode(_MRES16COLOR); /* 320 x 200  16 colors */
    srand(2);                         /* new random seed */
    for (i = 0; i < 100; i++)
        {
        x1 = rand() % 319;         /* random coordinates */
        x2 = rand() % 319;
        y1 = rand() % 199;
        y2 = rand() % 199;
        color = (rand() % 14) + 1; /* random color 1-15 */
        Line(x1, y1, x2, y2, color); /* draw a line */
        }
    while(!kbhit()); /* wait for key to be hit */

    _setvideomode(_DEFAULTMODE); /* restore video mode */
}

void Line(int x1, int y1, int x2, int y2, int color)
{
    _moveto(x1, y1); /* position at first endpoint */
    _setcolor(color);
    _lineto(x2, y2); /* draw line to second endpoint */
}
```

Listing 6-7. *The LINES.C program.*

The *Line()* function draws a line between the points (*x1,y1*) and (*x2,y2*) using a specified color. As you learned from PIXELS.C in Chapter 5, you must use a system of coordinates to specify pixel locations on the graphics screen. This program uses the 320-by-200, 16-color mode, with coordinates starting at (0,0) in the upper-left corner of the screen and ending with (319,199) in the lower-right corner.

After the program sets the video mode and initializes the random number generator with the QuickC library function *srand()*, a *for* loop executes. The body of the loop generates random sets of endpoints for lines. (The QuickC random number function *rand()* generates random integers between 0 and 32,767. To produce a random number between 0 and a number *n*, we use the expression *rand() % n*. Because the modulus operator gets the remainder by dividing the first number by the second, the result is a number greater than or equal to 0 [no remainder] and less than the second number.) A similar expression generates a random color from 1 through 15. (We can't use color 0 because that is the default background color—a line drawn in that color would be invisible.)

Finally, the program calls *Line()* and passes five parameters: the two pairs of end-point coordinates and the color number. Notice that commas must separate the parameters. The *Line()* function draws the line by first calling the QuickC graphics function *_moveto()* to position the cursor at the randomly specified point (*x1,y1*). Another graphics function, *_setcolor()*, sets the current drawing color to the value of *color*. Finally, the QuickC *_lineto()* function draws the line to the second endpoint (*x2,y2*). The *for* loop in *main()* then repeats the process to draw 100 random lines in random colors.

Recursion

Thus far, calling functions and returning values from them have been simple and straightforward matters. However, you can use function calls in a way that deviates slightly from the normal practice—with amazing results. Recursion is an idea that some find difficult to grasp at first, yet a little perseverance will lead you to a programming tool of great beauty, elegance, and power. Here's how it works: In C, any function can call any other function. In fact, a function can call itself—and that is the essence of recursion.

A classic example of recursion is the calculating of the factorial of a number. Recall that the factorial of a number is the product of all the integers between 1 and that number, inclusive. For example, the factorial of 4 (written by mathematicians as 4!) is $1 * 2 * 3 * 4$, or 24.

A program could calculate a factorial by the "brute force" method, using a *for* loop and multiplying the loop control variable by the previous total. But there is another way to calculate factorials. Consider that $4! = 4 * 3 * 2 * 1$, and that $3! = 3 * 2 * 1$. From this we can deduce that $4! = 4 * 3!$, or in general terms, that the factorial of a number n is equal to $n * (n - 1)!$, which in turn is equivalent to $n * (n - 1) * (n - 2)!$, and so on. Eventually we get to 0!, which by definition is equal to 1.

Figure 6-4a depicts the calculation of 4! Figure 6-4b then generalizes the calculation of a factorial. Note that you keep breaking down the expression by subtracting 1 from the current value of n, taking its factorial, and multiplying it by the preceding value. Eventually the expression becomes equal to $n - n$, or 0. But $0! = 1$, so we no longer need to break down n any further. Multiplying all the values together gives the factorial of the original number n. The RECURSE.C program (Listing 6-8) demonstrates how to use this recursive method to calculate factorials.

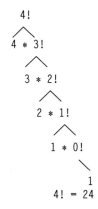

(A)　　　　　　　　BREAKING DOWN 4!

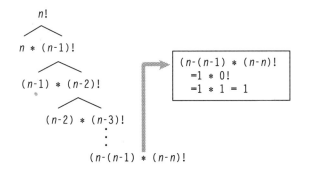

(B)　　　　　　　　BREAKING DOWN *n*!

Figure 6-4. *Breaking down factorial expressions.*

```
/* recurse.c -- demonstrates recursion */

int Factorial(int number);
int level = 1; /* recursion level */

main()
{
    int num, result;

    printf("Factorial of what number? ");
    scanf("%d", &num);
    result = Factorial(num);
    printf("Result is: %d\n", result);
}
```

Listing 6-8. *The RECURSE.C program.*

Listing 6-8. *continued*

```
int Factorial(int number)
{
    int result;

    printf("entering: ");
    printf("level %d. number = %d. &number = %d\n",
           level++, number, &number);

    if (number == 0)
        result = 1;
    else
        result = number * Factorial(number - 1);

    printf("exiting : ");
    printf("level %d. number = %d. &number = %d. ",
           --level, number, &number);
    printf("result = %d\n", result);

    return(result);
}
```

A Recursive Function at Work

Let's examine how the *Factorial()* function in RECURSE.C works. An *if* statement terminates the function and returns 1 if *number* is 0 (because 0! is 1). For any other value of *number*, the *else* branch executes

```
result = number * Factorial(number - 1);
```

This branch contains a recursive call because *Factorial()* is actually calling itself.

In RECURSE.C, the *main()* function makes the first call to *Factorial()* with the value of *number*. Because *number* initially is not 0, *Factorial()* executes the *else* branch and calls itself with *number − 1*. In this new call, execution again encounters the *else* branch, and another call to *Factorial()* results. Although this call uses the value *number − 1*, the value of *number* is now the value *number − 1* that *Factorial()* received from its previous call. So the actual value here in terms of the original *number* is $((number − 1) − 1)$, or *number − 2*. Next time around, the value will be $((number − 2) − 1)$, or *number − 3*, and so on.

As a result of the repeated calls of *Factorial()* to itself, the decreasing values passed with each call accumulate on the stack (because the values passed to a function call are not removed from the stack until the call terminates). Also, remember that each call to *Factorial()* creates a new set of the automatic variables *number* and *result*. These variables accumulate (one set for each call) until the function terminates. It is as though QuickC places a "bookmark" in each function call when the next call executes so that the compiler can keep track of what remains to be done in each.

The *printf()* statements in the program record the above process, as follows:

```
Factorial of what number? 4
entering: level 1. number = 4. &number = 4002
entering: level 2. number = 3. &number = 3990
entering: level 3. number = 2. &number = 3978
entering: level 4. number = 1. &number = 3966
entering: level 5. number = 0. &number = 3954
exiting : level 5. number = 0. &number = 3954. result = 1
exiting : level 4. number = 1. &number = 3966. result = 1
exiting : level 3. number = 2. &number = 3978. result = 2
exiting : level 2. number = 3. &number = 3990. result = 6
exiting : level 1. number = 4. &number = 4002. result = 24
Result is: 24
```

Notice the new address for each call's version of the *number* variable. This proves that separate automatic variables are being created. (The actual addresses the program returns may vary from setup to setup.)

The "turning point" in the recursive process occurs when *number* decreases to 0, the call *Factorial(0)* is made, and the *if* branch finally executes. Finally, the function returns to the caller (the preceding version of *Factorial()*), after assigning the value 1 to *result*. Now the preceding call can "pick up its bookmark" and replace the expression *Factorial(number – 1)* with 1, multiply it by the value of *number* that was saved in its automatic variable, and then return this value to its preceding caller. You can see this happening in the second half of the output listing: The calls move back through the recursion levels, back through the addresses of the accumulated automatic variables, with each *result* being multiplied by the preceding one, until the function returns to *main()* with the final result, 24.

Recursion and Stack Size

Some problems are naturally recursive: searching through directories and their sub-directories, parsing commands into subcommands, or working with tree structures. One thing to keep in mind, however, is that recursion uses a lot of memory for storing automatic variables and the stack. (The stack holds not only the parameters passed for each call but also the register values and return addresses.) Try running RECURSE.C with larger input numbers. You can use only numbers up to 7. After that, type *int*, which stores the result, overflows. If you rewrite the program to use *long* values, you can use numbers up to 16. With type *double*, you can generate some truly impressive factorials, but trying to generate 62! causes a stack overflow error. The stack, which by default can store 2048 bytes, simply cannot hold any more recursions. (You can specify a larger stack size by selecting Make from the Options menu and then selecting Linker Flags and typing a new value into the Stack Size area. Still, there is a limit in the small and medium memory models because the stack and the program data share one 64-KB segment. In Chapter 11, we also will show you how to use a compiler command-line switch to use memory models in which the stack has an entire 64-KB segment to itself.)

Noninteger Functions

The value returned by a function does not have to be an integer type. Functions can return a *float*, a *char*, or any other standard C data type. So far, we have declared and defined functions using a return data type, such as

```
int Expo(int number, int power)
```

An older style of C programming omits the return type when the function returns an *int* because the compiler defaults to *int* if no type is specified. We base our style on the new ANSI standard, which encourages declaring return types for all functions and using *void* for functions that do not return values. For example, we might define a function that calculates the cube root of a number as follows:

```
float Cube_root(int number)
```

This specifies that the *Cube_root()* function returns a value of type *float*. Remember that we also must declare this function in or before *main()*:

```
main()
    {
    char response;
    int x, y;
    float result;
    float Cube_root(int number);    /* function declaration */
```

The GETYN.C program (Listing 6-9) demonstrates the declaration and use of a noninteger function. It defines a function, *Getyn()*, that prompts for a yes or no answer, checks to be sure the character entered by the user is either a *y* or an *n*, and returns the entered character. We declare the function at the start of *main()* and define it as follows:

```
char Getyn(void)
```

because it returns a value of type *char*. Notice that this function does not use a parameter. Although many functions that return values, such as the *Expo()* function, require parameters, some functions receive their information not from the calling statement but from some other source. In the case of *Getyn()*, and indeed with the standard functions that read characters (*getch()*, *getche()*, and so on), the user supplies the value.

In the *Getyn()* function, a *while* loop prompts the user to enter *y* or *n*, a *getche()* gets a character, and an *if* statement checks to see whether the character is a *y* or an *n*. If it is either of the two characters, a *break* statement exits the loop, and the *return* statement returns the character. If the character is something other than *y* or *n*, a prompt asks the user to reenter a value, and then the loop repeats. Putting an input-type statement in a loop provides a framework for error checking.

168

```
/* getyn.c -- calls char function Getyn() */
/*            with error checking          */

#define TRUE 1

main()
{
    char ch;
    char Getyn(void);

    printf("Do you want to continue? ");
    if ((ch = Getyn()) == 'y')
        printf("Answer was y\n");
    else
        printf("Answer was n\n");
    printf("Value of ch is %c\n", ch);
}

char Getyn(void)
{
    char ch;

    while (TRUE)
        {
        printf(" (y or n) ");
        ch = getche();
        printf("\n");
        if ((ch == 'y') || (ch == 'n'))
        /* Valid response; break out of loop */
            break;
        /* Give error message and loop again */
        printf("Please reenter: ");
        }
    return(ch);
}
```

Listing 6-9. *The GETYN.C program.*

The *Getyn()* function is a handy tool that you can use in place of *getch()* or *getche()* whenever you want the user to enter a valid response to a yes-or-no question.

Local and Automatic Variables

A defined function, such as *Line()*, can contain its own variable declarations within its definition. Variables declared within a function definition are called "local" variables, and they are accessible only within the function in which they are declared. Outside the function braces, the variables don't exist. To be accessible to all the functions in your program, a variable must be declared globally—outside of any function. The extent of a variable's accessibility, or "visibility," is called the "scope" of a variable.

169

In Figure 6-5, note that variables defined in *Func1()* cannot be accessed from *main()*. They are "invisible" to *main()* or to *Func2()* or to any part of the program outside the definition of *Func1()*. For example, the definition of *Line()* in DBLBAR.C declares an *int* variable *pos*, which is used in the *for* loop. (See Listing 6-1 on p. 148.)

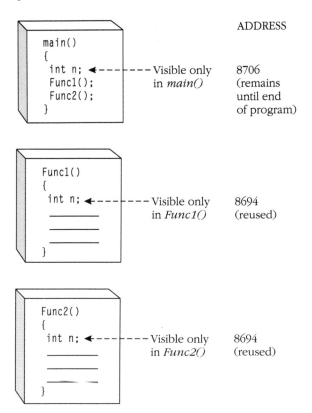

ADDRESS

```
main()
{
  int n;  ◄----┼--- Visible only      8706
  Func1();         in main()          (remains
  Func2();                            until end
}                                     of program)
```

```
Func1()
{
  int n;  ◄---┼--- Visible only       8694
  _____        in Func1()          (reused)
  _____
  _____
}
```

```
Func2()
{
  int n;  ◄---┼--- Visible only       8694
  _____        in Func2()          (reused)
  _____
  _____
}
```

Figure 6-5. *Local variables.*

Suppose the *main()* function in DBLBAR.C contained the following line:

```
printf("The variable pos in Line() has a value of %d\n", pos);
```

This line would produce a compiler error because *main()* doesn't "know" that a variable called *pos* exists—*pos* is the private property of the *Line()* function.

Similarly, if you declare a variable called *pos* within *main()*, it is private to *main()* and not accessible from within a function called by *main()*.

Because variables defined inside functions are local in C, you can use variables with the same name in different functions. Thus, many of your program functions can use a variable named *count*, yet QuickC maintains and refers to each one separately.

Variables Used in Functions Are Automatic

Another important characteristic of a local variable is that it is "automatic": The variable is created (meaning that internal storage is allocated and the address recorded) each time its function called. Conversely, the variable is destroyed and its internal storage released when the function ends and control returns to the calling statement. Only a local variable can be automatic (and temporary) because the compiler knows that it is valid only while the function executes. (A global variable must be stored permanently because the compiler must always assume that the program will need its value again.) Automatic variables permit more efficient storage allocation because the same block of memory can store many temporary variables as the program executes. C programs that use local, automatic variables also are smaller than comparable programs that make the same variables global.

The LOCAL.C program (Listing 6-10 on the following page) illustrates the way local variables work. (Again, refer to Figure 6-5.) The *main()* function declares an *int* variable, *n*, and prints its value and internal address. The program then calls *Func1()* and *Func2()*. Each of these functions also defines a variable called *n* and prints its value and address.

The program's output (which may vary from setup to setup) demonstrates that QuickC recognizes each variable's correct value and address without any confusion:

```
n in main(): val 12 address 3660
Calling Func1()
n in Func1(): val 8 address 3650
Calling Func2()
n in Func2(): val 20 address 3650
```

The Scope of Variables

In Pascal, you can "nest" function or procedure definitions within each other. A variable defined in a function or procedure is accessible not only to that function or procedure, but also to any definitions nested within the outer definition. This can make questions of the scope of certain variables rather complex. In C you cannot nest function definitions; therefore, a variable defined within a function is accessible only within that function.

If you've programmed in older versions of BASIC, you probably expect all variables to be global, that is, accessible throughout the program. You also might remember times that this "feature" created nasty bugs. For example, you might have used *count* as the control variable of a loop in one subroutine and then days later used another variable called *count* in a different subroutine. Depending on the order in which BASIC called the subroutines, hard-to-trace bugs probably resulted because BASIC remembered the last value in *count* when it started the new *count*. Rest assured that QuickC will never confuse the *count* of one function with the *count* of another.

```
/* local.c -- local variables defined */
/*            within functions        */

main()
{
    int n = 12;
    void Func1(void);
    void Func2(void);

    printf("n in main(): value %d; ", n);
    printf("address %d\n", &n);

    printf("Calling Func1()\n");
    Func1();
    printf("Calling Func2()\n");
    Func2();
}

void Func1(void)
{
    int n = 8; /* local variable */

    printf("n in Func1(): value %d; ", n);
    printf("address %d\n", &n);
}

void Func2(void)
{
    int n = 20; /* local variable */

    printf("n in Func2(): value %d; ", n);
    printf("address %d\n", &n);
}
```

Listing 6-10. *The LOCAL.C program.*

Also notice that *n* in *Func1()* and *n* in *Func2()* use the same address. This occurs because when *Func1()* ends, it discards its reference to the now useless local variable *n*. When the program calls *Func2()*, QuickC reuses the same address for the new *Func2()* local automatic variable *n*.

Notice that the address of the *n* in *main()* wasn't reused when the *n* in *Func1()* or *Func2()* was created. Variables declared in *main()* have no special status—the *n* in *main()* is as automatic and local as the variable in the other functions. Remember, however, that QuickC discards an automatic variable only when the function in which it is defined terminates. Because *main()* doesn't end execution until the program itself ends, its variables (including *n*) are not destroyed and reused.

Finally, notice that we declared both functions in LOCAL.C to have a *void* return type and a *void* parameter. This is in keeping with ANSI prototyping; it keeps you from mistakenly calling the function with an actual value (such as *int*) or trying to get a value back from the function. (Remember that if you don't declare the return type of a function, it defaults to *int*; if you don't declare a particular parameter's type, it also defaults to *int*. This accommodates the old style.)

The *auto* Storage Class

All variables declared within function definitions are, by default, automatic. Consider the following example:

```
void Plot_object()
{
    auto int length, width;
    ⋮
}
```

The variables *length* and *width* are automatic because they are declared within a function. The *auto* designation merely reminds us of this. Note that *auto* is not a data type. Rather, it (and the keywords *register*, *static*, and *extern*) is what is called a "storage class." It refers to the way in which QuickC manages the variable as the program runs. Specify the storage class before and in addition to the variable's data type (*int* in the previous example).

Static Variables

Occasionally you will need to have a variable retain its value after its function terminates. To do this, you must declare the variable with the *static* storage type, as follows:

```
static int total;
```

Now the value of *total* calculated during a previous call is still in storage when you call the function again. The *static* storage class is useful for keeping running totals, for example. Notice that a *static* variable is still local and accessible only within the function in which it is defined.

The STATIC.C program (Listing 6-11 on the following page) uses the function *Countline()* to count the words and characters in a line of text. (It simply counts a word whenever it encounters a space.) The *static* variables *chars* and *words* accumulate the counts. Because the variables are *static*, they retain the previous total each time the function is called.

A sample of the program's output follows:

```
Type some lines of text.
Start a line with a . to quit.

By now you should be able to
Words so far: 7. Characters so far: 28.
function very well in C!
Words so far: 12. Characters so far: 52.

.
```

```
/* static.c -- demonstrates a static variable */
/*            that holds count of lines,      */
/*            words, and characters           */

void Countline (void);

main()
{
    printf("Type some lines of text.\n");
    printf("Start a line with a . to quit.\n\n");

    while (getche() != '.')
        Countline();  /* accumulate word and line counts */
}

void Countline(void)
{
    static int words = 0; /* static variables */
    static int chars = 0;
    char ch;

    ++chars; /* count characters typed when function was called */

    while ((ch = getche()) != '\r')
        {
        ++chars;
        if (ch == ' ')
            ++words;
        }
        ++words; /* count last word */

    printf("\nWords so far: %d. Characters so far: %d.\n", words, chars);
}
```

Listing 6-11. *The STATIC.C program.*

External Variables

You can declare global variables in C when you want two or more functions to share relevant values or to communicate with each other by periodically changing the value of a common variable. A global variable in C is referred to as "external" because it is defined outside the function definitions in the program.

To declare an external variable, simply put its declaration outside of any function definition. External variables are usually placed after any *#include* and *#define* directives but before the definition of *main()*. In the following example, we declare *Scale* and *Palette* outside the function, making them external (global) and accessible throughout the program. The variables *length* and *width*, on the other hand, are local and accessible only within *main()*.

```
#include <stdio.h>
#define VERSION 1.0

float Scale = 1.5,        /* global variables */
      Palette = 1;        /* go here          */

main()
    {
    int length, width;  /* local variables */
    :                     /* go here        */
```

The EXTERNAL.C program (Listing 6-12) shows how you might use an external variable. We declare the variable *Length* before *main()* to make it an external variable. After the user supplies a value for *Length*, *main()* calls three functions: *Square()*, *Triangle()*, and *Circle()*. Each of these functions accesses and uses the value of *Length* to calculate the appropriate area.

```
/* external.c -- shows an external variable */

#define PI 3.14159

int Length; /* external (global) variable declared before main() */
void Square(void);
void Triangle(void);
void Circle(void);

main()
{
    printf("What length do you want to use? ");
    scanf("%d", &Length);
    Square();   /* calculate areas */
    Triangle();
    Circle();
}

void Square(void)
{
    float area;
    area = Length * Length;
    printf("A square with sides of %d has an area of %f\n",
           Length, area);
}

void Triangle(void)
{
    float area;
    area = (Length * Length) / 2;
    printf("A right triangle with sides of %d has an area of %f\n",
           Length, area);
}
```

Listing 6-12. *The EXTERNAL.C program.*   *(continued)*

175

Listing 6-12. *continued*

```
void Circle(void)
{
    float area;
    area = (Length * Length * PI);
    printf("A circle with radius of %d has an area of %f\n",
            Length, area);
}
```

Try to resist the temptation to make all your variables external; this invites the problems we discussed earlier. Variables used in only one function should remain local. Variables used by only two or three functions might be better handled as parameters passed from one function to another.

Register Variables

Let's look at one more storage type for variables, the *register* type. Microprocessors such as the 8088 and 80286 have several built-in storage locations called registers. A program can store and retrieve data from a register more quickly than it can from a location in regular memory, where C usually stores variables. As a result, you gain a performance advantage in a time-sensitive application by assigning a register to a frequently used variable.

The only problem with using registers is that usually there aren't enough registers to store all the data of a given operation. As shown in Figure 6-6, the IBM family of Intel microprocessors (8088, 8086, and 80286) have four general-purpose 16-bit registers that hold data being manipulated at the machine level.

In other languages, the compiler software determines which variables, if any, will be assigned registers. In C, however, you can tell the compiler to assign a register to a specific variable when you declare that variable, as follows:

```
register int count;
```

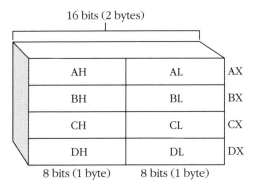

Figure 6-6. *General-purpose registers for the Intel 8086 family.*

This declaration tells QuickC to store the *count* variable in a CPU register. (You can't specify which physical register to use, however.) Because registers in the 8088, 8086, and 80286 cannot store variables with values larger than 2 bytes, only *char* and *int* variables can be accommodated. Additionally, you cannot declare external or static variables as *register* variables because registers cannot serve as permanent storage locations. Finally, QuickC assigns only two variables per function as register variables: You can make more declarations, but only the first two are honored. In fact, depending on the CPU workload, there is no guarantee that both, or even one, of the registers will be available. If speed is important in your program, try the declarations to see if they help.

Which variables should you declare to be register variables? Obvious candidates include loop control variables or variables that are part of statements performed in a loop. But even though most loops execute many times, you shouldn't specify these variables as *register* storage type. QuickC uses optimization techniques to try to produce the fastest machine code possible from your program, and one of its basic speedup techniques is the assigning of registers to variables in loops. Thus, you gain little by specifying these as register variables—in fact, you might even confuse the compiler and end up with less efficient code. The best variables to specify as *register* type are variables that are not involved with loops yet are used three or more times each time the function is called.

Putting It All Together: A Larger Program

To sum up our work with functions and function calls, we present the number game GETCLOSE.C (Listing 6-13), which uses 10 functions (counting *main()*). Although this program is much longer than previous programs, notice how the use of functions breaks this large, more complex program into manageable pieces. Look at the following listing; then we'll see how easy to understand this program actually is.

```
/* getclose.c -- a number game using */
/*                random numbers       */

#define TRUE 1
#define FALSE 0

/* Global variables */
int Number,    /* total number in current game    */
    Moves,     /* number of moves in current game */
    Target,    /* target number to reach          */
    Done,      /* true if game is over            */
    Score,     /* score of current game           */
    Wins = 0,  /* number of games won             */
    Losses = 0, /* number of games lost           */
    Total = 0; /* total score                     */
```

Listing 6-13. *The GETCLOSE.C program.*   *(continued)*

Listing 6-13. *continued*

```
char move;

/* Function prototype declarations */
void Intro(void);        /* tell player about game    */
char Getyn(void);        /* get yes/no response       */
int  Random(int num);    /* random between 1 and num  */
void New_target(void);   /* target number for game    */
char Get_move(void);     /* get player's move         */
void Do_move(void);      /* generate num from move     */
void Check_move(void);   /* won, lost, or continue?   */
void Show_score(void);   /* show score for game       */
void Show_total(void);   /* show total score          */

main()
{
    Intro();             /* print instructions */

    while (TRUE)         /* new games until user quits */
        {
        printf("\nDo you want to continue? ");
        if (Getyn() != 'y')
            break;   /* exit program */

        Done = FALSE;
        Number = Moves = Score = 0;
        New_target();        /* generate a target number */
        while (!Done)        /* play one game            */
            {
            Get_move();      /* user selects random number     */
            Do_move();       /* generate random number and add */
            Check_move();    /* win, lose, or continue?        */
            }
        Show_score(); /* score for this game */
        Show_total(); /* total score         */
        }
}

void Intro(void)
{
    printf("Welcome to Getclose\n\n");
    printf("The object of this game is to\n");
    printf("try to get as close to the target\n");
    printf("number as possible in as few\n");
    printf("moves as possible by choosing from\n");
    printf("various ranges of random numbers.\n");
    printf("You score if you get within 4 of the\n");
    printf("target. You get a 100-point bonus for\n");
    printf("hitting the target, but you get no score\n");
    printf("if you go over.\n\n");
}
```

(continued)

Listing 6-13. *continued*

```
char Getyn(void)
    /* Gets yes or no answer; repeats until valid entry */
{
    char ch;  /* character to read and return */

    while (TRUE)
        {
        printf(" (y or n) ");
        ch = getche();
        printf("\n");
        if ((ch == 'y') || (ch == 'n'))
        /* Valid response; break out of loop */
            break;
        /* Give error message and loop again */
        printf("Please reenter: ");
        }
    return(ch);
}

int Random(int num)
    /* Generates random number between 1 and num.   */
    /* Doesn't use library function srand() because */
    /* we don't want the same seed each time.       */
{
    long seconds, result;
    time(&seconds);    /* randomize with system time */
    return (abs ((int)seconds * rand() % num) + 1);
}

void New_target(void)
    /* Generates a new target number from 50 through 99 */
{
    Target = 50 + Random(49);
    printf("\nYour target for this game is %d\n", Target);
}

char Get_move(void)
{
    while (TRUE)
        {
        printf("\nPick a random number from 1 to\n");
        printf("a) 5  b) 10  c) 25  d) 50  e) 100 ");
        move = getche();
        if ((move >= 'a') && (move <= 'e'))
            {
            ++Moves; /* count the move */
            break;   /* valid response */
            }
```

(continued)

Listing 6-13. *continued*

```
        /* Invalid response; try again */
        printf("\nPlease type a, b, c, d, or e\n");
        }
}

void Do_move(void)
{
    int num = 0;   /* random value to obtain */

    switch (move)
        {
        case 'a' :
            num = Random(5);
            break;
        case 'b' :
            num = Random(10);
            break;
        case 'c' :
            num = Random(25);
            break;
        case 'd' :
            num = Random(50);
            break;
        case 'e' :
            num = Random(100);
            break;
        }
    Number += num;   /* add new number to total */
    printf("\n\nYou got a %d. Number is now %d. ", num, Number);
    printf("(Target is %d.)\n", Target);
}

void Check_move(void)
{
    int temp;

    if (Number > Target)
        {
        printf("\nYou went over! ");
        printf("No score this game.\n");
        Losses++;
        Done = TRUE; /* to break out of loop */
        }
    if (Number == Target)
        {
        printf("\nYou hit the target ");
        printf("for 100 bonus points!\n");
        Score = (100 / Moves) + 100;
        Total += Score;
        Wins++;
        Done = TRUE;
        }
```

(continued)

Listing 6-13. *continued*

```
    if ((Number >= (Target - 4)) && (Number < Target))
        {
        temp = 100 / Moves;
        /* Does player want to go for broke? */
        printf("\nTake %d points (y) or continue (n)? ", temp);
        if (Getyn() == 'y')
            {
            Score = temp;
            Total += Score;
            Wins++;
            Done = TRUE;
            }
        }
}

void Show_score(void)
{
    printf("\nYou scored %d points in %d move(s).\n", Score, Moves);
}

void Show_total(void)
{
    printf("You have won %d game(s) ", Wins);
    printf("and lost %d.\n", Losses);
    printf("Your total score is %d.\n", Total);
}
```

Overview of the Game

GETCLOSE.C is a number game in which you try to reach a randomly generated target number from 50 through 99 in as few moves as possible. Each "move" consists of choosing one of five possible ranges of random numbers: 1–5, 1–10, 1–25, 1–50, and 1–100. You start at zero, and each number you request is added to your total. Thus, each move brings your total closer to the target number. If you get within 4 of the target, you can settle for a score that depends on the number of moves you've made, or you can continue to try to hit the target exactly. If you actually hit the target number, you get a 100-point bonus. If you go over, however, you lose and score nothing. The program lets you play new games, and it keeps track of your total score and the number of games you have won and lost.

The strategy of the game involves deciding from how large a range you should pick the next random number. If you pick from the larger ranges, you can reach the target number in only a few moves, gaining you a high score. But the big ranges also present you with a greater chance of overshooting the target, giving you no points at all. (Playing the game is a little like playing blackjack, except that you have a random target and five different decks from which to choose cards.)

Playing the Game

Type in the program, run it, and play a few games to get an idea of the different operations the program performs. Then read the next section to explore the program's inner workings. The following is a sample game:

```
Welcome to Getclose

The object of this game is to
try to get as close to the target
number as possible in as few
moves as possible by choosing from
various ranges of random numbers.
You score if you get within 4 of the
target. You get a 100-point bonus for
hitting the target, but you get no score
if you go over.


Do you want to continue?  (y or n) y

Your target for this game is 93

Pick a random number from 1 to
a) 5   b) 10   c) 25   d) 50   e) 100 e

You got a 31. Number is now 31. (Target is 93.)

Pick a random number from 1 to
a) 5   b) 10   c) 25   d) 50   e) 100 d

You got a 13. Number is now 44. (Target is 93.)

Pick a random number from 1 to
a) 5   b) 10   c) 25   d) 50   e) 100 d

You got a 19. Number is now 63. (Target is 93.)

Pick a random number from 1 to
a) 5   b) 10   c) 25   d) 50   e) 100 d

You got a 13. Number is now 76. (Target is 93.)

Pick a random number from 1 to
a) 5   b) 10   c) 25   d) 50   e) 100 c

You got a 16. Number is now 92. (Target is 93.)

Take 20 points (y) or continue (n)?  (y or n) y

You scored 20 points in 5 move(s).
You have won 1 game(s) and lost 0.
Your total score is 20.
```

The *main()* Function

As you have seen, the *main()* function of a C program controls the overall flow of the program, and calls to various functions do the actual work. To explore GETCLOSE.C, look at the structure of *main()*. Even without knowing how the functions work, you can see the general structure of the program. First, it calls the *Intro()* function to explain the game briefly. (Notice that we commented each of the function prototype declarations in a block before *main()*. This quickly lets you understand the purpose of every function.)

The outer *while* loop permits unlimited games until the user decides to quit. At the start of each game, *New_target()* generates a new target number, and then the inner *while* loop processes the player's moves until the game ends. In this loop, *Getmove()* prints a menu and lets the user select a range of random numbers for the next move. The *Do_move()* function gets the random number and adds it to the player's current total; *Check_move()* then compares the current total with the target number and decides whether the player has won, lost, or can continue playing.

Finally, when the inner loop (which represents one game) ends, *Show_score()* displays the score of the last game, and *Show_total()* displays the total score and the games won and lost thus far.

You can also use the QuickC Calls menu to help you understand how the function calls work. First, compile GETCLOSE.C with Debug selected, and then move the cursor to the body of a function you want to examine. Use the Debug menu to set a breakpoint there, and then run the program. When the program stops at the breakpoint, pull down the Calls menu to see a list of all called functions. Then display the text of any listed function by selecting it. The Calls menu is especially useful for examining programs that nest function calls.

Modifying GETCLOSE.C

One of the best ways to improve your knowledge of C is to take a program such as GETCLOSE.C and try to add features to it. You might already have some ideas in mind from playing and studying the game. Here are some possibilities:

■ Give points for how close the player gets to the target number.

■ Generate a "poison number" between 1 and the target number minus 10. If the player gets within 4 of this number without going over, he or she loses.

■ Similarly, you could specify a "free number" that, when reached, is not counted as a turn (potentially improving the player's score).

Intermediate C Topics

7

Arrays

In programming, it is often advantageous to collect variables into sets or lists, so that many values can be stored and manipulated as a single conceptual unit. When all the variables in the set have the same data type, the collection is called an array. Arrays are used to organize values that range from the top ten scores in a video game to the payroll records for thousands of employees.

To visualize the advantage of arrays over simple variables, imagine that you run a business and that you want to store each employee's working hours in your computer. If you have even two employees, a year's worth of variables might look like this:

```
int emp1_jan_1, emp2_jan_1;
int emp1_jan_2, emp2_jan_2;
:                                        And so on for 362 intervening lines
int emp1_dec_31, emp2_dec_31;
```

Clearly, even with cut and paste, declaring this many variables would be a monumental undertaking. You can express the same number of variables as an array in C in a single line of code:

```
int employees[2][365];
```

Arrays let you organize data more concisely than do simple variables, as Figure 7-1 illustrates. Although the details of declaration, storage, and retrieval differ from language to language, the basic nature of an array does not. In its simplest form, an array consists of one or more variables of the same storage type (size and number of bytes), arranged one after the other, continuously upward in memory. All variables in an array are referenced by a single name, called an identifier.

Simple variables   Array

Figure 7-1. *Arrays provide superior organization over simple variables for many common C programs.*

How Arrays Are Stored in Memory

The elements in an array are stored consecutively in memory. An array consisting of only four *int* values, for example, is stored in memory as shown in Figure 7-2. Four *int* values (of 2 bytes each on the IBM PC) are arranged together in ascending order in memory. That is, the array begins with the leftmost *int*—the one lowest in memory—and continues upward in memory with one or more adjoining *int* values.

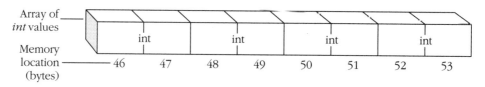

Figure 7-2. *An array of four* int *values as stored in memory.*

How to Declare Arrays

When you declare an array, you must tell the compiler how many items of which data type to set aside in memory for storage and the name to use when referencing that storage location.

The rules for declaring an array in C are relatively straightforward:

1. Declare the type (*char, float, int*, etc.).

2. Declare the variable name. Array names use the same naming conventions as other variable names.

3. Declare the number of items in the array by placing an integer constant expression inside square brackets; for example, [15].

You recall, of course, that an "integer constant expression" is any integer constant value or any combination of integer constant values and arithmetic operators. Thus, 15 is an integer constant value, and so are 3, 0x0F, and 'a'. The last is a character constant that C views as an integer constant. But 3.0 is a floating-point constant and thus illegal for specifying the array size. The expression 15 * 2 is a legal integer constant expression because it is one integer constant value multiplied by another.

Remember, you cannot specify the number of elements in an array with a variable. The following array declaration, for example, is illegal:

```
int line_num = 15;
int widths[line_num];
```

You cannot use the expression *line_num* to declare the number of elements in the array *widths*. The C compiler looks at only one small piece of a program at a time. It first sees *int line_num = 15* and generates code to store the value 15 in the variable *line_num*. When it reaches the array declaration, all it knows of *line_num* is that it currently contains the value 15; the QuickC compiler has no idea how that value will change as the program executes.

BASIC and Pascal Array Declarations

Declaring an array in C is similar to declaring an array in BASIC and Pascal. In BASIC, an array is declared as *widths%(15)*; in Pascal, the same array is declared as *widths : ARRAY [1...15] OF INTEGER*. In C, we declare this array as follows:

```
int widths[15];
```

All three of these declarations identify an array named *widths* composed of 15 integer variables. Each sets aside room in memory for 15 *int* values (30 bytes in the IBM PC because each *int* occupies 2 bytes). As you can see, declaring an array in C retains the simplicity of BASIC but is clearer than BASIC.

The *1...15* expression in the Pascal declaration tells the compiler that the elements in the array are represented by the numbers 1 through 15. In C, array elements are always numbered beginning with 0.

In C, a constant variable—that is, one declared with the ANSI keyword *const*—is not considered a constant value. Therefore, the following example is illegal:

```
int const line_num = 15;
int widths[line_num];
```

Using the *const* keyword declares to the compiler that you do not intend to change the value of *line_num*. It does not prevent a bug in your program from accidentally changing that value.

If you attempt to declare the size of an array with a variable, even a *const* variable, QuickC will print the following error message:

```
error C2057: expected constant expression
```

Examine the ARRAY1.C program (Listing 7-1). This "do-nothing" program demonstrates the correct way to declare arrays.

In this program, SIZEOARRAY is specified using *#define* as 26. The number of items in *ages* is therefore declared with 26 * 2, which is legal.

```
/* array1.c -- how to declare arrays legally */

#define SIZEOARRAY 26

main()
{
    char    initials[26];
    int     num_men[26], num_women[SIZEOARRAY];
    float   ages[SIZEOARRAY * 2];
}
```

Listing 7-1. *The ARRAY1.C program.*

Referencing and Using Array Items

The way you reference the items in an array (whether to store values in them or to fetch values from them) looks very much like the declaration. You merely state the identifier for the array and place the offset of the item within square brackets.

The offset is always measured from the beginning of the array, with the first item having an offset of 0. For example, the expression

```
widths[1] = 3;
```

stores the value 3 in the second item of the array named *widths*; that is, the item whose offset from the beginning of the array is 1.

Conversely, the expression

```
this_width = widths[1];
```

retrieves the value of the second item of the array *widths* and assigns that value to the variable *this_width*.

In C, the offset into an array can be the result of any expression that returns a value. It can be the value of a variable, the result of a computation or logical test, or even the returned value of a function call. The only restriction is that the array offset must be specified with an integer value. The following are legal specifications:

```
widths[1]──────────── Offset is a constant
widths[i]──────────── Offset is an int variable
widths[i++]────────── Offset is a computation
widths[getnum()]───── Return value of function call
widths['a']────────── Offset is a character constant
```

However, the following *float* type offset causes a compiler error:

```
widths[fltval]
```

Because there are no fractional memory locations, specifying an array's offset with a *float* causes the following QuickC error:

```
error C2108: nonintegral index
```

With a valid offset specification, an array element is no different from an ordinary variable of that type. You can perform the same operations with an array item as you can with any ordinary variable. Consider the following fragment, for example:

```
widths[1] = 3;
total   = widths[0] + widths[1] + widths[2];
```

In the first operation, the value 3 is stored in the second element of the array named *widths*. In the second, values stored in three array elements are added together. Notice that we use the same notation to access each—an offset in brackets.

An Example

Now that you have the basic rules for declaring arrays and accessing items in those arrays, examine the XMAS.C program (Listing 7-2 on the following page).

In XMAS.C, we declare the array *widths* to contain 20 items of type *int*. That array is then filled with values by the *for* loop; this is one way to store values in an array. Finally, each item in the array *widths* is passed to the function *Center_out()*; this is one way to access the values in an array.

Whenever you reference an array element, the value of that element becomes available for use—you can assign the value to other variables or pass it to a function.

Note, however, that passing an array element by giving its name and an offset merely passes a copy of that element, not the element itself. This is the same as the method for passing ordinary variables.

```
/* xmas.c -- fills an array with values, then passes */
/*          each of those values to a function       */

main()
{
    int i, j, widths[20];
    void Center_out(char character, int width);

    for (i = 0, j = 1; i < 18; ++i, j += 2)
        {
        widths[i] = j;
        }
    widths[i++] = 3;
    widths[i] = 3;

    for (i = 0; i < 20; i++)
        {
        Center_out('X', widths[i]);
        }

}

void Center_out(char character, int width)
{
    int i;

    for (i = 0; i < ((80 - width) / 2); ++i)
        {
        putch(' ');
        }
    for (i = 0; i < width; ++i)
        {
        putch(character);
        }
    putch('\r');
    putch('\n');
}
```

Listing 7-2. *The XMAS.C program.*

Bounds Checking Arrays in Your Code

In XMAS.C, the *for* loop prevents your specifying an offset beyond the end of the array *widths*:

```
for (i = 0; i < 20; ++i)
```

In many programs, however, the ability to exceed an array's bounds is not prevented by your code but is controlled by the user. For example, the SADD.C program (Listing 7-3) is a simple adding machine that lets the user enter as many as three numbers, one per line, and terminate entry with any non-numeric character such as an *x*.

```
/* sadd.c -- a small adding machine that illustrates */
/*           the need for array bounds checking      */

main()
{
    int offset = 0, i, result = 0;
    int stack[3];

    while (scanf("%d", &stack[offset]) == 1)
        {
        ++offset;
        }
    for (i = 0; i < offset; ++i)
        {
        result += stack[i];
        }
    printf("----------\n");
    printf("%d\n", result);

}
```

Listing 7-3. *The SADD.C program.*

Now run SADD.C and enter (on separate lines) the numbers *1*, *2*, and *3*, followed by an *x* character. The program displays the correct sum, which is 6:

```
1
2
3
x
----------
6
```

Now run the program again, but this time enter four numbers:

```
1
2
3
4
x
----------
20
```

The result shown is 20, which is wrong. But QuickC doesn't recognize that an error occurred and prints no error message. The C language itself, unlike Pascal and BASIC, contains no provisions to prevent offsets beyond the end of an array.

To understand why SADD.C referenced *stack[3]* even though no fourth item exists (remember that arrays begin with item 0), examine Figure 7-3a, which shows how the compiler translates into memory the declarations from SADD.C. As a bonus, we'll find out where the value 20 came from.

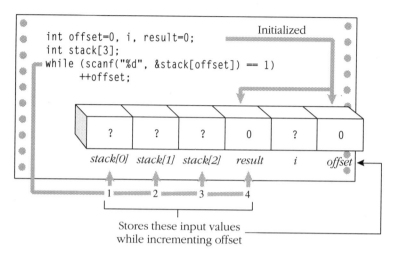

(A)

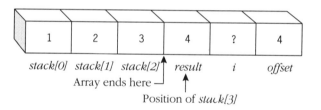

(B)

Figure 7-3. *Consequence of referencing beyond the end of an array.*

First, the variables *offset* and *result* are set to 0. Then the *while* loop fills out the items in the three-element array *stack*. The last value you entered was 4, which was the fourth value placed into *stack*. But *stack* contains no fourth item (that is, no *stack[3]*), so the fourth value is placed into *result* because *result* occupies the place in memory that follows the *stack* array—the place that would have been *stack[3]* had we declared it with the four items.

The arrangement depicted in Figure 7-3a occurs because QuickC places *auto* variables into memory from the top down. (It places *static* and global variables into memory from the bottom up.)

194

Now look closely at Figure 7-3b. Because *result* begins with a value of 4 instead of 0, the *for* loop adds 1, 2, and 3 to it, resulting in a sum of 10. The *for* loop continues (because *offset* is 4) by adding *stack[3]* to *result* (both reference the same address and the same value, 10), thus yielding the erroneous value 20.

To make programs less sensitive to improper user input, always provide code that detects array out-of-bounds conditions. You can do this simply by terminating the program when an error is detected, but writing your program so that it can recover from errors is better. The SADD2.C program (Listing 7-4) shows a common approach to array bounds checking that corrects the previous program's weakness.

In this revision of SADD.C, we use the preprocessor *#define* directive to create an "alias" for the size of the array *stack*. Thus, you can later easily change the number of items in *stack* by changing a single *#define* and then recompiling.

Next, we insert an *if* statement that checks a preincremented *offset* to be sure it does not exceed the number of items in *stack*, that is, *MAXSTAK*. If *offset* becomes too large, the *if* statement first causes a warning message to be printed and then breaks out of the *while* loop. The user gets an accurate sum for the numbers entered, despite the error, and any out-of-range numbers are simply ignored.

```
/* sadd2.c -- a small adding machine that includes */
/*            array bounds checking                 */

#define MAXSTAK 3

main()
{
    int offset = 0, i, result = 0;
    int stack[MAXSTAK];

    while (scanf("%d", &stack[offset]) == 1)
        {
        if (++offset >= MAXSTAK)
            {
            printf("Stack Full\n");
            break;
            }
        }
    for (i = 0; i < offset; ++i)
        {
        result += stack[i];
        }
    printf("----------\n");
    printf("%d\n", result);

}
```

Listing 7-4. *The SADD2.C program.*

How to Initialize Arrays

When you declare an *auto* array (an array declared inside a function and without the keyword *static*), it initially contains whatever values happen to be present in the allocated memory area, regardless of its type and size. (This also occurs when you create *auto* variables.) On the other hand, *static* arrays and arrays declared outside of functions always have their initial values set to zero. For example:

```
char Letters[26];————————————— Initialized to zeros

main()
{
    char vowels[5];————————————— Starts with garbage
    static char consonants[21];————— Initialized to zeros
```

When zero is not an appropriate initial value, you can give *static* and global variables starting values of your choice. To initialize an array:

1. Follow the right square bracket (]) in the array identifier with an assignment operator (=) and a left brace ({).

2. State the initializing values, separated by commas.

3. Finally, terminate your list of array initializers with a right brace (}) and the usual semicolon.

For example, to initialize the array *Letters* with the letters of the alphabet, you need simply declare it as:

```
char Letters[26] = { 'a', 'b', 'c', 'd', 'e',
                     'f', 'g', 'h', 'i', 'j',
                     'k', 'l', 'm', 'n', 'o',
                     'p', 'q', 'r', 's', 't',
                     'u', 'v', 'w', 'x', 'y',
                     'z' };
```

Or, for an array of numbers you could declare:

```
int Values[5] = { 12, 2, 44, 19, 7 };
```

In both of the above examples, the type of the initializing values matches the type of the array and is a constant value. This is mandatory. Values in array-initializing lists must be constant values or constant expressions, and those values must fit in the number of bytes declared for each array item. The array *Letters* is initialized with the type *char*, and *'a'* is a *char* constant. The array *Values* is initialized with type *int*, and *12* is an integer constant. A *float* array would have to be initialized with values of type *float*, such as 76.98, which is a floating-point constant.

The ASIMOV.C program (Listing 7-5) contains in the initialized array *Letters* the name of a famous Isaac Asimov novel. By entering the correct series of numbers, you can reveal that name.

```
/* asimov.c -- illustrates how to initialize an */
/*              array with starting values       */

#define MAXL 16
char Letters[MAXL] = { 'e', 'I', 'a', 'N', 'o', 'R', 'O', 'o',
                       'u', 't', 'o', 'R', 'l', 'o', 'B', 'b', };

main()
{
    int num, i;

    printf("Guess my identity with numbers.\n");
    printf("(Any non-number quits.)\n\n");

    while (scanf("%d", &num) == 1)
        {
        if (num <= 0)
            {
            printf("Guesses must be above zero\n");
            continue;
            }
        for (i = 1; i <= num; ++i)
            {
            printf("%c", Letters[(i * num) % MAXL]);
            }
        printf("\n");
        }
}
```

Listing 7-5. *The ASIMOV.C program.*

Quick Tip

The list of initializers for *Letters* ends with a trailing comma. That is not an error. Trailing commas in initializer value lists are optional but enable long lists to be rearranged easily with your text editor.

Letting the Compiler Supply the Size

When you declare the values for an initialized array, it is not always possible, or necessary, to state explicitly the number of items in the array. C provides an alternative. For example, the following declaration omits the size of the array:

```
int Primes[ ] = { 1, 2, 3, 5, 7, 11, };
```
└─────────────────────────────────── Number of items omitted

When you omit the size, the C compiler counts the initializers and dimensions the array as though you had declared the size to match that count.

```
int Primes[6] = { 1, 2, 3, 5, 7, 11, };
```

When the size of an array is omitted, you might expect bounds checking in your code to be difficult. Fortunately, you can use the *sizeof* operator to find the number of bytes in an array and thus specify, using *#define*, a bounds-checking value. When used with the preceding declaration, the expression

```
#define MAXL (sizeof(Primes) / sizeof(int))
```

gives *MAXL* a value of 6.

The *sizeof* keyword, when given the name of an array, yields the number of bytes in that array. The constant *MAXL*, then, is defined as the number of bytes in the array *Primes* (12 bytes) divided by the number of bytes in an *int* (2 bytes). The parentheses around the operand are optional, but their use is recommended when the operand is a data type.

Overinitializing and Underinitializing

One good reason to include the size of an array is that C permits a mismatch between the number of initializing values and the size you declare. When there are fewer initializers than there are elements in the array, the compiler fills the remaining locations with zero values. When there are too many initializers, the compiler complains and stops. Some compilers (especially under UNIX) issue a warning and truncate the array.

The UNDOVER.C program (Listing 7-6) demonstrates this behavior. As the program stands, it prints the following message:

```
The first 6 primes are: 1 2 3 5 7 11
```

```
/* undover.c -- illustrates the effect of underinitializing and */
/*              overinitializing arrays                          */

int Primes[6] = { 1, 2, 3, 5, 7, 11 };

#define NUMP (sizeof(Primes) / sizeof(int))

main()
{
    int i;

    printf("The first %d primes are: ", NUMP);
    for (i = 0; i < NUMP; ++i)
        {
        printf("%d ", Primes[i]);
        }
    printf("\n");
}
```

Listing 7-6. *The UNDOVER.C program.*

Now change *Primes[6]* to *Primes[8]* in the declaration and run the program again. This time it prints

```
The first 8 primes are: 1 2 3 5 7 11 0 0
```

The new result shows that underinitializing causes the compiler to fill the leftover items with zero values. Now change the declaration again, this time from *Primes[8]* to *Primes[3]*. This time the QuickC compiler stops and issues the message,

```
error C2078: too many initializers
```

Arrays and Functions

As you saw earlier in XMAS.C, passing one of an array's elements to a function is like passing an ordinary variable to a function. That is, a copy of the value of that element is passed, not the element itself.

However, when you pass whole arrays to functions, the situation changes. Although you are still passing by value, what you are actually passing is the address of the array (its location in memory). The effect of this is that you appear to be passing the array itself and that the array itself will be changed. (See the next chapter for further details. For now, we'll simply show you how to pass arrays to functions and how to use those arrays when they get there.)

Passing Arrays to Functions

To pass an array to a function, merely state the array's name (minus the offset) in the function call. For example, if you have declared an array as follows:

```
static int list[7] = { 5, 1, 3, 7, 2, 4, 6 }
```

you would pass that array to a function, called *Bub_sort()*, for example, by stating its name, as follows:

```
Bub_sort(list);
```

This tells the compiler to send the entire array named *list* to *Bub_sort()*.

At the receiving end, in *Bub_sort()*, you need to declare the type of the received array. To do so, declare an array in the normal C manner and leave the square brackets empty:

```
Bub_sort(int vals[])
{
    ⋮
```

This declares that a function named *Bub_sort()* will receive one argument, the int array *vals*. Because *Bub_sort()* is receiving an array—via the array's address—it receives the array itself and not a copy of that array. This allows *Bub_sort()* to change the original array.

The BUBSORT.C program (Listing 7-7) demonstrates the differences between passing array elements to functions and passing entire arrays.

```c
/* bubsort.c -- passes an array to a function,   */
/*              which affects the original array */

#define NUMINTS 6

main()
{
    void Bub_sort(int vals[]);
    void Triple(int x);

    int num = 2, i;
    static int list[NUMINTS] = { 6, 5, 4, 3, 2, 1 };

    printf("num before Triple = %d\n", num);
    Triple(num);
    printf("num after Triple = %d\n", num);
    printf("list[0] before Triple = %d\n", list[0]);
    Triple(list[0]);
    printf("list[0] after Triple = %d\n", list[0]);
    printf("Before sorting -> ");
    for (i = 0; i < NUMINTS; ++i)
        {
        printf("%d ", list[i]);
        }
    printf("\n");

    Bub_sort(list);
    printf("After sorting ->  ");
    for (i = 0; i < NUMINTS; ++i)
        {
        printf("%d ", list[i]);
        }
    printf("\n");

}
void Triple(int x)  /* function doesn't affect original */
{
    x *= 3;
}

void Bub_sort(int vals[NUMINTS]) /* function changes original */
{
    int i, j, temp;

    for (i = (NUMINTS - 1); i > 0; --i)
        {
        for (j = 0; j < i; ++j)
```

Listing 7-7. *The BUBSORT.C program.*   *(continued)*

Listing 7-7. *continued*

```
          {
          if (vals[j] > vals[j+1])
              {
              temp     = vals[j];
              vals[j]   = vals[j+1];
              vals[j+1] = temp;
              }
          }
      }
  }
```

This program first calls the *Triple()* function, passing it both an ordinary variable and one of the elements in the array *list*. The value of the original isn't changed in either case; only the value (a copy) of what is sent is changed.

Next, we pass the array *list* to the function *Bub_sort()* (a function that performs simple bubble sort). The program prints the array before and after the function call to demonstrate that the *Bub_sort()* function changes the values in the original array; it does not sort a copy.

Variations

When a function receives an array, the number of elements in the declaration of that array is usually omitted because the size specification is optional:

```
Bub_sort(int vals[])
```
└────── Size of array omitted

As we have seen, however, C does no array bounds checking on your behalf, so restating the size of the received array helps to clarify and document your program:

```
Bub_sort(int vals[NUMINTS])
```
└────── Restated for clarity

The type of the received array should also match that of the original. If the types do not match, your program might not work properly. The reason we say "might not" is that you might want to mismatch types intentionally. The HEXOUT.C program (Listing 7-8 on the following page) demonstrates such a planned mismatch. This program asks you to enter a floating-point number and then prints out that number, one byte at a time, in hexadecimal notation.

HEXOUT.C first reads a floating-point value into the array *fary* —a *float* type array consisting of only one element. That array is then passed to *Hexout()*. In *Hexout()*, we declare the type of the received array as *unsigned char*. This "deception" causes *Hexout()* to handle the array *fary* as if it were an array of single *unsigned* bytes, whereas the original was actually a 4-byte *float* type. We will explain this shortly. The data type deception illustrates one of C's primary strengths, the freedom of the programmer to change types in midstream.

```
/* hexout.c -- prints a floating-point variable in */
/*              hexadecimal format                  */

void Hexout(unsigned char chary[]);

main()
{
    float fary[1];

    fary[0] = 0;
    printf("Enter a floating-point number.\n");
    printf("(Any non-numeric entry quits.)\n\n");
    while (scanf("%f", &fary[0]) == 1)
        {
        Hexout(fary);
        }
    return (0);
}

void Hexout(unsigned char chary[])
{
    int i;

    for (i = 0; i < sizeof(float); ++i)
        {
        printf("%02X ", chary[i]);
        }
    printf("\n\n");
}
```

Listing 7-8. *The HEXOUT.C program.*

How Array Offsets Advance

When you reference an array element with an array name and an offset, QuickC invisibly converts the element offset to a bytes-in-memory offset. To illustrate this, let's look at how arrays of two different types are organized in memory. Figure 7-4 shows that an array of *char* type occupies 1 byte of memory for each element and that an array of *float* type occupies 4 bytes of memory for each element.

For the *char* array, *chary[4]*, each element occupies 1 byte, so each element offset specification corresponds to the bytes-in-memory offset. For the *float* array *fary[2]*, however, each element occupies 4 bytes, so each element offset specification corresponds to a bytes-in-memory offset of 4 bytes. In the latter case, when you specify

```
fary[1]
```

you are really telling the compiler to reference a value that is 4 bytes into the array *fary*. Because a *float* value occupies 4 bytes of memory, your element offset of 1 becomes a bytes-in-memory offset of 4 bytes.

This explains how, in the preceding program, HEXOUT.C, it is possible to print out a *float* one byte at a time. Inside the function *Hexout()*, the compiler thinks it is handling an array of *unsigned char* values, in which each element occupies a single byte. Thus, *i* increments in unmultiplied steps of single bytes.

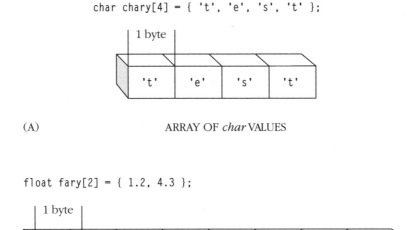

```
char chary[4] = { 't', 'e', 's', 't' };
```

(A)   ARRAY OF *char* VALUES

```
float fary[2] = { 1.2, 4.3 };
```

(B)   ARRAY OF *float* VALUES

Figure 7-4. *How offsets differ by number of bytes based on the type of the array.*

Multidimensional Arrays

In C you can easily create and use arrays of two, three, or many dimensions. Two-dimensional arrays correspond to such useful items as calendars, spreadsheets, and maps. This section begins with the rules for two-dimensional arrays and then applies them to arrays of three and more dimensions. Three-dimensional arrays apply to topics such as 3-D graphics, layered indexes, and solid topology. Arrays of many dimensions become useful in the arcane worlds of higher math and complex games.

Two-dimensional Arrays

Two-dimensional arrays represent rectangular grids of data. As illustrated in Figure 7-5 on the following page, they are organized in rows first and then columns. Because computer memory is linear, those rows and columns are stored in memory one row after the other.

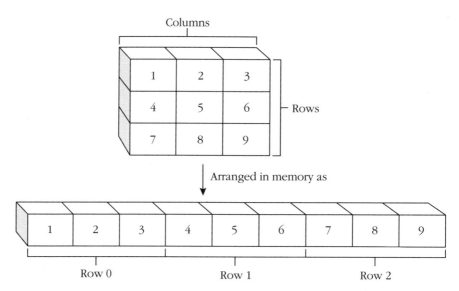

Figure 7-5. *Two-dimensional arrays are arranged in memory row by row.*

The rules for declaring a two-dimensional array are similar to those for declaring a one-dimensional array. They take the following form:

```
type name[rows][columns];
```

As with one-dimensional arrays, you must specify the number of rows and the number of columns as integer constant expressions. Thus, the expression

```
int week[7][8];
```

declares a two-dimensional array of type *int*, named *week*, with 7 rows (for 7 days) and 8 columns (for 8 working hours per day). You can fill it with any number of useful items, for example, the number of lines of code written per hour per day.

Referencing two-dimensional array elements is as simple as referencing elements of one-dimensional arrays. Specify the row and column with integer expressions:

```
int day  = 6, /* Saturday */
    hour = 2; /* 10:00 A.M. */

printf("Wrote %d lines of code.\n", week[day][hour]);
```

Initializing Two-dimensional Arrays

Before we examine the rules for initializing two-dimensional arrays, enter the MAGIC.C program (Listing 7-9). This program initializes an array of type *int* with scrambled numbers and then asks the user to rearrange those numbers in the correct order by continually swapping squares adjacent to the 0 with the 0. The object is to rearrange the numbers in ascending order with 0 at the top left, counting up row by row.

```
/* magic.c -- demonstrates use of a two-dimensional */
/*             array of type int                     */

main()
{
    static int square[3][3] = { 5, 8, 3, 4, 2, 0, 7, 1, 6 };
    int zrow = 1, zcol = 2;  /* location of the zero */
    int num, row, col, i, j, rowdist, coldist, flag;

    while (1)
        {
        printf("Swap what with zero?\n");
        printf("(Q to quit)\n");

        /* Print the square */
        for (i = 0; i < 3; ++i)
            {
            for (j = 0; j < 3; ++j)
                {
                printf(" %d ", square[i][j] );
                }
            printf("\n");
            }

        /* Enter the user number */
        if ((num = getch()) == 'Q')
            exit(0);
        num -= '0';
        if (num < 1 || num > 9)
            {
            printf("Not a legal number.\n\n");
            continue;
            }
        /* Find that square */
        for (row = 0; row < 3; ++row)
            {
            for(col = 0; col < 3; ++col)
                {
                if (num == square[row][col])
                    {
                    goto GOTIT;
                    }
                }
            }
GOTIT:
        /* Check for a legal move */
        if (row > 2 || col > 2)
            {
            printf("Bad Box Specification\n\n");
            continue;
            }
```

Listing 7-9. *The MAGIC.C program.*   *(continued)*

Listing 7-9. *continued*

```
        rowdist = zrow - row;
        if (rowdist < 0)
            rowdist *= -1;
        coldist = zcol - col;
        if (coldist < 0)
            coldist *= -1;
        if (rowdist > 1 || coldist > 1)
            {
            printf("Not A Neighbor\n\n");
            continue;
            }

        /* Make the move */
        square[zrow][zcol] = square[row][col];
        square[row][col] = 0;
        zrow = row;
        zcol = col;

        /* See if done, and solved */
        for (flag = 0, i = 0; i < 3; ++i)
            {
            for (j = 0; j < 3; ++j)
                {
                if (square[i][j] != ((i * 3) + j))
                    {
                    flag = 1;
                    break;
                    }
                }
            if (flag != 0)
                break;
            }
        if ((i * j) == 9)
            break;
        }
    printf("\n\aYOU GOT IT !!!\n");
}
```

We initialize the two-dimensional array in MAGIC.C by filling it row by row. When, for clarity, you want to specify where one row ends and the next begins, you can enclose each row's initializers in another set of braces:

```
static int square[3][3] = {
    {5, 8, 3},————————— Row 0
    {2, 4, 0},————————— Row 1
    {7, 1, 6}  ————————— Row 2
};
```

This amounts to specifying each row as its own subset of initializers, clearly a more readable arrangement.

To underinitialize a 3-by-3 array, we could use the following:

```
static int square[3][3] = { 5, 8, 3, 2, 4, 7, 1, 6 };
```
└────── One initializer short

Here the last column of the last row is omitted and thus is 0 by default. We also could underinitialize by a selected row, as follows:

```
static int square[3][3] = {
    {5, 8, 3},
    {2, 4},   ────────────────── Row 1 short
    {7, 1, 6}
};
```

Here we omit the third column of the second row, thus setting the value to 0.

Two-dimensional Arrays and Functions

As with one-dimensional arrays, you pass a two-dimensional array to a function by merely stating its name:

```
Make_move(board);
```

Again, this passes the two-dimensional array itself, not a copy.

For the receiving function, *Make_move()*, you must always declare the size of the columns. The number of rows—as with one-dimensional arrays that have only one row—is optional, as shown in the following legal example:

```
Make_move(field)
int field[][3];
```

The TTT.C program (Listing 7-10) is a somewhat unsophisticated tic-tac-toe game that will help you understand how to use two-dimensional arrays. It's an easy game to win. Forcing a tie, however, is difficult! For clarity, the declaration for *field* in *Make_move()* includes the number of rows.

```
/* ttt.c -- a tic-tac-toe game demonstrates */
/*          passing two-dimensional arrays   */
/*          to functions                     */

main()
{
    static char board[3][3] = {
        { '-', '-', '-' },
        { '-', '-', '-' },
        { '-', '-', '-' },
    };
```

Listing 7-10. *The TTT.C program.* *(continued)*

Listing 7-10. *continued*

```
    int row, col, ch;
    char Check_winner(char field[][3]);
    void Make_move(char field[][3]), Draw_field(char field[][3]);

    printf("You are X and make the first move.\n");
    while (1)
        {
        printf("Specify coordinate for your X\n");
        printf("(for example, a2, or Q to quit).\n");

        /* Print the square */
        Draw_field(board);

        /* Enter the user's coordinates */
        if ((row = getch()) == 'Q')
            exit(0);
        row -= 'a';
        col = getch() - '1';

        /* Check for a legal move */
        if (row < 0 || row > 2 || col < 0 || col > 2)
            {
            printf("Bad Square Specification\n\n");
            continue;
            }
        if (board[row][col] != '-')
            {
            printf("Sorry, Square Occupied\n\n");
            continue;
            }

        /* Make the move */
        board[row][col] = 'X';
        if ((ch = Check_winner(board)) != '-' || ch == 't')
            break;
        Make_move(board);
        if ((ch = Check_winner(board)) != '-' || ch == 't')
            break;
        }
    Draw_field(board);
    if (ch == 't')
        printf("It's a tie!\n");
    else if (ch == 'X')
        printf("You win!\n");
    else
        printf("I win!\n");
}
```

(continued)

Listing 7-10. *continued*

```
char Check_winner(char field[][3])
{
    int row, col;

    for (row = col = 0; row < 3; ++row, ++col)
        {
        if (field[row][0] != '-'                  /* horizontal */
                && field[row][0] == field[row][1]
                && field[row][1] == field[row][2])
            {
            return(field[row][0]);
            }
        if (field[0][col] != '-'                  /* vertical */
                && field[0][col] == field[1][col]
                && field[1][col] == field[2][col])
            {
            return(field[0][col]);
            }
        }
    if (field[0][0] != '-'           /* right diagonal */
            && field[0][0] == field[1][1]
            && field[1][1] == field[2][2])
        {
        return(field[0][0]);
        }
    if (field[0][2] != '-'             /* left diagonal */
            && field[0][2] == field[1][1]
            && field[1][1] == field[2][0])
        {
        return(field[0][2]);
        }

    for (row = 0; row < 3; ++row)            /* any moves left */
        {
        for (col = 0; col < 3; ++col)
            {
            if (field[row][col] == '-')
                {
                return('-');
                }
            }
        }
    return ('t');
}

void Make_move(char field[][3])
{
    int row, col;
```

(continued)

Listing 7-10. *continued*

```
    for (row = 2; row >= 0; --row)
        {
        for (col = 2; col >= 0; --col)
            {
            if (field[row][col] == '-')
                {
                field[row][col] = '0';
                return;
                }
            }
        }
}

void Draw_field(char field[][3])
{
    int row, col;

    printf("\n   1 2 3\n\n");
    for (row = 0; row < 3; ++row)
        {
        printf("%c ", 'a' + row);
        for (col = 0; col < 3; ++col)
            {
            printf(" %c ", field[row][col]);
            }
        printf("\n");
        }
    printf("\n");
}
```

Arrays of Three and More Dimensions

In C you can give an array an unlimited number of dimensions, but remember that the more dimensions an array has, the more unmanageable it becomes. You have already seen how two-dimensional arrays are declared, initialized, and passed to functions. The rules for using more dimensions are an extension of those same concepts.

Declaring Multidimensional Arrays

The general rule for declaring multidimensional arrays is as follows:

type name[exp][exp][exp][exp] ...

                     Fourth dimension, and so forth
                     Third dimension
                     Second dimension
                     First dimension

First, specify the type to be stored in each array item, and then name the entire array. Each *exp* is an integer constant expression that specifies the number of elements in that dimension. Each bracketed expression *[exp]* defines another dimension.

Think of a three-dimensional array as a cube (or as an array of two-dimensional arrays). Figure 7-6 shows a cube that corresponds to the following declaration of a three-dimensional array:

```
#define DEPTH  3
#define ROWS   3
#define COLS   3

int cube[DEPTH][ROWS][COLS];
```

— Size of each two-dimensional array

— Number of two-dimensional arrays (depth)

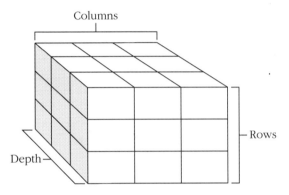

Figure 7-6. *A three-dimensional array can be thought of as a cube.*

Initializing Multidimensional Arrays

When you use a list of values to initialize a multidimensional *static* or global array, the compiler reads that list from left to right, filling the array row by row for each plane of the depth. The following declaration places the initializing values into *cube*, beginning with the value 1, as shown in Figure 7-7 on the following page.

```
int cube[3][3][3] = { 1, 2, 3, 4, 5, 6, 7, 8, 9,
    10, 11, 12, 13, 14, 15, 16, 17, 18, 19, 20, 21,
    22, 23, 24, 25, 26, 27 };
```

To specify the order for initializing, you can enclose any group with braces. Those braces correspond to the depth first, then to the rows and columns. You can therefore rewrite the above declaration more clearly as follows:

```
int cube[3][3][3] = {
    { {1,  2,  3}, {4,  5,  6}, {7,  8,  9} },
    { {10, 11, 12}, {13, 14, 15}, {16, 17, 18} },
    { {19, 20, 21}, {22, 23, 24}, {25, 26, 27} }
};
```

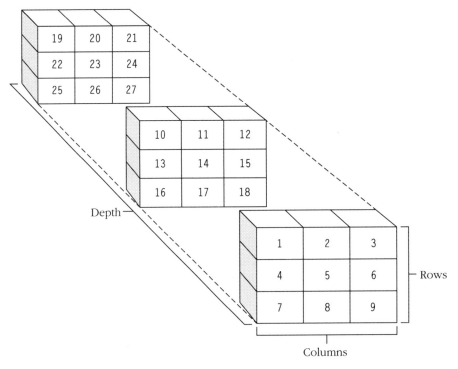

Figure 7-7. *Initializing a three-dimensional array.*

Here each inner set of braces encloses the list of initializers for a given row. Use this technique when you need to underinitialize a given row, column, or depth. Clearly, as you progress beyond three dimensions, initializing can become very confusing. Just remember the general rules, or, in despair, simplify your algorithm.

Using Multidimensional Arrays in Functions

To pass a multidimensional array to a function, you need to specify only the name of that array as an argument:

```
Draw_planes(cube);
```

On the receiving end—in the function *Draw_planes()*—you must specify the sizes of all but the leftmost dimension. That size is optional, as in the following:

```
int Draw_planes(int box[][3][3])
{
    ⋮
```

The BOX.C program (Listing 7-11) shows the initialization of a three-dimensional array and then prints out the result.

```
/* box.c -- demonstrates the result of initializing */
/*          a three-dimensional array              */

main()
{
    static int cube[3][3][3] = {
        1, 2, 3, 4, 5, 6, 7, 8, 9, 10, 11, 12,
        13, 14, 15, 16, 17, 18, 19, 20, 21, 22,
        23, 24, 25, 26, 27 };
    int plane;
    void Draw_plane(int box[3][3][3], int slice);

    for (plane = 0; plane < 3; ++plane)
        {
        Draw_plane(cube, plane);
        }
}

void Draw_plane(int box[3][3][3], int slice)
{
    int row, col;

    printf("Plane[%d] =\n", slice);
    for (row = 0; row < 3; ++row)
        {
        for (col = 0; col < 3; ++col)
            {
            printf( "%2d ", box[slice][row][col]);
            }
        printf("\n");
        }
    printf("\n");
}
```

Listing 7-11. *The BOX.C program.*

Advanced Topics and Tricks

In this section we discuss three advanced techniques that can be very handy:

- Negative subscripting

- Large and huge arrays

- Passing pieces of arrays

Negative Subscripting

Recall that unless you include code to perform bounds checking, C lets you reference items both beyond the end and before the beginning of an array. You have seen the consequences of referencing beyond an array's end. Referencing before its beginning is new, however, as Figure 7-8 on the following page demonstrates.

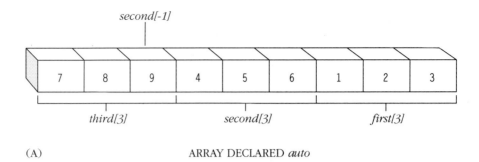

(A)   ARRAY DECLARED *auto*

(B)   ARRAY DECLARED *static*

Figure 7-8. *Effect of negative subscripting on* auto *and* static *arrays.*

If you declare three consecutive arrays in one of the following ways:

```
int first[3], second[3], third[3];
```

or

```
static int first[3], second[3], third[3];
```

and then reference with a negative subscript:

```
second[-1]
```

you actually reference either *third[2]* or *first[2]*, depending on whether the arrays are *auto* or *static*, as shown in Figure 7-8. QuickC places *auto* arrays into memory from right to left (top down) and *static* arrays from left to right (bottom up).

The L2WORDS.C program (Listing 9-11 on pp. 280–82) illustrates this technique.

Large and Huge Arrays

On the IBM PC an integer is 2 bytes long, so you have to be careful when you declare arrays larger than 32,767 elements. That is because 32,767 is the highest positive value a 2-byte integer can hold. If you successively reference the elements in an array with a loop,

```
int i;
for (i = 0; i < 40000; i++)
    printf("%dn", array[i]);
```

the 0th through 32,767th elements print out correctly, but the 32,768th element prints out as *array[-32768]*.

By default, *int* variables contain signed values, so they wrap to negative numbers when they exceed their highest positive value. Therefore, to reference elements in large arrays, use either *unsigned int* or *long* offsets.

Another problem occurs when arrays grow to more than 65,536 *bytes* total on the IBM PC. In this case, use the _*huge* keyword in the array declaration, as follows:

```
int _huge bigbox[100][100][100];
```

Here the keyword _*huge* is required because the total size in bytes of the array *bigbox* is $100 \times 100 \times 100$ times 2 (2 bytes per *int*), or 2,000,000. This tells the compiler to set aside more space for this array than the space reserved for ordinary variables. Whenever you use large arrays that require the _*huge* keyword, compile with the large memory model. That model will be discussed in greater detail in Chapter 12. (Of course, you will need lots of memory in your computer, too.)

Passing Pieces of Arrays

When you reference array elements with fewer dimensional offsets than were present in the declaration of that array, you are actually referencing the address of a subarray. If, for example, you declare:

```
int square[3][3];
```

and then later reference that array without specifying the second dimension:

```
Print_row(square[1]);
```

the compiler passes the address of *square*'s second row (a one-dimensional subarray) to *Print_row()*. Correspondingly, declare *Print_row()* to receive a one-dimensional array:

```
Print_row(int row[])
{
    ⋮
```

The Bitwise Operators, Tiny Arrays

Just as arrays can get larger and larger and more and more complex, it is also possible to go the other direction and store data in the individual bits of a single byte. You can manipulate individual bits of a byte by using the "bitwise" operators. Those operators are listed in the following table.

Operator	Description
&	The bitwise AND operator
¦	The bitwise OR operator
^	The bitwise exclusive-OR operator
~	The unary ones-complement operator
>>	The unary right-shift operator
<<	The unary left-shift operator

Each of these affects the individual bits in the bytes of a value, which can be either a constant or a variable. Remember, a *char* uses 8 bits, an *int* 16 bits, and a *long* 32 bits. First, we demonstrate the application of the bitwise operators, and then we discuss the logic of each.

The BITWISE.C program (Listing 7-12) lets you enter values interactively and then apply the bitwise operators to them. By running this program, you will better understand the discussion that follows. (Note that a set bit is represented with a *1* and a clear bit is represented with a *0*.)

```
/* bitwise.c -- demonstrates the bitwise operators */

#include <stdio.h>
void

main()
{
    unsigned int val1, val2, result;
    int ch;
    void Show(unsigned int val);

    while(1)
        {
        printf("\nval1: ");
        if (scanf("%d", &val1) != 1)
            break;

        printf("val2: ");
        if (scanf("%d", &val2) != 1)
            break;

        printf("\tval1   = ");
        Show(val1);
        printf("\tval2   = ");
        Show(val2);
        printf("Bitwise operator: ");
        while ((ch = getchar()) == '\n')
```

Listing 7-12. *The BITWISE.C program.*   *(continued)*

216

Listing 7-12. *continued*

```
            {
            continue;
            }
        if (ch == EOF)
            break;
        switch (ch)
            {
            case '&':
                result = val1 & val2;
                printf("Executing: result = val1 & val2;\n");
                break;
            case '¦':
                result = val1 != val2;
                printf("Executing: result = val1 ¦ val2;\n");
                break;
            case '^':
                result = val1 ^= val2;
                printf("Executing: result = val1 ^ val2;\n");
                break;
            case '~':
                result = ~val1;
                printf("Executing: result = ~val1;\n");
                printf("\tresult = ");
                Show(result);
                result = ~val2;
                printf("Executing: result = ~val2;\n");
                break;
            case '<':
                result = val1 <<= val2;
                printf("Executing: result = val1 << val2;\n");
                break;
            case '>':
                result = val1 >>= val2;
                printf("Executing: result = val1 >> val2;\n");
                break;
            case 'q':
            case 'Q':
                return(0);
            default:
                continue;
            }
        printf("\tresult = ");
        Show(result);
        }
}

void Bitout(unsigned char num[])
{
    int bytes = 2, i, j;
```

(continued)

Listing 7-12. *continued*

```
    /* IBM PC stores ints low/hi */
    for (i = bytes-1; i >= 0; --i)
        {
        for (j = 7; j >= 0; --j)
            {
            putchar((num[i] & (1 << j)) ? '1' : '0');
            }
        }
}

void Show(unsigned int val)
{
    void Bitout(unsigned char num[]);

    printf("%05u decimal; ", val);
    Bitout(&val);
    printf(" binary\n");
}
```

The Binary Bitwise Operators

The bitwise AND, the bitwise OR, and the bitwise exclusive-OR are binary operators. That is, like the addition operator, they operate on two values—not one. You can use them as follows:

```
result = val1 & val2;     /* bitwise AND           */
result = val1 ! val2;     /* bitwise OR            */
result = val1 ^ val2;     /* bitwise exclusive-OR  */
```

Or you can use them with the *op=* form:

```
result &= val1;    /* bitwise AND           */
resull !- val1;    /* bitwise OR            */
result ^= val1;    /* bitwise exclusive-OR  */
```

The Bitwise AND Operator

The bitwise AND operator, &, compares the bits in two values and produces a value based on the comparison of the same bits in each:

var1	&	var2	*yields*	Result
1		1		1
0		1		0
1		0		0
0		0		0

For the bitwise AND, the result bit is set only if the same bit in both values is set. Otherwise, the result bit is cleared.

The bitwise AND operator is useful for turning off (clearing) a selected bit in a variable. A typical application for the & operator is to turn off a blinking cursor when you are accessing screen memory directly:

```
var1 =  3;
var1 &= 0xFFFE;——— Turn off low bit
```

This results in the following calculation:

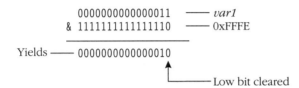

```
        0000000000000011    —— var1
      & 1111111111111110    —— 0xFFFE
      ─────────────────────
Yields —— 0000000000000010
                     ↑
                     └────── Low bit cleared
```

The Bitwise OR Operator

The bitwise OR operator, ¦, compares the bits in two values and sets the result bit for any bit that is set in either or both of the values:

var1	¦	var2	yields	result
1		1		1
0		1		1
1		0		1
0		0		0

For the bitwise OR, the result bit is set if *either or both* corresponding bits in both values are set. Otherwise, the result bit is cleared.

The bitwise OR operator is useful for turning on (setting) a selected bit in a variable. A typical application for the ¦ operator is to turn on the low bit of a character variable before sending that character to the printer:

```
var1 =  0;
var1 ¦= 1;——— Turn on low bit
```

This results in the following calculation:

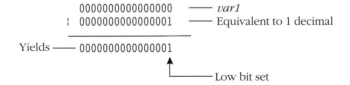

```
        0000000000000000    —— var1
      ¦ 0000000000000001    —— Equivalent to 1 decimal
      ─────────────────────
Yields —— 0000000000000001
                     ↑
                     └────── Low bit set
```

The Bitwise exclusive-OR Operator

The bitwise exclusive-OR operator, ^, compares the bits in two values and produces a set bit only if one bit or the other is set, but not both:

var1	^	var2	yields	Result
1		1		0
0		1		1
1		0		1
0		0		0

For the bitwise exclusive-OR, ^, the result bit is set if one or the other of the corresponding bits in the values is set, *but not both*. The bitwise exclusive-OR operator is useful for toggling (setting, clearing, setting, etc.) a selected bit in a variable. A typical application for the ^ operator is to toggle a flag in a game, thereby determining which of two players is to make the next move:

```
var1 = 0;
var1 ^= 1;
var1 ^= 1;
```

This results in the following calculations:

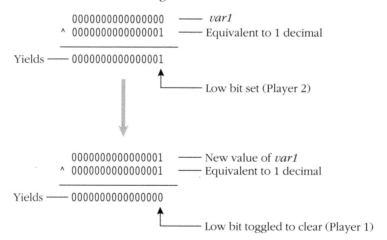

The Unary Bitwise Operators

The unary bitwise operators affect the bits of a single value. These operators are

Operator	Description
~	The unary ones-complement operator
>>	The unary right-shift operator
<<	The unary left-shift operator

The Unary Ones-Complement Operator

The ones-complement of a variable is derived by inverting all the bits in that value. If a bit is set, that bit changes to clear, and vice versa. In C, the ~ causes the bits in a value to be inverted, as follows:

```
var1    0000000000000111

~var1   1111111111111000 ———— Result
```

Two applications are common for the ones-complement operator. One is to set selected bits in a variable regardless of the number of bytes occupied by that variable. Suppose you have an *int* and you want all but the zeroth bit set. One way to do this is by:

```
number = 0xFFFE;
```

This does the job but pays the price of assuming an *int* always occupies 2 bytes of storage. Although that is true on the IBM PC, it is not the case on most 32-bit machines. The correct way to set all but the zeroth bit—and the portable way—is to use the ones-complement operator:

```
number = ~1;
```

The second common application for the ones-complement operator is turning off selected bits. One way to turn off the zeroth bit, while leaving all the other bits in a variable unchanged, is:

```
masks &= 0xFFFE;
```

But again, the ones-complement operator should be used for portability:

```
masks &= ~1;
```

The Unary Shift Operators

The shift operators move all the bits in a variable right or left by the number of bit positions specified. The shift operators are used as follows:

```
result = value << bits;
result = value >> bits;
```

Here the first line shifts the value in *value* left—from the low toward the high bit—by the number of bit positions specified by *bits*. The second line shifts *value* in the opposite direction—right, or from the high toward the low bit. For example:

```
val1         0000000000111000
val1 << 3    0000000111000000 ———— Left shift
val1 >> 3    0000000000000111 ———— Right shift
```

When shifting left, the bits on the right are filled with clear bits. With QuickC, the fill bits for a right shift are always set. For portability, however, always use *unsigned* variables when right-shifting.

The shift operators are useful for aligning a bit prior to an OR operation. Shifting also provides a quick way to multiply or divide by 2. Each bit you shift to the left multiplies a number by 2; each bit you shift to the right divides it by 2.

```
int val = 1;

val <<= 1;——— val now equals 2
val <<= 1;——— val now equals 4
val <<= 14;——— val now equals 0
```

In the final example, the operation shifts the set bit beyond the 16-bit range of an *int* value. A bit-shifting operation returns a value of the same type as the operand on the left side of the operator.

Summary of Bitwise Operators

If you haven't already done so, enter, compile, and run the BITWISE.C program (Listing 7-12 on pp. 216–18). Watching the actions of bits as the program applies each bitwise operator will give you a feel for bits and will lead you to develop sophisticated applications of your own. You will find the bitwise operators used a great deal in the hardware-specific chapters at the end of this book.

Addresses and Pointers

One of the chief strengths of C is its ability to manipulate individual areas of memory with almost the same precision that assembly language provides. This chapter discusses this ability in detail by showing you a new kind of variable called a pointer—a variable whose contents identify a memory address. Using pointers can greatly increase the speed at which your programs execute; pointers also let you access your computer's hardware directly and allow you to write subroutines that manipulate variables directly (via the address).

Addresses Reviewed

The concept of memory addresses is vital to C programming. Recall, for example, that all arguments passed to *scanf()* must be preceded by an ampersand (&). In the following expression:

```
scanf("%d", &num);
```

the *%d* tells *scanf()* to read an integer from the keyboard and to place that input value into the variable *num*, whose address is passed with the expression *&num*.

In the previous chapter, you also used addresses with arrays: When we pass an entire array to a function, it is passed as an address. For example, the code fragment

```
char choices[4] = {'Q', 'E', 'S', 'L'};
Get_move(choices);
```

passes the address of the *choices* array to the function *Get_move()*, rather than the individual elements of that array. When you use an array name without specifying an element in square brackets, the compiler uses the internal memory address of that array as its value.

One of C's strengths is the ease with which it lets you manipulate the values of variables by way of their addresses. This type of address manipulation, known as indirection, is accomplished with pointers.

What Is a Pointer?

A pointer, in its simplest form, is a variable whose value (contents) is an address, or a number corresponding to a specific location in memory. That is, if *address_var* is a pointer-type variable, and *num* is an integer variable, the expression

```
address_var = &num;
```

causes the address of the variable *num* to be placed into the pointer. This assignment ignores the actual value of *num*.

You can use pointers in your programs to:

- Save information from functions that return addresses

- Indirectly return more than one value from a function

- Speed up execution by manipulating pointers rather than large blocks of data

- Access and modify text screen memory

- Call functions using their addresses, thus creating more flexible code

- Access and manipulate strings

Before you can use a pointer, also called a "pointer to," you must declare it. Declaring a pointer is much like declaring an ordinary variable, the only difference being that you must always precede the pointer's name with the * character.

The following example declares two variables: an integer called *num* and a pointer called *address_var*.

```
int num, *address_var;
```

The * before *address_var* tells the compiler that *address_var* is a pointer whose contents will be an address. Because *address_var* is declared as type *int*, the compiler knows that *address_var* will contain the address of an integer variable. In the pointer declaration, the keyword *int* indicates the memory occupied by the referenced value, not the size of the pointer itself. Figure 8-1 illustrates this process.

In this example, we declare two variables and two pointers (Figure 8-1a). The variables are *num* (an *int*) and *fval* (a *float*). We also declare two pointers, *address_var* and *faddress_var*.

The pointer *address_var* can contain the address of a variable of type *int*; pointer *faddress_var* can contain the address of a variable of type *float*. The two assignment statements in Figure 8-1b store the addresses in the appropriate pointers. The result of the assignment is that *address_var* now holds the address of *num* (and thus points to *num*), and *faddress_var* holds the address of *fval* (and thus points to *fval*).

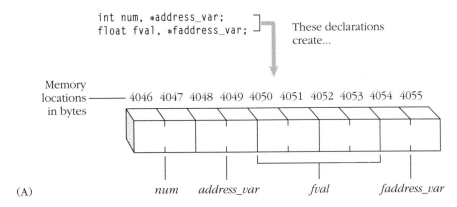

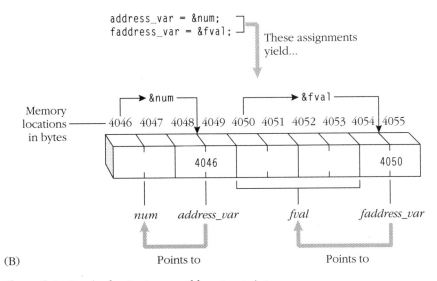

Figure 8-1. *Result of assigning an address to a pointer.*

Accessing Variables with Pointers

The ∗ operator (pronounced "star"), when used to signify a pointer, is called the indirection operator because it lets you access variables indirectly. When you use the ∗ operator in front of a pointer (other than in its declaration) you tell the compiler to fetch or store the value to which the pointer is pointing. For example, in the fragment

```
int num, *address_var;

address_var = &num;
*address_var = 3;
```

you first declare an *int* variable (*num*) and a pointer to an *int* (*address_var*). Next, the value you store in *address_var* is the address of the variable *num*. Finally, the ∗ in front of *address_var* tells the compiler to store the value 3 in the variable whose address is stored in *address_var*. Because the pointer *address_var* contains the address of *num*, that value is stored in *num*. (See Figure 8-2 on p. 230.)

The POINTER.C program (Listing 8-1) illustrates the procedure for declaring, assigning a value to, and using pointers.

```
/* pointer.c -- demonstrates pointer declaration, */
/*              assignment, and use               */

#define WAIT printf("(press any key)"); getch(); \
             printf("\n\n")

main()
{
    int num, *address_var;

    num = 0;
    address_var = &num;

    printf("The address of the variable ");
    printf("\"num\" is:  0x%04X\n", &num);
    printf("The value in the pointer ");
    printf("\"address_var\" is:  0x%04X\n", address_var);
    printf("The value in the variable ");
    printf("\"num\" is: %d\n", num);
    WAIT;
    printf("Since \"address_var\" points to \"num\"\n");
    printf("the value in ");
    printf("\"*address_var\" is: %d\n", *address_var);
    WAIT;
    printf("To verify this, let's store 3 in\n");
    printf("\"*address_var\", then print out ");
    printf("\"num\" and \"*address_var\"\n");
    printf("again.\n");
    WAIT;
```

Listing 8-1. *The POINTER.C program.*

(continued)

Listing 8-1. *continued*

```
    printf("Doing: *address_var = 3;\n\n");
    *address_var = 3;

    printf("The address of the variable ");
    printf("\"num\" is:  0x%04X\n", &num);
    printf("The value in the pointer ");
    printf("\"address_var\" is:  0x%04X\n", address_var);
    printf("The value in the variable ");
    printf("\"num\" is: %d\n", num);
    WAIT;
    printf("Since \"address_var\" points to \"num\"\n");
    printf("the value in ");
    printf("\"*address_var\" is: %d\n", *address_var);
    WAIT;

    printf("Now we will add 15 to \"num\" and print\n");
    printf("\"num\" and \"*address_var\" again.\n");
    WAIT;

    printf("Doing: num += 15;\n\n");
    num += 15;

    printf("The address of the variable ");
    printf("\"num\" is:  0x%04X\n", &num);
    printf("The value in the pointer ");
    printf("\"address_var\" is:  0x%04X\n", address_var);
    printf("The value in the variable ");
    printf("\"num\" is: %d\n", num);
    WAIT;
    printf("Since \"address_var\" points to \"num\"\n");
    printf("the value in ");
    printf("\"*address_var\" is: %d\n", *address_var);
    WAIT;

    printf("Doing: return (*address_var);\n\n");
    return (*address_var);
}
```

The output of this program follows. Compare it with the listing.

```
The address of the variable "num" is:  0x1388
The value in the pointer "address_var" is:  0x1388
The value in the variable "num" is: 0
(press any key)

Since "address_var" points to "num"
the value in "*address_var" is: 0
(press any key)
```

```
To verify this, let's store 3 in
"*address_var", then print out "num" and "*address_var"
again.
(press any key)

Doing: *address_var = 3;

The address of the variable "num" is: 0x1388
The value in the pointer "address_var" is: 0x1388
The value in the variable "num" is: 3
(press any key)

Since "address_var" points to "num"
the value in "*address_var" is: 3
(press any key)

Now we will add 15 to "num" and print
"num" and "*address_var" again.
(press any key)

Doing: num += 15;

The address of the variable "num" is:  0x1388
The value in the pointer "address_var" is: 0x1388
The value in the variable "num" is: 18
(press any key)

Since "address_var" points to "num"
the value in "*address_var" is: 18
(press any key)

Doing: return (*address_var);
```

In the POINTER.C program, the pointer *address_var* contains the address of *num* (as a result of the assignment *address_var* = &*num*) and therefore yields the value stored in *num*. That is, we indirectly access *num* via its address (*address_var* = 3). Because *address_var* contains *num*'s address, you can use *address_var* anywhere you would use *num*. For example, we could have ended the program with *return (num)* to produce the same result.

Passing Pointers to Functions

Until now, with the exception of arrays, we have passed arguments to functions by value. Thus, you might think we could write a function that squares the argument passed to it as follows:

```
Square(int num)
{
    num *= num;              ┌─────── Multiply by self
}              └─────────────┘
```

This function doesn't do us much good, however, because the variable *num* is a local variable to the function *Square()*, and the result is not accessible by other functions. Thus, calling *Square()* with

```
main()
{
    int val = 5;

    Square(val);
}
```

does not result in *main()*'s variable *val* being squared—the *main()* function doesn't "see" the variable *num*.

You can get around this by having *Square()* return a value, as follows:

```
main()
{
    int val = 5;

    val = Square(val);————— Value returned by Square()
}

Square(int num)
{
    num *= num;
    return (num);————— Square() returns value
}
```

Another approach is to use pointers. When you pass a pointer to a function, you still pass a copy of its value, but the value you pass is an address. Therefore, in *Square()*, you must declare *num* as a pointer because it will receive an address:

```
Square(int *address_var)————— Pointer receives an address
{
    *address_var *= *address_var;
}                    ————— Multiplication operator
```

This form of *Square()* receives an address as its argument. The pointer to hold that address, *address_var*, is declared as *int *address_var* because it receives the address of an *int* variable.

To use this new *Square()* function, we must pass it an address. We can do this in either of two ways. We can use the & operator, as follows:

```
main()
{
    int val = 5;

    Square(&val);————— Pass an address
}
```

Or we can pass a pointer:

```
main()
{
    int val = 5, *here;

    here = &val;
    Square(here); ——————— The value of here is the address of val
}
```

After making our declarations, we place the address of *val* into the pointer *here*. When we pass *here* to *Square()*, its value—the address of *val*—is what is actually passed. This results in *val* being squared.

The SQUARE.C program (Listing 8-2) summarizes this passing of pointers and addresses in an interactive quiz. In it, we've expanded on our original *Square()* routine. In the new *Square()*, we return two values from a single function. The first, returned by the *return* statement, is an error status—0 for a successful square and −1 for any attempt to square a number larger than 181 or less than −181 (the square root of 32,767, the largest signed *int* on the IBM PC). We return the second value with the pointer *where*.

```
/* square.c -- a quiz to demonstrate passing     */
/*              pointers and addresses in functions */

main()
{
    int val, count, guess, Square(int *where);

    for (count = 1; count < 255; ++count)
        {
        val = count;
        printf("What is the square of %d?\n"; val);
        if (scanf("%d"; &guess) != 1)
            return(0);              /* non-number exits  */

        if (Square(&val) != 0)     /* pass val's address */
            {
            printf("Range Error\n");
            exit(1);
            }
        if (val != guess)
            printf("Wrong. It is %d.\n", val);
        else
            printf("Right!\n");
        printf("Continue? ");
        if (getche() != 'y')
            break;
        }
}
```

Listing 8-2. *The SQUARE.C program.*   *(continued)*

Listing 8-2. *continued*

```
int Square(int *where)
{
    if (*where > 181 || *where < -181)
        return (-1);
    *where = (*where) * (*where);
    return (0);
}
```

In this program, we use a separate variable, *count*, in the *for* loop because the value of *val* is indirectly changed by the call to *Square()*. If we had used *val* as follows:

```
for (val = 1; val < 255; ++val)
```

you would be prompted only for the numbers 1, 2, 5, and 26, and then you would receive the message *Range Error*.

Pointers and Arrays

Pointers let you manipulate strings and arrays more succinctly and efficiently. We'll learn about strings in the next chapter. Here we will discuss the relationship between arrays and pointers, detailing potential pitfalls along the way.

Recall from the previous chapter that referencing an array by name, without an offset, yields the address of that array. What we didn't tell you was that the address of an array is the same as the address of the array's first element. For example, in the following array declaration:

```
int coins[4] = {25, 10, 5, 1};
```

the reference

```
Find_change(coins, amount);
```

causes the address of the array *coins* to be passed to the *Find_change()* function. Because the address of an array is the location in memory of its beginning, we can also reference that array with the expression

```
&coins[0]
```

Here the address operator & yields the address of the first item in the array *coins* and, therefore, the address of the array itself.

You can assign the address of another variable to a pointer by using the & operator (*address_var* = &*num*). Because each array element is a variable, the assignment

```
address_var = &coins[0];
```

stores in *address_var* the address of the first integer in the array *coins*.

Because &*coins[0]* and *coins* are equivalent, the following expression is the same as the previous one:

```
address_var = coins;
```

Now here comes the exciting part. When a value, say 1, is added to a pointer, it increments the address in that pointer by the number of bytes in the type to which it points. For example, in Figure 8-2 the variable *address_var* begins with a value that is the address of *coins[0]*. Notice what happens when we add 1 to *address_var*. Because *address_var* is a pointer to the type *int*, and because an *int* occupies 2 bytes (on the IBM PC), the value in *address_var* is increased by 2. The new value in *address_var* is thus the address of *coins[1]* (the next element in the array).

The CHANGE.C program (Listing 8-3) demonstrates how the pointer *coin_ptr* advances through the array *coins*, each step determined by the number of bytes for the type *int*. Compile the program with the Debug option set because we want to trace its execution.

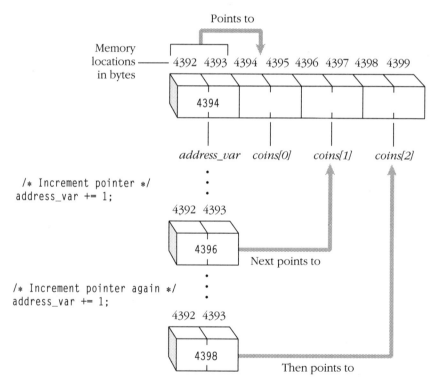

Figure 8-2. *The value of a pointer increases by multiples of the number of bytes in the data type to which it points.*

```
/* change.c -- a change-making program demonstrates */
/*             how pointers advance the correct      */
/*             number of bytes based on type         */

#define NCOINS (4)
#define CENT (0x9b)  /* IBM PC cent character */

main()
{
    static int coins[NCOINS] = {25, 10, 5, 1};
    int *coin_ptr, i = 0;
    int dollars, cents, pennies1, pennies2, count;

    printf("Enter an amount in dollars and cents and I will");
    printf(" give you change.\nAmount: ");
    if (scanf("%d.%2d", &dollars, &cents) != 2)
        {
        printf("I don't know how to change that!\n");
        exit(1);
        }
    pennies2 = pennies1 = (dollars * 100) + cents;

    coin_ptr = coins;
    for (i = 0; i < NCOINS; ++i)
        {
        count = 0;
        while ((pennies1 -= coins[i]) >= 0)
            ++count;
        printf("%4d %2d%c", count, coins[i], CENT);
        printf(" coins by array offset.\n");
        if (pennies1 == 0)
            break;
        pennies1 += coins[i];

        count = 0;
        while ((pennies2 -= *coin_ptr) >= 0)
            ++count;
        printf("%4d %2d%c", count, *coin_ptr, CENT);
        printf(" coins by pointer indirection.\n");
        if (pennies2 == 0)
            break;
        pennies2 += *coin_ptr;
        ++coin_ptr;
        }
}
```

Listing 8-3. *The CHANGE.C program.*

After you compile CHANGE.C, turn off screen swapping and specify the following four watch variables:

```
coin_ptr
*coin_ptr
i
coins[i]
```

(See pp. 116-18 if you've forgotten how to specify watch variables. You don't need to specify the types with a comma; the defaults are correct.) Now step through the program with the F8 function key. Observe that as *++i* followed by *coins[i]* steps through the array, so does *++coin_ptr* followed by **coin_ptr.* Figure 8-3 shows the screen as the program is being traced.

This equivalence between arrays and incrementing pointers is one of C's chief strengths. It can also be confusing and can lead to some unexpected bugs. In the CHANGE.C program, we perform bounds checking with the *for* loop. If we rewrite that loop without *i*, we need to do one of two things. One option is to put some stop value into our array, such as the last element (0) in the following:

```
int coins[5] = {25, 10, 5, 1, 0};
```

This approach is often used with string variables.

The other option requires that we add some means of detecting when the address in *coin_ptr* becomes too large, as follows:

```
for (coin_ptr = coins; coin_ptr < &coins[4]; ++coin_ptr)
```

```
 File  Edit  View  Search  Make  Run  Debug  Utility  Options              Help
|=|                         DEBUG: main                                    |=|
coin_ptr ♦ 0x609a:0x0042
*coin_ptr ♦ 25                              ▮
i ♦ 0
coins[i] ♦ 25
|=====================  C:\QC25\BOOKPROG\CHAP08\CHANGE.C  ================|=|
        {
        printf("I don't know how to change that!\n");
        exit(1);
        }
    pennies2 = pennies1 = (dollars * 100) + cents;

    coin_ptr = coins;
    for (i = 0; i < NCOINS; ++i)
        {
        count = 0;
        while ((pennies1 -= coins[i]) >= 0)
            ++count;
        printf("%4d %2d%c", count, coins[i], CENT);
        printf(" coins by array offset.\n");
        if (pennies1 == 0)
            break;
|=|
 <F1=Help> <F6=Window> <F5=Run> <F8=Trace> <F10=Step>    |      00024:001
```

Figure 8-3. *Incrementing a pointer moves it through an array in steps that correspond to the number of bytes in the data type.*

This approach is more common for situations where a stop value is not practical. In a database, for example, you might have 32 bytes available and want to use all 32 for a mailing address, with none reserved for a terminating value.

Pointer Arithmetic

QuickC permits fewer arithmetic operations on pointers than on other kinds of variables. Because pointers contain addresses as their values, whenever you change one, you reference a new location inside your computer's memory. Obviously, you don't want to reference random locations—not only would they be meaningless, but they might overwrite crucial memory locations and crash your PC.

To help avoid referencing meaningless addresses, C lets you perform only a handful of mathematical operations on pointers. They are:

Addition: You can add values to addresses (such as incrementing with ++). This is most useful with arrays.

Subtraction: You can subtract values from addresses (decrementing with −− and subtracting with −).

Comparison: You can compare one address with another to see if it is greater than, less than, equal to, or not equal to the other.

The operations allowed on pointers are a small set when compared to the operations allowed on numeric variables and array items. Let's examine why you cannot use the other arithmetic operations:

Multiplication: Doubling an address or even multiplying it by, let's say, 523 would yield a new address value that, at best, would be somewhere in your data and at worst would be beyond the end of your program, possibly in the code of another memory resident program (like QuickC or COMMAND.COM).

Division: Halving an address or even dividing it by, let's say, 10 would yield a new address value that, at best, would be somewhere inside your own code and at worst would be inside the MS-DOS interrupt vectors.

Bitwise operators: You cannot manipulate the bits in an address. This would result in a totally random address.

Unary negation: You can't reverse the sign of an address because addresses are always *unsigned*.

Quick Tip

C does not provide many safeguards against referencing incorrect addresses. QuickC, however, lets you compile with Pointer Check turned on. This provides a measure of safety by verifying that pointer values address program data, but it results in slower-executing programs.

Now let's look at the CHANGE2.C program (Listing 8-4). This rewrite of CHANGE.C illustrates the incrementing of pointers and the comparison of two pointers.

```c
/* change2.c -- modified to demonstrate passing */
/*              an address to a function         */

#define NCOINS (4)
#define CENT (0x9b)   /* IBM PC cent character */

main()
{
    static int coins[NCOINS] = {25, 10, 5, 1};
    int dollars, cents, pennies;

    printf("Enter an amount in dollars and cents and I will");
    printf(" give you change.\nAmount: ");
    if (scanf("%d.%2d", &dollars, &cents) != 2)
        {
        printf("I don't know how to change that!\n");
        exit(1);
        }
    pennies = (dollars * 100) + cents;

    Show_change(coins, &coins[NCOINS], pennies);
}

Show_change(int amts[], int *end, int due)
{
    int count;

    while (amts < end)     /* compare pointers */
        {
        count = 0;
        while ((due -= *amts) >= 0)
            {
            ++count;
            }
        printf("%4d %2d%c\n", count, *amts, CENT);
        if (due == 0)
            break;
        due += *amts;

        ++amts;            /* increment a pointer */
        }
}
```

Listing 8-4. *The CHANGE2.C program.*

The function *Show_change()* receives the addresses of the array *coins* and the fourth element in that array (one past its end). This introduces some new concepts: the interchangeability of the declaration *coins[]* and the declaration *coins*, and the importance of left versus right values.

The Interchangeability of *amts* and *amts[]*

In the following:

```
Show_change(int amts[])
{
```

the expression *int amts[]* tells the compiler that the function *Show_change()* will receive an array as its single argument. However, you can also use an array declaration of the form *amts* interchangeably with *amts[]*. The two are equivalent. In fact, if you declare an array as *amts[]*, you can use that array's name as though it were a pointer:

```
Show_change(int amts[])
{                              └─────── Declared as an array
    ⋮
    due = *amts;
             └─┴─────────────── but used as a pointer
```

and vice versa:

```
Show_change(int *amts)
{                          └─────── Declared as a pointer
    ⋮
    due = amts[i];
             └─┴─────────────── but used as an array
```

Note, however, that this interchangeability works only when the array is declared as one of a function's received arguments. An attempt to use that singular equivalence elsewhere results in either a syntax error or an lvalue error.

lvalue *vs* rvalue

An lvalue is any variable whose value can change (have a new value assigned to it). An rvalue is a variable whose value cannot change. The easiest way to differentiate between the two is to remember that an rvalue goes to the right of the assignment operator and an lvalue goes to the left. Why is this important?

Arrays are usually rvalues because of the way C generates its intermediate code. C treats an array as a label (just as the target of a *goto* is a label). As the address of a location, an array is a constant value much as the number 3 is a constant.

Confusing lvalues and rvalues when using array names is a common error for the beginning C programmer. Always remember that array names cannot be assigned to, incremented, or decremented, except when they are declared as one of the received arguments of a function, as follows:

```
char *Amount;──────────────── Global pointer, an lvalue
int Bills[4] = {20, 10, 5, 1};────── Array, an rvalue

Some_function(char amts[])──────── Equivalent to a pointer
{
    char *address_var,────────── Local pointer, an lvalue
         old_coins[];─────────── Syntax error

    ++Amount;────────────────── Legal
    ++Bills;─────────────────── Illegal operation on rvalue
    ++amts;──────────────────── Legal
    ++address_var;───────────── Legal
    ++old_coins;─────────────── Legal
}
```

In this sample program, *Amount* and *address_var* are pointers, values that can be incremented. Although *amts[]* is declared as an array, the interchangeability we discussed earlier permits us to increment it as though it were a pointer. On the other hand, *Bills* is not a function argument (it's a global array), so it is an rvalue that cannot be incremented. Finally, *old_coins[]* generates a syntax error because only arrays in function argument declarations can be used without specifying the size of their leftmost dimension. We could, however, have declared it as *old_coins*.

Type Casting Pointers and Addresses

Occasionally you will need to use a pointer in an arithmetic operation other than addition, subtraction, or comparison. Fortunately, C is very flexible, and it permits you to perform those other operations on pointers by using type casts (or simply "casts"). In Chapter 3 you used a type cast to convert one type to another: You can also use that technique with pointers. For example, suppose you need to divide a pointer's value by 2. You could use the method:

```
unsigned long temp;
int *point = some_address;

temp = (unsigned long)point;
temp /= 2;
point = (int *)temp;
```

First, we assign the address *some_address* to the pointer *int *point*. Next, we type cast the value in *point* (the address of *some_address*) to force a change to *unsigned long*, and then we store the resulting value in *temp*. Because it is legal to divide an *unsigned long*, we divide *temp* by 2. Then we cast that result, still an *unsigned long*, to the type *int *(meaning "pointer to an *int*"). Finally, we place the correctly typed new value in *point*.

```
/* peek.c -- demonstrates how to cast an int to a */
/*            pointer                             */

main()
{
    char *mem_ptr;
    unsigned int address;

    while (1)
        {
        printf("Examine what memory location?\n");
        printf("Enter location in decimal: ");
        if (scanf("%u", &address) != 1)
            break;

        mem_ptr = (char *)address;   /* cast */

        printf("The value in %u is 0x%02X\n",
                address, (unsigned char)*mem_ptr);
        }
}
```

Listing 8-5. *The PEEK.C program.*

The PEEK.C program (Listing 8-5) illustrates this use of type casting. PEEK.C asks the user for a number, then treats that number as an address and shows you the value stored at that address.

Far Pointers

So far, we've assumed that all pointers occupy 2 bytes of memory. Two bytes can represent only addresses in the range 0 through 65,535—not nearly enough to reference every location in the latest PCs. Fortunately, QuickC provides a 4-byte pointer, called a far pointer, that can address more than 4 billion bytes of memory.

In particular, far pointers are useful for directly accessing the text screen's memory and for producing sophisticated graphics output. In this section we'll show you how to manipulate text in video memory.

To declare a far pointer, add the keyword _far to the pointer declaration, as follows:

```
int _far *screenp;
```

Models and Pointers

The _far keyword is needed only when you compile with the small and medium memory models. The compact, large, and huge models make all the pointers far by default.

We must use a far pointer to access screen memory because that memory is located at 0xB0000000 (for machines with MDA) or 0xB8000000 (for machines with CGA, EGA, or VGA), locations that do not fit into a 2-byte pointer. (Two bytes can hold only four hex digits, not eight.) To place this hexadecimal constant into a far pointer, use the following type cast:

```
screenp = (int _far *)0xB0000000;
screenp = (int _far *)0xB8000000;
```

These casts tell the compiler to handle the constant 0xB0000000 (or 0xB8000000) as a far address and to assign that address to the far pointer variable *screenp*.

The SCRINV.C program (Listing 8-6) demonstrates a simple technique for manipulating text screen memory. Every time you press a key, the screen flips over. (Type *Q* to quit.) In the listing, adjust the constant assigned to *screenp* to suit your hardware: For EGA or VGA, replace 0xB0000000 with 0xB8000000.

SCRINV uses a pointer as if it were an array. We declare *screenp* as a far pointer:

```
int _far *screenp;
```

but we reference its elements using an offset in square brackets, as follows:

```
temp = screenp[i];
```

```
/* scrinv.c -- using a far pointer to access text */
/*             screen memory                       */

#define ROWS 25
#define COLS 80

main()
{
    int _far *screenp;
    int temp, i;

    do
        {
        /* Use 0xB0000000 for MDA */
        screenp = (int _far *)0xB8000000;

        for (i = 0; i < ((ROWS*COLS)/2); ++i)
            {
            temp = screenp[i];
            screenp[i] = screenp[(ROWS*COLS) - i - 1];
            screenp[(ROWS*COLS) - i - 1] = temp;
            }
        } while (getch() != 'Q');

}
```

Listing 8-6. *The SCRINV.C program.*

Quick Tip

We declared *screenp* as a pointer to an *int* because each character on your PC text screen is represented by 2 bytes of information—one byte is the character and the other is that character's attribute (normal, blinking, inverse, etc.). (We will discuss this organization and the various attributes in Chapter 14.)

Functions That Return Addresses

In Chapter 6, we demonstrated that functions can return values and that those values are of type *int* unless you declare otherwise. You can also declare functions that return addresses. The C library contains many functions of this type, and your functions can also take advantage of the speed and compactness this procedure offers.

You declare a function that returns an address the way you declare a pointer variable—with a type, a *, and a name. For example, the following function returns the address of a *char* type:

```
char *function(int arg)
{
```

This is like using a function as a pointer. Examine the *Range()* function:

```
char *Range(int key)
{
    static char   k2[] = {'a', 'b', 'c'},
                  k3[] = {'d', 'e', 'f'},
                  k4[] = {'g', 'h', 'i'};
    char *kp;

    if (key == 2)
        {
        return (k2);                         Address of k2[]
        }
    else if (key == 3)
        {
        return (&k3[0]);                     Address of k3[]
        }
    kp = k4;
    return (kp);                             Return the pointer value (an address)
}
```

Quick Tip

Be careful when casting pointers to integers. You should always type cast to an *unsigned long* because that type will be large enough to hold all addresses. Specifying *unsigned* will prevent addresses from being (wrongly) considered negative, which could lead to incorrect results.

This example demonstrates that you can return an address in three ways: as an array name (*k2*), as the address of the first element in an array (*&k3[0]*), or as a pointer variable (*kp*).

Now let's call the *Range()* function from the *main()* function:

```
main()
{
    char *keys;
    char *Range(int key);  ——— Range() will return the address of a char
```

Notice that you can only use the return value of *Range()* after you correctly declare it, both in its own declaration and in (or before) any functions that call it.

You can use a pointer value returned by a function the same way you use a pointer—with one exception. The address returned by a function is an rvalue. Thus, you can neither place it to the left of the assignment operator nor change it by computation. The following examples illustrate three correct ways to use the value returned by *Range()*:

```
keys = Range(2);——————————— Address assigned to keys (a pointer)

printf("%cn", Range(2)[1]);——— Address used as an array

printf("%cn", *(Range(2) + 1));——— Address used as a pointer
```

The first example assigns the address value returned by *Range()* to a pointer variable (*keys*). The second example uses the address returned by *Range()* as if it were an array, printing the second element. The third example uses the address returned by *Range()* as if it were a pointer, printing the value stored in that address plus 1.

The PHWORD.C program (Listing 8-7) asks the user for a telephone number and then, using the letters of the telephone dial, prints out all the possible words that can be made from that number.

```
/* phword.c -- generates all the possible words */
/*              in a phone number; demonstrates  */
/*              functions that return addresses  */

#define MAXD (7)    /* 7 digits max */

main()
{
    int digits[MAXD], ndigits = 0, line = 0;
    char *letters;
    signed char digit;
    int a, b, c, d, e, f, g;
    char *Range(int key);
```

Listing 8-7. *The PHWORD.C program.*   *(continued)*

Listing 8-7. *continued*

```
    printf("Enter phone number (7 digits): ");
    do
        {
        digit = getch() - '0';
        if (digit == ('-' - '0'))
            continue;
        if (digit < 0 || digit > 9)
            {
            printf("\nAborted: Nondigit\n");
            return(1);
            }
        digits[ndigits++] = digit;
        printf("%d", digit);
        } while (ndigits < 7);
    printf("\n");

    for (a = 0; a < 3; ++a)
     for (b = 0; b < 3; ++b)
      for (c = 0; c < 3; ++c)
       for (d = 0; d < 3; ++d)
        for (e = 0; e < 3; ++e)
         for (f = 0; f < 3; ++f)
          for (g = 0; g < 3; ++g)
                {
                printf("%c", Range(digits[0])[a]);
                printf("%c", Range(digits[1])[b]);
                printf("%c", Range(digits[2])[c]);
                printf("%c", Range(digits[3])[d]);
                printf("%c", Range(digits[4])[e]);
                printf("%c", Range(digits[5])[f]);
                printf("%c", Range(digits[6])[g]);
                printf("\n");
                if (++line == 20)
                    {
                    printf("Press any key for more");
                    printf(" (or q to quit): ");
                    if (getch() == 'q')
                        return (0);
                    printf("\n");
                    line = 0;
                    }
                }
}

char *Range(int key)
{
    static char keys[10][3] = {
        {'0', '0', '0'},
        {'1', '1', '1'},
        {'a', 'b', 'c'},
```

(continued)

Listing 8-7. *continued*

```
        {'d', 'e', 'f'},
        {'g', 'h', 'i'},
        {'j', 'k', 'l'},
        {'m', 'n', 'o'},
        {'p', 'r', 's'},
        {'t', 'u', 'v'},
        {'w', 'x', 'y'}
    };

    return (keys[key]);
}
```

The PHWORD.C program also illustrates another point about arrays. When you reference a multidimensional array with only a partial list of offsets, the value generated is the address of the portion you referenced. Thus, although *keys* in *Range()* is a two-dimensional array, referencing with only a single dimension, as follows:

```
return (keys[key]);
```

yields the address of only the row specified. In other words, it yields the address of a one-dimensional array that is a subset of the two-dimensional array.

Notice in PHWORD.C that *main()* screens your telephone number for illegal characters. The function *Range()* would be more portable if we checked for illegal values inside it and returned an error code. The trick is to return an error address that is always illegal. Defined in the standard header file stdio.h is the perfect value to convey address errors—*NULL*. This special zero address value is guaranteed to be illegal. By using *NULL* rather than 0, you ensure the portability of your programs.

The following is a rewrite of *Range()* that uses *NULL*:

```
#include <stdio.h>        /* for NULL */

char *Range(int key)
{
    static char keys[10][3] = ...

    if (key < 0 :: key > 9)
        {
        return (NULL);
        }
```

Quick Tip

The *extern* keyword tells QuickC that the variable or function named will be found elsewhere, either later in the current file or in another file that you plan to compile separately. It can also be used to tell QuickC that you plan to use a variable found in a library routine.

Now *Range()* does its own error checking. It can return *NULL*, even though it is declared *char **, because *NULL* is a special address value that is illegal regardless of the expected return type.

Dynamic Arrays

In the previous chapter, we explained that arrays in C must be dimensioned with integer constant expressions, and that you cannot, therefore, change the size of a declared array. But now that you have pointers at your disposal, the situation is different. By using standard C Library routines, you can allocate memory while the program is running (that is, "dynamically") and thus create arrays "on the fly." You can also use other C library routines to change the size of dynamically allocated arrays, again while the program is running.

The ability to create, change the size of, and discard arrays from within your running program opens a host of new programming possibilities. It frees your program from having to know ahead of time how many lines of text a user will type, for example, or how many characters it will receive via a modem. When you design a database, it is clearly better to allow users to add fields at will, rather than restricting them to a predetermined record structure. Games are generally more interesting when players can add characters at any time. Text editors are more powerful when the user can interactively define keyboard macros.

The standard library routines for the dynamic allocation and reallocation of memory are listed in Table 8-1. The return types for these functions are declared in the header file malloc.h. If you look at those declarations (using the Include option on the View menu), you will see that they are all declared as pointer type *void **. This new type, when applied to a function's return value, permits the returned address to be legally assigned to any type of pointer. This makes it very easy for us to create dynamic arrays of any type.

Table 8-1. Memory Allocation Library Routines

Function	Description
malloc()	Allocate memory
calloc()	Allocate calculated memory
realloc()	Reallocate memory
free()	Free allocated memory

The *malloc()* Memory Allocation Function

The *malloc()* function is the most frequently used library allocation function. It takes a single argument, the number of bytes of memory you wish to allocate (reserve), and returns the address of that memory. If *malloc()* cannot find as much free memory as you specify, it returns a *NULL* value. The correct form for using *malloc()*, including a check for failure, is as follows:

```
#include <stdio.h>————————————————————— For NULL
#include <malloc.h>———————————————————— For malloc() declaration
  ⋮
int *iptr;——————————————————————— To receive address
size_t bytes = 100;——————————————————— Number of bytes

if ((iptr = malloc(bytes)) == NULL)
    {
    /* handle error here */
    }
printf("Now let's fill the array iptr[]\n");
```

The parentheses in the *malloc()* expression force the result of the assignment—the value of *iptr*—to be compared to *NULL*. If *malloc* succeeds in allocating memory, *iptr* contains the address of that dynamically allocated memory.

Because the value of *iptr* evaluates as an address, you can use *iptr* as if it were an array. For example, the following expression is perfectly legal:

```
iptr[5]
```

The TOTAL.C program (Listing 8-8) asks you to type numbers, one per line, and dynamically builds an array of those numbers. When you enter a non-numeric character, the program displays your list of numbers from the array and totals them.

This program introduces two new elements to our memory allocation routines: *free()* and *realloc()*. The *free()* function releases memory that you reserve with *malloc()* or *realloc()*. The *realloc()* function copies memory into a larger or smaller block of memory.

The *free()* function takes a single argument, the address returned by *malloc()* or *realloc()*, and uses it to release that memory. Note that if you pass *free()* an address other than one returned by one of these functions, your program might crash.

The *realloc()* function takes two arguments: first, the address returned by *malloc()* or one returned from a previous call to *realloc()*; and second, a new size in bytes. The function copies the contents of the old memory to the new memory (truncating if the new size is smaller) and returns the address of the new memory. Like *malloc()*, *realloc()* returns a *NULL* address if it fails.

Quick Tip

Note in the above example that we declare *bytes* as type *size_t*. This type is defined in malloc.h as an *unsigned int* for QuickC. Because the type *size_t* is a part of the ANSI standard, you should use it rather than *unsigned int* to ensure the portability of your programs.

However, to transport programs written with *size_t* to different machines, you might need to use *#define* to make *size_t* an *unsigned int*.

```
/* total.c -- how to build an array on the fly */

#include <stdio.h>        /* for NULL   */
#include <malloc.h>       /* for size_t */

main()
{
    int *iptr, count = 0, i, total;
    size_t bytes = sizeof(int);

    /* Start the array with room for one value */
    if ((iptr = malloc(bytes)) == NULL)
        {
        printf("Oops, malloc failed.\n");
        exit(1);
        }

    printf("Enter as many integer values as you want.\n");
    printf("I will build an array on the fly with them.\n");
    printf("(Any non-number means you've finished.)\n");

    while (scanf("%d", &iptr[count]) == 1)
        {
        ++count;
        /* Enlarge the array */
        if ((iptr = realloc(iptr, bytes * (count + 1))) == NULL)
            {
            printf("Oops, realloc failed.\n");
            exit(1);
            }
        }
    total = 0;
    printf("You entered:\n");
    for (i = 0; i < count; i++)
        {
        printf("iptr[%d] = %d\n", i, iptr[i]);
        total += iptr[i];
        }
    printf("\nTotal: %d\n", total);
    /* Give back the memory */
    (void)free(iptr);
}
```

Listing 8-8. *The TOTAL.C program.*

The *calloc()* Memory Allocation Routine

QuickC supplies a companion routine to *malloc()* called *calloc()* (for "calculated allocate"). The *calloc()* function also allocates memory, but with a twist that makes it ideal for arrays. Instead of merely allocating a number of bytes, it takes a pair of arguments: the number of items and the number of bytes (*sizeof*) of each item. The form for using *calloc()* is as follows:

```
address = calloc(items, sizeof(item));
```

Like *malloc()*, *calloc()* returns the address of successfully allocated memory or *NULL* if insufficient memory is available.

The advantage offered by *calloc()* is that it initializes allocated memory to zero values, whereas *malloc()* can leave memory that is filled with garbage. The *free()* function also releases memory reserved by *calloc()*.

Advanced Pointer Techniques

Perhaps you've heard horror stories about C pointers and incomprehensible code. Well, some of those stories are true. Reading and understanding poorly written code is like trying to untangle a plate of spaghetti. C gives you the freedom to design many types of strange but useful constructs. But C also gives you the freedom to design the incomprehensible. This section discusses some of C's magnificent but potentially arcane constructs—those dealing with the more elaborate and sophisticated uses of pointers.

Arrays of Pointers

C lets you create arrays of any type of elements. Thus, you can even create an array whose elements are pointers. For example, to create an array, in which each item is a pointer to a *float*, simply declare the following:

```
float *array_name[10];
```

The * preceding the array name in this declaration tells the compiler that the array is an array of pointers; therefore, each element holds an address. The *float* signifies that all pointers will point to *float* variables.

You can use this technique for speeding up sorting routines, for example. Because an address in IBM PC memory occupies only 2 bytes (except for far pointers), while the data it points to occupies 4 bytes (for a *float*), it's faster to exchange two 2-byte addresses than to exchange the data. The advantage offered by arrays of pointers becomes even more evident when we use them with strings, as we do in the next chapter.

The REVERSE.C program (Listing 8-9) reads in lines of characters. The addresses of those lines are stored in an array of pointers to *char* values. (See Figure 8-4.) An empty input line causes the lines of text pointed to by the array of pointers to be printed in reverse order.

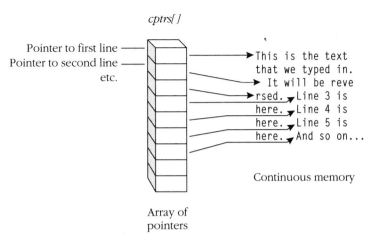

Figure 8-4. *An array of pointers, each element of which contains a line of text in allocated memory.*

```
/* reverse.c -- demonstrates an array of pointers */
/*              by reversing lines of text        */

#include <stdio.h>          /* for NULL    */
#include <malloc.h>         /* for size_t */

#define MAXL 20
#define HUNKSIZE 16

main()
{
    char *cptrs[MAXL];              /* array of pointers */
    char *cp;
    int count, i, j, ch;
    char *Getbyte(void);

    printf("Type in several lines of text, and I will\n");
    printf("print them back out in reverse order.\n");
    printf("(Any blank line ends input):\n");

    for (i = 0; i < MAXL; ++i)
        {
        cp = Getbyte();
        cptrs[i] = cp;             /* assign address to pointer */
        count = 0;
        while ((ch = getchar()) != '\n')  /* gather line */
            {
            *cp = ch;
            cp = Getbyte();
            ++count;
            }
```

Listing 8-9. *The REVERSE.C program.*

(continued)

Listing 8-9. *continued*

```
        *cp = '\0';
        if (count == 0)          /* all done if blank line */
            break;
        }
    printf("---------<reversed>---------\n");
    for (j = i-1; j >= 0; --j)
        {
        printf("%s\n", cptrs[j]);
        }
    }

char *Getbyte(void)
{
    static char *cp = NULL;
    static int bytes;
    static int hunk  = 1;

    if (cp == NULL)
        {
        if ((cp = malloc(HUNKSIZE)) == NULL)
            {
            printf("Panic: malloc() failed\n");
            exit(1);
            }
        bytes = 0;
        }
    else if ((++bytes % HUNKSIZE) == 0)
        {
        if ((cp = realloc(cp, (++hunk * HUNKSIZE))) == NULL)
            {
            printf("Panic: realloc() failed\n");
            exit(1);
            }
        }
    return (cp + bytes);
}
```

The fact that we can print an array of characters with *printf()* illustrates the correspondence between arrays of *char* values and strings. We will discuss that relationship in detail in the next chapter.

Pointers to Pointers

As you have seen, a pointer is a variable whose value is an address, and that address is usually the location in memory of another variable. However, in C, that other variable can also be a pointer. There is no limit to how far you can extend this "pointer-to-a-pointer" relationship—you can have pointers to pointers to pointers, and so on. Here, however, we'll minimize the danger of creating "spaghetti code" by restricting ourselves to pointers to pointers.

Figure 8-5 illustrates the relationship of a pointer to a pointer. The variable *pp* contains as its value the address of *p*. The variable *p* in turn contains as its value the address of *num*, an ordinary integer. Because *p* points to an *int*, *pp* is a pointer to a pointer to an *int*.

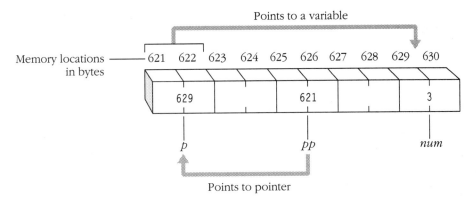

Figure 8-5. *Pointer to a Pointer: a variable whose value is the address of another pointer.*

The following example shows how to declare a pointer to a pointer.

```
int **pp, *p, num;
```
—— Pointer to an *int*
—— Pointer to a pointer to an *int*

The two * characters tell the compiler that *pp* is a pointer to a pointer and holds as its value the address of another pointer.

When accessing the values pointed to by *pp*, the number of * symbols determines which value is obtained. Consider the following initialization:

```
p = &num; —— Address of num
pp = &p; —— Address of p
```

Because *pp* points to *p*, *pp* yields the address stored in *p*, that of *num*. Placing another * in front of *pp* tells the compiler to fetch the value referenced by the pointer *p* to which *pp* points:

```
**pp
```

Because *pp* points to *p*, and *p* in turn points to *num*, *pp* fetches the value of *num*. Thus, all three of the following yield the value stored in the variable *num*:

```
**pp
*p
num
```

One useful application for a pointer to a pointer is in traversing arrays of pointers. The REVERSE2.C program (Listing 8-10) is a rewrite of the previous REVERSE.C. In this version, we replace the final *for* loop with a *while* loop that decrements *pp*, a pointer to a pointer.

```c
/* reverse2.c -- demonstrates a pointer to a pointer */

#include <stdio.h>        /* for NULL   */
#include <malloc.h>       /* for size_t */

#define MAXL 20
#define HUNKSIZE 16

main()
{
    char *cptrs[MAXL];
    char **pp;                       /* pointer to pointer */
    char *cp;
    int count, i, ch;
    char *Getbyte(void);

    printf("Type in several lines of text, and I will\n");
    printf("print them back out in reverse order.\n");
    printf("(Any blank line ends input):\n");

    for (i = 0; i < MAXL; ++i)
        {
        cp = Getbyte();
        cptrs[i] = cp;          /* assign address to pointer */
        count = 0;
        while ((ch = getchar()) != '\n')  /* gather line */
            {
            *cp = ch;
            cp = Getbyte();
            ++count;
            }
        *cp = '\0';
        if (count == 0)         /* all done if blank line */
            break;
        }
    printf("---------<reversed>---------\n");
    pp = &cptrs[i];
    while (pp >= cptrs)
        {
        printf("%s\n", *(pp--));
        }
}
```

Listing 8-10. *The REVERSE2.C program.*   *(continued)*

Listing 8-10. *continued*

```
char *Getbyte(void)
{
    static char *cp = NULL;
    static int bytes;
    static int hunk  = 1;

    if (cp == NULL)
        {
        if ((cp = malloc(HUNKSIZE)) == NULL)
            {
            printf("Panic: malloc() failed\n");
            exit(1);
            }
            bytes = 0;
        }
    else if ((++bytes % HUNKSIZE) == 0)
        {
        if ((cp = realloc(cp, (++hunk * HUNKSIZE))) == NULL)
            {
            printf("Panic: realloc() failed\n");
            exit(1);
            }
        }
    return (cp + bytes);
}
```

This program shows that a pointer to a pointer is decremented (or incremented) by the number of bytes in a pointer:

```
printf("%s\n", *(pp--))
```

The same

```
printf("%s\n", cptrs[i--])
```

Recall that the address in a pointer changes by a number of bytes that corresponds to the type to which it points. A *char* pointer changes by 1 byte, while a *float* pointer changes by 4 bytes. A pointer to a pointer changes by the number of bytes in an address because it points to a pointer, and thus to an address. Because *cptrs* is an array of pointers, and *pp* points to one of those addresses, decrementing *pp* causes it to point to the immediately preceding element in that array. Figure 8-6 on the following page illustrates this process.

Pointer Pointer

Pointers are so versatile that they can contain the address of almost anything. However, you cannot use pointers to obtain the address of the following C elements: constants (such as 5); variables declared with the keyword *register*; labels (the targets of *goto*); and keywords (such as *if*, *while*, and so on).

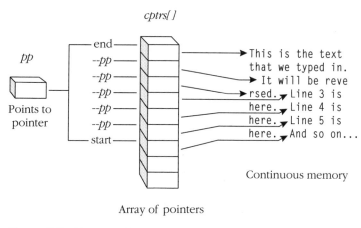

Figure 8-6. *Decrementing a pointer to a pointer moves it through an array of pointers.*

Based Pointers and Segments

When you write programs, you often face the need to make trade-offs between execution speed and code size. These trade-offs affect, among other things, the choice between near pointers and far pointers. Near pointers, it turns out, produce faster code than far pointers. They are thus both faster and smaller—two bytes rather than four. So why would you ever need to use far pointers?

As illustrated in Figure 8-7, your computer's memory is divided into a series of 64-KB units called segments. When you compile your program (using the small memory model), your executable code is placed into one segment, the CODE segment, and your variables are placed into another, the DATA segment. You can use near pointers to access the memory in only one segment, normally the DATA segment.

On the other hand, you can use far pointers to access storage at any location in your computer's memory, without being limited to a particular segment. A far pointer, in fact, combines a segment address and a near pointer, as shown in Figure 8-8. The

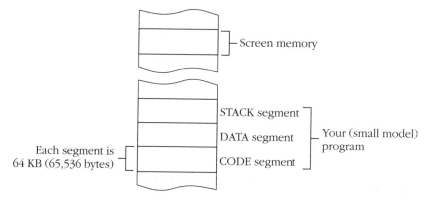

Figure 8-7. *Memory is organized into 64-KB segments.*

near pointer is an offset into the specified segment. It is the use of far pointers, for example, that enables you to access your video memory directly.

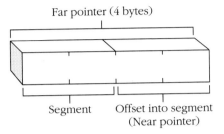

Figure 8-8. *Anatomy of a far pointer.*

For situations in which you want to use pointers to a known segment address, such as that of the segment that holds the video memory, QuickC 2.5 offers a faster version of the far pointer called a based pointer. The value of a based pointer is simply the offset (near) portion of a far pointer. To access memory with a based pointer, use the :> operator (a colon followed by a greater-than symbol):

segmentvar:>based_pointer

In this expression, *segmentvar* is the name of a segment declared with the *_segment* keyword, and *based_pointer* is the name of a based pointer declared with the *_based* keyword. The CLEAR.C program (Listing 8-11) illustrates the use of these new keywords. Running this program causes your screen to clear.

```
/* clear.c -- uses a based pointer and segment */
/*              to clear the text screen        */

#define ROWS 25
#define COLS 80

main()
{
    _segment screenseg;
    int _based(void) *cp;

    /* Use 0xB000 for Monochrome Display Adapters */
    screenseg = 0xB800;

    for (cp = (int *)0; cp < (int *)(ROWS * COLS); ++cp)
        {
        *(screenseg:>cp) = 0;
        }

    return (0);
}
```

Listing 8-11. *The CLEAR.C program.*

The *void* in parentheses following the *_based* keyword indicates that the segment for this base is declared elsewhere. The parentheses must be present and must not be empty. If the program uses the base with only one segment (as is true in Listing 8-11), you can place the segment name in the parentheses.

```
int _based(screenseg) *cp;
```

If you predeclare the segment name in this manner, you need not use the :> operator. Had the pointer *cp* been declared in CLEAR.C with such a fixed segment name, the statement body of the *for* loop could simply be

```
*cp = 0;
```

You can also declare a segment for a based pointer using the *_segname* keyword with a segment name. QuickC predefines four such names, which are listed below in Table 8-2.

Table 8-2.   Segment Names Reserved by QuickC

_CODE	The base is your code segment.
_CONST	The base is the constant segment for strings, or the string pool (described in the next chapter).
_DATA	The base is your data segment.
_STACK	The base is your stack segment.

To create a based pointer that expresses an offset into the DATA segment, for example, declare *cp* as follows:

```
int _based(_segname("_DATA")) *cp;
```

You can also assign your own names to segments your program used. Simply replace the name _DATA in the preceding declaration with a name of your own choosing, and initialize the declaration with the address of some data:

```
char _based(_segname("WORDS")) **wp =
    {
    "now", "is", "the", "time", "for", "all", "good"
    };
```

Pointers to Functions

It is often useful to know the address of a function. You declare a pointer to a function as follows:

```
int (*pointer_name)();
```

This declares the variable *pointer_name* to be a pointer *pointer_name*. The trailing parentheses tell the compiler that the pointer *pointer_name* contains the address of a function. The *int* specifies that the function pointed to returns an *int*.

To obtain the address of a function, merely state its name. However, be sure you declare the function before you take its address:

```
int (*funptr)();————— A pointer to a function declared
extern int Quit();————— A function declared

funptr = Quit;————— Address of Quit() assigned to funptr
```

In this example, *funptr* contains the address of *Quit()*, and we can call *Quit()* through *funptr*, as follows:

```
*funptr();
```

The preceding * tells the compiler to use the value to which *funptr* points (the address of *Quit()*). The trailing parentheses tell the compiler to call the function whose address we just fetched.

The CHOOSE.C program (Listing 8-12) goes one step further by creating an array of pointers to functions. First, the program asks you to choose a menu item. Then it translates your choice into an array offset and calls the function whose address is stored at that offset.

```
/* choose.c -- an array of pointers to functions */
/*             used to create a menu             */

void Choice1(), Choice2(), Choice3();
void (*Dochoice[3])() = {Choice1, Choice2, Choice3};

main()
{
    int ch;

    printf("Select 1, 2, or 3: ");
    ch = getch(); putch(ch);
    ch -= '1';
    if (ch < 0 || ch > 2)
        printf("\nNo such choice.\n");
    else
        Dochoice[ch]();

}

void Choice1(void)
{
        printf("\nThis is choice 1.\n");
}

void Choice2(void)
{
        printf("\nThis is choice 2.\n");
}
```

Listing 8-12. *The CHOOSE.C program.*   *(continued)*

Listing 8-12. *continued*

```
void Choice3(void)
{
        printf("\nThis is choice 3.\n");
}
```

Arrays of pointers to functions are best applied in interactive programs. Believe it or not, you'll find it easier to design word processors and complex games once you master this technique.

The following example illustrates the advantage of using an array of pointers to functions instead of a simpler *switch* statement. Examine the following fragment from a hypothetical text processor:

```
int (*commands[128])() = {
        ⋮
        Go_left,      /* L key (lowercase) */
        Mark_line,    /* M key (lowercase) */
        Next_search,  /* N key (lowercase) */
        ⋮
        };
```

This array has 128 pointers to functions, each of which corresponds to a key on the keyboard. Pressing L causes the text processor to call the *Go_left()* function, which moves the cursor left. If the user wants to change the meanings of two command keys—to the functions of L and N, for example—you need only use the following:

```
int (*temp)();——————————— Scratch pointer
int from, to;

from = 'l';
to   = 'n';
temp = commands[from];
commands[from] = commands[to];
commands[to] = temp;
```

Here we first declare a scratch variable to be used in the swap. We declare it as a pointer to a function because we will be swapping pointers to functions. We then assign to *temp* the address stored in *commands[from]*, where *from* is the offset that corresponds to the numeric value of the letter *'n'*. Because that array item is a pointer to the function *Next_search()*, we are saving the address of that function. We then copy the address in *commands[to]* into *commands[from]*. Finally, we assign the address saved in *temp* to *commands[to]*. The result of this exchange is that two command keys have swapped roles: Pressing N now causes the *Go_left()* function to be called, and pressing L causes the *Next_search()* function to be called.

Contrast this flexible form of programming with an inflexible *switch* statement, such as the following:

```
switch(key)
    {
    ⋮
    case 'l':
        Go_left();
        break;

    case 'm':
        Mark_line();
        break;

    case 'n':
        Next_search();
        break;
    ⋮
    }
```

Clearly, a program that a user can customize is more difficult to write, yet a versatile program is frequently worth the extra effort.

Untangling the Spaghetti

In the previous sections of this chapter you've seen some complicated declarations. You will see more of them in the chapters to follow, so we'll benefit by establishing some rules that will help us understand complex declarations.

The best approach is to start reading at the inside of a declaration with the pointer name (identifier) and then work your way outward. For example, to untangle the following declaration:

```
int (*name)();
```

follow the definition from the inside out: *name* is a pointer to a function of type *int*. Thus, this declaration is a pointer to a function that returns an *int*.

Let's try this same technique on a different declaration:

```
float (*name)[3];
```

In this example, *name* is a pointer to an array of three *float* variables. Contrast that declaration with the following:

```
float *name[3];
```

Here *name* is an array of three pointers to *float* variables. The difference lies in the parentheses. Be sure to obey the order of precedence for operators.

As an exercise in interpreting parentheses, try to decipher the following declaration from CHOOSE.C:

```
int (*funs[4])();
```

Here the * operator has a higher precedence than the [] operator, so * binds to *funs* first. Therefore, *funs* is a pointer variable, and four such pointers exist in an array; these pointers point to functions that return the type *int*. Thus, the declaration is an array of four pointers to functions that return *int* values.

9

Strings

A "string" is a sequence of ASCII characters—this sentence, for example, is a string. Strings give your programs life by enabling them to communicate with the user. Nearly all programs—from our simple *printf()* statements to the sophisticated dialogues of complex interactive programs—use strings of one type or another.

Unlike BASIC and Pascal, the C language has no built-in string-type variable. Instead, C uses the convention that a string is an array of type *char* whose final, or terminating, value is the special character '\0'—a 1-byte zero value. Figure 9-1 on the following page illustrates such an array.

We refer to this arrangement as a convention because nothing in C prevents you from handling strings in another manner. For example, you might store strings as arrays of *short* variables, using one byte to hold the character and the other to hold the character's attributes (more on this in Chapter 13). Or you might store strings as a value *length* followed by *length* number of characters. However, because you will most often handle strings in the conventional way, we will emphasize that method in our discussion of strings.

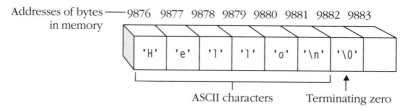

Addresses of bytes —— 9876 9877 9878 9879 9880 9881 9882 9883
in memory

| 'H' | 'e' | 'l' | 'l' | 'o' | '\n' | '\0' |

ASCII characters   Terminating zero

Figure 9-1. *In C, a string is an array of type* char *terminated by a zero value.*

Declaring and Initializing Strings

A string is merely an array of type *char*, and you initialize it the same way you would any other array. The following example fills the *char* array named *phrase* with ASCII character constants that spell the word *Hello* followed by an ASCII newline character:

```
char phrase[] = {'H', 'e', 'l', 'l', 'o', '\n', '\0'};
```

We made this array a conventional C string by adding a terminating zero value (the character constant '\0'). As with all arrays, string arrays can be initialized only if you use the keyword *static* or declare them globally—outside of all functions.

The HELLO.C program (Listing 9-1) illustrates the proper way to initialize string arrays. It also demonstrates the *printf()* format specifier %s, which tells *printf()* to print the associated argument as a string.

Because null-terminated *char* arrays so commonly represent strings in C, the language provides a built-in shorthand. When C finds text enclosed in full quotation marks (called *string constants*), it immediately stores that text as an array of type *char* and adds the terminating '\0'. This characteristic of C provides you an alternative way to initialize arrays.

```
/* hello.c -- legal ways to initialize strings as */
/*            arrays of char values                */

char Gphrase[] = {
    'H','e','l','l','o','\n','\0' };     /* global initialization */

main()
{
    static char loc_phrase[] = {
        'H','e','l','l','o','\n','\0' };    /* local initialization */

    printf("Global: %s", Gphrase);
    printf("Local:  %s", loc_phrase);

}
```

Listing 9-1. *The HELLO.C program.*

For example, you can create the same arrays as those declared in HELLO.C by substituting the following lines of code:

```
char Gphrase[] = "Hello\n";  ──────────── Global initialization
```

```
static char loc_phrase[] = "Hello\n";  ──────── Local initialization
```

As an aid in declaring long string constants, the compiler combines adjacent quoted strings into a single string constant. This feature lets you easily initialize long strings, as in the following example:

```
static char long_phrase[]  = "This is one long "
                             "sentence that the compiler "
                             "combines into a single string.";
```

C uses the rule that if nothing but white space (spaces, tabs, or newlines) separates two quoted strings, those strings are concatenated to form a single string. Thus, the above QuickC declaration is equivalent to the following:

```
static char long_phrase[]  =
"This is one long sentence that the compiler combines into a single string.";
```

Under pre-ANSI C, long string initializers can be emulated with the *#define* preprocessor directive. Recall that you can extend *#define* lines by ending each with a backslash and a newline character (that is, type \ and press Enter). Because this *#define* technique is portable to all compilers, we will use it throughout the rest of the book:

```
#define PHRASE \
"This is one long sentence that the compiler \
combines into a single string."
```

```
static char long_phrase[] = PHRASE;
```

A Constant Reminder

When you declare string constants, remember that it is illegal for a newline character to appear anywhere between double quotation marks. The following example is illegal:

```
static char long_phrase[] = "This is one
long sentence that the...";
```

and results in the following QuickC error message:

```
error C2001:
newline in constant
```

If you want to insert a newline character into a string constant, use the escape sequence for a newline character (\n) instead:

```
static char long_phrase[] = "This is one \nlong sentence that the..."
```

The String Pool and String Addresses

QuickC copies all of a program's quoted strings into a common area of memory called the string pool. They are copied there, one after the other, in the order that they occur in the program. (Figure 9-2 illustrates this process.)

The STRPOOL.C program (Listing 9-2) dumps the contents of the string pool to your terminal screen. Note in STRPOOL.C that any *char* array that ends with a zero value, such as *Cent_string*, is placed into the string pool.

We place nonprinting characters into quoted strings as we did with *printf()*—that is, a newline character, with \n; a carriage return, with \r; and a tab, with \t. Other special characters that you can place in string constants are the double quotation mark, with \"; the formfeed character, with \f; the backspace character, with \b; and the bell (beep) character, with \a.

You can include any character from the PC's extended character set in a string constant by using a \x followed by a two-digit hexadecimal number. For example, \x9B is used to represent the ¢ character. (QuickC's on-line help includes a handy table that lists these escape sequences.)

Notice also in the STRPOOL.C program that we assigned the address of a string to a pointer (*cp = Start*). Nowhere are pointers used more heavily than with strings.

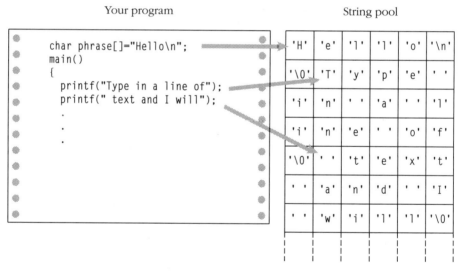

Figure 9-2. *Quoted string constants are placed one after the other into the string pool.*

```
/* strpool.c -- dumps the string pool to show how */
/*               quoted strings are stored         */

#define PHRASE \
"This is one long sentence that the compiler \
combines into a single string."

char Start[]        = "start";
char Long_phrase[]  = PHRASE;
char Short_phrase[] = "This is a short phrase";
char Cent_string[]  = "\x9b";
char End[]          = "^";

main()
{
    char *cp;

    printf("Dump of the string pool:\n");
    printf("----------------------\n");

    printf("\"");                     /* print leading quote */

    /*
     * Note that the address of a string can be
     * assigned to a pointer: cp = Start
     */
    for (cp = Start; *cp != '^'; ++cp)
        {
        if (*cp == '\0')            /* print '\0' as a quote */
            printf("\"\n\"");
        else if (*cp == '\n' )  /* print '\n' as '\' 'n' */
            printf("\\n");
        else
            printf("%c", *cp);
        }
}
```

Listing 9-2. *The STRPOOL.C program.*

Pointers and Initialized Strings

In the last chapter we assigned the address of an array to a pointer. We can also initialize a pointer to *char* with the address of a quoted "string constant," as follows:

```
char *str = "This is a phrase";
```

This example initializes the *char* pointer *str* to contain the address of the quoted string constant. Because the compiler places all string constants into the string pool, the address in *str* is that of the letter "T" (the first character of the *char* array) in the string pool.

Recall that an array declaration creates an *rvalue* and a pointer declaration creates an *lvalue*. Consider the following declarations:

```
char ary[] = "This is a phrase";
char *str = "This is another";
```

The *ary[]* declaration creates an *rvalue* (an address reference, such as a label) that cannot be changed with calculations.

The *str* declaration, on the other hand, creates an *lvalue* (a pointer variable whose value is an address), which can be changed with calculations. You can, for example, increment the pointer as follows:

```
++str;
```

The distinction between *lvalue* and *rvalue* can be a confusing one for beginning C programmers. Remember that an array name (such as *ary*) is a fixed location and cannot be changed; a pointer (such as *str*) is a variable and can be changed.

The BIFFRED.C program (Listing 9-3) demonstrates that you can use pointers to manipulate strings in the string pool. Examine the program before you run it. Can you predict what it will do?

```
/* biffred.c -- strings in the string pool can be */
/*              manipulated via pointers           */

char Start[] = "start";
char Name[]  = "My name is FRED\n";

main()
{
    char *cp;
    int pass;

    for (pass = 0; pass < 2; ++pass)
        {
        printf(Name);

        cp = Start;

        while (*cp != 'F')
            ++cp;

        *cp    = 'B';
        *++cp = 'I';
        *++cp = 'F';
        *++cp = 'F';
        }
}
```

Listing 9-3. *The BIFFRED.C program.*

266

Formatting Strings with *printf()*

So far, we've used *printf()* to print and format numbers (*int* with *%d* and *float* with *%f*, for example), individual characters with *%c*, and quoted strings with *%s*. The ability of *printf()* to print strings, however, goes far beyond the mere echoing of quoted string constants. In the following example:

```
printf("%s\n", ary);
```

the expression *ary* can be the address of any *char* type array that ends with the character constant value '\0'. It can be a quoted string constant such as

```
printf("%s\n", "This is a phrase");
```

or the address of a string from either a *char* array or a value in a pointer, as in the following examples:

```
char *str, ary[] = "This is a phrase";

str = ary;

printf("%s\n", ary);──────────────── Address of an array
printf("%s\n", str);──────────────── Value in a pointer
```

Because all quoted strings are placed into the string pool and replaced with their starting address in that string pool, it follows that the format specification in the control string of this example:

```
printf("%s\n", str);
```

────────────────── Control string

can also be expressed as either an array address or the value in a pointer, as follows:

```
char *str, ary[] = "This is a phrase.";
char *cp,  ctl[] = "%s\n";

str = ary;
cp  = ctl;

printf(ctl, ary);──────────────── Addresses of arrays
printf(cp, str);──────────────── Pointer values
printf(ctl, str);──────────────── Mixture of the two
```

The CONTROL.C program (Listing 9-4 on the following page) demonstrates this equivalence. This program asks you to type either an *l* or an *r*, and then it prints out a string with the corresponding left or right justification.

CONTROL.C shows how the *printf()* format specifier *%s* is used with various options to format strings. You can also combine options as in the following statement, which prints the first four letters of *computer* right-justified in a 25-character field.

```
printf("%25.4s\n", "computer");
```

```
/* control.c -- demonstrates string justification */
/*              using printf()                     */

char Some_text[] = "Some Text";
char Left_control[] = "<<%-15s>>";
char Right_control[] = "<<%15s>>";

main()
{
    char ch;

    while (1)
        {
        printf("Select l)eft, r)ight, or q)uit: ");
        ch = getch();
        putch(ch);

        printf("\n\n");

        switch((int)ch)
            {
            case 'l':
            case 'L':
                printf(Left_control, Some_text);
                break;
            case 'r':
            case 'R':
                printf(Right_control, Some_text);
                break;
            case 'q':
            case 'Q':
                exit (0);
            default:
                printf("Huh?");
                break;
            }
        printf("\n\n");
        }
}
```

Listing 9-4. *The CONTROL.C program.*

Table 9-1 lists formatting options that are available with %s. The value *num* must be a decimal integer. You can combine the last option, %.*num*s, with any of the others, to produce a specifier such as *%25.5s*, which right-justifies 5 characters of a given string within a 25-character field.

Table 9-1. Variations of the *printf()* %s Specifier

%s	Prints the string exactly as it is
%*num*s	Prints the string right-justified in a field of width *num*
%-*num*s	Prints the string left-justified in a field of width *num*
%.*num*s	Prints *num* characters of string

String Input and Output

The standard C Library contains several functions specifically designed to facilitate input and output of strings. In this section we discuss some that read from your keyboard or print to your screen. The next chapter ("Managing Files") deals with the file-handling counterparts to these functions. In Chapter 13, we will present additional routines that directly access the keyboard and screen hardware.

String Input with *scanf()*

We've already used *scanf()* several times. Now let's discuss it in detail. The *scanf()* function uses the same % specifiers that *printf()* does, but it uses them to read values, not to print them. Unfortunately, *scanf()* handles strings a little differently than does *printf()*. Whereas *printf()* prints the entire string to a terminating '\0', *scanf()* reads only space-delimited *words* of text. That is, for each %s in its control string, *scanf()* reads all characters up to, but not including, a space, tab, or newline. Therefore, *scanf()* is best used for reading words rather than lines of text.

The *scanf()* routine, when used with %s to read words of text, takes the form

```
scanf("%s", buf);
```

where *buf* is the address of a *char* array (buffer) into which *scanf()* places the text it reads from the keyboard. The array *buf* can be either a *char* array or a pointer to memory created by *malloc()*. (Note that you do not need to use an ampersand with an array name.) The *scanf()* function appends a terminating '\0' to the text in *buf*.

The short SCANLINE.C program (Listing 9-5 on the following page) illustrates a simple way to use *scanf()* for reading words of text from the keyboard. It asks you to type in a line of text and then uses *printf()* to print the words of that text, one word per line.

When you run SCANLINE.C, notice that it prints nothing until you press the Enter key. This is because *scanf()* is a "buffered I/O" routine. It reads from the standard input (the keyboard), but it "sees" nothing until you press the Enter key. (We discuss the concept of buffered versus unbuffered I/O in the next chapter.)

The *scanf()* function provides two variations for the %s specifier. (See Table 9-2 on the following page.) These let you read more than individual words.

Table 9-2. Variations of the *scanf()* %s Specifier

%*nums*	Reads *num* characters including space, tab, or newline characters (specify *num* as a decimal integer)
%[*range*]	Reads a specified range of characters

The following example reads 127 characters from the keyboard and places them into the array *buf*:

```
char buf[128];

scanf("%127s", buf); ——— %nums form
buf[127] = '\0';
```

This form of *scanf()* has two disadvantages. First, because newline characters can be read into *buf*, you can't easily tell whether *buf* contains a complete line or a partial line or a number of lines. Second, because this form does not append a terminating '\0' to the text, you must add it yourself.

```
/* scanline.c -- demonstrates how scanf() reads */
/*                the individual words of a line */

#define INTRO \
"Type in lines of text. They will be printed out\n\
one word per line, thus demonstrating scanf().\n\
(Type Ctrl-Z to quit.)\n"

main()
{
    char buf[512];     /* should be big enough */

    printf(INTRO);

    /*
     * scanf() returns the number of items
     * that its control string matched
     */
    while (scanf("%s", buf) == 1)
        {
        printf("%s\n", buf);
        }
}
```

Listing 9-5. *The SCANLINE.C program.*

For better control, use the more complex *scanf()* %[*range*] directive. Here *range* is any list of characters that you want to include in *buf*. The following example:

```
scanf("%[0123456789]", buf);
```

reads in only the digits 0 through 9. Anything else causes *scanf()* to stop reading and terminate *buf* with a *'\0'*.

You can construct a more useful variation of the *%[range]* directive using the ∧ character. When you use a ∧ as the first character in *range*, *scanf()* reads all characters up to, but not including, any characters in *range* and stops reading at the first excluded character. This version of *scanf()* also appends a terminating *'\0'* to the characters it reads. The following example shows how to use this variation:

```
scanf("%[^\n]", buf);————— Read all but a newline
scanf("%[\n]", dummy);————— Read only a newline
```

The first line tells *scanf()* to read all characters up to, but not including, the newline character and to place those characters into *buf*. The second line tells *scanf()* to read only a newline character (the one that terminated the first *scanf()*) and to place it into *dummy*. The *scanf()* function can be tricky to use (witness the need for the second statement), but with practice, you will find it a valuable programming resource.

The SCRANGE.C program (Listing 9-6) summarizes the *scanf()* function. It obtains several lines of text and then displays exactly what *scanf()* reads.

```
/* scrange.c -- illustrates scanf()'s control */
/*              directives                     */

main()
{
    char buf[512],    /* should be big enough */
         dummy[2];    /* used for \n and \0   */
    int num;

    do
        {
        printf("Running:\n");
        printf("\tscanf(\"%%d\", &num);\n");
        printf("\tscanf(\"%%[^\\n]\", buf);\n");
        printf("\tscanf(\"%%[\\n]\", dummy);\n");

        printf("\nType enough to satisfy this:\n");
        printf("(Set num equal to zero to quit)\n");

        scanf("%d", &num);
        scanf("%[^\n]", buf);
        scanf("%[\n]", dummy);

        printf("\n\tnum = %d\n", num);
        printf("\tbuf[] = \"%s\"\n", buf);
```

Listing 9-6. *The SCRANGE.C program.*   *(continued)*

Listing 9-6. *continued*

```
        printf("\n\n");

        } while (num != 0) ;

}
```

Lines of Text with *gets()* and *puts()*

Although we can use variations of *scanf()* to read lines of text, the QuickC library contains a pair of routines specifically tailored for reading and writing strings as lines of text. A line of text, in this case, is any string that includes a terminating newline. This is the most natural form of text entry because it corresponds to a line of text on the screen.

Although the newline, '\n', is used throughout C to represent the end of a line of text, it does not correspond to the characters produced or expected by your hardware. The Enter key, for example, actually produces the '\r' character. And printing a '\n' to your screen moves the cursor down but not to the left on the screen. Fortunately, *scanf()* and *gets()* convert an Enter keypress ('\r') to a newline ('\n'), and both *printf()* and *puts()* convert a newline ('\n') into a carriage return/linefeed combination ('\r' '\n') when writing to your screen.

The *gets()* (pronounced "get s") function reads all typed characters up to and including a newline (generated when you press Enter) and places those characters into a *char* array. The newline is then replaced with a '\0' to form a C string. The *puts()* (pronounced "put s") function displays a string and adds a newline to the end.

The DIALOG.C program (Listing 9-7) uses *gets()*, *puts()*, and *printf()* to carry on a simple conversation. Note that because the *gets()* function returns *NULL* if it fails, we must use the directive *#include <stdio.h>* to incorporate the definition of *NULL*.

```
/* dialog.c -- a conversation using gets() and puts() */

#include <stdio.h>        /* for NULL and BUFSIZ */

#define THE_QUESTION \
"And what is your view on the current price of corn\n\
and the stability of our trade import balance?"

main()
{
    char name[BUFSIZ],
        buf[BUFSIZ];
    extern char *gets();
```

Listing 9-7. *The DIALOG.C program.*   *(continued)*

Listing 9-7. *continued*

```
    name[0] = '\0';          /* clear the name */
    puts("\n\nHi there. And what is your name?");

    if (gets(name) != NULL && name[0] != '\0')
        {
        printf("\nPleased to meet you, %s.\n", name);
        puts(THE_QUESTION);
        /*
         * Force an extra <enter> before replying
         */
        do
            {
            if (gets(buf) == NULL)
                break;

            } while (*buf != '\0');          /* wait for empty line */

        puts("Sorry. I needed to think about that.");
        printf("Nice talking to you, %s.\n", name);
        }
    else
        puts("How rude!");

    puts("Goodbye.");
}
```

String-Manipulation Routines

As you can see, the string I/O routines in DIALOG.C are not very sophisticated. Fortunately, the QuickC library contains a host of functions that permit more complex string manipulations. We won't describe all of the functions here—see Appendix B, "C Library Guide," in *C for Yourself*—but we do list many of them in Table 9-3 on p. 277. We will, however, use many of these functions in one large program and then discuss those selected string-handling routines.

The ACME.C program (Listing 9-8) asks the user to fill out an employment application for a fictional company. It isn't particularly user friendly, and it terminates if you type something it can't understand.

```
/* acme.c -- illustrates an assortment of the   */
/*           C library string-handling routines */

#include <stdio.h>          /* for NULL */
#include <string.h>         /* for strchr(), et al */
#define NAME_PATTERN \
"first<space>last  or\n\
first<space>middle<space>last"
```

Listing 9-8. *The ACME.C program.*   *(continued)*

Listing 9-8. *continued*

```c
#define ADDRESS_PATTERN \
"number<space>street<comma><space>city<comma>"

char Buf[BUFSIZ];          /* global I/O buffer */
main()
{
    char *ocp, *cp, *first, *last, *street, *city;
    void Prompt(char *str), Cant(char *what, char *pattern);

    printf("Acme Employment Questionnaire\n");
    /*
     * Expect first<space>last or
     *         first<space>middle<space>last
     */
    Prompt("Full Name");

     /* Search forward for a space */
    if ((cp = strchr(Buf,' ')) == NULL)
        Cant("first name", NAME_PATTERN);
    *cp = '\0';
    first = strdup(Buf);
    *cp = ' ';

     /* Search back from end for a space */
    if ((cp = strrchr(Buf,' ')) == NULL)
        Cant("last name", NAME_PATTERN);
    last = strdup(++cp);

    /*
     * Expect number<space>street<comma><space>city<comma>
     */
    Prompt("Full Address");

     /* Search forward for a comma */
    if ((cp = strchr(Buf,',')) == NULL)
        Cant("street", ADDRESS_PATTERN);
    *cp = '\0';
    street = strdup(Buf);

     /* Search forward from last comma for next comma */
    if ((ocp = strchr(++cp,',')) == NULL)
        Cant("city", ADDRESS_PATTERN);
    *ocp = '\0';
    city = strdup(++cp);

    printf("\n\nYou entered:\n");
    printf("\tFirst Name: \"%s\"\n", first);
    printf("\tLast Name:  \"%s\"\n", last);
    printf("\tStreet:     \"%s\"\n", street);
    printf("\tCity:       \"%s\"\n", city);
}
```

(continued)

Listing 9-8. *continued*

```
void Cant(char *what, char *pattern)
{
    printf("\n\n\bFormat Error!!!\n");
    printf("Can't parse your %s.\n", what);
    printf("Expected an entry of the form:\n\n");
    printf("%s\n\nAborted\n", pattern);
    exit(1);
}

void Prompt(char *str)
{
    while (1)
        {
        printf("\n%s: ", str );
        if (gets(Buf) == NULL || *Buf == '\0')
            {
            printf("Do you wish to quit? ");
            if (gets(Buf) == NULL || *Buf == 'y')
                exit (0);
            continue;
            }
        break;
        }
}
```

The *strchr()* String Function

The first new function in ACME.C is *strchr()* (for "string character"). This routine requires two arguments—a string to search and a character to look for in that string:

```
strchr(Buf, ' ')
```
         └────┴──────── Search string for a space character

If *strchr()* finds the character in the string, it returns the address of that character. If it doesn't find the character, it returns *NULL*. Thus, we can handle the error as follows if the character is not in the string:

```
                    ┌───┬─────────────────── Search Buf for a space character
if ((cp = strchr(Buf, ' ')) == NULL)
   └──────────────────────┼────── Save address
                          └────── Then test for an error
```

In the example, *cp* is a pointer to *char* into which we assign the address returned by *strchr()*. If the result of that assignment (the value of *cp*) is *NULL*, the string *Buf* contains no space character.

Because *strchr()* returns the address of a string, you must either declare it in your program or use the statement *#include <string.h>* (as we did in ACME.C) to supply the declaration for *strchr()*.

The *strdup()* String Function

The second new function in ACME.C is *strdup()*. This is a Microsoft QuickC function that does not exist in other C libraries. When passed a string, *strdup()* makes a copy of that string and returns the address of the copy. Because this type of "string duplication" is not portable, we'll show you a version (Listing 9-9) that is. The implementation of this portable version of *strdup()* introduces two string-handling functions, *strlen()* and *strcpy()*.

```
#include <stdio.h>   /* for NULL */
#include <malloc.h>  /* malloc  */

char *
strdup(char *str);
{
    char *newstr;
    int bytes;

    bytes = strlen(str);
    if ((newstr = malloc(bytes + 1)) == NULL)
        return (NULL);
    (void)strcpy(newstr, str);
    return (newstr);
}
```

Listing 9-9. *The portable* strdup() *function.*

The *strlen()* String Function

The *strlen()* function counts the characters in a string (excluding the terminating '\0') and returns that count. For example, the assignments

```
static char word[] = "Biff";

bytes = strlen(word);
```

cause *bytes* to be assigned the value 4 because the string *word* contains four letters.

The *strcpy()* String Function

The *strcpy()* function copies its second argument (a string) into its first, a buffer large enough to hold that copy. The value returned by *strcpy()* is the address of its first argument. Because we wanted to ignore that return value in our version of *strdup()*, we type cast the call as type *void*:

```
if ((newstr = malloc(bytes + 1)) == NULL)
    return (NULL);
(void)strcpy(newstr, str);
```

To create the space for the copy, we call *malloc()* with the argument *bytes + 1*, the length of the string and its terminating '\0'. (Remember, *strlen()*, which gave us the value in *bytes*, does not count the terminating '\0'.)

Table 9-3.   QuickC Library String-Manipulation Functions

strlen(str)	Returns the length of a string *str*, not counting the terminating '\0'
strcat(s1, s2)	Concatenates the second string (*s2*) to the end of the first (*s1*)
strcmp(s1, s2)	Compares two strings (*s1* and *s2*); returns 0 if they are the same, otherwise returns the arithmetic difference of the first two nonmatching characters
stricmp(s1, s2)	Compares two strings without regard to case
strncmp(s1, s2, n)	Compares *n* characters in the two strings (*s1* and *s2*)
strcpy(buf, str)	Copies a string (*str*) into a char buffer *buf*, which must be large enough to hold both the string and its terminating '\0'
strncpy(buf, str, n)	Copies *n* characters of the string *str* into the buffer *buf*
strchr(str, ch)	Finds the first occurrence of a character (*ch*) in a string (*str*); returns the address of *ch* if found, otherwise returns *NULL*
strcspn(s1, s2)	Finds a substring in *s1* that begins with anything other than one of the characters in *s2*; returns the address of that substring if found, otherwise returns *NULL*
strstr(s1, s2)	Finds the first occurrence of the substring *s1* in the larger string *s2*; returns the address of that substring if found, otherwise returns *NULL*
strrchr(str, ch)	Finds the last ocurrence of a character (*ch*) in a string (*str*); returns the address of *ch* if found, otherwise returns *NULL*
strrev(str)	Reverses the characters in the string *str*; returns the address of that reversed string
strupr(str)	Converts a string (*str*) to uppercase characters
strset(str, ch)	Clears a string (*str*), converting all its characters to the character *ch*
strdup(str)	Duplicates a string (*str*), returning the address of the new copy
sprintf(str, cntl, args, . . .)	Formatted print into a string (*str*), converting *args* based on the control string *cntl*
sscanf(str, cntl, addrs, . . .)	Formatted convert, like *scanf()*, but converts from the string rather than from the keyboard

You should be aware that although *stricmp()*, *strcspn()*, and *strupr()* are supplied with the Microsoft QuickC library, they are not a part of ANSI C. Do not use them if you want your programs to be portable to other compilers and computers.

C vs BASIC String Functions

As you have seen, sophisticated C string handling can require complicated programming. The C library string-handling routines can emulate much of BASIC, but the corresponding statements are usually less straightforward:

```
A$ = B$————————— BASIC (assigns value of string B$ to A$)
first = strdup(Buf);——— C (duplicates Buf and assigns location of copy to first)
```

Some functions common to BASIC are missing from C. Among them are *LEFT$*, *MID$*, and *RIGHT$*. Listing 9-10 shows a C version of *LEFT$*. We leave it as an exercise for you to write C versions of the other two BASIC commands.

C offers two principal advantages over BASIC: It permits the programmer to extend string-handling library routines with customized routines, and it allows easy access to strings from pointers.

```
#include <stdio.h>    /* for NULL     */
#include <string.h>   /* for strdup() */

char *
leftstr(str, cnt)
char *str;
int  cnt;
{
    char *cp;

    if (strlen(str) < cnt !! cnt <= 0)
        return (NULL);
    if (strlen(str) == cnt)
        return (strdup(str));
    cp = strdup(str);
    cp[cnt - 1] = '\0';
    return (cp);
}
```

Listing 9-10. *The* leftstr() *function.*

Arrays and Strings

Because a string is nothing more than an array of type *char*, a two-dimensional array of type *char* can represent an array of strings. However, you must be sure to terminate each row (string) with a '\0' character, as follows:

```
char names[3][6] = {
        { 'J','o','e','\0' },
        { 'D','u','k','e','\0' },
        { 'O','z','z','i','e','\0' }
};
```

You also can take the easier route of using string constants (quoted strings) as array initializers:

```
char names[3][6] = { "Joe", "Duke", "Ozzie" };
```

Both forms create identical arrays, as illustrated in Figure 9-3. Also notice that under-initializing rows sets the trailing characters in rows 0 and 1 to '\0'.

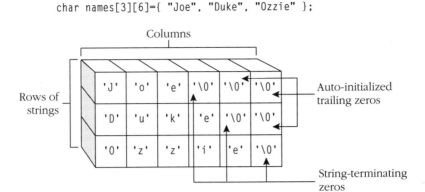

```
char names[3][6]={ "Joe", "Duke", "Ozzie" };
```

Figure 9-3. *A two-dimensional array of* char *values as an array of strings.*

As we've already seen, strings can be easily manipulated by pointers. Because of this, arrays of pointers to strings are often used in place of the two-dimensional arrays of *char.* The previous sample arrays, declared and initialized as an array of pointers, appear as follows:

```
char *names[3] = { "Joe", "Duke", "Ozzie" };
```
—————————————————————— Array of pointers

This pointer form also uses storage space more efficiently than the two-dimensional array. Compare the memory use of this form, depicted in Figure 9-4, with that of the preceding approach (shown in Figure 9-3).

The L2WORDS.C program (Listing 9-11 on the following page) illustrates one application for an array of pointers to strings. It asks you to enter a line of text, then it breaks that line into individual words and returns an array of pointers to the substrings that form those words. *Line2words()* assumes that spaces separate words, but

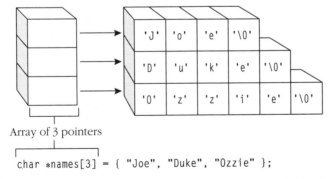

Array of 3 pointers

```
char *names[3] = { "Joe", "Duke", "Ozzie" };
```

Figure 9-4. *Arrays of pointers to strings use memory efficiently.*

it can take multiple words as a single word if you surround the words with double quotation marks. You might use a routine such as *Line2words()* if you are writing your own command-line interpreter (such as COMMAND.COM).

L2WORDS.C does a few tricky things: First, notice that we declare the function *Line2words()* as *char ***. This means that it returns a pointer to a pointer. That pointer contains the address of the first element of our array of pointers. The first element in that array points to the first word.

Second, notice that when the program prints words, it checks *list[i][-1]* (negative subscripting) to see whether the string has double quotation marks around it. If it does, the program replaces them when it prints the word.

```c
/* l2words.c -- employs an array of pointers to */
/*              strings to break a line of text */
/*              into its component words         */

#include <stdio.h>        /* for NULL and BUFSIZ */

main()
{
    char **Line2words(char *line, int *count);
    char **list;            /* pointer to pointer */
    char buf[BUFSIZ];       /* buffer for input */
    int count, i, quote_flag;

    printf("Enter a line of text and I will break\n");
    printf("it up for you.\n");

    if (gets(buf) == NULL)
        exit(1);

    list = Line2words(buf, &count);

    for (i = 0; i < count; i++)
        {
        quote_flag = 0;
        printf("<");
        if (list[i] != buf)
            {
            if (list[i][-1] == '"')    /* negative subscript */
                {
                ++quote_flag;
                printf("\"");
                }
            }
        printf("%s", list[i]);
```

Listing 9-11. *The L2WORDS.C program.*   *(continued)*

Listing 9-11. *continued*

```
        if (quote_flag)
            printf("\"");

        printf(">\n");
        }
}

#define MAXW 64

char **Line2words(char *line, int *count)
{
    static char *words[MAXW];
    int index;

    index = 0;          /* zero internal index */

    while (*line != '\0')
        {
        /* Turn spaces and tabs into zeros */
        if (*line == ' ' :: *line == '\t')
            {
            *(line++) = '\0';
            continue;
            }
        words[index] = line++;      /* found a word */

        /* Is it quoted? */
        if ( *(words[index]) == '"')
            {
            /* Yes, advance pointer to just past quote */
            ++words[index];

            /* Find next quote */
            while (*line && *line != '"')
                {
                ++line;
                }

            /* And turn it into a '\0' */
            if (*line)
                *(line++) = '\0';
            }
        else
            {
            /* Otherwise skip to next space */
            while (*line && *line != ' ' && *line != '\t')
```

(continued)

Listing 9-11. *continued*

```
            {
            ++line;
            }
        }
    if (++index == MAXW)
        break;
    }
    *count = index;        /* set count via pointer  */
    return (words);        /* return address of array */
}
```

The Arguments to *main()*—*argv* and *argc*

When you run a program from the command interpreter (COMMAND.COM under MS-DOS, or *sh* or *csh* under UNIX), you can specify arguments for the program on the command line. For example, when you run QuickC by entering

```
C>qc file.c
```

QuickC starts with the file named FILE.C already loaded. All C programs, including QuickC, retrieve arguments from the command line in the same way. That is, every C program begins execution with the function named *main()*, and that function, like any other, can receive arguments. Traditionally called *argc* and *argv*, these arguments are received by *main()* as follows:

```
main(int argc, char *argv[])
```

These arguments to *main()* contain all the information that you need to access the command-line arguments: *argc* is the number of command-line arguments, and *argv* is an array of pointers to those arguments.

The SHOWARGS.C program (Listing 9-12) shows how to access and use the arguments passed to *main()*. To run this program from within QuickC, you must first set the command-line arguments with Run / Debug on the Options menu.

When you run SHOWARGS.C with the following command-line preset in the Run / Debug dialog box:

```
kit makes lovely paper
```

the program prints the following:

argc = 5————— Five pointers in *argv*

```
argv[0] -> "C:\QC25\SRC\CHAP09\SHOWARGS.EXE"
argv[1] -> "kit"
argv[2] -> "makes"
argv[3] -> "lovely"
argv[4] -> "paper"
argv[5] -> NULL
```

The first string that *argv* (an array of pointers to strings) points to is the name of your program.

Because *argv* is an array of pointers to *char*, you often will see it alternatively declared as follows:

```
main(int argc, char **argv)
{                   └──────── A pointer to a pointer
```

Recall that this pointer to a pointer and the declaration *char *argv[]* are interchangeable.

```
/* showargs.c -- shows how to access the arguments */
/*               passed to main()                  */

#include <stdio.h>         /* for NULL */

main(int argc, char *argv[])
{
    int i;

    printf("argc = %d\n", argc);
    printf("\n");

    for (i = 0; i < argc; ++i)
        {
        printf("argv[%d] -> \"%s\"\n", i, argv[i]);
        }
    printf("argv[%d] -> NULL\n", i);
    printf("\n");
}
```

Listing 9-12. *The SHOWARGS.C program.*

The *main()* function is actually passed three arguments, but the third argument, called *envp*, is seldom used. Like *argv*, it is an array of pointers to strings and must be declared as follows:

```
main(int argc, char *argv[], char *envp[])
{
```

The strings to which the *envp* array elements point are your system's environment variables, such as *PATH*.

Take a moment to modify SHOWARGS.C so that it matches the SHOW2.C program (Listing 9-13 on the following page). After you run this program, choose DOS Shell from the File menu and type *set*. Compare the output produced by the MS-DOS command SET to that produced by SHOW2.C. (Type *exit* to return to QuickC.)

```
/* show2.c -- shows how to use main()'s envp argument */

#include <stdio.h>          /* for NULL */

main(int argc, char *argv[], char *envp[])
{
    int i;

    printf("argc = %d\n", argc);
    printf("\n");

    for (i = 0; i < argc; ++i)
        {
        printf("argv[%d] -> \"%s\"\n", i, argv[i]);
        }
    printf("argv[%d] -> NULL\n", i);
    printf("\n");

    for (i = 0; envp[i] != NULL; ++i)
        {
        printf("envp[%d] -> \"%s\"\n", i, envp[i]);
        }
    printf("envp[%d] -> NULL\n", i);
}
```

Listing 9-13. *The SHOW2.C program.*

Character Classification and Transformation

You often need to be able to classify individual characters of a string (such as uppercase versus lowercase) and then transform them (such as converting uppercase to lowercase). QuickC includes a standard C header file called ctype.h, which defines many classifying routines for characters (Table 9-4) and transforming them from one classification to another (Table 9-5). (Use the Include option on the View menu to examine it.) To access ctype.h, merely an *#include* directive to include it at the head of your program.

The routines in ctype.h are actually macros rather than functions. We'll describe macros in detail in Chapter 12. In the meantime, you can use these routines because they work like function calls.

Table 9-4. The Character-Classification Routines in ctype.h

Routine	Description
isalnum()	Tests for an alphanumeric character ('A' through 'Z', 'a' through 'z', and '0' through '9')
isalpha()	Tests for a letter ('A' through 'Z' and 'a' through 'z')
isascii()	Tests for an ASCII character (0x00 through 0x7F)
iscntrl()	Tests for a control character (less than 0x20 or equal to 0x7F)
isdigit()	Tests for a digit ('0' through '9')
isgraph()	Tests for printable character (inverse of *iscntrl()* but excludes space)
islower()	Tests for lowercase letter ('a' through 'z')
isprint()	Tests for printable character (inverse of *iscntrl()*)
ispunct()	Tests for punctuation character
iswhite()	Tests for white space ('\t', '\n', '\f', and ' ')
isupper()	Tests for uppercase letter ('A' through 'Z')
isxdigit()	Tests for a hexadecimal digit ('A' through 'F', 'a' through 'f', '0' through '9')

Table 9-5. The Character-Transformation Routines in ctype.h

Routine	Description
toascii()	Converts a non-ASCII character to an ASCII character (clears all but the low-order seven bits)
toupper()	Converts a lowercase character to an uppercase character
tolower()	Converts an uppercase character to a lowercase character

The Character-Classification Routines

Each of the character-classification routines in Table 9-4 takes a single argument—the character to classify—and returns a 1 for true or a 0 for false.

The WHATCHAR.C program (Listing 9-14 on the following page) prints all possible classifications for each character in a line of entered text. The program limits the line of text to 20 characters so that the output doesn't scroll off the screen.

The Character-Transformation Routines

The include file ctype.h also defines routines to transform characters. Each of the routines in Table 9-5 takes a single argument, the character to transform, and returns the transformed character, as in the following example:

```
ch = toupper('a');
```

Here *toupper()* is given a lowercase *'a'*. Because *'a'* is lowercase, *toupper()* transforms it to an uppercase *'A'* and assigns that value to the variable *ch*.

PART III: INTERMEDIATE C TOPICS

The INVERT.C program (Listing 9-15) uses both the character-classification and transformation routines to reverse a line of entered text. That is, it prints the line backward and inverts the case of each character.

```
/* whatchar.c -- demonstrates the character-classification */
/*               routines in ctype.h                        */

#include <stdio.h>        /* for NULL and BUFSIZ */
#include <ctype.h>        /* for iscntrl(), et al */
#define MAXL 20

main()
{
    char buf[BUFSIZ];
    int i;

    printf("Enter a line of text (20 chars max):\n");
    if (gets(buf) == NULL)
        exit(1);

    for (i = 0; i < MAXL; ++i)
        {
        if (buf[i] == '\0')
            break;
        printf("'%c' ->", buf[i]);
        if (isalpha(buf[i]))   printf(" isalpha");
        if (isascii(buf[i]))   printf(" isascii");
        if (iscntrl(buf[i]))   printf(" iscntrl");
        if (isgraph(buf[i]))   printf(" isgraph");
        if (isprint(buf[i]))   printf(" isprint");
        if (isdigit(buf[i]))   printf(" isdigit");
        if (isupper(buf[i]))   printf(" isupper");
        if (islower(buf[i]))   printf(" islower");
        if (ispunct(buf[i]))   printf(" ispunct");
        if (isspace(buf[i]))   printf(" isspace");
        if (isalnum(buf[i]))   printf(" isalnum");
        if (isxdigit(buf[i]))  printf(" isxdigit");
        printf("\n");
        }
}
```

Listing 9-14. *The WHATCHAR.C program.*

```
/* invert.c -- combines character classification */
/*              and transformation to invert text */

#include <stdio.h>        /* for NULL and BUFSIZ */
#include <ctype.h>        /* for toupper, et al  */

main()
{
    char buf[BUFSIZ];
    int i;

    printf("Enter a line of text and I will invert it.\n");

    if (gets(buf) == NULL)
        exit(1);
    /* Print the string backward */
    for (i = (strlen(buf) - 1); i >= 0; --i)
        {
        if (isupper(buf[i]))               /* upper to lower */
            putchar(tolower(buf[i]));
        else if (islower(buf[i]))          /* lower to upper */
            putchar(toupper(buf[i]));
        else
            putchar(buf[i]);
        }
    putchar('\n');
}
```

Listing 9-15. *The INVERT.C program.*

Managing Files

The QuickC library functions that handle file input and output are arranged in three categories, or levels, as illustrated in Figure 10-1 on the following page. At the top level are the buffered (stream I/O) routines; below those are the unbuffered (raw I/O) routines; and at the bottom are the direct BIOS interfaces. The lowest-level routines are not a part of portable C because they access PC-specific internal routines. The higher-level routines, however, are common to all C compilers. We will not cover the low-level BIOS routines in this book.

The top-level file I/O routines are called "buffered stream" routines because they read and write large blocks of information (buffering) and then pass a continuous series (stream) of bytes to your program.

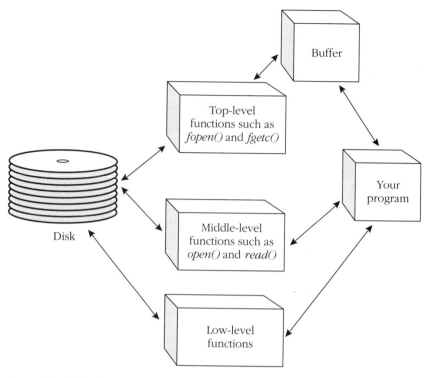

Figure 10-1. *The three levels of file I/O.*

The middle-level routines are termed "unbuffered" because they let your program access files directly. Reads and writes do not pass through an intermediate buffer; they pass directly between the operating system and your program. Middle-level routines can execute faster than the top-level routines, but they are more complex to use.

Both top-level and middle-level file routines have two modes—text and binary. Text mode is used with text files, or files that contain ASCII text (which is readable by persons). Binary mode is used with files that contain binary information, such as executable programs. In text mode, Ctrl-Z (a byte containing the value 0x1A) marks the end of a file. In binary mode, Ctrl-Z can be legally a part of the file; the operating system keeps track of file length.

Top-Level (Buffered) File I/O

All buffered file I/O functions require that you begin your program with *#include <stdio.h>*. That header file contains the definition for *FILE*, the data type that you use to manipulate files. The type *FILE* is used as shown on the following page.

```
#include <stdio.h>  /* for definition of FILE */
    ⋮
FILE *fp;
```

Remember, always use *#include <stdio.h>* for the definition of the type *FILE*. Then declare a file pointer to point to the data type *FILE*.

Opening Files with *fopen()*

Before you can access a file for reading or writing or both, you must first open that file. For buffered I/O routines (those that use a "file pointer"), open the file with the *fopen()* function, as follows:

```
fp = fopen(filename, activity);
```

                                     — Open to read, write, or both
                                     — Name of file to open

The *fopen()* function requires two arguments: the name of the file to open (a string or the address of a string) and an activity (also a string) as listed in Table 10-1. The activity determines whether the file is open for reading, writing, or appending. (In this case, "read" means to take information sequentially from a file, "write" means to put information sequentially into a file, and "append" means to add information to the end of a file.)

Table 10-1. Possible Modes (Activities) for *fopen()*

Mode	Description
"r"	Open for reading only. The file must already exist.
"w"	Open for writing only. Creates the file if it does not exist.
"a"	Open for appending (write-only, starting at the end of a file). Creates the file if it does not exist.
"r+"	Open for both reading and writing. The file must already exist.
"w+"	Open for both reading and writing. Creates the file if it does not exist.
"a+"	Open for both reading and writing, starting at the end of the file. Creates the file if it does not exist.

The *fopen()* function returns a value of type *FILE* *. In our example we assigned this value to file pointer *fp*, which we will use to access and manipulate the file. If *fopen()* fails, it returns *NULL*. Therefore, the complete call to *fopen()*, including error handling, is as follows:

```
fp = fopen("test.c", "r");
if (fp == NULL)
    {
    /* Handle error here */
    }
```

This opens the TEST.C file for reading (activity *"r"*). After the file pointer returned by *fopen()* is assigned to *fp*, we test *fp* to see if it is *NULL*. We test for an error here because it is possible, for example, that the file TEST.C does not exist.

Each open file requires its own file pointer. The following two open files, for example, require two separate file pointers:

```
#include <stdio.h>
   ⋮
FILE *fp_in, *fp_out;
   ⋮
fp_in = fopen("test.txt", "r");
fp_out = fopen("test.bak", "w");
```

In this example, *fp_in* is the file pointer for the file opened for reading (activity *"r"*), and *fp_out* is the file pointer for the file opened for writing (activity *"w"*).

File Access in BASIC and C

If you're used to BASIC file handling, you'll find that QuickC offers fewer "built-in" conveniences but ultimately provides more power and flexibility. In BASIC, you might open a random access file with the following statement, which specifies the file identification number and record length:

```
OPEN "C:\ACCT\TRANS" FOR RANDOM AS #1 LEN = 256
```

Before you can use the file, you have to use FIELD statements to associate whatever numeric or string variables you are going to use with the corresponding data fields in the file record. Because most versions of BASIC don't have a data type similar to the C *struct*, you have to manipulate numerous separate variables to move data to and from the file. The built-in random access support does allow you to get a record by its record number directly using the GET statement, however.

C has a different approach: A file can contain any valid C data type, such as a *struct*, which already has its fields defined, so you don't have to set up file data fields. On the other hand, file manipulation methods, such as random access, are not built into the C language per se. You can achieve random access, however, by converting a record number to an offset and then using the library function *fseek()* to position C's file pointer to the correct record. You can also use the *fgetpos()* and *fsetpos()* functions to manipulate the file pointer.

Also, because C uses function calls rather than BASIC's procedural commands to manipulate files, you can quickly check for errors by putting the function call in an *if* statement.

Reading Characters with *fgetc()*

There's more to reading a file than merely opening the file to read. To see what we mean, examine the STRINGS.C program (Listing 10-1), which reads a file one character at a time and looks for strings of five or more printable characters. The program takes a command-line argument, so before you run it, you must create the argument using the Run / Debug dialog box from the Options menu. In the Command Line box, type *c:\qc25\bin\qc.exe* (or the name of any existing file). Figure 10-2 on the following page shows the screen after you type the command.

```c
/* strings.c -- opens a file and searches it for */
/*              possible strings                  */

#include <stdio.h>        /* for FILE, BUFSIZ & EOF */
#include <ctype.h>        /* for isprint()          */

main(int argc, char *argv[])
{
    FILE *fp;
    char buf[BUFSIZ];
    int  ch, count;

    if (argc != 2)
        {
        fprintf(stderr, "Usage: strings file\n");
        exit(1);
        }
    if ((fp = fopen(argv[1], "rb")) == NULL)
        {
        fprintf(stderr, "Can't open %s\n", argv[1]);
        exit(1);
        }

    count = 0;
    while ((ch = fgetc(fp)) != EOF)
        {
        if (! isprint(ch) !! count >= (BUFSIZ - 1))
            {
            if (count > 5)
                {
                buf[count] = 0;
                puts(buf);
                }
            count = 0;
            continue;
            }
        buf[count++] = ch;
        }
}
```

Listing 10-1. *The STRINGS.C program.*

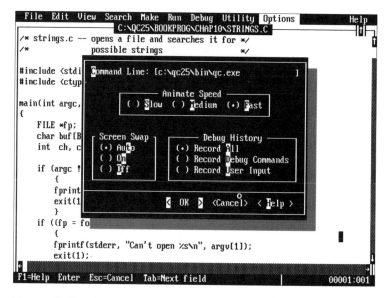

Figure 10-2. *The Run / Debug dialog box from the Options menu lets you enter a command line.*

When we run STRINGS.C on a large file such as QC.EXE, the program prints many screens of possible strings. For convenience, you might want to add a "paging" feature to the program.

STRINGS.C uses the *fgetc()* function, a file-oriented version of the *getchar()* routine we've used before. After it is passed a single argument (a file pointer), the function returns the next character read from the file pointed to. Assigning that character to a variable of type *int* lets us detect *EOF* (End Of File) easily.

```
int ch;

if ((ch = fgetc(fp)) == EOF)
    {
    /* Handle end of file here */
    }
```

Notice that STRINGS.C calls *fopen()* with the activity argument *"rb"*. This is a PC-specific extension of the normal "open for reading" argument. The *b* tells *fopen()* to open the file in binary mode but to do no character translation for us—that is, to give *fgetc()* every byte from the file as is. If we did not specify the *b*, *fopen()* would have opened the file in text mode. Had we used text mode, however, our program would not have read all of QC.EXE because the Ctrl-Z character, which is a legal byte in binary files, would have marked the end of the file. Table 10-2 shows the difference between these two modes.

Table 10-2. Text vs Binary Modes for *fopen()*

"t"	text mode	Translates carriage return/linefeed combinations into single linefeeds on input and makes the reverse translation on output. Ctrl-Z marks the end of the file.
"b"	binary mode	Suppresses the above translations. The operating system keeps track of the file's length.

Also notice that STRINGS.C ends without explicitly closing the file. C, like BASIC, closes all open files when you exit the program. This is true whether you exit *main()* with a *return* or terminate from within another function with an *exit()*.

Closing Files with *fclose()*

Although MS-DOS lets you have as many as 20 files open simultaneously, you might want to close each open file before you open another one. Closing a file writes everything to disk, updates the directory entry for that file, and frees a file pointer.

When you open files with *fopen()*, you can close them with *fclose()*, as follows:

```
if (fclose(fp) == EOF)
    {
    /* Unable to close file */
    }
/* fp may be reused here */
```

If *fclose()* cannot close a file (because the floppy disk containing that file was removed, for example), it returns *EOF*.

Line I/O with *fgets()* and *fputs()*

The standard C Library contains a pair of file-oriented routines called *fgets()* ("file get string") and *fputs()* ("file put string"). They are similar to the *gets()* and *puts()* pair we discussed in the last chapter: *fgets()* reads lines of text from files and *fputs()* writes lines of text to files. Use them as follows:

```
#include <stdio.h>
#define SIZE 512
   ⋮
FILE *fp_in, *fp_out;
char buf[SIZE];
   ⋮
/* Open fp_in for reading and fp_out for writing */
   ⋮
if (fgets(buf, SIZE, fp_in) == NULL)
    {
    /* Error reading or EOF */
    }
/* A line of text is now in buf */
   ⋮
```

(continued)

295

continued

```
if (fputs(buf, fp_out) == EOF)
    {
    /* Error writing */
    }
```

The *fgets()* function takes three arguments: the address of a *char* buffer, the maximum number of characters to read into that buffer, and a file pointer to a file opened for reading. In the example, *fgets()* reads a maximum of *SIZE* characters (up to and including the first newline character) and appends a terminating '\0' to the characters to form a string. The *fputs()* function requires two arguments: the address of a zero-terminated string (in *buf*) and a file pointer to a file opened for writing. In the example, *fputs()* writes the string in *buf* to *fp_out*—including any newline in that string. Note as well that *fputs()* does not add any newlines.

The *fputs()* and *fgets()* functions differ from their counterparts *puts()* and *gets()*. Each handles the newline character in a different way, as follows:

gets(buf) Reads characters from keyboard and places them into *buf*. Replaces the trailing newline character ('\n') with '\0'.

fgets(buf, len, fp) Reads a maximum of *len* characters from a file opened for reading. Places *len* or fewer characters (up to and including a newline) into *buf*. Retains the newline character and adds a terminating '\0'.

puts(buf) Prints the string in *buf* to the screen and adds a newline character to the output on the screen.

fputs(buf, fp) Prints (writes) the string in *buf* to the file (opened for writing) pointed to by the file pointer *fp*. Does not add a newline character to the output.

The CCOPY.C program (Listing 10-2) reads one file and writes to a second. The "C" preceding "COPY" (in the program name) signals that this version of COPY "crunches" its input—eliminating all empty lines, leading tabs, and spaces. You could use this program to prepare files before sending them over a slow modem.

```
/* ccopy.c -- copies a file, cutting blank lines and */
/*            leading space from lines of copy        */

#include <stdio.h>        /* for FILE, BUFSIZ, NULL */
#include <ctype.h>        /* for iswhite()           */

main(int argc, char *argv[])
{
    FILE *fp_in, *fp_out;
    char buf[BUFSIZ];
    char *cp;
```

Listing 10-2. *The CCOPY.C program.*   *(continued)*

Listing 10-2. *continued*

```
    if (argc != 3)
        {
        printf("Usage: ccopy infile outfile\n");
        exit(1);
        }
    if ((fp_in = fopen(argv[1], "r")) == NULL)
        {
        printf("Can't open %s for reading.\n", argv[1]);
        exit(1);
        }
    if ((fp_out = fopen(argv[2], "w")) == NULL)
        {
        printf("Can't open %s for writing.\n", argv[2]);
        exit(1);
        }

    printf("Copying and Crunching: %s->%s ...", argv[1], argv[2]);

    while (fgets(buf, BUFSIZ, fp_in) != NULL)
        {
        cp = buf;
        if (*cp == '\n')      /* blank line */
            continue;
        while (isspace(*cp))
            {
            ++cp;
            }
        if (*cp == '\0')      /* empty line */
            continue;
        if (fputs(cp, fp_out) == EOF)
            {
            printf("\nError writing %s.\n", argv[2]);
            exit(1);
            }
        }
    printf("Done\n");
}
```

To run this program you need to set its command line from the Run / Debug dialog box. The Command Line text box requires two filenames as arguments—first, the file to read, and second, the file to write to. For example, you might enter the filenames *strings.c temp*. The first name is the existing text file to be read. (Note that the *fopen()* in CCOPY.C uses *"r"* for text mode.) The second name is the new file that will be created (activity *"w"*).

Within a loop, *fgets()* reads a line of text from the first file, the program crunches that line, and *fputs()* writes the condensed line to the second file. After you run CCOPY.C, choose DOS Shell from the File menu and look at the newly created file using the TYPE command and Ctrl-S.

Error Detection with *feof()* and *ferror()*

Using *fgets()* has a drawback—it returns *NULL* both for *EOF* (which you expect) and for read errors (which you don't expect). However, you can differentiate between the two by using *feof()* and *ferror()*.

The *feof()* function tests a file opened for reading and associated with a file pointer to see if the end of that file has been reached. It returns true (nonzero) if the pointer is at the end of the file; it returns zero if the pointer is not at the end of the file. The *ferror()* function returns true if any error occurs—including reaching the end of file. The following example shows how to use *feof()* and *ferror()* together to differentiate between the two conditions:

```
if (feof(fp_in))
    {
    /* Reached end of file while reading */
    }
else if (ferror(fp_in))
    {
    /* Some read error has occurred */
    }
```

EOF is meaningful only when reading; use *ferror()* alone when writing to a file:

```
if (ferror(fp_out))
    {
    /* Some write error has occurred */
    }
```

Always include error-checking routines in your programs to protect yourself from careless users. Users sometimes remove floppy disks while the drive light is on or try writing to disks that are write-protected. Error detection lets you either take corrective action or notify users of their mistakes.

Block I/O with *fread()* and *fwrite()*

So far we've treated files as lines of text. However, you will often want to read and write files in specific blocks whose size is measured in bytes. (Executable program files and data files, for example, generally contain no meaningful lines of text.) To do this, the standard C Library provides a pair of routines called *fread()* and *fwrite()*. Their forms are nearly identical:

```
fread(buffer, size, count, fp_in);
```
A file pointer
How many *size* items
How many bytes per item
Address of (*size* * *count*) bytes buffer

```
fwrite(buffer, size, count, fp_out);
```
— A file pointer
— How many *size* items
— How many bytes per item
— Address of (*size* ∗ *count*) bytes buffer

Both routines require that you specify *#include <stdio.h>* to define *FILE* for the file pointer and to define the new type *size_t* for the variables *size* and *count*. QuickC defines the type *size_t* in the stdio.h header file as an *unsigned long*. Because it might be defined differently with other compilers, you should use *size_t* for portability.

Both functions return the number of bytes actually read or written. When that number is less than *size* times *count*, an error has occurred. In the case of *fread()*, however, that error can also indicate that you've reached the end of the file. Therefore, you need to use *feof()* to distinguish *EOF* file from other errors.

The UPPITY.C program (Listing 10-3) shows one way to use *fread()* and *fwrite()*. It reads an entire file into memory (using *malloc()* to obtain that memory), converts it to uppercase, and then writes the entire file to a new file having the .UP extension.

```c
/* uppity.c -- makes an uppercase copy of a file using */
/*             fread() and fwrite()                     */

#include <string.h>         /* for strrchr() */
#include <stdio.h>          /* for NULL      */
#include <malloc.h>         /* for malloc()  */
#include <ctype.h>          /* for isupper() */

#define HUNK 512

main(int argc, char *argv[])
{
    char *cp, newname[128], *np;
    FILE *fp;
    int  hunks = 0, bytes = 0, totbytes = 0;
    int  i;

    if (argc != 2)
        {
        printf("Usage: uppity file\n");
        exit(1);
        }
```

Listing 10-3. *The UPPITY.C program.*   *(continued)*

Listing 10-3. *continued*

```
    if ((fp = fopen(argv[1], "rb")) == NULL)
        {
        printf("\"%s\": Can't open.\n", argv[1]);
        exit(1);
        }
    if ((cp = malloc(HUNK)) == NULL)
        {
        printf("Malloc failed.\n");
        exit(1);
        }

    while ((bytes = fread(cp + (HUNK * hunks), 1, HUNK, fp)) == HUNK)
        {
        totbytes += bytes;
        ++hunks;
        if ((cp = realloc(cp, HUNK + (HUNK * hunks))) == NULL)
            {
            printf("Realloc failed.\n");
            exit(1);
            }
        }
    if (bytes < 0)
        {
        printf("\"%s\": Error reading.\n", argv[1]);
        exit(1);
        }
    totbytes += bytes;

    for (i = 0; i < totbytes; ++i)
        if (islower(cp[i]))
            cp[i] = toupper(cp[i]);

    (void)fclose(fp);

    if ((np = strrchr(argv[1], '.')) != NULL)
        *np = '\0';
    strcpy(newname, argv[1]);
    strcat(newname, ".up");
    if ((fp = fopen(newname, "wb")) == NULL)
        {
        printf("\"%s\": Can't open.\n", argv[1]);
        exit(1);
        }

    if (fwrite(cp, 1, totbytes, fp) != totbytes)
        {
        printf("\"%s\": Error writing.\n", argv[1]);
        exit(1);
        }
}
```

UPPITY.C continually reallocates memory for each *HUNK* (512 bytes) of the file read in. A more direct approach would find the size of the file and then read in that many bytes with a single *fread()*. You can do this with the *stat()* function. Unfortunately, to use *stat()* you must understand "structures," and we won't be describing those until the next chapter. Keep in mind that you might want to modify UPPITY.C when you learn how to use structures.

Predeclared File Pointers

When you run any QuickC program, five file pointers are always provided for five preopened files. Those file pointers are *stdin*, *stdout*, *stderr*, *stdaux*, and *stdprn*. (See Table 10-3.) Because these preopened file pointers are defined in stdio.h, you must include that header file if you want to use them.

Table 10-3. QuickC's Preopened File Pointers

stdin	The standard input. Your keyboard viewed as a file. Also, input to your program provided by redirection using <*file* from the MS-DOS command line.
stdout	The standard output. Your screen viewed as a file. Also, output to disk files provided by redirection using >*file* from the MS-DOS command line.
stderr	The standard error output. Always your screen. This file pointer is unaffected by redirection from the MS-DOS command line.
stdaux	The standard auxiliary. Usually your serial port or COM1. This file pointer provides easy access to your modem.
stdprn	The standard printer output. Usually your parallel port or PRN. This file pointer provides an easy way to generate hard copy from within a QuickC program.

To demonstrate the use of these file pointers, we revised CCOPY.C (the "crunch-and-copy program") to produce the CCOPY2.C program (Listing 10-4). This revision checks for the presence of a second (output) filename. If it is missing, *fputs()* directs the output to *stdout* (your screen).

```
/* ccopy2.c -- copies a file, cutting blank lines and   */
/*              leading space from lines of copy          */

/*              Modified to demonstrate stdout and stderr */

#include <stdio.h>        /* for FILE, BUFSIZ, NULL */
#include <ctype.h>        /* for iswhite()          */

main(int argc, char *argv[])
{
    FILE *fp_in, *fp_out;
    char buf[BUFSIZ];
```

Listing 10-4. *The CCOPY2.C program.*   (continued)

301

Listing 10-4. *continued*

```
    char *cp;

    if (argc < 2)
        {
        fprintf(stderr, "Usage: ccopy2 infile {outfile}\n");
        exit(1);
        }
    if ((fp_in = fopen(argv[1], "r")) == NULL)
        {
        fprintf(stderr, "\"%s\": Can't open.\n", argv[1]);
        exit(1);
        }
    if (argc == 3)
        {
        if ((fp_out = fopen(argv[2], "w")) == NULL)
            {
            fprintf(stderr, "\"%s\": Can't open.\n", argv[2]);
            exit(1);
            }
        }
    else
        fp_out = stdout;

    while (fgets(buf, BUFSIZ, fp_in) != NULL)
        {
        cp = buf;
        if (*cp == '\n')     /* blank line */
            continue;
        while (isspace(*cp))
            {
            ++cp;
            }
        if (*cp == '\0')     /* empty line */
            continue;
        if (fputs(cp, fp_out) == EOF)
            {
            fprintf(stderr, "Error writing.\n");
            exit(1);
            }
        }
    if (! feof(fp_in))       /* error reading? */
        {
        fprintf(stderr, "\"%s\": Error reading.\n", argv[1]);
        exit(1);
        }
}
```

Formatted File I/O with *fprintf()* and *fscanf()*

CCOPY2.C doesn't print error messages with *printf()*; instead, it uses the file-oriented version of *printf()*, called *fprintf()*, to send error messages to *stderr*, which is always your screen. This ensures that you will always see error messages, even when the program is printing its output to a file.

C's file-oriented counterpart to *scanf()* is called *fscanf()*. The *fprintf()* and *fscanf()* functions are identical to their nonfile brethren, with one exception: Each requires a file pointer as its first argument, as follows:

```
fprintf(fp_out, control, args ...);
```
Same as *printf()*
A file pointer

```
fscanf(fp_in, control, addresses ...);
```
Same as *scanf()*
A file pointer

Random Access with *fseek()*

Sophisticated applications, such as databases, must be able to move around in files (recall that files are continuous *streams* of bytes) reading and writing selected portions. The *fseek()* function lets a program access any file element by determining the position of the next read or write in a file, as follows:

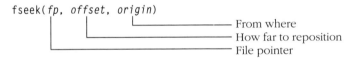

```
fseek(fp, offset, origin)
```
From where
How far to reposition
File pointer

The *offset*, in bytes, tells *fseek()* how far to move in the file; it must be a value of type *long*. The *origin* determines the point from which to measure *offset*; it can be any one of three values—the beginning of, current position in, or end of the file. Those values, which are defined in stdio.h appear in Table 10-4.

If *fseek()* cannot reposition in a file, it returns the value −1L. (The *L* is needed because *fseek()* returns the type *long*.) If *fseek()* is successful, it returns the new position in the file, measured in bytes from the beginning of the file.

Table 10-4. *origin* Positions for *fseek()*

SEEK_SET	From the beginning of the file; *offset* must always be positive.
SEEK_CUR	Relative to the current position. A negative *offset* moves toward the beginning of the file; a positive *offset* moves toward the end of the file. (You can move beyond the end of the file, thus enlarging the file.)
SEEK_END	From the end of the file; *offset* can be positive or negative. Movement is the same as SEEK_CUR, but relative to the end of the file.

The PHONE.C program (Listing 10-5) is a miniature telephone number database. When run without command-line arguments, the program asks you for numbers to add to its database file. Run with a command-line argument, it searches for an entry that matches the argument and prints the data it finds. This program assumes that you have a directory named \TMP.

```c
/* phone.c -- a telephone number mini-database that */
/*             demonstrates fseek()                  */

#include <stdio.h>            /* for FILE, BUFSIZ, NULL */

#define MAXL (128)
char Name[MAXL];
char Number[MAXL];
char File[] = "C:\\TMP\\PHONE.DB";
int  Count;
FILE *Fp;
int  Distance = (MAXL * MAXL);
void Find(char *str), Ask(void), Make(void);

main(int argc, char *argv[])
{
    if (argc == 1)
        Ask();
    else
        Find(argv[1]);

    return (0);
}

void Find(char *str)
{
    int i;

    if ((Fp = fopen(File, "r")) == NULL)
        {
        fprintf(stderr, "\"%s\": Can't read.\n", File);
        exit (1);
        }
    if (fread(&Count, sizeof(int), 1, Fp) != 1)
        {
        fprintf(stderr,"\"%s\": Error reading.\n", File);
        exit (1);
        }
    for (i = 0; i < Count; i++)
        {
        fread(Name, 1, MAXL, Fp);
        fread(Number, 1, MAXL, Fp);
```

Listing 10-5. *The PHONE.C program.*   *(continued)*

Listing 10-5. *continued*

```
        if (ferror(Fp))
            {
            fprintf(stderr, "\"%s\": Error reading.\n", File);
            exit (1);
            }
        if (strcmp(str, Name) == 0)
            {
            printf("Name: %s\n", Name);
            printf("Number: %s\n", Number);
            return;
            }
        }
    fprintf(stderr, "\"%s\": Not in database.\n", str);
    return;
}

void Ask(void)
{
    if ((Fp = fopen(File, "rb+")) == NULL)
        Make();
    else if (fread(&Count, sizeof(int), 1, Fp) != 1)
        {
        fprintf(stderr, "\"%s\": Error reading.\n", File);
        exit (1);
        }
    printf("Name: ");
    if (gets(Name) == NULL !! *Name == '\0')
        return;
    printf("Number: ");
    if (gets(Number) == NULL !! *Number == '\0')
        return;
    if (fseek(Fp, (long)(Distance * Count), SEEK_CUR) != 0)
        {
        fprintf(stderr, "\"%s\": Error seeking.\n", File);
        exit (1);
        }
    fwrite(Name, 1, MAXL, Fp);
    fwrite(Number, 1, MAXL, Fp);
    if (ferror(Fp))
        {
        fprintf(stderr, "\"%s\": Error writing.\n", File);
        exit (1);
        }
    if (fseek(Fp, 0L, SEEK_SET) != 0)
        {
        fprintf(stderr, "\"%s\": Error seeking.\n", File);
        exit (1);
        }
    ++Count;
```

(continued)

Listing 10-5. *continued*

```
    if (fwrite(&Count, sizeof(int), 1, Fp) != 1)
        {
        fprintf(stderr, "\"%s\": Error writing.\n", File);
        exit (1);
        }
    return;
}

void Make(void)
{
    if ((Fp = fopen(File, "wb+")) == NULL)
        {
        fprintf(stderr, "\"%s\": Can't create.\n", File);
        exit (1);
        }
    Count = 0;
    if (fwrite(&Count, sizeof(int), 1, Fp) != 1)
        {
        fprintf(stderr," \"%s\": Error creating.\n", File);
        exit (1);
        }
}
```

The PHONE.C program might seem more complex than it really is. We included many error-checking routines to prevent the user from making careless errors. Note, for example, that the program checks the first character of each input line for a null byte (*Name* == '\0'). An initial null byte indicates that the user pressed Enter without typing any information.

Moving with *rewind()*

Moving to the beginning of a file (rewinding) is so common in C programs that the standard C Library includes a special function to perform that task. The *rewind()* function takes a single argument—a file pointer for the opened file—and moves the position of the next read or write to the beginning of the file. A call to *rewind()*,

```
rewind(fp);
```

returns no value and therefore gives no indication of failure. In other respects, however, the above call to *rewind()* is identical to the following call to *fseek()* :

```
fseek(fp, 0L, SEEK_SET)
```
                   └──────── Move from beginning of file
          └──────────────── Offset must be a *long*

Determining Position in a File with *ftell()*

Moving through a file with *fseek()* often requires that you first know your current position in the file. When you pass a file pointer to the *ftell()* function, it returns your present position in that file. That position, a *long* value, is the measure in bytes from the beginning of the file. Consider the following code fragment.

```
if ((pos = ftell(fp)) == -1L)
    {
    /* Can't find position */
    }
/* Current position is pos bytes from beginning */
```

Used in that way, *ftell()* is identical to the following *fseek()* call:

```
if ((pos = fseek(fp, 0L, SEEK_CUR)) == -1L)
    {
    /* Can't find position */
    }
/* Current position is pos bytes from beginning */
```

As you progress in learning C, you will need to use functions that we have not discussed. For a complete summary of top-level (stream) I/O routines, refer to the section entitled "Input and Output Routines" in Appendix B of *C for Yourself*.

Middle-Level (Unbuffered) File I/O

Most of the top-level (buffered) stream file input/output functions have middle-level, unbuffered counterparts that permit direct access to disk files. Because they do not buffer data, they are frequently faster and more efficient, often allowing disk files to be read directly into a program's memory. (The top-level *fread()* function, for example, actually calls the middle-level *read()* to do its work.)

One disadvantage of the unbuffered routines is that they offer only the most basic of services. Although these routines offer a *read()* and a *write()*, there are no corresponding middle-level versions of *fgets()*, *fputs()*, *fscanf()*, *fprintf()*, or *fgetc()*. Another disadvantage is that you cannot use unbuffered functions in the same program that uses calls to top-level functions. If you mix them, as shown in Figure 10-3 on the following page, you risk losing synchronization of data. That is, if you first call *fgetc()* and then call *read()*, the *read()* will not begin with the next byte following the *fgetc()*. The *fgetc()* reads and buffers 512 bytes from the file, and then it returns the first one of those buffered bytes. The call to *read()*, however, reads a single byte directly from the disk.

Opening a File with *open()*

Unlike *fopen()*, *open()* returns its identifying value as a simple integer. This value, called a "file descriptor," is later passed to all other middle-level routines. To use the *open()* function, you must specify *#include <fcntl.h>* (not *<stdio.h>*, as you would with *fopen()*).

```
#include <fcntl.h>
    ⋮
int fd;─────────────────────────────── The file descriptor
    ⋮
if ((fd = open(filename, oflag)) < 0)
    {
    /* Handle error here */
    }
```

512-byte buffer

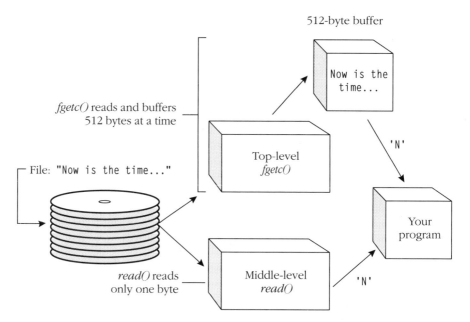

fgetc() reads and buffers 512 bytes at a time

File: "Now is the time..."

Top-level *fgetc()*

'N'

Your program

read() reads only one byte

Middle-level *read()*

'N'

Figure 10-3. *Data synchronization is lost when you mix buffered with unbuffered file I/O routines.*

The file descriptor, *fd*, is type *int*. The first argument, *filename*, is a string or the address of a string, and the second, *oflag*, is an *int* that supplies *open()* with a file activity (read, write, append, create) and a file mode (text or binary). The values for *oflag* are defined in fcntl.h, and their meanings are listed in Table 10-5. Note that you can combine *oflag* values by using the bitwise OR operator (¦). For example, the following declaration opens the file TEST.EXE for reading in binary mode:

```
fd = open("TEST.EXE", O_BINARY ¦ O_RDONLY)
```

If it fails, *open()* returns a negative integer value. Thus, all file descriptor values are greater than or equal to zero.

Of the possible values for *oflag*, you must use one of the first three activities in Table 10-5, (*O_RDONLY, O_RDWR,* or *O_WRONLY*); all others in the table are optional and can be added using bitwise OR. Unless specified otherwise, the mode is set for a text file; reads and writes begin at the start of the file; the file is not created if it doesn't exist; and the file is not truncated.

Table 10-5.   Values for *oflag* in fcntl.h

Value	Description
O_RDONLY	Accesses as read-only
O_RDWR	Accesses as read-write
O_WRONLY	Accesses as write-only
O_BINARY	Sets mode for a binary file
O_TEXT	Sets mode for a text file
O_APPEND	Opens for appending
O_CREAT	Creates file if it doesn't exist
O_EXEL	Returns error if file already exists
O_TRUNC	Truncates existing file to zero length

If you combine the *O_CREAT* value with *O_RDWR* or *O_WRONLY* to create a file, *open()* requires a third argument called *pmode* ("permissions" mode). Use the argument as follows:

```
fd = open(filename, oflag, pmode);
                    |     |_____ The permissions of the newly created file
                    |_____ (O_RDWR or O_WRONLY ¦ O_CREAT)
```

The possible values for *pmode*, listed in Table 10-6, determine whether the created file will be a read-only file, a write-only file, or a readable and writable file. (You must combine the two defined *pmode* values with a bitwise OR operator to create a readable and writable file.) Because *pmode* values are defined in sys\stat.h, you must specify the following include files to create a file with *open()*:

```
#include <fcntl.h> ──────── For oflag values
#include <sys\types.h> ──── For stat.h
#include <sys\stat.h> ───── For pmode values
```

Note that *#include <sys\types.h>* must precede *#include <sys\stat.h>* because the first contains the definitions needed by the second.

Table 10-6.   Values for *pmode* in sys\stat.h

S_IWRITE	Creates a writable file
S_IREAD	Creates a readable file

With MS-DOS, you cannot create a file that is write-only. Because all files are always readable, you can omit the *S_IREAD* value for *pmode*. (If you do use the value, MS-DOS ignores it.)

The following example is a complete call to *open()*, including all the *#include* directives:

```
#include <fcntl.h>
#include <sys\types.h>
#include <sys\stat.h>

int fd;

fd = open("TEST.EXE", O_RDWR¦O_BINARY¦O_CREAT¦O_TRUNC, S_IREAD¦S_IWRITE);
```

This example opens a file named TEST.EXE in binary mode for reading and writing. It creates the file if it doesn't exist and truncates it if it does.

Closing a File with *close()*

Just as the *fclose()* function closes a file based on a file pointer, the unbuffered *close()* library function closes a file based on a file descriptor, as follows:

```
if (close(fd) != 0)
    {
    /* Handle error closing here */
    }
```

A successfully executed *close()* returns a zero value; any nonzero return value indicates an error.

When your program exits, QuickC closes all files opened with the middle-level *open()*. Because you can have only 20 files open at one time, you should close files inside your program. Using *close()* to close a file frees its file descriptor for reuse.

Writing to a File with *write()*

The *write()* function is used to write to files. It is simpler to use than the top-level *fwrite()* function because it requires only three arguments, as in the following:

```
write(fd_out, buf, bytes)
```
                                          └────── Number of bytes to write
                                     └────────── Location of bytes to be written
                         └────────────── File descriptor for a file opened for writing

The expression *buf* is the address in memory of the first byte that you want to write to the file. That address can be any address expression, but it is usually the address of an array. The final argument, *bytes*, represents the number of characters you want to write to the file.

The *write()* function normally returns the number of bytes written (the same value as *bytes*). If *write()* fails, however, it returns a smaller or negative number.

The SCRSAVE.C program (Listing 10-6) demonstrates one way to use *open()* and *write()*. It copies the contents of the text screen into a local buffer, which is then written to a disk file. (The program will not overwrite an existing file.) For this program to run successfully, you will need to turn off the Pointer Check option. Choose Make from the Options menu, and then choose Compiler Flags to check the current status of pointer checking.

```c
/* scrsave.c -- demonstrates write() by saving the */
/*              text screen to a file               */

#include <stdio.h>        /* for stderr            */
#include <fcntl.h>        /* for O_CREAT : O_BINARY */
#include <sys\types.h>    /* for stat.h            */
#include <sys\stat.h>     /* for S_IREAD : S_IWRITE */

#define SCRCHARS  (25 * 80)
int Buf[SCRCHARS];

main(int argc, char *argv[])
{
    int *cp, *ep, fname[16];
    int _far *sp;
    int fd_out, bytes;

    if (argc != 2)
        {
        fprintf(stderr, "Usage: scrsave file\n");
        exit(0);
        }
    if (strlen(argv[1]) > 8)
        {
        fprintf(stderr, "\"%s\": Filename too long.\n", argv[1]);
        exit(1);
        }
    strcpy(fname, argv[1]);
    strcat(fname, ".SCR");
    if (access(fname, 0) == 0)
        {
        fprintf(stderr, "\"%s\": Won't overwrite.\n", fname);
        exit(1);
        }
    if ((fd_out = open(fname, O_WRONLY : O_CREAT : O_BINARY,
                    S_IREAD : S_IWRITE)) < 0)
        {
        fprintf(stderr, "\"%s\": Can't create.\n", fname);
        exit(1);
        }
```

Listing 10-6. *The SCRSAVE.C program.* *(continued)*

Listing 10-6. *continued*

```
      /* Copy the screen into a near buffer */
      ep = &Buf[SCRCHARS - 1];
      cp = Buf;
      /* Use 0xB0000000 for monochrome */
      sp = (int _far *)(0xB8000000);
      for ( ; cp < ep; ++cp, ++sp)
          *cp = *sp;
      /* Write it */
      bytes = write(fd_out, Buf, SCRCHARS * 2);
      if (bytes != SCRCHARS * 2)
          {
          fprintf(stderr, "\"%s\": Error writing.\n", fname);
          exit(1);
          }
      return (0);
}
```

Note that we copy the screen rather than write it directly because *write()* expects a normal pointer, whereas accessing the screen requires a far pointer.

Reading a File with *read()*

Use the *read()* function to read from files. It is a simpler function to use than *fread()* because it takes only three arguments, as follows:

```
read(fd_in, buf, bytes)
```
Number of bytes to read
Destination of bytes read
File descriptor for a file opened for reading

In this example, *buf* is either an array or the address of allocated memory. Be sure *buf* is large enough to hold the number of bytes specified by the argument *bytes*, however, because the compiler does not check this for you.

If the call to *read()* is successful, it returns the same value as *bytes*. If it returns a smaller value, then that value represents the number of bytes left in the file. A 0 return value signifies the end of the file, and a –1 return value shows that a read error has occurred.

The SCRREST.C program (Listing 10-7) reads a file, copying as much as a screenful of what it reads to text-screen memory. It works with any file type, but reading files created with SCRSAVE.C (Listing 10-6) is its most useful application. Before you run the program, choose Run / Debug from the Options menu, and be sure the Screen Swap option is set to Auto. For this program to run successfully, you will also need to turn off the Pointer Check option. Choose Make from the Options menu, and then choose Compiler Flags to check the status of pointer checking.

```
/* scrrest.c -- demonstrates read() by restoring */
/*              text screen from any file        */

#include <stdio.h>       /* for stderr              */
#include <fcntl.h>       /* for O_RDONLY : O_BINARY */

#define SCRCHARS  (25 * 80)
int Buf[SCRCHARS];

main(int argc, char *argv[])
{
    int *cp, *ep;
    int _far *sp;
    int fd_in, bytes;

    if (argc != 2)
        {
        fprintf(stderr, "Usage: scrrest file.scr\n");
        exit(0);
        }
    if ((fd_in = open(argv[1], O_RDONLY : O_BINARY)) < 0)
        {
        fprintf(stderr, "\"%s\": Can't open to read.\n", argv[1]);
        exit(1);
        }
    /* Read it */
    bytes = read(fd_in, Buf, SCRCHARS * 2);
    if (bytes < 0)
        {
        fprintf(stderr, "\"%s\": Error reading.\n", argv[1]);
        exit(1);
        }
    if (bytes == 0)
        {
        fprintf(stderr, "\"%s\": Empty file.\n", argv[1]);
        exit(1);
        }
    /* Copy the buffer to screen memory */
    ep = &Buf[bytes / 2];
    cp = Buf;

    /* Use 0xB0000000 for monochrome */
    sp = (int _far *)(0xB8000000);
    for ( ; cp < ep; ++cp, ++sp)
        *sp = *cp;

    return (0);
}
```

Listing 10-7. *The SCRREST.C program.*

Positioning with *lseek()*

The unbuffered *lseek()* function lets a program position its next read or write to begin anywhere in a file. Almost identical to the buffered *fseek()*, *lseek()* takes a file descriptor rather than a file pointer as its first argument. Therefore, use the *lseek()* function as follows:

```
#include <io.h>      /* defines lseek() */
#include <stdio.h>   /* for origin, etc. */

long newpos, offset = 100L;
int  fd;

newpos = lseek(fd, offset, origin);
```

From where (current, beginning, or end)
Move this many bytes
In this file (file descriptor)
New position in file

In this example, *fd* is a file descriptor for a file previously opened with *open()*. The second argument, *offset*, is the number of bytes to move in the file and must be of the type *long*. If *offset* is negative, the current position moves toward the beginning of the file. The last argument, *origin*, can be one of the three possible definitions that specify where the move begins. These definitions are the same as those used by *fseek()*, which were mentioned in Table 10-4 on p. 303. Also, as with *fseek()*, you must specify *#include <stdio.h>* to access those definitions.

After a successful repositioning, *lseek()* returns the new position in the file. A return value of −1L indicates an error. (Note that *lseek()* returns the type *long*.)

The VIEW.C program (Listing 10-8) is a simple file-viewing program that illustrates how to use *lseek()* to move through a file. Pressing + moves you forward in the file, pressing − moves you backward, and pressing *q* or *Q* ends the program.

```
/* view.c -- demonstrates lseek() by displaying */
/*            a file and moving around in it      */

#include <fcntl.h>           /* for open()       */
#include <stdio.h>           /* for SEEK_CUR, etc. */

#define HUNK 512
#define MOVE 512L

void Print(char *buf, int cnt);

main(int argc, char *argv[])
```

Listing 10-8. *The VIEW.C program.*   *(continued)*

Listing 10-8. *continued*

```
{
    char ch, buf[HUNK];
    long position = 0L;
    int  bytes, eofflag = 0, fd_in;

    if (argc != 2)
        {
        fprintf(stderr, "Usage: view file\n");
        exit(0);
        }

    if ((fd_in = open(argv[1], O_RDONLY)) < 0)
        {
        fprintf(stderr, "\"%s\": Can't open.\n", argv[1]);
        exit(1);
        }

    for (;;)
        {
        bytes = read(fd_in, buf, HUNK);
        if (bytes == 0)
            {
            if (! eofflag)
                {
                fprintf(stderr, "\n<<at end of file>>\n");
                ++eofflag;
                }
            else
                exit(0);
            }
        else if (bytes < 0)
            {
            fprintf(stderr, "\"%s\": Error reading.\n", argv[1]);
            exit(1);
            }
        else
            {
            eofflag = 0;
            position = lseek(fd_in, 0L, SEEK_CUR);
            if (position == -1L)
                {
                fprintf(stderr, "\"%s\": Error seeking.\n", argv[1]);
                exit(1);
                }
            Print(buf, bytes);
            }
```

(continued)

Listing 10-8. *continued*

```
        do
            {
            ch = getch();
            if (ch == 'q' !! ch == 'Q')
                exit(0);
            } while (ch != '+' && ch != '-');

        if (ch == '-')
            {
            position = lseek(fd_in, -2 * MOVE, SEEK_CUR);
            if (position == -1L)
                {
                fprintf(stderr, "\"%s\": Error seeking.\n", argv[1]);
                exit(1);
                }
            }
        }
    return (0);
}

void Print(char *buf, int cnt)
{
    int i;

    for (i = 0; i < cnt; ++i, ++buf)
        {
        if (*buf < ' ' && *buf != '\n' && *buf != '\t')
            printf("^%c", *buf + '@');
        else
            putchar(*buf);
        }
}
```

Finding Current Position with *tell()*

Notice that VIEW.C finds the current position in the viewed file with the following:

```
position = lseek(fd_in, 0L, SEEK_CUR);
```

Because the need to know the current position is so common, the QuickC library provides the *tell()* function. Similar to the top-level *ftell()* routine, *tell()* takes a single argument, a file descriptor, and returns the current position in the file associated with that file descriptor. Its syntax is as follows:

```
position = tell(fd);
```

The *position* is a value of type *long*, measured in bytes from the beginning of the file. If *tell()* fails for any reason, it returns a value of −1L.

The File System

Not only do programs read and write to files, they often need to manage the file system as a whole. By the file system, we mean the MS-DOS directory hierarchy and the naming of directories and files. For example, your program might need to create or remove a directory or file, or relocate in the directory hierarchy (change the working directory), or create unique temporary filenames. In this section we discuss the file system and the C Library routines that let you manipulate it. We also warn you of possible pitfalls and present a few routines that let you handle errors gracefully.

Directories

MS-DOS does not permit you to use *fopen()* or *open()* to open a directory. You can, however, create and remove directories or establish any directory as your current working directory. The routines for handling directories are listed in Table 10-7. All of the routines require that you include the header file direct.h, which contains their declarations.

Table 10-7. The Directory-handling Library Functions

chdir(path)	Changes the current working directory to *path*. Returns 0 if successful.
mkdir(path)	Creates a new directory named *path*. Returns 0 if successful.
rmdir(path)	Removes the directory whose name is *path*. Returns 0 if successful.
getcwd(buf, n)	Places the full pathname of your current working directory into the *char* buffer *buf* of length *n*. Returns *NULL* if an error occurs.

The directory-handling functions *chdir()*, *mkdir()*, and *rmdir()* take a single argument: a string or the address of a string that specifies a full pathname (such as C:\TMP\JUNKDIR), or a directory name relative to the current working directory (such as JUNKDIR). All three functions return 0 if they are successful; otherwise, they return −1. Consider, for example, the following code fragment:

```
#include <direct.h>

if (chdir("C:\\TMP") != 0)
    {
    /* chdir failed, so exit */
    }
if (mkdir("JUNKDIR") != 0)
    {
    /* mkdir failed, so exit */
    }
if (rmdir("JUNKDIR") != 0)
    {
    /* rmdir failed, so exit */
    }
```

The *#include <direct.h>* directive provides definitions for the three routines that follow it. The *chdir()* function changes the current working directory to C:\TMP. (Recall that in C you must use a double backslash to produce a single backslash in a literal string.) Next, inside C:\TMP, the program uses *mkdir()* to create a new subdirectory called JUNKDIR. The final call to *rmdir()* removes that same subdirectory.

The last routine in Table 10-7, *getcwd()* ("get current working directory"), takes two arguments and returns the address of a string. You can call this function using one of two forms. In the following form:

```
#include <direct.h>
#include <stdio.h>    /* for NULL */

char buf[512];
if (getcwd(buf, 512) == NULL)
    {
    /* Couldn't get current working directory */
    }
```

the *getcwd()* function is passed the address of a *char* buffer, *buf*, into which it places the name of the current working directory. The length *512* is the number of bytes in the buffer. (Remember that the buffer must be large enough for both the name and a terminating '\0'.)

The second form for calling *getcwd()* is as follows:

```
#include <direct.h>
#include <stdio.h>    /* for NULL */

char *name;
if ((name = getcwd(NULL, 0)) == NULL)
    {
    /* Couldn't get current working directory */
    }
```

This form passes to *getcwd()* the special zero address *NULL* and a length of zero. This causes *getcwd()* to allocate enough space for the name of the current working directory (plus 1 for the terminating '\0'), to copy that name into the newly allocated space, and to return the address of that space. Both forms of *getcwd()* return *NULL* if the operation fails.

The DIRX.C program (Listing 10-9) demonstrates all four of the directory-handling subroutines. It first creates a subdirectory in the current directory, then relocates to that subdirectory and creates a sub-subdirectory. Finally, it returns to the original directory and attempts to remove the first subdirectory it created. It fails at this point because MS-DOS does not permit removal of a directory that is not empty. If you run the program again, it will fail immediately—it cannot execute the first *mkdir()* because a directory with the specified name already exists.

```
/* dirx.c -- directory examples */

#include <direct.h>
#include <stdio.h>

#define SUBDIR "SUBDIR"
#define SUBSUBDIR "SUBSUB"

void Err(char *what, char *msg);

main()
{
    char *current_dir;

    if ((current_dir = getcwd(NULL, 0)) == NULL)
        Err("getcwd()", "Can't get current directory.");

    if (mkdir(SUBDIR) != 0)
        Err(SUBDIR, "Can't make directory.");

    if (chdir(SUBDIR) != 0)
        Err( SUBDIR, "Can't cd into directory.");

    if (mkdir(SUBSUBDIR) != 0)
        Err(SUBSUBDIR, "Can't make directory.");

    if (chdir(current_dir) != 0)
        Err(SUBDIR, "Can't cd back to.");

    if (rmdir(SUBDIR) != 0)
        Err(SUBDIR, "Can't remove directory.");
}

void Err(char *what, char *msg)
{
    fprintf(stderr, "\"%s\": %s\n", what, msg);
    exit (1);
}
```

Listing 10-9. *The DIRX.C program.*

Manipulating Files by Name

Several standard C Library routines make it easy for you to remove and rename files and also to create unique filenames from within a program. These routines (listed in Table 10-8 on the following page) are useful in databases, compilers, games, and any other program that needs to manipulate files.

319

Table 10-8. Routines That Manipulate Files by Name

unlink(path)	Removes (erases) the file whose name is specified by path. Returns 0 if the call is successful.
remove(path)	Same as *unlink()*.
rename(old, new)	Renames the file *old*, giving it the new name *new*. Also allows the renaming of directories. Files can be moved with this routine. Returns 0 if successful.
mktemp(tmplt)	Fills out the template *tmplt* with a filename that does not already exist.

The routines *unlink()* and *remove()* are identical. Each takes a single argument—the address of a string—and erases (removes from the disk) the file whose name is specified in that string. The filename that you specify can be either a full pathname such as C:\TMP\JUNK, which removes the file JUNK from the directory C:\TMP, or a relative pathname such as JUNK, in which case the called routine removes the file JUNK from the current working directory.

The *rename()* function can do more than merely rename files. It can rename directories and move files from one directory to another (but not from one disk to another). Consider the following example, in which JUNK is a file and DIR1 and DIR2 are directories:

```
rename("JUNK", "OLDJUNK");——————————— Rename a file
rename("DIR1\\JUNK", "DIR2\\JUNK");——— Move a file
rename("DIR1", "OLDDIR1");——————————— Rename a directory
```

The first line renames the file JUNK in the current working directory as OLDJUNK; the second line moves the file JUNK in the subdirectory DIR1 into the subdirectory DIR2. Note that you could have renamed JUNK during the move. The third line of the above example renames the directory DIR1 as OLDDIR1. It is important to note that directories, unlike files, cannot be moved.

The *mktemp()* function generates a unique filename that is guaranteed not to exist on your disk. Use it as follows:

```
#include <io.h>      /* defines mktemp() */
#include <stdio.h>  /* for NULL */

static char template[] = "C:\\TMP\\XXXXXX";

if (mktemp(template) == NULL)
    {
    /* No unique name possible */
    }
```

First we specify *#include <io.h>* for the definition of *mktemp()*. In that header file, *mktemp()* is defined as returning the address of a string (that is, *char **). We also must use *#include <stdio.h>* to define *NULL*, which *mktemp()* returns if it fails.

The filename template passed to *mktemp()* must take the form *baseXXXXXX*; that is, it may be any prefix, path, or part of a filename, ending with six *X* characters. The *mktemp()* function replaces the *X* characters with six digits, thus forming a unique name (one that does not already exist on the disk), such as 162301.

The FMENU.C program (Listing 10-10) uses all these file-handling routines within a small menu program. It enables you to rename a file or directory, move or remove a file, or create a unique file. You can use FMENU.C as the core of your own programs that let the user control files without exiting to MS-DOS.

```
/* fmenu.c -- demonstrates file renaming, etc. */

#include <direct.h>
#include <stdio.h>
#include <string.h>

#define MAXPATH (80)
char From_name[MAXPATH],
    To_name[MAXPATH];

int Input(char *prompt, char buf[])
{
    printf("%s: ", prompt);
    if (gets(buf) == NULL || *buf == '\0')
        return (0);
    return (1);
}
void Rename(void)
{
    printf("->Rename/move\n");
    if (!Input("From", From_name)) return;
    if (!Input("To", To_name)) return;
    if (rename(From_name, To_name) != 0)
        perror("RENAME");
    else
        printf("Renamed: \"%s\" -> \"%s\"\n",
                From_name, To_name);
}
void Remove(void)
{
    printf("->Remove\n");
    if (!Input("Remove", From_name)) return;
    if (!Input("Are you sure", To_name)) return;
    if (*To_name != 'y' && *To_name != 'Y')
        return;
```

Listing 10-10. *The FMENU.C program.*   *(continued)*

Listing 10-10. *continued*

```
        if (remove(From_name) != 0)
            perror(From_name);
        else
            printf("Removed: \"%s\"\n", From_name);
}
void Maketemp(void)
{
    printf("->Maketemp\n");
    if (!Input("In what directory", From_name))
        return;
    (void)strcat(From_name, "\\XXXXXX");
    if (mktemp(From_name) == NULL)
        printf("Can't create a unique name.\n");
    else
        printf("Created the name: \"%s\"\n", From_name);
}
void Quit(void)
{
    printf("->Quit\n");
    if (!Input("Are you sure", From_name))
        return;
    if (*From_name != 'y' && *From_name != 'Y')
        return;
    exit(0);
}

main()
{
    static void (*doit[])() = {Rename, Remove, Maketemp, Quit};
    int ch;

    while (1)
        {
        printf("-------------------------------------------------\n");
        printf("1) Rename/move a file or rename a directory\n");
        printf("2) Remove a file\n");
        printf("3) Make a unique filename\n");
        printf("4) Quit\n");
        printf("-------------------------------------------------\n");
        printf("Select: ");

        do
            {
            ch = getchar();
            } while (ch < '1' || ch > '4');
        getchar();      /* gobble trailing newline */
        printf("%c\n\n", ch);
        ch -= '1';
        doit[ch]();
        }
}
```

FMENU.C uses a technique we discussed in Chapter 8—an array of pointers to functions. Each menu choice corresponds to a function in that array, and each of those functions utilizes a different routine for file manipulation. Note that FMENU.C contains an error-printing routine you haven't seen before—*perror()*.

Printing Clear and Meaningful Diagnostics with *perror()*

All C programs use a system-defined global variable called *errno*, which is set and cleared with each system or I/O call. A standard C Library routine called *perror()* prints an appropriate error message based on the current value in *errno*. For example, suppose an *fopen()* for reading a file named JUNK fails because the file doesn't exist. In that case QuickC sets *errno* to 2, and *perror()*, when called as

```
perror("JUNK");
```

prints the following to the standard error output:

```
JUNK: No such file or directory
```

Using *perror()* helps your program generate clearer and more meaningful diagnostic messages. However, remember to call *perror()* immediately after a library routine returns an error. If you call another library routine before *perror()*, it might change *errno* and cause *perror()* to print an incorrect message. For example,

```
if ((fp = fopen(fname, "rb")) == NULL)
    {
    fprintf(stderr, "Program aborted because\n");
    perror(fname);
    exit(1);
    }
```

does not work because the call to *fprintf()* preceding *perror()* succeeds and thus sets *errno* to 0, which causes *perror()* to print the incorrect message *Undefined error*.

Advanced Error Handling

A program that can recover from any error is called "robust." Robust programs are not merely carefully written programs—they are programs that include library routines for handling all abnormal conditions and that issue clear diagnostic messages to the user. Table 10-9 lists the most useful routines for handling abnormal conditions.

Table 10-9. Abnormal-Condition Handlers and Diagnostic Routines

signal()	Traps errors that can terminate a program, such as Ctrl-C and floating-point exceptions
setjmp()	Prepares for a jump between functions
longjmp()	Executes a jump between functions

Signals

Signals are conditions that cause a program to terminate prematurely. The signals for MS-DOS are listed in signal.h: They include Ctrl-C, Ctrl-Break, and floating-point errors such as division by zero. A text editor is an example of a program that should not terminate if one of these conditions occurs. The user might, for example, be editing a temporary copy of a file, so you would want to write a user's changes to disk before exiting, no matter what.

To handle errors such as these, use the *signal()* function as follows:

```
#include <signal.h>

status = signal(sig, funct);
```

Function address or *SIG_IGN* or *SIG_DFL*
One of the signals defined in signal.h
SIG_ERR on error

Error-handling Philosophies: BASIC vs C

Most versions of BASIC build an error-handling mechanism into the language in the form of the ON ERROR GOTO *label* construct. When an error is encountered, control switches to the appropriate label or line number. Although you can turn this facility on and off, you don't have fine control of it.

To review the situation in C, each function is responsible for reporting errors back to its caller. This procedure is more flexible than that used by BASIC, but it admits some inconsistencies. Functions that return pointers (such as *fopen()*, which returns a pointer to the file opened) often return a null pointer, which can be tested against the predefined value *NULL*. Other functions return the value −1 to indicate an error and store the specific error number in the global variable *errno*, using error-number values defined in the include file errno.h. Still other functions cannot return error values because no values are reserved for that purpose: All values might conceivably be returned by normal operation. You can, however, use the function *ferror()* to find out whether an error occurred during input or output to a particular file. If you are not sure how a particular function handles error conditions, a fast way to find out is to use QuickC's on-line help facility discussed earlier in this book.

In return for the greater flexibility C provides, you must explicitly test for an error (usually by putting the function call in an *if* or *while* statement or by calling *ferror()*) and then call any error-handling functions.

The signal mechanism (discussed in this section) provides an additional, UNIX-compatible way to handle error conditions reported by the operating system. This mechanism is similar to the BASIC mechanism in that it establishes a global connection between a particular error condition and an error-handling function.

We specify #include <signal.h> for definitions of signal(), its return value, and all of the possible values for *sig*. The *signal()* function takes two arguments. The first specifies the type of error, the values of which are listed in signal.h and summarized for MS-DOS in Table 10-10 on the following page. The second argument is the name (or address) of a function to be called if *sig* occurs, or one of the two predefined values: *SIG_IGN* (ignore this signal) or *SIG_DFL* (resume the default action, that is, terminate the program). Figure 10-4 illustrates the use of *signal()*.

```
#include <signal.h>
int Sigflag = 0;     /* global */
main()
{
      extern int Funct();
  ①  if  (signal(SIGINT, Funct) == SIG_ERR)
          {
          printf("Signal() failed.\n");
          exit(0);
          }
      for (;;)         /* forever */
          {
          printf("Waiting for Ctrl-C\n");            ② ③
  ⑤
          if (Sigflag != 0)
              break;   ⑥
          }
} ⑦

Funct()
{
      ++Sigflag;
} ④
```

① Calling *signal()* sets up the program to handle the Ctrl-C interrupt.

② User presses Ctrl-C (or Ctrl-Break) during the perpetual *for* loop, which is printing *Waiting for Ctrl-C* at the time.

③ *Funct()* is immediately called and increments *Sigflag*.

④ *Funct()* returns and…

⑤ the *printf()* statement previously interrupted is then executed (again).

⑥ We check *Sigflag* and because it was set to a nonzero value when we called *Funct()*, we exit the perpetual *for* loop by breaking out of it.

⑦ Program ends.

Figure 10-4. *Analysis of* signal().

Table 10-10.   Signals Defined for MS-DOS

SIGABRT	Abnormal program termination. Terminates the program and exits with a return value of 3.
SIGFPE	Floating-point exception (such as division by zero or an invalid operation). Terminates the program.
SIGINT	Interrupt for keyboard. Sent when the user types the key sequence Ctrl-C. Terminates the program.

As a rule, the signal-handling function, *Funct()*, should not perform any I/O operation. Rather than handling the error itself, it should set a global flag variable, then return to let the main body of the code handle the error. The main program stops, and the signal-handling function, *Funct()*, is called with the signal number *sig* as its argument. When *Funct()* finishes and returns, the main program continues from the exact point at which it stopped.

Handling signals under MS-DOS is fairly simple because only six signals are defined, and only three of those actually do anything. However, if you move your code to XENIX or UNIX, you should be prepared to handle thirty or more signals, all of which can affect your program.

Jumping Between Functions with *setjmp()* and *longjmp()*

Sometimes when a signal occurs, your program might not be able to continue its main body of code. A signal caused by division by zero, for example, would result in a completely wrong answer should the program continue. For situations such as these, when you need to jump to an earlier stage of the program, the standard C Library offers two functions: *setjmp()* and *longjmp()*.

The *setjmp()* function prepares the program for an eventual jump to an earlier state:

```
#include <setjmp.h>

jmp_buf env;

if (setjmp(env) != 0)
    {
    /* We got here because of a longjmp()
       from someplace else */
    }
/* All prepared for a longjmp() */
```

We specify *#include <setjmp.h>* for the definition of *jmp_buf*. The variable *env* is declared as the type *jmp_buf* and is the buffer that will hold all the information QuickC needs to perform a jump between functions. Next, the call to *setjmp()* prepares for an eventual call to *longjmp()*. The result of this preparation is always 0. When *setjmp()* returns the value 0, you know that the program is set up for a later call to *longjmp()* but that the call has not occurred. A later call to *longjmp()* causes the program to call *setjmp()* again, but this time the call returns a nonzero value.

Use the *longjmp()* routine as follows:

```
longjmp(env, ret);
```

The program calls *longjmp()* with the same buffer *env* with which it called *setjmp()* earlier. The *ret* argument must be a nonzero number because it is the value returned by *setjmp()*. (Figure 10-5 illustrates this relationship.)

```
#include <setjmp.h>
jmp_buf Env;              /* global */
main()
{
①  if (setjmp(Env) != 0)
        {
        printf("Exiting at A\n");
        exit(0);  Ⓐ
        }

    printf("Calling Foo()\n");
    Foo();
②  printf("Exiting at B\n");
    exit(0);  Ⓑ
}

Foo()
{
    printf("In Foo()\n");

    longjmp(Env, 1);  ③
}
```

① The first call to *setjmp()* returns 0, so flow continues with the first line after the *if* statement.

② *Foo()* is called.

③ In *Foo()*, *longjmp()* returns us to ①. This time, however, *setjmp()* returns 1, so we exit at Ⓐ. Note that Ⓑ is never reached.

Figure 10-5. *Analysis of* setjmp() *and* longjmp().

11

Advanced Data Types

Many programs, such as databases, spreadsheets, catalogs, and indexes, group information in such a way that each item needs to be a different C data type. (See Figure 11-1 on the following page.) To facilitate writing these programs, C offers a "structure" type—a special array-like form in which each element can be a different type.

Another special storage requirement is the need to store different types of data, at one time or another, at the same place in memory. The street number in Figure 11-1, for example, could be numeric, such as 212, requiring an integer variable, or it could be alphanumeric, such as 212B, requiring a string variable. The C *union* data type solves this problem by letting you store different types at the same place in memory.

This chapter shows you how to program with structures and unions. It also discusses some less frequently used data types, *enum* and bit fields. Finally, it describes the *typedef* keyword, an alternative to the *#define* preprocessor directive that lets you create new types from old.

Figure 11-1. *To enter the information on an address/phone index card into a computer, you need to use a collection of different data types organized as a single conceptual unit.*

Structure—An Array of Different Types

An obvious limitation of arrays is that the variables in a single array must all be of the same type (all *char*, all *int*, and so on). However, you will frequently need to group variables of different data types together so that you can manipulate them as a single conceptual unit. The information on the index card in Figure 11-1 is a good example. Because all the different "types" of information actually relate to a single person, it is more convenient and conceptually sound to place all that information in a single array. Unfortunately, arrays cannot handle different data types. To group strings and integers, for example, you must use a structure, which can hold any mixture of types, including arrays, pointers, and integers.

Think of a structure as a special kind of array. However, whereas the variables in an array are called elements and are referenced by an index, the variables in a structure are called "members" and are referenced by name.

You declare a structure with the C keyword *struct*. The first step in setting up a structure is to declare a pattern, or template, for the variables it will contain and to give that pattern a name, sometimes called a tag. For example, a structure pattern that can contain the address-book information in Figure 11-1 appears at the top of the next page.

To declare a structure pattern, follow the keyword *struct* with the name of the pattern (*cardstruct*). Next, list the variables, or members, of the structure between a set of braces. Note that although this list resembles a list of variable declarations, you are not at this point allocating memory for storage of the structure's members—you are merely creating a template that reserves those names for future use.

```
                                        ─── Keyword
                              ─────────────── Name of pattern
                          ────────────────── Variables between braces
struct cardstruct {
    char *first, *last, *middle; ──── Member list start
    long street_num;
    char *street. *city, *state;
    long zip;
    int area_code;
    long phone; ──────────────────── Member list end
};
    ┌───────────────────────── Closing semicolon
    └───────────────────────── Variables between braces
```

Structure Variables

To reserve memory for a structure's members, you must declare structure variables that follow the pattern you defined. The following declaration sets aside memory for two structure variables (*card1* and *card2*) using the above *cardstruct* pattern:

```
struct cardstruct card1, card2;
```

This declaration starts with the keyword *struct*, as did the pattern, but this time *struct* is followed by the name of a previously declared pattern and then by the names of the structure variables. Remember, you manipulate *card1* and *card2* in the program—the pattern *cardstruct* merely declares new structures. This statement reserves memory (allocates enough storage) for the predefined members of those two structure variables, as shown in Figure 11-2.

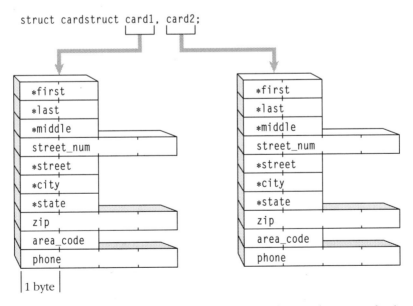

Figure 11-2. *Declaring structure variables sets aside enough memory for the variables defined by* cardstruct.

Accessing Structure Members

To access a member of a structure in C, specify the name of the structure variable that contains the member, then the . (pronounced "dot") operator, then the name of the member you need to access, as in the following example:

```
printf("%d\n", card1.area_code);
```
- Name of member of structure
- "Dot" operator
- Name of structure

This expression prints the value of the integer *area_code*, one of the member variables in the structure variable named *card1*.

You can manipulate members of structures as you would any C variables: You can assign values to them, use them in computations, and so on. The only difference is that you must reference each member variable with the name of its structure (*card1* or *card2*, for example), a dot, and then its own name.

The CARD.C program (Listing 11-1) demonstrates structures by prompting you to fill out information for a fictional address-book card; then it prints out the information you entered. CARD.C uses the members of the structure *card1* exactly as it would ordinary variables. It assigns values to them with the = operator and passes those values to *printf()* to be printed.

```
/* card.c -- demonstrates how to declare structures */
/*           and how to use structure members       */

#include <stdio.h>      /* for NULL and stdin */
#include <string.h>     /* for strdup()       */

#define MAXN 79

struct cardstruct {                    /* global pattern */
    char *first, *last, *middle;
    long street_num;
    char *street, *city, *state;
    long zip;
    int  area_code;
    long phone;
};

main()
{
    char *Str_Input(char *prompt);
    long Lint_Input(char *prompt);
    struct cardstruct card1;
```

Listing 11-1. *The CARD.C program.*

(continued)

Listing 11-1. *continued*

```
    card1.first      = Str_Input("First Name");
    card1.last       = Str_Input("Last Name");
    card1.middle     = Str_Input("Middle Name");
    card1.street_num = Lint_Input("Street Number");
    card1.street     = Str_Input("Street Name");
    card1.city       = Str_Input("City");
    card1.state      = Str_Input("State");
    card1.zip        = Lint_Input("Zip Code");
    card1.area_code  = (int)Lint_Input("Area Code");
    card1.phone      = Lint_Input("Phone Number");

    printf("\n\n");
    printf("%s %s %s\n", card1.first, card1.middle, card1.last);
    printf("%ld %s, %s, %s %ld\n", card1.street_num,
            card1.street, card1.city, card1.state, card1.zip);
    printf("(%d) %ld\n", card1.area_code, card1.phone);
}

char *Str_Input(char *prompt)
{
    char buf[MAXN+1], *ptr;

    printf("%s: ", prompt);
    if (fgets(buf, MAXN, stdin) == NULL)
        exit(0);
    buf[strlen(buf) - 1] = '\0'; /* strip '\n' */
    if (strlen(buf) == 0)
        exit(0);
    if ((ptr = strdup(buf)) == NULL)
        exit(0);
    return (ptr);
}

long Lint_Input(char *prompt)
{
    char buf[MAXN + 1];
    long num;

    printf("%s: ", prompt);
    if (fgets(buf, MAXN, stdin) == NULL)
        exit(0);
    if (sscanf(buf, "%ld", &num) != 1)
        exit(0);
    return (num);
}
```

Shorthand Structure Declarations

As a bit of shorthand, you can declare structure patterns and allocate storage for structure variables in a single statement, as follows:

```
                    ┌──────────────────── Name of pattern
struct cardstruct {
    /* list of members here */
} card1, card2;
  └────┘─────────────────────── Structures allocated storage
```

When you allocate storage for structure variables as a part of the declaration, the name of the pattern becomes optional and you can omit it:

```
            ┌──────────────────────── Name of pattern omitted
struct {
    /* list of members here */
} card1, card2;
  └────┘──────────────────── Structures allocated storage
```

You must use the pattern name, however, if you intend to declare additional structure variables using that pattern name later in the program:

```
struct cardstruct card3, card4;
```

Structure Assignment

When you declare structure variables with the same pattern, you can assign one to another, as follows:

```
card2 = card1;
```

This assignment copies the values of all *card1* members into the corresponding members of *card2*.

If you try to assign one structure variable to another when those structures are declared with different pattern names (even if their members are identical), QuickC returns the following error message:

```
error C2115: '=' : incompatible types
```

> ## Quick Tip
>
> One way to make a program such as CARD.C more robust, or user friendly, is to enable the program to handle telephone numbers that contain a hyphen (-) character. Consider the necessary revisions to CARD.C. Why is this enhancement difficult in a program that uses *scanf()* to parse user input?

If you need to assign values from one structure to another of a different pattern, you must assign the members individually. For example, if *card1* uses the pattern *cardstruct* and *memo* uses another pattern, *memostruct*, you could assign the members of one to the other in the following way:

```
card1.first  = memo.first_name;
card1.last   = memo.last_name;
card1.middle = memo.mid_name;
```

Passing Structures to Functions

Passing a structure to a function passes a *copy* of its members. This prevents the called function from changing the original structure. To pass a structure to a function, simply state the structure's name, as follows:

```
Showcard(card1);
```

In this example, a copy of the structure variable *card1*—including copies of all its members—is passed to the function *Showcard()*. Remember, structures differ from arrays in this regard: When you pass a structure to a function, you pass only a copy of that structure; when you pass an array, you pass the address of that array, thus allowing the original array to be changed by the called function.

In the receiving function (such as *Showcard()* below), you must declare the type of the received argument with *struct* and the pattern name (*cardstruct*). This tells the compiler that *Showcard()* is receiving a structure as its argument, and that the pattern for that structure is named *cardstruct*:

```
                                    ┌──────── Receive copy of structure
Showcard(struct cardstruct card)
{                        └──────────────── based on this pattern
    /* body of function */
}
```

The CARD2.C program (Listing 11-2 beginning on the following page) is a revised CARD.C program. In it, we fill out two cards and then print those cards using the *Showcard()* function.

Quick Tip

There are two drawbacks to passing structures to functions. First, not all compilers support the passing of structures, so if portability is important, you might want to avoid this technique. Second, as structures get larger, QuickC takes longer to copy them for each function call. This can become very time-consuming if it occurs in the middle of a loop. Thus, to speed the processing of your programs and enable the original to be changed, we advise you to use pointers to structures.

```
/* card2.c -- demonstrates structure assignment and */
/*            how to pass a structure to a function */

#include <stdio.h>      /* for NULL and stdin */
#include <string.h>     /* for strdup()       */

#define MAXN 79

struct cardstruct {                    /* global pattern */
    char *first, *last, *middle;
    long street_num;
    char *street, *city, *state;
    long zip;
    int  area_code;
    long phone;
};

main()
{
    int  i;
    void Showcard(struct cardstruct card);
    char *Str_Input(char *prompt);
    long Lint_Input(char *prompt);
    struct cardstruct card1, card2;

    for (i = 0; i < 2; i++) /* do twice */
        {
        printf("\nCard %d:\n\n", i + 1);

        card1.first      = Str_Input("First Name");
        card1.last       = Str_Input("Last Name");
        card1.middle     = Str_Input("Middle Name");
        card1.street_num = Lint_Input("Street Number");
        card1.street     = Str_Input("Street Name");
        card1.city       = Str_Input("City");
        card1.state      = Str_Input("State");
        card1.zip        = Lint_Input("Zip Code");
        card1.area_code  = (int)Lint_Input("Area Code");
        card1.phone      = Lint_Input("Phone Number");

        if (i == 0)
            card2 = card1;      /* structure assignment */
        }
    Showcard(card2);
    Showcard(card1);
}
```

Listing 11-2. *The CARD2.C program.*   *(continued)*

Listing 11-2. *continued*

```
void Showcard(struct cardstruct card)
{
    printf("\n\n");

    printf("%s %s %s\n", card.first, card.middle, card.last);
    printf("%ld %s, %s, %s %ld\n", card.street_num,
            card.street, card.city, card.state, card.zip);
    printf("(%d) %ld\n", card.area_code, card.phone);
}

char *Str_Input(char *prompt)
{
    char buf[MAXN + 1], *ptr;

    printf("%s: ", prompt);
    if (fgets(buf, MAXN, stdin) == NULL)
        exit(0);
    buf[strlen(buf) - 1 ] = '\0'; /* strip '\n' */
    if (strlen(buf) == 0)
        exit(0);
    if ((ptr = strdup(buf)) == NULL)
        exit(0);
    return (ptr);
}

long Lint_Input(char *prompt)
{
    char buf[MAXN + 1];
    long num;

    printf("%s: ", prompt);
    if (fgets(buf, MAXN, stdin) == NULL)
        exit(0);
    if (sscanf(buf, "%ld", &num) != 1)
        exit(0);
    return (num);
}
```

In CARD2.C, *Showcard()* receives a copy of *card1* from *main()*. Note that the members of the *Showcard()* structure, *card*, are accessed with the same "dot" notation as the originals in *main()*.

Pointers to Structures

Passing a pointer that references a structure, rather than passing a copy of the structure, to a function has two advantages. It permits the function to modify the members of the original structure. Also, far fewer bytes must be copied when a pointer is passed than when a structure is passed—the result is faster-executing code.

You declare a pointer to a structure the same way that you declare a pointer to any other type—by preceding its name with an asterisk (*), as follows:

```
struct cardstruct *cardptr;
```

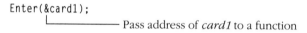

This example declares a pointer variable, *cardptr*, whose contents will be an address. The *struct cardstruct* in the declaration tells the compiler that *cardptr* will point to a structure variable based on the pattern *cardstruct*. (See Figure 11-3.)

Before you can use the pointer *cardptr*, it must be given a value. Because it is a pointer to a structure, we will assign it the address of the structure variable *card1* from CARD.C:

```
cardptr = &card1;
```

The & operator fetches the address of a structure. (Note that this differs from arrays, where the array name itself yields the address.) To assign the address of a structure variable to a pointer to a structure, declare both the pointer and the structure with the same pattern name. If you declare them with different pattern names, QuickC returns the following warning message:

```
warning C4049: '=' : indirection to different types
```

The & operator can also pass the address of a structure directly to a function:

```
Enter(&card1);
```
— Pass address of *card1* to a function

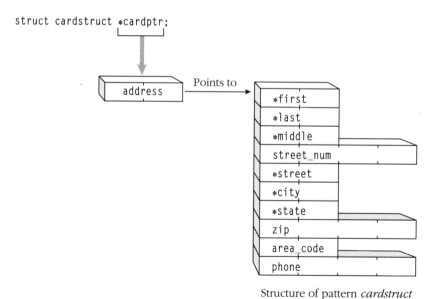

Structure of pattern *cardstruct*

Figure 11-3. *A pointer to a structure contains the address of a structure variable.*

We also must declare the received argument for the *Enter()* function as a pointer to a structure, as follows:

```
Enter(struct cardstruct *item)
    {                              Pointer to receive an address
```

Again, be sure that you declare the same pattern name for both the passed and the received structures.

Accessing Structure Members with a Pointer

To access the members of a structure with a pointer, you need to use a new symbol, –>. Called "to", –> is actually two characters—a "minus" character followed by a "greater than" character. The following code fragment illustrates the use of the –> operator. In it, the pointer *cardptr* accesses the *phone* member of the structure *card1*:

```
struct cardstruct {                 Define a pattern
    char *first, *last, *middle;
    int age;
};

struct cardstruct card1, *cardptr;
                                    Declare a pointer and
                                    a structure variable
                                    both of that pattern
cardptr = &card1;                   Assign address of card1 to cardptr
cardptr->phone = 5551212;           Access member of card1 via cardpter
                                    Points "to" member phone of card1
```

The CARD3.C program (Listing 11-3) is another revision of CARD.C. This modification has *Showcard()* receiving the address of a structure. Rather than printing a copy, it prints the original via a pointer to the structure.

```
/* card3.c -- demonstrates pointers to structures */

#include <stdio.h>      /* for NULL and stdin */
#include <string.h>     /* for strdup()       */

#define MAXN 79

struct cardstruct {                 /* global pattern */
    char *first, *last, *middle;
    long street_num;
    char *street, *city, *state;
    long zip;
    int  area_code;
    long phone;
};
```

Listing 11-3. *The CARD3.C program.*   *(continued)*

Listing 11-3. *continued*

```
main()
{
    int  i;
    void Showcard(struct cardstruct *card ptr);
    char *Str_Input(char *prompt);
    long Lint_Input(char *prompt);
    struct cardstruct card1, card2;

    for (i = 0; i < 2; i++) /* do twice */
        {
        printf("\nCard %d:\n\n", i + 1);

        card1.first      = Str_Input("First Name");
        card1.last       = Str_Input("Last Name");
        card1.middle     = Str_Input("Middle Name");
        card1.street_num = Lint_Input("Street Number");
        card1.street     = Str_Input("Street Name");
        card1.city       = Str_Input("City");
        card1.state      = Str_Input("State");
        card1.zip        = Lint_Input("Zip Code");
        card1.area_code  = (int)Lint_Input("Area Code");
        card1.phone      = Lint_Input("Phone Number");
        if (i == 0)
            card2 = card1;
        {
    Showcard(&card2);      /* pass addresses of structures */
    Showcard(&card1);

    return (0);
}

Showcard(struct cardstruct *cardptr) /* pointer receives an address */
{
    printf("\n\n");

    printf("%s %s %s\n", cardptr->first, cardptr->middle,
            cardptr->last);
    printf("%ld %s, %s, %s %ld\n", cardptr->street_num,
            cardptr->street, cardptr->city, cardptr->state,
            cardptr->zip);
    printf("(%d) %ld\n", cardptr->area_code, cardptr->phone);
}

char *Str_Input(char *prompt)
{
    char buf[MAXN + 1], *ptr;
```

(continued)

340

Listing 11-3. *continued*

```
    printf("%s: ", prompt);
    if (fgets(buf, MAXN, stdin) == NULL)
        exit(0);
    buf[strlen(buf) - 1] = '\0'; /* strip '\n' */
    if (strlen(buf) == 0)
        exit(0);
    if ((ptr = strdup(buf)) == NULL)
        exit(0);
    return (ptr);
}

long Lint_Input(char *prompt)
{
    char buf[MAXN + 1];
    long num;

    printf("%s: ", prompt);
    if (fgets(buf, MAXN, stdin) == NULL)
        exit(0);
    if (sscanf(buf, "%ld", &num) != 1)
        exit(0);
    return (num);
}
```

Arrays of Structures

Structures can be organized in arrays like any other type of variable. You declare an array of structures as follows:

```
struct cardstruct {
    /* members declared here */
} cards[3];
        └─────────────────────────── An array of three structures
```

This example declares an array of three structures (*cards[3]*) and defines the pattern *cardstruct* at the same time. If you had already defined the pattern, you could declare the same array as follows:

```
struct cardstruct cards[3];
```

Use an array of structures the same way you use any other array. For example, the following statement prints the *first* member of the second card:

```
printf("%s", cards[1].first);
```

The expression *cards[1]* accesses the second structure of the array, and the dot operator followed by a variable name yields the member named *first* from that structure.

To pass the address of one of the structures in the array *cards*, use the & operator followed by the structure's offset in square brackets:

```
                        ──── Address of
┌──────────────┐
&cards[i]
       └──────── the element with index i in the array of structures
```

The ROLO.C program (Listing 11-4) is a complete address book built from the earlier CARD.C program. It asks you to fill out the three cards in our array of structures. Then it prints out the information in those cards.

By combining this use of structures with the file-handling routines of PHONE.C (Listing 10-5 on pp. 304-306), you have the basis for a truly useful phone-index program. ROLO.C uses an array of three structures. Notice that the *cards* array consists of structures that themselves contain arrays.

```c
/* rolo.c -- demonstrates pointers to structures */

#include <stdio.h>     /* for NULL and stdin */
#include <string.h>    /* for strdup()       */

#define MAXN 79
#define MAXCARDS 3

struct cardstruct {                     /* global pattern */
    char first[MAXN],
         last[MAXN],
         middle[MAXN];
    unsigned long street_no;
    char street[MAXN],
         city[MAXN],
         state[MAXN];
    unsigned long zip;
    unsigned int area;
    unsigned long phone;
};

struct cardstruct cards[MAXCARDS];

main()
{
    int  i;
    void Input(struct cardstruct *cardp);
    void Showcard(struct cardstruct *cardptr);

    for (i = 0; i < MAXCARDS; ++i)
        {
        printf("\n<card %d of %d>\n", i + 1, MAXCARDS);
        Input(&cards[i]);
        }
```

Listing 11-4. *The ROLO.C program.*   *(continued)*

Listing 11-4. *continued*

```
    for (i = 0; i < MAXCARDS; ++i)
        {
        printf("\n<%d> ", i + 1);
        Showcard(&cards[i]);
        }
}

void Input(struct cardstruct *cardp)
{
    char *Str_Input(char *prompt);
    long Lint_Input(char *prompt);

    strcpy(cardp->first,Str_Input("First Name"));
    strcpy(cardp->last,Str_Input("Last Name"));
    strcpy(cardp->middle,Str_Input("Middle Name"));
    cardp->street_no = Lint_Input("Street Number");
    strcpy(cardp->street,Str_Input("Street"));
    strcpy(cardp->city,Str_Input("City"));
    strcpy(cardp->state,Str_Input("State"));
    cardp->zip = Lint_Input("Zip Code");
    cardp->area = (int)Lint_Input("Area Code");
    cardp->phone = Lint_Input("Phone Number");
}

char *Str_Input(char *prompt)
{
    char buf[MAXN + 1], *ptr;

    printf("%s: ", prompt);
    if (fgets(buf, MAXN, stdin) == NULL)
        exit(0);
    buf[strlen(buf) - 1 ] = '\0'; /* strip '\n' */
    if (strlen(buf) == 0)
        exit(0);
    if ((ptr = strdup(buf)) == NULL)
        exit(0);
    return (ptr);
}

long Lint_Input(char *prompt)
{
    char buf[MAXN + 1];
    long num;

    printf("%s: ", prompt);
    if (fgets(buf, MAXN, stdin) == NULL)
        exit(0);
    if (sscanf(buf, "%ld", &num) != 1)
        exit(0);
    return (num);
}
```

(continued)

Listing 11-4. *continued*

```
void Showcard(struct cardstruct *cardptr)
{
    printf("\n\n");
    printf("%s %s %s\n", cardptr->first, cardptr->middle,
            cardptr->last);
    printf("%ld %s, %s, %s %ld\n", cardptr->street_no,
            cardptr->street, cardptr->city, cardptr->state,
            cardptr->zip);
    printf("(%d) %ld\n", cardptr->area, cardptr->phone);
}
```

Arrays of Pointers to Structures

Not only can you create arrays of structures, you can also create arrays of pointers to structures. These arrays of pointers offer the advantage of increased efficiency. For example, when sorting, it is faster to swap two pointers than it is to exchange the vastly greater number of bytes of the structures themselves. The following statement declares an array of three pointers.

```
struct cardstruct *cardps[3];
```

Each array element points to a structure of the pattern *cardstruct*, as illustrated in Figure 11-4. You can initialize *cardps* (an array of pointers to structures) to contain the address of the corresponding elements in the array of structures *cards* as follows:

```
cardps[0] = &cards[0];
cardps[1] = &cards[1];
cardps[2] = &cards[2];
```

This lets you use the –> operator to indirectly reference the members of each structure in *cards* with the pointers in *cardps*. For example, the *street* member of the second structure of the array of structures *cards* can be indirectly referenced through the array of pointers to structures in *cardps*, as follows:

```
strcpy(cardps[1]->street, "Any St.");
```
————————————————————— Points "to" the member *street* of *cards[1]*

Structure Recursion and Linked Lists

Structures are so versatile that they can hold every possible type in C, including themselves. This remarkable ability to be self-inclusive opens whole new sets of programming possibilities. The most common of these is the technique shown in Figure 11-5 (on p. 346), which uses "linked lists."

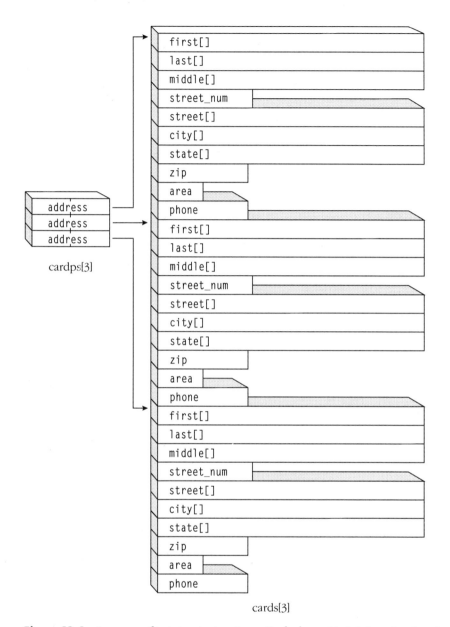

Figure 11-4. *An array of pointers to structures. Each element points to a structure in an array of structures.*

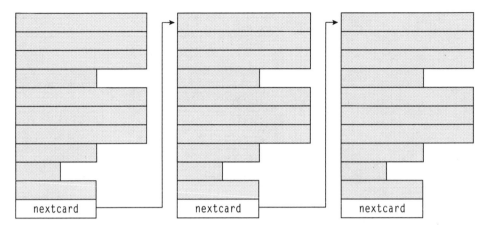

Figure 11-5. *In a linked list, each structure contains a pointer to another structure of the same type.*

A linked list is an arrangement of structures in which each structure contains a pointer to (the address of) its neighbor. For example, to declare such a linked list in ROLO.C, we must modify the structure pattern as follows:

```
struct cardstruct {
    char first[MAXN],
        last[MAXN],
        middle[MAXN];
    unsigned long street_no;
    char street[MAXN],
        city[MAXN],
        state[MAXN];
    unsigned long zip;
    unsigned int area;
    unsigned long phone;
    struct cardstruct *nextcard; ——— Added
};                               └——————— Pointer to another structure of this same pattern
```

The new member *nextcard* is a pointer to a structure, but it points to a structure of its own pattern. By declaring several structures of this pattern with

```
struct cardstruct card1, card2, card3, card4;
```

and then initializing the *nextcard* member of each to contain the address of its neighbor, you create a linked list:

```
card1.nextcard = &card2;
card2.nextcard = &card3;
card3.nextcard = &card4;
```

The ROLO2.C program (Listing 11-5) uses *malloc()* to build a linked list of structures while the program is running. Using this approach, we can add as many cards to our address book as we want (subject to the limit of the computer's memory).

```
/* rolo2.c -- demonstrates a linked list */

#include <stdio.h>      /* for NULL and stdin */
#include <string.h>     /* for strdup()       */
#include <malloc.h>     /* for malloc()       */

#define MAXN 79

struct cardstruct {                       /* global pattern */
    char first[MAXN],
         last[MAXN],
         middle[MAXN];
    unsigned long street_no;
    char street[MAXN],
         city[MAXN],
         state[MAXN];
    unsigned long zip;
    unsigned int area;
    unsigned long phone;
    struct cardstruct *nextcard;
};

main()
{
    int i;
    int Input(struct cardstruct *cardptr);
    void Showcard(struct cardstruct *cardptr);
    void Dumplist(struct cardstruct *head);
    struct cardstruct card, *first, *current;

    first = (struct cardstruct *)malloc(sizeof(struct cardstruct));
    if (first == NULL)
        exit(1);
    if (Input(&card) != 0)
        exit(1);
    *first = card;
    current = first;

    while (Input(&card) == 0)
        {
        current->nextcard =
            (struct cardstruct *)malloc(sizeof(struct cardstruct));
        if (current->nextcard == NULL)
            exit(1);
        current = current->nextcard;
        *current = card;
        }
    current->nextcard = NULL;

    Dumplist(first);
}
```

Listing 11-5. *The ROLO2.C program.*   *(continued)*

Listing 11-5. *continued*

```
void Dumplist(struct cardstruct *head)
{
    void Showcard(struct cardstruct *cardptr);

    do
        {
        Showcard(head);
        } while ((head = head->nextcard) != NULL);
}

void Showcard(struct cardstruct *cardptr)
{
    printf("\n\n");

    printf("%s %s %s\n", cardptr->first, cardptr->middle,
            cardptr->last);
    printf("%ld %s, %s, %s %ld\n", cardptr->street_no,
            cardptr->street, cardptr->city, cardptr->state,
            cardptr->zip );
    printf("(%d) %ld\n", cardptr->area, cardptr->phone);
}

int Input(struct cardstruct *cardp)
{
    char *Str_Input(char *prompt);
    long Lint_Input(char *prompt);

    printf("\n<new card> (Empty first name quits)\n");
    strcpy(cardp->first,Str_Input("First Name"));
    if (*(cardp->first) == '\0')
        return (1);
    strcpy(cardp->last,Str_Input("Last Name"));
    strcpy(cardp->middle,Str_Input("Middle Name"));
    cardp->street_no = Lint_Input("Street Number");
    strcpy(cardp->street,Str_Input("Street"));
    strcpy(cardp->city,Str_Input("City"));
    strcpy(cardp->state,Str_Input("State"));
    cardp->zip = Lint_Input("Zip Code");
    cardp->area = (int)Lint_Input("Area Code");
    cardp->phone = Lint_Input("Phone Number");
    return (0);
}

char *Str_Input(char *prompt)
{
    char buf[MAXN + 1], *ptr;

    printf("%s: ", prompt);
    if (fgets(buf, MAXN, stdin) == NULL)
        exit(0);
```

(continued)

Listing 11-5. *continued*

```
    buf[strlen(buf) - 1 ] = '\0'; /* strip '\n' */
    if ((ptr = strdup(buf)) == NULL)
        exit(0);
    return (ptr);
}

long Lint_Input(char *prompt)
{
    char buf[MAXN + 1];
    long num;

    printf("%s: ", prompt);
    if (fgets(buf, MAXN, stdin) == NULL)
        exit(0);
    if (sscanf(buf, "%ld", &num) != 1)
        num = 0;
    return (num);
}
```

Notice that the last structure in the list always has its *nextcard* member set to *NULL*. That's how the program marks the end of the linked list.

This program also illustrates two other interesting properties of structures. First, when you apply the *sizeof* operator to a structure or to a structure's pattern, it yields the total number of bytes for *all* the members of the structure:

```
malloc(sizeof(struct cardstruct));
```

Second, we had to type cast the value returned by *malloc()* to a type appropriate for the pointer to which the value is assigned:

```
first = (struct cardstruct *)malloc(sizeof(struct cardstruct));
```
Type cast to a pointer to a structure

Note that you must use the structure pattern name in the type cast, not the structure variable name. Had we omitted the type cast, QuickC would complain with:

```
warning C4049: '=' : indirection to different types
```

Initializing Structures with Starting Values

As in arrays, you can initialize static or global structures when you declare them. The type of the initializing value must, of course, match the type of the corresponding member. An attempt to initialize with the wrong type will yield the following QuickC warning:

```
warning C4047: "initializing" : different levels of indirection
```

The following structure is declared correctly:

```
static struct cardstruct card = {
    "Bob", ————————————————————— first
    "Roberts", ——————————————————— last
    "Mason", ————————————————————— middle
    42, —————————————————————————— street_no
    "Willow Way", ———————————————— street
    "Tonopah", ——————————————————— city
    "Nevada", ———————————————————— state
    84521L, —————————————————————— zip
    916, ————————————————————————— area
    5551212L ————————————————————— phone
};
```

As with arrays, if you specify fewer initializers than members, QuickC gives the trailing uninitialized members the default value zero.

Union—Multiple Types in the Same Space

You can think of a "union" as the opposite of a structure. While *struct* is a collection of many types, each with its own location in memory, a union is a collection of many types that all share the same location in memory. Thus, a union can contain different types at various times, but it can contain only a single type at any given time.

Although its uses are limited, a union is a blessing when you do encounter a need for one. For example, consider writing a function that needs to print either an *int* or a *float*, yet doesn't know ahead of time what type it will receive as its argument. Before we can show you how to write such a function, however, we need to cover the basics of declaring and using unions.

You declare a union as you would a structure, except you use the keyword *union* instead of *struct*:

```
                    ┌──────────── Name of pattern
union twotype {
    float ftype; ┐
    int   itype; ├──── Members
} one_of_many;   ┘
    └──────────────── Name of a union variable of pattern twotype
```

This example tells the compiler to reserve memory for the variable *one_of_many*, which will hold either a *float* or an *int*. Because the *float* is larger, *union* reserves 4 bytes—enough space to hold either type.

As a general rule, place the largest member first in a union declaration. Some compilers allocate memory based only on the first member, rather than searching all members for the largest. QuickC is well behaved in this regard, however. It allocates the correct number of bytes for a union, regardless of the order of the member declarations.

As with structure members, you access the members of a union with the "dot" operator. However, the compiler interprets the type of the union as the type specified by the member name, as follows:

```
one_of_many.ftype = 1.0;────── Interpret as a float
one_of_many.itype = 1;────── Interpret as an int
```

The UDEMO.C program (Listing 11-6) is a simple demonstration of how a union works. After asking the user to enter a type, it uses *scanf()* to read that type and *printf()* to echo it to the screen.

```c
/* udemo.c -- demonstrates a union at work */

#include <stdio.h>

char *Strings[6] = {
    "Quit",
    "line of text",
    "floating-point double value",
    "long integer value",
    "floating-point value",
    "integer value"
};

struct Unitstruct {
    union {
        char    wtype[BUFSIZ];
        double  dtype;
        long    ltype;
        float   ftype;
        int     itype;
    } manyu;
    int type_in_union;
};

main()
{
    struct Unitstruct one_of_many;
    void Inputval(struct Unitstruct *one_of_many);
    void Printval(struct Unitstruct *one_of_many);
    int Menu(void);

    while ((one_of_many.type_in_union = Menu()) != 0 )
        {
        Inputval(&one_of_many);
        Printval(&one_of_many);
        }
}
```

Listing 11-6. *The UDEMO.C program.*   *(continued)*

Listing 11-6. *continued*

```
void Inputval(struct Unitstruct *one_of_many)
{
    printf("\nEnter a %s: ", Strings[one_of_many->type_in_union]);
    switch(one_of_many->type_in_union)
        {
        case 1:
            fgets(one_of_many->manyu.wtype, BUFSIZ, stdin);
            break;
        case 2:
            scanf("%lf", &(one_of_many->manyu.dtype));
            while (getchar()!= '\n');
            break;
        case 3:
            scanf("%ld", &(one_of_many->manyu.ltype));
            while (getchar()!= '\n');
            break;
        case 4:
            scanf("%f", &(one_of_many->manyu.ftype));
            while (getchar()!= '\n');
            break;
        case 5:
            scanf("%i", &(one_of_many->manyu.itype));
            while (getchar()!= '\n');
            break;
        }
}

void Printval(struct Unitstruct *one_of_many)
{
    printf("The %s you entered\nwas: ",
            Strings[one_of_many->type_in_union]);
    switch (one_of_many->type_in_union)
        {
        case 1:
            fputs(one_of_many->manyu.wtype, stdout);
            break;
        case 2:
            printf("%lf", one_of_many->manyu.dtype);
            break;
        case 3:
            printf("%ld", one_of_many->manyu.ltype);
            break;
        case 4:
            printf("%f", one_of_many->manyu.ftype);
            break;
        case 5:
            printf("%i", one_of_many->manyu.itype);
            break;
        }
    printf("\n\n");
}
```

(continued)

Listing 11-6. *continued*

```
int Menu(void)
{
    int i;
    char ch;

    for (i = 0; i < 6; ++i)
        {
        printf("%d) %s\n", i, Strings[i]);
        }
    printf("Which: ");
    do
        {
        ch = getch();
        } while (ch < '0' || ch > '5');
    printf("%c\n", ch);
    return (ch - '0');
}
```

Unions and Functions

Although you can pass a structure as an argument to a function, you cannot pass a union to a function. Instead, you must pass the value of the type currently stored in that union. For example, the statement

```
printf("%f", one_of_many.ftype);
```
————————— Sends the *float* value in *one_of_many*

————————————— Expects a *float*

sends *printf()* the *float* value in *one_of_many*, which corresponds to the *printf()* format specifier *%f*. The compiler cannot manipulate a *union* variable (such as *one_of_many*) that lacks an associated "dot" and member name.

Unions Received by Functions

C permits you to use *union* as the type of an argument received by a function, but the procedure can be risky. The following function illustrates one way to declare a received variable in a subroutine as a union:

```
#define FLT 0   /* floating-point type */
#define INT 1   /* integer type        */

Printval(union twotype val, int type)
{
    switch (type)
        {
        case FLT: printf("%f", val.ftype); break;
        case INT: printf("%d", val.itype); break;
        }
}
```

This function receives two arguments: a union of two possible types and an *int* that specifies which of the two possible types is in that union.

But beware. Depending on how the compiler passes arguments to functions, this approach can fail. In QuickC, a *float* is 4 bytes and an *int* is 2 bytes; therefore, the stack (received arguments) resembles Figure 11-6a when passing a *float* and Figure 11-6b when passing an *int*. However, because the pattern for *twotype* reserves 4 bytes, passing an *int* to *Printval()* causes the *type* argument to appear in the wrong place.

You can resolve this dilemma by constraining union members to types that use the same number of bytes. That is, if you declare *twotype* as follows:

```
union twotype {
    float fval;
    long  ival;
};
```

it would contain either of two types, but each type requires 4 bytes. A better solution is to package a *union* and an *int* together inside a structure, as you saw earlier. That approach avoids the potential pitfalls of declaring a function that receives a barebones *union*.

Pointers to Unions

Pointers to unions behave like pointers to structures. You retrieve the address of a union with the & operator and the union variable name, as follows:

```
&one_of_many
```

Quick Tip

The UDEMO.C program illustrates a common technique for managing unions. Because a union contains no indication of the type it contains, unions are often made members of structures; another structure member indicates the type:

```
struct Unitstruct {
    union {
        char   wtype[BUFSIZ];
        double dtype;
        long   ltype;
        float  ftype;
        int    itype;
    } manyu; ───────────── The union
    int type_in_union; ───────── Indicator of type
};
```

By packaging a *union* and an *int* together in a structure like this, we are better able to keep track of the type stored in the union at any given time.

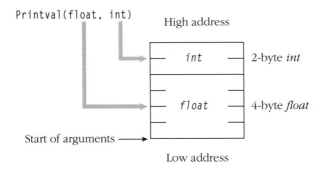

(A)

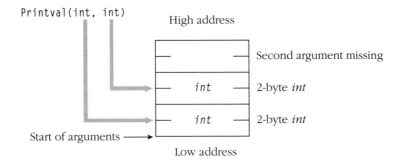

(B)

Figure 11-6. *Passing different-size data types to the same function can cause confusion.*

To fetch the address of a union member, specify the & operator, the union variable name, the dot operator, and the member name, as follows:

```
&one_of_many.ftype
```

As with structures, you can declare pointers to unions and manipulate values via the addresses in those pointers. Declare a pointer to a union as follows:

```
union manytype *up;
```
———— Pointer to a union of the pattern *manytype*

Place a value (an address) into that pointer in the following form:

```
up = &one_of_many;
```

To access the type of the value stored in the union whose address is in *up*, use the –> operator as follows:

```
up->ftype = 1.0;
```

Structures and unions are closely related. The main difference is that a structure holds many values simultaneously; a union holds only a single type of value at any one time. As you have seen, structures can include unions as members. Unions can also validly contain structures as members, a technique we demonstrate at the end of this chapter when we discuss bit fields.

Enumerated Data with *enum*

Many kinds of information are best represented by a finite list of discrete integer values—for example, the days of the week, the months of the year, or even the phases of the moon. Such kinds of information, in which every possibility is known in advance, lend themselves to enumeration—a listing of all possible values for a given topic or concept.

If you need to represent the days of the week in a program as discrete integers, you could make the following declarations and assignments:

```
int monday  = 0, tuesday = 1, wednesday = 2, thursday = 3,
    friday = 4, saturday = 5, sunday = 6;
```

and later use those values as follows:

```
pay_day = friday;
```

The previous approach, although reasonable, has a potential pitfall. Because the days of the week are *int* variables, the program might change their values and so render them meaningless. To avoid this problem, we can use the following preprocessor directives:

```
#define MONDAY 0
#define TUESDAY 1
    ⋮
```

The program can't change these values because they are integer constant aliases. But this is still not an ideal solution because you cannot group *#define* definitions under a single conceptual name.

The best solution uses the C enumerated data type, *enum*, whose members are constants grouped under a single name. To represent the days of the week using *enum*, first declare a pattern similar to a structure or union template:

```
                    ┌────────── Name of pattern
enum week_days {
    monday,      ┐
    tuesday,     │
    wednesday,   │
    thursday,    ├──── Members
    friday,      │
    saturday,    │
    sunday       ┘
} pay_day;
    └──────────── Enumerated variable
```

This example declares a pattern called *week_days*, an enumerated data type, and the enumerated variable *pay_day*. Note that the members don't need to be preceded by a type keyword because the members of *enum* are always of type *int*. Also notice that you don't need to assign the members any values: The declaration itself gives the members constant integer values, starting with 0 for *monday* and counting through 6 for *sunday*.

Another difference between *enum* and *struct* or *union* is that you access members of *enum* simply by stating the member's name without the dot operator or –> notation:

```
payday = monday;
```

Any attempt to change the value of an enumerated member (*monday = 5*, for example) results in the following QuickC error message:

```
error C2106: '=' : left operand must be lvalue
```

This reminds you that the members of an enumerated data type, like all other constants, are *rvalues* and can appear only to the right of an assignment operator.

Also note that you cannot use a pointer to change indirectly the value of an enumerated variable member. For example, the following assignment fails because you can't retrieve the address of a constant:

```
int *p;
```

```
p = &monday; ——— Can't take address of a constant
*p = 5;
```

This attempted assignment generates the following QuickC error message:

```
error C2101: '&' on constant
```

The TODAY.C program (Listing 11-7 on the following page) demonstrates one advantage to using *enum*—improved readability. The program asks you to specify the day on which you want to be paid. It then verifies that you specified a valid day.

The pattern *week_day* in TODAY.C shows that you can initialize an *enum* member to any integer value. Any uninitialized member, however, is assigned a value one higher than the member before it. For example, the declaration

```
enum folks {
    mo = -1,
    roseann,
    betsy = 0,
    kit,
    joey = 1
};
```

sets *mo* to –1, *roseann* and *betsy* to 0, and *kit* and *joey* to 1. This also shows that *enum* members can have duplicate values.

```
/* today.c -- demonstrates use of enum */

main()
{
    enum week_days {
        monday = 1,      /* start with 1 */
        tuesday,
        wednesday,
        thursday,
        friday,
        saturday,
        sunday
    } pay_day;

    static char *day_names[] = {
        "",
        "Monday",
        "Tuesday",
        "Wednesday",
        "Thursday",
        "Friday",
        "Saturday",
        "Sunday"
    };

    printf("What day do you want to be paid on?\n");

    for (pay_day = monday; pay_day <= sunday; ++pay_day)
        {
        printf("%d. %s\n", pay_day, day_names[pay_day]);
        }

    printf("Which (%d-%d): ", monday, sunday);

    do
        {
        pay_day = getch();
        pay_day -= '0';
        } while (pay_day < monday || pay_day > sunday);

    printf("%d\n\n", pay_day);

    printf("You selected %s\n", day_names[pay_day]);

}
```

Listing 11-7. *The TODAY.C program.*

Bit Fields

In Chapter 7, we discussed how to use bitwise operators to store data in the individual bits of bytes. Another, and simpler, way to store and access information in bits is with "bit fields."

Bit fields offer two advantages over the bitwise operators. First, you can access bit fields by name (such as *blink*) rather than by an obscure mask (such as *(1 << 15)*). Second, the compiler generates code for bit fields that you normally would have to write yourself. Examine, for example, the following bit field assignment:

```
blink = 1;
```

where *blink* is the name of the 16th bit of a 2-byte *int*. This statement is comparable to the following assignment using bitwise operators:

```
ch |= (1 << 15);
```

C's bit fields are especially handy when you need to manipulate items with built-in bit information. The characters in your screen memory are examples of such items. Recall that each screen character is represented by a 2-byte *int*. One byte is the character itself; the other is the attribute byte. (See Figure 11-7.)

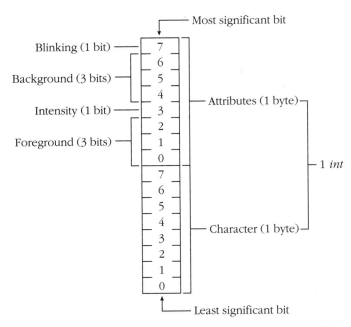

Figure 11-7. *One character in screen memory is represented by two consecutive bytes.*

The following is an example of one such screen *int* declared using bit fields:

```
                    ┌──────────────── One integer...
unsigned int character  :8, ┐
             foreground :3, │
             intensity  :1, ├── divided like this
             background :3, │
             blink      :1; ┘
          └──────────┴──────── Name for...this many bits
```

In this declaration, we tell QuickC to use the bits in one unsigned integer. Next, we specify the names for each group of bits in that integer, beginning with 8 bits, to which we give the name *character*, and continuing through all 16 bits until we end with *blink* as the name of the final bit.

You may name as many bits as there are in the enclosing variable, which must be an *int* or an *unsigned int*. Only integer types can be used as bit fields, and only integer constants can be used to declare the number of bits. Always declare the bits from the bottom up (from the least significant to the most significant bits). A colon separates the name for each group of bits from the number of bits assigned to it; a comma separates each *name :bits* from the next; and, of course, a semicolon must end the entire declaration.

If you declare fewer bits than there are in a type, the unused bits are simply ignored. If you declare more, an additional variable of the same type is allocated:

```
                    ┌──────────────── 8 bits
unsigned char character  :8,
             foreground :3,
             intensity  :1,
             background :3,
             blink      :1;
          │ ─────────16 bits total allocates two char variables
```

The *name :bits* combination is what defines a bit field as opposed to an ordinary variable. For example, the above declaration produces the same allocation as the following series of declarations:

```
unsigned char character  :8;
unsigned char foreground :3;
unsigned char intensity  :1;
unsigned char background :3;
unsigned char blink      :1;
```

In this example, the compiler gathers the bits from the declared bit fields into a compact unit, regardless of how many bit fields you declare.

Because you are not permitted to retrieve the address of a bit field, you usually will declare bit fields inside structures, as follows:

```
struct screen_char_struct {
    unsigned int character :8,
                 foreground :3,
                 intensity :1,
                 background :3,
                 blink      :1;
} screen_ch;
```
———————————————————— Structure variable whose members are bit fields

This approach has two advantages. First, you can access the individual bit fields with the usual *structure.member* notation. This improves readability:

```
screen_ch.blink = 1;
```

Second, you can access the address of a structure, but you cannot retrieve the address of a bit field. This lets you manipulate bit fields with pointers, which can increase the speed of your program:

```
&screen_ch
```
——— Retrieve the address of a structure

The SCRMENU.C program (Listing 11-8) demonstrates how to use bit fields to modify text-screen display. It lets you select an attribute; then it toggles the setting for that attribute for every character on the screen. For this program to run properly, you need to turn off the Pointer Check option in the Compiler Flags dialog box. To check the current status of pointer checking, choose Make from the Options menu and then choose Compiler Flags.

```
/* scrmenu.c -- uses bit fields to modify your text */
/*              screen's attributes                 */

char *Choice_Words[] = {
    "Quit",
    "Foreground",
    "Intensity",
    "Background",
    "Blinking"
};
enum Choices {
    Quit,
    Foreground,
    Intensity,
    Background,
    Blinking
};
```

Listing 11-8. *The SCRMENU.C program.*   *(continued)*

Listing 11-8. *continued*

```
/* Use 0xB0000000 for monochrome */
#define SCR_START (0xB8000000)
#define SCR_SIZE (25 * 80)

main()
{
    enum Choices choice;
    void Redraw(enum Choices field);

    printf("Select from the following by number:\n");

    for (choice = Quit; choice <= Blinking; ++choice)
        {
        printf("%d. %s\n", choice, Choice_Words[choice]);
        }

    printf("\nWhich: ");
    do
        {
        choice = getch();
        choice -= '0';
        if (choice < Foreground || choice > Blinking)
            continue;
        Redraw(choice);
        } while (choice != Quit);

}

void Redraw(enum Choices field)
{
    struct screen_char {
        unsigned int character  :8,
                     foreground :3,
                     intensity  :1,
                     background :3,
                     blink      :1;
    } scrchar, _far *sp, _far *ep;

    sp = (struct screen_char _far *)SCR_START;
    ep = sp + SCR_SIZE;

    while (sp < ep)
        {
        scrchar = *sp;
        switch (field)
            {
            case Foreground:
                scrchar.foreground = (scrchar.foreground)? 0 : 7;
                break;
```

(continued)

Listing 11-8. *continued*

```
        case Intensity:
            scrchar.intensity = (scrchar.intensity)? 0 : 1;
            break;
        case Background:
            scrchar.background = (scrchar.background)? 0 : 7;
            break;
        case Blinking:
            scrchar.blink = (scrchar.blink)? 0 : 1;
            break;
        }
    *(sp++) = scrchar;
    }
}
```

SCRMENU.C combines bit fields with *enum* and the *#define* preprocessor directive to virtually rid the body of the program of obscure constructs. Also, notice that we use a pointer to a structure to access the screen.

Advanced *typedef*

So far, we've used the *#define* preprocessor directive to create aliases, both for increased program clarity and as a shorthand method of entering repetitive code. We have also seen, in Chapter 3, that new types can be defined by using *typedef*. Superficially, *#define* and *typedef* appear to be interchangeable. To create simple aliases, you can use either one. Situations arise, however, in which *typedef* is suitable but *#define* is not.

For example, suppose you need to create a new type called *string*, an array of type *char*. Now suppose you attempt to create this new type with *#define*, as follows:

```
#define string char s[128]
```

You later would not be permitted to make the declaration

```
string str1, str2;
```

because the preprocessor would expand it to be

```
char s[128] str1, str2;
```

which is invalid. (Note the missing comma, among other things.) In situations such as this one, *typedef* is ideal. Rather than beginning with a *#define* directive, suppose you use the following:

```
typedef char string[128];
```

This creates a new type called *string*, which you can use later to declare variables of that new type:

```
string str1, str2;
```

Because we used *typedef* to define *string*, the compiler correctly translates this into

```
char str1[128], str2[128];
```

which is what we intended in the first place.

The secret to using *typedef* is to follow three simple steps. First, declare an ordinary variable of the type you want:

```
char s[128];
```
└──────────── Variable is an array of 128 *char* elements

Second, place the word *typedef* at the front:

```
typedef char s[128];
```

Third, replace the variable's name with the new type name:

```
typedef char string[128];
```

You can now use the newly defined type *string* exactly as you would one of C's built-in types, such as *int*.

In addition to doing what *#define* cannot, *typedef* also lends clarity to otherwise obscure constructs. For example, consider the following two pointers to functions:

```
int (*quit_fun)(), (*restart_fun)();
```

This could be confusing if it were to appear throughout your program. Using *typedef*, however, you can create a new type called *funptr*:

```
typedef (*funptr)();
```

Now you can use *funptr* throughout your program to declare variables of that new type, as follows:

```
funptr quit_fun, restart_fun;
```

Use *typedef* judiciously—it is the most easily abused concept in C. The indiscriminate use of *typedef*, rather than making your program more readable, can make it more obscure and (sometimes) indecipherable.

Large Projects

As your programs become larger and more complex, revising and maintaining them become less straightforward. Consequently, as your programming skills increase, you inevitably will find yourself looking for more efficient ways of handling programs. For example, you might want to

■ Use one function in several programs without having to retype it every time

■ Compile a program one way for testing and another for actual use—without having to rewrite it

■ Combine several .C files into a single program, while recompiling only those files that need to be changed

■ Transport one of your programs to another machine or compiler and compile it without having to rewrite it

This chapter offers solutions for these and other common programming needs. We'll discuss how to use the C preprocessor for conditional compilation and for creating macros. Next, we'll show you how to create and manage QuickC's "program lists." Finally, we'll show you how to develop custom C libraries and how to access them from within QuickC.

Advanced C Preprocessor

Although compiling under QuickC appears to be a single swift process, it is actually three processes combined into one. First, your C program is "preprocessed." In this phase, conditional compilation occurs, and other preprocessing directives are executed. For example, the directive *#define MAX 3* converts all instances of *MAX* to *3*. Second, the QuickC compiler translates your preprocessed code into machine language, or code that the computer can understand. Finally, your compiled machine code is combined (linked) with the precompiled code in the standard C Library of functions (such as *printf()*) to form the finished, executable program.

The C preprocessor recognizes only lines of text that begin with a pound symbol (#), such as those introduced by the directives *#define* and *#include*. Table 12-1 lists the complete set of the preprocessor directives.

Table 12-1. The Preprocessor Directives

Directive	Description
#define *x y*	Uses *x* as an alias for *y* throughout the program
#include *<file>*	Reads *file* from the INCLUDE subdirectory and inserts it into your program at this point
#include *"file"*	Reads *file* from the current working directory and inserts it into your program at this point
#ifdef *x*	If *x* is defined, compiles all program code between this and the next matching *#endif*, *#elif*, or *#else*
#if (*x*)	If the integer constant expression *x* is true (nonzero), compiles all program code between this directive and the next matching *#endif*, *#elif*, or *#else*
#ifndef *x*	If *x* is not defined, compiles all program code between this directive and the next matching *#endif*, *#elif*, or *#else*
#else	The inverse of the above three *if* directives: if the *#if* directive has a true result, compiles the program code before the *#else*; if the *#if* directive has a false result, compiles the code following the *#else*
#elif (*x*)	The *else if* extension for *#if* in a chain of conditions
#endif	Terminates the current matching *#if*, *#ifdef*, or *#ifndef*
#line *lineno "file"*	Sets the current line number to *lineno* and the current file to *file*
#pragma	Sets compiler-specific options
#define *x(y) z*	Defines preprocessor macros

Conditional Compilation

Occasionally, you will need to compile only part of your code—during debugging, for example, or when you compile different versions of a program for different users or different compilers. The C preprocessor offers an assortment of directives to facilitate this selective compiling process, called "conditional compilation."

#if and #endif

The most frequently used conditional directives are *#if* and *#endif*. The *#if* directive tests what is known as a restricted constant expression in your code to see if that expression is zero. If it is a nonzero (true) value, QuickC compiles all the code between that *#if* and its matching *#endif*. Use the directive as follows:

```
#define BYTES 4

#if (BYTES == 4)
/* Compile this code */
#endif
```

In this example, the expression *(BYTES == 4)* is a "constant expression" because it becomes *(4 == 4)* (the logical comparison of two integer constants). It is also a "restricted" constant expression, which is a constant expression that cannot contain:

■ *sizeof* operations

■ Enumerated constants

■ Type casts

■ Floating-point constants

Therefore, the following directives are valid:

```
#if (BYTES < 8)
#if ((6 * 9 / 3) != (2 % 1))
```

and the following are not:

```
#if (sizeof(int) == 4)─────── sizeof invalid

enum {true, false} yorn;
#if (true == 0) ─────────── Enumerated constant invalid

#if (NULL == (char *)0) ─────── Type cast invalid

#if (MIN < 4.2) ─────────── float constant invalid
```

One common use for the *#define* directive is in debugging. The program in Listing 12-1 on the following page, BUG.C, illustrates one possible way to use *#define* to change the behavior of your program. By using *#define* to define *DEBUG_LEVEL* to one of three possible values (0, 1, or 2) and then recompiling and running, you can cause the program to print one of three messages to your screen. For a debugging level of 0, nothing is printed; for 1, the calls to the subroutine *sub()* are documented; and for 2, entry into and exit from *main()* are printed.

```
/* bug.c -- shows how different levels of debugging */
/*          output can be produced using #if        */

#define DEBUG_LEVEL 2       /* 0 = none, 1-2 for debug */
#include <stdio.h>

main()
{
    int ret;

#if (DEBUG_LEVEL == 2)
    fprintf(stderr, "Entering main()\n");
#endif

#if (DEBUG_LEVEL == 1)
    fprintf(stderr, "Calling sub()\n");
#endif

    ret = sub();

#if (DEBUG_LEVEL == 1)
    fprintf(stderr, "sub() returned %d\n", ret);
#endif

#if (DEBUG_LEVEL == 2)
    fprintf(stderr, "Leaving main()\n");
#endif
}

sub()
{
    return (5);
}
```

Listing 12-1. *The BUG.C program.*

defined and #ifdef

You can use the *defined* keyword with the *#if* directive to detect whether or not a name has been specified in a *#define* directive:

```
#if defined(name)
```

If *defined(name)* determines that *name* was used in a *#define* directive, it evaluates to true. The keyword *defined* is used by the preprocessor only in this context; therefore, you can use it anywhere in your program without causing a conflict.

The *defined* variation of *#if* replaces the pre-ANSI directive *#ifdef*. That is, although the following are equivalent:

```
#if defined(name)
#ifdef name
```

the first form is preferable.

You can use the same technique to see if a name has not been specified with *#define*, as follows:

```
#if !defined(name)
#ifndef name
```

Again, the first form is preferable to the second.

The *defined* variation of *#if* is especially useful for writing programs that will be compiled on another type of computer or a different compiler. The BITOUT.C program (Listing 12-2) is an adaptation of the *Bitout()* function used in the BITWISE.C program (Listing 7-12 on pp. 216–18). After the user enters an integer, the program prints that integer in binary form. Note that it uses *#if defined* to print the bits one way on an 80286-based computer and another way on a 68000-based machine.

```c
/* bitout.c -- compiles one way on an IBM PC and */
/*             another on a 68000-based machine  */

#define CHIP_80286    /* don't define on a 68000 machine */
#include <stdio.h>

main()
{
    int num;

    printf("Enter an integer number and I will print"
           " it out in binary\nNumber: ");

    if (scanf("%d", &num) != 1)
        {
        fprintf(stderr, "Not an integer\n");
        exit(1);
        }
    Bitout(num);
}

Bitout(unsigned int num)
{
    int i, j;
    unsigned char *cp;
```

Listing 12-2. *The BITOUT.C program.*   *(continued)*

Listing 12-2. *continued*

```
    cp = (char *)&num;

#if defined(CHIP_80286)      /* IBM PC */
    for (i = 1; i >= 0; --i)
#endif
#if !defined(CHIP_80286)     /* otherwise 68000 machine */
    for (i = 0; i < 4; ++i)
#endif
        {
        for (j = 7; j >= 0; --j)
            putchar((cp[i] & (1 << j)) ? '1' : '0');
        }
    putchar('\n');
}
```

#else and #elif

We can simplify the two *#if* directives in BITOUT.C by using the *#else* directive:

```
#if defined(CHIP_80286)
    for (i = 1; i >= 0; --i)
#else
    for (i = 0; i < 4; ++i)
#endif
```

In this example, the preprocessor compiles the first *for* statement if *CHIP_80286* has been defined using *#define*; otherwise, it compiles the second *for* statement.

By using the *#elif* directive (which is similar to an *else if* construction), you can create a whole chain of conditions. The following series of directives, for example,

```
#if defined(CHIP_8086)
    for (i = 1; i >= 0; --i)
#elif defined(CHIP_80286)
    for (i = 1; i >= 0; --i)
#elif defined(CHIP_68000)
    for (i = 0; i < 4; ++i)
#else
    fprintf(stderr, "Unknown chip\n");
    return;
#endif
```

tells the preprocessor to compile the first *for* statement if *CHIP_8086* is defined, to compile the second *for* statement if *CHIP_80286* is defined, or to compile the third *for* statement if *CHIP_68000* is defined. If none of these is defined, the preprocessor compiles code to print an error and return.

Logical Operators and #if

Many of the preceding *#if* tests use similar code. You can take a coding shortcut by combining *#if* expressions using the C logical operators && and ¦¦. For example, you can shorten the previous *#elif* sequence by using the logical OR operator.

```
                              ┌──────────────────── Logical OR
#if defined(CHIP_8086) ¦¦ defined(CHIP_80286)
    for (i = 1; i >= 0; --i)
#elif defined(CHIP_68000)
    for (i = 0; i < 4; ++i)
#else
    fprint(stderr, "Unknown chip\n");
    return;
#endif
```

The *#if* directives and their corresponding *#endif* and *#elif* directives can be nested. However, when you nest them, we recommend that you use indents to show the levels of nesting, as follows:

```
#if defined(IBMPC)
#    if defined(CGA) ¦¦ defined(EGA)
        sp = (int far *)0xB8000000;
#    else
        sp = (int far *)0xB0000000;
#    endif
#else
    fprintf(stderr, "No screen memory\n");
    return;
#endif
```

In this example, if *IBMPC* is not defined, the last *#else* executes. If *IBMPC* is defined, the program checks to see whether either *CGA* or *EGA* (for the corresponding graphic adapter cards) is defined. If either is defined, we assign the address value 0xB8000000 (the location of screen memory for those cards) to the pointer *sp*. Otherwise, we use the address 0xB0000000 (the location of screen memory for the monochrome adapter).

You can avoid problems when using preprocessor directives by remembering two general rules. First, the # must always begin a line. Second, each directive can occupy only one line unless you extend it by typing a backslash and pressing Enter:

```
#if defined(EGA) \──────── Line extended
    ¦¦ \──────── Extended again
    defined(CGA)
```

Predefined Names

QuickC always predefines two names: _ _*FILE*_ _ and _ _*LINE*_ _. (Note that both have two leading and two trailing underscore characters.) The name _ _*FILE*_ _ is always the name of the C source file currently being compiled. It is a quoted string constant, so you can safely use it anywhere that strings are legal. The predefined name _ _*LINE*_ _ is an integer constant number that is always the current line number in the current file. You can use it anywhere as a legal integer constant.

These two predefined names are generally used to print meaningful diagnostics during debugging. The ERR.C program (Listing 12-3 on the following page) demonstrates their use for tracing the flow of a small program.

```
/* err.c -- illustrates __FILE__ and __LINE__ in */
/*          tracing a small program              */

#define ERR printf("Tracing: \"%s\" line %d\n",\
                    __FILE__, __LINE__);
main()
{
    ERR
    err1();
    ERR
    err2();
    ERR
}

err1()
{
    ERR
    err2();
}

err2()
{
    ERR
}
```

Listing 12-3. *The ERR.C program.*

By placing a *#define ERR* directive inside an *#if* branch, you can turn on and off custom tracing with a single change in code:

```
#define TRACE 0      /* change to 1 to turn on tracing */

#if (TRACE > 0)
#define ERR printf("Tracing: \"%s\" line %d\n",\
                    __FILE__, __LINE__ );
#else
#define ERR
#endif
```

If *TRACE* is defined as a value greater than 0, QuickC traces the program. If, on the other hand, *TRACE* is 0, then tracing is disabled.

#pragma Instructions to the Compiler

You can use the *#pragma* preprocessor directive to give instructions to the compiler (instructions that you must otherwise give as part of the MS-DOS command line or as QuickC's compile time options). Use it in the following way:

```
#pragma instruction
```

#pragma pack(1 ¦ 2 ¦ 4)

The *pack()* pragma tells the compiler to place structure members into memory on 1-byte, 2-byte, or 4-byte boundaries. Ordinarily, QuickC places structure members into memory so that *int* and *long* types always begin in an even address, which is equivalent to *pack(2)*. (See Figure 12-1a.) By using the *#pragma pack()* preprocessor directive, you can tell the compiler to store structures in a smaller space (see Figure 12-1b) or to spread them out into a larger space with *pack(4)*. (See Figure 12-1c.)

An extension to the *#pragma pack()* directive lets you turn packing on and off:

```
#pragma pack(1)──────── Set 1-byte packing
⋮
#pragma pack() no────── Turn packing off
⋮
#pragma pack() yes───── Turn packing back on
```

In the example, the first directive tells the compiler to pack all structure members to the nearest 1-byte boundary. Next, the *no* tells the compiler to stop packing and revert to its default even-byte boundary arrangement. Finally, the *yes* tells the compiler to resume packing on 1-byte boundaries.

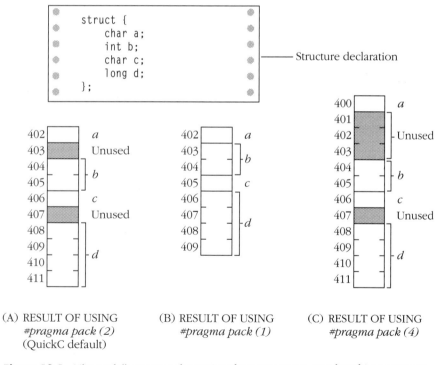

(A) RESULT OF USING
   #pragma pack (2)
   (QuickC default)

(B) RESULT OF USING
   #pragma pack (1)

(C) RESULT OF USING
   #pragma pack (4)

Figure 12-1. *The* pack() *pragma determines how structures are placed into memory.*

The PACK.C program (Listing 12-4) illustrates structure packing. When you run the program, notice the addresses it prints. Then change the *1* in *#pragma pack(1)* to *2* and compile and run PACK.C again. Finally, change that *2* to *4* and repeat the process.

```
/* pack.c -- demonstrates structure packing with */
/*           the #pragma pack() directive         */

#pragma pack(1)          /* 1, 2, or 4 */
main()
{
    struct {
        char ch1;
        int  int1;
        char ch2;
        long int2;
    } s;

    printf("ch1  -> %p\n", &(s.ch1));
    printf("int1 -> %p\n", &(s.int1));
    printf("ch2  -> %p\n", &(s.ch2));
    printf("int2 -> %p\n", &(s.int2));
}
```

Listing 12-4. *The PACK.C program.*

Preprocessor Macros

The *#define* preprocessor directive has a second form that is called a *#define* macro, or a preprocessor macro. The *#define* macro is an extremely powerful tool, used by programmers to place "in-line" code into a program in a manner that resembles a subroutine call. Take a moment to use QuickC's View Include feature to look at the stdio.h header file. Notice in line 107 of that file that the *getc()* function you have been using all along is not a function at all. It is actually a *#define* macro. Because it is a macro, the preprocessor expands each occurrence of *getc(stdin)* in your program to the following:

```
(--(_stream)->_cnt >= 0 ? 0xff & *(_stream)->_ptr++ : _filbuf(_stream))
```

Certainly, it is easier to type *getc(stdin)* than to type this complex code sequence.

> **Quick Tip**
>
> The Intel 80386 chip executes at its fastest if *int* and *long* types begin on 4-byte address boundaries. The Intel 80286 and earlier chips execute fastest when those types begin on even addresses. If file size is more important to you than execution speed, use the *#pragma pack(1)* directive.

The form for a #*define* macro is as follows:

```
#define TRIPLE(x) (x * 3)
```

In this example, the defined name is *TRIPLE* and the *(x)* is its formal argument. The expression *TRIPLE(x)* is defined as an alias for the expression *(x * 3)*. This means that anywhere in the program that you use the following expression:

```
TRIPLE(2)
```

the actual argument (here *2*) replaces every occurrence of the formal argument, *x*, in the original definition. This produces the following expansion:

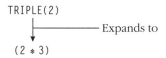

To illustrate further, examine the following macro definition for *MAX*, a macro that compares two values and yields a new value that is the higher of the two:

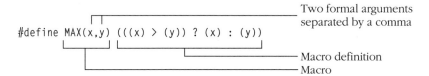

This example shows that macros can take more than one formal argument—but arguments must be separated from one another by commas. The *x* in the macro replaces each *x* in the macro definition with its corresponding actual argument, and each *y* replaces its corresponding *y*. If you use the above macro definition in your code and then use the following expression:

```
oldest = MAX(age1, age2);
```

with *int* variables *age1* and *age2*, the preprocessor expands the macro as follows:

```
oldest = (((age1) > (age2)) ? (age1) : (age2));
```

Potential Problems with Macros

Use preprocessor macros with care—actual arguments to macros can cause unexpected changes, such as the reading of an extra character. You should avoid using the following types of arguments because they can produce unwanted "side effects":

- Function calls

- Other macros

- The increment (++) and decrement (--) operators

- The assignment operator (=)

For example, consider the following *ISQ* macro:

```
#define ISQ(letter) ((letter) == 'q' !! (letter) == 'Q')
```

This macro detects whether a letter is an uppercase or lowercase *Q* and is useful for testing whether a user is quitting a program. You correctly use this macro as follows:

```
ch = getchar();

if (ISQ(ch))
    exit(0);
```

In the preceding code, *ch* is a *char* variable; therefore, the *if* statement expands to

```
if (((ch) == 'q' !! (ch) == 'Q'))
```

which is what you expect. However, if you use this macro incorrectly—for example, with a function call such as *getchar()*,

```
if (ISQ(getchar()))
```

it expands to an expression that doesn't do what you expect:

```
if (((getchar()) == 'q' !! (getchar()) == 'Q'))
```

This example illustrates a common problem. The first call to *getchar()* reads a character and compares the value to *'q'*. If that character is not a *'q'*, *getchar()* is called again to read a new character and to compare the new character to *'Q'*. This is not what you intended, however. You want *ISQ* to read only the first character and then to compare that character to both *'q'* and *'Q'*.

Macros and Semicolons

Never end a macro definition with a semicolon. For example, the following macro converts a printable character into a control character value:

```
#define CTRL(x) ('x' - '@');
```

The expression *CTRL(A)* expands to the expression *('A' - '@');* and yields the desired ASCII value 1 (Ctrl-A). However, the trailing semicolon causes a syntax error when you use the macro in an expression such as:

```
printf("And 'A' prints as %c\n", CTRL(A));
```

Note the syntax error that results when this expands to

```
printf("And 'A' prints as %c\n", ('A' - '@'););
```
                                              └──────── Wrong

Macros and Quotation Marks

As in normal *#define* directives, preprocessor macros do not substitute actual arguments inside double quotation marks. The following macro would, in principle, be a useful tool for debugging.

```
#define PERR(x) printf("The value of x is %d\n", x)
```

Unfortunately it won't work. Because the first *x* is inside full quotation marks, it isn't expanded. However, the final *x* is expanded:

```
int val = 5;
PERR(val);
```

Expands to

```
printf("The value of x is %d\n", val);
```

We can rectify this situation by using the preprocessor's "stringizing" operator, #. When placed before a formal argument in a macro definition, the # causes that argument to be expanded and quoted. Thus, the correct way to define *PERR* is as follows:

```
#define PERR(x) printf("The value of " #x " is %d\n", x)
```

Stringizing operator

This correctly expands as:

```
int val = 5;
PERR(val);
```

Expands to

```
printf("The value of " "val" " is %d\n", val);
```

The example works because the compiler joins adjacent quoted string constants into a single string. The result is that *printf()* correctly prints the following:

```
The value of val is 5
```

Using QuickC for Large Projects

Imagine you are writing a text editor program such as the one shown in Figure 12-2 on p. 379. With sufficient memory, QuickC can easily load and compile programs of this size. However, the larger a program is, the longer it takes to compile, load, and save. Therefore, you can manage large programs more easily when you break them into several smaller files by grouping the subroutines logically according to use. This approach has several advantages:

- When a program consists of several files, you need to recompile only those files that change.

- Grouping subroutines by usage lets you easily trace the logic of the program during debugging.

- Perfected subroutines that no longer need to be recompiled can be shared by many programs.

QuickC Program Lists

The QuickC "program list" feature compiles several small files or library modules and combines them into a single executable program. This lets you create complex, large programs from many small, easily maintained files. Before we examine this feature, enter and save the following three files: TEXED.C (Listing 12-5), KEYS.C (Listing 12-6), and FILE.C (Listing 12-7 on p. 380). These are three small pieces of our imaginary text editor in Figure 12-2. Although these modules don't do much, they demonstrate the basics of using QuickC program lists.

Next select Set Program List from the Make menu and enter *texed.mak* in the File Name text box. The first part of the filename, *texed*, is the name of your finished program. The second part, the extension *.mak*, signifies that this program list file is a "make" file. (We'll explain make files in the next section.)

```
/* texed.c -- main entry point to the editor; the */
/*            menu and signal handlers are here    */

main(int argc, char *argv[])
{
    char ch;

    while (1)
        {
        printf("\nTexEd Main Menu\n");
        printf("Select from:\n");
        printf("0) Quit\n\n");
        printf("1) Load File\n");
        printf("2) Save File\n");
        printf("3) Edit File\n");
        printf("Which: ");
        do
            {
            ch = getch();
            ch -= '0';
            } while (ch < 0 || ch > 3);
        printf("%d\n\n", (int)ch);
        switch(ch)
            {
            case 0: exit(0);
            case 1: Load_file(); break;
            case 2: Save_file(); break;
            case 3: Edit_file(); break;
            }
        }
}
```

Listing 12-5. *The TEXED.C file.*

After you enter the name *texed.mak*, QuickC prompts *'TEXED.MAK' does not exist Create?* A *Yes* response displays the Edit Program List dialog box. This box lets you specify the files in your program list. Enter the filenames TEXED.C, KEYS.C, and FILE.C. As you enter each filename, the name appears in the bottom window labeled Program List.

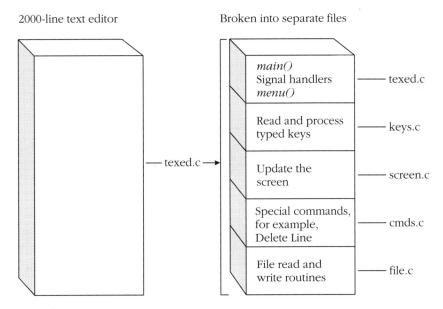

Figure 12-2. *A large program is often more manageable when split into smaller files.*

```
/* keys.c -- the keyboard input-handling routines */
/*           for the texed editor                 */

Edit_file()
{
    char ch;

    printf("\nYou are now in the editor.\n");
    printf("Press 'Q' to exit back to main menu.\n");

    do
        {
        ch = getch();
        putch(ch);
        } while (ch != 'Q');

    printf("\n\n");
}
```

Listing 12-6. *The KEYS.C file.*

```
/* file.c -- the file I/O routines for texed */

Load_file()
{
    printf("\nLoading ..... done.\n");
}

Save_file()
{
    printf("\nSaving ...... done.\n");
}
```

Listing 12-7. *The FILE.C file.*

After you enter all three files, your screen appears as in Figure 12-3. Now choose the Save List option to save your program list on disk and return to the main QuickC screen. You will now build your program from several files, not only from the one currently loaded.

To compile a program from a program list, display the Make menu, but this time, instead of selecting Compile File, select Build Program. Notice that each of your files is loaded in turn and compiled. After all three have been compiled, the linker combines your compiled files, along with any precompiled routines that you use from the standard C Library (such as *printf()*). This process creates a single, executable program.

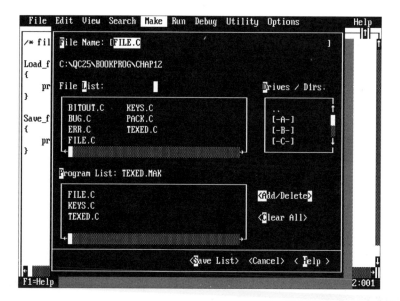

Figure 12-3. *The Edit Program List dialog box.*

Program List Files

Program list files contain rules and instructions that tell QuickC how to build your program. They are composed of four elements: comment lines (lines that begin with a # character), macros, dependencies, and link commands. Examine the following make file, TEXED.MAK. This is the kind of file that the NMAKE program uses.

```
PROJ      =TEXED
DEBUG     =1
CC        =qcl
CFLAGS_G        = /AS /W1 /Ze
CFLAGS_D        = /Zi /Zr /Gi$(PROJ).mdt /Od
CFLAGS_R        = /O /Ot /DNDEBUG
CFLAGS  =$(CFLAGS_G) $(CFLAGS_D)
LFLAGS_G        =/NOI
LFLAGS_D        =/INCR /CO
LFLAGS_R        =
LFLAGS  =$(LFLAGS_G) $(LFLAGS_D)
RUNFLAGS        =
OBJS_EXT =
LIBS_EXT =

.asm.obj: ; $(AS) $(AFLAGS) -c $*.asm

all:    $(PROJ).EXE

texed.obj:      texed.c $(H)

keys.obj:       keys.c $(H)

file.obj:       file.c $(H)

$(PROJ).EXE     texed.obj keys.obj file.obj $(OBJS_EXT)
        echo >NUL @<<$(PROJ).crf
texed.obj +
keys.obj +
file.obj +
$(OBJS_EXT)
$(PROJ).EXE

$(LIBS_EXT);
<<
        ilink -a -e "qlink $(LFLAGS) @$(PROJ).crf" $(PROJ)

run: $(PROJ).EXE
        $(PROJ) $(RUNFLAGS)
```

The NMAKE program is a powerful and complex tool included with the QuickC package. As you can see, every time QuickC creates a .MAK file for a program list, it does a lot of work on your behalf. We won't go into the details of this TEXED.MAK file here; the NMAKE section of your *Microsoft QuickC Tool Kit* manual will more than satisfy your curiosity. But you should appreciate the ways that QuickC makes building large products much easier.

Keeping Track of Changes

QuickC keeps track of which files have changed in a program list. To see how this works, first build the TEXED program: Select Build Program from the Make menu. Now load the KEYS.C file and change it by inserting a blank line anywhere. Save that file and select Build Program again. This time, QuickC recompiles the KEYS.C file, but it does not compile the other two .C files because they haven't changed.

This ability to know which files need to be recompiled makes QuickC a powerful tool for developing complex programs that are composed of many source files.

Header Files

Programs formed from separate .C files often share identical declarations. For example, examine the two files TEXED2.C and KEYS2.C in Listings 12-8a and 12-8b. These parts of a larger text editor program both use structures of the same pattern, and both use the *#define* directive to define the values *OK* and *ERROR*. (These listings are not intended to be compiled and run independently.) If you need to change the structures (by adding a member, for example) or the definition of *ERROR* (from 1 to −1, for example), you must make changes in both files (and possibly in many other files if the text editor program uses those values throughout).

Therefore, your program is easier to maintain if you gather such common definitions into a single, separate file called a header file, or an include file. Listing 12-9 shows one such header file for our text editor program. Now you can easily make changes that affect all files. Simply modify TEXED2.C and KEYS2.C to use the *#include* preprocessor directive, as shown in TEXED3.C and KEYS3.C, Listings 12-10a and 12-10b.

```
#define OK 1
#define ERROR 0
menu()
{
    struct key_struct {
        char key;
        unsigned char move;
    } *kp, *Read_key();
    int cur_key, cur_move;

    kp = Read_key();
    cur_key = kp->key;
    cur_move = kp->move;
    if (cur_key == ERROR)
        return (cur_move);
    return (cur_key);
}
```

Listing 12-8a. *The TEXED2.C file.*

Because we use double quotation marks with that directive (rather than angle brackets as with *#include <stdio.h>*), the compiler looks for the header file in our current working directory.

```
#define OK 1
#define ERROR 0
struct key_struct {
    char key;
    unsigned char move;
};

struct key_struct *Read_key()
{
    struct key_struct k;

    k.key = getch();
    if (k.key == ERROR)
        k.move = getch();
    return (&k);
}
```

Listing 12-8b. *The KEYS2.C file.*

```
#define OK 1
#define ERROR 0

struct key_struct {
    char key;
    unsigned char move;
};
```

Listing 12-9. *The texed.h header file.*

```
#include "texed.h"
menu()
{
    struct key_struct *kp, *Read_key();
    int cur_key, cur_move;

    kp = Read_key();
    cur_key = kp->key;
    cur_move = kp->move;
    if (cur_key == ERROR)
        return (cur_move);
    return (cur_key);
}
```

Listing 12-10a. *The TEXED3.C file.*

```
#include "texed.h"
struct key_struct *Read_key()
{
    struct key_struct k;

    k.key = getch();
    if (k.key == ERROR)
        k.move = getch();
    return (&k);
}
```

Listing 12-10b. *The KEYS3.C file.*

Variables in Header Files

You can also place declarations in header files that make variables global to all files. However, you cannot initialize variables in header files that are shared by more than one .C file. That is, in the header file texed.h,

```
char Last_key;————————— Valid
int  Upper_flag = 1;——————— Invalid
```

the declaration for *Last_key* is always valid because the variable is not initialized. The declaration for *Upper_flag* is not valid, however. The texed.h header file is specified by *#include* directives in several .C files and therefore cannot use initialized global variables.

You can declare and initialize a global variable only once in a program. If you want to declare and initialize a global variable in one file and access that variable from another file, you must make this an explicit operation by placing the *extern* keyword in the second file, as follows:

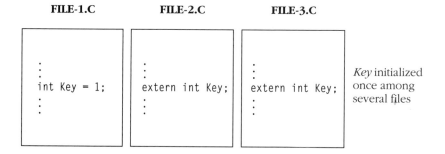

The *extern* keyword tells QuickC that the integer *Key* is located in another file. If a global variable is not initialized as part of its declaration, you can declare it in all files without the *extern* keyword, as follows.

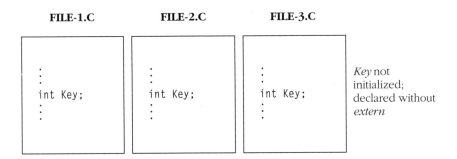

FILE-1.C   FILE-2.C   FILE-3.C

int Key;   int Key;   int Key;   *Key* not
                                     initialized;
                                     declared without
                                     extern

This is the same as declaring the global variable once in a header file and then specifying that header with *#include*, as follows:

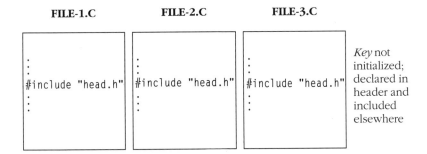

HEAD.H

int Key;

FILE-1.C   FILE-2.C   FILE-3.C

#include "head.h" #include "head.h" #include "head.h"   *Key* not
                                                            initialized;
                                                            declared in
                                                            header and
                                                            included
                                                            elsewhere

Libraries

In addition to listing .C files in a QuickC program list file, you can also list library (.LIB) files. Libraries are files that contain precompiled .OBJ files that you can use as part of a program.

During the course of your programming, you will develop many general subroutines that can be used in many programs. By placing those subroutines into a special library, you can access them through a QuickC program list without having to recompile them. For example, consider the following three subroutines: leftstr.c (Listing 12-11), midstr.c (Listing 12-12), and rightstr.c (Listing 12-13). (These subroutines, shown on pp. 387–88, are C analogs to the BASIC functions LEFT$, MID$, and RIGHT$.)

To create a library for these three subroutines, enter them using the QuickC editor, and then save each as an individual .C file. Now exit QuickC by selecting the DOS Shell command from the File menu, and compile each with QCL, as follows:

```
qcl /c /AS leftstr.c
qcl /c /AS midstr.c
qcl /c /AS rightstr.c
```

QCL is the command-line version of QuickC. The /c option tells QuickC to create an .OBJ file from the .C file, and /AS tells QuickC to use the small memory model.

After you generate the three .OBJ files, create a library for them by running the LIB program and answering its questions, as follows:

```
Library name: basic.lib
Library does not exist.  Create? (y/n) y
Operations: +leftstr.obj&
Operations: +midstr.obj&
Operations: +rightstr.obj
List file:
```

The first and second lines tell LIB to create a library named BASIC.LIB. In the three *Operations* lines, the + tells LIB that we are adding an .OBJ file to the library. The & following two of the lines is a signal that another operation will be specified. At the *List file* prompt, you simply press Enter because this library is small; you don't need to create a list of its contents. After a short wait, QuickC produces a library file named BASIC.LIB, which you can place into any program list. To return to the QuickC menu, enter *exit* at the MS-DOS prompt.

Now let's create a program to test our library and demonstrate how to use a library from a program list. Enter the TEST.C program (Listing 12-14 on p. 388) and save

---

Dependencies in Header Files

Because a change in a header file results in a change in a .C file, you might wonder if you can place header files into your QuickC program list as a dependency, as follows:

```
texed.obj : texed.c texed.h

keys.obj : keys.c texed.h
```

As this dependency is written, it tells QuickC (in our program list) to recompile TEXED.OBJ if either TEXED.C or texed.h changes and to recompile KEYS.OBJ if either KEYS.C or texed.h changes.

QuickC 1.0 allowed you to place header file dependencies into your program lists: It recognized and maintained them, but it did not treat header files as real dependencies. That means, for example, that TEXED.OBJ was not recompiled if only texed.h changed. This has been corrected in QuickC version 2.

---

it on disk. Next, choose Set Program List from the Make menu and enter TEST.MAK as the name of the program list.

After you press Enter and confirm that you want to create the file, the Edit Program List dialog box appears. Select *test.c* as the first item in the list. Notice that the name of the library is not displayed. That's okay; simply type *basic.lib* and add it to the list. Finally, save this program list.

```
/* leftstr.c -- a C version of BASIC's LEFT$ */

#include <stdio.h>

char *Leftstr(char *str, int cnt)
{
    static char *cp = NULL;
    char *malloc();

    if (cnt > strlen(str))
        cnt = strlen(str);
    if (cp != NULL)
        free(cp);
    if ((cp = malloc(cnt + 1)) == NULL)
        return (NULL);
    strncpy(cp, str, cnt);
    *(cp + cnt) = '\0';
    return (cp);
}
```

Listing 12-11. *The leftstr.c subroutine.*

```
/* midstr.c -- a C version of BASIC's MID$ */

#include <stdio.h>

char *Midstr(char *str, int where, int cnt)
{
    static char *cp = NULL;
    char *malloc();

    if (cnt > strlen(str + where))
        cnt = strlen(str + where);
    if (cp != NULL)
        free(cp);
    if ((cp = malloc(cnt + 1)) == NULL)
        return (NULL);
    strncpy(cp, str + where, cnt);
    *(cp + cnt) = '\0';
    return (cp);
}
```

Listing 12-12. *The midstr.c subroutine.*

```
/* rightstr.c -- a C version of BASIC's RIGHT$ */

#include <stdio.h>

char *Rightstr(char *str, int cnt)
{
    static char *cp = NULL;
    char *malloc();

    if (cnt > strlen(str))
        cnt = strlen(str);
    if (cp != NULL)
        free(cp);
    if ((cp = malloc(cnt + 1)) == NULL)
        return (NULL);
    strcpy(cp, str + strlen(str) - cnt);
    return (cp);
}
```

Listing 12-13. *The rightstr.c subroutine.*

```
/* test.c -- tests the routines in basic.lib */
/* Program list: test.c and basic.lib        */

#include <stdio.h>

main()
{
    static char string[] = "This is a test.";
    char *cp, *Leftstr(), *Midstr(), *Rightstr();

    printf("Testing: \"%s\"\n", string);

    if ((cp = Leftstr(string, 4)) == NULL)
        {
        printf("Error in Leftstr()\n");
        exit(1);
        }
    printf("Leftstr() returned: \"%s\"\n", cp);

    if ((cp = Midstr(string, 4, 5)) == NULL)
        {
        printf("Error in Midstr()\n");
        exit(1);
        }
    printf("Midstr() returned: \"%s\"\n", cp);
```

Listing 12-14. *The TEST.C program.*

(continued)

Listing 12-14. *continued*

```
if ((cp = Rightstr(string, 5)) == NULL)
        {
        printf("Error in Rightstr()\n");
        exit(1);
        }
    printf("Rightstr() returned: \"%s\"\n", cp);
}
```

At the QuickC editor, choose Build Program from the Make menu. Because we are compiling from a program list, we use Build Program to compile TEST.C and then combine it with the subroutines in BASIC.LIB.

One additional advantage offered by .LIB files is that you can place them in the directory specified by your LIB environment variable. From there, QuickC can find them no matter where you are in the directory hierarchy. The result of all this is that you need only one copy of common subroutines in a single library, and you can access those subroutines through a program list from any directory.

PART IV

Keyboard and Graphics

Keyboard and Cursor Control

Almost every PC program needs to get information from the keyboard and to display information on a monochrome or color screen. So far, our programs have used the standard C Library functions such as *getchar()*, *scanf()*, *putchar()*, and *printf()*, and occasionally we've used command-line arguments. These approaches to PC I/O produce portable code, but they also produce a bland interface that fails to take advantage of many PC capabilities. If you want your programs to do more than display mere text on the screen, study this and the next two chapters. You will learn how to use function keys and cursor control keys, how to control the location and appearance of text on the screen, and how to construct graphic figures.

In this chapter, we examine the keyboard and cursor control. We look at QuickC's numerous I/O functions and provide a more detailed discussion of the generic *getchar()* routine and the PC-specific *getche()* and *getch()* functions. We also describe scan codes, show how to use ANSI.SYS to redefine keys and to provide cursor control, and discuss BIOS routines. Finally, we use the *int86()* function to create a library of BIOS-based screen control and cursor control functions.

Keyboard Input Functions

You use the standard C I/O functions to read and to display a variety of input: characters, strings, integers, and floating-point numbers. But the standard input functions don't detect non-ASCII keys, such as the function keys. And they don't provide many of the input control features typically required by programs such as word processors, spreadsheets, and games. To get that control, we need to process input at a "lower" level than that of standard I/O functions.

Three QuickC routines read keyboard input character by character: *getchar()*, *getche()*, and *getch()*. Each routine reads one character at a time and reports its value to the calling program.

Input Examples

The programs on the opposite page illustrate how the three input functions respond to the same input—in each case, the input is the word *hat* followed by Enter.

The GETCHAR.C program (Listing 13-1) produces the following output:

```
Please enter a word.
hat<Enter>
1.. 2.. 3..  ──────────────── Counting delayed until you press Enter
3 characters altogether
```

Counting doesn't start until you type the word and press Enter. Next, look at GETCHE.C (Listing 13-2), which generates the following output:

```
Please enter a word.
h1.. a2.. t3.. <Enter>────── Immediate count
3 characters altogether
```

This time each letter is counted as it is typed. Finally, examine GETCH.C (Listing 13-3), which produces the following output:

```
Please enter a word.
1.. 2.. 3.. <Enter>──────── Input not displayed
3 characters altogether
```

This time the input is invisible; only the output is displayed.

The functions behave differently, and you use them for different purposes. The *getchar()* routine buffers and echoes input; *getche()* does not buffer input but echoes it; *getch()* neither buffers nor echoes input. Buffered input goes into a temporary storage area before being transferred to the calling program. (Pressing Enter "empties" the buffer.) Echoed input is displayed on the screen.

The *getchar()* routine handles arrow keys or function keys inconsistently from one system to another. Try using GETCHAR.C with these keys as input and see how your system responds. The *getche()* and *getch()* functions do read these keys in a consistent manner, however. Try GETCHE.C, for example, with an arrow key or function key as input. Each of these keys, as you'll see, is counted as two keystrokes, and characters other than those you typed are echoed on the screen. This is perfectly proper and reasonable behavior, as you'll see when we discuss scan codes.

```
/* getchar.c -- gets input with getchar() */

#include <stdio.h>
main()
{
    int count = 1;

    printf("Please enter a word.\n");
    while (getchar() != '\n')          /* here it is */
        printf("%d.. ", count++);
    printf("\n%d characters altogether\n", count - 1);
}
```

Listing 13-1. *The GETCHAR.C program.*

```
/* getche.c -- gets input with getche() */

#include <conio.h>      /* note different file included */
main()
{
    int count = 1;

    printf("Please enter a word.\n");
    while (getche() != '\r')    /* changed comparison */
        printf("%d.. ", count++);
    printf("\n%d characters altogether\n", count - 1);
}
```

Listing 13-2. *The GETCHE.C program.*

```
/* getch.c -- gets input with getch() */

#include <conio.h>
main()
{
    int count = 1;

    printf("Please enter a word.\n");
    while (getch() != '\r')
        printf("%d.. ", count++);
    printf("\n%d characters altogether\n", count - 1);
}
```

Listing 13-3. *The GETCH.C program.*

The *getchar()* Buffer

The program using *getchar()* doesn't receive the generated code until the routine's storage buffer is flushed. This occurs when you press Enter or when the buffer is filled. The *getchar()* buffer is 512 bytes, so normal keyboard input does not fill it.

Be aware that *getchar()* shares the input buffer with all the input functions of the stdio.h family. QuickC sets up this input buffer when any input function from that family is called. Thus, when your program calls both *scanf()* and *getchar()*, the routines use the same input buffer.

Differences in Usage

Pay attention to the differences among character input routines. First, *getchar()* requires stdio.h, whereas *getch()* and *getche()* require conio.h, the include file for console I/O functions. Second, *getch()* and *getche()* use \r instead of \n to represent the action of Enter, and they do not interpret Ctrl-Z as an end-of-file indicator.

The reason for these behavior differences is that *getchar()*, by default, reads input in text mode, whereas *getch()* and *getche()* read input in binary mode. In text mode, you may recall, the carriage return/linefeed combination is converted to a linefeed on input, and the linefeed is converted to a carriage return/linefeed on output. The binary mode makes no conversions. As a result, *getchar()* uses \n to detect the Enter key, but *getch()* and *getche()* must use \r.

Another difference is that *getchar()*, when used in the text mode, recognizes the Ctrl-Z character as marking the end of a file. This lets you simulate the end-of-file condition from the keyboard by entering Ctrl-Z. The binary mode used by *getche()* and *getch()* does not recognize Ctrl-Z (or any other character) to mark the end of a file. As a result, the following construction does not work for keyboard input:

```
while((ch = getche()) != EOF)     /* NO */
```

When you use *getch()* or *getche()* in such a loop, specify a keyboard character, such as \r or the Esc key, to indicate the end of input.

Although the *getchar()* input routine uses text mode by default, you can call QuickC's *setmode()* function to place *getchar()* in binary mode. (Refer to the Help menu for more information about *setmode()*). However, you cannot switch *getche()* and *getch()* to text mode.

Reminder

Don't mix buffered routines such as *getchar()* and *gets()* with unbuffered functions such as *getche()* and *getch()*. The buffered functions transmit characters from the input buffer when it is flushed; the unbuffered functions read keys as they are pressed. Thus, a program mixing buffered and unbuffered input functions might not process the characters in the order they were typed.

Table 13-1 summarizes the different behavior of the character input routines.

Table 13-1. Character Input Routines

	getchar()	*getche()*	*getch()*
Buffered	o		
Echoes	o	o	
Uses \n	o		
Uses \r		o	o
Uses stdio.h	o		
Uses conio.h		o	o
Text mode (default)	o		
Binary mode		o	o
Backspace editing	o		
Reads ASCII keys	o	o	o
Reads non-ASCII keys		o	o

Typical Uses for Character Input Routines

The primary advantage of using the buffered *getchar()* is that this routine lets users edit input with the Backspace key before they send it to the program. The non-buffered form, on the other hand, requires users to type less because they needn't press Enter. For example, suppose your program uses the following prompt:

```
Continue? <y/n>
```

With *getchar()*, the user must type *y* and press Enter, while *getche()* requires only a *y*. Likewise, the *getche()* function is useful in programs that use a typed character to select a menu item. Consider the following fragment:

```
while ((ch = getchar()) != 'q') /* oops example */
    switch (ch)
    {
        case 'a': ...
        case 'b': ...
        case 'c': ...
        default:  printf("Not a valid choice\n");
    }
```

To choose case *a*, the user types *a* and presses Enter. The loop processes the *a*, recycles and processes the \n generated by the Enter key, and prints the default message. Replacing *getchar()* with *getche()* eliminates the need to press the Enter key and hence the need to add programming to process the extraneous \n.

The nonechoed, nonbuffered *getch()* is useful, of course, when you don't want to display input on the screen. For example, you might use the *k* key to move an image on the screen. Also, a program that requires a user to type a secret password shouldn't display it on the screen.

Let's use *getch()* to construct a simple password program. A real application would ensure password security by also using encryption and periodic updating. In the PASSWORD.C program (Listing 13-4), we'll build the password into the program and concentrate on processing the user's input.

```c
/* password.c -- requires a password to complete the   */
/*               program; illustrates a use of getch() */

#include <stdio.h>
#include <conio.h>
#include <string.h>
#define GUESS_LIMIT 4
#define WORD_LIMIT 10   /* maximum length of password */
#define TRUE 1
#define FALSE 0

char *Password = "I'mOK";

main()
{
    int g_count = 0;            /* guesses taken    */
    int w_count;                /* letters accepted */
    int in_count;               /* letters entered  */
    char entry[WORD_LIMIT + 1];
    char ch;
    int correct, go_on;

    do
        {
        puts("Enter the secret password.");
        in_count = w_count = 0;

        /* The following loop accepts no more chars than entry[] */
        /* will hold but keeps track of total number typed       */
        while ((ch = getch()) != '\r')
            {
            if (w_count < WORD_LIMIT)
                entry[w_count++] = ch;
            in_count++;
            }
        entry[w_count] = '\0';
        if (in_count != w_count)
            correct = FALSE;       /* too many chars */
        else
            correct = (strcmp(entry, Password) == 0);
        g_count++;
        go_on = !correct && g_count < GUESS_LIMIT;
        if (go_on)
            puts("\nNo good; try again.");
        } while (go_on);
```

Listing 13-4. *The PASSWORD.C program.*   *(continued)*

Listing 13-4. *continued*

```
    if (!correct)
        {                           .
        puts("\nSorry, no more guesses.  Bye.");
        return(1);
        }
    puts("\nWelcome to Swiss bank account 2929100.");
    puts("Your current balance is $10,232,862.61.");
    return (0);
}
```

Notice the loop that obtains the user's input:

```
while ((ch = getch()) != '\r')
    {
        if (w_count < WORD_LIMIT)
            entry[w_count++] = ch;
        in_count++;
    }
```

Character and String Input in BASIC and C

If you are used to BASIC, you know that you can read a character from the keyboard (with no echo) using the INKEY$ function. This function is similar to C's *getch()*. C conveniently provides the alternative *getche()* function for character input with echo, while in BASIC you would need a separate PRINT statement to echo the input character. Note that neither the BASIC function nor the C functions mentioned recognize Ctrl-Z as a signal for the end of file.

Both BASIC and C provide generalized input functions that can handle a series of numeric or string variables. In BASIC, the INPUT statement lets you supply a prompt string and accept input into one or more variables. For example:

```
INPUT "Enter name and age: ", NAME$, AGE
```

The *scanf()* function in C is similar in that it allows you to receive input for a series of variables of different types. The *scanf()* function, however, allows you a much greater degree of control over the format of each input value, the interpretation of white space, and the characters used to separate input values. Unlike the INPUT function, *scanf()* makes no provision for a prompt string, so it is normally preceded by a *printf()* statement with the desired string.

In a typical trade-off for these two languages, BASIC's INPUT statement provides very rudimentary error checking and editing of the input line. Although *scanf()* rejects any input that does not match the specifications, it does not terminate or restart when it encounters bad input. The C programmer is responsible for error checking to determine whether the values entered are actually reasonable and complete.

This loop uses an *if* statement to prevent overflowing the array, yet it continues to read additional characters if the limit is exceeded. We could have made this loop stop at the character limit, but that would tell the illicit user the number of characters in the actual password.

The structure of the *do while* loop reflects the two conditions that terminate the loop: a correct password or an excessive number of attempts. If the loop ends and *correct* is still false, the program knows that the reason for termination was the number of attempts.

Reading Non-ASCII Keys

Some keys, such as the function keys, the cursor control keys, and Alt key combinations, have no ASCII code. How can a QuickC program read them? Before answering this question, we need to discuss the way in which the keyboard actually works.

The Keyboard Processor and Scan Codes

Information does not flow directly from the keyboard to a C program. Instead, pressing (or closing) a given key generates a "closure" code that indicates the physical location of the key. A microprocessor within the keyboard reads this code and generates a new code, called a "system code." It also reports the keyboard state— whether the user is holding down the Shift, Ctrl, or Alt key. Finally, it generates a third code (2 bytes called the "extended scan code") for the keystroke (or keystroke combination) and places it in a storage area called the "keyboard buffer." If the key is still "closed" after a predetermined period of time elapses, another keystroke is placed in the buffer. Thus, you can generate a string of characters by holding down a key. Releasing the key generates an "opening" code that tells the keyboard microprocessor that you are finished with that key. By default, the keyboard buffer holds a maximum of 16 extended scan codes.

The purpose of the keyboard buffer is to hold characters that are typed faster than an application can process them. It is distinct from the buffer created for the stdio.h input functions.

The *getch()* and *getche()* functions do not read the keyboard directly. Instead, they read the extended scan codes in the keyboard buffer. Because these codes are more extensive than the standard ASCII codes, programs can use them to identify function keys, cursor keys, and other keys lacking an ASCII code. (The only difference between *getch()* and *getche()* is that *getche()* echoes input; therefore, our next discussions about *getch()* actually apply to both functions.)

Using Scan Codes

Each extended scan code is 2 bytes. The first byte, the "ASCII byte," contains the ASCII code, if any, for the keystroke. The second byte, the "scan byte," contains a scan code for the key. This code is based on the physical position of the key on the keyboard and, in some cases, on whether the Shift, Ctrl, or Alt key is pressed.

The contents of an extended scan code reveal whether or not it represents an ASCII character. If the scan code represents an ASCII character, the ASCII byte is a nonzero value. However, if the scan code does not represent an ASCII character, the ASCII byte is set to zero, and the numeric value of the scan byte encodes the keystroke or keystroke combination. For example, in Figure 13-1, the uppercase Q character is represented by an ASCII byte of 81 because that is its ASCII code. The scan code of 16 means the Q key is the sixteenth key in the keyboard numbering scheme. The F1 key has no ASCII representation, so the ASCII byte is 0. However, because it is the 59th key on the keyboard, the scan byte is 59.

How does *getch()* use these extended codes? First, it looks at the ASCII byte. If the byte is nonzero, *getch()* knows it has found an ASCII character. It returns that value, skips the scan byte, and moves to the next ASCII byte. For example, it returns 0x41 for Shift-A, 0x61 for *a*, and 0x01 for Ctrl-A.

When the ASCII byte is 0, *getch()* lets the program know it has found a non-ASCII keystroke by returning a value of 0. Because *getch()* needs to know which non-ASCII character was pressed, it does not skip to the next ASCII byte; instead, it goes to the scan byte. Thus, the next call to *getch()* results in its reading the scan code that goes with the 0 ASCII byte. In other words, only one call of *getch()* is needed to read an ASCII keystroke, but two calls are needed to read a non-ASCII keystroke. Also, the scan codes are returned only for the non-ASCII keystrokes.

Suppose, for example, that you type the Shift-Q combination and then press the F1 key. The codes 81 16 00 59 are placed in the keyboard buffer. The first call to *getch()* returns the 81. The next call to the function skips to the 00 and returns that value, and the third call returns the 59. Thus, a program that plans to use the F1 key must look for return values of 0. When it encounters one, the program should check to see whether the next call returns 59. If so, F1 was pressed. The return value 0 is a flag that says, "Special processing required here."

Now, how does *getchar()* process non-ASCII characters? It copies ASCII values into the program buffer created by the standard I/O buffer. When it finds a 0 ASCII byte in the buffer, it skips to the next input character. The 0 ASCII bytes and the scan codes never make it to the I/O buffer, let alone to the program.

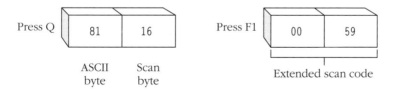

Figure 13-1. *Scan codes.*

A Scan Code Example

The SCANCODE.C program (Listing 13-5) demonstrates these functions by reading input. If the input is an ASCII character, the program prints the ASCII code. If the input is a non-ASCII character, the program prints the scan code.

The following is some sample output:

```
Press keys and see the codes!
Press the Esc key to quit.

Q has ASCII code 81─────────── Shift-Q
Scan code is 59─────────────── F1
t has ASCII code 116────────── Lowercase T
^T has ASCII code 20────────── Ctrl-T
```

What happens if you use *getch()* and *getche()* without checking for the 0 value? The routines would interpret the ASCII byte and scan byte as two ASCII bytes, thus interpreting 00 59 as code for Ctrl-@ and for the semicolon character, instead of F1.

```c
/* scancode.c -- displays ASCII or scan code    */
/* This program illustrates the use of getch()  */
/* to detect special keys, such as function keys */

#include <conio.h>
#define ESC '\033'       /* ESC key */

main()
{
    int ch;

    printf("Press keys and see the codes!\n");
    printf("Press the Esc key to quit.\n\n");

    while ((ch = getch()) != ESC)
        {
        if (ch != 0)
            {
            if (ch <= 32)    /* control characters */
                printf("^%c has ASCII code %d\n", ch + 64, ch);
            else
                printf("%c has ASCII code %d\n", ch, ch);
            }
        else              /* ch IS 0 */
            {
            ch = getch();  /* get scan code */
            printf("Scan code is %d\n", ch);
            }
        }
}
```

Listing 13-5. *The SCANCODE.C program.*

Scan Code Values

In this book we will use only scan codes contained in include file keys.h. When we need to use these keys, you can include keys.h, which is shown in Listing 13-6.

Not all keystrokes produce scan codes. For example, Shift, Ctrl, and Alt modify the scan codes that other keystrokes produce. The SCANCODE.C program shows this: When you press the Alt key, nothing happens until you simultaneously press a second key.

The operating system normally intercepts the Ctrl-Break combination as the code for terminating a program. Thus, *getch()*, *getche()*, and *getchar()* never read Ctrl-Break. (We will discuss how to handle Ctrl-Break later in this chapter.)

```
/* keys.h -- scan codes for several keys */

#define F1 59    /* function key F1 */
#define F2 60    /* function key F2 */
#define F3 61    /* and so on       */
#define F4 62
#define F5 63
#define F6 64
#define F7 65
#define F8 66
#define F9 67
#define F10 68
#define HM 71    /* Home key     */
#define UP 72    /* Up Arrow     */
#define PU 73    /* Page Up      */
#define LT 75    /* Left Arrow   */
#define RT 77    /* Right Arrow  */
#define END 79   /* End key      */
#define DN 80    /* Down Arrow   */
#define PD 81    /* Page Down    */
```

Listing 13-6. *The keys.h include file.*

Console I/O Functions

The *getch()* and *getche()* functions belong to the console I/O family of functions. These functions communicate with the console (the keyboard and screen) more directly than do the I/O functions of the stdio.h family. However, unlike the stdio.h family, console I/O functions are not in the standard C Library and are therefore not necessarily portable. The console I/O functions, which are declared in the conio.h header file, provide special services not offered by the standard I/O package:

```
cgets()
cprintf()
cputs()
cscanf()
```

(continued)

continued

```
getch()
getche()
putch()
ungetch()

kbhit()
inp()
outp()
inpw()
outpw()
```

The first eight functions in this list closely resemble the stdio.h functions with corresponding names. For example, *cgets()* resembles *gets()*, *cprintf()* is similar to *printf()*, and so on. We've already seen the *kbhit()* function. We'll discuss the *inp()*, *outp()*, *inpw()*, and *outpw()* functions in Chapter 14.

Character Output Routines

Now that we've used the character input routines, let's look at the console character output routines. The *putch()* function works much like *putchar()*. One difference is that *putchar()* is buffered and *putch()* is nòt. This means that *putch()* output goes to the screen directly; *putchar()* output goes to an intermediate storage area first. The second difference is that *putchar()* works in text mode by default, while *putch()* works in binary mode. The main practical consequence of this is in the handling of newlines. The C newline character (\n) represents the transference of the cursor to the beginning of the next line. This actually consists of two operations: a linefeed (LF) and a carriage return (CR). In QuickC, the newline character is represented by the LF character, ^J. Text mode produces the desired effect by mapping an LF to a CR/LF combination on the screen. In binary mode, no such mapping takes place, so you must explicitly generate both an LF and a CR character (\n and \r).

A third difference is that the text mode used by *putchar()* interprets a tab character (\t) as a tabbing instruction; the binary mode used by *putch()* interprets it as an ASCII value to be displayed. With the IBM character set, using *putch()* to generate a tab character results in a small circle on the screen.

The REKEY.C program (Listing 13-7) demonstrates how to use the console I/O functions *getch()* and *putch()* to map the characters you type to a different set of characters on the screen. Notice that we initialize the *Newchars* array to 26 letters. The construction *Newchars[ch - 'a']* causes the array index to be zero when *ch* is *a*. Array element 0 corresponds to the value *q*. Similarly, if *ch* is *b*, the index is 1; and the array value is the next letter in the initialization string, *w*. The initialization continues in this fashion, as shown in Figure 13-2.

The *toupper()* and *tolower()* QuickC macros (defined in ctype.h) convert cases; thus, we don't need to use another 26-element array for uppercase letters. Notice that the program explicitly translates Enter (read by *getch()* as \r) to an output of \r and \n.

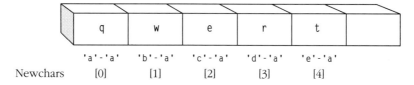

Figure 13-2. *The* Newchars[ch - a] *array.*

```
/* rekey.c -- transliterates typed input       */
/* This program illustrates getch() and putch() */

#include <stdio.h>
#include <conio.h>
#include <ctype.h>
#define ESC '\033'    /* the escape key */

/* Values to be assigned to the a, b, c keys, etc. */
char Newchars[] = "qwertyuiopasdfghjklzxcvbnm";

main()
{
    char ch;

    printf("Type characters and see them transformed.\n");
    printf("Press the Esc key to terminate.\n");
    while ((ch = getch()) != ESC)
        if (islower(ch))
            putch(Newchars[ch - 'a']);
        else if (isupper(ch))
            {
            ch = tolower(ch);
            putch(toupper(Newchars[ch - 'a']));
            }
        else if (ch == '\r')
            {
            putch('\n');
            putch('\r');
            }
        else
            putch(ch);
}
```

Listing 13-7. *The REKEY.C program.*

Console String I/O

Often you want to generate a string, or you want a program to read a string—for example, the name of a file. You can perform these activities character by character, but you can more conveniently use functions specifically designed to handle strings. The console functions *cgets()* and *cputs()* perform these tasks. In action, these functions are similar to *gets()* and *puts()*, but they exhibit some differences.

Like *gets()*, *cgets()* reads an input string into an array. However, the first element of the array holds the maximum allowable size of the input string, including a terminating null character. You must initialize this element correctly. The second element holds the actual number of bytes used, and it is set by *cgets()* after it reads the input. The string itself starts at the third element. Thus, the array must be 2 bytes longer than the maximum string size, including a null character, as shown in Figure 13-3.

The *cgets()* function reads input until it achieves the maximum length of the string (reserving space for the null character) or until the user presses Enter. The console beeps if you try to read beyond the limit, and you can't enter additional characters. The function will, however, let you use the Backspace key to correct input. This function returns a pointer to the beginning of the stored string; that is, if the array name is *str*, *cgets()* returns a pointer to *str[2]*.

The *cputs()* function takes a pointer to a string as its argument and displays that string on the console. Unlike *puts()*, *cputs()* does not append a newline character; therefore, you must explicitly include the \r\n combination to generate a new line. The function returns the last character written. It returns 0 if the string is a null string and −1 if an error occurs.

The short STRIO.C program (Listing 13-8) illustrates how the two functions work. Notice how we use *store + 2* as an argument for *cputs()*. We do this because the string starts at the location pointed to by *store + 2*. We kept the character limit small to make it easy to see what happens when you try to exceed it.

The following is a sample run of the program:

```
What's your name?
Steph
I'll remember you, Steph!
```

Note the \n\r at the beginning of the second *cputs()* statement. This prevents the message from being printed over the input line.

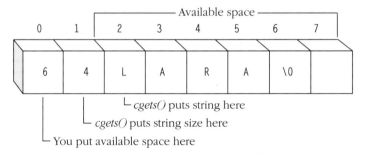

Figure 13-3. *Storage of an array read by* cputs().

```
/* strio.c -- uses cgets() and cputs() */

#include <conio.h>
#define MAXSIZE 6

main()
{
    char store[MAXSIZE + 2];

    store[0] = MAXSIZE; /* put limit in first element */
    cputs("What's your name?\n\r");
    cgets(store);
    cputs("\n\rI'll remember you, ");
    cputs(store + 2);
    cputs("!\n\r");
}
```

Listing 13-8. *The STRIO.C program.*

Instead of using *cputs(store + 2)*, we could have used *cputs(&store[2])*. Or, because the return value of *cgets()* points to the start of the string—not to the start of *store[]*—we could have declared a pointer and used it as follows:

```
char *start;
⋮
start = cgets(store);
⋮
cputs(start);
```

Formatted I/O

Finally, the *cscanf()* and *cprintf()* functions provide console analogues to the standard I/O functions *scanf()* and *printf()*. The main differences are that *cscanf()* and *cprintf()* work directly with the console, that *cprintf()* requires you to use the \r\n combination instead of \n, and that the console functions are less portable.

Keyboard Control with ANSI.SYS

Using *getch()* or *getche()* and the scan codes, a QuickC program can detect a function key or a cursor control key. But how can you turn that information into action? How, for example, can pressing the Left Arrow key be made to move the cursor one space to the left? There are three common techniques. One uses the ANSI.SYS driver provided with MS-DOS and PC-DOS, the second uses BIOS calls, and the third accesses video memory directly (DMA). Table 13-2 on the following page compares the three methods.

The first method is the simplest. Many terminals have internal hardware that lets you control cursor position and other screen attributes by sending "escape sequences" from your program to the terminal. These all begin with the ESC character, followed by different sequences corresponding to different actions. For example, the sequence *ESC[2B* moves the cursor down two lines in the same column. By using *printf()* to generate such a string, you can move the cursor around. The original IBM PC hardware design omitted this convenient feature.

Table 13-2. Cursor Control and Screen Control Methods

Method	ANSI.SYS	BIOS	DMA
Speed ranking	3	2	1
Ease-of-use ranking	1	2	3
Portability	ANSI-compatible	BIOS-compatible	Display-specific

MS-DOS version 2.0 came to the rescue, however, by providing the ANSI.SYS "driver" as a software fix. (A driver is software designed to handle specific hardware I/O devices.) The ANSI.SYS software intercepts output and examines it for escape sequences. When it finds a valid sequence, it performs the requested action. To use this method, you need ANSI.SYS up and running, and you need to know the proper escape sequences.

Starting ANSI.SYS

Running ANSI.SYS is not like running an ordinary program. You don't, for example, type *ansi*. Instead, you place this line in your CONFIG.SYS file:

```
DEVICE=ANSI.SYS
```

If the ANSI.SYS file is in a different directory from the CONFIG.SYS file, give the full pathname, as in the following example:

```
DEVICE=C:\DOS\ANSI.SYS
```

Now, when you boot your computer, ANSI.SYS is installed as part of MS-DOS.

Using ANSI.SYS Escape Sequences

One handy escape sequence lets you assign a string to a particular key. That is, it makes typing a single key have the same effect as typing the string. First, let's examine the format of the escape sequence required by ANSI.SYS:

```
ESC[ASCIIcode;"string";ASCIIcodep
```

Here ESC represents the escape character (ASCII 033). The first *ASCIIcode* represents the ASCII number of the key to which you assign the string. For non-ASCII keys, such as F1, use 0;*scancode*, where the number following the 0; is the scan code for the key. Next, *string* represents, in string form, the characters you want to assign to the key. For example, the string could be *DIR/W*. The final *ASCIIcode* lets you represent an assigned character in ASCII form instead of as a string. For example, you can use *13* instead of a carriage return. Finally, the character *p* terminates the escape sequence. You can use as many strings and ASCII codes as you like as

long as you separate them with semicolons. For example, you can represent CD by
"CD", by *"C"*;*68*, or by *67*;*68*, where 67 and 68 are ASCII codes for C and D. The
ASGNKEY.C program (Listing 13-9), for example, assigns meanings to keys F5
through F10. These meanings remain in effect until you reboot.

Because all the key assignments follow the same form, we use a macro to represent
the general form. In the macro, *printf()* displays the escape sequence. First comes
033, the octal code for ESC. Then come the left bracket and the *0;*, which indicate a
scan code. (The scan code itself is the variable *K* of the KASSIGN macro.) Next
comes another semicolon and a double quotation mark (escaped with a \ when used
within a string). Next, the string itself is represented by the variable *S* and closed
with another quotation mark. The sequence concludes with another semicolon, a *13*
(a carriage return), and a *p*.

Running this program changes the function key assignments, but you have to go to
MS-DOS before you can see the effects. Once you exit to MS-DOS, pressing F5
through F8 causes MS-DOS to list the specified types of files (**.c*, **.h*, and so on). The
F9 key lists your directories in the compact form (specified with the */W* option). The
F10 key switches to the root directory. The defining string uses \\ for root because a
single \ is an escape character in a C string. Because the code itself includes *13* for
Return, you don't press Enter when you use these function keys.

You can easily modify this program to read in the desired function key number and
the string interactively. But bear in mind that these assignments supersede existing
ones and remain in effect until you reboot. If, for example, you assign a function to
F1, you override the editing function given to it by MS-DOS.

```
/* asgnkey.c -- uses ANSI.SYS to assign meanings */
/*              to several function keys          */
/* Note: Requires that ANSI.SYS be installed      */

/* This macro assigns string S to key K */
#define KASSIGN(K, S) printf("\033[0;%d;\"%s\";13p", K, S)
#define F5 63
#define F6 64
#define F7 65
#define F8 66
#define F9 67
#define F10 68

main()
{
    KASSIGN(F5, "DIR *.C");
    KASSIGN(F6, "DIR *.H");
    KASSIGN(F7, "DIR *.OBJ");
    KASSIGN(F8, "DIR *.EXE");
    KASSIGN(F9, "DIR /W");
    KASSIGN(F10,"CD \\");
}
```

Listing 13-9. *The ASGNKEY.C program.*

Note that QuickC uses its own routines to read the keyboard, and it bypasses these function key definitions. Therefore, while you are using the QuickC environment, you still can press F5 to run a program. But if you call up an MS-DOS shell from QuickC, the new assignments apply.

Cursor and Screen Control

Now let's apply the ANSI.SYS method to a simple menu model. The goal is to write a program that clears the screen and displays a simple menu with one choice highlighted. The Up Arrow and Down Arrow keys move the cursor and highlighting to a different choice, and the Enter key selects the highlighted choice. To create the menu, we need more escape codes. Table 13-3 lists some representative examples from which we'll select the codes we need. Our program will use the various cursor control sequences to move the cursor. The highlighting of a choice is handled using the SGR (Set Graphics Rendition) escape sequence, which lets you specify character attributes. Each character to be displayed can be assigned an attribute that controls its presentation: color, reverse video, blinking, and so on. In Table 13-3, *ESC* represents the Escape character, and *num* is a numeric parameter for which you substitute a specific number. The numbering of rows and columns starts with 1. For all but the last code sequence, any omitted *num* is assumed to be 1.

To highlight a line of text, we must first print the escape code for highlighting on that line and then print the text. To confine highlighting to the menu line, we turn off highlighting at the end of the menu output.

To move the cursor and highlighting, we use *getch()* and the scan codes to detect when the arrow keys are pressed. If the Down Arrow key is pressed, for example,

Table 13-3. ANSI.SYS Escape Sequences

Name	Mnemonic	Escape Code	Description
Cursor Position	CUP	ESC[*num;num*H	Moves the cursor to the position specified by the numeric parameters. The first *num* is the line number; the second is the column number.
Cursor Up	CUU	ESC[*num*A	Moves the cursor up *num* lines in the same column.
Cursor Down	CUD	ESC[*num*B	Moves the cursor down *num* lines in the same column.
Cursor Forward	CUF	ESC[*num*C	Moves the cursor right *num* columns.
Cursor Back	CUB	ESC[*num*D	Moves the cursor left *num* columns.
Erase Display	ED	ESC[2J	Erases the entire display and homes the cursor.
Set Graphics Rendition	SGR	ESC[*num* m	Sets character attributes as indicated by *num*; possible values include 0 for normal, 1 for high intensity, 5 for blink, and 7 for reverse video.

the program moves the cursor and reprints the menu, changing the line that is highlighted. Listing 13-10 shows the completed MENU.C program, and Figure 13-4 on p. 413 shows the menu at work.

```
/* menu.c -- uses ANSI.SYS for cursor control and */
/*            for reverse video in a sample menu   */
/* Note: Requires that ANSI.SYS be installed       */

#include <conio.h>
#define ITEMS 5              /* number of menu items    */
#define UP 72                /* scan code for up arrow  */
#define DOWN 80              /* scan code for down arrow */
#define VIDREV "\033[7m"    /* reverse video attribute */
#define ATTOFF "\033[0m"    /* turn attributes off     */
#define ED()   printf("\033[2J")  /* erase display     */
#define HOME() printf("\033[H")   /* home the cursor   */
#define CUU(Y) printf("\033[%dA",Y)  /* cursor up      */
#define CUD(Y) printf("\033[%dB",Y)  /* cursor down    */

char *Menu[ITEMS] = {"Add a number to the list",
                     "Delete a number from the list",
                     "Clear the list",
                     "Sum the list",
                     "Quit"};
char *Heading = "Use arrow keys to highlight choice. "
                "Use Enter key to select choice.";

void Showmenu(int highlite);
int Getmesg(int mnum);

main()
{
    int messno = 0; /* message to be highlighted */
    ED();
    Showmenu(messno);
    while (messno != ITEMS - 1)
        {
        messno = Getmesg(messno);
        ED();
        switch (messno)
            {
            case 0 :
            case 1 :
            case 2 :
            case 3 : printf("...pretending to work ...");
                     printf("Hit any key to continue\n");
                     getch();
                     ED();
                     Showmenu(messno);
                     break;
```

Listing 13-10. *The MENU.C program.*   *(continued)*

Listing 13-10. *continued*

```
            case 4 : printf("Quitting!\n");
                    break;
            default: printf("Programming error!\n");
                    break;
            }
        }
}

/* Showmenu() displays the menu */
void Showmenu(int highlite)  /* receives message number to highlight */
{
    int n;
    char *start;

    HOME();
    printf("%s", Heading);
    for (n = 0; n < ITEMS; n++)
        {
        if (n == highlite)
            start = VIDREV; /* turn on reverse video */
        else
            start = ATTOFF;
        printf("\n\n%s%s%s", start, Menu[n], ATTOFF);
        }
    HOME();
    CUD(2 + 2 * highlite);
}

/* Getmesg() selects a menu item */
int Getmesg(int mnum)  /* receives current message number */
{
    char ch;

    while ((ch = getch()) != '\r')
        if (ch == 0)
            {
            ch = getch();
            switch (ch)
                {
                case UP   : if (mnum > 0)
                                {
                                CUU(2);
                                Showmenu (--mnum);
                                }
                            else
                                {
                                CUD(2 * ITEMS - 2);
                                Showmenu(mnum = ITEMS - 1);
                                }
                            break;
```

(continued)

412

Listing 13-10. *continued*

```
                case DOWN : if (mnum < ITEMS - 1)
                              {
                              CUD(2);
                              Showmenu(++mnum);
                              }
                           else
                              {
                              CUU(2 * ITEMS - 2);
                              Showmenu(mnum = 0);
                              }
                           break;
                }
        }
     return (mnum);
}
```

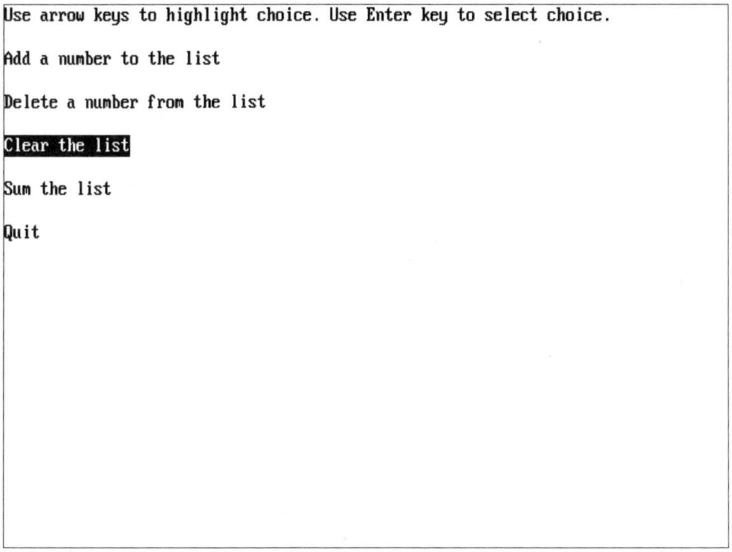

```
Use arrow keys to highlight choice. Use Enter key to select choice.

Add a number to the list

Delete a number from the list

Clear the list

Sum the list

Quit
```

Figure 13-4. *The MENU.C program at work.*

The MENU.C program first defines several macros using *printf()* and the escape codes to represent some of the ANSI.SYS sequences from Table 13-3 on p. 410. If you plan to use such macros often, create an include file for the macro definitions.

Because we are illustrating ANSI.SYS and not numeric analysis, the program does no actual calculation. However, the *switch* statement in *main()* provides the skeleton for controlling program flow. The *Getmesg()* function returns the index of the selected message, and the *switch* statement selects a response based on that value. The *switch* statement is in a loop, so you can make choices until you select *Quit*.

In *main()*, the *HOME()* macro uses the CUP escape code to home the cursor. Because we omitted the two numeric parameters, the default values of 1 are used, which effectively home the cursor.

The *Showmenu()* function displays the menu. It receives the array index of the element to be highlighted. That message then starts with highlighting turned on; the other messages have it turned off.

The *Getmesg()* function, as we mentioned, returns the array index of the selected item. It also handles the cursor movement. In this function, *getch()* checks for the Up Arrow and the Down Arrow keys. If, for example, the Down Arrow key is pressed, CUD moves the cursor down two lines to the next message. The array index is also incremented to tell *Showmenu()* which message to highlight. To keep the cursor inside the menu, we compare its position to the menu limits. If the cursor is on the bottom line of the menu, then pressing the Down Arrow key moves it to the top line.

This program works as designed, but it runs slowly, and the redrawing of the screen is not very smooth. The ANSI.SYS approach to cursor and screen control is relatively simple, but using BIOS calls or direct memory access gives better performance.

Watching the Keyboard in BASIC and C

The ANSI.SYS techniques discussed here allow you to achieve the functionality of the KEY statement in BASIC. The BASIC KEY *n, string* statement allows you to assign a string to the PC function key F*n*—that is, to create a simple "keyboard macro." The ANSI method is more general (it can be used with any key, not just a function key) and is not limited to assigning short strings.

BASIC statements such as ON KEY provide a very useful facility called "event-driven programming." After you use the KEY statement to assign a key number to one of the keyboard keys, any occurences of that key number while the program is running will be "trapped." The ON KEY(*n*) *subroutine* statement causes *subroutine* to be executed whenever the key that's assigned number *n* is pressed. This allows programs to respond to input immediately.

C has no such built-in facilities. You can, however, put the program in an outer loop that calls the *kbhit()* function to detect a key press. If a key is pressed, you can use *getch()* to read the key. After assigning the key to a variable of type *char*, you can use it in a *switch* statement that calls the appropriate function to handle the command received. This isn't true event-driven programming, because the response to a key comes only when the program is at the top of the loop, but QuickC programs run fast enough that the effect is often the same. The use of a special device driver or an environment such as Microsoft Windows can allow for true event-driven programming.

Using QuickC to Access the BIOS

One way to create programs that take advantage of the special capabilities of an IBM PC/XT, a PC/AT, or a compatible setup (without getting too involved in the hardware) is to use BIOS calls.

Background for the IBM BIOS

BIOS is an acronym for Basic Input/Output System. It consists of a set of assembly-language routines permanently stored in what is called the Read-Only Memory, or ROM, of the IBM PC. The computer can read and use information in ROM, but it cannot alter ROM. That permanence preserves the integrity of the routines.

The BIOS includes routines to read the keyboard, to control the video display, and to read from and write to disk drives. Most higher-level programming ultimately makes use of these routines. For instance, QuickC's *getch()* uses one of the keyboard routines, and many MS-DOS commands ultimately use the BIOS routines to do low-level work. In short, you can think of the BIOS as a built-in library of functions. All you need to do is find out what services are offered and how to use them.

The ultimate source of information about the BIOS is the *IBM Personal Computer Technical Reference Manual*. This manual includes assembly-language listings of all the routines. We'll describe those routines as we use them.

Using the BIOS

Two problems face the QuickC programmer who wants to use the BIOS. One is that the routines, which are written in assembly language, don't work the same as C functions, so you have to learn a little about assembly language and about the hardware to understand them. The second is that these BIOS routines are accessed not by function calls but by "interrupt signals." For this reason, these routines are commonly called "interrupt routines," or simply "interrupts." Let's clarify this topic first.

Interrupt Routines

The heart of a PC is its central processing unit, or CPU, but a PC contains other processors, too. For example, the keyboard processor handles keyboard input, and another processor handles data flow between the CPU and memory. To enable the CPU to keep in touch with its environment, an interrupt system was developed. Certain devices and assembly-language instructions can generate signals that take control of the microprocessor. The Intel 8086 family of microprocessors permits as many as 256 distinct interrupt signals, but fewer are actually used. When the CPU detects an interrupt signal, it "interrupts" its current activity and executes the set of assembly-language instructions identified with that particular signal.

Software Interrupts

In assembly language, generating interrupts is simple. For example, to generate interrupt signal 0x10 (the video I/O interrupt), you use the following instruction:

```
int 10h
```

What if one interrupt arrives while another interrupt routine is executing? This situation is handled by a priority ranking. A higher-priority interrupt can interrupt a lower-priority routine, but not vice versa.

C, as a general, portable language, doesn't have a built-in interrupt instruction. But the QuickC library offers several non-ANSI C functions designed to serve the same purpose. Seven of these functions make specific BIOS calls; they all have names beginning with _bios_ and are declared in the file bios.h. The dos.h file declares another 40 functions, most of which call specific MS-DOS functions. (Interrupt number 0x21 can be used to access many functions loaded into the system by MS-DOS; these are the MS-DOS system calls.) Five of the dos.h functions, however, are more general and can invoke a choice of interrupts. (Table 13-4 summarizes these functions.)

Table 13-4.
Interrupt-accessing Functions in Order of Decreasing Generality

Name	Use
intx86()	Invokes interrupts that require segment registers
int86()	Invokes interrupts that do not require segment registers
intxdos()	Invokes MS-DOS system calls that require segment registers
intdos()	Invokes MS-DOS system calls that do not require segment registers
bdos()	Invokes MS-DOS system calls that use only the DX and AL registers
bios...() family	Invokes specific BIOS interrupts
dos...() family	Invokes specific MS-DOS calls

How Interrupts Work

When you boot a PC, it sets up a table of addresses known as the "interrupt vectors." At the first address is the routine to be executed if interrupt signal 0 is detected. At the second address is the routine to be executed if interrupt signal 1 is detected, and so on. When an interrupt is detected, the corresponding address is found in the table, and the instructions beginning at that address are executed. At the end of those instructions, a "return from interrupt" instruction tells the microprocessor to resume its interrupted activity.

The operating system also uses the interrupt table. When MS-DOS or PC-DOS is first loaded, it adds its own batch of interrupt routines. Memory resident programs also work by storing their addresses in the interrupt vector table. Incidentally, MS-DOS can substitute its own version of a ROM-based BIOS routine by overwriting the appropriate interrupt vector with a new address. The ROM itself is unchanged, but when the interrupt is issued, the computer is directed to the new address instead. This method is sometimes used as a software "fix" for faulty BIOS routines. (The only way to update the actual BIOS is to get a newer version of the ROM chip.)

We will use the *int86()* function because it is generally applicable. As its name suggests, it generates a specified interrupt for the 8086 family of microprocessors. However, before we can use this function, we must examine the way in which interrupt routines use registers to transfer data.

Interrupts and Registers

Like C functions, interrupts pass information back and forth between the routine and the calling program. Instead of using arguments, however, interrupts use the microprocessor registers. The *int86()* function gets around this difference by using unions to pass the register information to and from the calling C program.

Registers are small work and storage areas built into the CPU. For example, the 8088 chip, the most commonly used member of the 8086 family, has 13 registers, each capable of holding 16 bits. Four of the registers are general-purpose registers used for arithmetic and logical operations; they are called AX, BX, CX, and DX. Four "segment" registers store the addresses of various memory segments; these registers are called CS, DS, SS, and ES. Four more "pointer/index" registers keep track of addresses used in a program; they are called SP, BP, SI, and DI. Finally, the instruction pointer (IP) contains the address of the next instruction to be executed. The processor also has nine "flags" that can be turned on or off. The flags can be considered to be individual bits in a flag register. Taken together, these are the resources open to an interrupt routine.

There is one further complication. Each of the four general-purpose registers can be considered to be two 8-bit registers. The AX register, for example, can be divided into the AH (H for high byte) and the AL (L for low byte) registers. Assigning a value to the AX register affects the whole register, but assigning a value to AL or AH affects only half the register. Similarly, the BX register is divided into the BH and BL registers, and so on. With this background about registers, let's see how *int86()* works.

The *int86()* Function

The *int86()* function will be our tool for initiating interrupt routines, initializing registers, and reading registers. Its library description begins with the following:

```
#include <dos.h>
int int86(intno, inregs, outregs);
int intno;          /* interrupt number */
union REGS *inregs; /* register values on call */
union REGS *outregs; /* register values on return */
```

This syntax summary says to include the dos.h header file when using this function. Also, *int86()* takes three arguments. The first is the number of the desired interrupt. The second is the address of a union containing the register values passed to the interrupt. The third is the address of the union into which the post-interrupt register values are copied.

To use *int86()*, you need to know how the type *union REGS* is defined in the include file dos.h. The two structures that can occupy the union give different views of the registers.

```
/* word registers */

struct WORDREGS {
        unsigned int ax;
        unsigned int bx;
        unsigned int cx;
        unsigned int dx;
        unsigned int si;
        unsigned int di;
        unsigned int cflag;
        };

/* byte registers */

struct BYTEREGS {
        unsigned char al, ah;
        unsigned char bl, bh;
        unsigned char cl, ch;
        unsigned char dl, dh;
        };

/* general purpose registers union -
 *   overlays the corresponding word and byte registers.
 */

union REGS {
        struct WORDREGS x;
        struct BYTEREGS h;
        };
```

The *WORDREGS* structure provides the 16-bit view. This structure has seven members representing the four general-purpose registers, two of the pointer registers, and the "carry" flag (which we won't use). These are the registers most commonly used by the interrupts. In this structure, for example, the *ax* member represents the AX register. (The *int86x()* function uses an additional structure to give access to more registers.)

The *BYTEREGS* structure gives the 8-bit view. This structure represents only the four general-purpose registers, with each register split into two 1-byte registers. Thus, the *ch* member of this structure represents the CH register, the high byte of CX.

The unusual part of the *int86()* function is the definition of the union *REGS*. It superimposes the word view and the byte view. For example, suppose you use the following declaration:

```
union REGS myreg;
```

To assign a value to the AX register, use a statement such as the following:

```
myreg.x.ax = 1026;
```

The *.x* notation specifies the *WORDREGS* member of *myreg*; therefore, *myreg.x.ax* is the *AX* member of that structure.

To assign a value to the BL register (the low byte of the BX register), use the following *.h* notation, which specifies the *BYTEREGS* member of the union:

```
myreg.h.bl = 22;
```

Recall that a union uses the same storage area for all its members. This means that *myreg.h.al* and *myreg.h.ah* overlie *myreg.x.ax*. To get the high byte of the *1026* that was assigned to *myreg.x.ax*, refer to *myreg.h.ah*. (See Figure 13-5.)

You now know enough theory to use *int86()*. However, you still need to know what values to pass as arguments to the BIOS routines. Let's look at a simple example.

```
union REGS myreg;
```

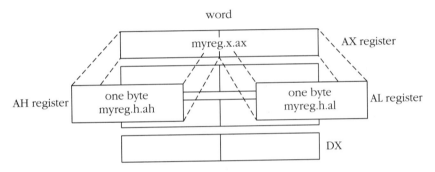

For a REGS union: .x means the 16-bit version
.h means the 8-bit version

Figure 13-5. *The* REGS *union.*

Interrupt 0x16—The Keyboard I/O Interrupt

Because we have been discussing the keyboard, let's look at interrupt routine 0x16, which reads the keyboard. The QuickC library provides the *_bios_keybrd()* function to access this specific routine. However, we will use *int86()* in order to demonstrate a more general approach to using interrupts.

Like many interrupts, 0x16 includes more than one subroutine. It has three subroutines; each is termed a "function" or "service." To select a particular function, you must place the "function code" number in the AH register before calling the interrupt. Let's take a look at what each function does.

Interrupt 0x16, Function Code 0—Get Character

This function reads the keyboard buffer if a character is present; otherwise, it waits until a keystroke is placed in the buffer. When it reads a key, it places the ASCII byte in the AL register and the scan byte in the AH register. (Note that the return values are written over the values we originally placed in AH and AL.) The code is removed from the keyboard buffer once it is read. The *getch()* function is based on this subroutine.

Interrupt 0x16, Function Code 1—Check Keyboard Buffer

This function checks to see if the keyboard buffer is empty or not. If it is empty, the "zero flag" (ZF) is set to 1; otherwise, the flag is cleared (set to 0). If a character is present, the ASCII byte is placed in AL and the scan byte in AH, but the code in the buffer is left there. The *kbhit()* function is based on this function.

Interrupt 0x16, Function Code 2—Get Keyboard Status

This function reports on the status of the Shift and Ctrl keys. Each of eight keys is assigned a particular bit in the AL register. If one of the eight keys is closed, the corresponding bit is set to 1. Table 13-5 shows the corresponding bits and keys.

Table 13-5. Keyboard Status Bits

Bit	Set to 1 if	Bit	Set to 1 if
0	Right Shift is closed	4	Scroll Lock is active
1	Left Shift is closed	5	Num Lock is active
2	Ctrl is closed	6	Caps Lock is active
3	Alt is closed	7	Insert mode is active

Reading ASCII and Scan Codes

Let's use function code 0 to construct a more general version of *getch()* that we'll call *Readkey()*. It will return both the ASCII and the scan bytes. Using it will give you a better picture of how the keyboard codes work and show you that using interrupts from QuickC is not all that difficult. The READKEY.C program (Listing 13-11) contains the *Readkey()* function.

The dos.h file defines the *union REGS* type and declares the *int86()* function. We define symbolic constants to represent the interrupt number and the function code number. Finally, we define a two-member structure called *SCANCODE* for holding the two keyboard codes. *Readkey()* uses the *reg* union to set the AH register to the proper function code, and then it calls *int86()*. Because preserving the original register values is unnecessary, the same structure stores both the input values and the returned values of the registers. Finally, the program copies the two relevant register values into the structure that the function returns.

The *int86()* syntax calls for two pointers to *union REGS* as arguments. In practice this usually calls for using the address operator applied to the appropriate union, as we have done here.

Having developed the *Readkey()* function, let's use it in the next program, SHOWCODE.C (Listing 13-12). This program reads a key, prints it (if it is printable), and displays both the ASCII and scan codes. Using this program can be instructive. The following, for example, is the output for the input series *m*, Shift-M, Ctrl-M, Alt-M, Enter, and Esc:

```
m: ascii = 109, scan =  50———— m
M: ascii =  77, scan =  50———— Shift-M
^M: ascii =  13, scan =  50———— Ctrl-M
 : ascii =   0, scan =  50———— Alt-M
^M: ascii =  13, scan =  28———— Enter
^[: ascii =  27, scan =   1———— Esc
```

```
/* readkey.c -- contains the Readkey() function */

#include <dos.h>
#define KEYINTR 0x16   /* keyboard read interrupt */
#define GETCHAR 0      /* read scancode function  */
struct SCANCODE {
                unsigned char ascii;  /* ascii code */
                unsigned char scan;   /* scan code  */
                };

struct SCANCODE Readkey()
{
    union REGS reg;
    struct SCANCODE scancode;

    reg.h.ah = GETCHAR;          /* specify function       */
    int86(KEYINTR, &reg, &reg); /* note use of & operator */
    scancode.ascii = reg.h.al;
    scancode.scan = reg.h.ah;
    return (scancode);
}
```

Listing 13-11. *The* Readkey() *function.*

```
/* showcode.c -- shows ASCII and scan codes for */
/*               keystrokes                      */

#include <stdio.h>
#include <dos.h>
#define KEYINTR 0x16   /* keyboard read interrupt */
#define GETCHAR 0      /* read scancode function  */
#define ESC '\033'     /* escape key              */
struct SCANCODE {
                unsigned char ascii;  /* ascii code */
                unsigned char scan;   /* scan code  */
                };
struct SCANCODE Readkey();
```

Listing 13-12. *The SHOWCODE.C program.*　　　　　　　　*(continued)*

Listing 13-12. *continued*

```
main()
{
    struct SCANCODE keys;

    printf("Press keys to see their scancodes.\n");
    printf("Press the Esc key to quit.\n");
    do {
        keys = Readkey();
        if (keys.ascii > 0 && keys.ascii < 040)
            printf("^%c: ascii = %3d, scan = %3d\n",
                    keys.ascii + 0100, keys.ascii,
                    keys.scan);
        else if (keys.ascii >= 40)
            printf(" %c: ascii = %3d, scan = %3d\n",
                    keys.ascii, keys.ascii, keys.scan);
        else
            printf("   : ascii = %3d, scan = %3d\n",
                    keys.ascii, keys.scan);
    } while (keys.ascii != ESC);
}

struct SCANCODE Readkey()
{
    union REGS reg;
    struct SCANCODE scancode;

    reg.h.ah = GETCHAR;
    int86(KEYINTR, &reg, &reg);
    scancode.ascii = reg.h.al;
    scancode.scan = reg.h.ah;
    return (scancode);
}
```

The scan code for the first four characters is the same (50) because the same primary key (the M key) was used in each case. The modifying key, if any, then caused the ASCII part of the code to be changed. Note that the ASCII part for Alt-M is 0. Also note that the Enter key has the same ASCII code as Ctrl-M but a different scan code. The scan code is different because a different physical key was pressed. Incidentally, if you need to write a program that discriminates between input of Ctrl-M and the Enter key, you can use *Readkey()* to check the scan code. (The *getch()* function cannot distinguish between the two keystrokes.)

The following represents another sample run:

```
  : ascii =   0, scan =  59———— F1
  : ascii =   0, scan =  94———— Ctrl-F1
  : ascii =   0, scan =  84———— Shift-F1
  : ascii =   0, scan = 104———— Alt-F1
^[: ascii =  27, scan =   1———— Esc
```

422

In this example, the scan code changes even though the same primary key was pressed each time. With ASCII characters, the ASCII code discriminates among different combinations, but with the control keys, the ASCII byte is always 0, so the scan code itself must change. Also, notice that these keystrokes are nonprinting; therefore, the program displays only the codes.

Finally, this example uses the following input: *1*, the End key, Shift-End, and Esc:

```
 1: ascii =  49, scan =   2———1
  : ascii =   0, scan =  79———End
 1: ascii =  49, scan =  79———Shift-End
^[: ascii =  27, scan =   1———Esc
```

Notice that Shift-End and *1* produce the same ASCII code (49) but different scan codes (2 and 79). We mention this because the QuickC editor uses the Shift-End combination to highlight a line. If the programming for QuickC relied on *getch()*, that would be impossible to do. Apparently QuickC, like our program, checks the scan code too. This lets it assign a different function to Shift-End.

Cursor and Screen Control with BIOS Calls

Now that you know how to use interrupts, we can extend that technique to cursor and screen control. To illustrate these applications, we will construct a rudimentary first step toward a word processor. With this program, you can do the following:

- ■ Start with a clear screen.

- ■ Enter text from the keyboard and see it on the screen.

- ■ Use the arrow keys to move the cursor.

- ■ Use the function keys to turn highlighting on and off.

- ■ Highlight or unhighlight existing text by moving the cursor over it.

To provide these features, we'll construct a library of approximately a dozen BIOS-based functions. Rather than jumping back and forth between program development and BIOS use, we'll develop the entire library first.

Incidentally, the QuickC Graphics Library, which we discuss in Chapter 15, provides an alternative means for implementing these features. Using the Graphics Library, however, produces executable programs substantially larger than those using the BIOS approach.

The Video I/O Interrupt

The first step is to find the appropriate interrupt routine. Interrupt 0x10, the video I/O interrupt, controls the display. Because maintaining a video display is more complex than monitoring a keyboard, this interrupt turns out to be much more involved than the keyboard I/O interrupt. It provides many subroutines, or functions, and many of them use several registers. Table 13-6 lists and describes the functions we use in this book. The table mentions "attributes" and "pages." Attributes, as we saw in our discussion of ANSI.SYS, determine how a character is to be displayed. A page is a screenful of display. Some video modes can store more than one page at once, although only one can be displayed at any given time. We discuss these terms further as needed.

When using *int86()* to call the MS-DOS video functions, you set AH to the appropriate function code number and initialize any other registers given in the description. The first argument to *int86()* should be *0x10*, the interrupt number.

Table 13-6.   Selected Video I/O Interrupt 0x10 Functions

FUNCTION CODE 0: Set the Display Mode

Action: Switches to desired mode and clears display.
Register setup: AH = 0

                     AL = Desired mode
Choose from the following modes:

Mode	Meaning	Mode	Meaning
0	40 x 25 B/W Text	13	320 x 200 Color EGA
1	40 x 25 Color Text	14	640 x 200 Color EGA
2	80 x 25 B/W Text	15	640 x 350 B/W EGA
3	80 x 25 Color Text	16	640 x 350 Color EGA
4	320 x 200 Color Graphics	17	640 x 480, 2-Color VGA
5	320 x 200 B/W Graphics	18	640 x 480, 16-Color VGA
6	640 x 200 B/W Graphics	19	320 x 200, 256-Color VGA
7	80 x 25 Monochrome		

FUNCTION CODE 2: Select Cursor Position

Action: Moves cursor to the specified row and column.
Register setup: AH = 2

                     DH = Row number

                     DL = Column number

                     BH = Page number

                     Numbering of rows and columns starts with 0, not 1.

FUNCTION CODE 3: Read Cursor Position

Action: Reports the row and column of cursor position.
Register setup: AH = 3

                     BH = Page number
Returns: DH = Row number

                     DL = Column number

                     CH, CL = Cursor type

(continued)

Table 13-6. *continued*

FUNCTION CODE 5: Select Active Display Page

Action:	Selects the page for modes supporting multiple pages.
Register setup:	AH = 5
	AL = Page number

FUNCTION CODE 6: Scroll Up an Area of the Screen

Action:	Scrolls up a section of the screen a specified amount.
Register setup:	AH = 6
	AL = Number of lines to scroll (0 in AL produces a blank window)
	BH = Blank-line attribute
	CH = Upper-left row number
	CL = Upper-left column number
	DH = Lower-right row number
	DL = Lower-right column number

FUNCTION CODE 8: Read Character and Attribute

Action:	Reports the character and attribute code at the current cursor position.
Register setup:	AH = 8
	BH = Page number
Returns:	AL = Character at cursor
	AH = Attribute at cursor

FUNCTION CODE 9: Write Character and Attribute

Action:	Writes a specified character and attribute to the current cursor position.
Register setup:	AH = 9
	BH = Page number (text modes)
	AL = Character
	BL = Attribute (text modes) or color (graphics modes)
	CX = Number of characters*

FUNCTION CODE 15: Return Current Video State

Action:	Reports the video mode, number of text columns, and current page value.
Register setup:	AH = 15
Returns:	AL = Current mode
	AH = Number of columns
	BH = Current active page number

* The character is written the indicated number of times starting at the current cursor position; the cursor position remains unchanged.

Developing a Library of C Functions

Our next step is to develop a set of C functions that use the video I/O interrupt. In this section, we will design several functions, each general enough to be useful for a variety of programs. We'll develop the functions individually but then collect them in one file so that they can share a common set of include files and definitions. You'll find the contents of this combined file, SCRFUN.C, in Listing 13-23 beginning on p. 435. Finally, we'll use the LIB utility to make a library of the video functions.

Setting the Cursor

First, we need two C functions: one to set the cursor and another to report the current cursor position. We use functions 2 and 3 of the video interrupt to develop our own *Setcurs()* and *Getcurs()* functions (Listing 13-13).

Pass the desired row, column, and page to *Setcurs()*, and it positions the cursor. Use *Getcurs()* to place row and column information in variables whose addresses we pass. What about the *page* variable? For now, use the default value of 0. The following SETCURS.C program (Listing 13-14) is a short example that uses *Setcurs()* to see if our programming is on the right track.

After you type in a row and column in the form *10 20*, the program places the cursor there and then prints a message starting at that location. It's not a spectacular program, but it shows that our function is working correctly. As we build this library with other functions, you might want to write similar test programs. With QuickC it doesn't take long to do so.

```
#include <dos.h>
#define VIDEO 0x10
#define SETCURSOR 2
#define GETCURSOR 3

/* Setcurs() -- sets cursor to given row, column */
void Setcurs(unsigned char row, unsigned char col, unsigned char page)
{
    union REGS reg;

    reg.h.ah = SETCURSOR;
    reg.h.dh = row;
    reg.h.dl = col;
    reg.h.bh = page;
    int86(VIDEO, &reg, &reg);
}
```

Listing 13-13. *The* Setcurs() *and* Getcurs() *functions.*

(continued)

Listing 13-13. *continued*

```
/* Getcurs() -- reports current cursor position */
void Getcurs(unsigned char *pr, unsigned char *pc, unsigned char page)
{
    union REGS reg;

    reg.h.ah = GETCURSOR;
    reg.h.bh = page;
    int86(VIDEO, &reg, &reg);
    *pr = reg.h.dh;  /* row number */
    *pc = reg.h.dl;  /* column number */
}
```

```
/* setcurs.c -- moves cursor, checks out Setcurs() */
#include <dos.h>
#include <stdio.h>
#define VIDEO 0x10
#define SETCURSOR 2
void Setcurs(unsigned char, unsigned char, unsigned char);

main()
{
    int row, col;

    printf("Enter row and column: (q to quit)\n");
    while (scanf("%d %d", &row, &col) == 2)
        {
        Setcurs(row, col, 0);
        printf("Enter row and column: (q to quit)");
        }
}

/* Setcurs() -- sets cursor to row, column, and page */
void Setcurs(unsigned char row, unsigned char col, unsigned char page)
{
    union REGS reg;

    reg.h.ah = SETCURSOR;
    reg.h.dh = row;
    reg.h.dl = col;
    reg.h.bh = page;
    int86(VIDEO, &reg, &reg);
}
```

Listing 13-14. *The SETCURS.C program.*

Setting the page to 0 worked fine in our example; however, we might need to use different video pages later, so let's look at that topic.

Getting and Setting the Page

The information displayed on the screen is read from a dedicated section of memory called video memory. The amount of memory available depends upon the video adapter. In some modes, video memory can hold two or more screenfuls of data. In those cases, you can divide video memory into separate pages, one page per screenful. This lets a program alter one page in memory while displaying the other on the screen. To set a page, we will use the *Setpage()* function (Listing 13-15).

By default, screen modes start at page 0, and we'll also use that page for a while. But to keep our programming general, we need a function that can tell our code which is the current page. We use function 15 to develop the QuickC *Getpage()* function (Listing 13-16). The interrupt function places the page number in the BH register, and the function returns that value to the program.

```
/* Setpage() -- sets page to given value */
#include <dos.h>
#define VIDEO 0x10
#define SETPAGE 5
void Setpage(unsigned char page)
{
    union REGS reg;

    reg.h.ah = SETPAGE;
    reg.h.al = page;
    int86(VIDEO, &reg, &reg);
}
```

Listing 13-15. *The* Setpage() *function.*

```
/* Getpage() -- obtains the currently active page */
#include <dos.h>
#define VIDEO 0x10
#define GETMODE 15
unsigned char Getpage(void)
{
    union REGS reg;

    reg.h.ah = GETMODE;
    int86(VIDEO, &reg, &reg);
    return reg.h.bh;
}
```

Listing 13-16. *The* Getpage() *function.*

Clearing the Screen

Another useful function is one that clears the screen (Listing 13-17). None of the interrupt functions specialize in that, but the Scroll Up function (function 6) can perform this task. Note in Table 13-6 that if register AL is set to zero, the entire designated area is cleared. However, several other registers must be set. To define the area to be cleared, give the coordinates of the upper-left and the lower-right corners.

The BIOS routine starts numbering with 0, unlike ANSI.SYS, which starts with 1. This means the upper-left row and column are 0, the lower-right row is 24, and the lower-right column is 79 (on an 80-by-25 display). The least straightforward register setting is the attribute setting for blank lines in register BH. An attribute is a value in the range 0 through 255 that modifies the display. We'll use the value 7, the normal attribute for "white-on-black." ("White" is white on a color display, but on a mono-chrome monitor "white" usually is green or amber.) Other values produce reverse video, blinking, underlining (on some monitors), and colors (on some monitors).

```
/* Clearscr() -- clears the screen */
#include <dos.h>
#define VIDEO 0x10
#define NORMAL 0x7
#define SCROLLUP 6
#define ROWS 25
#define COLS 80
void Clearscr(void)
{
    union REGS reg;

    reg.h.ah = SCROLLUP;
    reg.h.al = 0;       /* clear the window */
    reg.h.ch = 0;
    reg.h.cl = 0;
    reg.h.dh = ROWS - 1;
    reg.h.dl = COLS - 1;
    reg.h.bh = NORMAL;
    int86(VIDEO, &reg, &reg);
}
```

Listing 13-17. *The* Clearscr() *function.*

Quick Tip

If you are ambitious, you can generalize the *Clearscr()* function to work with 40-by-25 displays by using function 15 of the 0x10 interrupt to find the number of columns actually being used. A call to function 15 places that number of columns into the AH register. Subtract 1 from this number (to account for the fact that column numbering begins with column 0), save the result, and assign it to the DL register before you call function 6.

Reading and Writing Characters and Attributes '

Before we use BIOS routines to read from and write to the screen, you need to know how the video system works. The video adapter has its own memory, which it uses to represent the screen. Let's concentrate for now on the 80-by-25 text modes, the ones you probably use most often. All standard IBM video controllers (monochrome, CGA, EGA, MCGA, and VGA) use the same scheme for their 80-by-25 text modes, so this discussion applies to all.

You can think of an 80-by-25 screen as holding 2000 cells, each capable of displaying a character. Each cell is represented by 2 bytes in the video memory. One byte holds the code for the character, and the second byte holds the attribute, which determines how the character is displayed. When a program sends output to the screen, the characters actually are first stored in video memory. A microprocessor called a video controller then scans the video memory, mapping the characters it finds there to the screen. Video interrupt 0x10 functions 8 and 9, which read and write characters and attributes to the screen, actually work with the video memory. (The monochrome display system uses a different memory address from the others, but the BIOS calls adjust for that.)

The character code consists of the usual ASCII code plus extensions to the code that enable certain non-ASCII characters to be displayed on the screen. (IBM provides 128 such additional characters in its extended character set.) The attribute code also is simple, especially for black-and-white displays. Think of the attribute byte as a series of 8 bits, numbered 7 through 0, left to right. To generate the normal black-and-white display, set the bits to 00000111. To produce reverse video, set the bits to 01110000. Note that these binary values translate to 0x7 and 0x70, respectively.

In addition, you can intensify the foreground display by setting bit 3 to 1 or put the display in "blink" mode by setting bit 7 to 1. The attributes we've discussed here produce white-on-black (or black-on-white) characters for the monochrome display and for color-text displays. We discuss color-related attributes in Chapter 14.

To produce both normal and reverse video, our program must write the attribute as well as the character. We use video I/O function 9 instead of *putch()*, because the latter writes only characters, not attributes. Our *Write_ch_atr()* C function (Listing 13-18) uses that interrupt routine. This function writes the character-attribute pair *num* times to display a single pair several times in a row. We will use a *num* value of 1, but to preserve generality, we did not build that value into the function.

One of our program goals was converting normal text to reverse video by passing the cursor over it. You can do that simply by changing the attribute at the cursor location. Because no BIOS function merely changes an attribute, we need to write a character-attribute pair. One way to do this is to read the current character from the screen and then rewrite it using a different attribute. So let's start by devising a *Read_ch_atr()* function (Listing 13-19) to read the character and attribute at the current cursor location.

```
/* Write_ch_atr() -- writes characters and attributes */
#include <dos.h>
#define VIDEO 0x10
#define WRITECHATR 9
void Write_ch_atr(unsigned char ch, unsigned char atr, unsigned char page,
                  unsigned int num)
{
    union REGS reg;

    reg.h.ah = WRITECHATR;
    reg.h.al = ch;
    reg.h.bl = atr;
    reg.h.bh = page;
    reg.x.cx = num;
    int86(VIDEO, &reg, &reg);
}
```

Listing 13-18. *The* Write_ch_atr() *function.*

```
/* Read_ch_atr() -- reads character and attribute at */
/*                  cursor location                   */
#include <dos.h>
#define VIDEO 0x10
#define READCHATR 8
void Read_ch_atr(unsigned char *pc, unsigned char *pa, unsigned char page)
{
    union REGS reg;

    reg.h.ah = READCHATR;
    reg.h.bh = page;
    int86(VIDEO, &reg, &reg);
    *pc = reg.h.al;  /* character at cursor */
    *pa = reg.h.ah;  /* attribute at cursor */
}
```

Listing 13-19. *The* Read_ch_atr() *function.*

Because the function must return two values, we pass it the addresses of the two variables to which the values will be assigned. To read the character and attribute at the current cursor position on page 0 into the variables *ch* and *attr*, make this call:

```
Read_ch_atr(&ch, &attr, 0);
```

We also could have the function return a two-member structure.

Now we use the last two functions to produce the function our program requires. The *Rewrite()* function (Listing 13-20 on the following page) reads the current character and rewrites it with a potentially changed attribute.

If speed is an issue, which it usually isn't for keyboard input, you can speed up *Rewrite()* by having it use *int86()* to call the read and write BIOS functions directly instead of going through *Read_ch_atr()* and *Write_ch_atr()*.

```
/* Rewrite() -- changes attribute of on-screen character */
void Read_ch_atr(), Write_ch_atr(); /* used by Rewrite() */
void Rewrite(unsigned char at, unsigned char page)
{
    unsigned char ch, atr;

    Read_ch_atr(&ch, &atr, page);
    Write_ch_atr(ch, at, page, 1);
}
```

Listing 13-20. *The* Rewrite() *function.*

More Cursor Movement

We already have a function to set the cursor at a given row or column. But our primitive text editor really needs functions to move the cursor one column to the right when the Right Arrow key is pushed, and so on. We can use *Setcurs()* to create such functions. The *Cursrt_lim()* function (Listing 13-21) demonstrates how to construct a right-movement function.

Getcurs() and *Setcurs()* require the current page number; the *Cursrt_lim()* function uses *Getpage()* to obtain that information. Also, the function prevents the cursor from going past the column defined by *limit*. Our program will use a limit of 79, corresponding to the right side of the screen, but the numeric value is not built into

```
/* Cursrt_lim() -- moves cursor one space to the    */
                   right, but not past a set limit */
void Getcurs(), Setcurs();  /* functions used  */
unsigned char Getpage();    /* by Cursrt_lim() */

unsigned char Cursrt_lim(unsigned char limit)
{
    unsigned char row, col, page;
    unsigned char status = 1;

    Getcurs(&row, &col, page = Getpage());
    if (col < limit)
        Setcurs(row, col + 1, page);
    else
        status = 0;
    return status;
}
```

Listing 13-21. *The* Cursrt_lim() *function.*

the function. This variable limit lets you use the function with a program that confines the cursor to a section of the screen or with a program that uses a 40-column screen.

Also, the program uses a return value to tell the calling program whether the cursor reached its limit. This gives the calling program the option of responding in some way, such as beeping or moving the cursor to the beginning of the next line, whenever the limit is reached.

We can modify *Cursrt_lim()* to create functions corresponding to the other arrow keys. We'll show you these when we gather all the functions together into one file.

Putting the Library Together

By now we've created a small library of short, BIOS-based C functions. Before we use them in our intended sample program, let's reflect on how to organize this block of functions. One method is to give each its own file. Then, when we want to use a particular function in a program, we can add its filename to the QuickC program list. Or we can simply append the function file to the program file. Another approach is to consolidate all the functions into one file and to add that file to the program list. This is more convenient, but it might result in adding code to your program for functions it doesn't use. If you use the functions frequently, the most satisfactory approach is to make a library file for them. (This procedure was described in Chapter 12.)

Here's one way to make the library. Open the SCRFUN.C file from QuickC. Select the Compile File option from the Make menu. This produces a SCRFUN.OBJ file. Now go to MS-DOS and enter the LIB command. Answer the prompts as shown:

```
Library name: scrfun
Library does not exist.  Create? (y/n) y
Operations: +scrfun
List file: scrfun
```

The LIB command creates a library file called SCRFUN.LIB in the current directory. You can then copy it to your library directory. The LIB command also creates a text file called SCRFUN that lists the names of the functions in the library.

To help organize these functions, gather all the defined constants together into an include file. To this file, add function prototypes for all the functions. Then you can use this include file with your program. You still must incorporate the actual code by appending the source files or adding files to the program list or by using a library, but using the include file saves you the trouble of having to declare the functions. It also includes definitions useful to a program. We'll use the scrn.h include file (Listing 13-22 on the following page) for our programs.

```
/* scrn.h -- header file for BIOS video I/O functions */
/*           contained in scrfun.c and scrfun.lib      */

#define VIDEO 0x10
#define SETMODE 0
#define SETCURSOR 2
#define GETCURSOR 3
#define SETPAGE 5
#define SCROLL 6
#define READCHATR 8
#define WRITECHATR 9
#define GETMODE 15
#define NORMAL 0x7
#define VIDREV 0x70
#define INTENSE 0x8
#define BLINK 0x80
#define COLS 80
#define ROWS 25
#define TEXTBW80 2
#define TEXTC80 3
#define TEXTMONO 7

void Clearscr(void),
     Setvmode(unsigned char),
     Setpage(unsigned char),
     Setcurs(unsigned char, unsigned char, unsigned char),
     Read_ch_atr(unsigned char *, unsigned char *,
                 unsigned char),
     Write_ch_atr(unsigned char, unsigned char,
                  unsigned char, unsigned int),
     Rewrite(unsigned char, unsigned char),
     Getcurs(unsigned char *, unsigned char *,
             unsigned char);

unsigned char Getvmode(void),
              Getpage(void),
              Curslt_lim(unsigned char),
              Cursrt_lim(unsigned char),
              Cursup_lim(unsigned char),
              Cursdn_lim(unsigned char);

/* Macro definitions */

#define Home()        Setcurs(0, 0, Getpage())
/* The next four macros set cursor limits to the */
/* full screen                                   */
#define Curslt()      Curslt_lim(0)
#define Cursrt()      Cursrt_lim(COLS - 1)
#define Cursdn()      Cursdn_lim(ROWS - 1)
#define Cursup()      Cursup_lim(0)
```

Listing 13-22. *The scrn.h include file.*

434

The scrn.h file includes some function numbers that we won't use until later chapters. It also contains some constants that we'll use in our program. Finally, note the macros at the end of the file. The *Home()* macro homes the cursor, and the cursor-movement macros select a range corresponding to the entire screen.

For convenience, we've collected all the new functions together as shown in Figure 13-6 in a file called SCRFUN.C (Listing 13-23). We discuss both the *Getvmode()* and *Setvmode()* functions in Chapter 15.

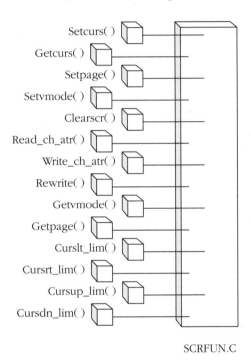

SCRFUN.C

Figure 13-6. *The SCRFUN.C program combines the functions we created previously.*

```
/* scrfun.c -- contains several video BIOS calls    */
/* Setcurs() sets the cursor position               */
/* Getcurs() gets the cursor position               */
/* Setpage() sets the current video page            */
/* Setvmode() sets the video mode                    */
/* Clearscr() clears the screen                     */
/* Read_ch_atr() reads the character and            */
/*               attribute at the cursor            */
/* Write_ch_atr() writes a character and            */
/*                attribute at the cursor           */
/* Rewrite() rewrites a screen character            */
```

Listing 13-23. *The SCRFUN.C program.*   *(continued)*

Listing 13-23. *continued*

```
/*          with a new attribute              */
/* Getvmode() gets the current video mode     */
/* Getpage() gets the current video page      */

/* The following functions use Setcurs() to move the */
/* cursor one position at a time up to a limit:       */
/*                                                    */
/* Curslt_lim() moves cursor one column left   */
/* Cursrt_lim() moves cursor one column right  */
/* Cursup_lim() moves cursor one line up       */
/* Cursdn_lim() moves cursor one line down     */
/*                                                    */
/* Programs using these functions should include the */
/* scrn.h file                                 */

#include <dos.h>
#include "scrn.h"

/* Sets cursor to row, column, and page */
void Setcurs(unsigned char row, unsigned char col, unsigned char page)
{
    union REGS reg;

    reg.h.ah = SETCURSOR;
    reg.h.dh = row;
    reg.h.dl = col;
    reg.h.bh = page;
    int86(VIDEO, &reg, &reg);
}

/* Gets current cursor row, column for given page */
void Getcurs(unsigned char *pr, unsigned char *pc, unsigned char page)
{
    union REGS reg;

    reg.h.ah = GETCURSOR;
    reg.h.bh = page;
    int86(VIDEO, &reg, &reg);
    *pr = reg.h.dh;  /* row number */
    *pc = reg.h.dl;  /* column number */
}

/* Sets page to given value */
void Setpage(unsigned char page)
{
    union REGS reg;

    reg.h.ah = SETPAGE;
    reg.h.al = page;
    int86(VIDEO, &reg, &reg);
}
```

(continued)

Listing 13-23. *continued*

```
/* Sets video mode to given mode */
void Setvmode(unsigned char mode)
{
    union REGS reg;

    reg.h.ah = SETMODE;
    reg.h.al = mode;
    int86(VIDEO, &reg, &reg);
}

/* Clears the screen */
void Clearscr(void)
{
    union REGS reg;

    reg.h.ah = SCROLL;
    reg.h.al = 0;
    reg.h.ch = 0;
    reg.h.cl = 0;
    reg.h.dh = ROWS - 1;
    reg.h.dl = COLS - 1;
    reg.h.bh = NORMAL;
    int86(VIDEO, &reg, &reg);
}

/* Reads the character and attribute at the cursor */
/* position on a given page                        */
void Read_ch_atr(unsigned char *pc, unsigned char *pa, unsigned char page)
{
    union REGS reg;

    reg.h.ah = READCHATR;
    reg.h.bh = page;
    int86(VIDEO, &reg, &reg);
    *pc = reg.h.al;  /* character at cursor */
    *pa = reg.h.ah;  /* attribute at cursor */
}

/* Writes a given character and attribute at the */
/* cursor on a given page for num times          */
void Write_ch_atr(unsigned char ch, unsigned char atr, unsigned char page,
                  unsigned int num)
{
    union REGS reg;

    reg.h.ah = WRITECHATR;
    reg.h.al = ch;
    reg.h.bl = atr;
```

(continued)

Listing 13-23. *continued*

```
        reg.h.bh = page;
        reg.x.cx = num;
        int86(VIDEO, &reg, &reg);
}


/* Rewrites the character at the cursor using */
/* attribute at                              */
void Rewrite(unsigned char at, unsigned char page)
{
        unsigned char ch, atr;

        Read_ch_atr(&ch, &atr, page);
        Write_ch_atr(ch, at, page, 1);
}


/* Obtains the current video mode */
unsigned char Getvmode(void)
{
        union REGS reg;

        reg.h.ah = GETMODE;
        int86(VIDEO, &reg, &reg);
        return reg.h.al;
}


/* Obtains the current video page */
unsigned char Getpage(void)
{
        union REGS reg;

        reg.h.ah = GETMODE;
        int86(VIDEO, &reg, &reg);
        return reg.h.bh;
}


/* Moves cursor one column left, but not past */
/* the given limit                            */
unsigned char Curslt_lim(unsigned char limit)
{
        unsigned char row, col, page;
        unsigned char status = 1;

        Getcurs(&row, &col, page = Getpage());
        if (col > limit)
            Setcurs(row, col - 1, page);
        else
            status = 0;
        return status;
}
```

(continued)

438

Chapter 13: Keyboard and Cursor Control

Listing 13-23. *continued*

```
/* Moves cursor one column right, but not past */
/* the given limit                             */
unsigned char Cursrt_lim(unsigned char limit)
{
    unsigned char row, col, page;
    unsigned char status = 1;

    Getcurs(&row, &col, page = Getpage());
    if (col < limit)
        Setcurs(row, col + 1, page);
    else
        status = 0;
    return status;
}

/* Moves cursor one row up, but not past */
/* the given limit                       */
unsigned char Cursup_lim(unsigned char limit)
{
    unsigned char row, col, page;
    unsigned char status = 1;

    Getcurs(&row, &col, page = Getpage());
    if (row > limit)
        Setcurs(row - 1, col, page);
    else
        status = 0;
    return status;
}

/* Moves cursor one row down, but not past */
/* the given limit                         */
unsigned char Cursdn_lim(unsigned char limit)
{
    unsigned char row, col, page;
    unsigned char status = 1;

    Getcurs(&row, &col, page = Getpage());
    if (row < limit)
        Setcurs(row + 1, col, page);
    else
        status = 0;
    return status;
}
```

Our small routines certainly create a big file! However, you need only compile it once. After that, you can use the .OBJ or .LIB versions. We assume that you create a library file called SCRFUN.LIB.

A Text Program

Finally, after much development, we have at hand all the tools we need for our program. The ROAMSCRN.C program (Listing 13-24) shows the results of our efforts.

```
/* roamscrn.c -- puts text on screen, positions  */
/*               cursor with arrow keys, uses F1  */
/*               and F2 to control reverse video  */
/* Program list -- roamscrn.c, scrfun.lib         */
/* User include files -- keys.h, scrn.h           */

#include <conio.h>
#include "keys.h"
#include "scrn.h"
#define BELL '\a'
#define ESC '\033'
#define PAGE 0

char *Heading =
"Use standard keys to enter text. Use arrow keys to "
"reposition cursor.\nUse F2 to turn on reverse video "
"and F1 to turn it off.\nPress the ESC key to quit.\n";

main()
{
    int ch;
    unsigned char atr = NORMAL;

    Clearscr();
    Home();
    printf("%s", Heading);
    while ((ch = getch()) != ESC)
        {
        if (ch == '\r')
            {
            putch('\n');
            putch('\r');
            }
        else if (ch != 0)
            {
            Write_ch_atr(ch, atr, PAGE, 1);
            if (!Cursrt())
                putch(BELL);
            }
        else
            {
            ch = getch();
            switch (ch)
```

Listing 13-24. *The ROAMSCRN.C program.*   *(continued)*

Listing 13-24. *continued*

```
            {
            case F1 : atr = NORMAL; break;
            case F2 : atr = VIDREV; break;
            case UP : Rewrite(atr, PAGE);
                        if (!Cursup())
                            putch(BELL);
                        break;
            case DN : Rewrite(atr, PAGE);
                        if (!Cursdn())
                            putch(BELL);
                        break;
            case LT : Rewrite(atr, PAGE);
                        if (!Curslt())
                            putch(BELL);
                        break;
            case RT : Rewrite(atr, PAGE);
                        if (!Cursrt())
                            putch(BELL);
                        break;
            default : break;
            }
        }
    }
}
```

Let's see how it works. The keys.h include file is the file we used earlier in this chapter; it defines the mnemonics for the function keys and the cursor control keys. The scrn.h include file is the one we just presented. We assume that you bring in the BIOS code by including the SCRFUN.LIB file in the program list, but you can also use one of the other methods we mentioned if you prefer.

The program begins with the attribute variable *atr* set to *NORMAL*. This is defined in scrn.h as 7, which is the normal attribute for white-on-black text. Next, the program clears the screen, homes the cursor, and prints an instructive heading. Finally, in the main part of the program, a large *while* loop uses *getch()* to read keyboard input until the Esc key is pressed to terminate input.

Next, the program inspects *ch*, the input character typed by the user. If *ch* has the value \r, the carriage return character generated by the Enter key, the program translates that value into a newline, that is, into \n\r. If the character is some other ASCII or extended ASCII value, the program uses *Write_ch_atr()* to display that character. Why not use *putch()* here? Because *putch()* has no provision for specifying the attribute. Notice, too, the following code fragment:

```
if (!Cursrt())
    putch(BELL);
```

The *Write_ch_atr()* function, like the BIOS call it uses, does not advance the cursor after writing the character. Therefore, we use *Cursrt()* to move the cursor. Recall that we created *Cursrt_lim()* to stop when it reaches the right side of the screen and that the macro *Cursrt()* uses the rightmost column as the limit. If the limit is reached, *Cursrt()* returns a value of 0, or false, causing the *if* statement to execute the *putch(BELL)* call. The action, then, is as follows: First the character is printed, and then the program attempts to advance the cursor one column to the right. If it can, fine; otherwise, the system beeps. If you like, you can replace the beeping instructions with a call to the *Setcurs()* function to relocate the cursor at the beginning of the next line.

Finally, this sequence of *if-else* lines processes the case in which *ch* is 0. This means the user entered a non-ASCII character. Another *getch()* call fetches the scan code for the key, and a *switch* statement checks for two of the function keys and for the arrow keys. Let's see what these keys do.

If the user presses F1, the attribute variable *atr* is set to *NORMAL*; if the user presses F2, *atr* is set to *VIDREV*. This constant, defined in scrn.h as 0x70, is the reverse video, or inverse video, attribute. The selected value for the variable *atr* is used in subsequent calls to *Write_ch_atr()* and *Rewrite()*. The attribute setting holds until another is selected.

Next, look at what happens when the Up Arrow key is pressed:

```
case UP : Rewrite(atr, PAGE);
          if (!Cursup())
              putch(BELL);
          break;
```

The *Rewrite()* function reads the character, if any, at the current cursor position and rewrites it using the current attribute. For example, if you have selected the reverse video attribute, then text passed over by the cursor is rewritten with that attribute. The cursor is then moved up a line unless it already is at the top line. In that case, the system beeps. The coding for the other arrow keys is similar.

All in all, the main program is fairly simple. Most of the work involved creating C functions to implement the various BIOS calls we needed to make.

Monitors
and Text Modes

Professional application programs, including QuickC itself, use a much fancier screen interface than we have used in our programs. In this chapter we produce some of those screen features in QuickC. First we must overcome the problem posed by the variety of different display systems. IBM supports several monitor/video controller systems: monochrome, CGA, EGA, MCGA, and VGA. In general, these systems use different hardware, and different memory and port addresses. They also provide different colors, resolutions, and graphics capabilities.

Writing programs that run on a range of video controller systems can be troublesome, especially if you want something fancier or faster than the teletype-like output produced by standard C library functions. This chapter concentrates on solving these problems for text-mode programs. We continue using BIOS calls, and we introduce direct memory access and ports. We also look at the IBM "graphics character" set, which lets you create screen graphics without leaving text mode.

Monitors and Controllers

IBM has developed several different video standards, each involving its own hardware video controller and corresponding monitors. In the PC series, the hardware controllers are on add-on cards called "adapters." In the new PS/2 series, however, the circuitry for controlling the monitor is built into the motherboard. We use the term "video controller" in this book to encompass both the adapter cards and the built-in control circuitry.

The most widely used video controller is the Monochrome Display Adapter, or MDA. When coupled with a monitor called the Monochrome Display, it produces a high-resolution, text-only display consisting of 25 rows of 80 characters each.

The next most commonly used controller is the Color Graphics Adapter, or CGA. It can be used with color or B/W monitors capable of either 40-by-25 or 80-by-25 text displays (but not with the Monochrome Display). It has seven separate modes of operation. Although the 80-by-25 display shows as many characters as the Monochrome Display, its lower resolution creates coarser text characters.

The Enhanced Graphics Adapter, or EGA, has also become popular. The EGA is compatible with the Monochrome Display, with normal CGA displays, and with a high-resolution monitor called the Enhanced Display (ED). Used with a Monochrome Display, it provides a graphics mode in addition to the text mode. Used with CGA-style monitors, it provides more colors than the CGA board does. Used with the Enhanced Display (or equivalent), it emulates the CGA modes with increased text resolution, and it provides three additional graphics modes.

The newest controllers are the Multi-Color Graphics Array (MCGA), found on the PS/2 Model 30, and the Video Graphics Array (VGA), found on the PS/2 Models 50, 60, 70, and 80. The MCGA matches CGA resolution but offers an enormously greater range of colors. The VGA emulates the EGA modes, adds three new graphics modes, offers higher resolution for all text modes, and provides more colors.

Table 14-1 summarizes some of the differences in features offered by the various video controllers we have introduced. Resolution is given in pixels, or picture elements, the elementary display elements from which characters and images are built. The size of a pixel depends on the controller and the mode. A pixel in mode 0, for example, is twice as wide as a pixel in mode 2. However, the VGA controller produces smaller pixels than the CGA controller, even when both are in mode 0. Also, not all monitors have sufficient resolution to support a controller's use of pixels. A CGA monitor, for example, is physically incapable of generating the higher resolution (smaller pixel) modes of the EGA and VGA. In general, all modes cannot produce the maximum number of colors; only a subset of available colors can be shown at any one time.

Table 14-1. Video Controllers

Name	Horizontal Resolution	Vertical Resolution	Colors	Modes	Monitors
MDA	720	350	2	1	MD
CGA	640/320	200	16	7	Color, B/W
EGA	640/320	350/200	64	12	ED, MD, Color, B/W
MCGA	720/360/640/320	400/480/200	262,144	11	PSM, ED, MD, Color, B/W
VGA	720/360/640/320	400/480/350/200	262,144	15	PSM, ED, MD, Color, B/W

Color = CGA color monitor   B/W = CGA black-and-white monitor
MD = Monochrome Display   ED = Enhanced Display
PSM = PS/2 monitor

Text Modes and Portability

Fortunately, all these video controllers support an 80-by-25 text mode, and that simplifies the task of writing programs to run with all combinations of controllers and monitors.

Controller Similarities

A comparison of 80-by-25 text modes for different hardware combinations shows both similarities and differences. In all cases, the screen is treated as an array of characters rather than as an array of pixels. That is, you can display or alter only entire characters, not the individual pixels that the characters comprise.

All controllers use 2 bytes of memory to represent each text-mode character. One byte holds the character's ASCII code, and the other byte holds the character's display attribute. All video controllers also contain random access memory (video RAM) in which character data is mapped to the display. That is, the controller periodically scans the video RAM to determine which characters it should display. Therefore, to change the screen display, you must change the appropriate bytes in the video RAM. Note that text-mode video RAM always consists of 4000 bytes: One screen holds 80 × 25, or 2000, characters, each represented by 2 bytes.

All controllers also maintain a table of character fonts called a "character generator." The controller uses these pixel patterns to physically represent characters on the screen. For example, ASCII code 72 in the video RAM tells the controller to put an *H* at a screen location, and the character font table specifies the particular "H" pixel pattern to use. (See Figure 14-1 on the following page.)

These similarities ease the task of writing text programs that are compatible with the various displays.

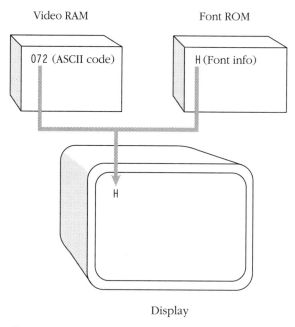

Video RAM

Font ROM

072 (ASCII code)

H (Font info)

H

Display

Figure 14-1. *Producing characters with the MDA.*

Differences between displays complicate the programming process. For example, one powerful video technique called "direct memory access" uses pointers to video RAM to directly alter RAM contents. However, the MDA uses a different video RAM address than other controllers, so your program must always test for its use. Another programming technique uses "ports" to access registers on the controllers. However, the various controllers have different numbers of registers, and each register has a different port address and performs a different function. This makes for very involved hardware programming.

Video controllers also contain differing amounts of video RAM. The MDA has only enough memory to hold one screenful, or page, of characters. The other controllers hold enough memory to hold four or more pages of text.

Most controllers offer different screen resolutions. Although all the controllers can display 2000 characters on the screen, some can generate more pixels than others. For example, the CGA screen consists of a matrix of 640 horizontal pixels (for 80 characters) by 200 vertical pixels (for 25 display lines). The net result is that each character is represented by an 8-by-8-pixel grid, or "character box." The MDA, on the other hand, generates 720 pixels horizontally and 350 pixels vertically, providing a 9-by-14-pixel character box. Thus, MDA characters look better than their CGA counterparts because each character is drawn with more detail, as shown in Figure 14-2.

Finally, the color displays can use the attribute byte to specify foreground and background colors for each character. Table 14-2 provides a summary of the different characteristics of video controllers operating in text mode.

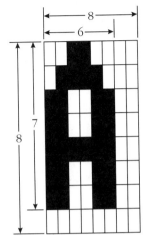

CGA resolution

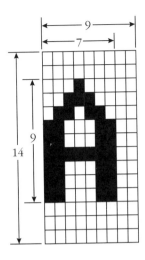

MDA resolution

Figure 14-2. *Character boxes.*

Table 14-2. Summary of Text-Mode Differences

Controller	Video RAM Starting Address	Pages	Character Box Size	Color
MDA	0xB0000	1	9 × 14	No
CGA	0xB8000	4	8 × 8	Yes
EGA (mode 7)	0xB0000	4/8*	9 × 14	No
EGA (modes 2, 3)	0xB8000	4/8*	8 × 14	Yes
MCGA	0xB8000	8	9 × 16	Yes
VGA	0xB8000	8	9 × 16	Yes

* For the EGA, available pages are determined by the amount of memory installed on the adapter. The standard EGA has 64 KB and four text pages. If memory is expanded to 256 KB, eight pages are available.

Device-independent Programming

When programming for the PC, you have the choice of programming for specific hardware or ignoring the hardware altogether. The direct memory access method discussed later in this chapter uses hardware information explicitly. To write device-independent programs that don't require explicit hardware information, use one or more of the following methods:

■ Program with the standard C Library output functions such as *printf()* and *putchar()*. This results in portable code, but it limits the positioning of text and doesn't permit the use of color.

- Use the ANSI.SYS escape sequences, as described in Chapter 13. However, if your program relies on the cursor-control keys, for example, you must use console I/O functions, which restrict portability. Also, using ANSI.SYS inhibits some special features of the EGA, such as the 43-line display. The ANSI approach works on all systems that recognize the standard ANSI codes; IBM PCs and clones must have the ANSI.SYS driver installed.

- Use IBM PC BIOS calls, as described in Chapter 13. The BIOS includes programs for all PC video controllers, and it selects the appropriate code for the display and controller you are using. That's why our examples in Chapter 13 didn't specify a monitor or controller. BIOS calls also support the use of more than one page of screen memory; but because the MDA has only one page, we suggest you restrict applications to page 0.

We thoroughly covered the first two choices in the last chapter. Although we also discussed BIOS calls, we skipped some of the detail until you understood more about the hardware. In the next section we will discuss BIOS calls in greater detail.

Working with BIOS Again: Attributes

In Chapter 13, we built a small library (SCRFUN.LIB) of BIOS-based C functions that are hardware independent. In fact, insulating the user from the hardware is one of the primary reasons for having a BIOS. For instance, we can use the same BIOS calls to control the way in which characters are displayed on an MDA, a CGA, an EGA, or a VGA monitor. The attribute of a character controls its appearance. Let's see how we can use the BIOS to investigate and control attributes.

An attribute is a 1-byte value in which the individual bits have particular meanings that affect the appearance of the associated character. For example, with the Monochrome Display Adapter, bit 7 of the attribute controls the blink function; bits 6, 5, and 4 control the background; bit 3 controls the intensify foreground function; and bits 2, 1, and 0 control the foreground—that is, the pixels constituting the character. (See Figure 14-3.) Table 14-3 lists the standard attribute values used by the MDA.

The other video controllers use bits 6, 5, and 4 to control the color of the background and bits 2, 1, and 0 to control the color of the foreground. Bits 7 and 3 serve the same function as they do for the MDA. Figure 14-4 shows the color that each bit controls.

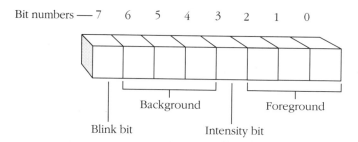

Figure 14-3. *Monochrome attribute bits.*

Table 14-3. Monochrome Attributes

Bit Pattern	Hex Value	Meaning
0000 0000	0x00	No display
0000 0111	0x07	Normal display
0111 0000	0x70	Reverse video
0000 0001	0x01	Underline
0111 0111	0x77	Whiteout
1xxx xxxx	0x80	Blink mode
xxxx 1xxx	0x08	Intensified foreground

Note: The last two entries are used with different modes. For example, 10000111 (0x87) is normal display with blinking, while 11110000 (0xF0) is reverse video with blinking. The x's indicate that those values don't affect blinking or intensity.

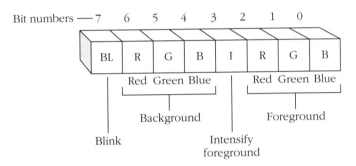

Figure 14-4. *Color attribute bits.*

To produce a blue character on a red screen, use an attribute of 01000001. This turns on the red background bit and the blue foreground bit. To make the foreground a bright blue, turn on the intensity bit with 01001001.

The EGA BIOS

The IBM BIOS was created long before the inception of the EGA. How then can you use BIOS routines to control the EGA? The EGA card comes with a set of BIOS interrupt 0x10 video I/O routines in its own ROM. Recall that the address of each interrupt routine is stored in the interrupt vector table. When you boot an EGA system, the entry for video interrupt 0x10 is loaded with the EGA BIOS address instead of the motherboard BIOS address. Thus, the old BIOS routines are bypassed and the new EGA-supplied ones are used.

If you set both the blue and the green foreground bits, the blue and the green phosphors on the display screen are simultaneously turned on, producing a color called cyan. Setting all three foreground bits turns on all three colors, which, by the laws of video color mixing, produces white. Similarly, clearing all three bits causes no pixels to be turned on, producing black. Therefore, the "normal" monochrome attribute of 00000111 also produces white-on-black characters for the CGA, EGA, and VGA. Table 14-4 shows the colors generated by the various 3-bit combinations.

Table 14-4.   Text Color Values

Bit Pattern	Hex Foreground	Hex Background	Color
000	0x0	0x00	Black
001	0x1	0x10	Blue
010	0x2	0x20	Green
011	0x3	0x30	Cyan
100	0x4	0x40	Red
101	0x5	0x50	Magenta
110	0x6	0x60	Dark yellow (brown)
111	0x7	0x70	White (light gray)

Note: The hex value 0x8 intensifies the foreground color, and 0x80 makes the character blink. Also, all attributes can be combined using logical operators.

Colors

All colors can be produced by combining three primary colors together in varying proportions. The three "additive" primary colors are red, green, and blue. For example, when you direct a beam of green light and a beam of red light toward a piece of white paper, the area where the beams overlap (or are "added") appears yellow.

A color video screen also creates colors by combining the additive primaries. Each pixel on a color screen contains individual red, green, and blue dots. Turning a pixel blue amounts to turning on the blue dots in the pixel. To produce yellow, you turn on the green and the red dots in a pixel; the eye perceives only the combined light, which is yellow.

The PC's system of using numbers to represent color imitates the physical color-mixing process. For example, in binary notation, the color number for red is 100 and the color number for green is 010. Turning on both the red and the green bits corresponds to specifying the binary number 110, which is the code for yellow.

Suppose you want a yellow character on a blue background. Because yellow is produced by combining red and green light (bits 2 and 1), and background blue is bit 4, the corresponding attribute is 00010110, or 0x16. (The actual colors you see depend on your monitor and its adjustments.)

It's more interesting to display the attributes on the screen than it is to read about them, so let's develop a program that changes the attribute bits to demonstrate how the colors change. First we must write a function that prints a string using a given attribute. Using the functions from our SCRFUN.LIB library, we produce the following *Print_attr()* function (Listing 14-1).

Print_attr() writes a character-attribute pair and moves the cursor one position to the right. *Print_attr()* has its limitations. First, it doesn't recognize the end of a line. Second, it doesn't have all the fancy formatting that *printf()* has. (You can modify the function to handle the end-of-line problem, and you can use the *sprintf()* function to do the formatting.)

Now let's use the *Print_attr()* string-displaying function in a program to display the various attributes. To demonstrate the role of each attribute bit, the program has you type the attribute byte as a binary number. The comments in the ATTRIB.C program (Listing 14-2 on the following pages) explain the workings of the various functions.

This program works with any of the previously mentioned standard video controllers. If you have a monochrome monitor, check to see what nonstandard combinations such as 00000100 produce. If you have a color monitor, enjoy the many color combinations.

```
/* Print_attr() -- prints the string str using */
/* attribute attr on the indicated page         */
/* It uses functions from the scrfun.c file.    */

void Print_attr(char *str, unsigned char attr, unsigned char page)
{
    while (*str != '\0')
        {
        Write_ch_atr(*str++, attr, page, 1);
        Cursrt();
        }
}
```

Listing 14-1. *The* Print_attr() *function.*

```
/* attrib.c -- illustrates character attributes */
/* Program list: attrib.c, scrfun.lib          */
/* User include files: scrn.h                   */

#include <stdio.h>
#include <conio.h>
#include "scrn.h"
#define PAGE 0
#define ESC '\033'
char *Format = "This message is displayed using an "
               "attribute value of %2X hex (%s).";
int Get_attrib(char *);
void Print_attr(char *, unsigned char, unsigned char);

main()
{

    int attribute;        /* value of attribute */
    char attr_str[9];     /* attribute in string form */
    char mesg[80];

    Clearscr();
    Home();
    printf("Enter an attribute as an 8-digit binary "
           "number, such as 00000111, and see a\n"
           "message displayed using that attribute. "
           "Hit Esc to quit.\n"
           "Attribute = ");
    while ((attribute = Get_attrib(attr_str)) != -1)
        {
        Setcurs(10,0,PAGE);
        sprintf(mesg, Format, attribute, attr_str);
        Print_attr(mesg, attribute, PAGE);
        Setcurs(2, 12, PAGE);
        printf("              ");  /* clear old display */
        Setcurs(2, 12, PAGE);
        }
    Clearscr();
    return (0);
}

/* The following function reads in a binary number    */
/* as a sequence of 1s and 0s. It places the 1 and 0 */
/* characters in a string whose address is passed as */
/* an argument. It returns the numeric value of the   */
/* binary number. Bad input is summarily rejected.    */
/* The function returns -1 when you press Esc.        */

int Get_attrib(char a_str[])  /* receives attribute as binary string */
{
    int attrib[8];
```

Listing 14-2. *The ATTRIB.C program.* *(continued)*

Listing 14-2. *continued*

```
    int index = 0;
    int ch;
    int attribute = 0; /* attribute as numeric value */
    int pow;

    a_str[8] = '\0';  /* terminate string */
    while ((index < 8) && (ch = getch()) != ESC)
        {
        if (ch != '0' && ch != '1')   /* bad input */
            putch('\a');
        else
            {
            putch(ch);
            a_str[index] = ch;        /* string form */
            attrib[index++] = ch - '0'; /* numeric */
            }
        }
    if (ch == ESC)
        return (-1);
    else              /* convert numeric array to a number */
        {
        for(index = 7, pow = 1; index >=0; index--, pow *= 2)
            attribute += attrib[index] * pow;
        return (attribute);
        }
}

/* The following function prints the string str using */
/* attribute attr on the indicated page.             */
/* It uses functions from the scrfun.c file.         */

void Print_attr(char *str, unsigned char attr, unsigned char page)
{
    while (*str != '\0')
        {
        Write_ch_atr(*str++, attr , page, 1);
        Cursrt();
        }
}
```

Attributes and Bitwise Operators

You can also manipulate attributes with the C bitwise operators that we discussed in Chapter 7. Suppose, for example, a program uses the following definitions:

```
#define NORMAL 0x07
#define VIDREV 0x70
#define BLINK  0x80
#define INTENSE 0x08
```

To set *mode* to an intense, normal attribute, we can use the bitwise logical OR operator, as follows:

```
mode = NORMAL | INTENSE;
```

Because an OR operation between 1 and anything else is 1, all bits set to 1 are left on. Now, suppose *mode* has already gone through several changes. At this point it might be normal, reverse video, have blinking on or off, and so on. To turn on the intensify mode regardless of the current state, use an instruction such as the following:

```
mode = mode | INTENSE;
```

The only bit this instruction can change is bit 3, the intensity bit, because all the other bits of *INTENSE* are 0, and an OR operation between 0 and any bit is merely that bit. (That is, 0 | 0 is 0, and 1 | 0 is 1.) Furthermore, this instruction always sets bit 3 to 1, regardless of its previous value. (0 | 1 is 1, and 1 | 1 is 1.) You can also use a combination assignment operator to rewrite the last C statement as follows:

```
mode |= INTENSE; /*unconditionally turns INTENSE on */
```

Sometimes an instruction must "toggle" a bit. That is, the instruction turns on an off bit or turns off an on bit. For this, we use the *exclusive-OR* operator (^). Recall that this operator produces a "true" value (1) if one operand or the other is "true" but not if both are "true." The following expression toggles the intensity bit:

```
mode = mode ^ INTENSE;
```

If the intensity bit in *mode* is initially off, the expression becomes 0 ^ 1, which is 1, or on. If the intensity bit in *mode* is initially on, the expression is 1 ^ 1, which is 0, or off. Again, we can simplify the statement with the following combination assignment operator:

```
mode ^= INTENSE;  /* toggles the intensity bit */
```

To see the toggling in action, modify the ROAMSCRN.C program (Listing 13-24 on pp. 440–41) by adding the following lines to the *switch* statement:

```
case F3 : atr ^= BLINK; break;
case F4 : atr ^= INTENSE; break;
```

The macros *F3* and *F4* are already defined in our keys.h header, and scrn.h defines *BLINK* and *INTENSE*. Note that F1 and F2 always reset the modes to *NORMAL* and *INVERSE*, so that if you want blinking inverse, the correct key sequence is F2 F3.

Direct Memory Access

Thus far, we've used BIOS routines to place the proper character and attribute bytes into video memory. This method offers two advantages—it saves us work and lets us write hardware-independent programs that run on the MDA, CGA, EGA, VGA, and MCGA. However, we can create faster programs by bypassing the BIOS and placing data directly into video memory. This programming technique is called "direct video memory access," which we will refer to as DMA for the remainder of this book. (Don't confuse this use of DMA with the DMA chip built into the IBM PC and compatibles, which performs a different function.)

DMA Basics

To copy information to or from a memory location, you need to use the address of that location. Often, you do so symbolically and indirectly by using variables and array names. Pointers provide a more obvious way to use addresses. So what do you use to access video memory?

Because video memory is a large block of bytes, it's natural to think of it as a large array. As you've learned, arrays can often be described by either array notation or pointer notation. But with video memory, you must use pointers. The reason is that the compiler chooses the physical addresses to which an array corresponds, but *you* can choose the physical address to which a pointer points. In particular, you can choose to have a pointer point to the beginning of video memory.

The specific address you use depends on the hardware. The MDA uses 0xB0000 (720,896 in decimal), and the CGA uses 0xB8000 (753,664 in decimal). The EGA and VGA use 0xB0000 for the monochrome mode and 0xB8000 for the color text modes.

To use the address, you must type cast the numeric value to the proper pointer type. Also, in the small and medium memory models, a data pointer is a 16-bit quantity. Neither of the addresses we need fits into 16 bits. The large memory model uses a 32-bit pointer, but not in a way that lets us make our simple assignment. So before we can assign the video RAM address to a pointer, we must first examine how the PC and QuickC handle memory addresses.

Segmented Memory

The PC has the same problem with large addresses that the small and medium models do. The 8086 chip normally uses a 16-bit register for addresses. However, this permits the register to address a maximum of 64 KB of memory, which falls far short of the address needed to access the video RAM.

As we noted in Chapter 12, the 8086 family of microprocessors uses segmented memory to overcome this problem. The maximum size of each segment is 64 KB, the size addressable by an address register. Typically, a program uses one segment for program code and a second segment for data.

Addresses for the program code are 16-bit addresses relative to the beginning of the program segment, and data addresses are relative to the beginning of the data segment. These relative addresses are called "offsets." In C, this offset is what is stored in a 16-bit pointer. The following statement:

```
printf("Address of x is %u\n", &x);
```

prints the offset, in bytes, of *x* from the beginning of a data segment. To keep track of where the code and data segments are, the PC uses special registers: the CS, or Code Segment register, and the DS, or Data Segment register.

To solve the problem of identifying the location of a segment by using only 16 bits, the PC divides the actual address of the segment by 16 (0x10 hex). For example, 0xB0000 divided by 0x10 is 0xB000. This result is called the "segment value." (See Figure 14-5.) Thus, the segment value 0xA000 corresponds to the segment address 0xA0000. As a result of this system, segments must start at addresses that are multiples of 16.

Suppose you want to specify the 0x20th byte of video memory. The absolute address of this byte is 0xB0020. The PC represents this by setting the data segment register DS to the segment value of 0xB000 and setting the data offset register to 0x20. The following equation expresses the relationship more generally:

```
absolute address = 0x10 * segment value + offset
```

Note that you can represent the same physical address in many ways. For example, the absolute address 0xB0020 also can be represented with a segment value of 0xB001 and an offset of 0x10.

C, Segments, and Offsets

As you already know, C has two classes of pointers—*near* and *far*. Near pointers, which are 16 bits, hold only the offset. Far pointers, which are 32 bits, use the high 16 bits to hold the segment value and the low 16 bits to hold the offset, as shown in Figure 14-6. Compact and large models use far data pointers by default. Small and medium models use near data pointers by default. However, you can use the non-standard C keyword _far to create far pointers in the small and medium models. To use the _far keyword in QuickC, be sure the Microsoft C language extensions are active. To check, select Make from the Options menu, choose Compiler Flags, and then look for the MS Extensions option.

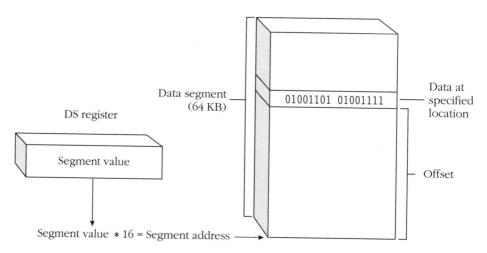

Figure 14-5. *Data addresses are represented by a segment value and an offset.*

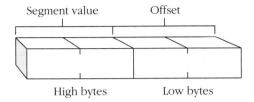

Figure 14-6. *Filling a far pointer.*

Using a Far Pointer

To access the video memory, we must declare a far pointer, initialize its high bytes to the segment value for the video RAM, and use its low bytes for the offset. Declare a far pointer by using the keyword *_far*, as follows:

```
unsigned short _far *far_ptr; /* far pointer */
```

This creates a 32-bit pointer that points to a 2-byte unit. Each 2-byte unit holds the ASCII code and the attribute of a single displayed character.

Next, let's set the pointer to an absolute screen address of 0xB0020. This corresponds to a segment value of 0xB000 (0xB0000 ÷ 0x10) and an offset of 0x20. To place the segment value into the high bytes, left-shift it 16 places; because the offset goes into the lower bytes, you needn't manipulate it at all.

```
far_ptr = (unsigned short _far *) (0xB000L << 16) | 0x20;
```

Notice that we used a type cast to convert the right side (type *long*) to the correct pointer type. Next, we used the *L* suffix to make the segment value type *long*. Otherwise, 0xB000 would be treated as type *int* (a 16-bit type on a PC), and the 16-bit left-shift would shift all the bits out of the *int* storage space, leaving only zeros. (See Figure 14-7 on the following page.)

Note also that the bitwise OR (|) operator combines the segment value and the off-set. Because one resides entirely in the upper bytes and the other is confined to the lower bytes, this has the same effect as addition but is faster.

Finally, note that the far pointer does not hold the absolute address. It holds two quantities: segment value and offset. If, for some reason, you want the absolute address, you can obtain it by using the following expression:

```
abs_addr = 0x10 * (far_ptr >> 16) + far_ptr & 0xFFFF;
```

The right-shift produces the segment value; multiplying by 0x10 gives the segment address; and the 0xFFFF mask screens the segment value of the pointer, leaving only the offset. The variable *abs_addr* should be type *long* or *unsigned long* so that it can hold the entire address.

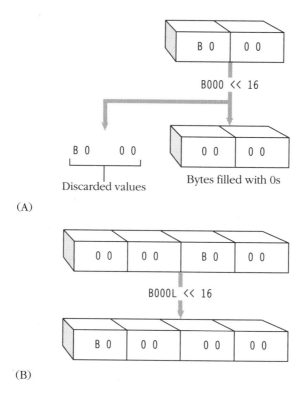

Figure 14-7. *A 16-bit left-shift discards all the values in an* int *(A), but the same operation on a long integer (B) places the value of the low bytes into the high bytes.*

Using Direct Memory Access—An Example

To use DMA to access video RAM, we must declare a far pointer and initialize it to point to the beginning of video memory. To do so, we must first decide which data type to reference. Think of one page of video memory as 2000 character-attribute units, with each unit describing a particular screen location. In QuickC, 2 bytes constitute a short value, so our pointer must be a far pointer to *unsigned short.* Use *typedef* to make *VIDMEM* a synonym for that type:

```
typedef unsigned short (_far * VIDMEM);
```

Then declare *screen* as a pointer of that type, as follows:

```
VIDMEM screen;
```

Next, you must decide which segment value to use. For the monochrome mode (mode 7), use 0xB000. For the CGA and CGA-compatible modes (0 through 6), use 0xB800. Because we must left-shift the segment value 16 bits to use it with a C far pointer, we represent our values as follows:

```
#define MONMEM ((VIDMEM) (0xB000L << 16))
#define CGAMEM ((VIDMEM) (0xB800L << 16))
```

458

The *L* suffix makes the addresses 32-bit quantities, and the type casting to type *VIDMEM* gives the numeric values the same type as the *screen* pointer.

Recall that in the character-attribute pair, the low byte holds the character and the high byte holds the attribute. Therefore, if *screen* is the pointer to the beginning of video memory, if *offset* is the character position we wish to set, and if *ch* and *attrib* are character and attribute values, we use the following statement:

```
*(screen + offset) = (attrib << 8) | ch;
```

The left-shift puts *attrib* into the high byte, and the bitwise OR operator combines the resulting values, as shown in Table 14-5. Note that in QuickC, *attrib* must be at least a 16-bit type. If it is an 8-bit type, the significant bits are lost. (Older versions of Microsoft C converted type *char* to *int* for calculation, and no bits were discarded.)

Table 14-5.   Manipulating Character and Attribute in RAM

Byte(s)	Bit Values	Hex Equivalents
attrib	00000000 00000111	0x0007
attrib << 8	00000111 00000000	0x0700
ch	01000001	0x41
(attrib << 8) ¦ ch	00000111 01000001	0x0741

Let's use this information in a simple program. The CH2000.C program (Listing 14-3) echoes any pressed ASCII key. However, instead of echoing it once, the program uses DMA to echo it 2000 times. Also, the program cycles through all possible attribute values, making the color version more spectacular than the monochrome version. (Use *CGAMEM* instead of *MONMEM* if you are using a CGA, EGA, or VGA display.)

The program first reads a character. The *for* loop displays the character at all 2000 positions. By using the increment operator on *attrib*, the program changes the attribute at each position and cycles through all 256 possibilities.

```
/* ch2000.c -- fills screen with 2000 characters */
/* This program demonstrates direct memory access */
/* of video memory.  It is set up for the MDA.     */
/* Assign CGAMEM instead of MONMEM to screen for   */
/* CGA and CGA-compatible modes.                    */
/* Press a key to fill the screen; press Esc to     */
/* quit.                                            */

#include <conio.h>
#include "scrn.h"
typedef unsigned short (_far * VIDMEM);
#define MONMEM ((VIDMEM) (0xB000L << 16)) /* monochrome */
```

Listing 14-3. *The CH2000.C program.*   *(continued)*

Listing 14-3. *continued*

```
#define CGAMEM ((VIDMEM) (0xB800L << 16)) /* CGA, EGA */
#define ESC '\033'
#define CHARS 2000
#define AMASK 0xFF    /* keep attribute in range */

main()
{
    unsigned ch;            /* character to be displayed */
    unsigned attrib = 7;    /* initial attribute         */
    VIDMEM screen;          /* pointer to video RAM      */
    int offset;             /* location on screen        */

    screen = MONMEM;        /* monochrome initialization */
    while ((ch = getch()) != ESC)
        {
        for (offset = 0; offset < CHARS; offset++)
            *(screen + offset) = ((attrib++ & AMASK) << 8) : ch;
        }
    return (0);
}
```

Notice how quickly the program fills the screen. To appreciate the speed of this program, rewrite it using the BIOS-based *Write_ch_atr()* function from SCRFUN.LIB and note the difference!

Making DMA More Compatible

CH2000.C is fast and simple, but it doesn't work with all controllers. The program needs to be able to choose the correct memory value itself. Function 15 of the BIOS 0x10 video I/O interrupt enables it to do so. Because this routine returns the current video mode, the program can use that value to select the correct video RAM address. Our SCRFUN.LIB library from Chapter 13 includes the *Getvmode()* function (Listing 14-4) based on that BIOS call. Note that the constant *GETMODE* is defined in the scrn.h file and that we have SCRFUN.LIB in the program list.

```
/* Getvmode() -- obtains the current video mode */
#include <dos.h>
#include "scrn.h"
unsigned char Getvmode()
{
    union REGS reg;

    reg.h.ah = GETMODE;
    int86(VIDEO, &reg, &reg);
    return reg.h.al;
}
```

Listing 14-4. *The* Getvmode() *function.*

Now rewrite CH2000.C as shown in the CH2001.C program (Listing 14-5). The mode constants *TEXTMONO*, *TEXTBW80*, and *TEXTC80* are defined in scrn.h; they represent mode 7 (monochrome), mode 2 (CGA 80-by-25 B/W), and mode 3 (CGA 80-by-25 Color), respectively.

```
/* ch2001.c -- fills screen with 2000 characters   */
/* This program demonstrates direct memory access   */
/* of video memory.  It uses the current video mode */
/* value to select the proper video RAM address.    */
/* Press a key to fill the screen; press Esc to      */
/* quit.                                             */
/* Program list: ch2001.c, scrfun.lib                */

#include <conio.h>
#include "scrn.h"
typedef unsigned short (_far * VIDMEM);
#define MONMEM ((VIDMEM) (0xB000L << 16)) /* monochrome */
#define CGAMEM ((VIDMEM) (0xB800L << 16)) /* CGA, EGA */
#define ESC '\033'
#define CHARS 2000
#define AMASK 0xFF

main()
{
    unsigned ch, mode;
    unsigned attrib = 7;
    VIDMEM screen;            /* pointer to video RAM */
    int offset;

    if ((mode = Getvmode()) == TEXTMONO)
        screen = MONMEM;
    else if (mode == TEXTC80 || mode == TEXTBW80)
        screen = CGAMEM;
    else
        exit(1);
    while ((ch = getch()) != ESC)
        {
        for (offset = 0; offset < CHARS; offset++)
            *(screen + offset) = ((attrib++ & AMASK) << 8) | ch;
        }
    return (0);
}
```

Listing 14-5. *The CH2001.C program.*

Paging

Now let's turn to a text topic that lies beyond the scope of the Monochrome Display Adapter—paging. The CGA, EGA, and VGA have enough memory to store more than one screenful, or page, of text. The 16-KB video memory of the CGA, for example, can hold four text pages. The BIOS supports the use of pages by providing routines for setting the page and for determining the current page number. Many other BIOS routines require page information. The SCRFUN.C file we developed in Chapter 13 contains two page-related functions—*Getpage()* and *Setpage()*, which are combined in Listing 14-6. As usual, the manifest constants are defined in scrn.h.

Paging is very fast, even compared to DMA, because the video RAM doesn't need to be rewritten. The video controller simply changes the section of video memory that it reads. A typical application for paging stores a help screen on one page while an application uses another page. This permits a rapid transition between the two screens without calling data from program memory or a disk file.

Let's develop a basic program that can switch back and forth between page 0 and a help screen on page 1. We could use BIOS calls to write the contents of the two screens, but direct memory access is faster. However, to use direct memory access, we need to supply the address of page 1. Because each page holds 2000 character-attribute pairs, or 4000 bytes, you might expect that page 1 is offset 4000 bytes from the beginning of video memory. But computers relate more to powers of 2 than to powers of 10, so the actual offset is 4096 bytes, 0x1000 in hex. (You can use the extra bytes between pages to display color in page borders.)

```
/* Getpage() -- obtains the current video page */
unsigned char Getpage()
{
    union REGS reg;

    reg.h.ah = GETMODE;
    int86(VIDEO, &reg, &reg);
    return reg.h.bh;
}

/* Setpage() -- sets page to given value */
void Setpage(unsigned char page)
{
    union REGS reg;

    reg.h.ah = SETPAGE;
    reg.h.al = page;
    int86(VIDEO, &reg, &reg);
}
```

Listing 14-6. *The* Getpage() *and* Setpage() *functions.*

We use the *VIDMEM* type pointer again to point to video memory. Because we define it to point to a 2-byte unit (the character-attribute pair), the offset in *VIDMEM* units is 2048 pairs, which is 0x800 in hex.

The HELP.C program (Listing 14-7) is fairly simple. The key points to note are its use of *Setpage()* to change pages and its use of direct memory access to write to the screen. The program uses two direct memory access modules. The writechr.c module (Listing 14-8 on the following pages) writes a character-attribute pair a specified number of times beginning at a specified memory location. The writestr.c module (Listing 14-9 on p. 465) is similar, but it writes a string once instead of writing a single character repeatedly. By choosing the appropriate memory location, you can use these functions to write to either page, no matter which one is currently displayed. For convenience, we've collected definitions of the colors in a file called color.h (Listing 14-10 on p. 465).

```
/* help.c -- uses paging and direct memory access */
/*           to display a help screen             */
/* Program list: help.c, writestr.c, writechr.c,  */
/*               scrfun.lib                        */
/* User include files: scrn.h, color.h            */

#include <stdio.h>
#include <conio.h>
#include "color.h"
#include "scrn.h"
typedef unsigned int (_far * VIDMEM);
#define CGAMEM ((VIDMEM) (0xB800L << 16))
#define PAGESIZE 2000
#define PAGEOFFSET 0x800L
#define ESC '\033'
#define ATTR1 (BG_BLUE : YELLOW)
#define ATTR2 (BG_YELLOW : BLUE)
#define ATTR3 (BG_RED : YELLOW : BLINK : INTENSE)
#define CH1 (unsigned short) '\xB1'
char *str1 = "Press ? key for help.";
char *str2 = "Press Enter key to return.";
char *str3 = "Press Esc key to quit.";
char *str4 = "\xB1HELP!\xB1";
void Write_chars(VIDMEM, unsigned short, unsigned
                 short, unsigned short);
void Write_str(VIDMEM, unsigned short, char *);

main()
{
    int ch;
    unsigned char page = 0;
    unsigned char mode;
```

Listing 14-7. *The HELP.C program.*   *(continued)*

Listing 14-7. *continued*

```
    mode = Getvmode();
    if (mode != TEXTC80 && mode != TEXTBW80)
        {
        printf("Only modes 2 and 3 supported. Bye.\n");
        exit(1);
        }
    Setpage(page);
    Write_chars(CGAMEM, '\0', ATTR2, PAGESIZE);
    Write_str(CGAMEM + 2 * COLS, ATTR1, str1);
    Write_str(CGAMEM + 22 * COLS, ATTR1, str3);
    Write_chars(CGAMEM + PAGEOFFSET, '\0', ATTR1,
            PAGESIZE);
    Write_str(CGAMEM + PAGEOFFSET + 20 * COLS, ATTR2,
            str2);
    Write_str(CGAMEM + PAGEOFFSET + 22 * COLS, ATTR1,
            str3);
    Write_chars(CGAMEM + PAGEOFFSET + 10 * COLS + 36,
            CH1, ATTR3, 7);
    Write_str(CGAMEM + PAGEOFFSET + 11 * COLS + 36,
            ATTR3, str4);
    Write_chars(CGAMEM + PAGEOFFSET + 12 * COLS + 36,
            CH1, ATTR3, 7);

    while ((ch = getch()) != ESC)
        {
        if (ch == '?' && page == 0)
            Setpage(page = 1);
        else if (ch == '\r' && page == 1)
            Setpage(page = 0);
        }
    Write_chars(CGAMEM, '\0', NORMAL, PAGESIZE);
    Write_chars(CGAMEM + PAGEOFFSET, '\0', NORMAL,
            PAGESIZE);
    return (0);
}
```

```
/* writechr.c -- writes char and attribute repeatedly */
/*              using DMA                              */
/* Write character ch with attribute attr num times   */
/* starting at location pstart -- uses array notation  */

typedef unsigned int (_far * VIDMEM);
```

Listing 14-8. *The writechr.c module.*   *(continued)*

Listing 14-8. *continued*

```
void Write_chars(VIDMEM pstart, unsigned short ch,
                 unsigned short attr, unsigned short num)
{
    register count;
    unsigned short pair;

    pair = (attr << 8) ¦ (ch & 0x00FF) ;
    for (count = 0; count < num; count++)
        pstart[count] = pair;
}
```

```
/* writestr.c -- writes string and attribute using DMA */
/* Write the string str with attribute attr at        */
/* location pstart -- uses pointer notation            */

typedef unsigned int (_far * VIDMEM);

void Write_str(VIDMEM pstart, unsigned short·attr, char *str)
{
    while (*str != '\0')
        *pstart++ = (attr << 8) ¦ (*str++ & 0x00FF);
}
```

Listing 14-9. *The writestr.c module.*

```
/* color.h -- defines the color attributes */
   /* Foreground colors */
#define  BLACK   0x0
#define  BLUE    0x1
#define  GREEN   0x2
#define  RED     0x4
#define  CYAN    0x3
#define  MAGENTA 0x5
#define  YELLOW  0x6
#define  WHITE   0x7
   /* Background colors */
#define  BG_BLACK   0x00
#define  BG_BLUE    0x10
#define  BG_GREEN   0x20
#define  BG_RED     0x40
#define  BG_CYAN    0x30
#define  BG_MAGENTA 0x50
#define  BG_YELLOW  0x60
#define  BG_WHITE   0x70
```

Listing 14-10. *The color.h include file.*

Most of the HELP.C program involves using the new *Write_chars()* and *Write_str()* functions, so let's examine them. The two functions are quite similar in behavior, but to illustrate different programming techniques, one uses array notation and the other uses pointer notation.

Write_chars() starts by combining the attribute and character into a 2-byte unit. It left-shifts the attribute into the high byte and places the character in the low byte. Next, the function performs a logical AND operation with the character and 0x00FF to limit the character to the range 0 through 0xFF, or 0 through 255. Next, a loop assigns the 2-byte pair to *num* consecutive locations in memory, beginning with the location that pointer *pstart* references. Recall that the notation *pstart[count]* is equivalent to *(pstart + count)*.

In the program, *Write_chars()* clears the two pages, setting them to yellow and blue, respectively. To clear the screen, the program sets the character part of the byte to a null character; the attribute sets the color.

The *Write_str()* function uses pointer notation to display a string. Like the preceding function, it combines the left-shifted attribute with a masked character value. In this case, *str* initially points to the first character in the string, so *str* represents the value of that character. The *while* loop continues until it reaches the terminating null character of the string. During each cycle, the increment operator advances the video memory pointer and the string pointer after they are used.

In the main program, note how we use addresses to specify locations on the screen. Consider, for example, the following statement:

```
Write_str(CGAMEM + PAGEOFFSET + 11 * COLS + 36,
          ATTR3, str4);
```

The address *CGAMEM* locates the beginning of the CGA (and EGA and VGA) memory. The *PAGEOFFSET* value is the offset to the beginning of the next page. Each line contains *COLS* characters, so the expression *11 * COLS* is the offset to the beginning of line 11 (the twelfth line, because numbering starts with zero). Finally, the *36* gives the offset, or the indention measured in character widths, from the left side of the display.

Note that the QuickC Graphics Library provides alternatives to many of our BIOS-based functions, including functions that clear the screen and set the page. However, using the Graphics Library produces final code noticeably larger than that of our examples. We use the Graphics Library only in graphics programs, in which its power and generality become evident.

Ports

Any discussion of hardware-dependent programming methods must mention "ports," which are information conduits between the CPU and the other devices and processors in a PC. In general, each processor or device has one or more registers of its own. Values placed in these registers can control the operation of the processor or, perhaps, test its state of readiness. In the PC, various registers are assigned "port addresses" that are completely separate from the memory address system and are handled differently. The CPU accesses registers through ports by using special port instructions. (See Figure 14-8.)

An 8086 CPU can address as many as 64,000 8-bit ports, but only a small fraction of that number (fewer than 200) are actually used. In assembly language, you access the ports with the instructions IN and OUT: IN reads a register; OUT writes to it. C does not contain these instructions, so QuickC supplies the non-ANSI *inp()* and *outp()* functions to serve the same purpose.

Reading Ports with *inp()*

As was mentioned in Chapter 13, the *inp()* and *outp()* functions are defined in conio.h. The following is the syntax for *inp()*:

```
#include <conio.h>

int inp(port)
unsigned port;    /* port number */
```

This function reads the register at port number *port*, which can be a value in the range 0 through 65,535. It then returns the byte it reads. With write-only ports, *inp()* returns the value 255, or all bits set to 1. However, a return value of 255 does not always signal a write-only register because 255 is also a valid register setting.

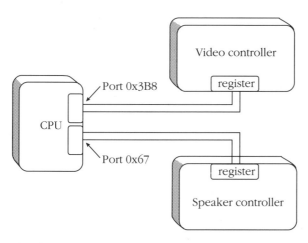

Figure 14-8. *Ports and registers.*

The short PORTINFO.C program (Listing 14-11) lets you access and read various ports. Note that it uses the return value of *scanf()* to terminate the input loop. We prompt for hexadecimal port numbers because technical manuals usually list them in that form. Note that *scanf()* returns a value equal to the number of successful reads. Therefore, if it reads a hex value, it returns 1. If it finds input that is not hex, such as the letter *q*, *scanf()* returns 0, and the loop terminates.

The following is a sample run:

```
Enter number (in hex) of the port you wish to read: 3da
Value returned for port 3da is 199 (decimal), c7 (hex)
Next port? (q to quit): 61
Value returned for port 61 is 49 (decimal), 31 (hex)
Next port? (q to quit): 42
Value returned for port 42 is 174 (decimal), ae (hex)
Next port? (q to quit): 3b8
Value returned for port 3b8 is 255 (decimal), ff (hex)
Next port? (q to quit): q
```

You may get different values from those in this sample run—some of the registers change values as you use the computer.

In the IBM PC and compatibles, the 0x3DA port reports status information about the MDA. Port 61 controls the speaker, and port 42 regulates the frequency of the 8253 timer chip. Finally, port 3B8 is the control port for the 6845 video controller on the MDA. (Because the last port is a write-only port, the reported value is not necessarily the true one.)

```c
/* portinfo.c -- reads port values */

#include <conio.h>
#include <stdio.h>

main()
{
    unsigned int portnum;
    int regvalue;

    printf("Enter number (in hex) of the port ");
    printf("you wish to read: ");
    while (scanf("%x", &portnum) == 1)
        {
        regvalue = inp(portnum);
        printf("Value returned for port %x is %d (decimal),"
               " %x (hex)\n", portnum, regvalue, regvalue);
        printf("Next port? (q to quit): ");
        }
    return (0);
}
```

Listing 14-11. *The PORTINFO.C program.*

As you can see, reading a register is a simple procedure. The difficult part is wading through the technical literature to see which port addresses correspond to which devices and to find out the meaning of the register settings.

Writing to a Port with *outp()*

You write to a port with the *outp()* function by using the following syntax:

```
#include <conio.h>

int outp(port, value)
unsigned port;              /* port number  */
int value;                  /* output value */
```

The function sends *value* to port number *port*. Although *value* is declared type *int*, you should use only numbers in the range 0 through 255. The function returns the same value it sends.

Although it is easy to write to a port, you must do so with caution. Sending incorrect values to some video controller registers, for example, can damage your monitor. Other ports can disable your keyboard, the system memory, the monitor, and so on. Do not use the experimental method when you write to ports! Before we write a sample program that uses port number 0x3B8, the MDA control register, study the function of each bit in the register as described in Table 14-6.

Table 14-6. Video Control Register Functions

Bit	Function
0	If this bit is 0, no communication is permitted between the CPU and the video display memory. (This prevents data from being changed.) If this bit is 1 (the default value), communication between the CPU and the video display memory is enabled. (This lets the CPU read from and write to memory.)
1, 2	Not used.
3	If this bit is 0, the display is disabled, which blanks the screen. The contents of video RAM, however, are unaffected. If this bit is 1 (the default value), the display is enabled, and data stored in video RAM is displayed.
4	Not used.
5	If this bit is 0, the blink attribute bit in video RAM controls the background intensity. If this bit is 1 (the default value), it controls blinking.
6, 7	Not used.

Let's write a short program that blanks the screen and then restores it. We can turn off the display by setting bit 3 to 0. Because this does not affect the video RAM, resetting bit 3 to 1 restores the display.

Ideally, we would use *inp()* to read and save the current register setting. Then we could use that value to restore the original setting when we were done. However, 3B8 is a write-only register, so we must use Table 14-6 to select the proper setting.

Clearly, we originally want bit 0 to be 1. Normally, bits 3 and 5 should be 1 also. Because the other bits don't affect the port, we can set them to 0. This makes our default setting 00101001 in binary, or 0x29 in hex. To turn the display off, set bit 3 to 0, which changes the setting to 00100001 in binary, or 0x21 in hex. The short BLANK.C program (Listing 14-12) demonstrates the results of our efforts.

```
/* blank.c -- blanks MDA screen */

#include <conio.h>
#define CONTROLREG 0x3B8 /* control register MDA */
#define DEFAULTSET 0x29
#define VIDEOOFF 0x21

main()
{
    outp(CONTROLREG, VIDEOOFF);
    getch();
    outp(CONTROLREG, DEFAULTSET);
}
```

Listing 14-12. *The BLANK.C program.*

As we mentioned, the port approach is hardware dependent. For example, changing the register number from 3B8 to 3D8 makes this program work with the CGA, but not with the EGA. By accessing the ports directly, you can make the video controllers do things that are impossible with BIOS calls alone. However, a new display adapter (and different port assignments) can render your program nonfunctional. Our BLANK.C program illustrates both these points.

But sometimes you must use ports. For example, there are no BIOS calls that control the speaker; therefore, if you want to play a little tune, programming the port is the only method available in C.

QuickC also provides the *inpw()* and *outpw()* functions for port communication. They work like *inp()* and *outp()* except that they transmit 1 word (2 bytes) at a time instead of a single byte.

The EGA and VGA

The normal text modes for the EGA and VGA systems are modes 3 and 4, which emulate the CGA 80-by-25 B/W and Color text modes. (Both systems also support mode 7 so that they can be used with a monochrome monitor.) All the applications we've discussed so far, aside from the port example, work with the EGA and VGA. These video controllers, however, have additional text capabilities that you might want to exploit.

Normally, when used with a high-resolution monitor, the EGA and VGA use more pixels per character than the CGA to achieve better-looking text. However, these controllers also can produce smaller characters by using the CGA 8-by-8-character grid instead of the normal 8-by-14 (EGA) or 9-by-16 (VGA) grid. This reduction lets us generate a 43-line screen with the EGA and a 50-line screen with the VGA. For simplicity, we'll use the term "extended-line" to describe either.

The EGA and VGA handle fonts differently than the MDA and CGA. The EGA and VGA store some standard fonts in ROM, much like the CGA and MDA. However, rather than scanning the ROM directly to get font information, the EGA and VGA first copy the fonts to a video RAM area beginning at memory location 0xA0000. Then they scan the RAM for font information. Thus, you can use BIOS calls to select a font, or you can even load a font of your own design. To access the extended-line mode, you must load the 8-by-8 font instead of the default (8-by-14 or 9-by-16) font.

To produce the extended-line display, you must reset several video controller registers. (New BIOS routines that come with these controllers simplify the process.) The LINES43.C program (Listing 14-13) sets up the extended-line mode. If ANSI.SYS is running, this program will not work properly—it displays the small characters, but it limits the display to 25 lines.

The program first sets the usual text mode. Next, it calls a new routine added to the EGA and VGA versions of interrupt 0x10. Routine 0x11, labeled *CHAR_GEN* in our program, specifies the character font to be used. Setting register AL to 0x12 selects the 8-by-8-pixel character set stored in the video ROM and resets the register settings to display 43 (or 50) lines.

```c
/* lines43.c -- leaves EGA in 43-line mode */

#include <dos.h>
#include <conio.h>
#define VIDEO 0x10
#define SETVMODE 0
#define CHAR_GEN 0x11    /* an EGA BIOS function number */
#define ROM8X8    0x12
#define BLOCK 0
#define TEXTC80 3

main()
{
    union REGS reg;

    reg.h.ah = SETVMODE;    /* set text mode */
    reg.h.al = TEXTC80;
    int86(VIDEO, &reg, &reg);

    reg.h.ah = CHAR_GEN;    /* char generator routine */
    reg.h.al = ROM8X8;      /* use 8x8 ROM character box */
    reg.h.bl = BLOCK;       /* copy to block 0 */
    int86(VIDEO, &reg, &reg);
}
```

Listing 14-13. *The LINES43.C program.*

Why did the program set BLOCK to 0? The EGA and VGA can simultaneously store as many as four fonts. Block 0 refers to the first font, block 1 to the second, and so on. Because block 0 is used unless you explicitly switch to another, we copied the font to that block.

If you run the LINES43.C program from within the QuickC environment, its effect ends when you return to the QuickC editor. If you run it from the MS-DOS environment, use the MS-DOS command MODE CO80 to restore the usual mode.

What happens if you set the extended-line mode and then run another program? Some programs reset the mode and undo the change. Some display the small characters but assume that only 25 lines can be displayed. Some, like QuickC, check to see the number of lines in use and display the full 43 (or 50) lines.

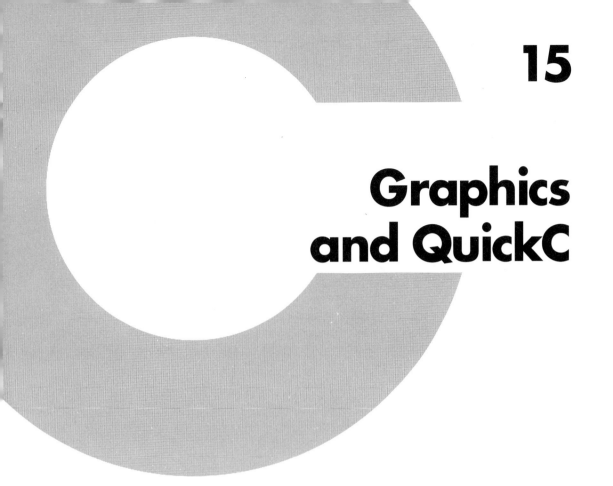

15

Graphics and QuickC

Generating computer graphics is one of the PC's most spectacular uses. All the video controllers listed in the preceding chapters—except the MDA—offer graphics modes that permit pixel-by-pixel control of the entire screen, enabling you to create figures and patterns and to set colors for individual pixels. QuickC supports these modes, and, beginning with version 1.01, it also supports the Hercules Graphics Card (HGC) graphics mode. The quality of graphics (and graphics programming in general) is hardware-dependent. The CGA, EGA, VGA, and HGC offer various graphics modes that are not compatible with one another. Fortunately, QuickC's extensive Graphics Library substantially simplifies graphics programming. We devote most of this chapter to exploring that library.

The Graphics Modes

First, let's review the available graphics modes. All of these modes are dependent on specific video controllers and displays. Table 15-1 on the following page shows which modes are available to various hardware systems.

Table 15-1. Graphics Modes

Mode	Adapters	Displays	Resolution	Colors per Palette	Palettes	Total Colors
4	CGA, EGA, VGA	B/W, CD, ED, VD	320 × 200	4	2	16
5	CGA, EGA, VGA	CD, ED, VD	320 × 200	4	1	4 gray
6	CGA, EGA, VGA	B/W, CD, ED, VD	640 × 200	2	1	2 B/W
8	HGC	MD	720 × 328	2	1	2 B/W
13	EGA, VGA	CD, ED, VD	320 × 200	16	User-definable	16
14	EGA, VGA	ED, VD	640 × 200	16	User-definable	16
15	EGA, VGA	MD	640 × 350	2	1	2 B/W
16	EGA, VGA	ED, VD	640 × 350	4/16	User-definable	16/64
17	VGA	VD	640 × 480	2	User-definable	262,144
18	VGA	VD	640 × 480	16	User-definable	262,144
19	VGA	VD	320 × 200	256	User-definable	262,144

Abbreviations: MD   Monochrome Display   ED   Enhanced display
                 B/W Black-and-white display   VD   VGA display
                 CD   Color display

Notes: For the EGA and VGA, mode 5 is the same as mode 4.

For mode 16, the number of colors available to the EGA depends on the amount of EGA memory. The lower figures correspond to 64 KB of memory; the higher figures correspond to 128 KB or more of EGA memory.

Modes and BIOS

In Chapter 14 we used the BIOS-based *Getvmode()* function from our SCRFUN.LIB library to obtain the current video mode. That library also provides the *Setvmode()* function shown in Listing 15-1.

You use this function to set mode 4, for example, with the following program lines:

```
if (Getvmode() != 7)  /* not the monochrome */
    Setvmode(4);
else
    {
    printf("Monochrome monitor does not use mode 4.\n");
    exit(1);
    }
```

The Graphics Library routines, however, simplify and enhance this procedure.

```
/* Setvmode() -- sets video mode to given mode */
#include <dos.h>
#include "scrn.h"

void Setvmode(unsigned char mode)
{
    union REGS reg;

    reg.h.ah = SETMODE;
    reg.h.al = mode;
    int86(VIDEO, &reg, &reg);
}
```

Listing 15-1. *The* Setvmode() *function.*

Modes and the Graphics Library

To run graphics programs, you must have appropriate hardware and software. For hardware, you need one of the controller-monitor combinations listed in Table 15-1. (QuickC version 2 additionally supports some Olivetti modes that we don't discuss here.) QuickC's Graphics Library provides the software. This library contains functions specifically designed to handle the various display interfaces and to provide a variety of graphics services. How you access this library depends upon how you initially set up your libraries. Let's run through the steps.

First, you should include the graph.h header file, which contains numerous definitions and function prototypes for the library. If, during the SETUP program, you answered *y* when asked if you wanted to include GRAPHICS.LIB in the combined libraries, you are done. QuickC will access the library functions automatically.

If you answered *n* to the query, you should create a program list for the graphics program and add GRAPHICS.LIB to it. The GRAPHICS.LIB file should be in a directory named in the *LIB* environment variable. (Note that the include file is graph.h, but the library is GRAPHICS.LIB; don't get confused and try to use graphics.h or GRAPH.LIB.)

With QuickC 1.0 you could place the graphics routines in the QuickC in-memory library when you invoked QuickC. This method is not supported in version 2.

Including GRAPHICS.LIB in the combined libraries is faster than keeping it separate, but the former method can require more disk space. The reason for this is that if you build combined libraries for several memory or emulation models, the SETUP program copies GRAPHICS.LIB into each combined library file.

If you don't remember or know how your libraries were set up, try running our examples without using a program list. If QuickC complains that the graphics functions in the program are undefined, you will have to create a program list that specifies GRAPHICS.LIB.

If you are using the Hercules Graphics Card or a clone, you need to run the MSHERC.COM program supplied with QuickC before you use routines from the Graphics Library. MSHERC.COM is a memory-resident program, so you have to run it only once during each computer session. Because HGC mode uses only two colors (black and white), some of the sample programs don't work well in that mode.

The following sections describe some of the mode-related functions of the graph.h header file.

The _setvideomode() Function

This more sophisticated version of our *Setvmode()* function takes as an argument the number of the desired mode. The graph.h file (Listing 15-2) contains the list of manifest constants that you can use.

```
/*  Mode constants from graph.h  */
/*  Arguments to _setvideomode() */
#define _DEFAULTMODE   -1
                         /* Restore screen to original mode */
#define _TEXTBW40       0  /* 40 x 25 text, 16-gray */
#define _TEXTC40        1  /* 40 x 25 text, 16/8-color */
#define _TEXTBW80       2  /* 80 x 25 text, 16-gray */
#define _TEXTC80        3  /* 80 x 25 text, 16/8-color */
#define _MRES4COLOR     4  /* 320 x 200, 4-color */
#define _MRESNOCOLOR    5  /* 320 x 200, 4-gray */
#define _HRESBW         6  /* 640 x 200, B/W */
#define _TEXTMONO       7  /* 80 x 25 text, B/W */
#define _HERCMONO       8  /* 720 x 348, B/W for HGC */
#define _MRES16COLOR   13  /* 320 x 200, 16-color */
#define _HRES16COLOR   14  /* 640 x 200, 16-color */
#define _ERESNOCOLOR   15  /* 640 x 350, B/W */
#define _ERESCOLOR     16  /* 640 x 350, 4- or 16-color */
#define _VRES2COLOR    17  /* 640 x 480, 2-color */
#define _VRES16COLOR   18  /* 640 x 480, 16-color */
#define _MRES256COLOR  19  /* 320 x 200, 256-color */
```

Listing 15-2. *Mode constants from graph.h.*

The *_setvideomode()* function has a few important features that *Setvmode()* lacks. For one thing, it keeps track of the original video mode, which means that you can use the *_DEFAULTMODE* argument to restore that mode. Another feature of *_setvideomode()* is that it has a return value. If the function succeeds in setting the requested mode, it returns a nonzero value. If the function fails, it returns a zero. Using the return value, we can rewrite our DMA (direct video memory access) example from Chapter 14 so that it doesn't need to first obtain the current mode. The relevant code in that example follows:

```
if ((mode = Getvmode()) == TEXTMONO)
    screen = MONMEM;
else if (mode == TEXTC80 || mode == TEXTBW80)
    screen = CGAMEM;
else
    exit(1);
```

After we add the *#include <graph.h>* line to the program, we can replace the preceding code with the following:

```
if (_setvideomode(_TEXTMONO))
    screen = MONMEM;
else if (_setvideomode(_TEXTC80) || _setvideomode(_TEXTBW80))
    screen = CGAMEM;
else
    exit(1);
```

This program attempts to set the MDA mode. If it succeeds, it sets the video display pointer to the MDA value. If it fails to set the MDA mode, it attempts to set either the CGA color 80-by-25 mode or the B/W equivalent. If either of those attempts succeeds, it sets the video display pointer to the CGA value. If none of these attempts succeed, the program exits. Notice the way the second *if* works. If *_setvideomode()* succeeds in setting the *_TEXTC80* mode, the function returns a true value. Because the first part of the logical *OR* expression is true, the whole expression is true, and thus the second half of the expression need not be evaluated.

The _getvideoconfig() Function

The Graphics Library also lets us retrieve a variety of information about the current mode. The *_getvideoconfig()* function fills a structure named *videoconfig* with mode-related information. The structure is defined in the graph.h file, as shown in Listing 15-3. The listing also shows the defined constants you can use with the *videoconfig* structure.

```
/* Video configuration information from graph.h */
struct videoconfig {
    short numxpixels;      /* number of pixels on X axis */
    short numypixels;      /* number of pixels on Y axis */
    short numtextcols;     /* number of text columns available */
    short numtextrows;     /* number of text rows available */
    short numcolors;       /* number of actual colors */
    short bitsperpixel;    /* number of bits per pixel */
    short numvideopages;   /* number of available video pages */
    short mode;            /* current video mode */
    short adapter;         /* active display adapter */
    short monitor;         /* active display monitor */
    short memory;          /* adapter video memory in K bytes */
};
```

Listing 15-3. *Video configuration information from graph.h.*   *(continued)*

Listing 15-3. *continued*

```
/* Videoconfig adapter values */
/* These manifest constants can be used to test adapter    */
/* values for a particular adapter using the bitwise AND    */
/* operator (&) */
#define _MDPA    0x0001 /* Monochrome Display Adapter (MDPA)  */
#define _CGA     0x0002 /* Color Graphics Adapter     (CGA)   */
#define _EGA     0x0004 /* Enhanced Graphics Adapter  (EGA)   */
#define _VGA     0x0008 /* Video Graphics Array       (VGA)   */
#define _MCGA    0x0010 /* Multi-Color Graphics Array (MCGA)  */
#define _HGC     0x0020 /* Hercules Graphics Card     (HGC)   */

/* Videoconfig monitor values */
/* These manifest constants can be used to test monitor     */
/* values for a particular monitor using the bitwise AND     */
/* operator (&) */
#define _MONO     0x0001  /* Monochrome */
#define _COLOR    0x0002  /* Color (or Enhanced emulating */
                          /* Color) */
#define _ENHCOLOR 0x0004  /* Enhanced Color */
```

When you pass *_setvideomode()* the address of a *videoconfig* structure, the function fills the structure with the indicated data. The MODEINFO.C program (Listing 15-4) cycles through the modes supported by QuickC and displays the mode-related information. When the program ends, the *_setvideomode(_DEFAULTMODE)* function call restores the original mode setting.

Notice in the output of MODEINFO.C that the *_getvideoconfig()* function returns 32 for the number of colors available in all text modes, including monochrome. This value indicates the range of values accepted by the *_settextcolor()* function, not necessarily the number of unique color options.

Because the actual mode values do not form a set of consecutive integers, the program holds the values in an array. However, the array indexes are consecutive, so they can be used in a loop.

```
/*  modeinfo.c -- sets modes and obtains information   */
/*  Demonstrates _setvideomode() and _getvideoconfig(). */
/*  You might need graphics.lib in the program list.    */

#include <conio.h>
#include <graph.h>
#define MODES 16
#define ADAPTERS 7
struct videoconfig Vc;
int modes[MODES] ={_TEXTBW40, _TEXTC40, _TEXTBW80, _TEXTC80,
    _MRES4COLOR, _MRESNOCOLOR, _HRESBW, _TEXTMONO,
    _HERCMONO, _MRES16COLOR, _HRES16COLOR, _ERESNOCOLOR,
```

Listing 15-4. *The MODEINFO.C program.*   *(continued)*

Listing 15-4. *continued*

```
       _ERESCOLOR, _VRES2COLOR, _VRES16COLOR, _MRES256COLOR};
char *Adapt(short), *Display(short);

main()
{
    int i;

    for (i = 0; i < MODES; i++)
        {
        if (_setvideomode(modes[i]))
            {
            _getvideoconfig(&Vc);
            printf("video mode is %d\n", Vc.mode);
            printf("number of columns is %d\n", Vc.numtextcols);
            printf("number of colors is %d\n", Vc.numcolors);
            printf("number of pages is %d\n", Vc.numvideopages);
            printf("adapter is %s\n", Adapt(Vc.adapter));
            printf("display is %s\n", Display(Vc.monitor));
            printf("the adapter has %dK of memory\n", Vc.memory);
            }
        else
            printf("mode %d not supported\n", modes[i]);
        printf("strike a key for next mode\n");
        getch();
        }
    _setvideomode(_DEFAULTMODE);
}

/* Adapt() returns a pointer to a string describing */
/* the adapter characterized by adapt_num           */
char *Adapt(short adapt_num)  /* receives videoconfig.adapter value */
{
    static char *anames[ADAPTERS] = {"Monochrome", "CGA", "EGA",
            "MCGA", "VGA", "HGC", "Not known"};
    char *point;

    switch (adapt_num)
        {
        case _MDPA : point = anames[0];
                    break;
        case _CGA  : point = anames[1];
                    break;
        case _EGA  : point = anames[2];
                    break;
        case _MCGA : point = anames[3];
                    break;
        case _VGA  : point = anames[4];
                    break;
        case _HGC  : point = anames[5];
                    break;
```

(continued)

Listing 15-4. *continued*

```
        default    : point = anames[ADAPTERS - 1];
        }
    return (point);
}

/* Display() returns a pointer to a string describing */
/* the monitor characterized by disp                  */
char *Display(short disp)  /* receives videoconfig.monitor value */
{
    static char *types[5] = {"monochrome", "color",
                             "enhanced color", "analog",
                             "unknown"};
    char *point;

    if (disp & _MONO)
        point = types[0];
    else if (disp & _COLOR)
        point = types[1];
    else if (disp & _ENHCOLOR)
        point = types[2];
    else if (disp & _ANALOG)
        point = types[3];
    else
        point = types[4];
    return (point);
}
```

The *Adapt()* function uses a *switch* statement to select the string that corresponds to the adapter value returned by *_getvideoconfig()*. The *Display()* function uses the manifest constants defined in graph.h and logical AND testing to identify the monitor. The returned values, being powers of 2, are such that *mode & _MONO* is zero (false) unless *mode* is *_MONO*, and so on.

CGA Graphics

We now have the tools to select a mode. The first mode we will explore is mode 4 (*_MRES4COLOR*) because all the IBM graphics video controllers support it. This is the medium-resolution CGA mode.

Because the graphics modes allow each screen pixel to be set individually, they require more video memory than do the text modes. The exact amount of memory, however, depends on how much information is needed to describe each pixel. For example, a black-and-white mode requires only 1 bit per pixel because the two possible values of the bit (0 and 1) can accommodate the two possible values for the pixel (off and on). With color modes, the amount of memory needed depends on the number of colors available to each pixel. With a fixed amount of memory, using more bits per pixel increases the color options but decreases the total number of pixels that can be mapped. The CGA 320-by-200 four-color mode (*_MRES4COLOR*) offers a typical compromise between resolution and color variety.

The Graphics Palette and Background

The CGA four-color mode represents each pixel with 2 bits of memory. This unit of memory can be set to a number in the range 0 through 3, thus providing a choice of four colors. Color 0 represents the background color, and the other three colors constitute the "palette." The background color and the palette are set in separate operations.

You can set the background color to any one of 16 values, numbers 0 through 15. The values 0 through 7 are the text foreground choices listed in the color.h file (Listing 14-10 on p. 465). The values 8 through 15 are the intensified versions of these same colors. Notice that the graphics background choice applies to the entire screen; the text background applies to only a particular character box. Thus, in the graphics mode, only one background color choice can be in effect at a time.

In CGA four-color mode, you can choose one of only two palettes, which are described in Table 15-2. Suppose you set the palette to 0 and the background to blue. When you set a bit pair in the video memory to 0, the corresponding pixel is set to blue. Setting the bit pair to 1, 2, or 3 produces the colors green, red, and dark yellow. Setting the video mode clears the display because it sets all the video display bits to 0. Thus, initially, the entire screen displays the background color.

Now suppose you create a pattern on the screen. If you select a different background color, the background for the entire screen changes, but the video display memory remains unchanged. Changing the background color essentially tells the controller how to interpret a 0 value in the video memory. Similarly, changing the palette actually tells the controller how to interpret values of 1, 2, or 3 in the video memory.

Table 15-2. Mode 4 Palette Choices

Palette	Color 1	Color 2	Color 3
0	Green	Red	Dark yellow
1	Cyan	Magenta	Light gray

The QuickC Graphics Library

Creating a graphics image requires several steps. First, set a graphics mode such as _MRES4COLOR. Then select a background color and a palette. Finally, set the appropriate bits in the video memory to the required values. To perform these tasks, you can use the BIOS video I/O routines or the QuickC Graphics Library functions, or you can directly access the video display memory and the controller registers. We will use the Graphics Library routines, but first let's briefly outline the other approaches.

The BIOS provides modest support for the graphics mode. It includes interrupt routines for selecting a background color and a palette. Other routines read a pixel from the screen, write a pixel to the screen, and generate text. After that, you are on your own. To draw a line, you first must figure out which pixels to turn on; then you must turn them on individually. The BIOS routines are also quite slow. The write-pixel routine, for example, takes a long time to fill a square.

On the other hand, the direct memory access approach is extremely fast. But the programming is difficult. First, because each byte of memory represents four separate pixels, you must use bitwise manipulations to alter only one of those pixels. Second, the CGA stores the bit pairs for the odd-numbered rows in a different section of memory from the even-numbered rows. To fill a solid figure on the screen, you must jump back and forth in the video display memory.

The Graphics Library overcomes the difficulties of the other two programming methods. Its drawing routines are much faster than the BIOS routines because they use direct memory access. The library functions are conveniently oriented toward end results, not internal representations. For example, the library provides functions to draw boxes and circles, and the functions describe the screen in terms of screen position, not in terms of memory location. Also, the library simplifies the creation of programs that work in more than one graphics mode. The EGA and VGA graphics modes, for example, use a different memory location (0xA0000) and different schemes for representing pixels and colors; the library makes those differences nearly invisible to the user. The main drawback in using the Graphics Library is the size it adds to a program. However, the speed, convenience, power, and monitor compatibility of the library approach easily compensate for the size liabilities.

Choosing in Modes

Let's explore the rudiments of graphics programming by creating a program that turns on a few pixels. Although we use the CGA medium-resolution mode 4, you might want to try the program in another mode. To make that easy to do, we use the following code with most of our examples:

```
#include <stdlib.h>
main (int argc, char *argv[])
{
    int mode = _MRES4COLOR;
    int ch;

    if (argc > 1)
        mode = atoi(argv[1]);

    if (_setvideomode(mode) == 0)
        {
        printf("Can't do mode %d.\n", mode);
        exit(1);
        }
```

This code fragment sets the mode to *_MRES4COLOR* by default. However, if you use a command-line argument (*argc > 1*), *mode* is set to that argument. The function *atoi()*, which is declared in stdlib.h, converts the argument from a string to a numeric value. To select a mode by this method, display the Options Run / Debug dialog box before running the program and then enter the desired mode number in the command-line field. For example, entering *16* causes the program to set mode 16 (*_ERESCOLOR*).

One convenient feature of the Graphics Library is that the same function calls work for all modes. Although different modes might require different argument values because the screen has more or fewer pixels, you can use *_getvideoconfig()* information to scale argument values accordingly. That is the approach we use.

Setting the mode also clears the screen, so you don't need to clear it explicitly. When you do need to clear the screen explicitly, you can use the Graphics Library function *_clearscreen()*.

Color Basics

Use the *_selectpalette()* function to choose a palette. This function takes the palette number as its argument and returns the former palette value. The Graphics Library supplements the two palettes provided by the BIOS with intensified versions of each. (See Table 15-3.) In all cases, color 0 is the current background color.

Table 15-3. Palette Values for *_selectpalette()*

Palette	Color 1	Color 2	Color 3
0	Green	Red	Dark yellow
1	Cyan	Magenta	Light gray
2	Light green	Light red	Yellow
3	Light cyan	Light magenta	White

To select a particular color from a palette, use *_setcolor()*. For example, if palette 0 is in effect, *_setcolor(2)* sets the color to red. (This function interprets color values differently in the EGA and VGA modes, as we'll see later.) When you call a drawing function from the Graphics Library, it draws with the currently defined color.

The Graphics Library function for setting the background color is *_setbkcolor()*. It takes a *long* color value as an argument and returns the color value of the background in effect when the function is called. The numeric value of the argument depends on whether you use *_setbkcolor()* in a text mode or in a graphics mode. This complication arises from the need to make the function compatible with the VGA graphics modes. Table 15-4 on the following page lists the color values and the manifest constant names defined in graph.h.

The graphics color values are not consecutive values. Therefore, it is often convenient to initialize an array to the values so they can be accessed consecutively with an array index. The DOTS.C program (Listing 15-5 on pp. 485–86) demonstrates this procedure.

Table 15-4. Background Color Values

Color	Text Color Value (dec)	Graphics Color Value (hex)	Manifest Constant
Black	0L	0x000000L	_BLACK
Blue	1L	0x2A0000L	_BLUE
Green	2L	0x002A00L	_GREEN
Cyan	3L	0x2A2A00L	_CYAN
Red	4L	0x00002AL	_RED
Magenta	5L	0x2A002AL	_MAGENTA
Dark yellow (brown)	6L	0x00152AL	_BROWN
White (light gray)	7L	0x2A2A2AL	_WHITE
Dark gray	8L	0x151515L	_GRAY
Light blue	9L	0x3F1515L	_LIGHTBLUE
Light green	10L	0x153F15L	_LIGHTGREEN
Light cyan	11L	0x3F3F15L	_LIGHTCYAN
Light red	12L	0x15153FL	_LIGHTRED
Light magenta	13L	0x3F153FL	_LIGHTMAGENTA
Light yellow	14L	0x153F3FL	_LIGHTYELLOW
Bright white	15L	0x3F3F3FL	_LIGHTWHITE

Physical Coordinates

The library drawing functions use coordinates to determine the location of images on the screen. Functions in the library use two forms of coordinates: physical coordinates and logical coordinates. Physical coordinates use the upper-left corner of the screen as their origin; logical coordinates let you select the origin. Most of the drawing functions use the logical coordinates. However, by default, the logical coordinates are the same as the physical coordinates, so let's start with a discussion of physical coordinates.

Both systems measure distances in pixels. The physical coordinate system uses the upper-left corner as the origin, that is, as the point whose coordinates are (0, 0). The column number, or x value, is listed first, and the row number, or y value, is listed second. The column values increase to the right, and the row values increase downward. Thus, for a 320-by-200 mode, the physical coordinates of the lower-right corner are (319, 199). Remember that pixel numbering starts with 0, so column 319 is the 320th column. (See Figure 15-1.)

A Simple Example

Let's write a small program that uses the _setpixel() function. This function takes two arguments—the horizontal and vertical location of a pixel—then sets that pixel to the color last set by _setcolor(). Our program uses the default logical coordinate system, whose origin is at the upper-left corner of the screen. If coordinates fall outside the drawing region, the function returns a value of –1.

Origin at upper-left corner (x = 0, y = 0)

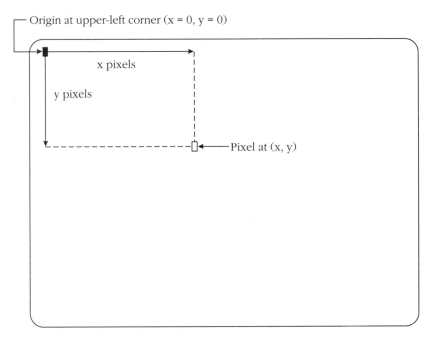

Figure 15-1. *Locating a pixel using physical coordinates.*

The DOTS.C program (Listing 15-5) uses nested loops to draw a rectangular pattern of pixels. Recall that you can override the default mode (*_MRES4COLOR*) with a command-line argument. After the program draws a pattern, you can type *p* to change the palette and type *b* to change the background. Each keystroke increments the palette or background number by one. (Palette changing works only in the CGA modes.) Remember that you must use one of the methods mentioned earlier for making the Graphics Library available to the program. To exit the program, press the Esc key.

```
/* dots.c -- illustrates the _setcolor(), _setpixel(), */
/*           and _selectpalette() functions from the   */
/*           QuickC graphics library                   */
/* You might need graphics.lib in the program list.    */

#include <conio.h>
#include <stdio.h>
#include <stdlib.h>
#include <graph.h>
#define ESC '\033'
#define BKCOLS 8      /* number of background colors */
#define PALNUM 4      /* number of palettes */
long Bkcolors[BKCOLS] = {_BLACK, _BLUE, _GREEN, _CYAN, _RED,
                         _MAGENTA, _BROWN, _WHITE};
```

Listing 15-5. *The DOTS.C program.*   *(continued)*

Listing 15-5. *continued*

```
main (int argc, char *argv[])
{
    struct videoconfig vc;
    unsigned int col, row;
    short color = 0;
    int bkc_index = 1;    /* blue background */
    short palette = 0;    /* red, green, brown */
    int firstcol, firstrow, lastrow, lastcol;
    int mode = _MRES4COLOR;
    int ch;

    if (argc > 1)
        mode = atoi(argv[1]);

    if (_setvideomode(mode) == 0)
        {
        printf("Can't do that mode.\n");
        exit(1);
        }
    _getvideoconfig(&vc);
    firstcol = vc.numxpixels / 5;
    firstrow = vc.numypixels / 5;
    lastcol = 4 * vc.numxpixels / 5;
    lastrow = 4 * vc.numypixels / 5;
    _selectpalette(palette);
    _setbkcolor (Bkcolors[bkc_index]);
    for (col = firstcol; col <= lastcol; ++col)
        {
        _setcolor((++color / 3) % vc.numcolors);
        for (row = firstrow; row <= lastrow; ++row)
            _setpixel(col, row);
        }
    while ((ch = getch()) != ESC)
        {
        if (ch == 'p')
            _selectpalette(++palette % PALNUM);
        else if (ch == 'b')
            _setbkcolor(Bkcolors[++bkc_index % BKCOLS]);
        }
    _setvideomode(_DEFAULTMODE);  /* reset orig. mode */
}
```

Program Notes

Drawing the pattern dot by dot is a slow process. But palette and background changes are practically instantaneous because they do not alter the video memory; they merely alter the interpretation of the bits already present.

The *Bkcolors* array is initialized to the first eight background colors. Later, the program steps through these nonsequential background color values by incrementing the array index.

486

The program uses mode-dependent information to draw the figure to scale. The _getvideoconfig() function obtains the number of pixels per row and column, and the program sizes the figure accordingly. The following code defines an area that covers 60 percent of the rows and of the columns:

```
firstcol = vc.numxpixels / 5;
firstrow = vc.numypixels / 5;
lastcol = 4 * vc.numxpixels / 5;
lastrow = 4 * vc.numypixels / 5;
```

Thus, in the 320-by-200 mode, the first column is 64 and the last column is 256, whereas in the 640-by-350 EGA mode, the first column is 128 and the last is 512.

The following statement changes the current color value:

```
_setcolor((++color / 3) % vc.numcolors);
```

This statement increments *color* each time the program writes a new column. However, because integer division is truncated, the expression *color / 3* increases only when *color* increases by 3. Thus, the columns change color every third column instead of every column. Unbounded incrementing causes color to exceed the valid range. Therefore, the code uses the modulus operator to produce a value in the range 0 through *vc.numcolors − 1*. For the *_MRES4COLOR* mode, where *vc.numcolors* is equal to 4, this range is 0 through 3. (Using *vc.numcolors* makes the program more portable among different video modes.)

EGA and VGA Considerations

Recall that the optional command-line parameter lets the program run in EGA and VGA modes. How does changing the mode affect the program? First, the row and column limits are set to reflect in pixels the new height and width of the screen. Second, the value of *vc.numcolors* is reset to the new mode. The *_MRES4COLOR* mode sets *vc.numcolors* to 4; the *_ERESCOLOR* mode reports a value of 16 if sufficient EGA memory is available, and it reports a value of 4 otherwise.

Those are the explicit provisions we made for other modes. In addition, some of the functions work differently. The *_selectpalette()* function, for example, is recognized only by the 320-by-200 four-color mode and the 320-by-200 black-and-white mode; other color graphics modes ignore it because they don't use the simple CGA palette system. The EGA and VGA graphics-mode palettes contain more than four colors and also let you select the palette colors individually. The default palette for the EGA and VGA modes is essentially the same as the background colors shown in Table 15-4 on p. 484. (The EGA/VGA brown, however, has a different tint than the CGA brown.) The function *_setcolor()* uses the same numeric values as those shown in the text color column of Table 15-4, except that it uses type *short* instead of type *long*.

Drawing Lines

Two minor modifications to the DOTS.C program produce major changes in its operation. First, we can speed up the program noticeably by using the *_lineto()*

function from the Graphics Library. This function takes a column coordinate and a row coordinate as arguments and draws a line from the current screen position to the specified position. Second, we can use the _moveto() function, which changes the current screen position to the column and row specified by its two arguments. This function lets you relocate your figurative drawing pen without drawing. Now modify DOTS.C to use these functions instead of _setpixel(). First, use the MS-DOS COPY command or, within QuickC, choose Merge or Save As from the File menu to create a copy of DOTS.C. Then, modify the copy by replacing the lines

```
for (col = firstcol; col <= lastcol; ++col)
    {
    _setcolor((++color / 3) % vc.numcolors);
    for (row = firstrow; row <= lastrow; ++row)
        _setpixel(col, row);
    }
```

with these lines:

```
for (col = firstcol; col <= lastcol; ++col)
    {
    _setcolor((++color / 3) % vc.numcolors);
    _moveto(col, firstrow);    /* new and improved */
    _lineto(col, lastrow);     /* version         */
    }
```

This change replaces the inner *for* loop of DOTS.C with two library functions that make this version of the program approximately 10 times faster than the original.

A Beautiful Example

One way to create interesting patterns is to key the color of a pixel to the value of its coordinates. Make another copy of DOTS.C and name it MOIRE.C. Alter the lines

```
for (col = firstcol; col <= lastcol; ++col)
    {
    _setcolor((++color / 3) % vc.numcolors);
    for (row = firstrow; row <= lastrow; ++row)
        _setpixel(col, row);
    }
```

so that they read as follows:

```
for (col = firstcol; col <= lastcol; ++col)
    {
    for (row = firstrow; row <= lastrow; ++row)
        {
        _setcolor(((row * row + col * col) / 20)
                    % vc.numcolors);
        _setpixel(col, row);
        }
    }
```

Note that the _setcolor() function has a new argument and that it has been moved to the inner loop.

This alteration produces a dramatic change in the display—complex, interlocking patterns called "moiré patterns." The change is even more impressive in the EGA and VGA modes because of their higher resolution and greater number of colors.

Although the _lineto()_ function draws much faster than _setpixel()_, the latter function offers more detailed control. As the MOIRE program shows, _setpixel()_ lets you create involved and intriguing displays.

Logical Coordinates

Many of the drawing functions, including the ones we've used, take logical coordinates rather than physical coordinates. By default, the two coordinate systems are the same, so we haven't made a distinction between the two. However, the _setlogorg()_ function lets you select another point as the origin of the logical coordinate system. To use the function, pass it the physical coordinates of the new origin. For example, using the call _setlogorg(100, 50)_ makes the point (100, 50) the new origin. Points to the left of the new origin have negative column values, and points to the right have positive values. Similarly, points above the new origin have negative row values, and points below have positive values. (See Figure 15-2.)

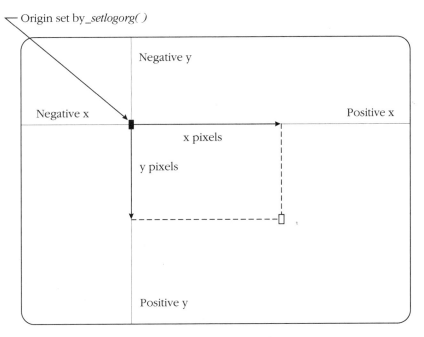

Figure 15-2. _Locating a pixel using logical coordinates._

Using logical coordinates can simplify specifying locations. For example, the center of the screen is a common choice as the logical origin because the signs of the coordinates signal the quadrant of the screen in which a point is located.

Drawing Rectangles

Now let's draw some rectangles. You could use _lineto(), but the Graphics Library contains a ready-made function for the task, _rectangle(). This function lets you do the following:

- Specify whether the rectangle is drawn in outline or as a filled figure.

- Specify the size and location of the rectangle.

- Select a color.

- Select a line-drawing style for outlined rectangles.

- Select a fill pattern for filled rectangles.

Function arguments determine the type, size, and location of the rectangle. The first argument specifies whether the rectangle is an outline or solid. The two values for this argument (from the graph.h file) are as follows:

```
#define _GBORDER        2    /* draw outline only */
#define _GFILLINTERIOR  3    /* fill using current */
                             /* fill mask          */
```

Outlined figures are drawn using the current line style, which is, by default, a solid line. Likewise, filled figures use the current fill pattern ("fill mask"), which is, by default, a solid color.

The remaining four arguments are the x and y logical coordinates of the upper-left corner of the rectangle and the x and y logical coordinates of the lower-right corner of the rectangle.

The drawing color (outline or fill pattern) is determined by the last color value passed to _setcolor(). The _setlinestyle() function specifies the line style, and _setfillmask() specifies the fill pattern. The _rectangle() function uses the last value set by these two functions, or, if they aren't used, it uses the default values.

The RECT.C program (Listing 15-6) illustrates logical coordinates, _rectangle(), and _setlinestyle(). Figure 15-3 shows output from the program.

Program Notes

Using logical coordinates, you can easily center rectangles on the screen. Merely assign the upper-left corner the negative coordinates of the lower-right corner. This program generates a series of centered rectangles by repeatedly scaling down the dimensions. Specifying this sequence of rectangles in the physical coordinate system is a more tedious task because you have to calculate all the coordinates.

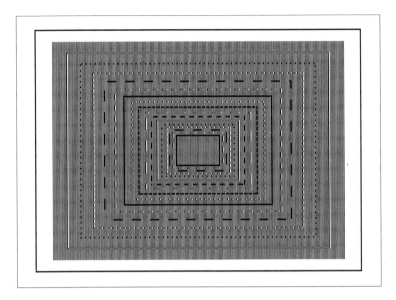

Figure 15-3. *Output of RECT.C.*

```
/* rect.c -- illustrates logical coordinates and      */
/*            the _rectangle() and _setlinestyle()    */
/*            functions                               */
/* You might need graphics.lib in the program list. */

#include <stdio.h>
#include <graph.h>
#include <conio.h>
#define STYLES 5
short Linestyles[STYLES] = {0xFFFF, 0x8888, 0x7777, 0x00FF, 0x8787};

main(int argc, char *argv[])
{
    struct videoconfig vc;
    int mode = _MRES4COLOR;
    int xcent, ycent;
    int xsize, ysize;
    int i;

    if (argc > 1)
        mode = atoi(argv[1]);
    if (_setvideomode(mode) == 0)
        {
        printf("Can't open that mode.\n");
        exit(1);
        }
```

Listing 15-6. *The RECT.C program.*   *(continued)*

491

Listing 15-6. *continued*

```
    _getvideoconfig(&vc);
    xcent = vc.numxpixels / 2 - 1;
    ycent = vc.numypixels / 2 - 1;
    _setlogorg(xcent, ycent);
    xsize = 0.9 * xcent;
    ysize = 0.9 * ycent;
    _selectpalette(1);
    _setcolor(3);
    _rectangle(_GBORDER, -xsize, -ysize, xsize, ysize);
    xsize *= 0.9;
    ysize *= 0.9;
    _setcolor(1);
    _rectangle(_GFILLINTERIOR, -xsize, -ysize, xsize, ysize);
    for (i = 0; i < 16; i++)
        {
        _setcolor(((i % 2) == 0) ? 2 : 3);
        _setlinestyle(Linestyles[ i % 5 ]);
        xsize *= 0.9;
        ysize *= 0.9;
        _rectangle(_GBORDER, -xsize, -ysize, xsize, ysize);
        }
    getch();        /* press a key to terminate */
    _setvideomode(_DEFAULTMODE);
}
```

The program draws the outer rectangle in outline; the next rectangle is drawn with the _GFILLINTERIOR option, so it is solid. Then the program draws a series of diminishing outline rectangles using a variety of line styles. The following statement:

```
_setcolor(((i % 2) == 0) ? 2 : 3);
```

chooses color 2 if the index *i* is even and color 3 if the index is odd; this prevents the use of color 1, which would not be visible against a background of the same color.

Line Styles

Now let's see how the rectangle-drawing loop cycles through a list of line styles.

The *_setlinestyle()* function takes one argument, a 16-bit "mask." This mask is a template in which each bit represents a pixel in the line being drawn. If a bit is set to 1, the corresponding pixel is turned on when the line is drawn. The pixel is set to the background color if the bit is 0. This template covers only 16 pixels, but you can visualize it as being moved along the entire line 16 pixels at a time.

The default line style is a solid line. That translates into a mask of sixteen 1s, or the hexadecimal value 0xFFFF. Now consider the following statement:

```
_setlinestyle(0x0F0F);
```

This function call creates a mask with the bit pattern 0000111100001111, which produces a pixel pattern of four pixels off, four pixels on, four off, four on—a dashed line. (See Figure 15-4.)

In RECT.C, the *Linestyles* array contains five line masks. The *for* loop near the end of the program cycles through these line styles as it draws a series of rectangles of decreasing size.

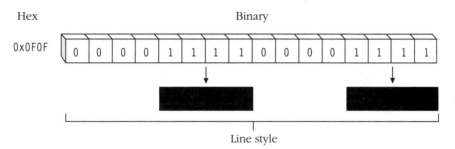

Figure 15-4. *A line style mask that produces a dashed line.*

The *_ellipse()* Function

The Graphics Library does not limit you to lines and rectangles. The *_ellipse()* function, for example, lets you draw ellipses. It takes the same argument list as *_rectangle()* and draws an ellipse that fits just inside the rectangular framework. The EGGS.C program (Listing 15-7) presents an example of this function and also illustrates what happens when solid figures overlap. (See Figure 15-5 on p. 495.)

```
/* eggs.c -- draws colorful eggs                              */
/* This program illustrates use of the video configuration    */
/* structure, the _ellipse() function, the effect of over-     */
/* lapping solid figures, and the use of logical coordinates. */
/* You might need graphics.lib in the program list.            */

#include <stdio.h>
#include <stdlib.h>
#include <graph.h>
#include <conio.h>
#define ESC '\033'

main(int argc, char *argv[])
{
    struct videoconfig vc;
    int mode = _MRES4COLOR;
    short xcent[3], ycent[3];  /* egg centers */
    short xsize, ysize;        /* egg limits */
    int egg;
```

Listing 15-7. *The EGGS.C program.* *(continued)*

Listing 15-7. *continued*

```
    if (argc > 1)
        mode = atoi(argv[1]);
    if (_setvideomode(mode) == 0)
        {
        printf("Can't open mode %d\n", mode);
        exit(1);
        }
    _getvideoconfig(&vc);
    xsize = 0.3 * vc.numxpixels;
    ysize = 0.3 * vc.numypixels;
    xcent[0] = 0.3 * vc.numxpixels;
    xcent[1] = 0.5 * vc.numxpixels;
    xcent[2] = 0.7 * vc.numxpixels;
    ycent[0] = ycent[2] = 0.4 * vc.numypixels;
    ycent[1] = 0.6 * vc.numypixels;

    _selectpalette(0);
    _setbkcolor(_MAGENTA);
    for (egg = 0; egg < 3; egg++)
        {
        _setlogorg(xcent[egg], ycent[egg]);
        _setcolor(egg + 1);
        _ellipse(_GFILLINTERIOR, -xsize, -ysize, xsize, ysize);
        }
    _settextposition(24, 0);
    _settextcolor(1);
    _outtext("Strike any key to terminate.");
    getch();
    _setvideomode(_DEFAULTMODE);
}
```

This program produces three colored eggs. When figures overlap, the figure drawn last prevails. Again, we use logical coordinates to simplify specifying the figures. The arrays *xcent* and *ycent* contain the coordinates for the centers of the three ellipses. The same command draws all three figures; however, the program changes the logical coordinates each time so that the ellipses are centered on different points.

We also use Graphics Library text functions in this program. Unlike *printf()*, these functions let you specify the location and color of the text. The *_settextposition()* routine positions the text on the screen. Unlike the graphics functions, the text functions measure positions in character rows and columns rather than in pixel columns and rows. Thus, our program positions text at row 24, column 0. The *_settextcolor()* function sets the color of the text. In the CGA graphics modes, you select the colors from the graphics palette. The EGA and VGA modes use the EGA and VGA palettes. In the color text modes, the colors follow the usual scheme—1 is blue, 2 is green, and so on. The *_outtext()* function takes as its argument of a pointer to a string and prints it using the location and color specified by the previous functions.

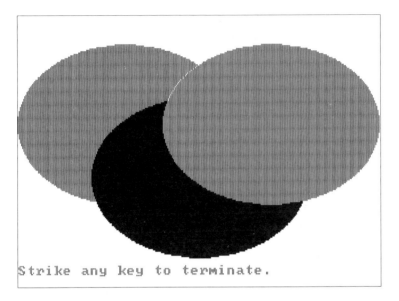

Figure 15-5. *Output of EGGS.C.*

Filling Figures: _*setfillmask()* and _*floodfill()*

Just as _*rectangle()* uses a line mask to determine the line style, _*rectangle()* and _*ellipse()* use a "fill mask" to determine the pattern that fills a figure. By default, this pattern is a solid color, but you can redefine the pattern with _*setfillmask()*. Recall how _*setlinestyle()* uses a 16-bit pattern to represent a 16-pixel section of line. The _*setfillmask()* function uses an 8-by-8-bit pattern to represent a pixel pattern. In particular, it uses an array of 8 bytes, with each byte representing one row.

To create a bit map, draw an 8-by-8 pattern of squares. Fill in the squares that represent foreground pixels. Then visualize each row as a binary number, each dark square representing a 1 and each unfilled square representing a 0. Take these eight binary numbers and convert them into a form recognized by C. (Hexadecimal notation is commonly used because each set of 4 bits corresponds to one hex digit.) After you initialize an array with those eight values, you can use the array as a fill mask.

Figure 15-6 on the following page shows a pattern that you can use repeatedly to create a bricklike pattern. The first row has a bit pattern of 1111 1111. The pattern 1111 corresponds to the hex value F; therefore, the entire byte is 0xFF. The remaining rows generate the values shown in the figure. Create a mask that uses these values with the following declaration:

```
unsigned char Mask[]= {0xFF, 0x80, 0x80, 0x80,
                       0xFF, 0x08, 0x08, 0x08};
```

Use this as the fill mask with the following statement:

```
_setfillmask(Mask);
```

495

directly before you call _rectangle() or _ellipse() with the fill parameter. The color of this mask is the same as the color of the figure.

To make the fill a different color from that of the outline, draw the figure in the outline mode, change the current color, and use the _floodfill() function to fill the figure. This function takes three arguments: a column position, a row position, and a color number. If the specified position falls within a closed boundary drawn in the indicated color, the interior of the figure is filled with the current fill pattern. If the point is outside the boundary, the exterior is filled. Do not specify a point that lies on the line.

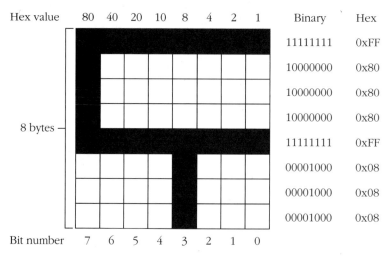

Figure 15-6. *A fill mask that creates a brick-wall pattern.*

The MASKS.C program (Listing 15-8) demonstrates how to use masks. Notice that this program looks better in the CGA mode than it does in either the EGA or VGA modes. That's because the patterns are larger at lower resolution and because the colors 1, 2, and 3 in the other modes don't look as good together as do the colors of the CGA palette 0. The program first draws a large rectangle and divides it into three parts. Then a *for* loop fills the parts using three separate masks and three different colors. (See Figure 15-7 on page 498.)

```
/* masks.c -- illustrates _setfillmask() and        */
/*             _floodfill()                          */
/* You might need graphics.lib in the program list. */

#include <stdio.h>
#include <stdlib.h>
#include <conio.h>
#include <graph.h>
```

Listing 15-8. *The MASKS.C program.*   *(continued)*

Listing 15-8. *continued*

```
unsigned char Inversemask[8];
unsigned char Masks[3][8] = {
            {0xff,0x00,0xff,0x00,0xff,0x00,0xff,0x00},
            {0xff,0x80,0x80,0x80,0xff,0x08,0x08,0x08},
            {0xaa,0xaa,0xaa,0xaa,0xaa,0xaa,0xaa,0xaa}};
main(int argc, char *argv[])
{
    struct videoconfig vc;
    int mode = _MRES4COLOR;
    short xc, yc;
    short box, i;

    if (argc > 1)
        mode = atoi(argv[1]);
    if (_setvideomode(mode) == 0)
        {
        fprintf(stderr,"Can't set mode %d\n", mode);
        exit(1);
        }
    _getvideoconfig(&vc);
    xc = vc.numxpixels / 2;
    yc = vc.numypixels / 2;
    for (i = 0; i < 8; i++)
        Inversemask[i] = ~Masks[1][i];
    _setlogorg(xc, yc);
    _selectpalette(0);
    _setcolor(1);
    _rectangle(_GBORDER, -xc + 1, -yc + 1, xc - 1, yc - 1);
    _moveto(-xc + 1, -yc / 3);
    _lineto(xc -1, -yc / 3);
    _moveto(-xc + 1, yc / 3);
    _lineto(xc -1, yc / 3);
    for (box = 0; box < 3; box++)
        {
        _setcolor(box + 1);
        _setfillmask(Masks[box]);
        _floodfill(0, (box - 1) * yc / 2, 1);
        }
    _settextposition(5, 10);
    _outtext("Press a key to continue");
    getch();
    _setcolor(3);
    _setfillmask(Inversemask);
    _floodfill (0, 0, 1);
    _setcolor(2);
    _setfillmask(Masks[0]);
    _floodfill(0, yc / 2, 1);
    _settextposition(5, 10);
    _outtext("Press a key to terminate");
    getch();
    _setvideomode(_DEFAULTMODE);
}
```

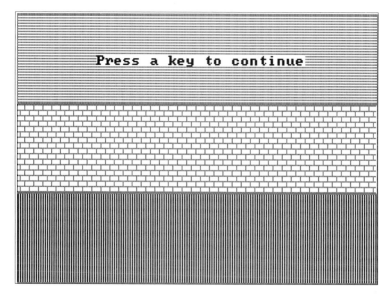

Figure 15-7. *Output of MASKS.C.*

Pressing a key initiates the second phase of the program, which illustrates what happens when you refill a figure. For example, the program overlays the bottom third of the rectangle with the mask used in the top third. Wherever the top mask has a bit set to 1, it covers the bottom pattern; wherever it has a bit set to 0, the bottom shows through. Thus, those portions of a mask set to 0 are "transparent."

The middle third of the rectangle demonstrates another aspect of superimposed masks. *Inversemask[]* is the opposite of *Masks[1][]*:

```
for (i = 0; i < 8; i++)
    Inversemask[i] = ~Masks[1][i];
```

The loop uses the bitwise ~ operator to create a mask containing the reversed bits of *Masks[1][]* (1s become 0s, and 0s become 1s). Superimposing the inverse mask on the original mask but using a different color produces a two-color pattern, as illustrated in Figure 15-8.

When you use *_floodfill()*, use a solid border; the pattern "leaks" through a border with gaps. If you superimpose one pattern on top of another, the boundary color (the third argument to the *_floodfill()* function) must be a different color from the original pattern. The *_floodfill()* function turns on pixels until it reaches pixels set with the specified boundary color. If the pixels from the first mask have the same color as the boundary, the fill function stops when it encounters them, and thus it does not fill the entire figure.

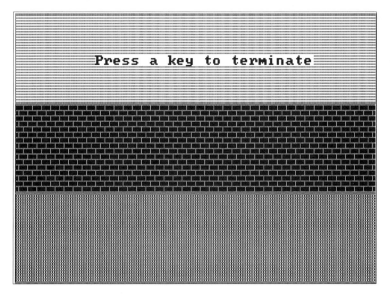

Figure 15-8. *More output of MASKS.C.*

Filling Other Shapes

You can use the *_floodfill()* function with any area enclosed by a solid boundary.
The ARROW.C program (Listing 15-9) provides an example. The program calls the
_lineto() function to draw a large arrow. Figure 15-9 on p. 501 shows the output.
Notice that the *Mask* pattern fills the interior of the figure, and the *Outmask* pattern
fills the exterior.

```
/* arrow.c -- fills inside and outside of a line    */
/*            drawing                                */
/* You might need graphics.lib in the program list. */

#include <stdio.h>
#include <graph.h>
#include <conio.h>
#define ESC '\033'
#define BKCOLS 16    /* use 16 background colors */
long Bkcolors[BKCOLS] = {_BLACK, _BLUE, _GREEN, _CYAN,
             _RED, _MAGENTA, _BROWN, _WHITE,
             _GRAY, _LIGHTBLUE, _LIGHTGREEN,
             _LIGHTCYAN, _LIGHTRED, _LIGHTMAGENTA,
             _LIGHTYELLOW,_BRIGHTWHITE};
char Mask[8] = {0x90, 0x68, 0x34, 0x19, 0x19, 0x34, 0x68,
            0x90};
char Outmask[8] = {0xff, 0x80, 0x80, 0x80, 0xff, 0x08, 0x08,
               0x08};
main(int argc, char *argv[])
```

Listing 15-9. *The ARROW.C program.*   *(continued)*

Listing 15-9. *continued*

```
{
    struct videoconfig vc;
    int mode = _MRES4COLOR;
    float x1, y1, x2, y2, x3, y3, y4, x5, y5;
    long bk = _BLUE;

    if (argc > 1)
        mode = atoi(argv[1]);
    if (_setvideomode(mode) == 0)
        {
        printf("Can't set mode %d.\n", mode);
        exit(1);
        }
    _getvideoconfig(&vc);

    x1 = 0.1 * vc.numxpixels;
    x2 = 0.7 * vc.numxpixels;
    x3 = 0.6 * vc.numxpixels;
    x5 = 0.9 * vc.numxpixels;
    y1 = 0.45 * vc.numypixels;
    y2 = 0.55 * vc.numypixels;
    y3 = 0.3 * vc.numypixels;
    y4 = 0.7 * vc.numypixels;
    y5 = 0.5 * vc.numypixels;
    _selectpalette(0);
    _setcolor(1);
    _moveto(x1, y1);
    _lineto(x2, y1);
    _lineto(x3, y3);
    _lineto(x5, y5);
    _lineto(x3, y4);
    _lineto(x2, y2);
    _lineto(x1, y2);
    _lineto(x1, y1);
    _setcolor(2);
    _setfillmask(Mask);
    _floodfill(x2, y5, 1);
    _setcolor(3);
    _setfillmask(Outmask);      /* restores default mask */
    _floodfill(5, 5, 1);
    _settextcolor(1);
    _settextposition(23, 0);
    _outtext("Press Enter to change background.");
    _settextposition(24, 0);
    _outtext("Press Esc to end.");
    while (getch() != ESC)
        _setbkcolor(Bkcolors[++bk % BKCOLS]);
    _setvideomode(_DEFAULTMODE);
}
```

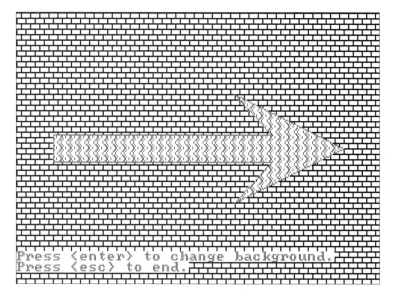

Figure 15-9. *Output of ARROW.C.*

This program uses a 16-element array to display all 16 background colors. In the CGA mode, the background extends beyond the area filled by the *Outmask* pattern. In the EGA and VGA modes, the background area is the same as the fill area.

Replicating Images

Sometimes you might want to use an image on the screen more than once. Rather than redrawing it several times, you can use the Graphics Library _getimage() and _putimage() functions to transfer the image from the screen to memory and then back to a different screen location.

The _getimage() Function

The _getimage() function copies a rectangular region into memory using the following format:

```
_getimage(xa, ya, xb, yb, storage);
```

In this syntax, *xa* and *ya* are the coordinates of the upper-left corner of the region to be copied, and *xb* and *yb* are the coordinates of the lower-right corner. The storage parameter is a far pointer to a block of memory large enough to hold all the pixel information.

Typically, you use the _imagesize() function to calculate the number of bytes required and then use *malloc()* to allocate the necessary memory, as follows:

```
char far *storage;
    ⋮
storage = (char _far *) malloc((unsigned int) _imagesize(xa, ya, xb, yb));
```

501

The _imagesize() function requires as arguments the same corner coordinates used by _getimage(). It returns type *long far*, so you must use a type cast to make it agree with *malloc()*.

The _putimage() Function

The _putimage() function copies a previously stored image from memory to a specified screen location using the following format:

```
_putimage(x, y, storage, action);
```

The *x* and *y* arguments are the coordinates of the upper-left corner of the desired position for the image. The *storage* argument is a pointer to the memory location containing the image. The *action* parameter describes how the new image interacts with any existing image at that location. The graph.h file contains a list of defined constants, or "action verbs," that can be used as *action* arguments. Table 15-5 lists and explains these constants.

Table 15-5.   Action Verbs for _putimage()

Action Verb	Meaning
_GAND	Combine the new and old images using a logical *AND*. That is, the final color for a pixel is *newcolor & oldcolor*.
_GOR	Combine the new and old images using a logical *OR*. That is, the final color for a pixel is *newcolor ¦ oldcolor*.
_GXOR	Combine the new and old images using a logical *exclusive-OR*. That is, the final color for a pixel is *newcolor ∧ oldcolor*.
_GPSET	Overwrite the old image and display the transferred image as it originally appeared. That is, the final color for a pixel is *newcolor*.
_GPRESET	Overwrite the old image and display the transferred image in inverted color. That is, the final color for a pixel is *~newcolor*.

The GETPUT.C program (Listing 15-10) demonstrates all the action verbs. It draws an image in the upper-left quadrant of the screen. Next, it fills the other three quadrants with striped patterns. Then it copies the original image five times to each of the other quadrants, using all five action verbs. The original image consists of vertical stripes of the palette colors 1, 2, and 3, and the backgrounds consist of horizontal stripes of the same colors. Therefore, this example shows all possible interactions. (See Figure 15-10 on p. 505.)

```
/* getput.c -- illustrates _getimage(), _putimage(), */
/*             the image-background interaction, and */
/*             the aspect ratio                       */
/* You might need graphics.lib in the program list.  */

#include <stdio.h>
#include <stdlib.h> /* declares malloc() */
```

Listing 15-10. *The GETPUT.C program.*   *(continued)*

Listing 15-10. *continued*

```
#include <graph.h>
#include <conio.h>
#define ESC '\033'

/* The following variables describe various */
/* coordinates and sizes. They are declared */
/* externally so that they can be shared     */
/* easily by several functions.              */
int X1, Yb1, X2, Y2, Xdelta, Xside, Yside; /* image */
int Xmid, Xmax, Ymid, Ymax;                /* background */
int Xps, Xpr, Xand, Xor, Xxor, Ytop, Ybot; /* copies */
int X[3], Y[3];
float Ar;     /* aspect ratio */

struct videoconfig Vc;
char Mask[8] = {0xFF, 0xFF, 0xFF, 0xFF, 0, 0, 0, 0};
void Initialize(void), Drawfig(void),
     Drawbackground(void), Drawcopies(void);

main(int argc, char *argv[])
{
    int mode = _MRES4COLOR;

    if (argc > 1)
        mode = atoi(argv[1]);
    if (_setvideomode(mode) == 0)
        {
        fprintf(stderr, "Can't handle mode %d\n", mode);
        exit(1);
        }
    Initialize();
    Drawfig();
    Drawbackground();
    Drawcopies();
    _settextposition(1, 1);
    _outtext("Press a key to end");
    _settextposition(3, 1);
    _outtext("_GPSET _GPRESET _GAND");
    _settextposition(11, 5);
    _outtext("_GOR _GXOR");
    getch();
    _setvideomode(_DEFAULTMODE);
}

void Initialize(void)
{
    _getvideoconfig(&Vc);
    Ar = (float) (10 * Vc.numypixels) /
         (6.5 * Vc.numxpixels);
```

(continued)

Listing 15-10. *continued*

```
    _setlogorg(0, 0);
    Xmid = Vc.numxpixels / 2;
    Ymid = Vc.numypixels / 2;
    Xmax = Vc.numxpixels - 1;
    Ymax = Vc.numypixels - 1;
    /* Locate three background rectangles */
    X[0] = Xmid;
    Y[0] = 0;
    X[1] = Xmid;
    Y[1] = Ymid;
    X[2] = 0;
    Y[2] = Ymid;
    X1 = 0.2 * Vc.numxpixels;
    Yb1 = 0.2 * Vc.numypixels;
    Xdelta = 0.033 * Vc.numxpixels;
    Xside = 3 * Xdelta;
    Yside = 3 * Ar * Xdelta;
    X2 = X1 + Xside;
    Y2 = Yb1 + Yside;
    /* Offsets for _putimage() */
    Xps = .05 * Vc.numxpixels;
    Xpr = .20 * Vc.numxpixels;
    Xand = 0.35 * Vc.numxpixels;
    Xor = .10 * Vc.numxpixels;
    Xxor = .30 * Vc.numxpixels;
    Ytop = .05 * Vc.numypixels;
    Ybot = 2 * Ytop + Yside;
    _selectpalette(0);
}

void Drawfig(void)
{
    _setcolor(1);
    _rectangle(_GFILLINTERIOR, X1, Yb1,
               X1 + Xdelta , Y2);
    _setcolor(2);
    _rectangle(_GFILLINTERIOR,X1 + Xdelta + 1, Yb1,
               X1 + 2 * Xdelta, Y2);
    _setcolor(3);
    _rectangle(_GFILLINTERIOR,X1 +  2 * Xdelta + 1,
               Yb1, X2, Y2);

}

void Drawbackground(void)
{
    _setfillmask(Mask);
    _setcolor(1);
    _rectangle(_GFILLINTERIOR, Xmid, 0, Xmax - 1, Ymid - 1);
    _setcolor(2);
    _rectangle(_GFILLINTERIOR, Xmid, Ymid, Xmax, Ymax);
```

(continued)

Listing 15-10. *continued*

```
    _setcolor (3);
    _rectangle(_GFILLINTERIOR, 0, Ymid, Xmid - 1, Ymax);
}

void Drawcopies(void)
{
    int quad;    /* quadrant used */
    char far *storage;

    storage = (char far *) malloc((unsigned)_imagesize(
            X1, Yb1, X2, Y2));
    _getimage(X1, Yb1, X2, Y2, storage);

    for (quad = 0; quad < 3; quad++)
        {
        _putimage(X[quad] + Xps, Y[quad] + Ytop,
                storage, _GPSET);
        _putimage(X[quad] + Xpr, Y[quad] + Ytop,
                storage, _GPRESET);
        _putimage(X[quad] + Xand, Y[quad] + Ytop,
                storage, _GAND);
        _putimage(X[quad] + Xor, Y[quad] + Ybot,
                storage, _GOR);
        _putimage(X[quad] + Xxor, Y[quad] + Ybot,
                storage, _GXOR);
        }
}
```

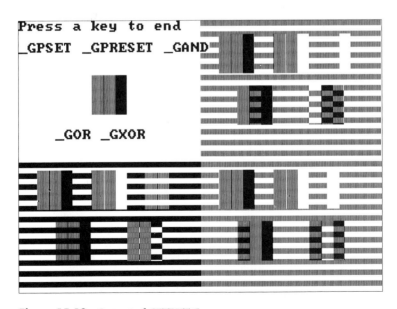

Figure 15-10. *Output of GETPUT.C.*

To recognize the precise interactions, you must understand the action of C's bitwise operators, and you must remember that the verbs operate on the palette numbers, not the color numbers. For example, if CGA palette 0 is in effect, and you select the color green, the action verbs use the palette number (1), not the color number for green (2). Because of this, the action verbs affect CGA mode colors differently than EGA or VGA colors. For example, when CGA palette 0 is used, palette number 1 is green. In the two-digit binary that represents CGA palette choices, the number is actually 01. When you apply the bitwise negation operator _GPRESET to the number, you get 10. In decimal, this is palette choice 2, or brown. Therefore, in CGA modes, _GPRESET converts a green image to brown. However, the EGA mode uses a 16-color palette. The default palette represents green with palette number 2, which is 0010 in binary. _GPRESET converts this to 1101 in binary, which represents intensified magenta. Therefore, in EGA modes, _GPRESET converts green not to brown but to intensified magenta—quite different from the CGA operation.

Aspect Ratios

The GETPUT.C program also illustrates how to make squares. In most modes, the pixel width is different from the pixel height, so you cannot make a square figure by creating a rectangle with equal numbers of horizontal and vertical pixels. To create square rectangles (or circular ellipses), you need to calculate the proper "aspect ratio." This is the ratio of the number of pixels in a vertical line to the number of pixels in a horizontal line of the same physical length. The aspect ratio is the product of two ratios:

- (screen height in pixels) / (screen width in pixels)
- (screen height in inches) / (screen width in inches)

The GETPUT.C program represents that ratio with the following code:

```
Ar = (float) (10 * Vc.numypixels) / (6.5 * Vc.numxpixels);
```

Then the program uses the aspect ratio to scale the number of *y* pixels:

```
Xside = 3 * Xdelta;
Yside = 3 * Ar * Xdelta;
```

This results in *Yside* and *Xside* representing equal lengths on the screen. Of course, the vertical and horizontal size settings on your monitor will also affect your results.

Simple Animation

You can use the _getimage() and _putimage() functions to create animation. The method is to erase the current image and to put a copy of the image at a slightly displaced location. To erase, you can superimpose a copy on the original using the _GXOR action verb. Because this operation combines like bits to produce an off bit, all bits get turned off.

The RACE.C program (Listing 15-11) uses this animation technique to stage a race across the screen. The contestants are three patterned circles.

```
/* race.c -- race of the patterned circles        */
/* Illustrates animation with _getimage() and      */
/* _putimage(), random number use with srand() and */
/* rand(), and system clock use with clock().       */
/* You might need graphics.lib in the program list. */

#include <stdio.h>
#include <stdlib.h>
#include <conio.h>
#include <graph.h>
#include <time.h>


#define END 25
#define FIGNUM 3
typedef char _far *PTFRCHAR;
PTFRCHAR Bufs[FIGNUM];
unsigned char Masks[FIGNUM][8] = {
            {0xFF,0x00,0xFF,0x00,0xFF,0x00,0xFF,0x00},
            {0xF0,0xF0,0xF0,0xF0,0x0F,0x0F,0x0F,0x0F},
            {0xAA,0xAA,0xAA,0xAA,0xAA,0xAA,0xAA,0xAA}};
short Xul[FIGNUM], Yul[FIGNUM];  /* figure locations */
short Xsize, Ysize;              /* figure size       */
struct videoconfig Vc;
void Initialize(void);
void Draw_n_store(void);
void Move_figs(void);
void Wait(double);

main(int argc, char *argv[])
{
    int mode = _MRES4COLOR;

    if (argc > 1)
        mode = atoi(argv[1]);
    if (_setvideomode(mode) == 0)
        {
        fprintf(stderr,"mode %d not supported\n",mode);
        exit(1);
        }
    Initialize();
    Draw_n_store();
    _settextcolor(2);
    _settextposition(1, 1);
    _outtext("Place your bets and press a key");
    _settextposition(25, 1);
    _outtext("Press a key again when done");
    getch();
    Move_figs();
    getch();
    _setvideomode(_DEFAULTMODE);
}
```

Listing 15-11. *The RACE.C program.*   *(continued)*

Listing 15-11. *continued*

```
void Initialize(void)
{
    int i;
    float ar;  /* aspect ratio */

    _getvideoconfig(&Vc);
    ar = (float)(10 * Vc.numypixels) / (6.5 * Vc.numxpixels);
      /* Set size, initial positions */
    Xsize = Vc.numxpixels / 30;
    Ysize = ar * Xsize;
    for (i = 0; i < FIGNUM; i++)
        {
        Xul[i] = 0;
        Yul[i] = (i + 1) * Vc.numypixels /
                (FIGNUM + 1);
        }
    _selectpalette(0);
    _setcolor(1);
      /* Draw finish line */
    _moveto(END * Xsize, 0);
    _lineto(END * Xsize, Vc.numypixels - 1);
}

void Draw_n_store(void) /* draw images, save them */
{
    int i;

    for (i = 0; i < FIGNUM; i++)
        {
        _setcolor(i + 1);
        _setfillmask(Masks[i]);
        _ellipse(_GFILLINTERIOR ,Xul[i], Yul[i],
                Xul[i] + Xsize, Yul[i] + Ysize);
        _ellipse(_GBORDER ,Xul[i], Yul[i],
                Xul[i] + Xsize, Yul[i] + Ysize);
        Bufs[i] = (PTFRCHAR) malloc((unsigned int)
                _imagesize(0,Yul[i], Xul[i] +
                Xsize, Yul[i] + Ysize));
        _getimage(Xul[i],Yul[i], Xul[i] + Xsize, Yul[i] +
                Ysize, Bufs[i]);
        }
}
void Move_figs(void)
{
    int i, j;
    static int dx[FIGNUM] = {0, 0, 0}; /* displacements */
```

(continued)

Listing 15-11. *continued*

```
      srand(clock());  /* use the current clock value */
                       /* to initialize rand()        */
   while (dx[0] < END && dx[1] < END && dx[2] < END)
      {
      for (i = 0; i < FIGNUM; i++)
         {
         /* Advance the figure one position if */
         /* rand() returns an even number      */
         if (rand() % 2 == 0)
            {
            /* Erase old image */
            _putimage(dx[i] * Xsize, Yul[i],
                      Bufs[i], _GXOR);
            /* Redraw in new position */
            _putimage((1 + dx[i]) * Xsize, Yul[i],
                      Bufs[i], _GPSET);
            dx[i]++;
            }
         }
      Wait(0.15);
      }
   for (j = 0; j < 5; j++)
      {
      for(i = 0; i < FIGNUM; i++)
         {
         /* Flash winning figure */
         if (dx[i] >= END)
            {
            Wait(0.2);
            _putimage(dx[i] * Xsize,Yul[i],
                      Bufs[i], _GPRESET);
            Wait(0.2);
            _putimage(dx[i] * Xsize,Yul[i],
                      Bufs[i], _GPSET);
            }
         }
      }
}

void Wait(double pause) /* wait for pause seconds */
{
   clock_t start, end;
   clock_t diff = (clock_t) (pause * CLK_TCK);
               /* convert seconds to "ticks" */
   start = clock();
   end = clock();
   while (end - start < diff)
      end = clock();
}
```

The race, in this program, goes to the luckiest because the program uses the *rand()* function to control the motion. At each movement opportunity, the program calls *rand()* to obtain a random number. If the function returns an even value, the circle moves ahead a step; otherwise, it remains in its current position.

The RACE.C program uses three action verbs. The *_GPSET* verb generates new ("moving") images. The *_GXOR* verb erases the old images. Finally, the program alternates between *_GPSET* and *_GPRESET*, creating a flashing image for the winner. (Ties are possible, in which case the cowinners flash.)

The program also features several standard C functions. The *rand()* function returns a random number in the range 0 through 32,767. Actually, it returns a "pseudorandom" number, meaning that eventually the function returns the same sequence of numbers. Also, *rand()* always starts with the same sequence of numbers unless you first use *srand()* to select a different starting point. The program uses the *time()* function to "seed" *srand()* with a different argument each time the program is called. As a result, the program always uses a different sequence of random numbers. (The *time()* function places the number of seconds elapsed since 00:00:00, January 1, 1970 [GMT] into the location it receives as an argument.)

Programs such as this can run into problems because different computers and different video modes run the animation at different speeds. What plods on one system may blur on another. To avoid this problem, RACE.C uses the system clock to run the animation at a constant rate. The *Wait()* function causes the program to pause for the number of seconds indicated by its floating-point argument. *Wait()*, in turn, uses a standard library function *clock()*. This function returns the current time in clock ticks, units that depend on the system and implementation. But the *CLK_TCK* macro, defined in the time.h file, is set to the number of time units per second. Thus, by multiplying the number of seconds by *CLK_TCK*, we get the equivalent number of time units. We type cast the result to type *clock_t*, since that is the return type for *clock()*. This type is defined in time.h; for QuickC it's type *long*. The *Wait()* function determines the current time and then enters a *while* loop until *delay* seconds have passed.

If you read the time.h file, you will see that *CLK_TCK* is defined as 1000, so you may think you can measure time to a thousandth of a second. However, the IBM PC/XT/AT clock runs at about 18.2 "ticks" per second, making the smallest measurable unit of time about 50 milliseconds.

EGA Graphics

As Table 15-1 on p. 474 suggests, the EGA offers more graphics capabilities than the CGA offers. The two adapters also map video memory to the display differently, but the QuickC Graphics Library functions hide those details from us. What QuickC can't hide are the different ways that the EGA graphics modes handle color.

The Palette

For comparison, let's quickly review the CGA palette. It has four colors numbered 0 through 3, and you can use the _setcolor() function to choose a particular color from the palette. Color 0 is the background color, and you set its value with the _setbkcolor() function by using one of the manifest constants in Table 15-4 on p. 484. The other three colors are chosen by using _selectpalette() to select one of the four preset combinations, listed in Table 15-3 on p. 483.

The EGA has a 16-color palette, using values in the range 0 through 15. Palette value 0 represents the background color. By default, the EGA color palette is set to the same colors shown in Table 15-4. As with the CGA, you can use _setcolor() to select a particular color from this palette; simply use the palette number as the argument. However, the EGA modes ignore the _selectpalette() function. Instead, these modes use the _remappalette() and _remapallpalette() functions to reassign colors to the palette values. That is, palette value 1, by default, is blue. But the remapping functions let you assign red, for example, to palette value 1. Note that although the palette-remapping functions don't work with the CGA, they do work if you are emulating CGA modes with an EGA or VGA.

The remapping functions provide you with a powerful tool. Suppose you've drawn and colored a figure, but you want to change the colors. Rather than redraw the figure and fill it again, you can remap the palette assignments and change the on-screen colors almost immediately.

Specifying Palette Values and Color Values

In the EGA graphics modes, each pixel is represented by 4 bits in the EGA video memory. These bits represent the palette value, which is a number in the range 0 through 15. If a particular pixel has a palette number of 3, for example, the EGA looks up the "color value" for that palette number and makes the pixel that color. The EGA color value, in turn, is a 6-bit number. Essentially, the palette number is an index to a table of color values, and the remapping functions alter that table.

The 6-bit EGA color values can generate 64 colors, but only mode 16 (_ERESCOLOR) makes all 64 available. The other modes use only 16 colors of the default palette; however, they let you select the palette number which will correspond to a given color. The total range of EGA colors uses the color values 0 through 63. However, the QuickC remapping functions use VGA color values for compatibility reasons. This complicates accessing all 64 EGA colors because, in the VGA representation, the EGA color values are not consecutive. However, you can use the manifest constants in graph.h to access the 16 colors of the default palette. (See Table 15-6 on the following page.) These are set to the VGA values shown in the second column. The EGA values are provided for your information. (Later we will show you how to access all 64 colors.)

Table 15-6.   VGA Color Values for the Default Palette

#define Name	VGA Color Value	EGA Color Value		
	Hex	rgb	RGB	Octal
_BLACK	0x000000L	000	000	000
_BLUE	0x2A0000L	000	001	001
_GREEN	0x002A00L	000	010	002
_CYAN	0x2A2A00L	000	011	003
_RED	0x00002AL	000	100	004
_MAGENTA	0x2A002AL	000	101	005
_BROWN	0x00152AL	010	100	024
_WHITE	0x2A2A2AL	000	111	007
_GRAY	0x151515L	111	000	070
_LIGHTBLUE	0x3F1515L	111	001	071
_LIGHTGREEN	0x153F15L	111	010	072
_LIGHTCYAN	0x3F3F15L	111	011	073
_LIGHTRED	0x15153FL	111	100	074
_LIGHTMAGENTA	0x3F153FL	111	101	075
_LIGHTYELLOW	0x153F3FL	111	110	076
_BRIGHTWHITE	0x3F3F3FL	111	111	077

Setting the Palette

The QuickC Graphics Library contains two functions for setting the EGA palette. One, called _remappalette(), lets you assign a color value to a particular palette value. You can use it, for example, to change palette value 3 from cyan to magenta.

The function uses VGA color values, for which it's convenient to use the graph.h constants. To make palette value 3 represent magenta, use the following call:

```
_remappalette(3, _MAGENTA);
```

The second function, called _remapallpalette(), lets you remap all the palette values simultaneously. Its argument is an array of the desired color values. Because the VGA color values are type *long*, initialize a type *long* array to the desired VGA color values.

The RINGS.C program (Listing 15-12 beginning on p. 514) presents an interesting example of palette remapping. It initializes the *newpalette* array to light blue for all but three palette values. Palette value 0 (which represents the background) is assigned gray, and palette values 1 and 8 are assigned the colors red and light red. Then _remapallpalette() sets the palette to the values provided by *newpalette*. Next, a *for* loop draws a series of concentric circles:

```
for (index = 2; index < 16; index++)
    {
    xmax /= 1.4;
```

```
ymax /= 1.4;
_setcolor(index);
_ellipse(_GFILLINTERIOR, -xmax, -ymax, xmax, ymax);
}
```

If the palette weren't reset, this code would produce concentric rings of different colors. However, with the new palette, all but two rings are light blue, and all but those two rings blend into a featureless background.

Next, the program enters a loop that shifts the color values in *newpalette* by one array element; then it remaps the palette. The first pass through this loop assigns red to palette value 2 and light red to palette value 9. On the screen, this produces the illusion that each ring has moved one position inward. (See Figure 15-12 on the following page.) One final program feature lets you use the keys 2 through 7 to change the ring colors—by changing the color assignments for *newpalette*. Press the Esc key to end the program.

EGA Color Values

The QuickC Graphics Library doesn't use the EGA color values explicitly, but here's how they work. Each of the 64 EGA colors is represented by a 6-bit color value. The left 3 bits represent low-intensity red, green, and blue, respectively. The right 3 bits represent the same series of colors, but with normal intensity. The sequence rgbRGB represents this order symbolically. The binary value 000001, for example, has the B bit (normal-intensity blue) set.

How then does the EGA form the intensified colors—light blue, light red, and so on? The CGA forms them by adding low-intensity white to the standard colors. Low-intensity white is 111000 in EGA notation, so light blue, for example, is 111001. Table 15-6 defines brown as 010100, or red plus low-intensity green. This produces a different tint than the corresponding CGA color, which is yellow, or 000110.

The EGA has other combinations with no CGA equivalents. For example, 001000 would be a low-intensity blue, and 010100 would be a mixture of low-intensity green and normal-intensity red. Altogether, the 6-bit representation permits 64 combinations, corresponding to the integers 0 through 63. Another way of looking at the EGA color value is that each color is described by 2 bits, permitting four intensity settings for that color: off, low, normal, and high intensity, as shown in Figure 15-11 on the following page. The rgb bits are sometimes referred to as the "⅓" intensity bits, and the RGB bits as the "⅔" intensity bits. Setting both gives full intensity. Note, however, that the actual ratios of intensities depend on the display's brightness and contrast settings. (The rgbRGB system is also reflected in the EGA hardware, which uses six wires, one for each bit, to communicate color information to the monitor.)

EGA color value bits r g [b] R G [B]   Blue intensity

Bit values —

0	0	0 (off)
1	0	1/3 (low intensity)
0	1	2/3 (normal)
1	1	1 (high intensity)

Figure 15-11. *The EGA supports four intensities for blue.*

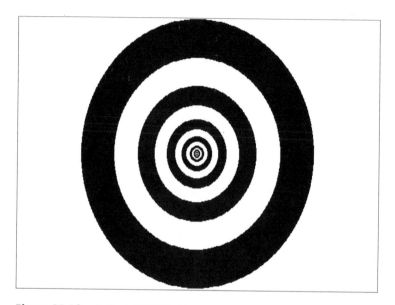

Figure 15-12. *Output of RINGS.C.*

```
/* rings.c -- shoots colored rings                    */
/* This program illustrates _remapallpalette() and    */
/* how it can be used to produce the appearance of     */
/* motion. The program is intended for EGA modes 13,   */
/* 14, and 16, or VGA mode 18.                         */
/* You might need graphics.lib in the program list.    */

#include <stdio.h>
#include <stdlib.h>
#include <conio.h>
#include <graph.h>
#define ESC '\033'

long Colors[16] = {_BLACK, _BLUE, _GREEN, _CYAN,
                   _RED, _MAGENTA, _BROWN, _WHITE,
                   _GRAY, _LIGHTBLUE, _LIGHTGREEN,
```

Listing 15-12. *The RINGS.C program.*   *(continued)*

Listing 15-12. *continued*

```
                  _LIGHTCYAN, _LIGHTRED, _LIGHTMAGENTA,
                  _LIGHTYELLOW, _BRIGHTWHITE };
#define SIZE 4
int Ok[SIZE] = {13, 14, 16, 18};
int mode_not_in (int m, int ar[], int n);

main(int argc, char *argv[])
{
    struct videoconfig vc;
    float aspect;
    short xmax, ymax;
    long int newpalette[16];
    long int temp;
    int index;
    int hot1 = 1;  /* first colored ring  */
    int hot2 = 8;  /* second colored ring */
    int mode = _ERESCOLOR;
    int ch;

    if (argc > 1)
        mode = atoi(argv[1]);
    if (mode_not_in(mode, Ok, SIZE))
        {
        fprintf(stderr,"Requires EGA or VGA mode\n");
        exit(1);
        }
    if (_setvideomode(mode) == 0)
        {
        fprintf(stderr,"%d mode unavailable\n", mode);
        exit(2);
        }
    _getvideoconfig(&vc);
    _setlogorg(vc.numxpixels / 2 - 1, vc.numypixels / 2 - 1);
    aspect = (10.0 * vc.numypixels) / (6.5 * vc.numxpixels);
    ymax = vc.numypixels / 2 - 2;
    xmax = ymax / aspect;
    for (index = 2; index < 16; index++)
        newpalette[index] = _LIGHTBLUE;
    newpalette[0] = _GRAY;
    newpalette[hot1] = _RED;
    newpalette[hot2] = _LIGHTRED;
    _remapallpalette(newpalette);  /* set initial palette */
    _setcolor(1);
    _ellipse(_GFILLINTERIOR, -xmax, -ymax, xmax, ymax);
    /* Draw concentric circles */
    for (index = 2; index < 16; index++)
        {
        xmax /= 1.4;
```

(continued)

Listing 15-12. *continued*

```
            ymax /= 1.4;
            _setcolor(index);
            _ellipse(_GFILLINTERIOR, -xmax, -ymax, xmax, ymax);
            }
    do
        {
        while (!kbhit())
            {
            temp = newpalette[15];
            for(index = 15; index > 1; index--)
                newpalette[index] = newpalette[index - 1];
            newpalette[1] = temp;
            _remapallpalette(newpalette);
            hot1 = hot1 % 15 + 1;  /* index of colored ring */
            hot2 = hot2 % 15 + 1;
            }
        ch = getch();
        if (ch > '1' && ch < '8')  /* reassign colors */
            {
            newpalette[hot1] = Colors[ch - '0'];
            newpalette[hot2] = Colors[ch - '0' + 8];
            }
        } while (ch != ESC);
    _clearscreen(_GCLEARSCREEN);
    _setvideomode(_DEFAULTMODE);
    }

int mode_not_in (int m, int ar[], int n)
{

    int not_in = 1; /* returns 1 (true) if m not in ar[] */

    while ( n-- > 0 )
        if (ar[n] == m)
            {
            not_in = 0;
            break;
            }
    return (not_in);
}
```

The program illustrates a useful graphics programming technique—declaring an array to hold the standard color values. This use of the following array lets a program access the nonsequential VGA values with sequential array indexes:

```
long Colors[16] = {_BLACK, _BLUE, _GREEN, _CYAN,
                _RED, _MAGENTA, _BROWN, _WHITE,
                _GRAY, _LIGHTBLUE, _LIGHTGREEN,
                _LIGHTCYAN, _LIGHTRED, _LIGHTMAGENTA,
                _LIGHTYELLOW, _BRIGHTWHITE};
```

Accessing All 64 EGA Colors

The _ERESCOLOR_ mode lets you use all 64 EGA colors. However, to do so with the QuickC remapping functions, you must use the VGA color code for these colors. Although the graph.h list of manifest constants provides 16 of these codes, 48 EGA colors are unrepresented. To access them, you need to generate their VGA codes.

The VGA uses 6 bits to describe the intensity of each of the three primary colors. Six bits produce 64 intensity levels for each primary color, so the total number of combinations is $64 \times 64 \times 64$, or 262,144 colors. The VGA stores this information in a 4-byte unit. The leftmost byte is set to 0, the next byte contains the 6-bit code for blue intensity, the next byte contains the 6-bit code for green intensity, and the last byte contains the 6-bit code for red intensity. Each of these color bytes has its leftmost 2 bits set to 0. (See Figure 15-13.)

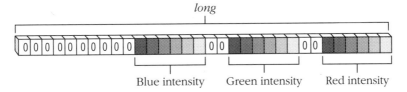

Figure 15-13. *VGA color value storage.*

How does this compare to the EGA system? Consider the color blue. The EGA rgbRGB system can generate four levels of blue: 000000, 001000, 000001, and 001001. These levels represent 0, ⅓, ⅔, and full intensity. The VGA has 64 levels of intensity, represented by a blue byte in the range 0 through 63. Zero intensity is 0. The ⅓ level is 21 decimal, or 0x15 hex. The ⅔ intensity level is 42 decimal, or 0x2A hex. The full level is 63 decimal, or 0x3F hex. Extending this analysis to red and green produces the list of correspondences shown in Table 15-7. Hex is the natural base to use for VGA values because two hex digits can represent one byte. Thus, the first two hex digits represent the blue intensity, the second two hex digits represent the green intensity, and the final two hex digits represent the red intensity.

Table 15-7. EGA Bit to VGA Byte Conversion

EGA Color Bit Setting	VGA Equivalent	Color
000 001	0x2A0000	Blue (2/3 intensity)
000 010	0x002A00	Green (2/3 intensity)
000 100	0x00002A	Red (2/3 intensity)
001 000	0x150000	Blue (1/3 intensity)
010 000	0x001500	Green (1/3 intensity)
100 000	0x000015	Red (1/3 intensity)

Because Table 15-7 lists all the EGA color bits as VGA values, you can now combine them to represent any EGA color. For example, cyan is blue plus green, or 0x2A2A00. For another example, consider light blue, which is 111001 in EGA notation. We can sum the VGA equivalents as follows:

EGA	VGA	Color
001 000	0x000015	Blue (1/3 intensity)
010 000	0x001500	Green (1/3 intensity)
100 000	0x150000	Red (1/3 intensity)
000 001	0x2A0000	Blue (2/3 intensity)
--------	--------	----------------------
111 001	0x3F1515	Light blue

The final value, 0x3F1515, matches VGA _LIGHTBLUE in Table 15-6 on p. 512.

Defining Nonpalette Colors

You can use this information to construct a header file (Listing 15-13) to supplement the graph.h color value constants.

```
/* egacolor.h -- VGA equivalents for base EGA colors */
#define r 0x000015L      /* 1/3 intensity red    */
#define g 0x001500L      /* 1/3 intensity green */
#define b 0x150000L      /* 1/3 intensity blue   */
#define R 0x00002AL      /* 2/3 intensity red    */
#define G 0x002A00L      /* 2/3 intensity green */
#define B 0x2A0000L      /* 2/3 intensity blue   */
```

Listing 15-13. *The egacolor.h program.*

The constants in egacolor.h provide the base color values. To generate any other EGA color, use the bitwise *OR* operator with these values. For example, a color whose rgbRGB representation is 101010 has the VGA value $r \mid b \mid G$. What color is this? Well, 111000 is dim white (dark gray), and 101010 replaces the faint green of 111000 with a brighter green. The result is a greenish gray.

The SCAPE.C program (Listing 15-14) demonstrates how to define other colors in terms of the base colors. It draws a simple scene, shown in Figure 15-14 on p. 520, using colors that are not in the default palette.

```
/* scape.c -- uses nondefault EGA colors            */
/* You might need graphics.lib in the program list. */

#include <stdio.h>
#include <graph.h>
```

Listing 15-14. *The SCAPE.C program.* (continued)

Listing 15-14. *continued*

```
#include "egacolor.h"
#include <stdlib.h>
#include <conio.h>
#define SKY (b | B | g)
#define OCEAN b
#define SAND (R | g | b)
#define SUN (R | G | r | g)

main(int argc, char *argv[])
{
    struct videoconfig vc;
    int mode = _ERESCOLOR;
    short xmax, ymax, sunx, suny, sunsizex, sunsizey;
    float ar;

    if (argc > 1)
        mode = atoi(argv[1]);
    if (_setvideomode(mode) == 0)
        {
        fprintf(stderr,"mode %d not supported\n", mode);
        exit(1);
        }
    _getvideoconfig(&vc);
    xmax = vc.numxpixels - 1;
    ymax = vc.numypixels - 1;
    sunx = 0.7 * xmax;
    suny = 0.2 * ymax;
    ar = (float)(10 * vc.numypixels) / (6.5 * vc.numxpixels);
    sunsizex = xmax / 30;
    sunsizey = ar * sunsizex;
    _remappalette(1, SKY);
    _remappalette(2, OCEAN);
    _remappalette(3, SAND);
    _remappalette(4, SUN);
    _setcolor(1);
    _rectangle(_GFILLINTERIOR, 0, 0, xmax, 2 * ymax / 5);
    _setcolor(4);
    _ellipse(_GFILLINTERIOR, sunx - sunsizex, suny -
             sunsizey, sunx + sunsizex, suny + sunsizey);
    _setcolor(2);
    _rectangle(_GFILLINTERIOR, 0, 2 * ymax / 5, xmax,
               2 * ymax / 3);
    _setcolor(3);
    _rectangle(_GFILLINTERIOR, 0, 2 * ymax / 3, xmax, ymax);
    getch();
    _setvideomode(_DEFAULTMODE);
}
```

Figure 15-14. *SCAPE.C uses nondefault colors. (Trust us.)*

Automatic Color Value Conversion

A second approach to using nonpalette colors is to write a function that converts an EGA value to the corresponding VGA value. This lets us map the simple EGA color values into the complicated VGA color values that the library functions use. Listing 15-15 presents a function that takes an EGA color value as an argument and returns the corresponding VGA color value.

```
/* egatovga.c -- converts EGA color values to VGA */
/*                color values                     */

long Ega_to_vga(int egacolor)  /* receives EGA color value */
{
    static long vgavals[6] = {0x2a0000L, 0x002a00L,
                              0x00002aL, 0x150000L,
                              0x001500L, 0x000015L};
    /* Array holds VGA equivalents to EGA bits */
    long vgacolor = 0L; /* vga color value */
    int bit;

    /* Convert each bit to equivalent, and sum */
    for (bit = 0; bit < 6; bit++)
        vgacolor += ((egacolor >> bit) & 1) * vgavals[bit];
    return (vgacolor);
}
```

Listing 15-15. *The* Ega_to_vga() *function.*

The program's *egacolor >> bit* operation shifts a specified bit to position 0. The subsequent *& 1* operation then masks all the other bits. This gives the expression the value 1 if the bit is 1; otherwise, it is 0. The result is multiplied by the VGA equivalent for the bit, and the loop obtains a running total.

A Palette-Mapping Example

Now we can look at all of the 48 hidden EGA colors. The ALLCOLOR.C program (Listing 15-16) uses *Ega_to_vga()* and *_remappalette()* to display all the EGA colors. It divides the screen vertically into two rectangles. The left rectangle fills with blue, and the right with red. Windows at the bottom of each rectangle show the current color value. Pressing G advances the color value of the left rectangle by 1 (it remaps palette value 1 to the next color value). Similarly, the H key advances the color value of the right rectangle. Shift-G and Shift-H decrement the color values. Using this program, you can thus match any two of the 64 colors side by side and see the sometimes subtle distinctions.

```
/* allcolor.c -- shows _ERESCOLOR 64-color palette    */
/* You might need graphics.lib in the program list.   */

/* Press <g> to advance left palette, <G> to go back.  */
/* Press <h> to advance right palette, <H> to go back. */
/* Press <Esc> to quit.                                */
#include <stdio.h>
#include <graph.h>
#include <conio.h>
#define MAXCOLORS 64
#define ESC '\033'
long Ega_to_vga(int);    /* color value conversion */

main(int argc, char *argv[])
{
    struct videoconfig vc;
    int mode = _ERESCOLOR;
    int xmax, ymax;
    int c1 = 1;
    int c2 = 4;
    char left[11];
    char right[11];
    int lpos, rpos;
    char ch;

    if (argc > 1)
        mode = atoi(argv[1]);
```

Listing 15-16. *The ALLCOLOR.C program.*   (continued)

Listing 15-16. *continued*

```
if (_setvideomode(mode) == 0)
    {
    fprintf(stderr,"%d mode not supported\n", mode);
    exit(1);
    }
_getvideoconfig(&vc);
_setlogorg(vc.numxpixels / 2, vc.numypixels / 2);

xmax = vc.numxpixels / 2 - 1;
ymax = vc.numypixels / 2 - 1;
lpos = vc.numxpixels / 32 - 5;
rpos = lpos + vc.numxpixels / 16;
_setcolor(1);
_rectangle(_GFILLINTERIOR, -xmax, -ymax, 0, ymax);
_setcolor(4);
_rectangle(_GFILLINTERIOR, 1, -ymax, xmax, ymax);
sprintf(left, "<-G %2d g->", c1);
sprintf(right, "<-H %2d h->", c2);
_settextcolor(6);
_settextposition(0, 0);
_outtext("Press Esc to quit");
_settextposition(24, lpos);
_outtext(left);
_settextposition(24, rpos);
_outtext(right);
while ((ch = getch()) != ESC)
    {
    switch (ch)
        {
        case 'g': c1 = (c1 + 1) % MAXCOLORS;
                  _remappalette(1, Ega_to_vga(c1));
                  break;
        case 'G': c1 = (c1 - 1) % MAXCOLORS;
                  _remappalette(1, Ega_to_vga(c1));
                  break;
        case 'h': c2 = (c2 + 1) % MAXCOLORS;
                  _remappalette(4, Ega_to_vga(c2));
                  break;
        case 'H': c2 = (c2 - 1) % MAXCOLORS;
                  _remappalette(4, Ega_to_vga(c2));
                  break;
        }
    sprintf(left, "<-G %2d ->g", c1);
    sprintf(right, "<-H %2d ->h", c2);
    _settextposition(0, 0);
    _outtext("Press Esc to quit");
    _settextposition(24, lpos);
    _outtext(left);
    _settextposition(24, rpos);
```

(continued)

Listing 15-16. *continued*

```
        _outtext(right);
        }
    _setvideomode(_DEFAULTMODE);
}

long Ega_to_vga(int egacolor)   /* receives ega color value */
{
    static long vgavals[6] = {0x2A0000L, 0x002A00L, 0x00002AL,
                              0x150000L, 0x001500L, 0x000015L};
    long vgacolor = 0L; /* vga color value */
    int bit;

    for (bit = 0; bit < 6; bit++)
        vgacolor += ((egacolor >> bit) & 1) * vgavals[bit];
    return (vgacolor);
}
```

In ALLCOLOR.C, the following code does the remapping:

```
case 'g': c1 = (c1 + 1) % MAXCOLORS;
          _remappalette(1, Ega_to_vga(c1));
          break;
```

When *g* is pressed, the program increments by one the color value (*c1*) for the left rectangle. The modulus operator limits the final value to the range 0 through 63. The *Ega_to_vga()* function converts the EGA color value to a VGA color value, which is then used as an argument to *_remappalette()*. Notice how fast the colors change using the remapping approach.

Remapping the Entire Palette

The RINGS.C program (Listing 15-12 beginning on p. 514) demonstrated how to use the *_remapallpalette()* function to reassign the 16 default colors to different palette values. Now let's use the function with all 64 EGA colors.

First, we must initialize a 64-element array to the VGA color values for the EGA colors and then initialize a 16-element array to the color values for a particular palette. Thus, the 64-element array supplies color values for the *palette* array, and we can use the *palette* array with *_remapallpalette()* to remap the palette.

To see how this works, let's apply the approach to our MOIRE.C program; the resulting program is REMOIRE.C (Listing 15-17 beginning on the following page). After it draws a pattern, the program begins remapping the colors. Press any key to stop the remapping; and then press any key (except Esc) to restart it. To terminate the program, press the Esc key while the program is paused.

```
/* remoire.c -- adds palette remapping to moire.c   */
/* You might need graphics.lib in the program list. */

#include <conio.h>
#include <stdio.h>
#include <stdlib.h>
#include <graph.h>
#define ESC '\033'
#define MAXCOLORS 64
#define PALCOLORS 16
long Ega_to_vga(int);

main (int argc, char *argv[])
{
    struct videoconfig vc;
    unsigned int col, row;
    long colors[MAXCOLORS];
    long palette[PALCOLORS];
    int index;
    int shift = 1;
    int firstcol, firstrow, lastrow, lastcol;
    int mode = _ERESCOLOR;


    if (argc > 1)
        mode = atoi(argv[1]);

    if (_setvideomode(mode) == 0)
        {
        printf("Can't do that mode.\n");
        exit(1);
        }
    /* Create array of all 64 color values */
    for (index = 0; index < MAXCOLORS; index++)
        colors[index] = Ega_to_vga(index);
    /* Create array of 16 palette choices */
    for (index = 0; index < PALCOLORS; index++)
        palette[index] = colors[index];
    _remapallpalette(palette);
    _getvideoconfig(&vc);
    firstcol = vc.numxpixels / 5;
    firstrow = vc.numypixels / 5;
    lastcol = 4 * vc.numxpixels / 5;
    lastrow = 4 * vc.numypixels / 5;

    for (col = firstcol; col <= lastcol; ++col)
        {
        for (row = firstrow; row <= lastrow; ++row)
            {
            _setcolor(((row * row + col * col) / 20 )
                    % vc.numcolors);
```

Listing 15-17. *The REMOIRE.C program.*   *(continued)*

Listing 15-17. *continued*

```
            _setpixel(col, row);
            }
        }
    _settextposition(1, 1);
    _outtext("Press a key to stop or start.");
    _settextposition(2, 1);
    _outtext("Press Esc while paused to quit.");
    do
        {
        while (!kbhit())
            {
            /*  Set palette array to new color values */
            for (index = 1; index < PALCOLORS; index++)
                palette[index] = (colors[(index + shift)
                                    % MAXCOLORS]);
            _remapallpalette(palette);
            shift++;
            }
        getch();  /* pause until key is pressed */
        } while (getch() != ESC);

    _setvideomode(_DEFAULTMODE);  /* reset orig. mode */
}

long Ega_to_vga(int egacolor)  /* receives ega color value */
{
    static long vgavals[6] = {0x2A0000L, 0x002A00L, 0x00002AL,
                              0x150000L, 0x001500L, 0x000015L};
    long vgacolor = 0L; /* vga color value */
    int bit;

    for (bit = 0; bit < 6; bit++)
        vgacolor += ((egacolor >> bit) & 1) * vgavals[bit];
    return (vgacolor);
}
```

The following code initializes the arrays:

```
/* Create array of all 64 color values */
for (index = 0; index. < MAXCOLORS; index++)
    colors[index] = Ega_to_vga(index);
/* Create array of 16 palette choices */
for (index = 0; index < PALCOLORS; index++)
    palette[index] = colors[index];
```

The first loop initializes *colors* to the VGA color values. The second loop sets *palette* to the first 16 EGA colors. Note that this is not the default EGA palette. (Compare the values with those in Table 15-6 on p. 512.)

The following code reassigns the colors to *palette*:

```
do
    {
    while (!kbhit())
        {
        /* Set palette array to new color values */
        for (index = 1; index < PALCOLORS; index++)
            palette[index] = (colors[(index + shift) % MAXCOLORS]);
        _remapallpalette(palette);
        shift++;
        }
    getch();   /* pause until key is pressed */
    } while (getch() != ESC);
```

Because *shift* is initialized to 1, the first pass through this loop sets the palette array to the second through seventeenth elements of *colors*. When *shift* is incremented, the next pass moves the palette one element further into *colors*.

This example showcases the speed of remapping compared to the time the program originally took to color the screen.

VGA Graphics

Now let's look at some programs that use VGA features exclusively. The VGA supports all EGA modes and provides three additional modes. Modes 17 and 18 offer even a higher resolution (640 by 480 pixels) than does EGA mode 16. Mode 17 uses a 2-color palette, and mode 18 uses a 16-color palette. Mode 19 uses only medium resolution (320 by 200 pixels) but offers a 256-color palette. Furthermore, you can select the colors used in these modes from 262,144 color values. By choosing a suitable palette, you can construct images with much more realistic shadings of color than you can get from the CGA or EGA palettes. (The MCGA supports only mode 19 of these three VGA modes.)

To use these modes, you need the proper video display controller (VGA, MCGA, or a clone) and the proper monitor. Unlike the CGA and EGA adapters, which control display colors with digital signals, the VGA and MCGA use analog signals. Thus, they cannot be used with CGA or EGA display monitors. (The popular multisync monitors, however, can handle both digital and analog signals and can be used with all these adapters. Some automatically switch between digital and analog modes; others require you to set a switch manually.)

The 256-Color Palette

The 256-color palette makes mode 19 the most interesting of the new VGA modes, and because both the MCGA and the VGA support it, mode 19 is also the most general. The COL256.C program (Listing 15-18) displays the 256-color default palette. It draws a rectangular border and then uses *_moveto()* and *_lineto()* to divide the screen into a 16-by-16 array of rectangles. Finally, the program uses *_floodfill()* to display all 256 colors.

The call to *setcolor()* in the final nested *for* loop sets the palette value (the
_setcolor() argument) to each value from 0 through 255: This series of values con-
stitutes the full range of palette values in this mode.

```
_setcolor(row * ROWS + col);
```

```
/* col256.c -- show 256 colors in mode 19          */
/* You might need graphics.lib in the program list. */

#include <stdio.h>
#include <graph.h>
#include <conio.h>
#define ESC '\033'
#define ROWS 16
#define COLS 16

main()
{
    struct videoconfig vc;
    int mode = _MRES256COLOR;
    short xmax, ymax;          /* screen size */
    short xcs[ROWS][COLS];     /* coordinates of the */
    short ycs[ROWS][COLS];     /* 256 rectangles     */
    short row, col;

    if (_setvideomode(mode) == 0)
        {
        fprintf(stderr, "%d mode not supported\n", mode);
        exit(1);
        }
    _getvideoconfig(&vc);

    xmax = vc.numxpixels - 1;
    ymax = vc.numypixels - 1;

    /* Compute an interior point for each rectangle */
    for (col = 0; col < COLS; col++)
        for (row = 0; row < ROWS; row++)
            {
            xcs[row][col] =  col * xmax / COLS + 5;
            ycs[row][col] =  row * ymax / ROWS + 5;
            }

    /* Draw outside boundary */
    _setcolor(1);
    _rectangle(_GBORDER, 0, 0, xmax, ymax);

    /* Draw gridwork */
    for (col = 1; col < COLS ; col++)
```

Listing 15-18. *The COL256.C program.*   *(continued)*

Listing 15-18. *continued*

```
        {
        _moveto(col * (xmax + 1) / COLS, 0);
        _lineto(col * (xmax + 1) / COLS, ymax);
        }
    for (row = 1; row < ROWS;  row++)
        {
        _moveto(0, row * (ymax + 1) / ROWS);
        _lineto(xmax, row * (ymax + 1) / ROWS);
        }

    /* Fill in rectangles with palette colors */
    for (col = 0; col < COLS; col++)
        for (row = 0; row < ROWS; row++)
            {
            _setcolor(row * ROWS + col);
            _floodfill(xcs[row][col], ycs[row][col], 1);
            }

    /* Terminate program */
    getch();
    _setvideomode(_DEFAULTMODE);
}
```

Changing the Palette

You can use the *_remappalette()* and *_remapallpalette()* functions to change the
palette settings. Of course, you must use the VGA color value system to do so. Recall
that the color value is represented by a 4-byte number. The low byte represents the
red intensity level and can have any value from 0 through 63. Similarly, the next byte
describes 64 levels of green intensity, and the third byte describes 64 levels of blue
intensity. Therefore, we can represent any of the 262,144 available colors by the following form:

```
colorvalue = blue << 16 ¦ green << 8 ¦ red;
```

The shift operators use type *long* values to place the intensity values in the correct
bytes. For example, to generate a color that is "nearly" a blend of blue at half intensity, green at one-quarter intensity, and red at three-quarter intensity, use the following color value assignment:

```
colorvalue = 32L << 16 ¦ 16L << 8 ¦ 48L
```

We say "nearly" because, using 63 to represent full intensity, you can't specify precisely half, quarter, and three-quarter intensities with integers.

The VGAMAP.C program (Listing 15-19) extends COL256.C to demonstrate the
remapping techniques for mode 19. It starts by showing the default palette. Pressing a
key initializes a 256-element array to a new palette. (This array is declared externally
so that it won't use up stack space.) The first 64 elements are set to the 64 levels of

blue; the second 64 are set to the green levels; and the third 64 elements are set to the red levels. The final 64 are set to some of the red-blue (magenta) blends. (With 64 choices for each color component, there are 64 × 64, or 4096, red-blue blends.) These illustrate the shadings possible by varying only one of the three color components. The program uses _remapallpalette() to reset the palette to the new color values in this array.

When you press another key, the program uses *rand()* to generate a randomly placed rectangle. It then selects random blue, green, and red intensity levels, constructs a color value from them, and sets the rectangle to that color. This process continues until you press a key. Subsequent key presses (except the Esc key) toggle the random remapping on and off. Press the Esc key to terminate the program. Notice that the _remappalette() function uses a *short* argument for the palette value, *palval*, and a *long* argument for the color value, *colorval*.

A color intensity range of 64 levels makes extremely subtle color variations possible. The ALLVGA.C program (Listing 15-20 on pp. 531–33) modifies the ALLCOLOR.C program (Listing 15-16 on pp. 521–23) so that you can investigate these color possibilities. Rather than using one key to step through the 262,144 values, we use one key to control the blue level, one to control the green level, and one to control the red level.

```
/* vgamap.c -- remaps the VGA mode 19 palette      */
/* You might need graphics.lib in the program list. */

#include <stdio.h>
#include <graph.h>
#include <conio.h>
#define ESC '\033'
#define PALSIZE 256
#define ROWS 16
#define COLS 16
#define MIDBLUE 0x190000L
long newpal[PALSIZE]; /* array of color values */

main()
{
    struct videoconfig vc;
    int mode = _MRES256COLOR;
    short xmax, ymax;
    short xcs[ROWS][COLS];
    short ycs[ROWS][COLS];
    short row, col;
    long colorval;        /* VGA color value */
    long index;           /* looping index   */
    short palval;         /* palette value   */
    int c_base;  /* color base -- blue, green, or red */
    int ch;
```

Listing 15-19. *The VGAMAP.C program.*   *(continued)*

Listing 15-19. *continued*

```
if (_setvideomode(mode) == 0)
    {
    fprintf(stderr, "%d mode not supported\n", mode);
    exit(1);
    }
_getvideoconfig(&vc);
xmax = vc.numxpixels - 1;
ymax = vc.numypixels - 1;
for (col = 0; col < COLS; col++)
    for (row = 0; row < ROWS; row++)
        {
        xcs[row][col] =  col * xmax / COLS + 5;
        ycs[row][col] =  row * ymax / ROWS + 5;
        }
_setcolor(1);
_rectangle(_GBORDER, 0, 0, xmax, ymax);
for (col = 1; col < COLS ; col++)
    {
    _moveto(col * (xmax + 1) / COLS, 0);
    _lineto(col * (xmax + 1) / COLS, ymax);
    }
for (row = 1; row < ROWS;  row++)
    {
    _moveto(0, row * (ymax + 1) / ROWS);
    _lineto(xmax, row * (ymax + 1) / ROWS);
    }

for (col = 0; col < COLS; col++)
    for (row = 0; row < ROWS; row++)
        {
        _setcolor(row * ROWS + col);
        _floodfill(xcs[row][col], ycs[row][col], 1);
        }
getch();

/* Initialize newpal[] to 64 shades of blue, 64 shades of
   green, 64 shades of red, and 64 shades of magenta */
for (index = 0; index < 64; index++)
    {
    newpal[index] = index << 16;
    newpal[index + 64] = index << 8;
    newpal[index + 128] = index;
    newpal[index + 192] = index : MIDBLUE;
    }
_remapallpalette(newpal);
getch();

/* Set squares and colors randomly -- ESC
   terminates loop, and other keystrokes toggle
   it on and off */
```

(continued)

Listing 15-19. *continued*

```
    do
        {
        while (!kbhit())
            {
            palval = rand() % PALSIZE;
            colorval = 0L;
            for (c_base = 0; c_base < 3; c_base++)
                colorval += ((long) rand() % 64) << (c_base * 8);
            _remappalette (palval, colorval);
            }
        ch = getch();
        if (ch != ESC)
            ch = getch();
        } while (ch != ESC);
    _setvideomode(_DEFAULTMODE);
}
```

```
/* allvga.c -- shows _MRES256COLOR 256K colors      */
/* You might need graphics.lib in the program list. */

#include <stdio.h>
#include <stdlib.h>
#include <graph.h>
#include <conio.h>
#define FULLBRIGHT 64
#define ESC '\033'
char label[2][7] = {"ACTIVE", "      "};

main(int argc, char *argv[])
{
    struct videoconfig vc;
    int mode = _MRES256COLOR;
    int xmax, ymax;
    static long colors[2] = {_BLUE, _RED};
    char left[11];
    char right[11];
    int lpos, rpos;
    char ch;
    unsigned long blue = _BLUE >> 16;
    unsigned long green = 0L;
    unsigned long red = 0L;
    long color;
    short palnum = 0;

    if (argc > 1)
        mode = atoi(argv[1]);
```

Listing 15-20. *The ALLVGA.C program.*   *(continued)*

Listing 15-20. *continued*

```
if (_setvideomode(mode) == 0)
    {
    fprintf(stderr,"%d mode not supported\n", mode);
    exit(1);
    }
_getvideoconfig(&vc);
_setlogorg(vc.numxpixels / 2, vc.numypixels / 2);

xmax = vc.numxpixels / 2 - 1;
ymax = vc.numypixels / 2 - 1;
lpos = vc.numxpixels / 32 - 5;
rpos = lpos + vc.numxpixels / 16;
_remappalette(2, _RED);
_setcolor(1);
_rectangle(_GFILLINTERIOR, -xmax, -ymax, 0, ymax);
_setcolor(2);
_rectangle(_GFILLINTERIOR, 1, -ymax, xmax, ymax);
sprintf(left," %6lxH ", colors[0]);
sprintf(right," %6lxH ", colors[1]);
_settextcolor(6);
_settextposition(1, 1);
_outtext("Press Tab to toggle panels, Esc to quit.");
_settextposition(2, 1);
_outtext("B increases blue level, b decreases it. ");
_settextposition(3, 1);
_outtext("G and g control green, R and r red.      ");
_settextposition(24, lpos);
_outtext(left);
_settextposition(24, rpos);
_outtext(right);
_settextposition(5, 7);
_outtext(label[0]);
_settextposition(5, 27);
_outtext(label[1]);
while ((ch = getch()) != ESC)
    {
    switch (ch)
        {
        case '\t': _settextposition(5, 27);
                   _outtext(label[palnum]);
                   palnum ^= 1;
                   blue = (colors[palnum] << 16) & 0x3F;
                   green = (colors[palnum] << 8) & 0x3F;
                   red = colors[palnum] & 0x3F;
                   _settextposition(5, 7);
                   _outtext(label[palnum]);

                   break;
```

(continued)

Listing 15-20. *continued*

```
            case 'B':  blue = (blue + 1) % FULLBRIGHT;
                       colors[palnum] = blue << 16 |
                             green << 8 | red;
                       _remappalette(palnum + 1, colors[palnum]);

                       break;
            case 'b':  blue = (blue - 1) % FULLBRIGHT;
                       colors[palnum] = blue << 16 |
                             green << 8 | red;
                       _remappalette(palnum + 1, colors[palnum]);

                       break;
            case 'G':  green = (green + 1) % FULLBRIGHT;
                       colors[palnum] = blue << 16 |
                             green << 8 | red;
                       _remappalette(palnum + 1, colors[palnum]);

                       break;
            case 'g':  green = (green - 1) % FULLBRIGHT;
                       colors[palnum] = blue << 16 |
                             green << 8 | red;
                       _remappalette(palnum + 1, colors[palnum]);

                       break;
            case 'R':  red = (red + 1) % FULLBRIGHT;
                       colors[palnum] = blue << 16 |
                             green << 8 | red;
                       _remappalette(palnum + 1, colors[palnum]);

                       break;
            case 'r':  red = (red - 1) % FULLBRIGHT;
                       colors[palnum] = blue << 16 |
                             green << 8 | red;
                       _remappalette(palnum + 1, colors[palnum]);

                       break;

            }
        sprintf(left," %6lxH ", colors[0]);
        sprintf(right," %6lxH ", colors[1]);
        _settextposition(24, lpos);
        _outtext(left);
        _settextposition(24, rpos);
        _outtext(right);
        }
    _setvideomode(_DEFAULTMODE);
}
```

Fonts

QuickC version 2 expands the Graphics Library to include several font-related functions. A font is a set of text characters that share a common style, or typeface. For instance, the text in this book is set in a particular font called ITC Garamond. The listings, however, use a different font, one called Letter Gothic monospace. If you compare the regular text and the listings, you can see differences in how the characters are formed. Fonts can differ in size as well as in style. The section headings in this book, for example, use a larger font size than the regular text. They also use a darker, thicker variety of ITC Garamond called ITC Garamond Bold.

QuickC's font capabilities apply to the fonts that appear on the screen. Normally, QuickC uses the standard font provided by the video controller. However, by using the font functions, you can specify fonts from special font files introduced with QuickC version 2. The following sections provide an introductory look at fonts.

What You Need in Order to Use Fonts

The QuickC fonts are part of the graphics package. This means that you can use them in graphics modes but not in text modes. Thus, you need a system that supports graphics modes, and you need to have the GRAPHICS.LIB library available, just as you do for all the preceding examples in this chapter.

The font functions are in the GRAPHICS.LIB file, but the fonts themselves are in separate files. These files have a .FON extension. The SETUP program places these files in the \QC25\SAMPLES directory. (If you skipped that step, you can find these files on the distribution disks.) You need to tell your programs which font files to use, so you'll need to know where the files are. The simplest way to do this is to copy them into the current directory so that you can refer to them by name without providing a directory path. This is the method we'll use.

The font files are in the same format as the .FON and .FNT font files used with Microsoft Windows. Thus, QuickC programs can also use Microsoft Windows screen fonts, including those provided by other vendors.

Font Choices

Computer-generated fonts come in two varieties: "bit-mapped" and "vector." Bit-mapped (or raster-mapped) fonts represent a character as a pixel pattern, much like that shown in Figure 14-2 on p. 453. Displaying a particular bit-mapped character consists of looking up a bit pattern and turning the corresponding screen pixels on or off as needed.

Vector fonts, on the other hand, represent characters with mathematical formulas that describe the lines and arcs needed to draw the character. Displaying a particular vector character consists of looking up the proper formulas and then calculating which screen pixels to turn on or off.

Vector fonts sound more complicated than bit-mapped fonts, but they have the advantage of being "scalable." That is, the same font can be used to construct characters of different sizes; the program just scales the mathematical formulas accordingly. The bit-mapping method, on the other hand, requires a separate pattern for each font size. The resulting fonts, however, do have a more solid look.

QuickC version 2 comes with three font families of each type. The bit-mapped fonts are called Courier, Helv (for Helvetica), and Tms Rmn (for Times Roman). Each comes in several sizes. (See Table 15-8.) The vector fonts are Modern, Script, and Roman. Figure 15-15 shows samples of the fonts.

Table 15-8. QuickC Font Library

Typeface	Mapping	Size in Pixels (height x width)	Spacing	File
Courier	Bit	13 × 8, 16 × 9, 20 × 12	Fixed	COURB.FON
Helv	Bit	13 × 5, 16 × 7, 20 × 8, 13 × 15, 16 × 6, 19 × 8	Fixed	HELVB.FON
Tms Rmn	Bit	10 × 5, 12 × 6, 15 × 8, 16 × 9, 20 × 12, 26 × 16	Fixed	TMSRB.FON
Modern	Vector	Scaled	Proportional	MODERN.FON
Script	Vector	Scaled	Proportional	SCRIPT.FON
Roman	Vector	Scaled	Proportional	ROMAN.FON

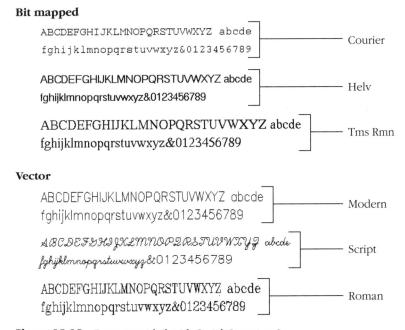

Figure 15-15. *Fonts provided with QuickC version 2.*

Note that the font sizes are given in pixels (height × width). This means that the on-screen size depends on the graphics mode. For example, CGA graphics mode 4 uses much larger pixels than VGA graphics mode 18. Thus, a 13 × 8 Courier character is much larger in the CGA mode than in the VGA mode. Also, the character will be shaped differently in the two modes because the pixels have different proportions.

Steps for Using Fonts

To use fonts, follow these steps:

1. Use the _registerfonts() function to register the fonts you plan to use. This builds an information table that describes the registered fonts.

2. Use _setvideomode() to select a graphics mode.

3. Use the _setfont() function to select one of the registered fonts to be the current font. This causes the program to read the font file to get the mapping information for the selected font.

4. Use _moveto() to indicate where text is to appear.

5. Use _outgtext() to display text.

6. When the text portion of the program is complete, use _unregisterfonts() to free the memory used for the font table.

Let's look at an example to see how to execute these steps. Listing 15-21 displays *Hello!* eight times using the Tms Rmn bit-mapped font and the Roman vector font. Figure 15-16 on p. 538 shows the output for the high-resolution VGA mode 18.

```
/* fonts.c -- illustrates font capabilities        */
/* You might need graphics.lib in the program list. */

#include <conio.h>
#include <graph.h>
#include <string.h>
#define NFONTS 8      /* number of fonts to be displayed */

main(int argc, char *argv[])
{
    int mode = _ERESCOLOR;
    int i, imod, j, nfonts;
    struct videoconfig vc;
    char report[50];
    unsigned char *fontcalls[NFONTS] =
        {
        "t'tms rmn'h10w6b",
        "t'tms rmn'h20w12b",
        "t'tms rmn'h30w18b",
```

Listing 15-21. *The FONTS.C program.*   *(continued)*

Listing 15-21. *continued*

```
        "t'tms rmn'h40w24b",
        "t'roman'h10w6b",
        "t'roman'h20w12b",
        "t'roman'h30w18b",
        "t'roman'h40w24b"
        };
    if (argc > 1)
        mode = atoi(argv[1]);
    if (_setvideomode(mode) == 0)
        {
        printf("Can't set mode %d.\n", mode);
        exit(1);
        }
    _getvideoconfig(&vc);
    if ((nfonts = _registerfonts("*.FON")) < 0)
        {
        _outtext("Can't register fonts -- bye!");
        exit(1);
        }
    sprintf(report, "%d fonts were registered.", nfonts);
    _settextposition(23, 0);
    _outtext(report);
    for (i = 0; i < NFONTS; i++)
        {
        imod = i % (NFONTS / 2);
        if (_setfont(fontcalls[i]) >= 0)
            {
            _setcolor(imod % vc.numcolors + 1);
            j = (i < NFONTS / 2) ? 0 : vc.numxpixels / 2 ;
            _moveto(j, (imod * vc.numypixels) / (NFONTS / 2 + 1));
            _outgtext("Hello!");
            }
        else
            {
            _settextposition(24,0);
            sprintf(report,"Can't set font %s: press a key.",
                    fontcalls[i]);
            _outtext(report);
            getch();
            }
        }
    getch();
    _setvideomode(_DEFAULTMODE);
    _unregisterfonts();
}
```

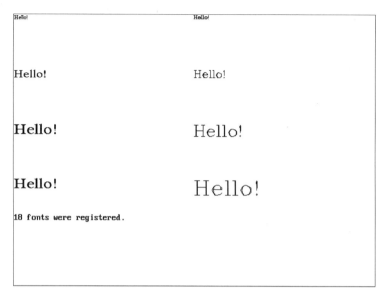

Figure 15-16. *Output of the FONTS.C program.*

Registering the Fonts

The *_registerfonts()* function takes one argument, the address of a string containing the name of the font file. For example,

```
_registerfonts("MODERN.FON")
```

registers the Modern font. To register a font in another directory, use the directory pathname, as in

```
_registerfonts("C:\\WINDOWS\\HELVD.FON")
```

Recall that the backslash character has a special meaning in C, and so a double backslash character is needed in a string to represent an ordinary backslash. Because the DOS environment is not case sensitive, you can use either uppercase or lowercase. Uppercase is used in the listings in this book.

One nice feature of *_registerfonts()* is that it recognizes wildcard notation. Thus, we can use the statement

```
_registerfonts("*.FON");
```

to register all the fonts in the current directory.

The *_registerfonts()* function returns the number of fonts registered, 18 in our example. Note that there is just one file for, say, the Helv fonts (HELVB.FON), but it contains six separate sizes (see Table 15-8 on p. 535) and counts as six fonts. That explains why we were able to register 18 fonts from only six files.

Setting a Graphics Mode

We use _setvideomode() to select EGA mode 15 by default, but by using a command-line argument, you can select other graphics modes.

Selecting a Font

The _setfont() function sets the current font. It takes as an argument a string constructed from "option codes." The *fontcalls* array contains pointers to eight such option-code strings, so that we can use a loop to select eight different fonts. The loop prints four Tms Rmn examples in the left column and four Roman examples in the right column. (Incidentally, the FONTS.C program uses the fact that QuickC version 2, following ANSI C rules, lets you initialize automatic arrays and structures.)

Let's look at one of the option strings. The first one is

```
"t'tms rmn'h10w6b"
```

The *t* option specifies the name of the desired font; the name is placed within single quotes. In this case, the name is *tms rmn*; note that the space is part of the name. The *h* option indicates the desired height of the font in pixels. Here, *h10* requests a font 10 pixels high. Similarly, *w6* requests a font width of 6 pixels. Finally, the *b* option asks _setfont() to find the best fit from the registered fonts.

Let's see how these requests are interpreted. The Tms Rmn font is available only in the sizes given in Table 15-8, unless you have other font files at the program's disposal. Thus, the font closest to the 10 × 6 we requested is the 10 × 5 font. The 20 × 12 request in the second option string exactly matches one of the available fonts. The 26 × 16 font is the closest match to both the 30 × 18 and the 40 × 24 requests, so the program selects it twice. You will notice in Figure 15-16 that the last two output strings in the left column are both 26 × 16.

In choosing the best fit, _setfont() tries to match, in order of precedence, the height, typeface, width, and spacing (fixed or proportional).

The Roman font is a vector font, and so _setfont() is able to create fonts that exactly meet the size specifications. You may notice, however, that the scaled Roman characters (those in the right column of Figure 15-16) are not as well formed as those displayed in Tms Rmn.

If we omitted the *b* option from our example, only one of the four Tms Rmn requests would succeed. If _setfont() is not able to set a font, it returns a nonzero value and leaves the previously selected font as the current font. If it is successful, _setfont() returns zero.

The option letters can be uppercase or lowercase, and they can be specified in any order. Table 15-9 on the following page summarizes the choices.

Table 15-9. _setfont() Options

Option	Meaning
t'*fontname*'	Specifies the typeface for the font. The names of the fonts provided with QuickC version 2 are as follows: courier helv tms rmn modern script roman
h*y*	Specifies the character height, with *y* the height in pixels
w*x*	Specifies the character width, with *x* the width in pixels
f	Specifies a fixed-spaced font only
p	Specifies a proportionally spaced font only
v	Specifies a vector-mapped font only
r	Specifies a raster-mapped (bit-mapped) font only
b	Requests the best fit from the registered fonts; best fit is based, in descending order, on matching the height, typeface, width, and spacing.
n*x*	Specifies the font number *x*, where *x* is its registration number.

Displaying Text

The FONTS.C program uses _moveto() to locate text. Recall that the command _moveto(x,y) sets the position to *x* pixels horizontally and *y* pixels vertically from the origin. By default, the origin is the upper-left corner of the display. The program then uses _outgtext() to display a string at that location. More precisely, the upper-left corner of the first character box coincides with the *x,y* location.

To set the spacing between strings, we called the _getvideoconfig() function to obtain information about the number of *x* and *y* pixels for the current video mode.

Note the difference between _outtext() and _outgtext(). To set the position for the _outtext() function, we use _settextposition(), which measures position in *y,x* instead of *x,y* and which indicates the size in characters rather than pixels. Also, _outtext() uses the system font, not the font selected by _setfont().

Cleaning Up

A call to _unregisterfonts() frees the memory used to register the fonts. Once this is done, you cannot use _setfont() again unless you call _registerfonts() again.

Other Font Functions

The QuickC font library has two more functions. The _getfontinfo() function takes the address of a *struct_fontinfo* variable and fills it with information about the current font. The _getgtextextent() function takes a string as its argument and returns its width in pixels for the current font.

To learn more about fonts, consult QuickC's on-line help for descriptions and examples of the font functions.

Presentation Graphics

Another QuickC version 2 enhancement is the Presentation Graphics Library. This set of functions helps you create charts of the following types:

- Pie charts
- Bar charts
- Column charts
- Line charts
- Scatter charts

Each of these chart types comes in two varieties, and each variety can be customized as to size, colors, fonts, and other properties.

What You Need for Presentation Graphics

To generate presentation graphics, you first need hardware that supports one of the graphics modes. Although the functions work with the CGA graphics modes, the output looks much better if you use the higher-resolution modes of other adapters.

Next, you need to have the supporting libraries available. As is the case with the other examples in this chapter, you will need access to GRAPHICS.LIB. In addition, you will need access to PGCHART.LIB, the library file containing the presentation graphics functions. Like GRAPHICS.LIB, PGCHART.LIB will have been combined with your other libraries if you chose that option when running the SETUP program. Otherwise, you will have to place PGCHART.LIB in a program list.

As before, your programs should include the graph.h file. In addition, charting programs should include pgchart.h.

Steps for Using Presentation Graphics

Normally, you take the following steps when using presentation graphics:

1. Include graph.h and pgchart.h, and make sure your program has access to GRAPHICS.LIB and PGCHART.LIB.

2. Use _setvideomode() to select one of the graphics modes.

3. Use _pg_initchart() and _pg_defaultchart() to initialize the charting functions and set up the basic chart type.

4. Place the plotting data into suitable arrays.

5. Use one of the QuickC charting functions to create and display a chart.

6. Pause the program long enough for the result to be viewed.

7. Use _setvideomode(_DEFAULTMODE) to restore the original display mode.

The following sections show how these steps apply to some basic examples.

A Pie Chart

A pie chart consists of a circle divided into slices. Each slice represents some proportional part of the whole, and the size of the slice reflects the relative size or importance of that part. For instance, each slice could reflect the sales for a different salesperson. The CHART1.C program (Listing 15-22) shows an example, and Figure 15-17 shows the output of CHART1 using mode 17 (_VRES2COLOR).

You are already familiar with including files and setting graphics modes and with using *getch()* to pause a program, so let's look at the charting actions.

```
/* chart1.c -- a simple pie chart                       */
/* Program list (maybe):  graphics.lib and pgchart.lib */

#include <stdio.h>
#include <conio.h>
#include <graph.h>
#include <pgchart.h>
#define AGENTS 4
float far Balloons[AGENTS] = { 2000, 1500, 1700, 1600 };
char far *Agents[AGENTS] = { "Bozo", "Foofoo", "Popo", "Woowoo" };
short far explode[AGENTS] = { 1, 0, 0 , 0 };

main(int argc, char *argv[])
{
    chartenv env;           /* chart environment structure */
    int mode = _ERESCOLOR;
    int i;

    if (argc > 1)
        mode = atoi(argv[1]);
    if (_setvideomode(mode) == 0)
        {
        printf("Can't set mode %d.\n", mode);
        exit(1);
        }
    _pg_initchart();
    _pg_defaultchart(&env, _PG_PIECHART, _PG_PERCENT);
    if (_pg_chartpie(&env, Agents, Balloons, explode, AGENTS) != 0)
        {
        _setvideomode(_DEFAULTMODE);
        _outtext("No can do");
        exit(1);
        }
    getch();
    _setvideomode(_DEFAULTMODE);
}
```

Listing 15-22. *The CHART1.C program.*

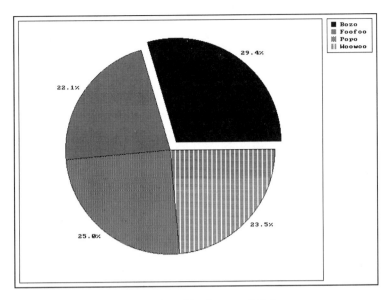

Figure 15-17. *Pie chart produced by the CHART1.C program.*

Initializing the Chart

Initializing the charting package is simple. The *_pg_initchart()* function takes no arguments; it initializes the package, and returns zero if successful, a nonzero value if it is unsuccessful.

The *_pg_defaultchart()* function is more involved. Its first argument is the address of a *chartenv* structure. The pgchart.h file contains the structure template and the *typedef* for this type. The next two arguments are type *short* values specifying the chart type and style. We've used macros defined in pgchart.h for those two arguments. (We will discuss these macros shortly.) The function initializes the *chartenv* structure to default values, which are determined by the last two arguments. In addition, the function returns zero if successful and a nonzero value if not.

Note that the *_pg_defaultchart()* function requires that we first create a *chartenv* structure to hold the information. We did so by declaring *env* at the beginning of the program.

The pgchart.h file defines five macros that can be used for the chart type argument. Of the following, we chose *_PG_PIECHART* because we want the program to create a pie chart.

```
_PG_BARCHART
_PG_COLUMNCHART
_PG_LINECHART
_PG_SCATTERCHART
_PG_PIECHART
```

The two possible styles, or varieties, of pie chart are those charts that include percentages and those without them. Again, the pgchart.h file defines macros for these choices:

```
_PG_PERCENT
_PG_NOPERCENT
```

Other macros define the style choices for the other chart types.

At this point, the chart design is established. You can modify the contents of the *env* structure to customize the chart appearance. We'll look at how to do that in the next example.

Readying the Data

The chart-display functions expect to be passed pointers to the data for the chart. Naturally, this data should be in the proper form. The pie chart function requires three arrays of data.

One array holds the numeric data to be charted. It should be a type *float* array. In the CHART1.C program, the *Balloons* array holds the data. It has been set to the balloon sales figures for four salespersons. We have used the *_far* keyword because the display function prototypes call for far pointers. In general, numeric data items are called "values."

The second array holds pointers to strings that identify the "categories" used. Categories are non-numeric data, such as persons, months, or states, used in the chart. In our example, the *Agents* array is initialized to the names of the four balloon salespersons. (More precisely, it is initialized to the addresses of the strings.) The first name in this array corresponds to the first sales figure in the *Balloons* array, the second name to the second sales figure, and so on. The pie chart function identifies each slice by the agent's name and scales the slice according to the agent's sales.

The third array determines which slices, if any, are "exploded." An exploded slice is one that is slightly detached from the rest of the pie. This array should be of type *short _far*. To explode a particular slice, set the corresponding element to 1; otherwise, set the element to 0. The CHART1.C program, for example, sets the first element of the *explode* array to 1; this will explode Bozo's slice of the pie.

Displaying the Pie Chart

The *_pg_chartpie()* function creates and displays the pie chart. It takes five arguments. The first is the address of the type *chartenv* structure containing chart parameters; *&env* fits the bill. The second is the name of the array containing pointers to the categories; we use *Agents*. The third argument is the name of the array containing the values; we use *Balloons*. The fourth argument is the name of the array with the explosion data—*explode*, in this case. The fifth and final argument is the number of items to be plotted. We use the defined constant *AGENTS* here and in dimensioning the arrays to ensure that the same value is used in all those places.

A Bar Chart

Our second example uses the same data to create a bar chart, that is, a chart made up of horizontal bars whose lengths reflect relative values. You'll also see how to use the *chartenv* structure to alter the chart's appearance. Listing 15-23 presents the example, and Figure 15-18 on the following page shows the results.

```
/* chart2.c -- a bar chart                          */
/* Program list (maybe):  graphics.lib and pgchart.lib */

#include <stdio.h>
#include <conio.h>
#include <graph.h>
#include <pgchart.h>
#include <string.h>
#define AGENTS 4
float _far Balloons[AGENTS] = { 2000, 1500, 1700, 1600 };
char _far *Agents[AGENTS] = { "Bozo", "Foofoo", "Popo", "Woowoo" };

main(int argc, char *argv[])
{
    chartenv env;
    int mode = _ERESCOLOR;
    int i;

    if (argc > 1)
        mode = atoi(argv[1]);
    if (_setvideomode(mode) == 0)
        {
        printf("Can't set mode %d.\n", mode);
        exit(1);
        }
    _pg_initchart();
    _pg_defaultchart(&env, _PG_BARCHART, _PG_PLAINBARS);
    strcpy(env.maintitle.title, "CLOWNS AT WORK");
    env.maintitle.titlecolor = 6;
    strcpy(env.xaxis.axistitle.title, "BALLOON SALES");
    strcpy(env.yaxis.axistitle.title, "SALESPERSON");
    env.yaxis.axistitle.titlecolor = 3;
    env.xaxis.axistitle.titlecolor = 3;
    if (_pg_chart(&env, Agents, Balloons, AGENTS) != 0)
        {
        _setvideomode(_DEFAULTMODE);
        _outtext("No can do");
        exit(1);
        }
    getch();
    _setvideomode(_DEFAULTMODE);
}
```

Listing 15-23. *The CHART2.C program.*

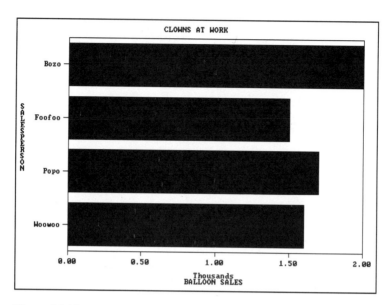

Figure 15-18. *Bar chart produced by the CHART2.C program.*

For the most part, the program is much like CHART1.C. Let's examine the main differences.

Initializing the Chart

Again, we use *_pg_initchart()* and *_pg_defaultchart()* to initialize the charting package and the *chartenv* structure *env*. This time, however, we use the argument *_PG_BARCHART* to set up a bar chart instead of a pie chart. There are two styles of bar chart, represented by the following macros from pgchart.h:

```
_PG_PLAINBARS
_PG_STACKEDBARS
```

The difference between these two styles is apparent only when multiple values are plotted. For instance, if you plot balloon sales and kazoo sales for each salesperson, the plain bars style places the balloon and kazoo bars side by side for each salesperson, while the stacked bars style places the bars end to end.

Once the *env* structure variable is initialized, we modify its contents by using member names obtained from the structure definition in pgchart.h. For instance, the statement

```
strcpy(env.maintitle.title, "CLOWNS AT WORK");
```

copies the string *CLOWNS AT WORK* into the structure location used to hold a title for the chart. We use a similar technique to establish labels for the horizontal and vertical axes. We also assign color numbers for the title and labels.

546

Readying the Data

We can use the same value and category arrays that we used in the previous program. One difference is that we don't need the *explode* array, because only pies can be exploded.

Displaying the Bar Chart

To create and display the bar chart, we use the *_pg_chart()* function. You can also use the same function to create column charts (vertical bar charts) and line charts. The second argument to *_pg_defaultchart()* determines which form is created.

The *pg_chart()* function takes four arguments. They are the same arguments used by *_pg_chartpie()*, with the omission of the explosion data argument.

A Line Chart with Multiple Values

For our final example, we'll see how to make a line chart and how to extend the number of value sets to be plotted. To create a line chart, we merely change the arguments to the *_pg_defaultchart()* function. But when we increase the number of value sets, we must also alter the way in which we represent data, and we must use a new function. Listing 15-24 shows the example, CHART3.C, and Figure 15-19 on the following page shows its output. Let's look at the changes.

```
/* chart3.c -- a line chart                    */
/* Program list (maybe): graphics.lib and pgchart.lib */

#include <stdio.h>
#include <conio.h>
#include <graph.h>
#include <pgchart.h>
#include <string.h>
#define AGENTS 4
#define ITEMS 3
float far Novelties[ITEMS][AGENTS] = { {1000,1500,1700,1600},
                                       {2000,1500,1300,1400},
                                       { 500, 800,1000,1200} };
char _far *Agents[AGENTS] = {"Bozo", "Foofoo", "Popo", "Woowoo"};
char _far *Items[ITEMS] = {"Balloons", "Kazoos", "Videos"};

main(int argc, char *argv[])
{
    chartenv env;
    int mode = _ERESCOLOR;
    int i;

    if (argc > 1)
        mode = atoi(argv[1]);
```

Listing 15-24. *The CHART3.C program.*   *(continued)*

Listing 15-24. *continued*

```
    if (_setvideomode(mode) == 0)
        {
        printf("Can't set mode %d.\n", mode);
        exit(1);
        }
    _pg_initchart();
    _pg_defaultchart(&env, _PG_LINECHART, _PG_POINTANDLINE);
    strcpy(env.maintitle.title, "CLOWNS AT WORK");
    env.maintitle.titlecolor = 6;
    strcpy(env.yaxis.axistitle.title, "SALES");
    strcpy(env.xaxis.axistitle.title, "SALESPERSON");
    env.yaxis.axistitle.titlecolor = 3;
    env.xaxis.axistitle.titlecolor = 3;
    if (_pg_chartms(&env, Agents, (float far *) Novelties, ITEMS,
        AGENTS, AGENTS, Items) != 0)
        {
        _setvideomode(_DEFAULTMODE);
        _outtext("No can do");
        exit(1);
        }
    getch();
    _setvideomode(_DEFAULTMODE);
}
```

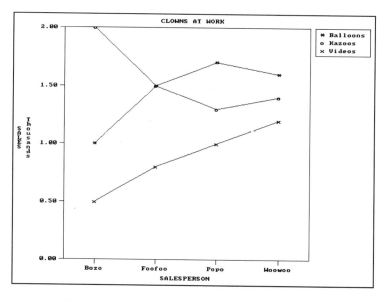

Figure 15-19. *Line chart produced by the CHART3.C program.*

Initializing the Chart

To indicate that we want a line chart, we use _PG_LINECHART_ as the second argument to _pg_defaultchart()_. The two possible styles for line charts are dots connected by lines and dots only. The pgchart.h file represents these choices with the following macros:

```
_PG_POINTANDLINE
_PG_POINTONLY
```

Readying the Data

We are using the same categories as before (the four salespersons), so the _Agents_ array is unaffected. However, we are now representing sales for three items. We do this by initializing an array of pointers to the address of three strings, each describing a particular sales item. The charting program will use this information to label a line chart for each sales item.

This time we have three value sets: balloon sales, kazoo sales, and video sales. We represent this with a two-dimensional array: three arrays of four _float_ values each. Thus, _Novelties[0]_ represents the array of balloon sales, _Novelties[1]_ represents the kazoo sales, and so on. And _Novelties[0][0]_ represents Bozo's balloon sales.

Displaying the Line Chart

The _pg_chartms()_ function charts multiple values. It takes seven arguments:

```
_pg_chartms(&env, Agents, (float _far *) Novelties, ITEMS,
        AGENTS, AGENTS, Items)
```

The first and second arguments, as before, are the address of the _chartenv_ structure and the array of pointers to the category strings. The third argument is the array of values. The function expects a one-dimensional array, so we use a type cast to convert _Novelties_ to the proper type. To determine how to interpret the array, the function needs to know the number of value series and the number of values each series contains. These are the next two arguments: _ITEMS_ and _AGENTS_. You might want to plot only some of the data, however, and so the next argument indicates how many of the categories are to be used. We opted to use all of them. The final argument is the array of pointers to the strings labeling the items to be plotted. Like the other array arguments, it should be a far array.

Charting Epilogue

The examples in the preceding sections should give you a feel for the types of charts available. There are several more charting functions, most of which report or modify specific settings of the charting environment. The _chartenv_ structure contains many members and submembers that delineate the appearance of the graph. You can explore these topics further using the QuickC Help facility.

PART V

Advanced
C Topics

16

QuickC and Assembly Language

One of the most important and interesting additions Microsoft made to version 2 of QuickC is the in-line assembly facility. This enhancement lets you tap the power and speed of assembly language easily and quickly by inserting assembly code into your QuickC programs. In this chapter, we will look at this new feature. Of course, we don't have space in this book to teach assembly language, but we can show you how in-line assembly code works and outline the way to use it with your QuickC programs. If you already know assembly language, you'll find the in-line feature easy to use. If you don't know assembly language, you can run the examples in this chapter to see whether assembly language is something you would want to study further.

The in-line facility isn't meant for writing separate assembly modules that you can call from C. For that you need to use the *Microsoft Macro Assembler* or the new *Microsoft QuickAssembler*. The latter has been designed to work in the same integrated environment as QuickC and is included with QuickC version 2.51. This chapter also takes a brief look at QuickAssembler.

Assembly Language

Assembly language is the natural language for a computer. Its set of instructions relates directly to the computer's hardware capabilities; assembly language is, therefore, specific to particular processors or families of processors. For instance, the IBM line of personal computers is based on the Intel 80x86 family of microprocessors (the 8088, 8086, 80186, 80286, 80386, and the new 80486). This family has a common assembly language, although the more powerful chips use some instructions that are unavailable to their less potent brethren. Assembly-language instructions accomplish tasks such as copying values from memory to registers, adding register contents, comparing register contents, shifting bit values, and making program execution jump from one instruction to another. In short, assembly language lets you—indeed, makes you—control a computer by providing detailed, step-by-step directions to the hardware. In return, it gives you fine control and the potential to write speedy, compact programs.

Assembly language has advantages and disadvantages compared to higher-level languages such as C. In general, assembly-language programs run faster and use less space than high-level languages. They also can perform actions that are difficult or impossible to do in high-level languages. In these respects (speed, compactness, and power), QuickC fares better than most high-level languages. C is designed to be fast and compact, and QuickC, as you have seen, lets you make BIOS calls, access ports, and directly access memory. Nonetheless, assembly language can perform these tasks better and faster.

The main disadvantage of assembly language is that it is tied to a particular family of hardware. It's no easy task to convert an assembly-language program so that it will work on a different family of computers. If you include assembly-language code in a C program, don't expect it to run on a different processor.

Also, programming in assembly language is more tedious and exacting than programming in C. High-level languages, such as C, have a task-oriented design. They provide constructs, such as *for* loops and *if-else* statements, that offer solutions to common programming tasks. Assembly language, on the other hand, is designed to express the capabilities of the hardware; it's up to you to organize these capabilities into forms that match your programming needs.

Assemblers and In-Line Code

The traditional technique for assembly-language programming is to use a text editor to write the assembly code and then use a program called an "assembler" to convert the code to an executable program. Microsoft's Macro Assembler (MASM) is the most widely used assembler for PCs. Microsoft's new QuickAssembler modernizes the user interface by providing an integrated environment. To use an assembler, you need to know not only assembly language but also various assembler directives. These directives inform the assembler about such matters as memory models, where to store data, where to store program code, and so on. By following the same standards that QuickC uses in producing executable code, you can write complete assembly modules that can be assembled into object files (that is, files having the extension .OBJ) and then used as C functions.

In-line assembly code offers a much simpler, but less flexible, alternative. You can use the Microsoft keyword *_asm* in your source code to insert assembly-language instructions directly into a C program. That's what "in-line" means. Let's look at a simple example of in-line code: setting the video page to 1. Listing 13-15 showed how to set the video page to a general value using QuickC's *int86()* function. The following shows a slightly simpler version that only sets the page to 1:

```
#include <dos.h>
    ⋮
union REGS reg;
reg.h.ah = 5;  /* set AH register to 5 */
reg.h.al = 1;  /* set AL register to 1 */
int86(0x10, &reg, &reg);  /* invoke interrupt 0x10 */
```

Recall that the code works by calling a video interrupt. This requires first that registers be set to the proper value. Here we use the *reg* structure to assign the correct values to the AH and AL registers. Then the *int86()* function invokes the BIOS video interrupt.

Here is the equivalent in-line assembly code:

```
_asm       mov ah, 5   /* put 5 into the AH register */
_asm       mov al, 1   ; set AL register to 1
_asm       int 10h     ; invoke the video interrupt
```

The *_asm* keyword indicates that the rest of the line (excluding comments) is assembly code. The assembly-language command *mov ah, 5* means move the value 5 into the AH register. The *int 10h* command means to invoke interrupt 0x10. With assembly language, we can set register values directly and invoke interrupts directly. Note that assembly language uses an *h* suffix to indicate hexadecimal values. With QuickC in-line assembly code, you can use either C-style comments or assembly-style comments, in which a semicolon marks the rest of the line as a comment.

If you prefer, you can put all the assembly code on one line, as long as you precede each instruction with *_asm*:

```
_asm       mov ah, 5   _asm    mov al, 1   _asm    int 10h
```

You can also use braces to indicate that a block of code is assembly language. For instance, we can rewrite the previous example as follows:

```
_asm {
    mov ah, 5
    mov al, 1
    int 10h
    }
```

Alternatively, you can place the opening brace on the next line. We use a backslash to escape the subsequent newline, but even that is optional:

```
_asm \
{
    mov ah, 5
    mov al, 1
    int 10h
}
```

In short, QuickC makes it easy for you to include in-line assembly code in your programs.

The C Connection

One especially nice feature of the QuickC in-line assembler is that it lets you use many C elements, including variable names, labels, function names, and macros. For instance, we could modify the preceding example so that the page value is given by a C variable, as follows:

```
unsigned char page;    /* one-byte quantity */
⋮
_asm    {
        mov ah, 5
        mov al, page
        int 10h
        }
```

Unlike C, however, assembly language is not case conscious, so *page* and *PAGE* would be considered equivalent.

The in-line assembler recognizes the following list of C elements, all of which, aside from the constants, are termed C "symbols":

■ Named constants, such as *#define* and *enum* constants

■ Variable names

■ *typedef* names

■ Labels

■ Function identifiers

■ Macros

■ Comments

The in-line assembler places the following restrictions on C symbols:

■ You can use no more than one C symbol per assembly-language instruction. For instance, *mov house, home* is invalid if both *house* and *home* are the names of C variables.

■ Although you can use a pointer variable to represent an address, you can't use the indirection operator to indicate a value. For example, *mov ax, *ptr* doesn't work; neither does array notation.

■ In-line assembly language does not recognize the C convention that the name of an array represents the address of the first element.

■ Functions must be prototyped before they are used.

You should be aware that assembly language lets you do things with registers that can conflict with C usage. For instance, QuickC uses the DI and SI registers (see Chapter 13) for type *register* variables. Thus, if you declare *register* variables and your assembly-language routine uses these registers, it should save the register values and restore them when the routine finishes. Also, QuickC uses the BP and SP registers to manage the stack, so your routine should also save and restore their values. Finally, QuickC uses the ES and DS segment registers for memory management; again, save and restore the values for those registers. The examples show how to do this.

The following sections give some simple examples that explore the usefulness of in-line code.

An In-Line Code Example: Block Initialization

Suppose you want to initialize all the elements of an array to the same value. If it's a *char* array, you have several choices. You can use a C loop to initialize each element, you can use the *memset()* function, or you can use in-line assembly language. Because there are non-assembly alternatives, the main reason for using assembly language here would be to save time. Let's investigate each of these three methods and see how well they perform.

The CHARCOPY.C program (Listing 16-1 on the following page) uses all three methods to initialize an array of 4000 characters. To make the times measurable, we do each initialization 200 times.

We use a new function here: *memset()*. The *memset()* function, which is declared in memory.h, takes three arguments: the address of a byte, a byte value, and the number of bytes to set. Accordingly, the function call *memset(sample, 'T', SIZE)* in Listing 16-1 sets *SIZE* consecutive bytes to *'T'*, beginning with the byte referenced by *sample*. Because *sample* is an array name, the compiler interprets it as the address of the first byte of the array.

The *clock()* function, as you may recall from Chapter 15, returns a time from the system clock. The macro *CLK_TCK*, defined in time.h, provides the number of clock units per second. This makes the expression *(end - start) / (double)CLK_TCK* represent the seconds elapsed between the setting of *start* and the setting of *end*. The type cast to *double* gives us a fractional result instead of an integer result.

```
/* charcopy.c -- initializes character blocks */

#include <stdio.h>
#include <time.h>    /* clock() prototype, clock_t definition */
#include <memory.h>    /* memset() prototype */
#define SIZE 4000
#define LIMIT 200
char sample[SIZE];

main()
{
    clock_t start, end;
    double t1, t2, t3;
    register int i,j;
    char *arr_add = sample;

    start = clock();
    for (j = 0; j < LIMIT; j++)
        for ( i = 0; i < SIZE; i++)
            sample[i] = 'S';
    end = clock();
    t1 = (end - start) / (double)CLK_TCK;

    start = clock();
    for (j = 0; j < LIMIT; j++)
        memset(sample, 'T', SIZE);
    end = clock();
    t2 = (end - start) / (double)CLK_TCK;

    start = clock();
    for (j = 0; j < LIMIT; j++)
        _asm \
        {
            push di
            push es
            mov  ax, ds
            mov  es, ax
            mov  di, BYTE PTR arr_add
            mov  al, 'E'
            mov  cx, SIZE
            rep  stosb
            pop  es
            pop  di
        }
    end = clock();
    t3 = (end - start) / (double)CLK_TCK;

    printf("t1 = %0.2f, t2 = %0.2f, t3 = %0.2f\n", t1, t2, t3);
}
```

Listing 16-1. *The CHARCOPY.C program.*

Now let's look at the assembly-language portion of the listing. If you don't know assembly language, this discussion should give you a feel for how it works. The code is based on the assembly instruction *rep stosb*, which repeatedly stores a value in consecutive bytes. Like many assembly instructions, this one requires that we first set up certain registers. We need to place the number of bytes to be set in the CX register; the *move cx, SIZE* instruction does that. The byte value to be copied goes into the AL register; the instruction *mov al, 'E'* puts the ASCII code for 'E' into that register. Providing the final bit of information, the starting address of the array to be filled, is more involved. The *stosb* instruction requires a full 32-bit address, with the segment value placed in the ES register and the offset placed in the DI register. (You may want to review the section in Chapter 14 on segmented memory.) In the default small memory model, all data is stored in the segment described by the DS register, so we have to copy the value of DS to ES. Assembly language can't do that directly, so we copy DS to AX and then copy AX to ES. The offset we want is the address of the *sample* array. Assembly language doesn't recognize the C convention that the name of a C array is its address, so we can't use *sample* here. But the QuickC in-line assembler does recognize ordinary variables. Therefore, the program initializes a pointer *arr_add* to the proper address, and we use *arr_add* in the assembly code. The *BYTE PTR* prefix indicates that *arr_add* is the address of a single byte.

One more point: Using the *rep stosb* instruction required us to use the DI and ES registers, the contents of which should be preserved. The assembly-language method for doing this is to use the *push* and *pop* instructions. The *push* instruction places the indicated value in a temporary storage area called the stack. Conceptually, each time you *push* a new value, it goes on top of the stack and pushes the preceding top value down one position. The *pop* command removes the top value from the stack, placing it in the indicated location. So to save registers, you first *push* them at the start of the assembly code. Then, at the end, you *pop* the values back in the opposite order. That is, the stack is a FILO (First In, Last Out) design.

How much time did we save by using assembly language? Here is a sample output:

```
t1 = 4.10, t2 = 0.22, t3 = 0.44
```

The assembly-language version was about nine times faster than the *for* loop, but the *memset()* function was even faster! The moral here is: Don't assume that using assembly language guarantees you more speed.

You're probably wondering how a function call can beat the speed of assembly language, the processor's own language. The answer is that *memset()* also uses assembly language, but it does so more cleverly than we did. It turns out that the *rep stosb* instruction has a variant form: *rep stosw*. This form initializes data one word at a time instead of one byte at a time, so it can do the job twice as fast.

Round Two

We can rewrite CHARCOPY.C using *rep stosw* to match the speed of *memset()*, but *memset()* already does the job, so we have no need to do so. Suppose, however, that we want to initialize a block of 16-bit integers? There is no integer equivalent to *memset()*, but we can easily modify CHARCOPY.C to do the job. The INTINIT.C program (Listing 16-2) shows the result.

```
/* intinit.c -- initializes a block of integers */

#include <stdio.h>
#include <time.h>
#define SIZE 2000
#define LIMIT 200
int sample[SIZE];                /* change array type */

main()
{
    clock_t start, end;
    double t1, t2;
    register int i, j;
    int *arr_add = sample;       /* change pointer type */

    start = clock();
    for (j = 0; j < LIMIT; j++)
        for ( i = 0; i < SIZE; i++)
            sample[i] = 12345;
    end = clock();
    t1 = (end - start) / (double) CLK_TCK;
    printf("%d %d\n", sample[0], sample[SIZE - 1]);

    start = clock();
    for (j = 0; j < LIMIT; j++)
        _asm \
        {
            push di
            push es
            mov  ax, ds
            mov  es, ax
            mov  di, WORD PTR arr_add ; change type
            mov  ax, 23451
            mov  cx, SIZE
            rep  stosw                ; change command
            pop  es
            pop  di
        }
    end = clock();
    t2 = (end - start) / (double)CLK_TCK;
    printf("%d %d\n", sample[0], sample[SIZE - 1]);
    printf("C time = %0.2f, assembly time = %0.2f\n", t1, t2);
}
```

Listing 16-2. *The INTINIT.C program.*

In the C portion of the listing, we simply had to change the array and pointer types. In the assembly-language portion, we now use *WORD PTR* to indicate that *arr_add* now points to an integer, and we replace *stosb* with *stosw*. We also added a couple of *printf()* statements to verify that the blocks were set to the right values. Here is a sample of the program output:

```
12345 12345
23451 23451
C time = 2.30, assembly time = 0.22
```

Again, assembly language provides about a tenfold speed increase, and this time there is no C library alternative. Also note that by using *stosw*, we have matched the speed of *memset()*.

A Far Pointer Example

The INTINIT.C program initialized a block of integers to a given value. We can use the same technique to initialize a screen of text. This involves one new element: Video memory requires a far pointer (see Chapter 14), and so the program will have to be able to handle a 32-bit address.

Recall that the *stosw* instruction requires that you place the segment address value into the ES register and the offset into the DI register. In INTINIT.C we used the following assembly-language instructions to store the beginning address of the destination array:

```
mov   ax, ds
mov   es, ax
mov   di, WORD PTR arr_add
```

This uses the current data-segment value for ES and the 16-bit pointer *arr_add* for DI. Now suppose we make *screen* a 32-bit pointer to the beginning of video memory. Assembly language provides the instruction *les*, which loads the segment portion of a 32-bit pointer into ES and the offset into the indicated register, so we can replace the preceding code with the following:

```
les  di, DWORD PTR screen
```

Here *DWORD PTR* identifies *screen* as a 32-bit (double-word) pointer. The offset is placed in DI, and the segment value in ES.

The VIDEO.C program (Listing 16-3 on the following page) uses this approach to initialize the screen. Recall that in text mode each character on the screen is represented by a 2-byte unit of video memory, with 1 byte holding the character and the other the attribute. For comparison, we use a C *for* loop to perform the same task and time the results.

After setting the screen to *S* and then *T*, our system reported the following times:

```
C time = 2.36, assembly time = 0.55
```

```
/* video.c -- uses far pointers in assembly */

#include <stdio.h>
#include <time.h>
typedef unsigned short (_far *VIDMEM);
#define MONMEM   ((VIDMEM) (0xB000L << 16))
#define CGAMEM   ((VIDMEM) (0xB800L << 16))
#define GETMODE  0xF
#define VIDEO    0x10
#define SIZE     2000
#define LIMIT    100

main()
{
    clock_t start, end;
    double t1, t2, t3;
    register i, j;
    unsigned char mode;
    VIDMEM screen = CGAMEM;        /* CGA text mode */
    unsigned short value1 = 'S' ¦ (0x41 << 8);
    unsigned short value2 = 'T' ¦ (0x62 << 8);

    start = clock();
    for (j = 0; j < LIMIT; j++)
        for (i = 0; i < SIZE; i++)
            *screen++ = value1;
    end = clock();
    t1 = (end - start) / (double)CLK_TCK;
    screen = CGAMEM;       /* reset pointer */
    start = clock();
    for (j = 0; j < LIMIT; j++)
        _asm \
        {
            push di
            push es
            les  di, DWORD PTR screen
            mov  ax, value2
            mov  cx, SIZE
            rep  stosw
            pop  es
            pop  di
        }
    end = clock();
    t2 = (end - start) / (double)CLK_TCK;
    printf("C time = %0.2f, assembly time = %0.2f\n", t1, t2);
}
```

Listing 16-3. *The VIDEO.C program.*

562

The results for Listing 16-3 show that the assembly version rewrites the video memory about four times faster than the C version for the test system, a 6-MHz AT clone (80286 CPU) with a Paradise VGAPlus video card. Because the program did 100 rewrites, the times for a single rewrite are about 0.006 and 0.024 second each. However, these are the times taken to rewrite the video memory, not to rewrite the actual screen. The screen is rewritten whenever the hardware scans the video memory. Depending on the monitor, this is done from 50 to 70 times a second, meaning that the screen is redrawn approximately every 0.017 second. For our example, this means the C loop takes slightly longer to set the video memory than the time between scans. The assembly code, on the other hand, resets the video memory approximately three times per scan.

Rewriting video memory several times per screen rewrite has no practical value, but it does mean the computer has time to do one rewrite plus some other actions between screen rewrites. This means, for example, that you can determine when the video controller does a vertical retrace, rewrite the screen, perform some sort of calculation, and prepare for the next retrace. You can see why assembly language is invaluable if you need to do screen animation.

CGA Snow

If you run the preceding program on a CGA monitor, you'll probably see a lot of interference, or "snow." The problem arises because the CPU sends data to the video RAM at the same time that the CGA controller reads the RAM. (The other controllers don't have this problem.) One way to eliminate the interference is to avoid writing to video RAM while the controller is scanning. Instead, wait for the horizontal retrace, which occurs when the electron beam in the monitor is reset for the next scan across the screen.

The CGA has a read-only port with port address 0x3DA that reports the horizontal retrace status. When retrace is occurring, bit 0 is set to 1; otherwise, it is set to 0. The usual trick is to use two consecutive loops. The first loop waits until the end of the current retrace, because you don't want to start, say, after the retrace is 80 percent finished. The second loop waits until the end of the horizontal scan. At that point, the monitor is about to start the retrace, and that is when we write to video memory. The VIDCGA.C program (Listing 16-4 on the following page) revises Listing 16-3 to write one character during each retrace. Because the program writes a single character at a time instead of a block, we replace *rep stosw* with an assembly loop that uses *stosw* once each cycle.

Our system produced the following timing:

```
Slow no-snow time = 7.18
```

Clearly, snow-free direct memory access in CGA mode costs dearly in time, but if you must write only during retraces, assembly language is the way to go.

```
/* vidcga.c -- waits for horizontal retrace */

#include <stdio.h>
#include <time.h>
typedef unsigned short (_far *VIDMEM);
#define MONMEM  ((VIDMEM) (0xB000L << 16))
#define CGAMEM  ((VIDMEM) (0xB800L << 16))
#define SIZE    2000
#define LIMIT   100
main()
{
    clock_t start, end;
    double t;
    register i,j;
    unsigned char mode;
    VIDMEM screen = CGAMEM;       /* CGA text mode */
    unsigned short value = 'E' | (0x41 << 8);

    start = clock();
    for (j = 0; j < LIMIT; j++)
        _asm \
        {
            push di
            push es
            les  di, DWORD PTR screen
            mov  cx, SIZE
            mov  dx, 03DAh     ; load controller port address

    wait1:  in   al, dx       ; read port
            test al, 1         ; test if retracing
            jnz  wait1         ; if so, wait till done
            cli                ; turn off interrupts

    wait2:  in   al, dx       ; read port
            test al, 1         ; test if retracing
            jz   wait2         ; if not, wait till it is

            mov  ax, value     ; load character
            stosw              ; move to video memory
            sti                ; turn on interrupts

            loop wait1         ; next character

            pop  es
            pop  di
        }
    end = clock();
    t = (end - start) / (double)CLK_TCK;
    printf("Slow no-snow time = %0.2f\n", t);
}
```

Listing 16-4. *The VIDCGA.C program.*

More Assembly-Language Instructions

Let's look at some of the assembly-language instructions that were introduced in the VIDCGA.C program. The *in* command reads a port value into the register. The port address has to be in the DX register, and the contents must be read into AX, AL, or AH. Because *stosw* also must use the AX register, we have to reset AX to *value* within each cycle.

The *test* command lets us compare two values. If the two values are the same, a CPU bit called the zero flag is set to 1; otherwise the flag is cleared to 0. The *jnz* command causes the processor to jump to the following label if the zero flag is 1, while *jz* causes it to jump to the following label if the zero flag is 0. Thus, the segment

```
wait1:      in   al, dx        ; read port
            test al, 1         ; test if retracing
            jnz  wait1         ; if so, wait till done
```

is a loop that continues as long as the port value in AL remains 1. Here *wait1:* labels a particular line of code, and *jnz* jumps to that line.

The *cli* instruction causes the processor to ignore most interrupts until the *sti* instruction restores the processor's alertness. This ensures that nothing else interrupts the copying of the character to video memory. This is a fine detail that we couldn't accomplish in C.

To create a loop controlling the writing of all 2000 characters, we introduce the assembly instruction *loop*. To use it, first set the CX register to the desired number of iterations. You also need to set up a label to establish the bounds of the loop. Here we let it share the *wait1:* label with the first inner loop.

Creating Assembly Functions

You may want to convert a particularly useful block of assembly code into a C function. To do so, create the usual C function header and arguments, and then use in-line assembly within the function body. For instance, the INTSET.C program (Listing 16-5 on the following page) uses the assembly code from INTINIT.C to create an *Intset()* function for initializing an array of integers.

What makes creating an assembly function so easy is the fact that the QuickC in-line assembler recognizes most C identifiers. In particular, it recognizes the formal arguments to the function. This lets us use those variables in the assembly-language portion of the program.

```
/* intset.c -- uses an assembly-language function */

#include <stdio.h>
void Intset(int *loc, int val, unsigned int num);
void Showsample(int ar[], int n);
#define SIZE 100
int sample[SIZE];

main()
{
    int value;

    puts("Enter an integer value:");
    while (scanf("%d", &value) == 1)
        {
        Intset(sample, value, SIZE);
        Showsample(sample, SIZE);
        puts("Enter next value; enter q to quit:");
        }
    puts("Bye");
}
/* Intset() initializes a block of num integers at */
/* address loc to the value val */
void Intset(int *loc, int val, unsigned int num)
{
    _asm \
    {
        push di
        push es
        mov  ax, ds
        mov  es, ax
        mov  di, WORD PTR loc
        mov  ax, val
        mov  cx, num
        rep  stosw
        pop  es
        pop  di
    }
}
void Showsample(int ar[], int n)  /* print array contents */
{
    int i;

    for (i = 0; i < n; i++)
        {
        printf("%6d ", ar[i]);
        if ( i % 10 == 9 )
            putchar('\n');
        }
}
```

Listing 16-5. *The INTSET.C program.*

Functions with Return Values

You can use the QuickC in-line assembler to create functions that have return values. If you are familiar with the QuickC conventions for return values, you can take some shortcuts. For example, if the return value of a function is a single word, as is the case with types *int*, *short*, and *unsigned int*, the compiler places the return value in the AX register. Thus, when we write an in-line assembly function that returns an *int* value, we can place the answer in the AX register and dispense with *return*. The SUMARR.C program (Listing 16-6) shows an example that sums the elements of an integer array.

```
/* sumarr.c -- uses an assembly-language function */

#include <stdio.h>
int Sum_arr(int ar[], int n);
#define SIZE 100
int sample[SIZE];

main()
{
    int i;
    int sum;

    for (i = 0; i < SIZE; i++)
        sample[i] = i + 1;
    sum = Sum_arr(sample, SIZE);
    printf("sum = %d\n", sum);
}
int Sum_arr(int ar[], int n)
{
    _asm \
        {
        mov  ax, 0              ; initialize sum to 0
        mov  cx, n              ; set counting register to n
        mov  bx, WORD PTR ar    ; copy pointer
    start:
        add  ax, WORD PTR [bx]  ; add pointed-to value
        add  bx, 2              ; increment pointer
        loop start              ; repeat loop
        }
    /* QuickC uses the AX register for return values */
}
```

Listing 16-6. *The SUMARR.C program.*

We've used *loop* again, this time using *start:* as a label. Before the loop we copy the array address to the BX register. In the loop we add *[bx]* to the AX register. The notation *[bx]* means the value found at the address *bx*; it's the assembly-language equivalent of *ar*. Next, we add 2 to the BX register; this advances the pointer to the next array element. Unlike C, address addition in assembly language is by bytes. Thus, if an address points to a 2-byte object, we have to add 2 explicitly.

The assembly *add* instruction adds two values and places the results of the addition in the lefthand location; thus, the loop keeps a cumulative total in AX. And when the loop finishes, the desired result is in the proper register for *int* returns, so no further action is needed.

On our system, the *Sum_arr()* function is about three times faster than the C equivalent, so again we've achieved a speed gain.

Calling a Function from Assembly Language

You can call C functions from assembly language. The technique is to use the assembly instruction *call* followed by the name of the function, as shown in Listing 16-7.

```
/* howdy.c -- calls a C function from assembly language */

#include <stdio.h>
void Howdy(void);

main()
{
    _asm call Howdy      ; assembly function call
}
void Howdy(void)
{
    puts("Howdy");
}
```

Listing 16-7. *The HOWDY.C program.*

We declared *Howdy()* before using it so that QuickC would know that *Howdy* is a function name, not a variable name.

What if the function takes arguments? To call it from assembly language, you first must place those arguments on the stack in accordance with the conventions followed by QuickC functions. That is beyond the scope of this book. But one of the charms of the in-line assembler is that you can return to ordinary C if the assembly-language coding gets too difficult for you.

Function Concerns

Microsoft C functions should follow certain standards regarding registers. The AX, BX, CX, and DX registers are regarded as workspace. You can use them freely and not worry about saving their values. This also means, however, that if you call a C function from assembly language, the called function may change the values of those registers. You can't, for example, rely on CX to have the same value after a function call as before. Thus, placing a function call in a loop controlled by the CX register can produce unwanted results. Also, C functions don't bother to preserve the values of the ES register and of the flags register. But you should preserve the values of any other registers your code uses. The simplest way is to *push* the register values at the start of the code and to *pop* them at the end.

As we mentioned earlier, QuickC uses the AX register for 2-byte return values. To return 4-byte values, such as *long* values, QuickC places the 2 high-order bytes in DX and the 2 low-order bytes in AX. Longer values, such as *double* and *struct* objects, are handled by returning a pointer to a value in memory. The segment value goes into DX, and the offset goes into AX.

Sound Programming

Let's use assembly language to make some sounds. The PC provides very little programming support for controlling the speaker. Instead of using BIOS calls, you need to read from and write to several ports that control the speaker. We've already seen that the assembly-language instruction *in* reads ports. To send information to ports, use *out*. The NOTES.C program (Listing 16-8) plays a sequence of notes of increasing frequency. It uses C to let you enter integer values for starting and ending frequencies and for the time separation between notes. Then it uses in-line assembly language to do the actual work.

```
/* notes.c -- sounds the speaker */

#include <stdio.h>
main()
{
    void Sound(int, int, int);
    int first, last, delay;

    while (scanf("%d %d %d", &first, &last, &delay) == 3)
        Sound(first, last, delay);
}
void Sound(int start, int stop, int pause)
{
    long time;
    _asm \
    {
            sub bx, bx          ; initialize bx to 0
    loop1:  add bx, start       ; sound with frequencies
            cmp bx, stop        ;    from start to stop
            ja  exit            ; exits when bx exceeds stop
            mov al, 0B6h        ; initialize channel 2 of
            out 43h, al         ;    timer chip
            mov dx, 12h         ; divide 1,193,182 hertz
            mov ax, 34DEh       ;    (clock frequency) by
            div bx              ;    desired frequency
                                ; result is timer clock count
            out 42h, al         ; low byte of count to timer
            mov al, ah
            out 42h, al         ; high byte of count to timer
            in  al, 61h         ; read value from port 61h
            or  al, 3           ; set first two bits
            out 61h, al         ; turn speaker on
```

Listing 16-8. *The NOTES.C program.* *(continued)*

Listing 16-8. *continued*

```
          sub ah, ah         ; set ah to 0
          int 1Ah            ; get clock count in CX:DX
          add dx, pause      ; add pause time to it
          adc cx, 0
          mov WORD PTR time[0], dx    ; result is target time;
          mov WORD PTR time[2], cx    ;   keep in local variable
loop2:    int 1AH                     ; now repeatedly poll clock
          cmp dx, WORD PTR time[0]     ;   count until the target
          jb  loop2                   ;   time is reached
          cmp cx, WORD PTR time[2]
          jb  loop2

          in  al, 61h        ; get port value
          xor al, 3          ; clear bits 0-1 to turn
          out 61h, al        ;   speaker off
          jmp loop1
    exit:
    }
}
```

To run the program, enter values for the frequency of the first note, the frequency of the last note, and the delay between notes. For example, enter

```
100 2000 2
```

Enter non-numeric values to terminate the input loop.

We won't discuss this program in detail; the comments describe what the assembly code does. It is based on a sample program provided with QuickAssembler.

Doing the Impossible

We've said that you typically would use in-line assembly language to speed up or to compact some critical code, or to accomplish something that would be difficult or impossible to do with ordinary C. So far, our examples have produced speed increases. Let's look at an assembly-language example that enables you to check for an integer overflow condition—something that you cannot do with C.

The 80x86 processors maintain several flags that monitor the register operations, reporting on such things as overflows, registers being set to zero, and the like. The flag values are kept in a flags register. To find the values, you use the *pushf* instruction to place the current values on the stack. You can then pop the values off into a register or variable. The FLAGS.C program (Listing 16-9) does precisely that.

The following is a sample output:

```
flags = 0000000100000110
```

```
/* flags.c -- shows current flag settings */

#include <stdio.h>
char *Itobs(int, char *);
main()
{
    unsigned short flags;
    char bflags[17];

    puts("Here are the current flag settings:");
    _asm \
    {
        pushf
        pop flags
    }
    printf("flags = %s\n", Itobs(flags, bflags));
}

char *Itobs(int n, char *ps)  /* converts n to binary string */
{
    int i;

    for (i = 15; i >= 0; i--, n >>= 1)
        ps[i] = (01 & n) + '0';
    ps[16] = '\0';
    return (ps);
}
```

Listing 16-9. *The FLAGS.C program.*

Figure 16-1 identifies the 8086 flags. By comparing the figure with the sample output, we see that the interrupt flag and the parity flag are set. The final 1 in the output doesn't correspond to a particular flag. The meanings and uses of these flags we leave to books about assembly language. Note, however, that you can use the carry and overflow flags to check for integer overflow conditions. (Don't convert this code to a function call: The act of calling the function can change some flag settings.)

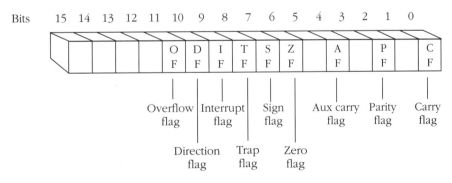

Figure 16-1. *In the flags register, flag settings are associated with individual bits.*

QuickC and QuickAssembler

Microsoft's QuickC/QuickAssembler combination (QuickC version 2.51) provides another way to mix C with assembly language. With QuickAssembler you can create separate assembly-language modules that C programs can call as functions. Here are the steps:

1. Using the QuickC editor, write the C part of the program, saving it in one or more files that have the .C extension. Put the filenames in a program list.

2. Use the same editor to write the assembly modules. These modules should conform to C conventions, and they should be saved in files that have the .ASM extension. Add the names of these files to the program list.

3. Initiate compiling as usual. QuickC compiles the .C files, producing object files that have the .OBJ extension. QuickAssembler assembles the .ASM files, producing more object files that have the .OBJ extension. The Microsoft linker then combines the object files and library functions to form the executable file, which has the .EXE extension.

Let's modify our INTSET.C program (Listing 16-5 on p. 566) so that the integer-setting function is an assembly module rather than a C function that uses in-line assembly. First, we remove *Intset()* from the file so that only the pure C code remains. We'll change a couple of names too. The result is shown in the INTQUICK.C program (Listing 16-10).

```
/* intquick.c -- uses a QuickAssembler module */

#include <stdio.h>
void Intaset(int *loc, int val, unsigned int num);
void Showsample(int ar[], int n);
#define SIZE 100
int sample[SIZE];
main()
{
    int value;

    puts("Enter an integer value:");
    while (scanf("%d", &value) == 1)
        {
        Intaset(sample, value, SIZE);
        Showsample(sample, SIZE);
        puts("Enter next value; enter q to quit:");
        }
    puts("Bye");
}
void Showsample(int ar[], int n)
{
    int i;
```

Listing 16-10. *The INTQUICK.C program.* (continued)

Listing 16-10. *continued*

```
    for (i = 0; i < n; i++)
        {
        printf("%6d ", ar[i]);
        if (i % 10 == 9)
            putchar('\n');
        }
}
```

Next, we create the assembly module, Listing 16-11, which replaces the in-line version (Listing 16-12). The core assembly code is the same, so let's look at what is new.

```
        .MODEL  small,c   ; small memory model, C format
        .CODE             ; following is stored in code segment
Intaset PROC  USES di es,  loc:PTR WORD, val:WORD, num:WORD
                          ; Intaset is name of a procedure
                          ; save and restore di, es registers
                          ; loc is address of a word (integer)
                          ; val and num are words (integers)
        mov ax, ds
        mov es, ax
        mov di, WORD PTR loc
        mov ax, val
        mov cx, num
        rep stosw
        ret               ; VERY IMPORTANT
Intaset ENDP              ; end of procedure definition
        END               ; end of module
```

Listing 16-11. *The Intaset module.*

```
/* Intset() initializes a block of num integers at */
/* address loc to the value val */
void Intset(int *loc, int val, unsigned int num)
{
    _asm \
    {
        push di
        push es
        mov  ax, ds
        mov  es, ax
        mov  di, WORD PTR loc
        mov  ax, val
        mov  cx, num
        rep  stosw
        pop  es
        pop  di
    }
}
```

Listing 16-12. *The* Intset() *function.*

Assembly Module Basics

We've already used assembly instructions with in-line code. Access to an assembler lets us do more: We can use a variety of assembler "directives," instructions to the assembler that tell it how to put programs together. The directives in our example are *.MODEL*, *.CODE*, *PROC*, *USES*, *ENDP*, and *END*.

For the assembly module to interact correctly with the C program, both have to use the same conventions. The first line accomplishes much toward that end:

```
.MODEL  small,c   ; small memory model, C format
```

As the comment suggests, this *.MODEL* directive tells the assembler to use the small memory model and to follow C conventions. In particular, this lets the assembler know how function arguments will be passed to the module.

Now look at the next line:

```
.CODE             ; following is stored in code segment
```

In general, the assembler places data and code in different segments. This directive announces that the following module goes into the code segment.

The next line does a lot:

```
Intaset PROC  USES di es,  loc:PTR WORD, val:WORD, num:WORD
```

First, it establishes that *Intaset* is the name of a "procedure," the assembly-language equivalent of a function. Thus, calls to *Intaset()* in a C program get transferred to this section of code. Next, *USES di es* tells the assembler that the procedure uses the DI and ES registers. Accordingly, the module saves and restores the register values for us, so we can drop the *push* and *pop* instructions we had in the in-line version. Next is a list of values being passed to the procedure. This is the assembly-language equivalent of declaring the formal arguments to a function. In this case, *loc* is a pointer to a word, and *val* and *num* are words. A word in assembly comprises 16 bits; it corresponds to the *int* type in the calling C program.

The next six lines of code are the same as those in the in-line version. Then comes a very important line:

```
ret             ; VERY IMPORTANT
```

The *ret* instruction tells the program to return to the calling function. Unlike C functions, assembly modules do not automatically return program flow to the calling program. Remember to use *ret*, or you may find your code behaving quite strangely.

The last two lines of code mark the end of the procedure and the end of the module, respectively. In general, you can have several procedures within a single module, so you could have several *ENDP* directives. The *END* directive marks the end of the whole module, however, so your module has only one.

What have we gained by using an assembly module instead of in-line code? Because both versions do the same job with essentially the same assembly instructions, there is no significant difference in power or speed. But on our system, the .OBJ code for the in-line version uses 410 bytes, whereas the QuickAssembler .OBJ code uses only 138 bytes. (These figures are generated with debugging turned off.)

More generally, the use of assembly modules gives you access to the full capabilities of assembly language. For instance, the assembler offers macro definitions that are much more powerful than those of C. In addition, the assembly directives give you precise and powerful control over the way in which the program is set up. For example, the *PROC* and *ENDP* directives let you modularize the code. We could rewrite our sound program, NOTES.C, to use separate procedures: one to set up the frequency loop, one to sound the speaker, and one to create the pause. These modules could then be used together or separately in other programming projects.

If you want (or need) to use small amounts of assembly code occasionally, then in-line code is quick, convenient, and works well. One advantage, at least for short programs, is that you can keep all your code together in one file. If you plan to do a lot of mixed-language programming, however, you'll probably want to use the QuickC/QuickAssembler combination. QuickAssembler provides on-line help for all the assembly instructions and directives.

Exploring Further

To give you further insight into the uses of assembly-language routines, the final section of this chapter offers three quick examples. Each presents a useful assembly-language routine with a minimum of explanation.

Text Transfer

The SCRNBUF.C program (Listing 16-13 on the following page) uses assembly language to copy blocks of text, including string attributes, back and forth between screen memory and a buffer. The main assembly-language tool is *movsw*, which works much like *stosw* except that it copies an array of values to the destination array, instead of a single value. The *lds* instruction works much like *les*, except that it places the segment value in the DS register—the location at which *movsw* expects to find the segment value for the source array. The *Move_word()* function works much like the library's *movedata()* function; both routines can move data across segments. The *Move_word()* function explicitly uses far pointers, however, whereas *movedata()* requires that you provide segment values and offsets separately for each memory block.

```
/* scrnbuf.c -- transfers text between screen and a buffer */

#include <stdio.h>
#include <conio.h>
typedef unsigned short (_far *VIDMEM);
#define MONMEM  ((VIDMEM) (0xB000L << 16))
#define CGAMEM  ((VIDMEM) (0xB800L << 16))
#define SIZE    2000
unsigned short _far buffer[SIZE];
void Move_word(short _far *source, short _far *target);

main()
{
    register i;
    VIDMEM screen = CGAMEM;         /* CGA text mode */
    unsigned short attrib = 0x41 << 8;

    for (i = 0; i < SIZE; i++)
        buffer[i] = (' ' + i % 91) | attrib;
    Move_word(buffer, screen);
    while (getch() != 'q')
        {
        Move_word(screen, buffer);
        for (i = 0; i < SIZE; i++)
            buffer[i] += (1 << 8);
        Move_word(buffer, screen);
        }
}

void Move_word(short _far *source, short _far *target)
{
    _asm \
    {
        push di
        push es
        push si
        push ds
        les  di, DWORD PTR target  ; pointer to target
        lds  si, DWORD PTR source  ; pointer to source
        mov  cx, SIZE
        rep  movsw
        pop  ds
        pop  si
        pop  es
        pop  di
    }
}
```

Listing 16-13. *The SCRNBUF.C program.*

White-Noise Generation

Listing 16-14 presents an assembly-language routine that produces "white noise" (a kind of hiss) by turning the speaker on and off at irregular intervals. The argument to *White_noise()* controls the duration of the noise.

```
/* noise. c -- makes white noise */

#include <stdio.h>

main()
{
    void White_noise(int);
    int count;

    while (scanf("%d",&count) == 1)
        White_noise(count);
}

void White_noise(int count)
{
    unsigned char setting;

    _asm \
    {
                mov   dx, 140h      ; initial delay count
                in    al, 61h
                mov   setting, al   ; save port setting
                sub   bx, bx        ; initialize count to 0

        sound:  xor   al, 2         ; toggle speaker on and off
                out   61h, al
                add   dx, 9248h     ; vary delay count
                mov   cl, 3         ;   by adding a value
                ror   dx, cl        ;   and then rotating bits
                mov   cx, dx
                and   cx, 1ffh
                or    cx, 10

        awhile: loop awhile
                add   bx, 1         ; increment count
                cmp   bx, count
                ja    nomore        ; quit if count exceeded
                jmp   sound         ; else repeat sound loop

        nomore: mov   al, setting
                out   61h, al       ; restore port setting
    }
}
```

Listing 16-14. *The NOISE.C program.*

Note Generation

The SONG.C program (Listing 16-15) modifies the *Sound()* function (see Listing 16-8 on pp. 569–70). The new function, *Sing()*, takes an array address as an argument. The array should contain pairs of values that specify note frequency and duration and should be terminated with a pair of zeros. The function then plays the sequence of notes represented by the array.

```
/* song.c -- plays a sequence of notes */

#include <stdio.h>
#define NOTES 9
int Notes[2 * NOTES] = {512, 12, 480, 6, 427, 6, 384, 12, 341, 6,
                        320, 12, 288, 12, 256, 12, 0, 0};
void Sing(int *input);

main()
{
    int first, last, delay;

    Sing(Notes);
}

void Sing(int *input)
{
    long time;

    _asm \
    {
            mov bx, WORD PTR input  ; copy pointer

    loop1:  mov cx, WORD PTR [bx]    ; copy note value to cx
            cmp cx, 0
            jz  exit                ; exits when cx = 0
            mov al, 0B6h            ; initialize channel 2 of
            out 43h, al             ;    timer chip
            mov dx, 12h             ; divide 1,193,182 hertz
            mov ax, 34DEh           ;    (clock frequency) by
            div cx                  ;    desired frequency
                                    ; result is timer clock count
            out 42h, al             ; low byte of count to timer
            mov al, ah
            out 42h, al             ; high byte of count to timer
            in  al, 61h             ; read value from port 61h
            or  al, 3               ; set first two bits
            out 61h, al             ; turn speaker on

            add bx, 2               ; advance pointer to duration
            sub ah, ah              ; set ah to 0
            int 1Ah                 ; get clock count in CX:DX
            add dx, WORD PTR [bx]    ; add pause time to it
```

Listing 16-15. *The SONG.C program.*   *(continued)*

578

Listing 16-15. *continued*

```
        adc cx, 0
        mov WORD PTR time[0], dx    ; result is target time;
        mov WORD PTR time[2], cx    ;   keep in local variable

loop2:  int 1AH                     ; now repeatedly poll clock
        cmp dx, WORD PTR time[0]    ;   count until the target
        jb  loop2                   ;   time is reached
        cmp cx, WORD PTR time[2]
        jb  loop2

        in  al, 61h      ; get port value
        xor al, 3        ; clear bits 0-1 to turn
        out 61h, al      ;   speaker off
        add bx, 2        ; go to next note
        jmp loop1
        exit:
    }
}
```

17

Debugging

Ever since that fateful day in the 1940s when a moth flew into the back of a computer and caused a vacuum tube to short-circuit, programmers have been beset by bugs. Most errors, however, are not *ex machina;* they are caused, in myriad ways, by programmers themselves.

One common type of program error can be classed as the misuse of symbols. For example, you can mistype words and operators, misemploy keywords, and jumble syntax. You detect most of these errors before a program ever runs. Logic errors, the second major class of errors, are more insidious. These often carry through to an operational program, producing mysterious behavior.

Fortunately, the situation is not hopeless. The QuickC compiler helps detect many kinds of errors, and the debugger can actually help trace errors in logic. In this chapter, we try to increase your awareness of common types of errors. Many of the errors we show might seem obvious because we present them as the central attractions in short programs. However, in the context of a large and complex program, these errors are much more difficult to notice.

Debugging, or the finding of errors, can be a challenging, frustrating, rewarding, and time-consuming process. It requires a different mind-set than programming. Programming is an inventive, creative process. Although debugging can also require creativity, it is primarily an investigative process. You must transform yourself from a designer into a sleuth.

Keyboard-Entry Errors

With each line of code you enter from the keyboard, you run the risk of mistyping a word and creating an error. Fortunately, the compiler detects most of these errors.

The MISIDENT.C program (Listing 17-1) is an error-laden program. When you compile it, QuickC returns the following message:

```
misident.c(3) : fatal error C1021: invalid preprocessor command 'defne'
```

The 3 in parentheses identifies the line number that contains the error. Within its integrated environment, QuickC also places the cursor on the offending line.

```
/* misident.c -- careless typing */

#defne BIG 3

main()
{
    char ltr;
    integer num;

    num = 2 + BIG;
    lrt = 'a';
    printf("%c %d\n", ltr, num);
}
```

Listing 17-1. *The MISIDENT.C program.*

You can get further information about an error by placing the cursor on the error message (using the F6 key or the mouse to move to the Error window) and pressing F1 for help. Doing so with the previous message produces this information:

```
Error: C1021   bad preprocessor command 'string'
The characters following the number sign (#) do not
form a valid preprocessor directive.
```

When you compile a program, QuickC first runs a preprocessor to process the # statements. The preprocessor recognizes a limited set of directives, and *#defne* is not among them. Note that compilation stops immediately—before the compiler checks for program errors.

To correct the error, replace *#defne* with *#define* and compile the program again. This time the compiler generates the error messages that follow.

```
misident.c(8) : error C2065: 'integer' : undefined
misident.c(8) : error C2146: syntax error : missing ';'
before identifier 'num'
misident.c(8) : error C2065: 'num' : undefined
misident.c(11) : error C2065: 'lrt' : undefined
```

QuickC opens an error window that shows several messages at a time. You can re-size the window or you can use the scroll bars to see more messages.

This example illustrates one of the virtues of declaring variables. Because *lrt* was undeclared, the compiler quickly spotted the "typo" as an error. It also shows how a simple error can produce several different error messages. The compiler fails to recognize *integer* as a type; therefore, it fails to understand that the statement is a type declaration. It detects a syntax error and views *num* as undefined.

Defensive Programming

One way to reduce errors such as typing *lrt* for *ltr* is to use recognizable words as identifiers. If you scan through a long program, you can easily misread *lrt* for the in-tended *ltr*. But if you use a name such as *letter*, mistypings such as *lerret* or *lettre* are much more likely to catch your eye.

An Anomalous Example

The compiler does not catch all typos. The BADSIGN.C program (Listing 17-2) is an interesting example of this.

```
/* badsign.c -- uncaught typo */

main()
{
    int i;
    int j = 1;

    for (i = 0; i < 10; i++)
        {
        j =+ 10;            /* transposed += */
        printf("%4d ", j);
        }
    printf("\n");
}
```

Listing 17-2. *The BADSIGN.C program.*

This program is meant to print the numbers 1, 11, 21, 31, and so on by incrementing *j* by 10 during each loop cycle. Instead, it prints the following:

```
10 10 10 10 10 10 10 10 10 10
```

What happens is that the program uses =+ instead of +=. In the early days of C, the addition assignment operator was written =+, so at that time, the program would have run as intended. Later, after the switch was made from =+ to +=, this program might have run correctly but with a compiler warning message. If the compiler was not tolerant of anachronisms, it might have rejected the program altogether for using an unknown operator.

QuickC runs the BADSIGN program with no complaints about anachronisms or unknown operators—but the program produces unwanted results. The reason the program runs is that the new ANSI standards for C recognize the + character as a valid unary operator, so QuickC reads the assignment statement as follows:

```
j = +10;
```

That is, the compiler assigns *positive 10* to *j*. Under the old standard, the + could be used only as a binary operator to indicate addition. This particular error was easy to localize because *j* was printed within every loop cycle. If *j* were not printed, finding the problem could be more difficult. The moral here is: Don't be certain that the compiler will catch all mistypings.

One final point: C, unlike many popular languages, is case sensitive; as a consequence, the three identifiers *porter*, *Porter*, and *PORTER* are all distinct. If you aren't used to this convention and QuickC rejects what you consider a valid identifier, check your usage of case.

Syntax Errors

Syntax errors occur when you use valid symbols in an invalid manner. Because the compiler must recognize and enforce valid syntax, it will always catch these errors. However, it might not correctly interpret what you were trying to do.

Misuse of Operators

The POWER.C program (Listing 17-3) might be written by a FORTRAN programmer who is accustomed to using the exponentiation operator of that language.

```
/* power.c -- attempts to raise to a power */

main()
{
    int number;

    number = 10**3; /* raise 10 to 3rd power? */
    printf("%d\n", number);
}
```

Listing 17-3. *The POWER.C program.*

Interestingly enough, QuickC doesn't complain that the FORTRAN exponentiation operator (**) is unknown. Instead, it returns the following error message:

```
power.c(7) : error C2100: illegal indirection
```

The C compiler interprets the operation *10**3* as *10 * (*3)*, that is, 10 times the value at the address 3. The indirection operator should, of course, be applied to a pointer, and 3 is an integer. Therefore, the compiler complains that you used the operator incorrectly.

A Scrambled Operator

In the CONDITN.C program (Listing 17-4), we reverse the order of the *:* and the *?* in the conditional operator. The compiler finds the error, but the error message is not very illuminating:

```
conditn.c(8) : error C2143: syntax error : missing ';' before ':'
```

If you follow QuickC's analysis blindly and insert a semicolon before the colon, you receive the same error message when you compile again:

```
conditn.c(8) : error C2143: syntax error : missing ';' before ':'
```

The moral here is: The compiler is much better at detecting syntax errors than it is at figuring out exactly what went wrong. QuickC is reliable in *locating* a syntax error; however, you must take the analysis with a grain of salt. If the problem doesn't seem to be in the indicated line, carefully read its immediate neighbors.

```
/* conditn.c -- attempt to use conditional op */

main()
{
    int n, m;

    n = 2;
    m = (n != 2) : 0 ? 1;   /* almost right */
    printf("%d\n", m);
}
```

Listing 17-4. *The CONDITN.C program.*

Another Anomalous Example

The human capacity to err far exceeds the capabilities of compilers to respond helpfully. The DOWHILE.C program (Listing 17-5 on the following page) provides an example. When you compile this program, QuickC places the cursor on the *VOOOM* line and returns the following message:

```
dowhile.c(12) : error C2061: syntax error : identifier 'printf'
```

Apparently, the compiler doesn't recognize *printf()* as the name of a function. Because the compiler accepted the first *printf()* without complaint, this is a puzzling message. Indeed, not one of the lines near the reported error seems wrong.

The error lies in our misuse of the *do* loop. DOWHILE2.C (Listing 17-6 on the following page) shows the correct version of the command.

```
/* dowhile.c -- misuses a do loop */

main()
{
    int i = 0;

    do while (i < 10)
        {
        printf("Happy Fourth of July!\n");
        i++;
        }
    printf("VOOOM\n");
}
```

Listing 17-5. *The DOWHILE.C program.*

```
/* dowhile2.c -- correct use of a do loop */

main()
{
    int i = 0;

    do
        {
        printf("Happy Fourth of July!\n");
        i++;
        } while (i < 10) ;
    printf("VOOOM\n");
}
```

Listing 17-6. *The DOWHILE2.C program.*

The first version had no obvious error near the marked line. But sometimes it is not enough to look at nearby lines. The compiler thinks in terms of statements, and the entire *do* loop counts as a single statement. In that sense, the error *was* near the marked line—it was in the immediately preceding statement, which happened to cover several lines. The moral here is: If QuickC shows an error in a line following an extended statement and you don't see a mistake in the marked line, check the syntax of the entire preceding statement.

Macro Problems

When you use macros, the meaning of an error message might not be obvious. The compiler preprocessor first replaces the macros with the corresponding code. Next, it tries to compile the program. Thus, these compiler error messages refer to the substituted code, not your original code. This can be confusing, especially if you are using a system macro with which you are not familiar. The BADPUTC.C program (Listing 17-7) looks innocent enough:

```
/* badputc.c -- misuses putc() */

#include <stdio.h>

main()
{
    FILE *fp;
    int ch;

    if ((fp = fopen("junk", "w")) == NULL)
        exit(1);

    while ((ch = getchar()) != EOF)
        putc(fp, ch);
    fclose(fp);
}
```

Listing 17-7. *The BADPUTC.C program.*

However, the compiler places the cursor on the *putc()* line and delivers the following barrage of messages:

```
badputc.c(14) : error C2223: left of '->_cnt' must point to struct/union
badputc.c(14) : error C2223: left of '->_ptr' must point to struct/union
badputc.c(14) : warning C4047: 'argument' : different levels of indirection
badputc.c(14) : warning C4024: '_flsbuf' : different types : parameter 1
badputc.c(14) : warning C4047: 'argument' : different levels of indirection
badputc.c(14) : warning C4024: '_flsbuf' : different types : parameter 2
```

These comments don't even seem to relate to our code. We don't use ->_cnt, _ptr, and so on. However, *putc()* is a macro defined in stdio.h, and we can use the /P option of the QCL compiler-linker to see what a file looks like after the preprocessor finishes with it.

Here's the proper command line:

```
qcl /P badputc.c
```

QuickC gives the processed file the same basename as the original, but it adds a .I extension. Listing 17-8 shows part of that processed file. We add comments to indicate the location of the *getchar()* and *putc()* macros.

```
/* badputc.i -- preprocessed badputc.c       */
/* Not shown are all the stdio.h contents that */
/* come at the top of the file.               */
```

Listing 17-8. *The BADPUTC.I file.*

(continued)

587

Listing 17-8. *continued*

```
main()
{
    FILE *fp;
    int ch;

    if ((fp = fopen("junk", "w")) ==((void *)0))
        exit(1);

    /* Original was while ((ch = getchar()) != EOF) */
    while ((ch = (--((&_iob[0]))->_cnt >= 0 ? 0xff &
        *((&_iob[0]))->_ptr++ : _filbuf((&_iob[0])))) != (-1))

    /* Original was putc(fp, ch); */
        (--(ch)->_cnt >= 0 ? 0xff &
        (*(ch)->_ptr++ = (char)(fp)) : _flsbuf((fp),(ch)));

    fclose(fp);
}
```

Now that we see the actual code that is passed to the compiler, the message

```
badputc.c(14) : error C2223: left of '->_cnt' must point to struct/union
```

makes sense. The preprocessed code contains the following expression:

```
--(ch)->_cnt
```

Because the macro uses the -> operator with a pointer to a structure, this code suggests that *ch* should be a pointer to a structure. It isn't, so the compiler reports an error. However, note that *fp* is a pointer to a structure. If we switch *fp* with *ch* in the code, the code makes sense. That's our mistake—we should have used *putc(ch, fp)* rather than *putc(fp, ch)*.

This example illustrates one of the dangers of macros: They offer no provision for function prototyping or for checking the types of arguments. The example also illustrates the usefulness of viewing a file's preprocessor listing.

Run-Time Errors

The most difficult errors to detect are those that the compiler misses. These errors can be inadvertent, such as the =+ error, or they can arise from logical errors in the design of the program.

Function Argument Problems

If you don't use function prototypes, C does not try to match the types you pass to the expected types. Problems here can produce odd results, as the SUMNUMS.C program (Listing 17-9 on p. 590) demonstrates.

The *getc()* Macro

The previous *getc()* and *putc()* macros might be a little obscure. Let's take a closer look at the *getc()* macro definition in QuickC 2.0. (The *getc()* definition in version 2.5 works similarly.)

```
#define getc(f)    (--(f)->_cnt >= 0 ? 0xff & *(f)->_ptr++ : _filbuf(f))
```

This defines *getc()* as a conditional expression having the form *A ? B : C*. If A is nonzero, the entire expression has the value of the B expression; if A is zero, the entire expression has the value of the C expression. The first operand (A) for the conditional expression is as follows:

```
--(f)->_cnt >= 0
```

Loosely translated, this means, "Decrement the *_cnt* member of the structure pointed to by *f*, and check whether the result is greater than 0." From the definition, *f* is the argument to *getc()* and is a pointer to type *FILE*:

```
extern FILE {
    char *_ptr;
    int   _cnt;
    char *_base;
    char _flag;
    char _file;
    } _NEAR _CDECL _iob[];
```

This structure, which is defined in stdio.h, describes the file and the I/O buffer in use. The *_cnt* member describes the number of characters left in the buffer. If the number is greater than zero, then a character remains to be read, and the entire expression has the value of operand B, or:

```
0xff & *(f)->_ptr++
```

The first part (*0xff*) is a mask to limit the final value to a byte. The second part (*(f)->_ptr++*) is the value referenced by the *_ptr* member of the structure pointed to by *f*. The *_ptr* member points to the current location in the buffer. Thus, if *_cnt* indicates that a character remains to be read, *getc()* evaluates to the buffer character currently pointed to. The increment operator then moves the pointer to the next buffer location. If, however, no characters remain, the entire expression has the value of the final operand:

```
_filbuf(f)
```

This is a "hidden" C function (one that the compiler uses but that is not part of the public library of C functions); it copies characters from the file to the buffer, reinitializes *_ptr* to point to the beginning of the buffer, and resets *_cnt* to the number of characters in the buffer. It also returns the value of the first character in the buffer or of EOF if the end of file has been reached. Therefore, if the buffer is empty, you can call this function to refill it.

```
/* sumnums.c -- mismatches types in function arguments */
/*                  No function prototyping              */

int Sums();

main()
{
    float a = 10.0;
    float b = 20.0;
    int c;

    c = Sums(a, b);
    printf("Sum of %.1f and %.1f is %d\n", a, b, c);
}
int Sums(int x, int y)
{
    return (x + y);
}
```

Listing 17-9. *The SUMNUMS.C program.*

After the program initializes *a* to 10.0 and *b* to 20.0, it passes the two values to *Sums()* to be added. The final output is as follows:

```
Sum of 10.0 and 20.0 is 0
```

Clearly, this is false. To see what went wrong, compile in the Debug mode and set watch variables for *a* and *x*. Use the F8 key to step through the program. At first, the value of *a* is undefined, but after the declaration is executed, variable *a* contains the correct value of 10. However, when the *Sums()* function is entered, *x* is set to 0. Therefore, the problem must occur in the passing of arguments.

Knowing how C passes arguments can provide insight into the nature of this problem. Consider the call *Sums(a, b)*. First, QuickC converts *float* types to *double* when passing them as arguments. On a PC, this means that *a* and *b* are now 8-byte quantities. Next, the arguments are put into a memory area called the stack. The last argument, *b*, is pushed onto the stack first. (See Figure 17-1.)

When the called function executes, it reads the values off the stack and assigns them to its formal parameters. It uses the declared types of the formal parameters to determine how many bytes to read. And this is where the problem arises. Because the formal parameters *x* and *y* are declared to be type *int*, the *Sums()* function reads 2 bytes off the stack for the value of *x* and the next 2 bytes for the value of *y*. (It should read 8 bytes for *x* and 8 bytes for *y*.)

The net result of this process is that the first 2 bytes of *a* are assigned to *x* and the next 2 bytes of *a* are assigned to *y*. This leaves 4 bytes of *a* and all 8 bytes of *b* unread, as illustrated in Figure 17-2 on p. 592. Consequently, it is not surprising that the function gets the wrong values from the stack.

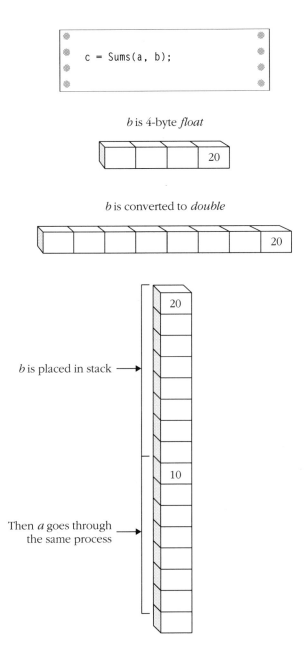

Figure 17-1. *Passing arguments by means of the stack.*

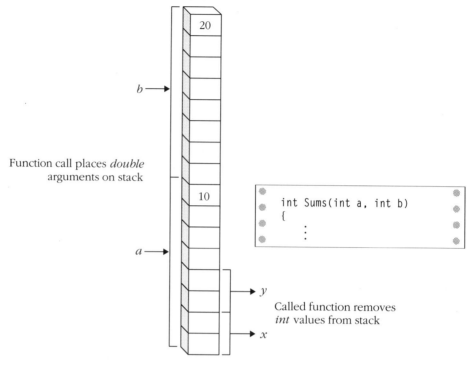

Figure 17-2. *Misaligned data.*

Function Prototyping to the Rescue

The SUMNUMS2.C program (Listing 17-10) adds function prototyping to SUMNUMS.C.

```
/* sumnums2.c -- mismatches types in function arguments */
/*              Function prototyping                     */

int Sums(int, int);

main()
{
    float a = 10.0;
    float b = 20.0;
    int c;

    c = Sums(a, b);
    printf("Sum of %.1f and %.1f is %d\n", a, b, c);
}
int Sums(int x, int y)
{
    return (x + y);
}
```

Listing 17-10. *The SUMNUMS2.C program.*

The program now generates the correct output:

```
Sum of 10.0 and 20.0 is 30
```

With function prototyping, *a* and *b* are converted to type *int* before going onto the stack, and *Sums()* can retrieve the correct values. (See Figure 17-3.)

This is a convenient feature, but it can lead to another kind of error by not alerting you to a type mismatch if you're using a version of QuickC prior to 2.5. After all, the fact that you are passing the wrong type of argument can indicate a programming error. Or you might lose part of the data when converting from *float* to *int*. To use function prototyping but remain aware of mismatched types, select a higher warning level.

```
int Sums(int, int); /* function prototype */
   :
float a = 10.0      /* floating-point values */
float b = 20.0
float c;
   :
c = Sums(a, b)      /* function call */
```

Prototyping causes *a* and *b* to be converted to *int* values 10 and 20

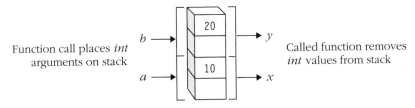

Function call places *int* arguments on stack

Called function removes *int* values from stack

Figure 17-3. *Passing arguments with function prototyping.*

Warning Levels

QuickC issues both error messages and warnings. Errors are mistakes that prevent a source file from compiling. Warnings alert you to usages that might be wrong but that don't prevent compilation. QuickC maintains five warning levels. Level 0 informs you only of errors. Level 1, the default, displays warning messages for those conditions most likely to cause problems, such as mixing levels of indirection in a pointer expression. Level 2 displays more warning messages, adding situations that are not usually serious problems, such as failure to declare as *void* a function that lacks a return value. Warnings that relate to omitted function prototypes are included at Level 3. Level 4 provides the most extensive range of warnings, including such "nonerrors" as non-ANSI keywords. To select warning levels, choose Make from the Options menu, choose Compiler Flags, and then set the warning level.

To see the effect of these warning levels, compile SUMNUMS2.C using all five levels. Level 0 produces no warnings, but level 1 alerts you to the fact that the arguments supplied for *Sum()* do not match those specified in its prototype. Level 2 produces five warnings, and level 3 yields the following list:

```
sumnums2.c(8) : warning C4136: conversion between different floating types
sumnums2.c(9) : warning C4136: conversion between different floating types
sumnums2.c(12) : warning C4051: type conversion - possible loss of data
sumnums2.c(12) : warning C4051: type conversion - possible loss of data
sumnums2.c(12) : warning C4061: long/short mismatch in argument :
    conversion supplied
sumnums2.c(12) : warning C4061: long/short mismatch in argument :
    conversion supplied
sumnums2.c(13) : warning C4016: 'printf' : no function return type, using
    int as default
sumnums2.c(13) : warning C4071: 'printf' : no function prototype given
sumnums2.c(14) : warning C4035: 'main' : no return value
```

The first two warnings refer to the declarations for *a* and *b*. The reason for the warning is that C floating-point constants are always type *double*, yet *a* and *b* are declared type *float*. Because *float* uses fewer bytes, the potential exists for a partial loss of data. These warnings did not appear at lower levels.

The second two warnings refer to the two conversions that take place in the *Sums()* function call as a result of function prototyping. Because the values change from *float* to *int*, the conversion might lead to a partial loss of data. The third pair of warnings describes the type mismatch that was first revealed at level 1.

The seventh warning tells us that we haven't declared the return type for the *printf()* function, and the eighth warning laments the lack of a prototype for *printf()*. Fix these by including the stdio.h file.

The final warning informs us that *main()* has no return value. Because we did not explicitly declare a type for *main()*, the compiler assumes that *main()* is type *int*. Therefore, it expects *main()* to have an integer return value. To avoid this warning, provide a return value at the end of the function. Neither this warning nor the eighth warning was displayed at level 2.

The highest warning sensitivity, level 4, adds no additional warnings in the case of SUMNUMS2.C. Warnings at this level are especially significant to developers, who are concerned about the portability of their code.

Common Run-Time Errors

Some programming errors arise from the design of the C language itself. After we discuss ways to avoid such errors in simple contexts, we will demonstrate how to detect them in more complex contexts.

The Misleading *if* Statement

We begin with an error that almost every C programmer has made more than once. The LINE_CNT.C program (Listing 17-11) counts lines of input. It reads each character to EOF, which is signaled by obtaining Ctrl-Z with *getchar()*. A newline character increments the line count (*lines*).

```
/* line_cnt.c -- an overly active line counter */

#include <stdio.h>

main()
{
    int ch;
    int lines = 0;

    while ((ch = getchar()) != EOF)
        if (ch = '\n')
            lines++;
    printf("There were %d lines\n", lines);
}
```

Listing 17-11. *The LINE_CNT.C program.*

The following is a sample run:

```
Cat
Hat
Bat
^Z
There were 12 lines
```

The problem is that we used the assignment operator (=) instead of the is-equal-to relational operator (==). Consider this statement:

```
if (ch = '\n')
    lines++;
```

The conditional expression assigns the character $\n$ to *ch*, giving it the numeric value of 10 (the corresponding ASCII code). The entire expression $ch = '\n'$ now has the value 10, which, being nonzero, is interpreted as being true. Thus, *lines* is incremented for every character, regardless of its value. Because this is a legal construction, QuickC returns no syntax error message.

Knowing about this potential error is not enough to protect you from occasionally making it, especially if you are a Pascal programmer accustomed to using = for comparison. It is not an eye-catching error. How, then, can we detect it in a large program listing?

The telltale sign is an *if* branch or *while* loop that always executes, even when you think it shouldn't. The use of = instead of == isn't the only possible cause, but it is the first you should look for.

The Debug facility can help find this type of bug. Suppose we didn't know what was wrong with Listing 17-11. We could select the Debug option, set a watch on *ch*, and use the *c* modifier (separated from *ch* by a comma) to display the value of *ch* as an ASCII character.

As we first trace through the program, *ch* is undefined. After it is declared (but not initialized), it has a garbage value. Next, if we enter the word *Cat* as input, we see *ch* take the value *C* as we enter the *if* statement. When control goes to the *lines++;* statement, we see that *ch* now is *'\n'*. Therefore, *ch* is being assigned a new value, and that tells us to look for an incorrect assignment statement.

Examining Arrays, Part 1

One of the most common tasks for a *for* loop is to process the elements of an array. The INDEXER.C program (Listing 17-12) is a simple example that is meant to initialize three arrays, calculate the number of elements in the second array, and display the contents of that array. Instead, it prints the character *3* until you press Ctrl-Break. The reason for this failure is that the program increments *size* rather than *index*. Thus, *index* remains at 1, while the comparison limit grows. (Eventually, the loop halts when *size* exceeds the maximum *int* value and becomes negative.)

```
/* indexer.c -- uses indexes to display an array */

#include <stdio.h>
int Code1[] = {2, 4, 6, 8};
int Code2[] = {1, 3, 7, 9};
int Code3[] = {5, 10, 15, 20};

main()
{
    int index;
    int size = (sizeof Code2) / (sizeof (int));

    for (index = 1; index <= size; size++)
        printf("%3d ", Code2[index]);
    putchar('\n');
}
```

Listing 17-12. *The INDEXER.C program.*

This is a C error that is inherent in the language. Most languages increment the loop variable for you, thus preventing you from making the mistake. C, as usual, chooses flexibility over the more restrictive but trouble-free approach.

If you don't catch this error in the code, however, how can you spot it later? One way is to monitor the program as it runs. The Debug option provides a simple method. If you have problems in a loop, set a watch on the loop index. Making *index* a watch variable and tracing through the preceding program soon reveals that *index* does not change, so you turn to the update portion of the *for* control statement.

Examining Arrays, Part 2

Fixing the error in the loop index results in the INDEXER2.C program (Listing 17-13). Running the revised program produces the following output:

```
3   7   9   5
```

Because the values should be 1, 3, 7, and 9, the program still fails. The new problem is the array index range. Array numbering starts with 0, not 1. Thus, the correct limits for the loop are as follows:

```
for (index = 0; index < size; index++)
```

The original limits print the last three members of the array and the first element of the array that followed *Code2* in memory.

```
/* indexer2.c -- uses indexes to display an array */

#include <stdio.h>
int Code1[] = {2, 4, 6, 8};
int Code2[] = {1, 3, 7, 9};
int Code3[] = {5, 10, 15, 20};
main()
{
    int index;
    int size = (sizeof Code2) / (sizeof (int));

    for (index = 1; index <= size; index++) /* increments index */
        printf("%3d ", Code2[index]);
    putchar('\n');
}
```

Listing 17-13. *The INDEXER2.C program.*

The index limit error is easy to make, especially if you are accustomed to languages such as FORTRAN, which start numbering with 1. This error is difficult to detect because C does not check for bounds errors. (Pascal gives a run-time error message when an index becomes too large or small; C doesn't.) You can use Debug to trace the array index, but that doesn't help if you forget the proper limits.

You can prevent this error by habitually using a standard form for the *for* loop. For example, if an array has *size* elements, use either of the following:

```
for (index = 0; index < size; index++) /* OK */
```

```
for (index = 0; index <= size - 1; index++) /* OK */
```

Don't alternate between the two forms. If you do, you increase your chances of producing an incorrect hybrid form, such as the following:

```
for (index = 0; index <= size; index++) /* NO */
```

Mirror Words

The BACKWARD.C program (Listing 17-14) is designed to print a word in normal order and then reverse the order of the letters.

A quick look at the program suggests that its output should be as follows:

```
trap backward is part
```

And, indeed, the program prints that out. But it doesn't stop there. It keeps on printing. Some of the output is garbage, some appears to be words and phrases spelled backward. What went wrong?

The first things to check when a loop unexpectedly becomes infinite are the loop's control statements. In this case, they look reasonable:

```
(index = SIZE - 2; index >= 0; index--)
```

SIZE is the number of elements, so *SIZE - 1* is the index of the terminating null character, and *SIZE - 2* is the index of the final character in the word. Each loop decrements the index by 1, thus moving back a character. When *index* reaches 0, the loop should display the last character and stop. But it doesn't. In this loop, the obvious variable to examine is *index*. Compile the program in the Debug mode, set a watch on *index*, and trace through the program step by step. The value of *index* follows this sequence: 3, 2, 1, 0, 65535, 65534, and so on. The *index* variable never becomes less than 0, so the loop never ends. Why not? Because *index* is declared an *unsigned int*. Change the type to *int*, and the program works properly. What at first looked like a looping error turns out to be a type error.

The moral here is: Be careful when comparing unsigned quantities to zero. For example, if *index* is unsigned, *index = 0* is always true, and *index < 0* is always false. But *index <= 0* can be either true or false.

```
/* backward.c -- the backward word displayer */

#include <stdio.h>
#define SIZE 5
char Word[SIZE] = "trap";

main()
{
    unsigned int index;

    printf("%s backward is ", Word);
    for (index = SIZE - 2; index >= 0; index--)
        putchar(Word[index]);
    putchar('\n');
}
```

Listing 17-14. *The BACKWARD.C program.*

Operator Priorities

Because C has so many operators, you might at first have difficulty in remembering all the operator priorities. Certainly, multiplication has a higher priority than addition, but how do the increment operator and the indirect value operators compare? Does *ps++ mean (*ps)++ (use the pointed-to value and then increment the value) or *(ps++) (use the pointed-to value and then increment the pointer)? The second choice is the correct one; if you think the first interpretation is correct, you won't get the results you expect.

For another example of priorities, consider the binary shift operator used in the SHIFTADD.C program (Listing 17-15).

```
/* shiftadd.c -- shifts and adds numbers */

main()
{
    int x = 0x12;
    int y;

    y = x << 8 + 2;
    printf("y is 0x%x\n", y);
}
```

Listing 17-15. *The SHIFTADD.C program.*

From appearances, this program should left-shift x 8 places and then add 2. Because each hex digit represents four binary digits, a left-shift of 8 in binary is a two-digit shift left in hex, so $x << 8$ is 0x1200. Adding 2 gives 0x1202. But when you run the program, it prints a value of 0x4800. Addition has a higher priority than shifting; therefore, QuickC interprets the code as: Add 2 to 8 and do a 10-bit left-shift.

You can find this type of error by using the Debug mode: Trace the values as they are calculated and compare them using Quickwatch to calculations you perform by hand or with the *assert()* macro we discuss later.

The best way to solve the problem is to avoid it in the first place. If you're not sure of priorities, look them up. The QuickC Help menu provides quick access to this information. Another method is to use parentheses to clarify your intent:

```
y = (x << 8) + 2;
```

Scanning Problems

The IBMIQ.C program (Listing 17-16 on the following page) reveals one of the most common C errors. The following dialogue is a sample of the program output:

```
Enter your first name: -> Mortimer
Enter your IQ: -> 88
Well, Mortimer, my IQ is -1!
run-time error R6001
- null pointer assignment
```

```
/* ibmiq.c -- a short dialogue */

#include <stdio.h>
char Name[80];
int Iq;

main()
{
    printf("Enter your first name: -> ");
    scanf("%s", Name);
    printf("Enter your IQ: -> ");
    scanf("%d", Iq);
    printf("Well, %s, my IQ is %d!", Name, 2 * Iq - 1 );
}
```

Listing 17-16. *The IBMIQ.C program.*

Notice that the computer claims an IQ of −1 rather than the 175 you might expect from glancing at the program. Also, QuickC does not issue the run-time error message until after the program ends. These errors occur because in the second *scanf()* call, the program uses *Iq* rather than the correct *&Iq*.

Most programmers make this kind of error through carelessness. For example, two lines above the incorrect statement, the program uses *Name* as an argument. And because *Name* does not need the & operator, it's easy to forget that *Iq* does.

Let's look at the mechanics of this error and at the error message itself. The following sequence of events occurs. First, *Iq* starts with the value 0 because external variables are initialized to 0. The *scanf()* function interprets 0 as the address 0; that is, it thinks it received a pointer to *NULL*. It then places the input value 88 at that address rather than in *Iq*. (See Figure 17-4.) Therefore, *Iq* remains 0, and the program calculates the machine's IQ as −1. Then the program ends. However, the C null pointer never points to valid data. To be sure of this, QuickC sets aside a "null block," which is not to be modified or allocated for other purposes. QuickC also includes postmortem code in each program that checks the null block to see if it has been altered. If it has, something is wrong, and QuickC displays the null pointer error message.

Note that the postmortem code doesn't detect data written to non-null locations. For example, if we initialize *Iq* to 200, the program still fails to work properly, but because address 200 is outside the null block, QuickC returns no error message. Thus, in general, you might not detect this kind of error unless you notice suspect data in the output. Unfortunately, this error can also overwrite legitimate data.

Function prototyping won't help here. If you try an error level of 3 or 4, the compiler still doesn't complain about using a nonpointer as an argument. Looking at the function prototype in stdio.h shows us why:

```
int _FAR_ _cdecl scanf(const char _FAR_ *, ...);
```

```
int Iq;    /* Iq happens to be initialized to 0 */
           /* and to have adress 3400          */
```

scanf("%", &Iq) is the same as *scanf("%s", 3400)*
so a value of *88* is placed in location 3400.

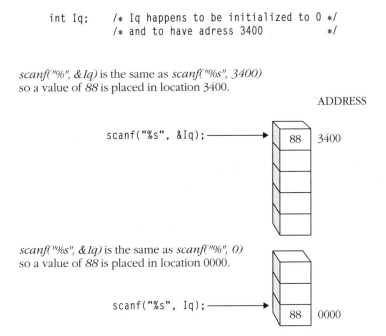

Figure 17-4. *Entering forbidden territory.*

The *scanf()* function is one of those rare functions that take a variable number of arguments. The first argument is always a string, but the others can be different types. Therefore, the prototype doesn't limit the nature and number of the remaining arguments: It type-checks only the first argument.

(The _cdecl keyword ensures that C functions use C calling conventions even if the /Gc compiler flag is set. That flag enables the Pascal and FORTRAN calling sequence for programs that use mixed-language modules.)

References

The BADREF.C program (Listing 17-17 on the following page) provides an example of a more subtle pointer error. The following is a sample run of the program:

```
Enter your first name: -> Fillmore
The second letter of your name is i

run-time error R6001
- null pointer assignment
```

This program gives the correct answer, but it also produces the null pointer error message, which means that data has been written in the null block. The program uses two pointers to assign data. First, in the call

```
scanf("%s", Name);
```

the *Name* variable is a pointer. This variable isn't a pointer to the null block, however, because the compiler allocates the space for *Name*.

Now look at the following assignment:

```
*Pt_ch = Name[1];
```

This tells QuickC to copy the contents of *Name[1]* to the location pointed to by *Pt_ch*. The program allocates space for the pointer *Pt_ch*, but it never specifies where *Pt_ch* points. Therefore, *Pt_ch* becomes an "unreferenced" pointer—it doesn't refer to a known location. As in the preceding example, because *Pt_ch* has an initial value of 0, the data is copied to the null block.

The unreferenced pointer is an insidious error. If such a pointer is initialized to a value that doesn't point to the null block, the postmortem program will not detect it. However, there is an effective method for preventing this kind of error. When you compile a program, enable the Pointer Check feature. To do this, select Make from the Options menu, and then select Compiler Flags. This adds code to your program that checks to see if each pointer is referenced before it is used. Recompile BADREF.C using this option. The following is a sample run:

```
Enter your first name: -> Fillmore

run-time error R6012
- illegal near-pointer use
```

This time, instead of generating incorrect results, the program halts when it attempts to use the unreferenced pointer. If you compiled in the Debug mode, the cursor marks the guilty line of code when you return to the editing screen.

Obviously, the Pointer Check mode makes for safer programs. Unfortunately, it slows program execution, thus sacrificing one of C's strengths. Typically, you use this mode only when you suspect pointer problems (such as when you receive a null pointer warning). Once you rectify the problem by initializing the pointer to point to previously allocated memory, turn off the pointer check and recompile.

```
/* badref.c -- misuses a pointer */

#include <stdio.h>
char Name[80];
char *Pt_ch;

main()
{
    printf("Enter your first name: -> ");
    scanf("%s", Name);
    *Pt_ch = Name[1];
    printf("The second letter of your name is %c\n", *Pt_ch );
}
```

Listing 17-17. *The BADREF.C program.*

Design Errors

So far we have focused on the misuse of the C language. However, you can write programs that use nothing but valid C statements but that fail because of design errors. The DIGSUM.C program (Listing 17-18), for example, contains a design flaw.

```
/* digsum.c -- sums digits in input */

#include <stdio.h>

main()
{
    int ch;
    int digits = 0;  /* number of digits in input */
    int others = 0;  /* number of nondigits in input */

    while ((ch = getchar()) != EOF)
    if (ch <= '0' && ch >= '9')
        others++;
    else
        digits++;
    printf("digits = %d, others = %d", digits, others);
}
```

Listing 17-18. *The DIGSUM.C program.*

The program examines input. Characters that are less than 0 or greater than 9 are considered nondigits, and the program lists them as *others*; the program lists values within that range as *digits*. The following is a sample dialogue:

```
2b
4c
^-Z
digits = 6, others = 0
```

The program counts all input, including the newlines, as digits. The problem lies in the following test condition:

```
if (ch <= '0' && ch >= '9')
```

The expression is always false because it asks if *ch* is simultaneously less than *'0'* and greater than *'9'*, which is impossible. You must use the logical OR operator (¦ ¦) to express the test condition properly.

Other than its flaw in logic, this program contains no C errors, and QuickC compiles it with no objections. The error becomes apparent when you analyze the output.

You can ferret out this kind of logic error (expressing a test condition incorrectly) by using Debug to trace the program step by step. When you see that the program takes the wrong branch each time, you know to inspect the test condition.

Small Programs

Often, with small programs, you can locate errors merely by examining the code, especially if the behavior of the program suggests likely sources of difficulty. By becoming familiar with common errors and the effects they produce, you will learn to detect errors quickly.

If a simple inspection fails to turn up the error, don't spend a lot of time poring over the code. Instead, gather more evidence. First, trace the values of key variables as a program runs. This gives you an inside view of program execution and can help uncover clues that let you deduce what is wrong. Traditionally, C programmers do this by embedding *printf()* statements at key locations. However, you need not use this method—QuickC's Debug mode is a quicker and more powerful technique.

If your problem seems array related, check your use of indexes. If it's loop related, check your loop conditions, paying close attention to the starting and ending values.

If pointers are involved, check to see whether they are referenced properly. You should always assign a pointer an address before you use it.

Test conditions that combine two or more relationships are breeding grounds for errors, and you should put them high on your list of items to be checked.

Large Programs

The difficulty of finding errors rapidly increases with program size. The Debug mode lets you watch the progress of several variables, but a large program can have so many things going on that Debug is of little help. Also, large programs often use complex interdependencies that make it difficult for you to visualize details.

The key to debugging large programs is the same as the key to writing large programs—modularity. If you don't use a modular approach when you develop a large program, you greatly decrease your chances of debugging the result. Using the modular approach, you break a program into smaller, more manageable pieces; as a result, you can localize most problems with only a few debugging techniques.

Stub Functions

The "stub function" debugging technique is based on the top-down method of programming. Begin debugging by testing the highest level of program organization. Suppose that your *main()* function contains the overall organization of the program and calls upon other functions to handle the details. These second-level functions, in turn, might subdivide the work into further functions.

With this method, you replace the second-level functions with simple, error-free routines called stub functions. For example, suppose one second-level function takes an array and an array size as arguments and performs a complex calculation.

Replace it with the following stub function:

```
void Complex_calc(double array, int size)
{
    printf("Function Complex_calc was called with "
            "arguments %u and %d\n", array, size);
}
```

Do this with all second-level functions to concentrate on how *main()* works. Does it perform the proper sequence of steps? Does it pass the correct arguments? Use the Debug mode to trace the order in which the statements execute. If *main()* works properly, replace the stub functions with the originals one by one until a problem occurs. If necessary, you can use stubs within stubs.

Drivers

Another debugging method is the bottom-up approach. Here you start with the most basic functions. However, instead of testing them in the complex final environment, you use small programs called "drivers" to test the functions.

For convenience, design your driver so that it can feed a variety of values to the function to be tested. The MATHTEST.C program (Listing 17-19) offers an example of such a driver.

```
/* mathtest.c -- driver for Do_math() */

#include <stdio.h>
double Do_math(double);

main()
{
    double input, result;

    printf("Enter a number: ");
    while (scanf("%lf", &input) == 1)
        {
        result = Do_math(input);
        printf("input = %.2e, result = %.2e\n", input, result);
        printf("Next number (q to quit): ");
        }
}

#include <math.h>

double Do_math(double x)
{
    return (sin(x) * exp(-x));
}
```

Listing 17-19. *The MATHTEST.C program.*

The following is a sample run:

```
Enter a number: 0
input = 0.00e+000, result = 0.00e+000
Next number (q to quit): 1
input = 1.00e+000, result = 3.10e-001
Next number (q to quit): -2
input = -2.00e+000, result = -6.72e+000
Next number (q to quit): q
```

Actually, any non-numeric input (not just *q*) causes *scanf()* to return a value other than 1 and thus terminates the loop.

Notice that the driver function echoes the input value to let you know that the *Do_math()* function receives the intended value. That is good programming practice when you use *scanf()* for input, because *scanf()* gives you two opportunities to make mistakes: You can omit the & operator or use the wrong format specifier. (For example, because *input* is a *double* value, we must use *%lf* for input rather than *%f*.)

The *assert()* Routine

The *assert()* macro is another tool for locating logic errors in a large program. Use this macro to test whether certain conditions are in fact true. The *assert()* macro takes an expression as an argument. If the expression is true, the program continues. If it is false, the program halts and prints a message identifying the file and line number of the incorrect assertion. The TESTER.C program (Listing 17-20) is a short example that illustrates how *assert()* works.

The program calculates the hypotenuse of a right triangle by finding the square root of the sum of the squares of the remaining sides. We deliberately introduce an error into the calculation so that *sumsq* contains a negative value. Because *sumsq* must always be positive or zero, we specify that with the *assert()* statement. When you run the program, it halts at the *assert()* statement and displays the following message:

```
Assertion failed: sumsq >= 0, file c:\qc25\tester.c, line 15
```

By placing *assert()* statements at strategic locations in a large program, you can localize logic errors, which enables you either to find the error or to use Debug more productively.

One convenient feature of *assert()* statements is that once you fix your mistakes, you can recompile and eliminate the statements from the compiled program without altering your source code. To do so, merely place the following definition in your program:

```
#define NDEBUG /* turns off assert() macros */
```

This causes the *assert()* macro to be defined as a blank.

```
/* tester.c -- demonstrates the assert() macro */

#include <assert.h>
#include <stdio.h>
#include <math.h>

main()
{
    float s1 = 3.0;
    float s2 = 4.0;
    float sumsq;
    float hypot;

    sumsq = s1 * s1 - s2 * s2;
    assert(sumsq >= 0);
    hypot = sqrt(sumsq);
    printf("Hypotenuse is %.2f\n", hypot);
}
```

Listing 17-20. *The TESTER.C program.*

A Final Word of Advice

QuickC offers you many powerful tools for debugging your programs. However, the ultimate tool in debugging is your own mind. Become familiar with common programming errors and study how to detect or prevent them. Most importantly, write your programs in a structured, modular form so that you can easily trace or localize the errors.

Appendix A

Some Resources for C Programmers

Much has been published on C for every level, from beginner to expert. The following is a list of a few books and magazines that have proved useful and that can supplement and extend your grasp of the topics discussed in this book.

Fundamental and Comprehensive Books

Barkakati, Nabajyoti / The Waite Group. *The Waite Group's QuickC Bible.* Indianapolis, Ind.: Howard W. Sams, 1988.

A comprehensive guide to every library function in QuickC. Includes usage guidelines and complete sample programs for each function.

Barkakati, Nabajyoti / The Waite Group. *The Waite Group's Essential Guide to Microsoft C.* Indianapolis, Ind.: Howard W. Sams, 1988.

A concise, easy-to-use pocket reference guide to all Microsoft C functions.

Costales, Bryan. *C From A To Z.* Englewood Cliffs, N.J.: Prentice–Hall, 1985.

Recommended by Allen Holub as "the best introduction to the language that [I have] seen." One of the few books used in the University of California at Berkeley's course on the C language.

Kernighan, Brian W., and Dennis M. Ritchie. *The C Programming Language.* Second edition. Englewood Cliffs, N.J.: Prentice–Hall, 1988.

This new edition of the definitive description of the C language reflects the draft ANSI proposals. The writing is terse but very clear, providing a synopsis of C language features and their typical uses.

LaFore, Robert / The Waite Group. *The Waite Group's Microsoft C Programming for the PC.* Revised edition. Indianapolis, Ind.: Howard W. Sams, 1989.

This bestselling tutorial has been updated to include coverage of the QuickC compiler. Its approach is example driven, with chapters on using C for graphics and other applications.

Waite, Mitchell, and Stephen Prata / The Waite Group. *The Waite Group's New C Primer Plus.* Revised edition. Indianapolis, Ind.: Howard W. Sams, 1989.

This new edition of the world's bestselling introductory primer on C is fully compatible with the new ANSI standard, UNIX-based C, and the Microsoft C Compiler. It contains quizzes and exercises.

Books on Advanced Topics

Chesley, Harry, and Mitchell Waite / The Waite Group. *Supercharging C with Assembly Language.* Reading, Mass.: Addison–Wesley, 1987.

This book shows you how to determine which parts of a program would benefit from recoding in assembly language for the ultimate in speed and efficiency. Includes many specific code examples.

Feuer, Alan. *The C Puzzle Book.* Englewood Cliffs, N.J.: Prentice–Hall, 1982.

This book poses tricky and interesting questions that challenge your understanding of the subtle points of C.

Hansen, Augie. *Proficient C.* Redmond, Wash.: Microsoft Press, 1987.

Insightful advice on solving real problems with C. Written for both advanced-level and intermediate-level programmers.

Jaeschke, Rex. *Solutions in C.* Reading, Mass.: Addison–Wesley, 1986.

This book covers the finer points of C that programmers must master to avoid subtle pitfalls in the handling of pointers, structures, and other elements. For advanced programmers.

Kernighan, Brian W., and P. J. Plauger. *Software Tools.* Reading, Mass.: Addison–Wesley, 1976.

A classic and a cornerstone of modern program design. This book shows how to create versatile software tools that can be combined to solve programming problems. The language used, RATFOR, can easily be translated into C. If you are familiar with Pascal, you might want to try *Software Tools in Pascal,* also by Kernighan and Plauger (Reading, Mass.: Addison–Wesley, 1981).

Koenig, Andrew. *C Traps and Pitfalls.* Reading, Mass.: Addison–Wesley, 1989.

This unique book is a systematic survey of the typical errors made by C programmers and includes general advice to help you minimize errors and ambiguities.

Prata, Stephen / The Waite Group. *Advanced C Primer ++.* Indianapolis, Ind.: Howard W. Sams, 1986.

This sequel to *C Primer Plus* provides a complete tutorial that covers advanced topics, such as I/O operations, memory management, and the use of assembly language with C. Focuses on the IBM PC family.

Periodicals

Don't neglect the many programmer-oriented magazines that feature C projects. Among these publications are the following:

BYTE. Subscription Dept., P.O. Box 6807, Piscataway, NJ 08855-9940.

This monthly magazine often has articles about the use of C for various applications and reviews of products of interest to C programmers. Source code available on its BIX electronic network.

Computer Language. P.O. Box 11333, Des Moines, IA 50347-1333.

This monthly has many feature articles on C programming and reviews of commercial C libraries and other add-on products. Source code available on CompuServe and other bulletin boards.

Dr. Dobb's Journal of Software Tools. P.O. Box 3713, Escondido, CA 92025-9843.

Dr. Dobb's is the hacker's delight with the funny name. Material on C, assembly language, unusual programming tricks, and so forth. Source code available on CompuServe.

PC Magazine. P.O. Box 51524, Boulder, CO 80321-1524.

This IBM PC–specific magazine has a languages column that often features C programs. This monthly magazine also maintains a bulletin board offering many utilities and other programs.

PC Tech Journal. P.O. Box 52077, Boulder, CO 80321-2077.

This monthly is, as the name suggests, specific to the IBM PC and MS-DOS. Besides having material on C, it also offers much news and technical features about MS-DOS, OS/2, and other aspects of the PC programming environment.

Programmer's Journal. 150 North 4th Street, Springfield, OR 97477.

This IBM PC–specific magazine often features C programs. Published bimonthly.

Differences Between QuickC Versions 2 and 1

This appendix describes the major differences between QuickC version 2 and QuickC version 1. If you are using QuickC 1.0 with this book or are converting from version 1.0 or 1.5 to version 2, use this appendix to find out which features are not available and what basic internal changes have occurred. (References to version 2 apply to versions 2.0 and later.) Overall, the main change is that QuickC version 2 provides full .EXE disk-based compilation and linking, as found in the full Microsoft C Professional Development System, whereas earlier versions of QuickC compile and link in memory. This brings QuickC more in line with Microsoft C and eliminates some of the problems that occur with in-memory compilation.

The major external changes in QuickC version 2 are

- A new hypertext-based help system

- A customizable editor

- New windows

- A considerably enhanced graphics library

Changes in the User Interface

Users upgrading from QuickC version 1 will find the overall feel of the user interface for QuickC version 2 to be the same. Many menu items are identical, as are most of the keys (or mouse actions) used for navigating through the program's various features. The new version, however, provides significant enhancements, which are discussed in the following sections.

New Learning Aid

Microsoft provides a colorful overview of C called LEARN with QuickC version 2. This on-line review offers a series of short lessons that help you become familiar with the important QuickC keys; the use of the menus, dialog boxes, and windows; the writing, compiling, and running of a program; and basic debugging. This system provides a quick way to become familiar with the operation of QuickC. It is not designed to be a detailed guide to the C language and the various tools included with the compiler.

Expanded Help System

In addition to the context-sensitive help and topical help that are available in QuickC version 1, QuickC version 2 offers help with the current menu selection or dialog box. A new indexed help display lets you browse alphabetically through topics or consult a table of contents. The new help system provides expanded help on library functions (including sample programs that show usage) and new "hypertext" links that let you jump to related topics at the touch of a key or mouse button.

New Windows

In QuickC version 2 you can move more quickly and easily among a larger variety of windows. QuickC version 1 had windows for the source file, program output, error messages, and help. The new version adds windows for the contents of local variables, machine register contents, and a notepad. You can now cut and paste text between windows (including the Help window). This means that you can paste sample code from the Help system into the edit window and run it.

Customizable Editor

The QuickC editor is still fully supported in QuickC version 2. If you prefer another editor, however, you can attach it to the QuickC environment through a menu option and use it instead. You can also create a "key file" with your own key assignments to override the defaults, or you can use one of the Microsoft-supplied files to configure the QuickC editor to work like the Microsoft Editor (ME), Brief, Epsilon, or EMACS.

New Compiler Features

QuickC version 2 changes the way compiling and linking are done, supports all memory models, lets you use in-line assembly-language code, and lets you compile programs to run under OS/2 or Microsoft Windows. QuickC version 2.5 introduced a number of enhancements to provide compatibility with Microsoft C version 6 and to strengthen ANSI compliance.

Incremental Compiling and Linking

QuickC version 1 compiles to RAM by default, rather than to disk, which is the more common approach. In-memory compilation, a process in which code for the most frequently used run-time library functions is loaded into memory, results in very fast linking. With version 1 of QuickC, you can also create Quick Libraries and load them into memory. Although this technique yields extremely fast compilation benchmarks, it is also limited by the amount of available memory. Further, the in-memory compiler requires you to keep track of the functions that are not in RAM and that must therefore be loaded from libraries on disk. (You have to add those libraries to the program list.)

With QuickC version 2, the wizards at Microsoft have achieved even greater compiling and linking speed, but they have found a way to do this while compiling to disk. Their "magic" involves incremental compilation and linking, meaning that only the changed parts of your program are recompiled and relinked. Program lists, which are very frequently needed in QuickC version 1, are needed in QuickC version 2 only for programs that have multiple source files. Further, this incremental linking takes advantage of expanded memory (LIM EMS) if it is available.

More Memory Models

QuickC version 1 supports only the medium memory model in the integrated environment. (The command-line QCL compiler supports all models.) In its integrated environment, QuickC version 2 supports five of the popular memory models (small, medium, compact, large, and huge). Even the "tiny" model—for writing .COM programs—is available to users of version 2.5. This means that you can now write programs of all sizes with QuickC without sacrificing the integrated environment.

QCL, Microsoft Windows, and OS/2

QuickC version 1 does not support Microsoft Windows or OS/2. In QuickC version 2, you can use the QCL (command-line) compiler to compile programs that run under Microsoft Windows. You can also use QCL (in conjunction with the Microsoft C Professional Development System version 5.1 or later) to compile "bound" applications that will run in both real and protected mode under OS/2.

Compatibility with Microsoft C Version 6

QuickC version 2.5 introduces several new capabilities to the compiler. Among them are fastcall protocols for passing parameters in registers to certain types of functions, support for based pointers, and the ability to store and manipulate 10-byte *long double* values.

Assembly-Language Support

QuickC now offers two ways to build programs that include assembly language: an in-line assembler and the new Microsoft QuickAssembler.

In-Line Assembly Language

With the built-in in-line assembler, you can embed assembly-language code in your C functions by using the *_asm* keyword. The additional instructions used by the 80286 and 80287 processors are generated with the */G2* command-line compiler switch. The constants, variables, *typedef* statements, functions, and macros in your C code can be referenced within the assembly-language block. You can even use in-line assembly-language code as the definition for a C macro. In-line assembly language is not meant to be used to write separate assembly modules, but if you need to use small amounts of assembly-language code in your C programs, the in-line assembler is quick and convenient.

QuickAssembler

Versions 2.01 and 2.51 of QuickC come with the Microsoft QuickAssembler, which allows you to program in assembly language directly from the QuickC environment. With QuickAssembler you can create separate assembly-language modules that C programs can call as functions. The QuickAssembler enables you to develop mixed-language programs and even stand-alone assembly-language programs. Like QuickC, QuickAssembler provides on-line help for all the assembly-language instructions and directives.

New Libraries and Graphics Features

The run-time library has been considerably expanded in QuickC version 2, mainly in the area of graphics. The Presentation Graphics Library makes it much easier to create business charts and graphs, even pie charts in full color. Other functions let you display text in a variety of fonts, including all your Microsoft Windows fonts. Scaling functions combine with automatic sensing of graphics hardware to make it easy to write programs that run on the wide range of graphics hardware found in PCs today.

Index

*Italic page numbers refer to figures
and listings*

Special Characters

THE WAITE GROUP

Mitchell Waite is President of the Waite Group, a San Francisco, California-based developer of technical and computer books. He is also an experienced programmer, fluent in a variety of computer languages. Waite is a coauthor of **MICROSOFT MACINATIONS,** published by Microsoft Press, and of *UNIX Primer Plus* and *C Primer Plus,* published by Howard W. Sams.

Stephen Prata, Ph.D., is Professor of Physics and Astronomy at the College of Marin in Kentfield, California, where he teaches C and UNIX. Prata is coauthor of several Waite Group books, including *UNIX Primer Plus, C Primer Plus,* and *UNIX System V Primer,* all published by Howard W. Sams.

Bryan Costales is Senior Systems Programmer at EEG Systems Laboratory. He is the author of *C From A to Z,* from Prentice-Hall (Simon & Schuster), and coauthor of *UNIX Communications,* published by Howard W. Sams.

Harry Henderson is a freelance technical writer and editor. He has edited and contributed to computer books for the Waite Group, Blackwell Scientific, and Wadsworth. In addition, he is the editor for *Tricks of the UNIX Masters* and *The UNIX Bible,* Waite Group books published by Howard W. Sams.

The manuscript for this book was prepared and submitted to Microsoft Press in electronic form. Text files were processed and formatted using Microsoft Word.

Cover design by Thomas A. Draper
Interior text design by Darcie S. Furlan
Illustrations by Becky Geisler-Johnson
Principal typography by Lisa Iversen and Katherine Erickson
Color separations by Wescan Color Corp.

Text composition by Microsoft Press in Garamond Light with display in Futura Bold, using the Magna composition system and the Linotronic 300 laser imagesetter.

Printed on recycled paper stock.

THANK YOU FOR YOUR PURCHASE OF
The Waite Group's
Microsoft QuickC Programming!

Because The Waite Group values the comments of its customers, we would appreciate your taking a few minutes—*after you have spent some time with Microsoft QuickC Programming*—to answer these questions. If you would like more information on products from The Waite Group or Microsoft Press, please turn this card over, check the box(es) and fill in your name and address in the upper left corner.

1) What was most influential in your decision to purchase this book? Please rank by order of influence, #1 being the most influential factor.
___ A) Tutorials
___ B) Examples
___ C) Reputation of Microsoft Press
___ D) Reputation of The Waite Group
___ E) Companion disk

2) What specific computer experience did you have before using this book? Please check only one.
___ A) Beginner
(no previous computer experience)
___ B) Some experience with IBM PCs
(applications, etc.)
___ C) Beginning programmer
(some experience with BASIC or another programming language)
___ D) Power user (lots of applications, some utilities, and batch files)
___ E) Advanced programmer
(know C, PASCAL, etc.)

3) How did you use this book? Please check all that apply.
___ A) Self-study at home
___ B) Work-related use
___ C) Computer course in school
___ 1) high school
___ 2) vocational institution
___ 3) college or university

4) How would you rate the content of this book?
___ Excellent   ___ Fair
___ Very Good   ___ Below Average
___ Good   ___ Poor

5) Mark an L for things you liked and D for things you disliked:
___ Content   ___ Listings   ___ Illustrations
___ Pace   ___ Cover   ___ Writing Style
___ Format   ___ Index   ___ Accuracy
___ Price   ___ Examples   ___ Construction

6) Where did you purchase your copy of this book?
___ Bookstore   ___ Software store
___ Catalog   ___ Other

7) What other computer-related books and topics are you interested in?
_____
_____

8) How many Waite Group books do you own? ___ What are your favorite Waite Group books?
_____

9) What other programming languages do you know?
_____

10) We would like to hear any additional comments you have about any portion of the book:
_____
_____

Be assured that The Waite Group will use this information only in developing future products that you need. We appreciate your comments.

ORDER CARD

For information on the Companion Disk for Microsoft QuickC Programming, 2nd ed. and ordering information within the U.K., please see page xii.

YES... please send me _____ copies of the Companion Disk for Microsoft QuickC Programming, 2nd ed. at $19.95 each (U.S. funds only) . . . . $ _____

Sales Tax: Add the applicable sale tax in the following states: CA, CT, DC, FL, GA, ID, IL, KY, ME, MA, MN, MO, NE, NV, NJ, NY, NC, OH, SC, TN, TX, VA, and WA. Microsoft reserves the right to correct tax rates and/or collect the sales tax assessed by additional states as required by law, without notice. . . . . $ _____

Postage and Handling Charges: $2.50 per disk set (domestic orders)
$6.00 per disk set (foreign orders) . . . . $ _____

Please check correct box: ☐ 5.25-inch format   ☐ 3.5-inch format
097-000-448   097-000-451   **TOTAL** $ _____

NAME _____

ADDRESS _____
(___) _____
DAYTIME PHONE NUMBER

CITY _____   STATE _____   ZIP _____

Payment: ☐ Check/Money Order   ☐ VISA   ☐ MasterCard   ☐ American Express
(13 or 16 numbers)   (16 numbers)   (15 numbers)

Credit Card No. [ ] [ ] [ ] [ ] [ ] [ ] [ ] [ ] [ ] [ ] [ ] [ ] [ ] [ ] [ ] [ ]
1 2 3 4 5 6 7 8 9 10 11 12 13 14 15 16
_____
EXP. DATE

CARDHOLDER SIGNATURE _____   **Please allow 2-3 weeks for delivery.**

NAME (please print clearly)

COMPANY

ADDRESS

CITY   STATE   ZIP

☐ **Yes,** please send me a catalog
of products from The Waite Group.
☐ **Yes,** please send me a catalog
of products from Microsoft Press.

The Waite Group, Inc.
100 Shoreline Highway, Suite A-285
Mill Valley, CA 94941

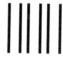

BUSINESS REPLY MAIL
FIRST-CLASS MAIL   PERMIT NO. 108   BELLEVUE, WA

POSTAGE WILL BE PAID BY ADDRESSEE

MICROSOFT PRESS
ATTN: MICROSOFT QUICKC
        PROGRAMMING, 2ND ED.
        COMPANION DISK OFFER
21919 20th AVE SE
PO BOX 3011
BOTHELL WA 98041